THE SUICIDE OF AN ELITE

THE SUICIDE OF AN ELITE

American Internationalists and Vietnam

PATRICK LLOYD HATCHER

STANFORD UNIVERSITY PRESS   STANFORD, CALIFORNIA   1990

Stanford University Press
Stanford, California
© 1990 by the Board of Trustees of the
Leland Stanford Junior University
Printed in the United States of America

CIP data appear at the end of the book

TO MY MOTHER AND BROTHER

Preface

THE WARS ALL NATIONS FIGHT have roots in the past; and the United States, too, went to war driven by historical demons. Victorious in all previous conflicts, Americans could not understand the defeat in Vietnam. The generation that lost tried, perhaps understandably, to forget; and lamentably, successor generations who want to know what went wrong have heard mainly about accidents or conspiracies, explanations that satisfy only the converted. This book attempts to look beyond self-serving one-cause explanations and, by relying mainly on primary sources, to challenge the conventional wisdom.

For the sake of limiting the war in the minds of the general public, the U.S. mislabeled it. The nation of Vietnam was not the sole locale of combat; the war would properly have been called the Southeast Asian war, since it embraced, at a minimum, the four states of old Indochina—North Vietnam, South Vietnam, Cambodia, and Laos—in addition to Thailand and the Philippines. The multiplicity of combatants, confused and divided (especially after forces like the South Koreans and Australians arrived in Vietnam), tested the American desire for a collective security response. Since there was no dependable sense of community for collective action in Southeast Asia in the 1960's, it is not surprising that Americans could not agree on the boundaries of the conflict.

Americans managed, more than fought, the war. To manage the war, the Pentagon of the 1960's housed a new type of technocrat, epitomized by Secretary of Defense Robert McNamara. From his office the Secretary assigned to the U.S. military the nation-building of South Vietnam—an impossible mission.

McNamara was the supreme allied manager, but he did not command the war's major institution. In the Southeast Asian war, the armed services, which in previous military campaigns had supervised combat operations, were outmaneuvered by the National Security Council (NSC); its staff replaced the Generals. With the help of the Central Intelligence Agency (CIA), the Agency for International Development (AID), and the Office of the Secretary of Defense (OSD), the NSC fought and lost the Southeast Asian war. The NSC gained primacy among the new security agencies Congress authorized between 1947 and 1961 because it set the President's war agenda. In that agenda, with the concurrence of Presidents Kennedy and Johnson, the NSC pursued a military, political, and economic intervention in Vietnam, an intervention from which it demanded results rapid enough to avoid a domestic reelection debate over a foreign military campaign. But it was impossible to accomplish that three-fold intervention in the midst of war; and, in large measure, the war's outcome can be explained in terms of the attempt to do so.

In other words, the United States fought, and lost, for specific reasons. No accident excuses the war or its aftermath; nor were there conspiracies. The NSC designed a war that many people, in and out of government, knew about and believed in. Moreover, Americans were the real revolutionaries of this war, for they, unlike the leadership of either Saigon or Hanoi, planned to induce the South Vietnamese, by force if necessary, to accept their rights to physical, political, and economic liberty.

Who were these Americans? Few of them held elected office, preferring appointments to the executive branch. An eclectic group, they stressed merit over birth or bank account, and commonality came from their belief in postwar internationalism. These men's access to power in Washington dates from 1947, at which time they silently began to overhaul U.S. foreign and defense strategies. Typical of successful American reformers with limited goals, they introduced changes near the top of American society, not at the bottom. Nor did this group of internationalists hesitate to use power, a commodity that postwar America possessed in abundance. Determined to block a Leninist elite in the Soviet Union, an elite seen as expansionist, they updated a Lockean view of reform, applied it to global politics, and fought the Cold War with the acquiescence of a majority of Americans. From the late 1940's to the early 1960's, internationalists experienced both successes and setbacks, both relatively minor by global standards. The policies did not work in Vietnam. The enemy would not allow them to win, but the internationalists refused to lose. Compromise, if ever it had been a possibility, escaped them; therefore, a peripheral struggle was escalated into the center of global politics.

Before defeat brought a halt, internationalists experimented in South Vietnam with tactics new to them. The NSC, not the CIA, staged a coup. AID helped with land reform. OSD planned the civic action. But nothing worked. Military operations kept getting in their way. To read the cables, memos, diaries, and oral histories of that group is to study the suicide of an elite. Debating the needs of strangers, a Tory wing of internationalism preferred economic reform first, political reform later, while their Whig associates reversed those priorities. Choosing from among the globe's lesser evils, evils they assigned ranks, internationalists believed that when necessary they could determine, with no other guide, the national self-interest of the United States even in the most complex of global politics. The roots of the Southeast Asian defeat are entangled in the misjudgments of these influential policymakers about American self-interest in that struggle.

The postwar internationalists and their institutions are the subjects of this book. The Introduction presents my major arguments about the war. I separate the following nine chapters into three parts: Part I, military issues; Part II, political issues; and Part III, economic issues. The first chapter of each part places the specific issues—either military, political, or economic—in a general global setting; the second chapter emphasizes the specific Vietnamese locale for those issues; and the third chapter looks at the issues within the specific U.S. setting. These three parts are followed by a concluding chapter that summarizes my findings.

I am grateful to the *Wall Street Journal* for permission to reprint the quotations that open each of the three parts of this book, from the January 11 and March 14, 1985, issues of the *Wall Street Journal*, © 1985 Dow Jones & Company, Inc.

In writing this book I have had the help of many generous people, including Richard Abrams, Paul Seabury, Douglas Pike, William Muir, Gregory Grossman, Gene Tanke, Mappie Seabury, Grant Barnes, John Feneron, and Nancy Atkinson. What praise there might be I share with them; the faults I reserve for myself.

P.L.H.

Contents

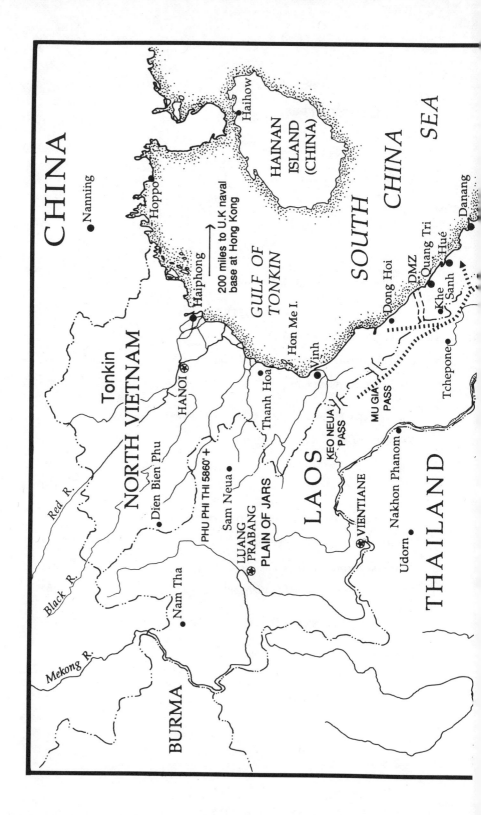

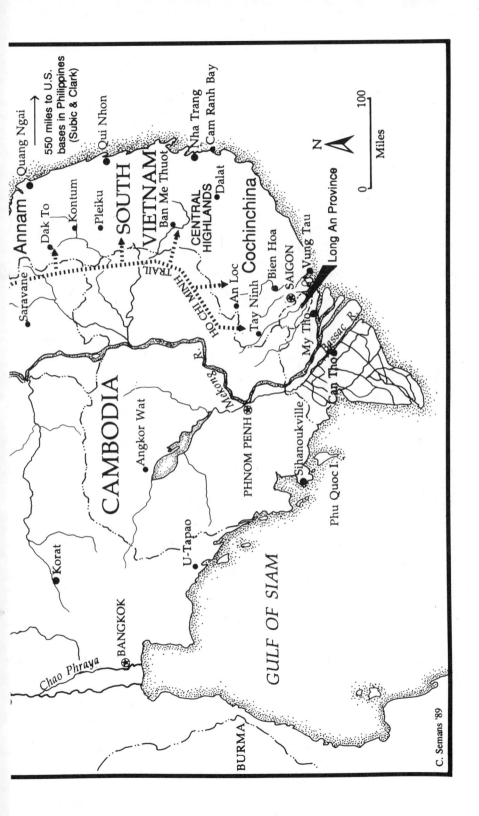

C. Semans '89

THE SUICIDE OF AN ELITE

INTRODUCTION

[America] goes not abroad in search of monsters to destroy. She is the well-wisher to the freedom and independence of all. She is the champion and vindicator only of her own. She well knows that by once enlisting under other banners than her own, *were they even the banners of foreign independence*, she would involve herself beyond the power of extrication, in all the wars of interest and intrigue, of individual avarice, envy, and ambition, which assume the colors and usurp the standard of freedom. The fundamental maxims of her policy would insensibly change from liberty to force. . . . She might become the dictatress of the world. She would be no longer the ruler of her own spirit.

John Quincy Adams,
July 14, 1821

Governments can err, Presidents do make mistakes, but the immortal Dante tells us that Divine Justice weighs the sins of the coldblooded and the sins of the warmhearted in a different scale. Better the occasional faults of a government living in the spirit of charity than the consistent omissions of a government frozen in the ice of its own indifference.

John Fitzgerald Kennedy,
September 5, 1960

The Design of the War

The acts of extraordinary courage to which we pay tribute were
not performed with any hope of reward. They began with a soldier doing his duty—but they went so far beyond the call of
duty that they became a patriot's gift to his country.
    President Lyndon B. Johnson, awarding the Medal of Honor to
                Lieutenant Charles Williams, June 23, 1966.

FOR AMERICANS, their war in Vietnam occurred by design,
not by accident. Therefore, any account should stress continuity, not aberration. For the Vietnamese, their revolution—or, more precisely, "militarized mass insurrection"—took place in their fatherland, by accident
rather than by design. Yet the Vietnamese were at the same time recipients of the American war design—and from the Vietnamese perspective
the Americans designed an aberration. The conflict was part of a lengthy
revolution for the Vietnamese; it was a shorter war for the Americans;
and the American war design damaged both participants severely. For
the Vietnamese, their revolution commenced with the Japanese occupation of 1941, when Japan's samurai imperialists began to risk all for control of the Pacific basin's rim, around whose western half they planned
their version of *zaibatsu* reordering. The Japanese phase brought about a
quick succession of Vietnamese battle deaths. In quick succession another
Vietnamese contingent followed the anti-Japanese martyrs to second-
generation graves, dying in order to defeat the returned French. Following the ignominious French departure, many more Vietnamese were to
die fighting over the role of the Americans in part of their fatherland.
After these last non-Asian outsiders were gone, still more Vietnamese
died, fighting this time to secure their tribe's control of all of old Indochina, with its mix of local outsiders, that is, non-Vietnamese.[1]

How a people could remain at war for over forty years bewilders
Americans, of whose system of government General George C. Marshall
reportedly quipped that it could not fight a Seven Years' War.[2] And indeed, if we do not include the advisory period of 1961–64, Marshall was
correct: for Americans the Vietnam war began in 1965 and ended in 1972.
In order to illustrate the problems inherent in America's longest war, this
study will focus on those Americans who decided the issues, particularly
in the last year of the advisory period, 1964, and the first year of the big-

unit period, 1965. Those twenty-four months bracket the period during which the major American actors set their nation's war agenda. In the main, these internationalists assembled in Washington, D.C.

The New Internationalists

In his book on the Roman republic, Ronald Syme wrote that "a democracy cannot rule an empire." Yet the success of that ancient republic in regulating an enlarged community suggests that a powerful modern republic might likewise be able to regulate parts of a confederation, even if the effort causes great problems. Syme further suggests that an empire, and presumably a confederation as well, cannot be ruled through a single individual. Who then would rule? Syme's answer is simple: "There is always an oligarchy somewhere, open or concealed." Years after Syme's explanation appeared, C. Wright Mills suggested that an American oligarchy ruled as a concealed power elite. In much the same way, it has been suggested that an oligarchy rules the USSR, although no one has claimed that the oligarchs in question conceal their power.[3]

In comparative history, categories are helpful, but not if forced beyond recognition. For example, the Roman, British, and Soviet empires have one important dimension in common—an almost closed ruling class. In Rome it was the senatorial class of the first century B.C., in Britain, the landed nineteenth-century aristocracy; and in the USSR, the Leninist party of this century, the new class. Disconcerted by the absence of such a class in the United States, foreign scholars have tried to classify this nation as "an unconscious imperial power." But in the midst of the Vietnam war, Secretary of State Dean Rusk, well aware of attacks on Americans as empire-builders, privately insisted, "There is no imperium in Americans—at least not in the postwar period."[4] And U.S. history will bear him out: most Americans with oligarchical pretensions—and there have been a few—have seen the personal risks of exercising global power as too large; they have instead engaged their energy in the private sector, where the rewards have occasionally matched their ambitions.[5]

What clouds the debate is the simple fact that when Americans accidentally inherited a great deal of global power after World War II, they tried to manage that power with part-time help in a temporary, ad hoc arrangement that defied imperial logic. The directors of American power in the world were on short-term loan from law firms, corporate boardrooms, research universities, and so forth. Their institutional support was an underpaid class of civil servants, who more nearly resembled Ming dynasty scholar-officials than Roman, British, or Soviet oligarchs.

Amazingly, the civil servants and their temporary supervisors muddled through.

In coming to terms with this legacy of immense power, these temporary supervisors made a "covenant with power." This covenant was and is uniquely American. Because it fails to fit the empire analogy, it will at first seem awkward to those accustomed to the imperial metaphor. But the idea of a covenant has a long pedigree within American history. And since the dean of American diplomatic historians, Samuel Flagg Bemis, adopted the concept in 1943, it has given many historians a key to the workings of state policy.[6]

Those who made this new covenant were the internationalists who supervised the postwar use of American power. In most respects, their covenant with power was open. Members were recruited on the basis of merit and had to operate in full view of Congress and the media. Most critically, their senior supervisor, the U.S. President, had to undergo intense public scrutiny every four years and was allowed power for only eight before having to retire to an American version of the farm to which Lucius Quinctius Cincinnatus returned having served the Roman Republic in time of danger—a Gettysburg country estate or a Texas cattle ranch. In other words, American internationalists were not members of that concealed and closed oligarchy imagined by C. Wright Mills. If anything, the President and his advisers more nearly resembled Thomas Carlyle's aristocracy of talent and Leslie Stephen's intellectual aristocracy.

Why have such a covenant, even if open? Because after World War II it could address two issues that worried Americans. The first was primarily domestic: Would the new economic gains disappear in a return to the conditions of the 1930's, another world depression? The second was mainly international: Would the new peace disappear in a return to the conditions of the 1940's, another world war?[7] America's internationalist elite understood both of these issues. They saw the connection between them, but concentrated on designing policies to prevent the spread of revolution abroad, leaving much of the domestic economic debate to other elites. Internationalists hoped to eliminate anxiety about foreign issues, by working to increase the global bounty so that more of the world's people could feast. They saw this as being in America's own self-interest; if all the world feasted, both in body and in spirit, then people might be safe at home. Two of these men, Adlai Stevenson and Harlan Cleveland, had warned that rising expectations around the world could lead to revolution, and that the way to prevent revolution was to fulfill as many national and international expectations as possible.[8]

As an elite, American internationalists predate the 1940s.[9] Nevertheless, prior to World War II, powerful unilateralists such as Senator William E. Borah blocked access to positions of power from which internationalists could make enduring, substantive changes.[10] It may be true that American internationalism triumphed as an intellectual construct early in this century. But in this book I will examine not the idea but the reality, which is that governments take circuitous, incremental routes in groping toward new policies.[11]

Some diplomatic historians have emphasized the difference between Wilsonian (or altruistic) internationalism, which lost its trial by fire by 1920, and self-interest internationalism, which triumphed in 1947 in the creation of the American national security state.[12] Sometimes, of course, the difference was only a matter of nuance. For example, Dean Acheson, the self-interest internationalist par excellence, endorsed François de Callières's advice that "open dealing is the basis of confidence," adding that it expressed "a very different idea from President Wilson's ill-considered maxim, 'open covenants openly arrived at'."[13] This was only a minor difference, but when added to many other minor disagreements with the Wilsonian faith it made for a new internationalism.

The growth of American internationalism ranks as a miracle of political leadership: a small internationalist elite, operating in both major American political parties, converted a staunchly unilateralist state—the America of 1783 to 1939—to the assertive internationalism of the 1960's. Over many decades several generations of internationalists met great resistance and experienced mainly defeat in their efforts. Their first permanent success came in the 1930's after the Democratic party had chosen as its presidential candidate someone who could learn to share internationalist views. This successful candidate, Franklin Roosevelt, consolidated key positions for internationalists and helped convert his new majority party to that view of national security policy.[14] This conversion assured internationalists access to the seats of government power when the Democratic party obtained the right to regulate the convenant. In the 1950's, when Republican internationalists captured their party's nomination, and then the presidency, for Dwight Eisenhower, the internationalist elite from both parties consolidated its control of American national security policy. It would be fair to say that since 1947 internationalism has never left office—the offices it dominates being the Departments of State, Defense, and Treasury, the Central Intelligence Agency, the National Security Council, and certain national newspapers, like the *New York Times*. Name recognition followed for many—John Foster Dulles, James Reston, Dean Rusk, Henry Kissinger, Cyrus Vance, George Marshall, Robert McNamara, Richard Helms, Douglas Dillon, Lucius Clay, George Kennan, Paul Nitze.

An ambitious mid-1960's survey analysis attempted to define American internationalists and anti-internationalists (isolationists or unilateralists). It concluded that internationalists generally supported foreign aid, immigration, tariff reduction, NATO, and U.N. activities. Anti-internationalists generally took the opposite view in these five areas. Anti-internationalism, according to the survey, was "a complex attitude that can be arrived at by different routes [and is] more common among those who are, by any criterion and for any reason, parochial." This attitude was found among those who held "radical doctrines of the extreme right and extreme left, and attitudes critical of democratic beliefs and practices." Anti-internationalism was described also as "characteristically xenophobic and belligerent in its posture toward foreign affairs" and as being marked by "a disavowal of responsibility and a strong urge to disengage oneself from obligations toward others." Internationalism, in contrast, was more common among persons "open to experience" and "cosmopolitan in their perspective." [15]

One must not draw too sweeping a character study from these data, for "the distinction between 'locals' and 'cosmopolitans' is too often overdrawn." The U.S. population "is not made up exclusively of nationalists (locals) or internationalists (cosmopolitans)." Furthermore, the distinction cut across party lines. For example, within Republican ranks, Robert Taft and Barry Goldwater, but not Arthur Vandenberg and Dwight Eisenhower, distrusted internationalism; and within the Democratic party, a senior Senator, Mike Mansfield, distrusted internationalists, while a junior Senator, John Kennedy, supported them. Within the bureaucracy, too, the split continued. For example, General Curtis LeMay was the Goldwater of the military, and General Maxwell Taylor was the Pentagon's uniformed internationalist. [16]

Curiously enough, internationalists met no serious challenge from isolationists in converting the American political center to an interventionist global policy. In fact, more often than not, isolationism was simply a code word for anti-Europeanism; in isolationists' imagery, America was too virtuous to practice world politics à la Europa. In the postwar period, American commentators as diverse as Walter Lippmann and William Appleman Williams had already demolished the myth of an American history marked by splendid isolation. [17] In place of the old isolationist myth they proposed a unilateralist "reality"—an America that had always been able to operate without consultation or compromise, and without being either drawn into the quarrels of others or driven by others' concerns. This unilateralist view, in fact, had exerted a powerful influence on the imagination of American elites since the administration of George Washington. The fact that American unilateralism in foreign affairs had worked for a very long time—the whole of the nineteenth century—did not pass without notice.[18]

Described in this manner, the pre–World War II past looked much like the postwar era. In both periods, the United States had pursued an activist, interventionist policy in world affairs. The only difference, perhaps, was that prewar American leaders had limited their "foreign actions" to North America, the West Pacific, and the Caribbean basin, whereas postwar leaders saw the whole globe as a suitable arena for American action.[19] This interpretation, however, overlooks a crucial ingredient—the nature of collective action, or collective security.

When America's postwar leaders disregarded Washington's farewell warning not to "entangle our peace and prosperity in the toils of European ambitions, rivalship, interest, humor, or caprice," they set out on a historic change of course.[20] They assumed that it was safe, and even desirable, to link their nation's future to the future of other nations, so long as those nations had a demonstrable self-interest in the new relationship.

Internationalism: Agencies for Action

By 1946, when internationalist experts began to argue that their activist approach was necessary in order to deal with the postwar ambitions of the Soviet Union, the American public generally deferred to them. By 1947 these influential figures had decided that Soviet-American conflict would continue as a permanent feature of global relations, and in that year George Kennan furnished a basis for managing it in his doctrine of containment, an anticommunist manifesto.[21] Like Wilson's early notions of internationalism, Kennan's containment doctrine was an intellectual abstraction. To use it as a basis for a policy meant defining strategies for implementing it. The new internationalism assumed the need for four basic strategies: collective security agreements, limited-war theory, selective political intervention abroad, and global economic development. Each strategy led to policies intended to place military, political, and economic constraints on the Soviet Union.

The manifesto for those who would place military constraints on the Soviet Union was NSC Memorandum 68, accepted by President Truman in 1950.[22] Its chief architect was Paul Nitze, and during the Vietnam war, when Nitze once again held a position of influence, NSC-68 found its bureaucratic enforcer in an overhauled behemoth, the Defense Department of Robert McNamara. Within the Office of the Secretary of Defense—a domain for civilian strategists, and the key management unit within the Defense Department—McNamara gave new defense-policy tasks to three units: the Directorate of Defense Research and Engineering, the Office of the Assistant Secretary of Defense for Systems Analysis, and the Office of the Defense Comptroller.[23] These units managed limited-war activities under the shield of collective security arrangements—in Vietnam it would be the Southeast Asia Treaty Organization (SEATO).

The political constraints to be applied against the Soviet Union were designed in 1947 and 1948 by George Kennan. At this time, he had not yet become the Princeton scholar who argued that political containment could be achieved through the State Department, with its embassies and consulates playing diplomatic chess games. In fact, Kennan rivaled any Potomac activist in his belief that the United States should intervene, overtly or covertly, in the politics of other nations whenever that seemed necessary to forestall a Soviet gain. Many like-minded internationalists agreed, although they considered the State Department bureaucracy hopelessly moribund, stuck in the Eurocentric world of the nineteenth century. They were looking for an agency that might furnish "new modes of conduct in foreign policy to supplement the traditional alternatives of diplomacy and war."[24] In their view this agency would have to push aggressively for political constraints against Soviet meddling, which internationalists perceived as already occurring on a global scale. They found what they were looking for when Congress created the Central Intelligence Agency in late 1947. Initially, the CIA had no covert or extralegal mission. One of the first to recommend a peacetime role for covert intelligence, Secretary of War Robert Patterson, simply suggested that others study the feasibility of this idea. From feasibility study to reality took twelve months. In 1947 Truman ordered the State Department to house covert intelligence activities. Within three weeks of that order, Secretary of State George Marshall asked for and received a reversal by the President. On December 14, 1947, the National Security Council adopted NSC Directive 4/A, which gave responsibility for covert activities to the CIA. But that directive settled only the battle over where the internationalists would house the activity. Kennan, as chief author of NSC Directive 10/2, actually launched the first large-scale, covert operations—intervention in the 1948 Western European elections.[25] Adopted in June 1948, NSC 10/2 made political constraint of the Soviet Union a government policy.

The third constraint, economic containment, did not depend on Kennan's manifesto. In fact, Truman's fellow Midwesterner, a Kansan named Clark Clifford, had written the main text for it a year prior to Kennan's highly publicized "Mr. X" article in *Foreign Affairs*. Clifford's "American Military Firmness versus Soviet Aggression"—prepared for a White House that did not yet house a National Security Council or a National Security Adviser—suggested economic weapons as the chief means of constraining the Soviets.[26] The internationalists eagerly adopted his suggestion, and by the time of the Kennedy-Johnson war in Vietnam, they had created a new instrument for economic intervention, the United States Agency for International Development (AID). As a child of the 1960's, AID displayed much of the hope and suffered much of the despair of that decade.

In order to coordinate the military, political, and economic constraints—to be planned respectively by the Office of the Secretary of Defense (OSD), the CIA, and the State Department's AID—the internationalists created a new clearinghouse for the national security state. Appropriately enough, they named it the National Security Council (NSC). Henceforth, only one-third of America's intrastate relations would fall under the rubric of foreign policy; the second and third parts would consist of military and economic arrangements. The internationalists conceived of all three parts working together to produce "national security policy"—a label "self-consciously used to denote a much expanded vision."[27] In fact, by the time of the Vietnam war, to assure a fair hearing for all economic constraints (the State Department supervised only the AID), the Secretary of the Treasury regularly attended NSC meetings. By that time also, the statutory members—the President, the Vice President, and the Secretaries of State and Defense—were joined by key nonstatutory advisers such as the National Security Adviser, the Chairman of the Joint Chiefs of Staff, and the Director of Central Intelligence.[28]

As with other federal organizations, the National Security Council had a predecessor—the old State-War-Navy Coordinating Committee (SWNCC) that dated from 1944, renamed the SANACC when in 1947 the Air Force received equal standing with the Army and Navy. The internationalists folded the SANACC into the NSC structure as an advisory board; it was finally absorbed in 1949.[29] Not only did the NSC possess a pedigree, but its establishing legislation, the National Security Act of 1947, also had an ancestor. This was a 1945 report authored by Ferdinand Eberstadt, a Wall Street friend of the then Secretary of the Navy (and later first Defense Secretary), James Forrestal. Eberstadt's committee—the Committee on the National Security Organization—recommended the essential institution of "self-interest" internationalism, a National Security Council of key policymakers coordinating national security issues. The committee suggested that the NSC would act as a clearinghouse in "waging peace, as well as war." Nor did the committee stop here; they went on to recommend a Joint Chiefs of Staff and a central agency for intelligence.[30]

The NSC crowned this organizational triumph of internationalism, but other components shared the same parentage: the new CIA and the Joint Chiefs of Staff (JCS) as well as the NSC derived their legitimacy from the passage of this security package. The NSC and JCS became "strategic legislatures."[31] Little could those 1947 creators have known that their creations would assume this role. But in the years that followed 1947, the creators helped to modify their handiwork, adding and subtracting as events demanded.

Just such a demand arose two years after passage of this legislation. Having created a National Military Establishment as a sister to the National Security Council, the act's authors created a Secretary of Defense, who was so weak that the most he could accomplish was to encourage the armed forces to cooperate. In 1949 Congress strengthened the office of the Secretary of Defense by amending the act, converting the National Military Establishment into an executive department, the Department of Defense (DOD), with the Departments of Army, Navy, and Air Force reduced from executive departments to military departments within the DOD.[32] From 1949 to Robert McNamara's rise to power in 1961, the power of the Defense Secretary grew. With McNamara, the position came to dominate the cabinet.

When the Secretary of Defense was granted adequate authority in 1949, the internationalists could bring forward civilian strategists to formulate a new look for American national security policy. But they found that they did not always have to place these strategists at the Pentagon, for the NSC quickly became the focal point of coordination for the State, Defense, and Treasury Departments and the CIA.[33]

Although the NSC remained the pinnacle of the new internationalist structure, different presidents used it in different ways. For Truman it helped bring order out of the immediate postwar chaos, whereas for Eisenhower the NSC worked like the old army staff system he knew so well. Kennedy found it unwieldy; he much preferred making ad hoc committees out of its separate parts. And Johnson used the NSC as he had employed important Senate committees, making it find political compromises that protected his flanks.[34]

Under these four Presidents, the National Security advisers did not de facto outrank any cabinet members, nor did they try to overreach their authority. In that respect, in the 1960's and the Vietnam war, neither McGeorge Bundy nor Walt Rostow saw their assignments politicized as they were for Henry Kissinger and Zbigniew Brzezinski in the 1970's. While it is true that the latter two clashed with career diplomats, thus causing a great deal of Potomac gossip, the deeper institutional struggle, which pitted the NSC staffer against the career foreign service officer,[35] had begun before they arrived on the scene.

When these struggles were still in embryo, the first four postwar Presidents were making policy for the national security state according to personal preference. Truman experimented; and, given the newness of superpower status, most of his decisions set precedents. Eisenhower educated, following the staff model he had used as Supreme Allied Commander. Kennedy innovated, using ad hoc arrangements and performing many functions himself. Johnson bargained and compromised, bringing in the Senate's rule of seniority; for example, Dean Rusk's importance as senior cabinet official rose under Johnson, whereas it had declined under Kennedy.[36] No specific national security policy gained total acceptance or passed unchanged from one administration to another. Policy-making in this area was like that in any other—political "horse-trading" that led to "muddling through."[37] Nevertheless, at bottom the policymakers shared the same internationalist assumptions and the four strategies that flowed from them—collective security, limited war, political intervention, and economic development.

In implementing specific features of their general agenda, internationalists found their protector in the powerful executive branch. Since the four Presidents from 1945 to 1968 shared internationalist aspirations, no rival camp of unilateralists could block the national security activists as long as presidential power continued to expand. Soon dwarfing the legislative and judicial branches, the postwar executive branch enjoyed its greatest influence in the twenty-five internationalist years after 1945. The Vietnam debacle, more than any other event, reversed that influence, at least temporarily. In fact, even measured against domestic events, the only close competition would be the Watergate fiasco.

At the apex of its influence, the internationalist-dominated executive branch needed something beyond new organizations such as the National Security Council. It also required a legal method for making national security policy quickly. In the dawning space age, treaty-making appeared as slow as steamship travel, especially if one's traveling companions were U.S. Senators. Dusting off an old legal device that dated from the Second Congress, the internationalists breathed new life into the executive agreement. From the birth of the republic until 1930 the unilateralists, predecessors of the internationalists, had signed only 25 treaties and 9 executive agreements; by 1972, however, the triumphant internationalists had signed 947 treaties and 4,359 executive agreements. And more than the number and ratio of treaties to executive agreements had changed; the purpose and intended duration of the agreements also had altered radically. The internationalists, in making claims for executive power, could cite the 1936 Supreme Court decision in United States v. Curtiss-Wright Export Corporation et al., in which Justice George S. Sutherland, writing for the majority, suggested that "the president alone has the power to speak or listen as a representative of the nation." Strict constitutionalists objected, insisting that the effort to broaden presidential power was based on constitutional myths. But internationalists favored a broad interpretation, and in the decades following World War II, their interpretation triumphed.[38]

Global Reordering: Lockean Versus Leninist

Armed with executive agreements, preferably those that could deal with "cold" and not "hot" war, these executive-branch activists prepared to compete with their main challengers—Soviet elites who also planned a global reordering, along Leninist rather than Lockean lines.[39] For each side, reordering meant establishing ideologically congenial institutions in allied, client, and nonaligned states. American internationalists, privately too sophisticated to endorse simplistic anticommunist campaigns, set out to prevent the spread of Leninism. To them, Lenin and his followers represented the "doers" among the scribblers on the radical left, the people who had known what was to be done and did it. In similar fashion, Soviet internationalists, too sophisticated to see their efforts as simply anticapitalist, looked for concrete political manifestations of U.S. Lockean designs.[40] Where American experts saw *apparatchik* class control through a single, powerful party as proof of Leninist triumph, Soviet experts saw middle-class control through multiple legal and market mechanisms as proof of Lockean incursions. Imported Leninism would show itself in a command economy commanded by a *nomenklatura* of party planners; imported Lockean manifestations came from a controlled economy controlled by a bourgeoisie of crafty consumers. Lockeans expected to find the key institutions that supported Leninist control in the police and military functions; Leninists expected to find the key institutions that supported Lockean control in the law and market functions.[41]

These two internationalist elites did not allow ideology to cloud their vision of international politics, blocking opportunities that a nonideological world haphazardly made available. First and foremost Americans and Russians alike remained self-interested. For example, if the Soviets witnessed France, with its Lockean-like institutions, irritating American internationalists, they could and did make efforts to encourage General de Gaulle. If the Americans witnessed China, with its Leninist-like institutions, irritating Soviet internationalists, they would make efforts to encourage Chairman Mao. If Marshall Tito defected from the Soviet sphere, American internationalists such as Kennedy would welcome the Yugoslavs, even with their modified Leninist institutions, into a special relationship. If Colonel Nasser defected from the American sphere, Soviet internationalists would embrace the Egyptians, even with their modified Lockean institutions.[42]

With respect to Yugoslavia and Egypt, the competing superpower elites would have preferred a less contaminated relationship; but, the world being an imperfect place, each side grudgingly accepted what they could. When working for reordering in the underdeveloped world, in places such as Indochina, however, each power strove to build copies of their own native institutions, ones deemed necessary for the recipient elites. In fact, both America and the USSR usually thought that the assisted nation's relative backwardness would help them, for they hoped not to find, and therefore not to have to tolerate, any institutions already contaminated by Soviet-American competition. Yet even here disappointment awaited, for the term "backward" meant nonindustrial, not nontraditional. Many recipients of Soviet and American reordering, though fairly uncontaminated with the competing elite's institutions, nevertheless had strong traditional institutions, which they could not or would not adapt to the imposition of Lockean or Leninist industrialism. In many ways, Vietnam represents such a situation.

While the influence of the pragmatic Locke on American "doers" in the domestic arena can hardly be denied, that in itself does not prove that when American leaders intervened in places such as Vietnam, decisions were based on concepts derived from Locke. It is one thing to conclude that Locke influenced the elite virtuosi of America's revolutionary century, or to suggest that educated Americans of the first four decades of the nineteenth century found in Locke a major explanation for democratic practices in their domestic century.[43] It is quite another thing to claim that in their international century, educated Americans carried Locke's ideas abroad to justify the political and economic interventions; but in fact, they did.

While the influence of the pragmatic Lenin on North Vietnamese "doers" in the domestic arena can hardly be denied, that does not in itself prove that when the northern leaders intervened in South Vietnam, they made decisions based on concepts derived from Lenin. It is one thing for Ho Chi Minh to praise Lenin in a *Pravda* article.[44] It is quite another to claim that in its struggles with other Vietnamese factions, the people in the faction headed by Ho Chi Minh carried Lenin's ideas into their political and economic battles. But in fact, they did.

There exists no better area in which to examine the differences between Leninists and Lockeans than in their contrasting concepts of property and politics; they differed specifically over land ownership, as well as over the role of political parties. Lockeans conceived of property in terms of private ownership. Leninists saw it in terms of collective ownership.[45] When Lockeans came to Vietnam they worked at turning its peasant-dominated, rural-based economy into one of privately owned farms; this was American-style land reform. When Leninists triumphed in Vietnam—the northern half first—they worked at turning the same peasant-dominated, rural-based economy into one of collective farms; this was Soviet-style land reform.[46] With regard to political parties, the two elites offered sharply contrasting models. Lockeans stressed the desirability of having several political parties, each limited in power, and thus forced to bargain for compromises. Leninists stressed the necessity of one party, unlimited in power, able to control counterrevolutionary forces without having to compromise the people's programs.[47] The Vietnamese received forceful instruction in both political styles, for neither instructor was hesitant about breaking the back of the tradition-bound mandarin model.

Leninist ideology tends to legitimize certain people, whereas Lockean ideology tends to legitimize certain policies. Leninist leaders find it necessary to consult their ideology frequently, and with some sophistication, lest in discarding a part of the ideology they give up their own claim to power.[48] But Lockean policies, expressed in legislation, tolerate clashes between leaders with widely differing interpretations of the Lockean ideology. Therefore, the rise and fall of any set of leaders has only minimal reference to modifications in the ideology.

By the time Lockeans focused their attention on Vietnam, Leninists were already at work there. Rushing to catch up, the Americans organized a collective security agreement in the Southeast Asia Treaty Organization (SEATO). Lacking a regional sense of community on which to build, SEATO became a weak imitation of its more successful model, NATO. The Lockeans created these globe-girdling treaties and bilateral agreements as segments forming an arc around Leninism's citadel, the Soviet Union.

As the postwar Lockeans took Southeast Asia into their global calculations, they discovered a long-enduring war evolving from phase to phase. By then it was in its second phase, rejection of the returned French; Americans thus found themselves caught between the aspirations of a critical ally, France, and several unknown Vietnamese factions. Considering France vital to Europe and NATO, the United States refused to force France out of Indochina. They watched and waited. Disaster came for the French in 1954 at Dien Bien Phu, a military defeat of great psychological importance.

Both then and later, even after the Tet offensive of 1968—a psychological defeat of military importance—Lockeans remained faithful to their view of collective security and limited war. They stood with their ally

France until it lost, but they would not use "tactical" nuclear weapons at Dien Bien Phu, as a few had suggested to President Eisenhower. Nor later, in their own war design, would the Lockeans march north to the Red River as General MacArthur had a decade earlier marched to his disaster on the Yalu River in Korea under an unwatchful Truman administration. This is not to say that they did not have disagreements about minimum and maximum efforts. But it was a split among gentlemen; Lockeans tried to keep their differences to themselves, always fearing the return of unilateralism in any of its postwar disguises, such as libertarianism.[49]

Vietnam: Whig and Tory Internationalism

However, as soon as internationalists agreed that Leninist involvement in Vietnam had to be checked, they began to argue among themselves over competing designs for reforming Vietnam. One group insisted that the war could not be won unless first they forced political reform in Saigon. The opposing group insisted that in order to win the war, economic reform had to receive first priority regardless of who ruled in Saigon. A third group, frustrated by both these agendas, argued that security ought to come first, because that was all that could be guaranteed. A few internationalists argued for pursuing all three agendas simultaneously, but most thought they should be pursued in sequence, each in due time. Unfortunately, as General Marshall had warned, time was the one thing they would not have. Presidential politics would set time limits to U.S. participation in any foreign conflict.

Distinguishing between security, political, and economic designs poses problems, and U.S. policymakers themselves often blurred the distinctions. In seeking to clarify the policy-making process, it will be useful to identify two types of internationalists: Whigs, who emphasized political reform, and Tories, who emphasized economic reform. (Each group expected that the security design, implemented simultaneously, would support its own priority.) Of course, the use of these labels simplifies their complex historical derivation.[50] Here, the Whig label simply refers to American internationalists who, when intervening in the domestic affairs of another state, concentrated their energy on the political order of that state. When they did not like what they saw politically, they forcefully suggested changes. When rebuffed, the Whigs had a trump, a coup sponsored by their agency of last resort, the CIA. In American popular culture during the 1950's and 1960's, with its James Bond novels and movies, espionage was presented as heroic and exciting, and there was little political will to investigate or restrain CIA operations in Vietnam. The Tory label, as used here, simply refers to American internationalists who, when intervening in the domestic affairs of another state, concentrated their energy on its economic order. When they did not like what they saw economically, they too forcefully suggested changes. When rebuffed, Tories also held a trump, the ability to withdraw financial assistance through their agency of first resort, the Agency for International Development. American popular culture had a record of generous support for private philanthropy abroad. In the 1950's and 1960's, when the U.S. government began to engage in public philanthropy abroad, the popular culture supported AID projects in Vietnam.

I believe that a historical work should attempt to use terms that connect events to a past. Others might object that the connections are too ambiguous and that therefore terms from the social sciences ought to be substituted, terms such as "developmentalist" in lieu of "Tory" and "constitutionalist" in lieu of "Whig." In this vocabulary the former would refer to an economic reformer or modernizer, and the latter to a political reformer or modernizer. Thus recast, the terms would float free, disconnected from the past. But this work will retain the terms with historical connections, links with the Anglo-American past that are rich in meaningful insights, especially into the symbolic power of land ownership issues.

It is worth considering for a moment why the Whig and Tory labels, which may seem novel and arbitrary, are preferable to more commonly used labels. For example, are not Whigs and Tories simply "liberals" and "conservatives"? The answer is no. Even on certain issues in domestic politics, this latter pair of labels cannot be made to fit well; in global politics they become meaningless. Once unshackled from domestic constraints, American internationalists of both Whig and Tory persuasions accepted the liberal challenge of making the United States "the foremost exponent of liberty and justice" along with the conservative challenge of promoting "the politics of degree, priority and place, insistence, course, proportion, season, form, office, and custom."[51] In other words, internationalists were reformers, not revolutionaries, and they were ideologically eclectic. The term "liberal internationalism," understood to include "an ideological commitment to democratic humanism," also is inadequate. For, as we shall see in the Vietnam intervention, democratic humanism embraces concern for both economic security rights (Tory) and political-security rights (Whig). The terms "left" and "right" internationalism suffer from the same lack of descriptive powers as "liberal" and "conservative."[52]

If liberal versus conservative and left versus right will not suffice, neither will "realist" versus "idealist," labels that political scientists in particular have used to distinguish between political players.[53] However, using these terms adds a degree of confusion because the idealist players do not really play, at least not in Vietnam. In other words, one of the two ideal types, the idealist, seldom if ever makes an appearance in the circle of power, often preferring instead to remain outside. Therefore, internationalism has housed mainly realists, especially following the aftermath of the last global war. But a more important reason for rejecting these labels is that through popular misuse, they have acquired connotations of "good" and "bad," depending upon the context. To pursue ideals and moral values is good; but an "idealist" is not the only person who can resign rather than support an immoral policy, or a losing argument for what later appears to have been the "better" policy. Likewise, to understand self-interest is good; but a "realist" is not the only person who can understand the self-interest of a nation, or recognize the need to choose the lesser of the two evils and use force in defense of that choice.

Labels that carry value judgments, though perhaps helpful in specific cases, are almost never helpful when used to explain postwar American national security policy. For example, President Kennedy is often remembered for two international episodes: he traveled to West Berlin to denounce the wall of shame there, and he approved the abortive Bay of Pigs invasion of Cuba. Similarly, Lyndon Johnson challenged the American people to travel with him in a conquest of poverty while almost simultaneously dispatching the 82nd Airborne Division on an uninvited trip to the Dominican Republic. Both the Kennedy and Johnson administrations arrived in Washington, D.C., labeled by the media "left-liberal-idealist." In 1968, the American electorate chose what was usually called a "right-conservative-realist" administration led by Richard Nixon. Yet of all political people, it was Nixon who made the left-liberal-idealist aspirations for a reconciliation with China a reality. And besides giving American voters an accommodation with his old nemesis-of-convenience, "Red China," Nixon also gave them the Christmas bombing of North Vietnam's cities and "the incursion" into Cambodia. To explain such apparent contradictions and to illuminate specific features of American postwar internationalism, we need some terms that are relatively value-neutral.[54] The terms Whig and Tory, in the twentieth-century American context, certainly seem to carry less baggage, fewer inhibitors of clarity. But clarity in terminology does not necessarily result in clarity about specific policies. What a value-neutral policy, as opposed to a label, did for both Whigs and Tories, as the terms are used here, was to allow them to base decisions on the national self-interest, as they defined that interest.

New, self-interest internationalism possesses a checkered history, one that contains successes and failures. Internationalists introduced Americans to the Marshall Plan and the Alliance for Progress, but also they allowed America's accommodations with Francisco Franco's Spain and Anastasio Somoza's Nicaragua. These accommodations were tolerated not primarily because they were considered morally sound, but most of all because they appeared to be in the interest of the United States. When Franco departed, the internationalists decided that supporting Franco's royal successor was even more in the U.S. interest, and embraced him. When Somoza departed hastily for Miami, the internationalists serving President Jimmy Carter—many of them, like Cyrus Vance, former members of the Kennedy-Johnson team—hesitated in half-embrace of Somoza's successors, then finally rejected them as not serving U.S. interest. Earlier, the same Vance had (as Deputy Secretary of Defense) helped President Johnson capitalize on the Gulf of Tonkin resolution—an example of pure self-interest.[55] Later, as Secretary of State, Vance would resign in indignation over Carter's rescue attempt in Iran.

These examples do not prove that American policymakers fail to apply moral standards in making policy; generally speaking, they do, and at least they have not rejected what has seemed to them at the time to be moral conduct in the international arena. Also, self-interest and moral judgment can complement each other. The Marshall Plan, for example, is often cited with pride by internationalists as a successful combination of self-interest and public philanthropy. But in difficult situations—as in Vietnam, where the just cause seemed split up and scattered among competing camps—U.S. internationalists allowed Vietnamese national self-interest, something they believed they could discern, to be their primary guide.

We can best see the difference between Whig and Tory internationalists, however, not in negative definitions but in their choice of preferred action. Whig internationalists favor supporting political action: writing constitutions, organizing trade unions, establishing newspapers, assisting church groups, running libraries, encouraging legal studies, and holding elections of all sorts. In search of data on which to base policy, the questions Whigs ask are political: How many newspapers publish daily issues? Are radio and television stations government organs? How many dissenting religions built how many churches, temples, synagogues, or mosques? How do voters register, how often do they have the right to vote, on what issues are they allowed to vote, and do they have the right to a secret ballot? How are candidates selected and how do parties function? How is an individual represented in court, what is the right of appeal, and how does due process work? Who controls the police, is torture a method of interrogation, and what rights does an accused person have? What is the right of assembly and of petition?

Tory internationalists prefer to support economic action. They are interested in providing hybrid seeds or chemical fertilizers, in promoting dry farming techniques, in augmenting human labor with machines, in reforming banking and trading practices, in introducing textiles and other minimum-technology industries, in upgrading health and sanitation practices, and in offering new transportation and power-generating facilities. Tories ask economic questions: How many flush toilets are there in a community? How do individuals get unpolluted drinking water, and how do communities dispose of sewage? How many doctors and dentists are there per capita, and do they reach rural households? What diet does the population receive in the form of calories per capita, vitamin content, and mix of fresh vegetables and fruits? In a peasant-based economy, dependent upon irrigation, how do farmers move water to fields or paddies? What is the figure for the gross national product, and what is the prediction for productivity gains in the agricultural and industrial sectors? How is the population housed—type of roof, dirt or covered floors, ventilation, number of persons per room? What methods of birth control would keep the population growth lower than productivity gains, and how would imported medical technology change life expectancy figures? How do individuals transport themselves—by foot, by horseback, by bicycle, by motorcycle, by automobile?

We know that internationalists asked these questions about Vietnam, for the cables they sent are full of them. More surprisingly, the largest American agency in Vietnam—the Military Advisory Command Vietnam, whose major task was to deal with security issues—found its personnel absorbed with problems of political and economic intervention, described as civic action and pacification. Finding the security intervention burdensome enough, however, it never solved those other problems.

How did such questions and tasks come to dominate the American agenda in Vietnam? In fact, they grew out of the competition with Leninists. Those competitors had something to sell, their ideal of a modern community, which they thought could be realized if certain requirements were met. The American Lockeans had a competing ideal of modernity to sell but, unlike the Leninists, differed among themselves over what would be required to make the ideal a reality. Most of their differences concerned views about liberty. To Whigs political liberty was both the crowning achievement of a civilization and, in smaller degree, the sine qua non for progress toward that achievement. Tories, though inclined to agree that political liberty was the highest human achievement, believed that it sprang from, or at least rested heavily upon, economic liberty.

Interestingly, in a life's work almost contiguous with the lives of these first Whig and Tory internationalists, Abraham Maslow offered an explanation of human nature that could encompass both views. In Maslow's psychology, which was influential throughout the social sciences by the 1960's, all individuals and peoples recognize a hierarchy of needs.[56] At the bottom are the needs for food, drink, clothing, shelter, safety, sex, and companionship. As these needs are satisfied, persons begin to demand the fulfillment of increasingly complex and sophisticated needs. At the top of the hierarchy Maslow placed what he called needs for "self-actualization": when freed of concern for basic needs, individuals can develop their talents and stretch their horizons to the fullest extent possible. Not surprisingly, Tory internationalists committed themselves to fulfilling the earlier, more basic needs faster and better than the Leninists.[57] Whig internationalists, on the other hand, worked at beating the Leninists by contriving measures that would make self-actualization a real possibility.

Whigs and Tories also differed in their views of what they were offering to others. Whigs saw Tories as offering other nations market institutions that encouraged selfish—not self-interested but selfish—motivations.[58] Although aware that these acquisitive instincts were approved in their own society, and unashamed of that fact, Whigs did not think they should export so unmajestic a vision of human destiny—a Tory shopping mall for the globe. For that vision, Whigs substituted parliaments and courthouses. Roger Hilsman gives a fair example of the Whiggish penchant for celebratory rhetoric: "The State Department analysis also argued that the idea that Vietnam existed for the benefit of the people, that a government could really *care*, was as revolutionary in most of Asia as anything the Communists had to offer."[59] In the other camp, Tories did not find a majestic or inspiring call to arms in democratic political institutions. For them, democratic politics seemed as plebian as one could get, certainly nothing to celebrate, and based on compromises that always yielded a second-best solution for the people involved. Tory internationalists such as John Kennedy never tired of quoting Winston Churchill: "Democracy is the worst form of government—except all those other forms that have been tried from time to time."[60] Selling the "worst best thing" did not excite Tories.

Despite this split, each camp within American internationalism tolerated the bias of the other in the beginning—better that than a return to ad hoc unilateralism. Moreover, even within the smallest state in which they intervened, internationalists quickly discovered that more tasks existed than they could possibly manage; this meant that both Whigs and Tories would have enough room for maneuver. Also, both camps contained minimalists and maximalists, depending on the specific issue. For example, when discussing land reform, minimalist Tories only favored encouraging a policy of private land ownership, whereas maximalist Tories joined minimalist Whigs, both favoring a land redistribution program with compensation to former owners. All opposed maximalist Whigs, who would tolerate land confiscation by the aided government. But during the first years in South Vietnam, growing irritation led to a collision. Tories, unable to rely on Vietnamese political stability while trying to restructure South Vietnam's economy, grew impatient of what they saw as Whig meddling in Saigon politics. Whigs, unable to rely on Vietnamese economic stability, saw Tory market schemes as creating new winners and losers who did not yet understand the political constraints essential to self-interest politics in a democracy: one does not shoot the new loser or confiscate the property of the replaced elite or exile the sons of opponents, and one must be willing to accept media criticism from a free press, tolerate religions one personally considers heretical, and accept an election loss in the future. Finally, the third group of internationalists—those who thought that the only goal possible for the United States was to help furnish physical security to South Vietnam—blamed both Tories and Whigs for imposing their agendas.

Even with these differing agendas, the internationalists postponed their collision over Vietnam for nine years, from 1955 to 1963. In the years following the French debacle, Tory preferences dominated Vietnam policy; and although certain Whig decorations adorned the Saigon government, in fact Ngo Dinh Diem remained the autocratic mandarin he had always been, a perfect match for the northern autocrat in Hanoi, Ho Chi Minh. Therefore, in 1963 when the final Tory-Whig collision occurred over Vietnam policy, a Whig ascendancy began, only to exhaust itself in a desperate after-the-fact search for a successor to Vietnam's last mandarin. Quickly exhausted, and under relentless Tory criticism for their political failures, Whigs accepted defeat in the form of a Vietnamese dictatorship by military committee.

By then it was late 1963. In the following twelve months, a time in which Lyndon Johnson manipulated domestic opinion concerning the war, all hopes of the South Vietnamese winning the competition for themselves vanished. By then governance in Saigon was rotating between chronically insecure military committees. Ambassador Lodge once cabled President Johnson from Saigon that General Nguyen Khanh, leader of the second of these military committees, felt so unsafe in the presidential palace that he changed his place of domicile every night.[61] Johnson, safely returned to the White House in his own landslide election victory in November 1964, decided that the United States should win the competition that these committees could not win for themselves. But Johnson lost his way in trying to win for the Saigon factions in the years between the 1964 Tonkin Gulf Resolution and the 1968 Tet offensive. He did not have to hear this from student protestors or the press. His own council of "wise men" told him.[62] Many of them—Dean Acheson, George Ball, Clark Clifford, Douglas Dillon—were the founding architects of internationalism.

How could these internationalists, these truly dedicated public officials who were generally competent and sometimes brilliant, have stumbled into a catastrophe of such magnitude? On a priority list of global targets being contested with Leninists, Gamal Abdul Nasser's Egypt ranked higher than Ngo Dinh Diem's South Vietnam.[63] Yet internationalists watched Egypt drift into the Leninist camp, biding their time for a reversal to occur. Even more strikingly, after witnessing the sudden triumph of Leninism in Cuba, the internationalists burned their collective hands once at the Bay of Pigs and then settled for attacking Fidel Castro with words, not bullets. Why then, were they willing to sacrifice so much blood and treasure in Vietnam?

One explanation offered for the tragedy has been this: "Of the two forces responsible for inducing Americans to assume the burdens of international leadership after World War II, anticommunism rather than liberalism came to play the stronger part." If we replace, "liberalism" with "anticolonialism," it becomes easy to agree with the conclusion that "Vietnam became the apotheosis of that error."[64] Internationalists, seeing themselves forced to choose between colonialism and communism, often chose colonialism as their lesser evil. They thought also they could nudge the major colonial powers—mainly Lockean-influenced states in their domestic politics—out of their empires more easily than they could ever dislodge Leninists. And in that assessment they were usually correct. Yet in Vietnam internationalists often fell into the trap of playing the colonial mentor-in-transition, an unwelcome role that substantially assisted in their undoing.

Another explanation lies in the way "the administrative man" makes decisions. In complex bureaucracies, whether Lockean or Leninist, such people seek decisions through collegial compromises. In choosing a new policy, they choose one that meets minimum requirements, one that "satisfies" rather than "maximizes." Where there are many such bureaucrats of "bounded or limited rationality," preference for a simple formula that will lead to consensus often overrides the need for complex analysis. At those times their guideline tends to be "Do what we did last time if it worked, and the opposite if it didn't."[65] Thus if an American-supported coup worked in Guatemala in 1954, it ought to work in South Vietnam in 1963. Between 1955 and 1965, a series of small incremental decisions concerning Vietnam policy added layer upon layer to an internationalist consensus. Once committed by these various "muddling through" decisions, internationalists fought to protect their turf from unilateralists, and from other opponents whom President Johnson called "nervous Nellies."[66] Although willing to debate heatedly in private, when it came to the public arena—and criticism of a policy which all had partially shared in implementing—they hoisted the consensus flag behind a wall of stone. And the tougher the fight, the higher the wall. Some social scientists have described this phenomenon as "groupthink." But one should not assume that debate behind the stone wall could not be heated, even if the disputatious dissenters later became prisoners of the very consensus they and their opponents had hammered out of conflicting positions.[67]

It is probable that the internationalists would have become prisoners of consensus regardless of the specific issues or political parties involved, because of a legalistic interpretation of the collective security treaties they managed to obtain. Concern for their reputation as guarantor in Vietnam put them into the prisoner's dilemma: antagonistic states, lacking trust in each other, often are damned if they do risk cooperation and damned if they don't. If "the United States seeks to establish a reputation as a country that actually does carry out [its] guarantees, despite short-run cost,"[68] then it had to fulfill its contracts, costs be damned. Among the documents collectively known as the Pentagon Papers, a memorandum written in March 1965 by John McNaughton, Assistant Secretary of Defense for International Affairs, ranks the importance of various guarantor aims in the percentage terms favored by Secretary McNamara:

> 60%—To avoid a humiliating U.S. defeat (to our reputation as a guarantor).
> 20%—To keep SVN (South Vietnam) and the adjacent territory from Chinese hands.
> 10%—To permit the people of SVN to enjoy a better, freer way of life.
> Also—To emerge from crisis without unacceptable taint from methods used.
> Not—To "help a friend," although it would be hard to stay in if asked out.[69]

Of course, internationalists argued privately, along Whig and Tory lines, about how to pursue the top, or 60 percent, priority—whether through political or economic interventions. Clearly, however, individuals in both camps were warning each other about their collective reputation as executors of America's guarantee.

The Dissonance of Internationalism

American internationalists often found that their actions contradicted what they told themselves they believed. According to Leon Festinger's theory of cognitive dissonance, the only way out of this dilemma is to change either one's actions or one's beliefs, in order to make them more congruent over time. For example, strategic bombing of cities caused dissonance for internationalists. In the case of Germany and Japan during World War II, and in Korea and Vietnam in postwar Asian combat, internationalists did not want to target civilians. Nevertheless, once at war they did so. They eliminated the dissonance (coming from the clash of earlier beliefs with current actions) by adjusting their attitudes about targeting civilians, suggesting that some civilians who directly suffered war's horrors would influence their government to compromise. Internationalists came to believe that this would end hostilities more quickly, resulting in fewer overall deaths and less total destruction, hence the least bad outcome.[70] Though social psychology offers other explanations of attitude change, the cognitive dissonance theory seems particularly appropriate here. This is because the majority of internationalists were primarily intellectuals specializing in matters of national security policy. They were not politicians. As intellectuals, they were uncomfortable with discrepant cognitions and bothered by incongruities between their beliefs and their actions. Thus Acheson, Ball, and Clifford wanted an ordered world to reflect their ordered minds. So did McNamara and Nitze. Nevertheless, a minority of internationalists were primarily extroverted politicians, with much less interest in self-reflection. Johnson, Kennedy, and Lodge—and especially Johnson—exemplify this minority group. When inconsistencies in their policies surfaced, the extroverted politicians either tolerated them or made whatever practical adjustments seemed likely to preserve their power. In American politics, to survive was to adjust. Admittedly, cognitive dissonance is not the best explanation for their behavior.[71]

Festinger was not the only social scientist who theorized about cognitive changes in attitudes or about the ability of individuals to reduce dissonance in their belief systems. In the immediate postwar world, many journal articles, written mainly by psychologists, appeared on aspects of this subject. But it was not until 1967 that political scientists applied these theories to major case studies in the political arena. One of the best examples of that showed up in a case study of John Foster Dulles, a late convert to internationalism. The authors found that Dulles was able to reduce any dissonance concerning his view of the Soviet Union by holding to a fairly rigid belief system and ignoring new evidence about the Soviets that might contradict aspects of his beliefs. Later internationalists of the Kennedy and Johnson administrations tended to be less rigid, hence more likely to suffer from aspects of cognitive dissonance once they witnessed the contradictions in policies they pursued.[72]

These internationalists of the 1960's accepted William James's challenge to find a moral equivalent of war. And many of them—like Walter Lippmann and Arthur Schlesinger, Jr., who was influenced by James— found their war-substitute internationally in aiding the global growth of Lockean political and economic institutions.[73]

But what happened to Tory belief in the rule of law when Tory actions in another state helped modernize a police force that routinely used American-furnished equipment to torture political prisoners? Tories could applaud the economic liberty granted by the military governments they assisted in South Korea and yet be appalled at the police brutality of the regime. In reverse, what became of the Whig belief in the fair treatment of minorities if Whig actions in another state helped install a majority that quickly spent American funds on oppression of the displaced minority? Whigs could applaud the political reforms occurring in Malaysia and yet be saddened by the Malay treatment of its Chinese minority. In both the Whig and Tory camps there existed both high and low members, the high Tory and Whig being more orthodox than their low cousins.

Since 1947, the internationalists had known that in many ways it was their best-intended actions that often gave others the means to perpetrate gross violations of certain essential values of American society. Having learned that international life was neither fair nor just, they sought a way of making their actions congruent with what they believed. And many found their way in the writings of another Anglo-Saxon theorist who brought religion back into politics.

Internationalism's Confessor

Unlike Locke, Reinhold Niebuhr wrote theological tracts that influenced opinionmakers of a global power whose civil war had long ended. Among his many works, the two that had their greatest impact on internationalists were *Moral Man and Immoral Society* and *Children of Light and Children of Darkness*, the latter a series of public lecture-sermons delivered at Stanford University in 1944 and published in 1946. Numerous citations reflect his influence: Dean Acheson in his memoirs, Stanley Karnow in his journalism, Arthur Schlesinger, Jr., in his historical essays, Ernest W. Lefever (an ordained minister also) in his political analysis, Adlai Stevenson (twice the Democratic party's presidential candidate in the 1950's, and the Kennedy-Johnson Ambassador to the United Nations in the 1960's) in his letters, and Felix Frankfurter in his public papers. Niebuhr came into contact with, and influenced, persons across the whole spectrum of America's opinion-making elite, from George Kennan to Martin Luther King. Arnold Wolfers's important work, *Discord and Collaboration: Essays on International Politics,* contains an introduction by Niebuhr, and Niebuhr's imprimatur was proudly displayed in the advertising for other books, such as *The Moral Issue in Statecraft* by Kenneth Thompson. Niebuhr's view of American history became so influential that one American historian has ranked him in a pantheon that includes Frederick Jackson Turner, Charles Beard, and Richard Hofstadter.[74]

This influence was not confined to intellectuals and academics. When the great popularizer of American internationalism, Henry Luce, in an essay in his own *Life* magazine, called citizens to action on behalf of "the American century," Niebuhr rebuked him for jingoism and "egotistic corruption." Luce recanted in the face of this minister's wrath, but others—like *New York Times* reporter James Reston, who, in his bestseller *The Prelude to Victory,* envisioned an American millennium—continued to preach a global mission. No extremist, not even in the defense of liberty, Niebuhr mistrusted those who would attempt to Americanize the globe through simple missionary fervor. Like Niebuhr, Herbert Butterfield, another Anglo-Atlanticist, preached moderation in defense against aggression. Like Niebuhr, he abhorred the idea of a modern crusade, which he feared would destroy more than it defended. But both Niebuhr and Butterfield believed in action—moderate action.[75]

If Niebuhr was the internationalist movement's chief moral philosopher, another scholar, Hans J. Morgenthau, was its most respected political philosopher. Morgenthau was an academic whose influence grew to the point that Secretaries of Defense cited him in their annual reports to the nation. At Niebuhr's funeral, in 1961 at New York City's Cathedral Church of St. John the Divine, Morgenthau honored his deceased colleague for rediscovering Burckhardt's "political man" and "the tragedy which is inherent in the political act."[76] Both Niebuhr and Morgenthau influenced not only their own generation but the one to follow, as one can quickly discover from the neorealist social science literature that appeared in the 1960's.[77]

Insisting that a distinction existed between the moral behavior of individuals and of social groups, Niebuhr made himself the philosopher of Christian pessimism.[78] Arguing that nations cannot act in a spirit of self-sacrifice, since their governments are trustees for individuals, he held governments exempt from the unselfish standards of conduct set for individuals. This did not mean that no standards applied; it meant only that the standards were different. Niebuhr quoted Hugh Cecil's warning that unselfishness is "inappropriate to the action of a state" because "no one has the right to be unselfish with other people's interests." Updating Alexander Hamilton's precept that "the rule of morality is not precisely the same between nations as between individuals," Niebuhr concluded that "power cannot be wielded without guilt, since it is never transcendent over interest." He wrote: "Our American nation, involved in its vast responsibilities, must slough off many illusions [derived from] the experiences and the ideologies of its childhood. Otherwise either we will seek escape from responsibilities which involve unavoidable guilt, or we will be plunged into avoidable guilt by too great confidence in our virtue."[79]

George Bernard Shaw suggested that the St. Joans who enter politics must sooner or later burn, for religious and political goals make an inflammatory mixture. A saint must be religious while a statesman must be reponsible. In his postwar histories, the old Tory of Blenheim Palace, Winston Churchill, reminded readers that although the Sermon on the Mount may be the touchstone for individual Christian ethics, it is "not on those terms that ministers assume their responsibilities of guiding states."[80] Niebuhr gave American internationalists a philosophical justification to heed these warnings. In practical terms, he gave them much greater license to act. They no longer needed to believe that international goals, by definition, had to embody moral values. Within internationalist circles, an amoral attitude toward international politics became acceptable.

But a problem remained. As members of a policy-making elite that wanted to gain adherents from the next generation, and as opinion-makers who depended on the general public's day-to-day deference to their expertise in conducting the nation's complex national security policy, American internationalists had to find explanations for apparently amoral, or immoral, actions. Here again, Niebuhr provided crucial support. He justified choosing between the lesser of two evils, with only one caveat: there should be some likelihood that the lesser evil could be reformed, to some degree, over a span of time that was appropriate to the task. This, of course, was a condition of choice that the postwar world seemed to possess in abundance. He also said it was defensible to choose between competing just causes, even if this choice would allow representatives of the chosen cause to persecute their competitors (as in Korea, for example). Believing that action was better than nonaction, Niebuhrian internationalists, such as McGeorge Bundy, warned their audiences that "in politics as elsewhere all that is needed for bad men to triumph is for good men to do nothing."[81] Good men had to act, and in acting they could choose between bad, worse, and worst. And therein lay the escape route from cognitive dissonance. Confronted with evidence that many choices made in Vietnam had produced "bad" results, the Niebuhrian disciples could answer that they had prevented the "worst" results, and if within a few years luck granted them some good, better, and best choices, they believed they could tilt the scales toward a Lockean revolution.

Vietnam: Choices, Costs, Confusion

The choices made in Vietnam certainly produced contradictory results. The internationalists shored up an autocrat, Ngo Dinh Diem, while
trying at the same time to install institutions of liberty such as courts of
law. They introduced new agricultural seeds, fertilizers, and pesticides to
Vietnamese farmers only to witness absentee landlords from South Vietnam's urban centers exploit the gains made by the labor of the peasant
majority. They helped displaced Catholic Vietnamese from the North, almost one million of them, to resettle in the South. Later the internationalists watched helplessly while some of these former refugees exploited their
new positions of influence to harm the non-Catholic majority. And after
the Catholics lost their Saigon protector, Ngo Dinh Diem, internationalists watched some Catholics once again become members of a persecuted
minority. Here were the makings of a tragedy. In the beginning both
Catholics and non-Catholics possessed just causes. But helping either
group led to persecution of the other. Helping neither left both in dire
straits. And helping both equally posed insurmountable problems of esti-
mating equality of assistance, particularly given the two groups' different
demands.

Significantly, Vietnam was the scene of the first Lockean struggle with
Leninism in which both camps attempted nation-building in the midst of
real war. (The nation-building competition in the two Koreas, for example, ceased until cold war confrontations replaced hot combat.) In
Vietnam both sides initially thought it would be possible to battle and
build simultaneously. But it was not. The Leninists, who learned this
early, adjusted their efforts accordingly. For example, they instituted land
reform by returning land to the tillers, thus postponing collectivization.
The Lockeans, however, tried to reform a wartime society from top to
bottom. In doing so they became extremists of the kind that even Niebuhr
abhorred. In applying their various Lockean strategies—collective security, limited war, political intervention, and economic containment—the
Lockeans stretched each one to the extreme. But since the assumptions
behind those strategies had no roots in the regional values of Southeast
Asia, the strategies failed.

The chief planning agency for the internationalists was the civilian-
dominated National Security Council, but their major action-agency in
Vietnam was the U.S. Army. In other words, intelligence agents from the
CIA, diplomats from the State Department, and technical planners from
AID employed the U.S. Army. With an Army Colonel coordinating signals with Vietnamese Colonels and Generals for the coup that ended
in the murder of Ngo Dinh Diem; with Army Captains assisting in civic

action programs that brought U.S. military dentists and doctors to village peasants; and with Army Privates forming cordons around hamlets so their inhabitants could be issued identification cards in order to vote, U.S. soldiers found themselves assigned the Lockean restructuring mission. And on these soldiers, the refinements of Abraham Maslow, Leon Festinger, and Reinhold Niebuhr were entirely lost.[82]

We know that this confusion existed because the soldiers themselves left a record of it in their letters, diaries, and novels. One might argue that, in most wars, soldiers cannot be expected to understand the grand design, for they find it difficult enough to know the immediate danger. Even so, it would seem one could expect, at a minimum, that military leaders not be confused. In Vietnam this expectation was not met. When Douglas Kinnard, himself a retired U.S. Army General, interviewed 173 Army general officers who had held command positions in Vietnam between 1965 and 1972, a majority admitted they had been confused about the war. Certainly they had no zeal for nation-building or other civic tasks.[83]

Yet some armies are born with, and maintain in their youth, a revolutionary zeal. Often, along with zeal, comes an organization built for civic tasks. But armies age and organizations change; and armies in their maturity tend to become either praetorian or professional forces.[84] Oliver Cromwell's seventeenth-century New Model Army functioned as a force for revolution; its successor, the British Army of today, has had centuries in which to transform itself into a professional army. Leon Trotsky's Red Army of the 1920's functioned as a force for revolution; its successor, the Soviet Army of today, has had decades in which to transform itself into a praetorian force.

Unluckily, the American Army functioned as a citizen force trying to be a professional army. Although its war chief, Robert McNamara, thought it a fit organization for implementing social change at home and abroad, others doubted its ability to perform such assignments to any level of competence. While the U.S. Army could win many battles for an ally, strategists debated whether it could win a revolution for an ally. Trying to win the Vietnamese revolution for the government of South Vietnam meant the application by the United States of extreme measures.

This extremism took the form of what Isaiah Berlin calls monism, a tendency to assert the "unity or harmony of human ends" in such a manner that "all truly good things are linked to one another in a single, perfect whole; or, at the very least, cannot be incompatible." Berlin's monists, like our internationalists, are lost once they discover an "all-embracing system guaranteed to be eternal," a discovery that encourages the discoverers to become "ruthless fanatics, men possessed by an all-embracing coherent vision."[85] For America in Vietnam, this vision became an international version of Louis Hartz's view of America's domestic extremism—irrational Lockeanism. And internationalism's global vision found its way into the old American tradition of political sermons, jeremiads, this time delivered by a new breed of reformer-turned-extremist. Among many of these visible reformers were those who, like the early puritan settlers, castigated themselves and others once their war-errand, as if by default, went against them.[86]

PART ONE

MILITARY CONSTRAINTS

Dean Rusk, Secretary of State, 1961–69:
"Mr. Rusk readily concedes the right to question the wisdom of collective security and the morality of applying that concept in Vietnam. 'But it still leaves us with a basic question,' he says firmly. 'If we don't believe in collective security, how *do* we prevent World War III?'"

Wall Street Journal, Mar. 11, 1985, p. 14.

Harold Brown, Secretary of the Air Force, 1965–69, Secretary of Defense, 1977–81:
"It is very difficult for the U.S. to sustain a protracted conventional war for interests that aren't obviously vital to the American public." *Wall Street Journal*, Jan. 14, 1985, p. 8.

CHAPTER ONE

The Limits of Collective Combat

THIS CHAPTER WILL examine the postwar development of two key military strategies of American postwar internationalism: collective security and limited war. Along the way, it will also describe the major units of the Washington bureaucracy that implemented them: the Department of Defense (DOD), which came to have primary responsibility for collective security, and the National Security Council (NSC), which became the primary policy instructor in limited-war theory.

Collective Security

Until the mid-twentieth century the idea of collective security never attracted general American support. Since the days of the founding fathers, a haphazard, ad hoc activism under unilateralist principles had allowed national leaders to muddle through in international politics; and the few who infrequently raised security issues appeared generally satisfied. To be sure, the United States had allied itself with certain combatant states in both world wars, but it had always been the latecomer, and had viewed these alliances as temporary departures from the norm, much as Pitt's England had viewed its coalitions against Napoleon's France.

This attitude changed near mid-century, when American leaders decided that they required a "strategy in the missile age."[1] In April 1949 they signed, and their Senate ratified, the North Atlantic Treaty, a document that involved the United States in its first entangling alliance of modern times. It was no coincidence that in August of that year the Soviet Union first successfully tested an atomic bomb. In fact, the probability of such a Soviet test had dominated internationalist concerns since the breakup of the wartime coalition.[2] That Soviet science was catching up with them had shocked the Lockeans in Washington almost as much as the earlier American nuclear success had depressed the Leninists in Moscow.

As they began to face what one German philosopher called "the new fact," the leadership on both sides decided to create collective security systems.[3] Americans soon discovered that a multinational security system strains the patience of all. If installed by the force of the strongest member, it tests even that member's patience.[4] If collaborative, by the nature of the shared sense of community membership it is even more likely to exasperate the most powerful member. While pleading for support for collective security, Robert McNamara warned his colleagues of this fact: "Even where these states subscribe in principle to the policy of collective security, we should not expect that there will always be unanimity as to how and by whom that policy should be implemented in any particular situation."[5] In the two halves of postwar Europe, only the new superpowers—the United States and the USSR—had the power to exercise hegemony. There are two interpretations of how they obtained that power. In essence, each superpower either installed a system by force of arms or joined one that expressed existing community ties.

In the first interpretation, there was no preexisting Atlantic community, and no corresponding Soviet community in Eastern Europe. Instead, two victors emerged from World War II, each with the opportunity to make an old-fashioned grab for empire. The two giants were old twentieth-century antagonists, having been only allies-of-convenience during hostilities. Each had won a victory in a segment of both World War II theaters—Europe and Asia. The geographic winnings of each were the terrain nearest its own domain, winnings that were consolidated by armies of occupation. In this interpretation Americans took the best geographic prizes—Western Germany and all of Japan. U.S. leaders organized their global gains around these two former industrial giants after finding it impossible to organize them around preferred allies—the United Kingdom, France, and Chiang Kai-shek's China. In Europe the concept of Atlanticism was a mere camouflage for a German-American military alliance against the Soviet Union. In the Pacific no camouflage could disguise the unilaterally imposed Japanese peace treaty and the U.S.-Japanese military alliance, both blatantly anti-Russian. In like manner, the Soviet Union had invested its World War II real-estate winnings not in a community but in a military alliance that was overtly anti-American.

Those who hold to this first interpretation believe that two armed camps faced each other, each hostile to any gains by its adversary. Only the balance of nuclear terror preserved the peace. Hence it followed that nuclear weapons played a positive as well as a negative role. If the mere existence of nuclear arsenals prevented a third world war, then such weapons were worth the price—the danger that in a tense situation, a misjudgment might someday lead to their use. Thus the leadership of the Atlantic alliance could tolerate a public bemoaning of nuclear weapons while at the same time privately admitting that the West's lead in nuclear technology made it unnecessary to rely on the more expensive alternative—large standing armies.[6] From this interpretation, it could be argued that American internationalists made their North Atlantic strategy work by successfully maintaining a Janus-faced posture for over a quarter of a century.

Many internationalists, however, rejected this sort of realpolitik. They preferred to see the NATO countries as united not primarily by tanks, destroyers, and jet fighters but by shared values. Thus Henry Cabot Lodge argued that he was converted to the cause of collective security because "the Soviet Union, under Stalin, shared neither the basic tenets of the Atlantic community nor our vision of the United Nations." Lodge's active service to the cause included his joining Canada's Lester Pearson, Belgium's Paul Henri Spaak, France's Raymond Aron, and Harvard's President James Conant in heading the communities' Atlantic Institute in Paris, an institution whose North American cousin, the Atlantic Council, has listed among its members the most important American internationalists of the postwar period.[7] Through the pages of its journal, *The Atlantic Quarterly*, the Council has kept the community torch burning on the American side of the ocean. Even in Turkey, NATO's outpost on the Black Sea, Atlanticism was celebrated as late as the 1980's by small teams of lecturers who visited the villages of Anatolia.

President John Kennedy surpassed Ambassador Lodge in the passion of his appeals to a sense of community. In 1963, he flew to Germany, on the eastern rim of the Atlantic basin. "I have crossed the Atlantic, some 3,500 miles, at a crucial time in the life of the Grand Alliance," he told a crowd at the Bonn airport. He insisted that Atlantic unity, "forged in a time of danger . . . must be maintained in a time of peace," because "economically, militarily, politically, our two nations and all the other nations of the Alliance are now dependent on one another." He reminded his audience that "your liberty is our liberty; and any attack on your soil is an attack upon our own." He admitted that this was so "out of necessity," but then quickly added "as well as sentiment," maintaining that "in our approach to peace as well as war, our fortunes are one."[8] Two days later in a Frankfurt church, birthplace of the first German Assembly, Kennedy added that it was "not in [the U.S.] interest to try to dominate the European councils of decision." He said the United States looked forward to "a Europe united and strong, speaking with a common voice, acting with a common will, a world power capable of meeting world problems as a full and equal partner."[9] The President carried this theme to Italy and Britain, and finally gave a European television address in which he stressed the importance of the Atlantic community.

Although both Lodge and Kennedy insisted that an Atlantic community of interests existed, they did not define its exact boundaries. In fact, its fuzzy perimeter looks probably more like a cultural trace than a line on a cartographer's map. One might attempt to locate it by dispatching four surveyors, by land and sea, to the north, east, west, and south of Greenwich in Britain. When they all reached cities where no libraries contained the works of John Locke, where no citizens had ever heard of him, and where no legal or political institutions reflected his influence, they would know that they had just crossed the invisible frontier of Atlanticism. By repeating the trip several times, each time traveling on a different azimuth, the four surveyors could draw a rough outline of the community's frontier, behind which was housed a time-honored Atlantic republican tradition. Nevertheless, with or without such an outline, not everyone agreed with Kennedy and Lodge. Some saw fantasies, others saw darker motives—de Gaulle telling Roosevelt that Atlanticism represented nothing more than America's "will to power . . . cloaked in idealism." Whether fantasy or will to power, we know that "if men define situations as real, they are real in their consequences." And in that sense, for American internationalists in the 1950's and 1960's, Atlanticism was indeed real.[10]

A more scholarly concept of the Atlantic community can be found in studies of comparative civic cultures. This definition grants that the nations of the Atlantic basin possess a variety of civic cultures, which differ considerably in their political dimensions. Yet it claims that all have a fundamental similarity: all try to adhere to Lockean-like principles concerning the rights of individuals and the proper role and scope of government. In the 1830's Alexis de Tocqueville discovered several Lockean principles at work in the first new Atlantic nation, the United States. In his discussion of *moeurs*—"the sum of the moral and intellectual disposition of men in society . . . the habits of heart . . . (and) the sum of ideas that shape mental habits"—he awakened the Atlantic world to what became, over the next hundred years, an Atlantic political culture.[11] At least American internationalists came to think that this was so.

Yet in the 1960's, when the authors of an ambitious multivolume study of comparative political culture began to examine nations beyond the Atlantic basin, they found almost no evidence of regional communities cohering around shared political cultures.[12] Nowhere was this clearer than in their study of developing areas. Compared with the citizens of West Germany, Italy, the United States, and Britain, the peoples of Thailand, Indochina, Malaysia, and the Philippines had no sense whatever of regional community. One possible explanation for this lack is that the values of various national groups may converge as the structures of their societies become more alike. For example, industrial societies grow to value smaller families and more years of formal education, whereas nonindustrial societies do not. Nor do nonindustrial societies have values that might encourage their societies to converge with neighboring states. The pragmatic preferences of industrialism, while originating in the structure of developed society, also help to make possible a transnational community. Some European scholars share this theory of convergence and apply it to the Atlantic alliance. For another means of stating the convergence hypothesis, one could turn to a theory of collective behavior. Thus it has been suggested that "the democratic countries of northwestern Europe and North America have institutionalized—with varying degrees of finality—this principle of differentiation under formulae such as 'separation of church and state,' 'civil control of military power,' 'separation of church and school,' 'academic freedom,' 'freedom of expression,' etc." This is another way of describing transnational values that converge in a regional civic community.[13]

The internationalists, however, assumed that the sense of community they found in the North Atlantic basin could be replicated in other regions—in fact, anywhere in the world. Flushed with their success with NATO, they designed an arc of collective security treaties around the Soviet land empire. And within each signatory nation they expected to establish a sense of shared regional values that would make citizens willing to fight in defense of a transnational community. By the beginning of the Kennedy-Johnson years, the ideal of collective security on a multilateral basis had swept aside old unilateralist principles. Some American allies—Japan, for example—had to settle for a bilateral association with the United States, and internationalists accepted that as a second best to a regional association. This was a necessary compromise for Japan because its postwar Asian neighbors still viewed it as the aggressor in World War II. Therefore with Japan, as with Southeast Asia, internationalists found it difficult to create a Pacific community, at least one in which the United States also could hold joint membership. (The cultural difficulties to be expected were made clear in Ruth Benedict's *The Chrysanthemum and the Sword*, the product of research commissioned by early defense internationalists in order to educate themselves about the relatively unknown culture they were about to conquer in 1945.) But Japan, unlike the states of Southeast Asia, had an advanced industrial economy, and economic institutions that in many ways reflected American models. But since it did not share North America's and Western Europe's sense of cultural community, Japan had to rely largely on its sense of similar economic institutions to sustain the special relationship with the United States. And Japan did sustain it, thereby underwriting a shared self-interest in the power structure of the North Pacific basin.

Nevertheless, the 1950's and 1960's remained Eurocentric decades for American internationalists. Only after they had lost the war in Vietnam did they discover the Pacific basin. And then it was Asian internationalists, mainly Japanese, who instructed Americans about the region. For example, when the Asian Club, headquartered in Tokyo, decided to publish a quarterly journal dedicated to basin problems, they chose as its title *Asia Pacific Community*, modeling it on the Atlantic Council's journal, *The Atlantic Quarterly*. By 1985 Pacific basin citizens from the Asian crescent were fond of quoting President McKinley's Secretary of State, John Hay, that "the Mediterranean is the ocean of the past, the Atlantic Ocean of the present, but the Pacific is the ocean of the future."[14]

When the shock waves of the 1960's roiled that ocean of the future, it was mainly NATO and the Japanese pact that survived. In the 1980's former Secretary of Defense Harold Brown wrote, "For more than thirty years, the basic U.S. approach to security has been a collective, coalition approach." Brown suggested that some of the formal alliances, like NATO and the one with Japan, "have proven durable," while others, like SEATO, "though valuable in their time" have not survived the shocks of global strife.[15] By the end of the Kennedy-Johnson years the gravest shocks to collective security pacts came from the Vietnam war.

A Super Secretary for Collective Defense

During this period of strain, Robert S. McNamara, the cabinet man some called the "super Secretary," tried to block any unraveling of mutual commitments. In 1968, the year in which the Tet offensive occurred, he published *The Essence of Security*, in which he warned that "the new international situation is far too complicated and threatening for abandonment of collective defense."[16] In McNamara's view, the principle of collective defense had to be defended by an effort in Vietnam. And he believed he could direct such an effort. After all, he had experience in managing the world's largest organization, the U.S. Department of Defense. During his tenure as Secretary he had brought that supposedly unmanageable giant under the discipline of the managerial revolution.[17] He vigorously employed the power granted his office by the reorganization legislation of 1953 and 1958. That of 1953 had created a strong Chairman of the Joint Chiefs of Staff, a single and senior military voice; the 1958 legislation empowered the Secretary to combine units of all services into commands that reported to him.

Armed with these powers, McNamara quickly dispossessed the military leaders of their roles "within the Pentagon in management and strategic planning" and gave those roles to civilian analysts.[18] Together they lost the best-managed war ever fought by a great power. But before McNamara lost that external struggle, he did win the internal one. He indirectly merged the three services by assigning all combat forces to unified or specified commands. Thus "by the end of 1961, with the creation of STRIKE Command, virtually all combat forces had been assigned to unified and specified commands who report directly to the secretary through the JCS."[19] In the beginning, McNamara designed the defense of Vietnam to be carried out through one existing command, the Pacific Command based in Hawaii. Before long, deciding that even this arrangement was too cumbersome, he bypassed Hawaii and dealt directly with his Vietnam representatives at the Military Assistance Command Vietnam (MACV). Because of the preponderance of land forces committed, MACV, though officially a joint command of the three services, was always commanded by an Army General. The Army Generals, however, wanted to avoid the sort of feuding that General MacArthur had engaged in during World War II with the U.S. Navy—which, in military terms, had "owned" the Pacific in the way that the Army "owned" Europe. Seeing McNamara's action as a breach of military etiquette, the various Army Generals who at one time or another commanded MACV—notably Paul Harkins, William Westmoreland, and Creighton Abrams—tried to soothe the feelings of their nominal Navy bosses in Hawaii, Admiral Harry Felt and, later, Admiral U. S. Grant Sharp. These Admirals therefore saved their rancor for McNamara alone.[20]

Rampaging over traditions, particularly command traditions, caused only part of the anger that military leaders aimed at their "whiz kid" boss. To the military, stealing their budget prerogatives was an even more heinous crime. McNamara had done this by creating his program budget, a budget that required marginal-utility analysis, or cost analysis. In the words of one observer, "Whoever makes the analysis gains enormous, if not virtually complete, authority over future DOD . . . programs as well as budgets."[21]

No one had to guess who that "whoever" was; from 1961 to 1965 it was Charles Hitch, McNamara's own Assistant Secretary of Defense–Comptroller. A previous RAND Corporation economist, Hitch had made known as early as 1960 what management devices he would be likely to employ; and McNamara allowed him to father the Planning-Programming-Budgeting System used in McNamara's Pentagon.[22] Program-budgeting mattered greatly, not only to the prerogatives of the entrenched military but to the four basic strategies of internationalism. As one scholar of budgetary politics has noted, the procedures of program-budgeting "have important consequences for our defense policies."[23] In creating his defense technocracy, McNamara gave internationalists what Tocqueville called "administrative despotism."

An illustration of McNamara's budget power is worth giving here. In 1962 McNamara convinced Kennedy that one of the U.S. Air Force's major strategic weapons, the Skybolt missile, should be canceled. Although Alain Enthoven and his colleagues made a persuasive case against the Skybolt missile as an unnecessary weapon that the U.S. Air Force wanted mainly to extend the usefulness of manned bombers, the fact remains that its cancellation caused heavy political damage to Atlanticism, in the following manner. Aware that British leaders had based their strategic plans on buying this weapon, both McNamara and Kennedy tried to assuage Prime Minister Harold Macmillan with an offer to sell the British Polaris missiles in lieu of the canceled Skybolt. Macmillan found himself forced to accept this American offer. In response, Charles de Gaulle, enraged by what he considered Britain's constant deference to the United States, vetoed Britain's application for membership in the Common Market. The French President decided that Britain wanted to be treated like a permanently anchored, offshore American aircraft and missile platform.[24] McNamara had had his way, but so had de Gaulle. And while disturbing the Atlantic community, de Gaulle was also disturbing the collective security arrangements within SEATO, of which France was a chartered member. Ambassador Henry Cabot Lodge's cables from his Saigon embassy rang with denouncements of Fifth Republic meddling.[25] In the 1950's internationalists had hoped that having France in both NATO and SEATO would help bring stability to Europe and Asia; but in the 1960's de Gaulle had created his own definition of stability.

McNamara, however, who found little free time within his Pentagon world, allowed others to deal with de Gaulle. With his Assistant Secretary of Defense–Comptroller telling him what funds were available, with his Assistant Secretary of Defense–Systems Analyst telling him which of the many possible weapon systems to buy with said funds, with his Assistant Secretary of Defense–International Security Affairs telling him where to place these systems internationally, and with his Director of Research and Engineering showing him how to improve these weapon systems within the collective defense effort, McNamara had lots of internationalist advice to process. When he lost one top assistant, Charles Hitch, he could replace him with what appeared to be a brilliant interchangeable part—Robert N. Anthony, a former Harvard Business School professor who, like Hitch, also had prewritten his management formula in book form.[26] Thus the McNamara machine kept on designing.

McNamara's four key assistants designed various collective security systems for him to use specifically in Vietnam. One such defensive plan required sensors associated with a barrier system—dubbed the McNamara Line. Basically this consisted of an electronic battle line composed of acoustic and seismic devices (ACOUBUOY's, ADSID's, ACOUSID's, etc.) that would allow Allied weapons to engage identified enemy targets crossing into South Vietnam.[27] The idea was that Allied troops would defend in depth behind the barrier, allowing time for the South Vietnamese to deal with their internal rebels. Since internationalists in McNamara's Defense Communications Planning Group (DCPG) convinced him that the major problem in defending South Vietnam was to prevent infiltration from the North, isolating the South was seen as the solution. But strategists who followed MacArthur tried in vain to replicate his World War II success with island isolation. Certainly they failed to repeat it on two peninsulas, Korea and Indochina.[28] The McNamara Line in South Vietnam proved an even costlier mistake than the attempt to isolate the battlefield of South Korea. A state can isolate an island if its navy can dominate the surrounding sea, but an air force cannot isolate a connected land formation by dominating the surrounding air space. Persuasive air-power enthusiasts, however, persuaded the aging MacArthur to try in Korea, much to his undoing. A decade later air strategists convinced McNamara and President Johnson, and with similar results. Both peninsular wars indicated that only ground troops can win a ground war; high technology weapons may help, but they cannot do the whole job.

An Obsolete Inheritance: NSC-68

The McNamara Line failed largely because of the obsolete strategy behind it. The strategic culprit was a National Security Council document, NSC-68. Drafted in 1950, not by the NSC staff but by an ad hoc group of state and defense officials headed by Paul Nitze, it presented a sweeping conception of Lockean defense against all Leninist incursions that left little room for maneuver.[29] Standing or falling everywhere at once would have taxed Ciceronian Rome, let alone the American republic of the 1960's. But they, the Lockean internationalists, tried. They failed to understand that NSC-68's purpose was to rearm the United States in 1950, nothing more and nothing less.

Watching over the attempt in Vietnam to prove the wisdom of the document that he had "spearheaded" through the bureaucracy was Paul Nitze.[30] He served McNamara as Assistant Secretary of Defense for International Security Affairs from 1961 to 1963, when he resigned to accept the job of Secretary of the Navy. Resigning that post in 1967, he succeeded Cyrus Vance as Deputy Secretary of Defense. Among internationalists,

Nitze is the quintessential survivor, having served not only Truman, Kennedy, and Johnson, but also Eisenhower, Nixon, and Reagan. Nitze does not neatly fit any category. One can perhaps best discover the strategist behind the public figure in three of his published interviews. In one of them he suggests that "the origin of NSC-68 was the Russian explosion of the nuclear device in the fall of 1949." Nitze suggests also that his handiwork "involved a much broader approach than merely increasing our nuclear capability."[31]

One might assume that by "broader approach" Nitze meant he would have advised the many Presidents he served to hold the Leninists to their gains as of 1950, militarily constraining them through collective security pacts. One would certainly assume that Nitze survived the 1960's as the "hawk's hawk" on Vietnam. But Nitze denies it. Although he concurred with plans to interdict the flow of military supplies coming from the North to the South, especially those coming via the sea lanes, he insists that he was "very much opposed to getting ourselves that deeply involved in Vietnam."[32] Surprisingly, Nitze was a minimalist when it came to Vietnam affairs, less rigid than those who were disposed to treat NSC-68 as strategic writ.

Nitze's Navy aide, Captain Elmo Zumwalt, confirms that among Kennedy-Johnson appointees his boss was a "dove" in the sense that he "opposed massive American intervention on the ground in southeast Asia."[33] By 1968 and Tet, this Navy Captain had become an Admiral, the senior Admiral on the joint Military Assistance Command Vietnam headquarters staff. Following twelve months of Saigon duty, Zumwalt completed his active naval service as the Chief of Naval Operations (CNO), the senior U.S. Navy billet.

Perhaps it was obvious from the start that Secretary of the Navy Nitze and his aide, the Admiral-to-be, would follow in the tradition of American navalists. Command of the seas ranked first with Zumwalt because of training in a very old tradition, but Nitze possessed a sophistication that blocked parochial interests. Although a product of State Department training—he served in the 1940's in the arena of economic containment, first as Deputy Director of the Office of International Trade Policy and then as Deputy to the Assistant Secretary of State for Economic Affairs—Nitze trained himself to be a military expert, and concluded his career as a specialist in nuclear arms control.[34] And although he was perhaps prejudiced in favor of the military aspects of containment, Nitze understood the usefulness of political and economic weapons as well. Like his contemporaries George Kennan and Clark Clifford, he saw all three constraints as the means of forging collective security measures with other states. Yet simultaneously, while these three men were working for President Truman on collective security arrangements, they had to consider ways to avoid having these arrangements lead to an unlimited war.

Limited-War Theory

If collective security as a global chart for the pilots of American state-craft proved difficult to follow, limited-war theory almost shipwrecked the lot, for it clashed with traditional attitudes. Americans were slow to anger, but once aroused they were quick to demand unconditional surrender, a total victory. And in past conflicts the nation, often in a war frenzy, had appeared willing to risk everything for that victory.

It was no less a personage than General of the Army Douglas MacArthur who tested this American lack of patience with compromise. On March 20, 1951, in the midst of commanding all United Nations forces fighting in Korea, he wrote a letter to Congressman Joe Martin that concluded, "There is no substitute for victory"—a line that became the war chant of all those who resisted changing the venerable American way of war.[35] After Martin read the letter aloud to his fellow congressmen, the American public, which usually deferred to experts, joined the great debate over how to change the conditions under which Americans would fight.

Change came slowly at first but gained momentum as more opinion-makers contemplated nuclear war. Beginning with Bernard Brodie, who published *The Absolute Weapon: Atomic Power and World Order* in 1946, civilian strategists began to suggest the acceptability of conditional surrender and of fighting for limited-war goals. During the 1950's other academic internationalists came out in favor of reducing American ambitions in any future combat.[36]

Many Americans, including MacArthur, believed that accepting anything less than victory was appeasement.[37] But others, many of them influenced by Reinhold Niebuhr, had second thoughts. Since Niebuhr suggested that individuals possessed limited rationality and that "nations are too selfish and morally too obtuse and self-righteous to make the attainment of international justice without the use of force possible," perhaps whatever force was applied should be only such force as was necessary for minimum purposes.[38] In other words, Niebuhrians generally were minimalists, seldom maximalists.

Dean Acheson, the trainer of many internationalists, quoted Niebuhr's statement that "there is always an element of moral ambiguity in historic responsibilities." He approved of Niebuhr's warning that "our survival as a civilization depends upon our ability to do what seems right from day to day without . . . alternate moments of illusion and despair."[39] With

President Truman preparing to leave the White House, the Democratic shadow President, Adlai Stevenson, recalled to Niebuhr his Potomac popularity, writing to him in 1952, "Just the other day I was talking about you with one of your myriad admirers in Washington."[40] Those admirers were scattered throughout the national security organizations, especially the Defense Department and the National Security Council.

If the Defense Department had a difficult mission in managing collective security, the National Security Council had twice as much trouble supervising the design of limited-war actions. In the beginning, this supervision meant housing internationalists as they battled with unilateralists. Internationalists began to win in 1952, when Truman relieved MacArthur of his command in Korea. MacArthur was America's Cromwell in Asia, and with his triumphant return, the policy-making battlefield switched from Korea to the chambers of the Armed Services and Foreign Relations Committees. In testimony before these committees two other "old soldiers," Generals of the Army George C. Marshall and Omar N. Bradley, supported the internationalists' position. By the manner in which he questioned them, Senator William Fulbright helped focus the attention of Americans on the complexities of limited war. He obtained from Marshall an admission that the unconditional surrender of Germany and Japan in World War II had not led to satisfactory results.[41] Although less loquacious than Marshall in his testimony, Bradley provided the more famous quote. Citing the Joint Chiefs of Staff (JCS) as his source, he told Congress that MacArthur's strategy "would involve us in the wrong war, at the wrong place, at the wrong time, and with the wrong enemy."[42]

The first National Security Council, Truman's, nevertheless remained aloof from this feud, largely because the antagonists represented the American military titans from World War II, but also because initially Truman mistrusted the NSC, seeing in it two threats, one presidential and the other personal. First, Truman feared a possible denigration of the power of the presidency; second, he feared a possible denigration of himself as an accidental chief supervisor of the covenant. He had the same task as the early Roman consul Fabius Maximus Cunctator, who had to contain the forces of the Roman Republic's enemy, Hannibal, by a cautious, defensive strategy. But even as Fabius had surprised Rome by taking charge of Roman statecraft, so Truman surprised Washington by taking charge of the NSC. Initially, others in Washington, especially Secretary of Defense James Forrestal, envisioned the NSC as an organization dominated by the Defense Department and charged with coordinating security policies. But other Washingtonians, especially Secretary of State George Marshall, were determined that this Defense Department domination should not come about. Marshall succeeded at blocking Forrestal. Truman watched and supervised their struggle, but bided his time.[43]

Truman did so because he planned a different solution. James B. Webb, his Director of the Bureau of the Budget, had suggested that Truman should make the NSC serve as a "further enlargement of the Presidential staff," thus eliminating the possibility of domination by either the State Department or the Defense Department. Truman accepted this advice and appointed Admiral Sidney W. Souers as the first executive secretary of the NSC. To mark his territory as distinct from that of his cabinet barons, Truman also housed the NSC secretariat in the Executive Office Building.[44] By such measures Souers and his staff became presidential retainers.

Souers possessed several qualities that appealed to Truman and therefore reduced his suspicions of the NSC. To begin with, Souers had been Truman's successful Director of the Central Intelligence Group (CIG), the organization that spanned the time from the demise of the wartime Office of Strategic Services (OSS) to the birth of the peacetime Central Intelligence Agency (CIA). Next, Souers counted among his Potomac River friends many men of influence—notably Special Assistant to the President Clark Clifford, Admiral William Leahy, and Secretary James Forrestal. Also reassuring was the fact that, prior to active military service, Souers had been a pillar of the Democratic party in St. Louis. But his greatest attribute, surrounded as he was by powerful personalities demanding larger fiefdoms, was a self-effacing style. Aware of this delicate situation, Souers insisted that the executive secretary of the NSC "must be willing to forgo publicity and personal aggrandizement."[45]

With Souers in place Truman allowed the NSC to make recommendations to him, but avoided attending many of their meetings. Then suddenly in 1950 the first postwar Asian-rim struggle began. With his police action in Korea to supervise, Truman ordered the NSC senior staff to meet weekly, with himself often presiding. He also asked each nonstatutory member of the NSC—the heads of the Treasury, the JCS, and the CIA—to nominate an individual from his organization to join the NSC senior staff. With Clifford leaving the White House to join a Washington law firm, it was the new Presidential Special Assistant, Averell Harriman, and the enlarged NSC senior staff who became Truman's assistants in designing and supervising America's first limited war in the twentieth century. And the Korean example served as a model for later NSC staffs as they struggled to limit the Vietnam war. But before that later war began, the Eisenhower administration had to accept the NSC and to dedicate itself to limited-war theory, a thorny issue for some Republicans.

Only slowly did the NSC of Eisenhower's two administrations begin implementing any of the key internationalist beliefs. Since Eisenhower himself had converted to internationalism, the White House remained a safe preserve. Secretary of State John Foster Dulles, however, seemed to his critics to pose a real threat to the internationalist preference for limited-war strategy. When Dulles talked loosely about a "rollback" in Eastern Europe, some were shocked; any liberation there would have meant engaging the nuclear-armed Leninist Army. But such loose talk remained only talk. In fact, Dulles professed a type of Niebuhrian Christian pessimism when among other internationalists, people who knew better than to take his public preaching seriously. In addressing the Commission on a Just and Durable Peace, Dulles said that "to secure unity, it may be necessary to compromise ideals." However, he also offered a possible way around this dilemma: "On the other hand, it may be possible to maintain ideals but only at the expense of the division of the world into spheres of influence."[46] Though Dulles disliked accepting spheres of influence, the Leninists gave him no other reasonable option.

Even when Dulles approved the old American maxim of "all or nothing," rechristened as "massive retaliation," internationalists watched him distance himself from his own creation. Paul Nitze was in the audience for Dulles's 1954 speech at the Council on Foreign Relations, whose fashionable Manhattan offices offered a Hudson River cure for Potomac River fever. Sitting at a table near the Secretary of State, Nitze recalls how he and other internationalists "were all immediately shocked by the extreme reliance that Mr. Dulles was proposing to put upon massive retaliation." Not one to remain silent when shocked, Nitze "immediately sat down and wrote a paper on this and took it to Bob Bowie, who was then the Director of the Policy Planning Staff."[47] Nitze claims that Bowie "took this up with Mr. Dulles, and Mr. Dulles himself was somewhat concerned about the extreme position he had taken in that 1954 speech." Indeed, Dulles later published an article in the Council's *Foreign Affairs* in which he retreated somewhat from his primary reliance on massive retaliation.[48]

During the time Dulles was shocking the internationalists, the staff of the National Security Council had begun to learn its job. Complaining publicly that in national security policy-making the Truman administration had "failed to bring into line its crisscrossing and overlapping, and jealous departments and bureaus and agencies," Eisenhower commanded his political soldiers to bring order out of chaos.[49] To accomplish this, he made Robert Cutler the first Special Assistant for National Security Affairs. Cutler and his successor Gordon Gray were the predecessors of Kennedy's McGeorge Bundy and Walt Rostow, Rostow following Bundy as Johnson's National Security Adviser.

Under Eisenhower the NSC came to consist of two major boards, the Planning Board and the Operations Coordinating Board. The latter was

Eisenhower's contribution. The Special Assistant for National Security Affairs presided over the Planning Board, the unit that examined policy recommendations, attempted to resolve differences, and prepared policy papers. The Operations Coordinating Board, according to Robert Cutler, helped "to coordinate, to 'ride herd on,' and report to the council on the performance by the departments and agencies charged with responsibility to carry out national-security policies approved by the President."[50]

Initially this latter board had as its chairman the Under Secretary of State. But by 1960 Eisenhower decided that State Department officials, then under Secretary of State Christian Herter's leadership, might have been less than fair to the other NSC participants. Ike therefore made his last National Security Adviser, Gordon Gray, chairman of both boards. Presidents Kennedy and Johnson inherited the Eisenhower organization. Although some critics have censured the General for applying a military staff system to national security policy-making, not all have concurred with this censure. Beginning in the last year of Lyndon Johnson's presidency, the Institute for Defense Analysis, an independent Washington research center, made a major team effort to document the history of the NSC from Truman to Tet. Their research suggests that Eisenhower was more flexible than previously supposed, and had gone so far as to use a select group of advisers for specific and important problems. In other words, Kennedy's much-noted executive committees had in fact been an Eisenhower creation.[51]

Besides identifying Eisenhower's innovative use of the NSC, the Institute for Defense Analysis study also recognized the NSC as the critical new organ of the national security state. So had Senator Henry Jackson. In the latter years of the Eisenhower administration, Jackson's senate subcommittee held hearings concerning the NSC. This subcommittee's 1961 report came at a propitious time; Kennedy's people drew on it in their reorganization of the NSC. In fact, McGeorge Bundy told Jackson's subcommittee that the new team intended to eliminate "the distinction between planning and operations that governed the administrative structure of the NSC staff."[52] And in February 1961, by executive order, President Kennedy abolished the Operations Coordinating Board.

These moves did not bode well for the adoption of carefully considered policies. But action, not reflection, marked the Kennedy-Johnson NSC, especially in policies dealing with Vietnam. And as Vietnam policies soured, the streamlined NSC, by then a model of what the military in the 1960's called a "lean and mean" organization, cracked the presidential whip. It was only then that outgoing State Department cables dealing with "important" matters had to come to the White House for clearance before dispatch. There would be no loose ship for the presidential sailor from Hyannisport. But even on a tight ship, standing watch over any limited war required a highly skilled crew—capable of exerting a maximum effort for minimalist goals.[53] If an American Lockean allowed an incident with an Asian Leninist to escalate into nuclear war, of what importance were the three remaining strategies of internationalism? Careful consideration would help, but it was in short supply. There were plenty of competent technicians available, and both Kennedy and Johnson spent lavishly on them and their solutions. The real problems, however, proved resistant to technical solutions, for they posed questions of political judgment that could never be answered with certainty.

For key NSC members such as Walt Rostow, the problem of limiting the Vietnam war resembled the earlier problem of limiting the Korean conflict.[54] In that first Asian test, the theorists had believed that keeping Stalin's Russia and Mao's China out of the Korean conflict had ranked as priorities one and two. Obviously someone had succeeded with the first, but failed with the second. Why? Conventional wisdom had it that Mao's China came into the conflict only because of MacArthur's march to the Yalu River, Mao's industrial border with North Korea. But how far into the middle of the Korean peninsula would the Chinese Leninists have tolerated an advance by the United Nations? That is a difficult question.

Would China have intervened if United Nations forces had stopped on October 7, 1950, after driving the invading North Koreans back across the old boundary, the 38th parallel? Probably not; there is no evidence that Chinese forces had crossed the Yalu by that date. Would China have intervened if the U.N. forces had obtained a more defensible border slightly north of this parallel, something they did by October 10? That remains unknown; but again, Chinese forces remained on their own territory when the U.N. forces crossed that line. Would China have intervened if the U.N. forces had stopped after capturing the North Korean capital of Pyongyang? Here the problem becomes more complex. The U.N. forces captured Pyongyang on October 19, but Mao had secretly dispatched his first volunteers on October 16. In other words, some Chinese troops were in North Korea by the time its capital fell.[55] But they were not yet fighting against U.N. forces.

Above Pyongyang the Korean peninsula narrows, affording a defender the shortest front possible. Would Mao, China's Lenin, have allowed even that front to fall to the U.N. forces without striking? How would Mao know the limits of that fateful move by U.N. forces to the narrow front above Pyongyang, what with the Yalu and Tumen Rivers the next available U.N. defensive—or worse yet, U.N. offensive—line?[56] Perhaps the most a Niebuhrian minimalist would contemplate was taking Pyongyang; the least, regaining the old boundary. But MacArthur was not a Niebuhrian, maximalist or minimalist.

Within the Kennedy-Johnson national security apparatus, Allen Whiting had asked and answered many of these questions about Korea, and he began to ask the same questions about Vietnam. Whiting wanted to know what sort of action would force Mao's People's Liberation Army to cross China's southern agrarian border to help defend their sometime client, North Vietnam.[57] Would an incursion into Cambodian sanctuaries force it? What about cutting the Ho Chi Minh Trail in Laos? Bombing the North, mining its harbors, arming the Meo tribesmen in northern Laos? As it turned out, none of these actions impelled China to intervene with major military forces.

General Bruce Palmer, at one time Westmoreland's deputy and subsequently the Army Vice Chief of Staff, later suggested that it would have been best to defend behind the DMZ on a line that ran through Laos. Would this have forced the Chinese into the fray? Palmer suggested also that U.S. leaders erred in assuring Ho Chi Minh that the United States would not attack North Vietnam with ground troops, arguing that ambiguity on the matter would have better served U.S. interests. But would forcing North Vietnam into keeping a large strategic reserve at home have caused the Chinese to intervene? Finally, Palmer suggests that all that was needed was a "constantly visible and credible amphibious presence off the coast of North Vietnam." But would that have forced China's hand? Walt Rostow and William Westmoreland at one time suggested that Washington and Saigon emulate MacArthur at Inchon and land in North Vietnam at Vinh.[58] Such a plan would have taken the war into the North, at the same time keeping it out of North Vietnam's Red River Delta—even maximalists thought a move into this region would invite a reprise of MacArthur's disaster at Korea's Yalu River. This plan the minimalist Niebuhrians succeeded in rejecting. For the remainder of the war, however, they worried. Where were the limits?

CHAPTER TWO

Collective Security: One for All and All for One

WHILE WORRYING ABOUT limiting local wars, internationalists had to work on building and maintaining an American consensus in favor of collective security treaties. In making their case, the internationalists argued from a central theme, namely, that the failure of Allied nations to organize effective collective security was what had allowed Germany, Italy, and Japan to launch the last great war. By the Eisenhower years internationalists had succeeded in establishing the North Atlantic Treaty Organization (NATO), the Central Treaty Organization (CENTO), the Southeast Asia Treaty Organization (SEATO), and the Australia–New Zealand–United States (ANZUS) treaty.[1] The geographic limits of each of these American-sponsored pacts were intended to abut against those of neighboring pacts, so that a global arc would be formed around the last European land empire, the Soviet Union. However, because of the enormous geographic and cultural differences along an arc that stretched from Norway through Turkey to Korea, there were bound to be some gaps in coverage. These the internationalists tried to fill in various ways: with the bilateral agreement with Taiwan, for example, and the congressional resolution dealing with Israel.

The internationalists gained a noteworthy diplomatic success by convincing the United Nations to condemn the North Korean attack of June 25, 1950, as an act of aggression. Building on this success, the United Nations created a military command in South Korea and approved the appointment of an American, General Douglas MacArthur, to command U.N. forces in the Northeast Asian Pacific basin rim. Of critical importance were the United Nations' Security Council Resolution of June 27, 1950, and the later General Assembly Resolution of October 7, 1950, which, by condemning North Korean aggression and calling for a collective response, reinforced American internationalists in their strong commitment to an activist internationalism.[2] By 1953, the last year of the Korean

War, many Americans were angrily questioning whether its costs were justified, or equitably shared. (Within the U.N. forces, U.S. and South Korean troops had done most of the fighting, and the United States had met most of the debt payment.) But the internationalist consensus survived this debate without major damage, in part because internationalists now claimed new evidence for the worthiness of collective security pacts. In Korea, they argued, force had stopped force in a hot war, proving the validity of U.S. promises to join in a collective response to future aggression.

Most American leaders thought that the United States and its allies had preserved a noncommunist Northeast Asia as a quadrant of the Pacific basin rim. Along this rim were Okinawa, Japan, Taiwan, and South Korea—several islands and the southern tip of a peninsula. To make its future commitment visible, the United States stationed small Army, Air Force, and Marine commands in all four areas. But the key military ingredient in the strategy for Northeast Asia was naval. American military strategies based the 7th Fleet in these waters to command various aircraft carrier battle groups committed to defending the connecting seas and straits. These battle groups were like movable islands.

To the south of this fleet-among-islands was the Southeast Asian quadrant of the Pacific basin. Along its rim another war, contemporary with the American-led U.N. effort in Korea, had involved the French, who were fighting to preserve their empire in Indochina. As American domestic bitterness over Korea began to take root, many internationalists began to see the French effort as part of the same struggle in Asia. As early as June 20, 1950, Assistant Secretary of State Dean Rusk made this clear in congressional testimony. In answering Chairman John Kee, of the House Committee on Foreign Affairs, Rusk affirmed Kee's assertion that the Vietnam war was "very much like the operation in Korea." As Rusk put it: "There are raids across the 38th parallel in Korea and there are agents, supply trains, and some arms coming across into Indochina."[3] Rusk gave this mild testimony on linkages between the northern and southern Pacific rims five days before the outbreak of hostilities in Korea— and months before the rise of Senator Joseph McCarthy, who began to link all world strife to disagreements between the United States and the Soviet Union.

Despite the rhetoric of politicians, continuity, not discontinuity, marked American security policy in the postwar years. Scholars noted this continuity immediately upon the close of the fifteen-year stewardship of the Truman and Eisenhower internationalists. So did Paul Nitze, who had helped Acheson to form America's postwar security policy, and then helped in the transition to Dulles; Nitze described Dulles's alterations to this policy as basically cosmetic.[4] Like Nitze, most highly positioned internationalists in both parties survived both Dulles's rhetoric and McCarthy's witch-hunts. But rhetorician and hunter, with help from their followers, did manage to decimate the lower ranks of Asian specialists in the government. And in this respect, Dulles and McCarthy had a real impact. As one member of the later Johnson team argued, part of the general American ignorance about Chinese interests in Vietnam resulted from this purge of suspect experts.[5]

However, before these China specialists were driven from government service, they had helped Acheson expand George Kennan's European-centered containment design to cover Asia. In August 1949, Secretary of State Dean Acheson testified before a congressional committee that the United States had to "do the best we can to prevent the spread of this Communist menace throughout Southeast Asia."[6] Not all aspects of this Asian emphasis satisfied everyone. Indeed, George Kennan himself made clear in his memoirs that he left government service in August 1950 because of deep differences with the Acheson team at State. He wrote: "There is no logical stopping point in the development of a system of anti-Russian alliance until that system has circled the globe and has embraced all the non-communist countries of Europe, Asia, and Africa."[7] But Acheson took pride in having inserted most of "the stoppers on the east, west, and south" to contain Soviet power in the heartland of Eurasia.[8] And what the Acheson team of internationalists left "unstopped," Dulles and his team of internationalists completed. One of their "stoppers" became the Southeast Asia Treaty Organization (SEATO), which was supposed to provide collective security for the last quadrant of the Pacific basin rim.

In Southeast Asia, however, the United States had little geopolitical and military experience to draw upon. The western Pacific is distinctly different from the eastern Pacific in that the western half contains many islands, large and small. To reach Japan in World War II the U.S. military employed these islands with some strategic mastery, in contrast to the American military's prewar penchant for costly frontal assaults, or what the British strategist B. H. Liddell Hart called the direct approach. In the Pacific war the United States discovered the indirect approach, which avoided the political and military dangers of invading Japanese strongpoints. In effect, in the Pacific "the United States made its greatest military efforts in areas outside the productive and population centers" because "of military limitations."[9] Therefore, the China-Burma-India theater, to the great dismay of General Stilwell, became the backwater war for Roosevelt's strategists. Given this historical background, Southeast Asia was an unlikely locale for a U.S.-sponsored collective security pact.

Nevertheless, Dulles took the patchwork quilt of mainland and island ex-colonies, once ruled by North Atlantic rim powers, and pushed and shoved a gun-shy post-Korea internationalist establishment into rounding off the Southeast Asian quadrant of the global containment arc. In congressional testimony in April 1954 Dulles argued that Leninism's larger purpose was "not only to take over Indochina but to dominate all of Southeast Asia"—not only Vietnam, Laos, and Cambodia but also Malaysia, Thailand, Indonesia, the Philippines, Australia, and New Zealand.[10] As late as 1958 he suggested that the fate of Berlin, Lebanon, Taiwan, and Korea depended on the system of collective security organized by the United States. Yet for Dulles the troublesome area remained Asia. In the same 1958 speech he emphasized that in Asia "international Communism now controls a great population and land mass represented by the China Mainland, Tibet, North Korea, and North Vietnam." As opposed to this solid mass of Leninists, Dulles worried about the way that "the non-Communist countries are scattered about the rim of this great mass."[11] And it was on this rim that collective security marked its Asian Rubicon.

How to cement the Northeast to the Southeast Asian quadrant became the problem. Revived trade—a Lockean co-prosperity sphere—became the Pacific rim answer. American planners envisaged a restored Japanese industrial base that would furnish finished and semifinished goods to Southeast Asia, which was rich in natural resources.[12] They hoped that this economic connection would relieve the giant American economy of its one-way aid programs while helping in the establishment of Asian political models similar to the Atlantic basin Lockean models. This trading scenario would depend on economic revival of the Pacific crescent of the global containment arc in much the same manner as the trading scenario for the Atlantic basin had depended on the economic revival of the European crescent.[13]

The economic revival began modestly in Japan. For example, "Americans also started to buy [Japanese] fertilizer and consumer goods destined for South and Southeast Asian non-communist countries as part of the American foreign aid effort." Then the Korean War became an economic catalyst. Revival of the Japanese automotive industry, for instance, was greatly assisted by the U.S. purchase, during the worst part of the Korean war, of 7,095 trucks.[14]

As this Pacific trading region began to come to life in the 1950's, it became a cornerstone of U.S. Pacific strategy. When the Democratic party recaptured the executive branch of the U.S. government in 1961, internationalists held fast to the major subordinate positions at the Departments of State, Defense, and Treasury and the Central Intelligence

Agency. Once Kennedy and Khrushchev had placed Berlin and Cuba in perspective, Southeast Asia became the major point of Lockean versus Leninist contention. In South Vietnam, Kennedy moved from the observer phase of the long Eisenhower years into a more active adviser phase. This phase did not long outlast his truncated presidency: although Johnson used most of 1964 to postpone decisions until after the November elections, as soon as he was back in the White House he moved into a combatant phase, a Southeast Asian war for collective security.

Yet the rationale for action in Vietnam remained the same for Johnson as it had for Kennedy. LBJ's Secretary of Defense, Robert McNamara, reemphasized the old ordering of containment priorities, stating that American military assistance programs were "oriented mainly toward those countries on the periphery of the major Communist nations where the threats are greatest and in which the indigenous resources are least." For the Secretary of Defense, the primary "forward defense" nation was South Vietnam, "which now faces the most serious and direct action."[15] And McNamara's was not the only military voice to rank Vietnam as a military security problem. The Army Chief of Staff, General Harold K. Johnson, noted that by 1964 forty-seven nations, including South Vietnam, were hosting U.S. Military Assistance Advisory Groups, but noted that "in South Vietnam, it was evident that the war was not being won."[16]

While his Army Chief of Staff was warning of South Vietnam's possible defeat, the President was searching for a politically safe way to involve American troops in Vietnam so as to appear not to have suffered defeat. In other words, Lyndon Johnson wanted cover. The internationalists' long-held tenet of collective security appeared ideal for the purpose, and so Johnson launched his "More Flags" program.[17] After sending a cable to selected U.S. embassies, on April 23, 1964, he made a public call for international assistance for South Vietnam. The U.S. Ambassadors receiving the cable discovered that their President wanted pressure applied to allied states all along the global containment arc. Johnson wanted to obtain visible allied presence on Southeast Asia's rim, where the dikes of containment appeared breeched in Vietnam.

When the Saigon government of General Nguyen Khanh was unable to organize a complementary diplomatic effort to help obtain this collective security shield, the Washington task force assigned to the Vietnam problem wrote a draft statement for Khanh. In its American-directed hunt for collective security allies, however, the Khanh government notably failed. But so did Johnson's Ambassadors. In a memorandum to Johnson on June 15, Secretary Rusk enclosed a status report of third-country aid to South Vietnam and added in his own hand, "There is still not enough progress."[18]

The seriousness of this failure for Johnson's collective security hopes was shown in presidential anger. On July 2 U.S. Ambassadors in Tokyo, Bonn, London, Rome, Brussels, Ottawa, Copenhagen, Bangkok, Taipei, Karachi, and Athens—with information copies to Saigon and Paris—got a taste of Texas rancor. Johnson began, "I am gravely disappointed by the inadequacy of the actions by our friends and allies in response to our request that they share the burden of Free World responsibility in Vietnam." He concluded four pages later, instructing the Ambassadors to personally "undertake this task in working with the highest possible levels of the government to which you are accredited." He added, "If it would assist you to have from me a letter directed to the Chief of State or the Chief of Government, I stand ready to give you one." He would, he promised, personally "review reports of the progress being made responsive to this cable at regular intervals," and warned that he hoped "to see evidence of your success in the near future."[19] The message was clear.

Still, William H. Sullivan, of the National Security Council staff, did not believe that everyone at the U.S. mission in Saigon had received a clear warning, and sensed that some of them still preferred unilateralism to collective action. To correct for this error, Rusk had previously dispatched a "For the Ambassador from the Secretary" cable on May 1 in which he highlighted the "problem of engaging more flags."[20] On June 24, in a memorandum to McGeorge Bundy, Sullivan stated that "there is ample indication that our own mission, specifically the military element, look upon third-country assistance with very little zeal." He surmised that "this is partly because of their experience in allied commands, such as Korea, in which the care and feeding of these third-country elements has always proved far more trouble than it is worth."[21]

Sullivan aimed his blast at a U.S. Saigon mission headed by a New England Brahmin, Henry Cabot Lodge, Jr., who was carrying on his own feud with the senior U.S. military commander in Saigon, General Paul Harkins.[22] The arrival of General William Westmoreland in January 1964 helped defuse this situation. Westmoreland served as Harkins' deputy until June, and then replaced him; Lodge found this South Carolina Brahmin more to his taste. Lodge insisted on the support of his military mission, and Westmoreland gave it. In a cable to Washington dated April 29, 1964, Lodge stated that he had led the discussion of possibilities for additional assistance from countries of the free world, and informed the Secretary of State that the Military Advisory Command Vietnam representative (Westmoreland) had made positive suggestions.

Lodge—the politician from the internationalist wing of the Republican party—believed, as did Johnson, that it was necessary to transform any appearance of U.S. unilateral combat in Vietnam into that of a collective security effort. Lodge thought it absolutely essential for the American public to believe in this tenet of Southeast Asian policy. The Ambassador warned his mission team "that psychologically it is most important that others share with us the casualties of the U.S. effort here." Lodge lectured his subordinates that "because of the great potential impact on U.S. public opinion which foreign sharing of the dangers could have, the U.S. should finance military manpower contributions from other countries if this is needed," and he pressured General Khanh's government in Saigon to participate actively in finding more flags.[23] Even with the Republican convention and the November elections on the horizon, Lodge willingly, after vacating his post in Saigon to General Maxwell Taylor, toured Western Europe for the Johnson collective security campaign, trying to obtain European help in Vietnam. In an August 24 memorandum to the President, Carl Rowan, as Director of the U.S. Information Agency (USIA), reported on the public and media success of Lodge's Western European travels.[24] But contrary to the Rowan memo, success eluded the Lodge mission to Europe. Again, rhetoric had substituted for action.

In many ways the USIA, an organization for persuasion, was the agency of first choice for Whigs who wanted to intervene abroad. Usually they turned to the CIA, an organization for preemption, only as an action agency of last resort. And the USIA (run by Rowan out of Washington) had a Saigon office, the Joint United States Public Affairs Office (JUSPAO), directed by Barry Zorthian, an activist who intervened in almost every area. His office hosted the afternoon media briefings—which the press corps came to call "the Five O'Clock Follies"—and he escorted Westmoreland to Malaysia, where the General studied how the British had successfully dealt with the insurgency there. Interestingly, Westmoreland met Sir Robert Thompson, who, more than anyone, had been responsible for that success. Westmoreland noted that Thompson had led the police, not the military. Unfortunately for them, the leaders in Saigon and Washington had failed to appreciate the potential effectiveness of police units for pacification plans. Instead most pacification tasks went to the regular military, and the American military at that.

Zorthian became involved in this pacification effort, particularly when the role of the military somehow backfired. Normal military operations backfired enough, particularly if the American forces employed munitions such as napalm. In order to counteract the negative effects of such incidents, Robert Manning, the State Department's Assistant Secretary for Public Affairs, suggested to Westmoreland and Zorthian that certain Americans, returning from military service in Vietnam, appear on television and radio to give the American public a positive report on U.S.

efforts to help South Vietnam maintain its freedom.[25] This kind of public relations campaign, of course, was exactly what Lodge had undertaken in his tour of NATO countries.

Interestingly, it was not Lodge who initiated the European diplomatic blitz in 1964. That spring and summer, like messengers in classical Greek drama, various internationalists crossed and recrossed the Atlantic, carrying warnings to the Europeans about salvaging the concept of collective security by coming to the rescue in Vietnam. On May 12, Secretary of State Rusk publicly asked NATO members to give greater support to South Vietnam. On the day before, West German Chancellor Ludwig Erhard had received Secretary of Defense McNamara. As summarized in the cable from the U.S. embassy in Bonn, McNamara's entreaty was blunt indeed. He warned Erhard that the U.S. public was asking why, if Vietnam was so important to the free world, the United States had to continue to defend it alone. Then McNamara applied what was the clincher for the Germans: "If the U.S. ever had to pull out and Vietnam were lost to the communists, Germany would suffer as would we."[26]

McNamara rubbed a raw nerve. Of the powerful states allied with the United States and located along the containment arc, the Federal Republic was the most exposed. Hence collective security remained a basic tenet of faith to the West Germans. But the German faith remained regional, whereas the American practice was global. Faced with the simultaneous need to satisfy both their larger ally and their own population, the West Germans found a way to slip quietly through the net of commitment. The route they chose was medical aid.

Medical assistance to South Vietnam had carried a high priority as early as 1962, when the Commander-in-Chief of the Pacific (CINCPAC), gave the mission of "medical civic action" to MACV. In 1963 Kennedy had congratulated his Surgeon General for the work of Public Health Service surgical teams in Vietnam. By 1964 the U.S. embassy was making various calls for medical assistance; for example, in a May 4 cable Ambassador Lodge insisted that "to augment present capacity in Vietnam to handle battle casualties, third country assistance on large scale essential."[27] Word of this medical requirement had reached several world capitals, including Bonn, where it suggested to the Germans a way out of their dilemma. The Federal Republic offered to station its 3,000-ton hospital ship S.S. *Helgoland* off the coast of Vietnam, where it could show the German flag while providing humanitarian medical aid.

This offer failed to satisfy Lodge and his Saigon staffers. On May 19 he fumed via cable that they "would much prefer Federal Republic medical assistance in form of traumatic surgical teams." While not rejecting the ship offer, Lodge was playing a political game; he knew where he wanted the Germans stationed—in the provincial capitals of South Vietnam. In the end, German and American diplomats reached a compromise: the S.S. *Helgoland* came, a few German medical teams worked on South Vietnamese soil, and the Federal Republic gave Saigon financial assistance.[28] But the West Germans succeeded in making their presence nearly invisible.

American diplomats pressured leaders in other capitals near the containment arc. Their efforts to involve South Korea exemplified the problems they faced in trying to orchestrate global acceptance of a complex, unpopular, and perplexing view of the world. As early as March 18, 1964, State Department officials cabled the American embassies in Seoul, Saigon, Taipei, Tokyo, and the United Nations, asking for their views on a South Korean role in South Vietnam.[29] This brought an immediate reaction from American official circles in Tokyo. Since the mid-1950's U.S. internationalists had hoped for a rapprochement between Japan and South Korea, so that together the two states could hold down the northern end of the global containment arc. Now, delicate negotiations to normalize the relations between the two states had reached a turning point. Ambassador E. O. Reischauer made this clear the day following the State Department inquiry, when he cabled that "proposals for use Republic of Korea (ROK) forces Vietnam would be grist for mill elements Japan opposing ROK-GOJ [Government of Japan] normalization, and any public announcement or discussion such proposals would be most untimely at this critical juncture ROK-GOJ talks."[30] Untimely grist for the mill or not, Lodge, in Saigon, wanted allies "who would share in the really dangerous work." He informed Washington officials that South Korea "has well qualified personnel for the type of work where our men are getting killed and wounded. Why not use a few of them here?"[31]

As with the response of West Germany, the South Korean flag flew in South Vietnam. Unlike the West Germans, however, the South Koreans did want a presence there. As early as 1954, Korea's Syngman Rhee had offered to dispatch Korean troops to fight in Vietnam against the communists. The authoritarian nature of his government in Seoul made it relatively easy for him to convince the South Korean public that South Vietnam's present fate had previously been theirs. But it is probably that any South Korean government, authoritarian or not, would have seen its own national interest in holding U.S. commitments not exclusively on the safer, offshore islands but on the Asian continental rim as well.

Other reasons existed for a relationship between Seoul and Saigon. Both governments were modified versions of what the Japanese call a *bakufu*, or military "tent" government. In that form of Asian rule, the key constituents are the leading generals. In Seoul it appeared that General

Park Chung Hee, the Korean daimyo, convinced his military colleagues that an American-Korean partnership in Vietnam was the price necessary to block the slow American withdrawal from South Korea. And by dispatching Korean troop units to Vietnam, the military elite would gain a magnificent opportunity to force the United States to modernize the South Korean armed forces. By 1968 two South Korean divisions were in South Vietnam. In other words, Park's gamble paid handsomely.[32]

While Park gambled and won, Johnson was losing in his global effort. As the failure to gain meaningful support for collective security became more apparent, the definition of "more flags" broadened. For example, a gift of 1,000 tons of petroleum products from the Shah's government in Tehran became another "flag" by the middle of July. The team headed by Ambassador Maxwell Taylor, recently retired as an Army General, modified the departed Lodge's approach. Taylor cabled Washington that "since main purpose of 'more flags' effort is political, we would prefer Iranian aid arrive in form better lending itself to publicity and national identity." He believed that "barrels are therefore better than bulk delivery," and that these "barrels should bear some such inscription as 'provided to the people of Vietnam by the people of Iran' in English and Farsi and displaying Iranian national colors." (That Saigonese in particular, and Vietnamese in general, would not recognize the Iranian colors or read Farsi or English seems to be a minor point.) The subordinate leadership's assumption that Iranian officials' traveling to Saigon and presenting the gift would "serve as [an] example to Pakistani and other Moslem countries which [are] generally unresponsive thus far" indicated the desperate nature of their attempts to appease Johnson.[33]

And Johnson remained a hard taskmaster. No one escaped his grip; to come to Washington that summer of 1964 meant to embrace a "more flags" posture. Prime Minister Tunkee Abdul Rahman, of Malaysia, met Johnson there on July 22 and 23, and the Texan corralled him. In the joint statement issued following their discussions, "the President noted with appreciation the contribution Malaysia has made to the common cause in Vietnam by providing equipment, training, and advice based on her own experience in combating Communist terrorism."[34] If the West German profile remained low and mainly off the coast, the Malaysian profile remained ephemeral and over the horizon. As late as 1966 the Commander-in-Chief of the Pacific, Admiral U. S. Grant Sharp, noted that all Malaysian forces were fully committed in their own country.[35]

If the government of Malaysia seemed unresponsive, the Taiwan government of Chiang Kai-shek was not. Chiang was willing to place his forces back in Vietnam, where they had been at the end of World War II to help the British accept the surrender of the Japanese. In October 1961, to be exact, President Ngo Dinh Diem indicated to U.S. Ambassador Frederick E. Nolting, Jr., that his Saigon government would view favorably the support of a division of Nationalist Chinese troops.[36] Though always reluctant to accept outside intervention, Diem nevertheless hoped that some Nationalists would help balance the all-too-intrusive American presence. But American officials remained nervous about giving any role to Chiang's troops. They could not forget that "unleashing" Chiang's forces had been a favorite slogan of those American unilateralists who would have "unlimited" the Korean War. Nevertheless, after the murder of Ngo Dinh Diem, General Kanh also expressed interest in getting Nationalist Chinese assistance; this led to one of the more bizarre episodes in the "More Flags" program.

In 1964 CIA agents in Saigon and Manila were watching the movements of an ethnic Chinese citizen of South Vietnam by the name of Father Hoa, whom Khanh allowed to control the Hai Yen sector in South Vietnam and who had high-level contacts in Manila, Saigon, Taipei, and Washington, D.C. The CIA warned Washington officials that if Father Hoa arrived in Washington the U.S. government was to "emphasize his status as citizen of RVN [Republic of Vietnam] rather than his Chineseness." They considered this critical because Hoa was likely to presume that the "recent U.S. proposal to install 112 CHINAT [Chinese Nationalist] officers and men in Sea Swallow haven at Hai Yen gives him very special relationship vis-à-vis U.S. government and outside GVN [Government of Vietnam] channels." CIA officials feared this eventuality even though "General Khanh endorsed proposal to bring in CHINATS when originally broached by Father Hoa, and later approved in principle detailed plans prepared by U.S. officials." The CIA warned that other South Vietnamese leaders might "have reservations about turning Chinese loose to act independently in Father Hoa's fief."[37] Well, other internationalists wanted even more of Chiang's troops. For example, CIA Director John A. McCone suggested bringing three Chinese Nationalist Divisions into Vietnam, though Lodge scotched the idea by applying his narrower view of revolutionary Asian combat: "I would be interested in the feasibility of introducing—not Chinese Nationalist Divisions—but small parties of Chinese Nationalist night fighters who would go after the VC."[38] Discounting night fighters and Father Hoa, Washington-based internationalists blocked any proposals for Chiang's forces to play a major role in Vietnam. But they invited every other American ally to contribute, a contribution that they hoped to use militarily in Vietnam and politically in Washington.

As a Washington example, on July 20 William Bundy for State, John McNaughton for Defense, and Michael Forrestal and McGeorge Bundy, of the National Security Council, initialed a TOP SECRET cable from Dean Rusk to Maxwell Taylor in Saigon. The cable contained a draft Presidential statement expressing gratitude that "our United States effort [in Vietnam] is increasingly being joined by that of our Free World allies," and then announcing another "proposed U.S. military personnel increase" in South Vietnam.[39] Almost before the U.S. mission in Saigon could comment on this message, Washington cabled again: "Opinion at highest level here now is that news of increase in U.S. military assistance to South Vietnam would better come from Saigon than Washington."[40] Here, internationalists had stumbled across a fact of domestic political life. Even in times of declared war, presidential candidates (even incumbents) have an aversion to announcing troop increases in combat zones prior to elections. When the war is undeclared and the U.S. side can be seen as losing, aversion is too mild a word.

Johnson's presidential style did not permit admitting defeat, whether that defeat was declared or undeclared. Nor did the style of the internationalists permit them to rethink the application of the collective security argument for Vietnam.[41] Therefore, in spring and summer of 1964 Johnson and his advisers followed a steady-on-course approach to Vietnam. From April to July he and his emissaries struggled to sell Vietnam, as a global test of collective security, to American allies locked into existing regional pacts. They failed, not for lack of trying but because their logic simply did not convince. Then, as the situation worsened, the North Vietnamese suddenly granted Johnson's ambassadors a short respite from presidential pressure by engaging U.S. ships in the Gulf of Tonkin.

The Tonkin Gulf naval engagement is most often remembered today as having enabled Johnson to obtain a congressional resolution he could use to justify a U.S. combat role in Vietnam. But at the time, in 1964, it also helped gain much-needed international backing for Washington and Saigon. Averell Harriman wrote to Dean Rusk that the U.S. counterstrike in the Gulf "gained the respect of many countries . . . and the acquiescence of others who are reserving judgment."[42] In other words, the Tonkin engagement worked where calls for collective security had failed.

Soon after Johnson's reelection, the cables again carried "more flag" scenarios. For example, Ambassador Taylor informed Washington on November 14, 1964, that while the "floods in central provinces constitute a serious disaster," there appeared to be no need for more American logistical units to assist in repair work. But he was quick to recommend "using this situation as a means of trying to obtain third country military engineers," mainly to repair flood-damaged bridges along lines of communication.[43]

Reminiscing about the collective security efforts of 1964, Chester Cooper, a Johnson appointee, wrote that it required "the application of considerable pressure from Washington to elicit any meaningful commitments." He went on to cite two reasons for the lassitude and lack of interest of the Saigon regime—political jockeying at home, and belief that "the program was a public relations campaign directed at the American people." In fact, Cooper estimates that "only a few countries came forward with anything very consequential."[44]

This failure of other countries to contribute had an inordinately high price tag for Americans. As in Korea a decade earlier, it was chiefly the United States that fought and financed the collective security effort in Vietnam. In this war, however, large amounts of money were going to the various allies, in return for very modest efforts, a circumstance that distressed many Americans. Cooper recalls that according "to official Administration estimates, the war in South Vietnam provided South Korea with 20 percent of its foreign exchange earnings in 1969." A 1,500-man engineering troop unit of Filipinos was paid $39 million, or $26,000 per person, between 1967 and 1979, and approximately 10 percent of the Philippines' foreign exchange income in those years came from various projects associated with the war in Vietnam. Nor did Thailand lose in the cash flow; its 11,000 troops cost the United States almost $50 million annually.[45] Henry Cabot Lodge had suggested earlier that the United States should pay for the flags if necessary; that certainly is what happened.

One of the few Asian military organizations that the United States did not buy happened to be the British-trained Gurkha Brigade, professional soldiers from faraway Nepal. The British government planned their retirement from the British Army, and they were available for service in Vietnam, but the United States declined to pay for them—partly, it has been suggested, because of the "American antipathy toward the use of mercenaries."[46] Despite this antipathy, many units engaged by the Americans looked more like mercenaries than allies. And Johnson's mixed force of mercenaries and allies—"allies," since there is no evidence that Australian or New Zealand combat forces received American financing—had reached a total of only 467 persons in 1964. But with Texas diligence, Johnson had bought or arm-wrestled the total up to 64,802 by the end of his presidency in 1968. South Korea accounted for 50,003 of the total force.[47]

In pursuing the "More Flags" program, internationalists mortgaged the integrity of what collective security meant to the American public. Most Americans, regardless of whether they approved of interventionist policies, never understood collective security to mean an exercise in public relations, or the purchase of soldiers of fortune, or partisan party policies, or the advancement of an internationalist ideology over unilateralist or pacifist views. Taking a pragmatic view, they recognized that the collective security action could come in one of four ways. The first two were widely understood: global defense under United Nations auspices, as in the Korean conflict, and regional defense sanctioned by the U.N. charter, as in the Berlin crisis with NATO as the setting. The third and fourth were recognized mainly by internationalists: bilateral agreements between the United States and a state, like Taiwan, that did not belong to a regional defense association, and unilateral U.S. action, as in the Cuban missile crisis, that could be supported by regional opinion. In the Cuban missile crisis the United States invoked the authority of the Organization of American States (OAS), and President Kennedy dispatched ranking envoys to NATO capitals to brief European community leaders.

As for securing global security through the United Nations, by the 1960's many Americans believed that this organization existed as an intense, media-covered debating platform rather than as an action agency. But hope for the United Nations had not vanished. A Gallup poll taken in July 1964 revealed that 58 percent of the Americans polled approved of the creation of a U.N. army to deal with the Vietnam problem; 19 percent disapproved; and 23 percent had no opinion.[48] Unfortunately for those who hoped for a U.N. army, after the success of the U.N. Korean resolution, neither the Americans nor the Russians absented themselves again from their blocking positions at the U.N. Security Council. And as an arena for arranging collective world action, the U.N. General Assembly seemed even less promising. Only by interminable debate and public posturing could a nation or a group of states hope to defeat or deflect a hostile resolution; to pass one that was positive became almost impossible. Besides, resolutions alone carried little validity. In 1963 it appeared enough for the Kennedy administration that an international commission oversaw the shadow war in Laos, with its tripartite government, and the frontier quarrel between Cambodia and South Vietnam. These facts most Americans could understand.

Furthermore, since 1947 internationalists had persuasively argued that friendly neighboring states, under Article 52 of the U.N. charter, could link themselves together through collective security pacts.[49] To convince those who suspected that the United States would not pledge its real support, these American activists were willing to link U.S. interests to regional interests in Western Europe, the Middle East, Southeast Asia, and Northeast Asia. The last region to be organized for collective defense was Southeast Asia, under SEATO. And although SEATO was modeled after NATO, the first and most successful regional pact, SEATO failed to work in a crisis. Why?

Some of the reasons are historical. The North Atlantic rim states had a deep-rooted sense of shared community; the southeast Pacific rim states did not. This is one reason why U.S. internationalists had to organize SEATO unilaterally; there existed no real sense in which regional co-organizers could take a forceful lead. In contrast to the states that organized NATO, the southeast Pacific rim states had recently undergone a series of traumas—Japanese occupation, Allied liberation, and national revolutions culminating in independence—all in one decade. Furthermore, what appeared clear to Washington—the threat of Leninist subversion of the states on the southeast Pacific rim—did not appear at all clear in Kuala Lumpur or Jakarta. In that region, a revival of Japanese imperialism or North Atlantic colonialism seemed a greater danger than any threat posed by the unknown world of Moscow. As for Peking, China had existed as the giant of Asia long before the North Atlantic powers had begun warning Pacific rim peoples about the threat of Chinese imperialism; and it seemed certain that China would remain the Asian giant long after the ideological quarrels of the twentieth century had subsided. Learning to live with whoever rules the Middle Kingdom had been an Asian fact of life for millennia. What was worse for Washington, leaders in the region watched Pakistan join France (both SEATO members) in rejecting the U.S. interpretation of Asian security problems.

The Collapse of Consensus

It slowly dawned on some in Washington that SEATO members did not possess a communal sense of danger great enough for them to implement U.S. prescriptions for collective security in the region. As early as June 1962, Senator Mike Mansfield gave a public address in which he said, "We have allies under SEATO to be sure, but allies either unwilling or unable to assume but the smallest fraction of the burdens of the alliance." Mansfield gave copies of this and other public warnings to Johnson in 1963 shortly after he had become President. Johnson had the NSC staff review Mansfield's charges, but as 1964 wore on it became increasingly difficult to make conciliatory replies to the Montana Senator's continued attack.[50] Despite considerable effort, no one could sway the Montanan; he seemed as fixed in his assessment as Johnson. To make matters worse, internal administration reports began to confirm Mansfield's charges that SEATO was a collective security failure.[51] Secretary of State Rusk thus began to walk a narrow path between slowly dawning reality and persistent presidential pressure. On April 6 Rusk received a memorandum on SEATO in particular, and general regional disharmony in general, from his Director of Intelligence and Research. On April 20 Rusk stated that other countries besides the United States were "prepared to be helpful in [furnishing] resources in South Vietnam," for there were already "a few military personnel in South Vietnam from other countries." Yet he did not "envision organized combat units at the present moment from other countries."[52]

Between the dawning reality and presidential pressure there was very little area in which to maneuver. The strain Johnson placed on other regional pacts indicated that whereas internationalism to the United States was global, to allies it remained regional. Requesting states of the North Atlantic rim to lock their regional security with that of the southeast Pacific rim states overreached the capacity of member nations. Even Britain and France, members of both NATO and SEATO and old hands at empire in Southeast Asia, remained unsympathetic. Britain quietly so, always ready to reopen the Geneva Conference on Indochina, for, as in the Korean conflict, the British Foreign Office quietly sought ways to ensure that the United States would concentrate on what they considered vital, the Atlantic rim security zone. The French government simply distanced itself as far as possible from U.S. actions in what de Gaulle considered an unmitigated disaster.[53]

Without a global collective security arrangement tied to the United Nations or an effective regional collective security arrangement through SEATO, the only options were bilateral treaties or unilateral action. In theory, a bilateral defense treaty with South Vietnam, like the one between America and Japan, remained an option. In other words, assisting South Vietnam need not necessarily bring a return to the pre–World War II pattern of conducting American foreign policy through unilateral action. But Mansfield feared that it would. He had been saying so since June 1962. To him, the actions of the United States in Vietnam confirmed his suspicions that, if blocked, internationalists would revert to unilateralism in order to have their way. In a Michigan State University commencement speech in 1962 Mansfield proposed that U.S. leaders "actively, intensely, and continuously [search for] every possibility of minimizing the unilateral activity of the United States in Southeast Asia."[54] Later, in the famous Mansfield resolution, he was to suggest American troop reductions in NATO. Simply stated, by the 1960's Mansfield wanted neither internationalism nor unilateralism.

In his own way, Mansfield was as wrong as Johnson. The United States could certainly aid a state invaded by another state, even without a bilateral treaty, simply by invitation. Even internationalists recognized this. To them the Truman Doctrine was based on the invitations from Greece and Turkey made before NATO existed. Internationalists also applauded Truman's pressure of the Soviets regarding Iran. In each situation, especially Turkey's, they saw a legitimate strategy of self-interest.[55] For internationalists, a unilateral action occurred only when the government of a foreign nation had not invited the United States to assist, especially if that nation had made this noninvitation clear to all other states that recognized it as the legal government. Internationalists justified the U.S. intervention in South Vietnam as having come via an invitation.

Internationalists never considered U.S. involvement in Vietnam as unilateral action. They reserved that sort of action for cases of the gravest sort—that is, cases involving national survival itself. Some of Johnson's advisers, notably Walt W. Rostow, considered South Vietnam vital to U.S. national security interests, though other internationalists questioned whether U.S. entry there was like the missile crisis in Cuba—that is, whether it was worth risking consequences of that order of magnitude. Johnson hoped that successfully invoking multilateral collective security would confer approval on his war in a way that bilateralism might not and unilateralism would not. The flaw in this strategy became clear over the years, as his administration tried to maintain the Vietnam collective security charade in the face of relentless media coverage.

Johnson's strategy can be explained partly by his reading of American politics. In some ways one could characterize Vietnam in 1964 as the winter of Johnson's discontent, saved by no sun of Yankee Camelot. Despite successes by Johnson on the domestic legislative front, international political gloom hung in the humid air of Washington. By September of that year Rusk cabled Saigon about the "considerable public pessimism here."[56] President for less than ten months by July, facing a general election in November, and losing a foreign test of endurance—Johnson's discontent had substantive causes. Perhaps his glorious summer could be found in collective security. He knew, for example, that if his administration were to support a higher intensity of combat, the political explanations for this shift would require a solid base. When troop levels in Vietnam remained low, composed in the main of career military men and volunteers instead of draftees, a President could postpone political problems. When casualty levels and violence also remained low, making no decision might be the wisest choice. But LBJ knew also that with body counts of the American dead climbing higher because of troop-level increases, and with bombing strikes on North Vietnam escalating the violence, postponement would be seen as indecisiveness. And Johnson kept alert to the public mood on these key issues. The following examples may illustrate his consuming political motives.

Many of Johnson's critics sniped at him from the relative safety of Congress. Mansfield broke early, hoping for a Johnson conversion. Senator Wayne Morse characterized the United States as an outlaw in Vietnam. And when, in early May, Johnson heard of criticism mounting in Chairman Carl Vinson's House Armed Services Committee, he counter-attacked in all directions. When critics charged that U.S. flyers in Vietnam flew in poorly equipped aircraft, Johnson vented his wrath on McNamara. McGeorge Bundy found himself ordered to cable McNamara that "the President is himself determined that U.S. flyers in South Vietnam shall have the best possible equipment for achieving their missions."[57] The poor-equipment charge did not stay buried. It appeared again in an obscure newspaper, the Jeannette, Pennsylvania, *News Dispatch* of October 5. A citizen charged that his son "was forced to fly in a 16-year-old helicopter (America's oldest one is 17 years old and in a museum)." Johnson had the news item sent to Bundy with the following postscript: "The President wanted you to see this news clipping."[58]

Forever watching the barometer of American politics, Johnson wanted his news clippings to reflect approval. This would be essential in any escalation to a U.S. combat role. When such a role seemed the likely choice of last resort, it had to be postponed until after the November elections of 1964. Then, when implemented, the escalation required a satisfactory political explanation. To Johnson, collective security explained it in terms that had been tried successfully in the past. If it were to be war, it had to be a collective security war. At the minimum, he thought, a war in Vietnam required an explanation that stressed the defensive nature of the U.S. effort: it was a response to outside aggression. The President's explanation to the American people about how North Vietnam had invaded South Vietnam would be reinforced when regional states, and others beyond the region, came to the rescue of the attacked state. By 1964 the deference paid by the American people to the internationalists and their collective defense pacts encouraged Johnson to hope that his Vietnam policy would receive national, regional, and transregional approval.

With regard to national approval, the American people generously deferred to the internationalists from 1947 onward in the belief that three general conditions for collective security would be met. First, they assumed that responsible American leadership would link the destiny of Americans to that of other peoples in regional pacts only for defensive, not offensive, purposes. Second, although the United States would lend great weight to any collectivity, essentially the pact nations themselves would perceive their keenest national interest—military security—to be interlocked with the interests of other states in their region. Third, the regional-pact states would genuinely desire a U.S. presence and would willingly allow their governments to enter into long-term contracts on a mutual basis of self-defense.[59]

In Vietnam, however, only the first condition proved valid, and it could not support the weight of the demands placed on it. Internationalists relied on a consensus of the American public in favor of collective security through a series of defensive regional alliances, but the war in Vietnam was not a collective security war; and saying that it was only made the public brand internationalists as liars.[60] Over this issue the consensus about the propriety of the American intervention in Vietnam began to break, first in the internationalist camp and then, slowly, in the nation at large. By the time of the Tet offensive in 1968, it was dead.

The consensus collapsed for several reasons, of course. Here I have dealt with only one: the misuse of the concept of collective security. Johnson at first chose to defend his actions in South Vietnam as based on collective security agreements. But Vietnam was not a collective effort, and calling it one only denigrated the concept. In reality, Vietnam at first was a bilateral effort, by South Vietnam and the United States. And after the departure of Ngo Dinh Diem it became mainly a unilateral effort—a series of Saigon military committees acting on U.S. orders. In fact, this had been true, by default, in the Korean War. But even in Korea, and especially in Vietnam, the internationalists, usually hardheaded realists, became romantics, taking literally D'Artagnan's call of one for all and all for one, applying it on a global scale. They refused to see the Asian international situation for what it was. The internationalists would have been better off to avoid slogans from French literature, especially when operating outside the region in which Alexandre Dumas was part of the cultural heritage. Internationalist efforts might have resulted in a different outcome if they had replaced the literary slogan with a historical symbol—France's great seventeenth-century statesman, Cardinal Richelieu. He, opponent to the heroes of Dumas's fiction, in reality was an activist intervener in the regional politics of his day, one who could think the unthinkable and act upon it. He too joined collective security pacts, his being against the Austrian Hapsburgs; but Richelieu dealt differently with the English Stuarts, since that royal house was more open to French suggestions of bilateral negotiations. Richelieu never confused bilateral arrangements with collective security pacts; American internationalists did. When the public looked behind the musketeer cloak of collective security in Vietnam, they found a bankrupt strategy. Thus began their withdrawal of deference.

CHAPTER THREE

The Southeast Asian War

FROM THE BEGINNING, administration spokesmen in Washington referred to the war in Southeast Asia as the "Vietnam" war. However, even before the Tonkin Gulf naval engagements and the bombing of North Vietnam, U.S. leaders, frustrated by the indecisive nature of protracted guerrilla tactics, had greatly expanded the geographical reach of the war.[1] In order to define more accurately the greater Southeast Asian war, one has to count the occasions when U.S. advisers and their Vietnamese counterparts launched cross-border military operations from South Vietnamese soil, flew military air missions from Thai air fields, sailed naval ships from Philippine bases—operations that at various times targeted not only South Vietnam but also Cambodia, Laos, and North Vietnam. In a cable of May 1964, Secretary of State Dean Rusk alerted Ambassador Lodge that the "situation in Southeast Asia is clearly moving toward basic decisions" and that "the present activity with regard to Cambodia, Laos and Vietnam illustrates that the central issue of pressure for the communist North will have to be faced not just by us but by other allies."[2] By the time the Americans pushed their defensive frontier into neighboring Cambodia and Laos, they had discovered that Ho Chi Minh had pushed his offensive frontier there already. In 1970, when the Nixon administration ordered combined U.S. and Vietnamese forces into Cambodia, a chilling reality dawned on the American people: this was no limited war. But the Kennedy-Johnson escalations in the 1960's differed only in size, scope, and secrecy from those later made by Nixon; the two Democrats had ordered their forces to scout the infiltration trails before Nixon's combat units arrived. Before Nixon, their Army units had infiltrated across international borders, their Air Force units had flown air strikes beyond South Vietnam, and their Navy units had chartered seaborne landings through other nations' territorial waters.

In fact, most of the planning for these military moves had occurred under Kennedy. In December 1963 Secretary of Defense McNamara reminded the new President, Lyndon Johnson, that planning for covert action into North Vietnam had reached the point where Johnson could select from among several options. In a memorandum of December 11 Mike Forrestal of the NSC staff surveyed for Johnson the covert operations, planned or implemented, in South Vietnam, Cambodia, Laos, and North Vietnam.[3] Earlier that month Senator Mike Mansfield had warned the President not to assume that the war "can be won in South Vietnam alone." He foresaw the nightmare of "a war which will, in time, involve U.S. forces throughout Southeast Asia."[4]

The Cambodian War

In Cambodia in 1964 the royal Khmer government of Prince Norodom Sihanouk existed in close proximity to the southern lands of its ancestral enemy, Vietnam. For hundreds of years this blood feud, a miniature version of the older Franco-German enmity, had been the source of violence. Like their larger European counterparts, Cambodia and Vietnam argued over the location of the border and over control of a great river—for them, the Mekong. To Cambodians the Vietnamese were the Prussians of Southeast Asia; or, in Asian terms, if China was the big dragon at the center of Asia, then Vietnam was the little dragon in its southeast corner. Through that corner of Asia flowed the Mekong River, the region's Nile or Amazon. It drains a huge international basin before fanning out to form the Mekong Delta in southern South Vietnam, where a maze of tributaries forms a latticework of rich bottomland. In the southern war-migration of the seventeenth century, the ethnic Vietnamese drove the Khmers and Chams out of this region, later known as Cochinchina, and made it the new frontier of their regional empire. By the turn of the twentieth century French engineers, with their penchant for digging canal systems, had turned it into an export-oriented rice bowl.

From the beginning this "immigrant South" differed from Vietnamese settlements in the northern Tonkinese delta and in the highlands of imperial Annam. In those areas, productive land was scarcer, and a feudal tradition of landlord paternalism and population pressure had restricted production of crops. The leaders in Tonkin and Annam faced three critical distributive issues, "water, communal land, and taxes," whereas in Cochinchina the settlers had to deal with only one—taxes.[5]

In this fertile region American internationalists found the seeds of trouble as waterborne fighters and weapons took primacy over farmers and harvests. On January 2, 1964, Rusk announced the discovery of a large arms cache in the Mekong Delta area, consisting of weapons and munitions of Chinese communist manufacture. State Department intelligence analysts confirmed Rusk's charges, and soon estimated that the bulk of weapons furnished to the Viet Cong from outside sources came into South Vietnam via the Mekong Delta. The analysts offered various arms-cache findings as evidence.[6] When General Joseph Stilwell, Jr., speaking for the U.S. Military Advisory Command Vietnam (MACV), briefed the U.S. press corps in Saigon of substantially the same facts, he struck sensitive nerves in Washington; MACV quickly announced that Stilwell did not mean to imply "collusion on part of Cambodian government."[7]

Any further communist infiltration raised the possibility of a major clash along the river border. At first, in fact, General Khanh's new Saigon government had wanted harmonious relations with Phnom Penh, and as late as March 9, 1964, Ambassador Lodge had assessed Khanh's Cambodian policy as conciliatory.[8] But on that date Sihanouk torpedoed any bilateral South Vietnamese–Cambodian conference on frontier issues; most offensive of all, he expressed willingness to discuss the frontier problem only with the Democratic Republic of North Vietnam (DRV), and had proposed diplomatic recognition of only the DRV. Although he reported that Khanh still followed a moderate course in Cambodian relations, Lodge believed an explosion was likely if minor border and river confrontations continued. As he put it in a March 15 cable, "Stopping traffic in Mekong is clearly a card that Khanh can play."[9]

Lodge was not the only internationalist to note this. On December 5, 1963, the Commander-in-Chief of the Pacific (CINCPAC), Admiral Harry Felt, had recommended to the Joint Chiefs that "strict control of Mekong and other waterways should be a priority objective." McNamara, whom Paul Nitze and General Lyman Lemnitzer had warned of this problem as early as 1961, took Felt's recommendation to Johnson. He told the President that although in agreement with the CINCPAC assessment of the situation, he was pessimistic about the chances of controlling so vast a sea and river infiltration system. Nevertheless, McNamara took up the challenge by dispatching a special U.S. naval team to South Vietnam.[10]

Blocking seaborne infiltration by the direct use of force quickly fell afoul of internationalist concern for legalities, because an international protocol already regulated maritime and inland navigation of the Mekong. In fact, it was the Secretary of Defense who alerted his subordinates to this river convention by advising them to consider its Article 2, which authorized the various river states to make thorough inspections of all river traffic if such measures were necessary to enhance general security.[11] In early March, Roger Hilsman, at State, reminded Cambodian officials, such as Nong Kimny, that in the U.S. interpretation of international law, inspection measures now were necessary. Shortly thereafter, on March 10, a crowd sacked the U.S. embassy in Phnom Penh, a sacking that Lodge characterized as Sihanouk-inspired.

River relations worsened during the spring and summer. During a cabinet meeting in early September, Saigon ministers expressed a strong desire to cut the riverine path to the Viet Cong, regardless of Cambodian reactions. The U.S. country team in Saigon, while applauding the decision, encouraged the Saigon government to emphasize that all its measures were defensive, concerned only with Vietnamese internal security, and not reprisals against Phnom Penh. On that same day, Rusk cabled Lodge, expressing frustration over the situation. The Deputy Chief of Mission at Phnom Penh, Herbert Spivak (the senior remaining U.S. diplomat in Cambodia after the U.S. embassy sacking) had explained to Rusk that shipping destined to go upriver to the Viet Cong could easily be rerouted from the Mekong to the seaport at Sihanoukville, whence it could be sent on to the Viet Cong by overland and downriver transport.[12]

Simultaneously with Rusk, the Joint Chiefs of Staff were describing the problem in stark military terms. If river controls were intensified, the opponent could enlarge the water arena by shipping to Sihanoukville, thence by land to Phnom Penh, and then down the Mekong and Bassac Rivers and associated waterways. The downriver passage was ideal for infiltration, which could be carried out during the hours of darkness in scattered small, shallow-draft river craft. To prevent this sort of traffic, military planners proposed installing searchlights, net booms, and heavy machine guns at checkpoints along the Mekong and Bassac Rivers.[13] They planned to use two strategically placed "nets." One, consisting of U.S. naval vessels in the open sea, would catch large "fish" trying to enter the Mekong; the other, a riverine force, would catch small fry slipping downstream. By fall the American navy, working with its Saigon counterpart, had planned coastal surveillance flights and the integration of coastal force junkmen into the regular South Vietnamese navy.[14]

While debating what to do about the Mekong River problem, U.S. policymakers were also plagued with the question of how to deal with armed clashes along the Cambodian-Vietnamese border. A partial list of these 1964 border-related incidents would include the following. March 19: Army of South Vietnam (ARVN) incursion and firefight takes place in Cambodia at Chantrea, with U.S. advisers present. May 7–8: An ARVN incursion and firefight occurs in Cambodia near the Rach Boa River. June 4: A United Nations Security Council meeting discusses incidents on Cambodian territory in the vicinity of the Cambodian–South Vietnamese border. July 28: A telegram from the Cambodian government to the

United Nations accuses Washington and Saigon of spreading poisonous chemicals over Cambodia by aircraft. August 6: At the United Nations, Cambodia charges that Americans in uniform joined South Vietnamese soldiers in firing into Cambodia. September 3: Cambodia charges that South Vietnam had launched a "major attack" near Koh Rokar and thereby penetrated Cambodian territory. October 24: Cambodian antiaircraft gunners shoot down a U.S. C-123 aircraft over Cambodian territory. October 25: Cambodian antiaircraft gunners fire on a U.S. helicopter searching for a missing U.S. officer presumed to be dead inside Cambodia.[15]

The Chantrea incursion of early 1964 typified these bitter border battles, and is thus worth describing briefly. On the morning of March 19 an ARVN armored cavalry troop scouted along the Cambodian border as part of a larger operation. The troop's U.S. adviser remained close to its lead elements as it sought out the source of ground fire drawn by a South Vietnam Air Force (VNAF) plane. The American adviser saw two men run from cover as his ARVN cavalry formation approached them; within seconds, he estimated, about one hundred more men "rose from the ground" and ran. The cavalry troop gave chase and engaged in a firefight. The U.S. adviser later told his commander that until a Cambodian flag appeared at his rear he did not know he had entered Cambodia. Then, before the troop could withdraw, its forward air controller—aboard a circling VNAF TO-1A aircraft piloted by an American—ordered a bomb and napalm strike nearby. Upon moving forward to exploit the air strike, ARVN infantrymen found a small village behind the tree line. Next, an American-piloted helicopter landed with its four-man American crew and three senior American advisers, including the 7th ARVN Division's senior American adviser. All disembarked, on Cambodian soil. After a brief consultation, the senior ARVN commander ordered the cavalry troop back to Vietnamese territory. As they left Cambodia, the American troop adviser recorded one suspected enemy dead, several dead livestock, and ten houses burning. The debriefing report indicated that the cavalry troop captured two prisoners. One, who admitted under interrogation that he was a Viet Cong platoon leader, was executed by ARVN forces; the other was held for later detailed interrogation.[16]

In their response to similar incidents, American internationalists revealed the internal divisions that made policy-making so difficult. Within internationalist ranks, Whigs and Tories alike agreed that military security was essential to the realization of the next internationalist goal in a developmental sequence. For Whigs, that next goal was political liberty—an intangible thing that bombs and bullets could neither create nor destroy. For Tories, it was economic liberty—which could be achieved only through an infrastructure of physical assets that would be extremely vulnerable to the destructive force of modern weapons. On the question of how to limit the war in Vietnam, Whigs tended to be minimalists; they hoped to hold the enemy at bay mainly through diplomatic means, and to use the minimum military force necessary to achieve military security. Tories, on the other hand, preferred to keep the enemy as far away as possible from fixed economic assets, and to do so they were willing to use the maximum amount of military force needed, short of provoking a general war with China or the Soviet Union.

Given these predispositions, Whig minimalists saw the Chantrea incursion as a coordinated American-Vietnamese raid into Cambodia, whereas Tory maximalists saw it as a U.S.-Vietnamese application of the doctrine of hot pursuit. For the former it was unjustified; for the latter it was justified. The difference between the two viewpoints was debated throughout the war. Most Whigs argued that even the hot-pursuit doctrine could not be stretched to cover the facts—the duration of the incursion after the sighting of the Cambodian flag, the use of napalm against an inhabited village, and the shooting of a prisoner. These actions, they believed, tended to discredit American internationalism. As Whig minimalists squirmed at the growing media attention being paid to incidents such as the Chantrea incursion, Mike Forrestal, of the National Security Council, presented the minimalist case and suggested to McGeorge Bundy that someone should chastise the U.S. military for the Chantrea incident— perhaps a head or two should roll. General Maxwell Taylor blocked any such reprisals, but the exchange soured civil-military relations.

In order to avoid future Chantreas, key White House and Pentagon managers decided to centralize their control over details of the war. Henceforth, for example, they—and not commanders in the field— would select exact targets, the exact explosives to be used on them, and the exact time of the strike. This, of course, made civil-military relations even worse, especially among the military who were doing the dying.[17] Yet it was not the Whigs who were most insistent on running the war from Washington; the command to do so came from the Secretary of Defense, Robert McNamara, a Tory whose management style emphasized the centralizing theme.

In the early stages of Johnson's Southeast Asian war, centralization brought some benefits. Through joint operations planned at the top, leaders in Washington and Saigon amassed a considerable body of evidence that confirmed Viet Cong use of Cambodian sanctuaries. Three Viet Cong prisoners, captured in three separate engagements in early May 1964, for example, admitted receiving orders to withdraw across the Cambodian border upon sighting ARVN forces; one said his troop unit commander had contacted local Cambodian officials, who told him that sanctuary would be given to Viet Cong who were not seen carrying weapons.[18] Battle reports also confirmed Viet Cong cross-border operations. On April 4, 1964, for instance, two Viet Cong battalions, challenged by ARVN armor and infantry at the Vietnamese hamlet of Tan Lap, withdrew to a point two kilometers away and "waved to GVN [Government of Vietnam] forces once they reached Cambodia."[19] Aerial photography in early March 1964 confirmed the location of a heavily defended Viet Cong (VC) military complex straddling the border. It consisted of approximately 9 square kilometers of extensive command, storage, and supply facilities, along with foxholes, automatic weapons emplacements, and trenches—all interconnected by an elaborate canal system and trail network.[20] The ARVN sweep of March 19 against Chantrea had been intended to destroy this complex. Finally, joint ARVN-US crater analysis of incoming mortars in an early September 1964 border firefight confirmed that the shells came from mortar positions inside Cambodia.[21]

From vantage points along this hostile border, American Special Forces—the Green Berets assigned to counterinsurgency tasks—reported incursions into South Vietnam by the Khmer Kampuchea Kro (KKK), a Cambodian bandit group that terrorized the border communities; and U.S. analysts in Saigon told Washington that they had a "substantial amount of information indicating direct RKG [Royal Khmer Government] involvement in KKK activities in delta."[22] Thus teams of U.S. Special Forces (SF) joined teams of ethnic hill and border peoples (the Civilian Irregular Defense Group, CIDG) in a twilight war against Cambodian frontier patrols—crossing and recrossing the border with regularity, and holding a watch on the Mekong.

The October 23, 1964, crash of an American C-123 aircraft in Cambodia—brought down by either Cambodian or Viet Cong antiaircraft fire—is a typical case of a border-crossing operation led by U.S. Special Forces. SF personnel (5 in number) led a 102-man CIDG to the crash location in hopes of recovering the last missing body (the others having been recovered by U.S. helicopters on the day of the crash). The C-123 had attempted an aerial resupply of the SF camp at Bu Prang; too late did the crew discover that they had overflown an enemy camp and, in the rain and thunder storms of the monsoon season, received lethal ground fire. By the time the SF-CIDG team arrived at the crash site, Cambodians had disassembled most of the aircraft and had taken the pieces to Phnom Penh for public display. A Cambodian Army major told the SF-CIDG team that they were on Khmer territory. The Cambodians insisted that the Americans and Vietnamese depart, which they did—shadowed by elements of a Cambodian Army battalion.[23]

Unfortunately for the plans of internationalists, what began in 1964 as a river and border problem became by the end of Johnson's tenure a most unintended tragedy: the beginnings of Cambodian disintegration. Between 1964 and 1968 Prince Sihanouk and his appointees had, in the eyes of the Cambodian opposition, managed to wreck the frail Khmer economy. Under pressure from former centrist supporters, the Prince recalled General Lon Nol and made him Prime Minister in April 1968, three months after the Tet offensive. Because Lon Nol was known to have had contact with U.S. agents throughout the 1960's—even after Cambodia had broken off diplomatic relations with the United States in 1964—the Khmer Rouge opposed him and spread rebellion to the Cambodian provinces of Kompong Speu, Kampot, and Kirisom. To make things worse, the Laotian Pathet Lao, a Leninist group, took control of areas on the Laotian-Cambodian border, and temple raids and threats of hostilities increased on the Thai-Cambodian border. For Cambodia, vultures seemed to be gathering at every compass point.[24]

The Laotian War

By early 1964 that landlocked slice of Indochina known as Laos, though still a backwater to the U.S. media, had become crucial to the designs of American maximalists. These leaders wanted to widen the Vietnam war in response to actions of Hanoi, which in their view had already expanded the combat into a Southeast Asian war. Blocked by jungle-encrusted mountains from easy access to the American-dominated Pacific Ocean, underdeveloped and underpopulated in comparison to neighboring states, not yet launched into what social scientists call modern nation-building, Laos bewildered internationalists.

The Kennedy minimalists, believing they knew what it would cost to project American power into Laos, had already attempted a diplomatic solution. They planned to use Laos as a buffer, a lock on the back door to South Vietnam. In this they thought they had international support. The Laotian accords of the Geneva Conference of 1962—cochaired by Great Britain and the Soviet Union—had guaranteed Laotian neutrality; and in April 1963 special emissary Averell Harriman persuaded Khrushchev to issue a statement supporting the accords. But the diplomatic solution failed because Hanoi could not afford to have the back door to the South closed after Kennedy's successes at starting to close the front door, the coastal sealanes. In Vietnam, Ngo Dinh Diem knew this as early as August 1961, when there was fighting around Saravane, a Laotian point only 80 kilometers from Quong Nam province in South Vietnam. Diem warned Ambassadors Nolting (Saigon) and Harriman (Geneva) that what many could put together in Geneva, a few could undo in Hanoi.[25] He was correct.

The undoing was accomplished largely through Hanoi's use of the Ho Chi Minh Trail, a network of footpaths and unpaved roads that stretched for approximately 550 miles under the dark canopy of the jungle. Some analysts estimate that if one counted all the feeder, side, and duplicate parts of the trail, it would total 12,000 miles. Traffic on the trail started from various North Vietnamese border positions and funneled into Laos across the Bannakai and Mu Gia mountain passes. Hanoi gave command of the trail to a unit it named Group 559, which by 1968 grew to number 50,000. Another 50,000 North Vietnamese army engineers and 12,000 infantry and antiaircraft artillerymen were used along the trail, and perhaps a million people traveled down it during the war. About this situation the Laotian government could do nothing. In fact, government in Laos in 1964 represented a compromise, a royal troika of praetorian right, neutralist center, and Pathet Lao left trying to govern a frail and fractured tribal kingdom of rural hill people and river-valley folk. By themselves, the three princes who ruled Laos could do nothing to block use of the Ho Chi Minh Trail or to force the North Vietnamese from that portion of Laotian territory.[26]

By 1964 American maximalists were ready to push their solution. In Niebuhrian terms, they argued that since the North Vietnamese had violated Laotian territory and Vientiane, the Laotian administrative capital, could not eject them, there was justification for applying military force to expel an aggressor. Planners in Washington and Saigon envisaged a two-pronged attack. The Americans would make air strikes—expensive in the machinery required but cost-effective in the manpower saved. The Vietnamese would make cross-border raids—expensive in the manpower required but cost-effective in the machinery saved. With this division of capital-intensive and labor-intensive tasks, the Americans generally took to the air and the South Vietnamese to the ground—Laotian air and ground.

As he had in Cambodia, President Johnson began to widen the war in Laos almost immediately. In an "Eyes Only" cable of December 6, 1963, Rusk asked Ambassador Lodge in Saigon and Admiral Harry Felt in Honolulu for a field report, saying that Johnson had expressed "deep concern that our efforts in Vietnam be stepped up to highest pitch." In fact, Felt had already provided his report, in a December 5 cable that received immediate and wide Washington distribution. Drawing on complaints from General Paul Harkins about overly detailed management control from Washington, Felt advanced a strong argument, which ran as follows: The United States already was sponsoring cross-border operations into Laos under CIA auspices (the maximum the Kennedy minimalists had said they could accept). But because these operations were being conducted by indigenous people whose leaders lacked aggressiveness, they had failed to get results. To succeed, "U.S. advisors should be permitted to accompany the patrols for a certain distance into Laos without continuous referral for approval to higher headquarters." If cross-border patrols were to penetrate deeply enough to provide useful information, they would need air resupply. And finally, although tactical air reconnaissance should first be used to locate the exact areas of VC activity, "Washington D.C. restrictions prevent current use of U.S. aircraft for low-level time-sensitive tactical photography." These were telling points, and internationalists, especially the minimalists, squirmed.[27] Concerned about the presence of U.S. advisers on any probes, Whig minimalists persuaded Johnson to agree only to develop detailed plans while obtaining a field assessment of the likely political consequences in Vientiane. These minimalists wanted to know "what must be done overtly and what Lao Government might agree to."[28] Johnson gave this task to his fellow Southerner, Secretary of State Dean Rusk.

Rusk soon discovered that on Laotian issues U.S. internationalism was a house divided. For example, in a long memorandum to the President on March 13, McNamara recommended that the United States authorize hot pursuit by U.S. aircraft, as well as South Vietnamese ground operations, over the Laotian frontier. This maximalist suggestion was followed on March 14 by a surprising recommendation from Roger Hilsman, the leading State Department minimalist. In a letter to Rusk, he recommended among other things that in order to solidify the commitment of Laos's neighbor state of Thailand to U.S. aims in Southeast Asia, the United States should "imply clearly that we are prepared to introduce U.S. ground forces into Laos if necessary." McGeorge Bundy obtained a copy of the Hilsman letter for Johnson's perusal.[29] At this, some internationalists remembered that Kennedy had dispatched 500 U.S. troops to northern Thailand in early 1962 following the Pathet Lao–North Vietnamese military victory at Nam Tha, Laos.

Even with Hilsman's apparent defection to Felt's camp, Defense and State internationalists disagreed on a Laotian solution. Generally they held opposite opinions, even on Hilsman's suggestion for stationing American troops in Thailand; the Pentagon opposed it as sending too weak a military signal, and the State Department favored the plan because its object appeared political rather than military. Ambassador Leonard Unger in Vientiane, who represented the U.S. government to a royal retinue of warring princes, launched the State Department's counterattack. Any arrangement would have to maintain a delicate balance between Prince Boun Oum Na Champassak for the rightists, Prince Souvanna Phouma for the neutralists, and his half-brother Prince Souphanouvong for the leftists. Unger, a firm minimalist, believed that Prince Souvanna Phouma and his neutralist followers represented the only realistic hope for Laos, and that any U.S. tilt to either right or left in Laos might rekindle the ambitions of the military royal-right; in 1962 Kennedy internationalists had pressured this faction into accepting Souvanna Phouma's neutralist leadership. And, as Unger feared, the Laotian right did act to upset the balance of power within the government. On April 19 they attempted a coup; this allowed the Pathet Lao to claim that rightists thereby had canceled the earlier, laboriously negotiated Plain of Jars Agreements that had set up the earlier power-sharing troika.[30] Unknown to Souvanna Phouma, by the time of the attempted coup U.S. policy toward Laos had already undergone a change.

The change in U.S. policy came about when, on March 17, Washington maximalists persuaded the National Security Council to issue NSC Memorandum 288, authorizing South Vietnamese ground operations into Laos for border control purposes. This memorandum marked the beginning of an in-house power struggle between minimalists and maximalists over how to define a limited war in Southeast Asia. By this time the coalitions were thoroughly mixed: some Whigs, such as Hilsman, had joined the Tory-dominated maximalist camp; and on the issue of ground operations in Laos, President Johnson, a Tory, favored the Whig-dominated minimalist camp.

On May 5, however, internationalists from the Defense and State Departments reached an agreement that meant partial victory for Unger and the minimalists. Washington would authorize only small Vietnamese patrols, not exceeding one hundred men, not accompanied by U.S. advisers, resupplied by unmarked aircraft, in the Laotian area of Tchepone between Route 9 and the 17th parallel. Questions of low-level aircraft reconnaissance and patrols to other Laotian locations were deferred for later consideration.[31]

Meanwhile, since the attempted coup in April, both minimalists and maximalists had worked feverishly to restore Souvanna Phouma's influence as the one politician who could balance forces on the left and right in Laotian politics. But with the central government stretched between the administrative capital of Vientiane on the southern Mekong to the royal capital of Luang Prabang on the northern banks of the 1,000-mile-long Laotian Mekong, Unger feared for the permanence of this arrangement.

The key problem was Johnson's possible reconsideration of low-level air reconnaissance. On May 11 Unger warned internationalists in Washington, Saigon, and Honolulu that "coalition government prospects hang in balance" and that if any "recon flights become known and are attacked by Pathet Lao, U.S. and GVN [Saigon] will have to deny knowledge any such action, including to Souvanna." Unger commiserated with Souvanna's nearly hopeless task: "He is now trying to keep communists quiescent while he undertakes [to] work out governmental reorganization under right-wing pressure."[32]

The pressure for expanding the raids into Laos also increased. In the first week of May 1964, Henry Cabot Lodge reported from Saigon that his chief military and intelligence advisers, General Paul Harkins and Mr. Peer De Silva, argued at the weekly group meeting that because North Vietnam maintained troops in Laos along Route 9, MACV and CIA Saigon needed more intelligence on their operations. By May 18 the group orchestrated by Admiral Felt could perceive the tide turning. On that date administration officials advised the Commanding General of MACV to prepare U.S. aircraft, now ready at Vietnamese bases, for low-level reconnaissance over Laos once Washington sent the signal. Minimalists insisted that, at the least, the U.S. mission in Saigon inform General Khanh and obtain his blessings for such flights.[33]

To the disappointment of minimalists, Khanh did more than bless the proposals. On May 30 the CIA reported that Khanh proposed cutting off and occupying "southern Laos somewhere near the 17th parallel." Further, he thought "action should be taken in concert with the Thai, who would seize and defend the remainder of the Mekong river valley north of the 17th parallel."[34] These suggestions were too extreme even for maximalist Tories to countenance.

In early June, low-level reconnaissance aircraft—given the code name YANKEE TEAM—began flying missions, and within days antiaircraft weapons of either the Pathet Lao or the North Vietnamese Army had shot down a YANKEE TEAM plane, leading the United States to bomb the antiaircraft site. In a June 9 letter to President Johnson, Senator Mansfield posed several rhetorical questions: "What happens if other U.S. reconnaissance planes are shot down? And if we cannot stop the attrition by air, must we not do it by land forces or suffer the ignominious consequence?"[35]

Only silence answered Mansfield; meanwhile, Laos emerged as yet another battlefield in Johnson's Southeast Asian war. On June 11 an American-furnished T-28 aircraft bombed the old neutralist–Pathet Lao headquarters area in Khang Khay on the Plain of Jars. A few bombs exploded at the extensive Chinese Communist mission, killing one Chinese and wounding five others. Immediately, Souvanna Phouma made an urgent call for a June conference in Zurich, and representatives of the Geneva Conference Co-Chairmen and the International Control Commission visited Khang Khay. Johnson paid a costly human price for these Laotian raids; the CIA reported that the Pathet Lao had captured a U.S. Navy pilot, Lieutenant Klusmann, whom they had shot down on June 6.

According to CIA sources, the Pathet Lao executed him on June 26 in Khang Khay.[36]

Charges and countercharges punctuated the Laotian debate. Prince Souphanouvong took his case to Chen Yi in Peking in August and to Moscow officials in September. On December 8, to counter the princes on the left, General Phoumi Nosavan read a royal White Paper before the nineteenth session of the U.N. General Assembly. His subject was North Vietnamese interference inside Laos. By mid-December, however, the debate had only academic interest, for by then the United States had begun its BARREL ROLE operations: air strikes by U.S. planes flown by U.S. pilots against infiltration targets in Laos.

Coincidentally with the Laotian debate, the Johnson internationalists were directing Saigon forces and CIA-controlled groups in and out of Laos. The maximalist faction inside the Johnson administration did not hold together well during this storm of increased Laotian activity. When McNamara opposed Maxwell Taylor's August proposal that U.S. aircraft launch major air operations in the Laotian panhandle, even the President became aware that maximalists were fighting each other. The minimalist ranks split also. For example, John T. McNaughton, of McNamara's civilian staff at Defense, heard that minimalists such as Mike Forrestal, at NSC, hoped that Taylor's recommendations would "be approved in toto." Even the Joint Chiefs split: General LeMay of the Air Force and General Wally Greene, Commandant of the Marine Corps, favored extensive U.S. air strikes, but General Wheeler and his Army and Navy cochiefs refused to commit their support to increased air operations. In August and September, LeMay circulated a RAND memorandum that highlighted "the function of Laos and Cambodia in providing supply routes and safe haven for the insurgents." (The RAND Corporation was the favorite Air Force "think tank," a private-sector organization contracted to perform classified or unclassified research.) But the Tory CIA director, John McCone, opposed LeMay, and his CIA analysts warned Johnson that the proposed air strikes could do little to dampen infiltration activity. In the end, the President tilted toward Taylor.[37]

Johnson held back one key element; he would not approve U.S. ground advisers' entering Laos. But the new Commander-in-Chief of the Pacific (CINCPAC), Admiral U. S. Grant Sharp, gave Johnson no rest. On June 30, 1964, the Admiral replaced Felt as leader of the loyal military opposition, and he did not admit defeat. In August Sharp cabled that "participation of U.S. advisors at all planning and operating echelons is essential" and that "U.S. advisor participation should include going into Laos on both air and ground operations." Again in September he recommended that "U.S. advisors should accompany ARVN ground forces."

The United States had already begun FARMGATE, a special covert program of air strikes against Communist-held targets in South Vietnam, in which U.S. Air Force pilots flew South Vietnamese marked aircraft. Sharp recommended using FARMGATE against targets in Laos.[38] By late September his persistence won the air argument but not the ground debate.

The internationalists had hard evidence that the North Vietnamese were using Laos as an infiltration route to the South. As with Cambodia, that evidence came from high-resolution photography, interrogation of prisoners, translations of captured documents, agent reports, and information furnished by units of the U.S. Special Forces assigned to border areas. The U.S. Special Forces, which earlier had played a role in Laos as WHITE STAR teams, were seen by MACV as a key source of information. To facilitate their use with ARVN ground probes into Laos, MACV formed a composite detachment at Nha Trang by reassigning the most experienced Special Forces troops from units in South Vietnam; and on June 2 MACV requested that U.S. training centers send small assault teams and larger detachments capable of performing more varied missions. In their enthusiasm for the role the Special Forces could play, especially with a Special Force Group Headquarters located on the northeastern Pacific rim in Okinawa, MACV and CINCPAC were no match for General Khanh. Whereas the American military had authorized 684 spaces for Special Forces personnel in Vietnam and envisaged a moderate rate of increase. Khanh called for 10,000 Special Forces to "cover the whole Cambodian-Laotian frontier." Lodge cabled this figure to Rusk, McNamara, Harriman, and Bundy with the wry postscript, "This man obviously wants to get on with the job."[39]

By September 1964, Tory maximalists had persuaded Johnson that he could win a limited war by expanding it. In a terse, State-Defense cable, dated September 9, to the U.S. Ambassadors in South Vietnam, Laos, and Thailand, the United States approved US-GVN-RLAF (Royal Laotian Air Force) air strikes at Laotian targets with U.S. high-performance aircraft. The internationalist authors of the cable asked the three U.S. Ambassadors "whether we should inform Souvanna before undertaking, or go ahead without informing him." The cable ended on an ominous note: "Believe it would be desirable [that] Bangkok be represented at meeting, in view possible Thai involvement in some operations."[40]

These events of 1964 set the pattern for a continuing expansion of the war into Laos. By 1968, when Johnson announced that he would not run again for President, U.S. involvement was substantial. The CIA had financed a military unit of Meo tribesmen in northern Laos, as well as an airline (Air America), some of whose pilots flew throughout Laos in T-28 fighter bombers as well as civil aircraft. American-financed radar sites dominated key terrain in Laos at places such as Muong Phalane and Phu Phi Thi—both of which the Pathet Lao and North Vietnamese had captured by 1968. (The Phu Phi Thi site was on a 5,860-foot peak in Laos 17 miles from the North Vietnamese border; and before its capture, it was garrisoned with about a dozen Americans and a detachment of Meo Special Forces.) The loss of U.S. aircraft mounted steadily until 1969, when the figures included 80 aircraft lost in northern Laos and just under 300 in southern Laos. By 1968 the United States was directing the Royal Laotian military, the ARVN, VNAF, various CIA-trained Meo guerrillas, and U.S. Special Forces teams. In Laos they faced some 40,000 North Vietnamese troops and unknown numbers of the native Pathet Lao, the local Leninist army that the North Vietnamese directed. For these Laotian operations, the Chinese offered support to the North Vietnamese, and the Thais sold to the United States rights to their air bases and support facilities.[41]

The North Vietnamese War

The American internationalists made a distinction between North Vietnam and the three other Mekong River states—South Vietnam, Laos, and Cambodia—that were involved in the Southeast Asian war. In their scenarios, North Vietnam was the main source of supplies for the guerrilla war in the South. Internationalists did not deny the existence of southern rebels, for they knew that there were southerners who joined southern units to aid, direct, organize, and train southern forces to overthrow the regime in South Vietnam. Recognizing this, they believed that with persistent U.S. help, the Government of South Vietnam (GVN) could prevent its indigenous southern rebels from receiving outside assistance, and could then bring the southern resistance under a modicum of control. Since the largest percentage of Leninist assistance to the southern rebels came through North Vietnam, the northern regime became the critical target of GVN and U.S. reaction.[42]

The internationalists' record does not reflect any unease about the early U.S. counterstrikes at the Hanoi regime. Initially internationalists designed their strikes as reactive; they were supposed to block a specific enemy activity in an appropriately measured way. But as their patience began to run out, and Johnson and his advisers became more frustrated, measured responses were often replaced with raids of vengeance that made little strategic sense. What Johnson attempted—by listing as many targets as possible—was to shift the balance of power by using as much force as necessary to guarantee that the U.S.-GVN coalition would not lose the war. Force of that magnitude, however, was more than even Tory maximalists could accept. Some limits had to be set and maintained. And as the following discussion will illustrate, that was more easily said than done.

Covert action aimed at North Vietnam dated from the Kennedy era. The CIA air-dropped sabotage teams into North Vietnam (DRV) as early as 1961.[43] Many internationalists viewed these CIA operations as haphazard, and at the Vietnam Policy Conference in Honolulu on November 30, 1963, the internationalist conferees directed CIA (Controlled American Source Saigon, or CAS Saigon) and MACV to organize a combined twelve-month program for covert operations against the DRV. In mid-December Secretary McNamara forwarded the CIA-MACV plan to the new President, and Johnson selected a Marine Corps Major-General, Victor Krulak, to chair an interdepartmental group with the task of ordering the plan's recommendations according to risk. Krulak returned the risk analysis on January 2, 1964. On January 16 Johnson approved covert actions as ranked, with a February 1 starting date under the code name OPLAN 34A. The authors of OPLAN 34A conceived of a three-phase operation that would increase the damage to North Vietnamese assets until costs outweighed benefits for the Leninist Lao Dong leadership in Hanoi.

To assure that Johnson did not waver in his resolve to limit strikes on the North, Ambassador Lodge sent the President a cable on February 20, 1964, in which he argued that enemy terrorism aimed at Americans—and only that—warranted "swift retaliation" against the DRV. (Lodge, who had urged this view on Kennedy in October 1963, suggested that Undersecretary Averell Harriman should have a copy of the October memorandum if Johnson wanted to review it.) Typically for anyone serving as the U.S. Ambassador in Saigon, Lodge raised the sanctuary issue in regard to North Vietnam. In the Korean War, internationalists had denied that the Japanese islands gave U.S. forces a sanctuary equivalent to the North Korean sanctuary in Chinese Manchuria. Now, in the Vietnam war, internationalists said that the Philippine Islands and Thailand did not provide a sanctuary for U.S. forces, at least not one equal to that enjoyed by the Vietnamese enemy. General Matthew B. Ridgway, who had had to design victory in the Korean War after the MacArthur-Truman debacle in strategy, admitted that the unspoken acceptance of sanctuaries on both sides was one cost of limited war. But in 1964 Ridgway's words went unheeded.[44] North Vietnamese forces, of course, did have a sanctuary in southern China and the Vietnamese-Chinese border area; even Niebuhrian maximalists recognized it. What Lodge could not accept was the minimalist view that placed most, if not all, of North Vietnam within the sanctuary. He argued, "We let them [DRV] have a sanctuary from which they operate against us, whereas we not only have no sanctuary, but do not operate against them in any significant way."[45] This thesis persuaded Johnson, and the attacks proceeded on schedule.

A month after the Lodge cable, Defense Secretary McNamara described OPLAN 34A to the President as "a very modest covert program operated by the South Vietnamese (and a few Chinese Nationalists) . . . a program so limited that it is unlikely to have any significant effect."[46] And yet by late March of 1964, a series of OPLAN 34 missions led Hanoi to charge that the United States planned to extend the war into the North. As many key internationalists knew, the United States and the GVN had indeed planned limited intelligence collection, psychological warfare, and punitive raids into the North. Yet Lodge, even in his SECRET cables to Washington, characterized as pure propaganda the Radio Hanoi and DRV News Agency reports of an American plan to extend the war.[47]

Across the Potomac River from the White House, maximalists in the Joint Chiefs of Staff responded more directly. In their March manifesto they urged McNamara to change the status of the strikes from covert to overt, and, more important, to design them to be counterstrikes that would bring specific military results instead of representing only punitive raids of vengeance in an ideological war (à la Lodge). Admiral David McDonald was the most vehement, with the other Chiefs supporting much of his position on making the strikes militarily effective. Krulak's successor on the Joint Staff, General Rollen Anthis, proclaimed, in the presence of civilian Pentagon and CIA officials such as Ray Cline, that if the United States could not "make the high jumps in South Vietnam," it "should pole vault into the North."[48] McNamara was able to keep the Joint Chiefs quiet during March because General Khanh, absorbed in trying to run his new government in Saigon, wanted no part of overt strikes at the North. Within a month, however, as he was losing his grip over his own governing military committee, Khanh requested that the United States "redouble covert operations right away."[49] This even the maximalists refused to grant Khanh. By accident his opportunity to redouble operations came from the U.S. Navy.

Since U.S. and GVN army and air force personnel dominated OPLAN 34A planning, only the minor naval resources required to perform coastal infiltration and coastal raids were involved in those operations. The American high-seas navy, effectively the major source of military power in the Pacific basin, was given only one operation of its own—the De Soto patrols. These sea patrols were conducted by U.S. Navy destroyers in the Gulf of Tonkin, beyond the 3-mile territorial waters of the DRV; they observed shipping and tried to intercept communications of the Hanoi military and political forces. As De Soto patrols usually avoided close proximity to the DRV's coast by observing a 6- to 9-mile limit, the location of certain DRV islands off their continental coast brought the destroyers to within 4 miles of the coasts of certain islands. While De Soto patrols ranged off the DRV coast and its islands, Kennedy and Johnson stationed the large movable U.S. islands—aircraft carrier battle groups—along the GVN coast. By May of 1964 the U.S.S. *Kitty Hawk* and its escorting vessels patrolled just beyond the horizon east from Hue, the old imperial capital of Annam. From here the *Kitty Hawk's* aircraft flew cover for YANKEE TEAM air reconnaissance over Laos. By July the JCS ordered CINCPAC to maintain one attack carrier on station off South Vietnam as a continuing requirement. The *Kitty Hawk* rotated this duty with its companion carriers, the U.S.S. *Constellation* and the U.S.S. *Ticonderoga*. By mid-July the cruiser *Oklahoma City*, flagship of the U.S. 7th Fleet, paid a goodwill visit to the port of Saigon, having steamed up the dangerous channel of the Saigon River past the Rung Sat secret zone, a mangrove swamp often used by the Viet Cong. In Saigon the 7th Fleet Commander, Vice Admiral Roy L. Johnson, informed reporters that the attack carriers of his three carrier battle groups stood within easy striking distance of any western Pacific Ocean target. By August 3 the *Ticonderoga* and the *Constellation* were steaming south again from their sanctuary in British Hong Kong. CINCPAC alerted the two carriers to prepare for reprisal strikes against North Vietnam.

Earlier that summer Secretary Rusk had suggested that flights from the *Kitty Hawk* should range over GVN territory to the 17th parallel, and that the carrier should then steam north into international waters, coming within 30 miles of China's Hainan Island. But his suggestion was rejected in the NSC, where Mike Forrestal explained to McGeorge Bundy that this might send the wrong signal to the leaders of the People's Republic of China (PRC). It fell to the two warships departing from Hong Kong to send a signal more dramatic than Rusk's suggestion—sixty-four sorties were flown from their decks against North Vietnamese torpedo boat bases and an oil storage depot near Vinh, following the August 4 naval engagements in the Gulf of Tonkin. General William Westmoreland cabled Admiral Sharp and General Wheeler with his assessment that both North Vietnam and China had received the American signal.[50]

An occasion on which U.S. jets fought Mao's MIG's in early 1965 illustrates how Johnson's war oozed across Southeast Asian borders regardless of signals. Counterstrikes north of the North Vietnamese city of Vinh raised the risk of aircraft losses, especially following the August raids. China always remained off-limits, even after August 15, 1964, when new "hot pursuit" engagement rules authorized U.S. forces to pursue attacking ships and aircraft into North Vietnamese territorial waters and airspace. The JCS tried to bring both Hainan Island and the southern provinces of mainland China into the geography covered by the hot-pursuit rules, but here Tories and Whigs stood firm; limits were limits. In combat, however, rules are easily bent or broken. By the first week of April 1965,

Vietnamese MIG's scored their first "kills" of American F-105 jets. By the following week American jets—evading the MIG's that often traversed the Tonkinese Red River corridor under the control of Ground Controlled Intercept Radar—flew instead over Hainan Island. There they met Chinese MIG's in what one Reuters correspondent reported as the "Hainan Island Air Battle." The PRC had signaled back.[51]

Both sides sent signals (many of them misunderstood), but the U.S. naval power that began in 1964 continued to increase in the region. And as American warships approached the southern rim of the Pacific basin, they could find sanctuary in the safe harbor at British Hong Kong to the north and the U.S. naval base at Subic Bay in the Philippines to the east. On these warships, marine landing teams prepared for any emergencies, using their sanctuary base at Okinawa to rotate marine units from sea duty to shore tasks. It was the Whig ambassador, Henry Cabot Lodge, who wanted this naval flotilla berthed even closer to the Vietnamese coast, perhaps at Cam Ranh Bay. Although the NSC responded negatively to this naval-basing strategy, by May 1964, the Joint Chiefs had cast their naval future with Lodge, requesting "an austere naval facility" at Cam Ranh Bay.[52]

As internationalists stationed these land, air, and sea assets in Southeast Asia in the spring and early summer of 1964, their respective commands used them to make an increasing number of military counterstrikes throughout all of Indochina. Because internationalists had classified and compartmentalized many separate operations—such as De Soto patrols, FARMGATE, and OPLAN 34A—no one individual, group, or military command coordinated their daily activities. This fact, more than any other, led to the Gulf of Tonkin affair of August 1964 and the controversial congressional resolution that followed.

The story behind the Gulf of Tonkin Resolution is a long one, but worth retelling here because it illustrates so well the way in which peace-oriented internationalist assumptions were translated into a disastrous war policy. The question of how to secure congressional support for the Southeast Asian effort was a major preoccupation of the Johnson team from its earliest months in the White House. In an NSC discussion of June 10, 1964, Johnson's advisers saw timing as critical: Congress should not be presented with a proposed resolution until the politically important civil rights bill had cleared the Senate floor. They wanted to offer a resolution that was "general in tone" only after "careful congressional soundings indicate rapid passage by a very substantial majority." The President's men foresaw domestic political costs in this effort, and therefore recommended that Johnson present a resolution only when he saw it as necessary to focus attention on "the defense of Southeast Asia in the coming summer."[53] Far off in Saigon, Lodge worried that sudden governmental changes by Khanh could throw off Washington's careful political timing of the resolution. He visited Khanh on June 12 to explain this concern, and afterward cabled Rusk with assurances that Khanh would not organize his government without first consulting Lodge.[54]

As the summer wore on, planning for the congressional resolution on Southeast Asia was handled by high-level staff members as part of routine contingency planning. Thus in offering recommendations on Vietnam, veteran presidential advisers such as Nitze and Harriman often referred to past congressional resolutions that had been preplanned on the executive side of government and later offered to the Congress for advice and consent. In one memorandum the basic precedents for success were said to be "the Formosa Resolution, the Middle East Resolution and, in a sense, the Vandenburg Resolution."[55] Still, Johnson hesitated to make the formal congressional approach.

In July, debate within the administration became more urgent. In a cable dated July 20, Rusk told Lodge that Washington feared Khanh might still be trying to involve the United States in overt northern ventures. In early May—in a dramatic statement of his views to a joint American delegation that included McNamara, Lodge, Taylor, and Harkins—Khanh had advocated attacking the North.[56] CIA analysts insisted that Khanh was using "March North" propaganda only as a means to maneuver against internal forces in the GVN. But in late July, Ambassador Taylor, having replaced Lodge, reported that whatever his motives, Khanh indeed had launched a deliberate campaign to associate the United States in a "March North" policy with full knowledge that it would cause embarrassment to the United States.[57]

And embarrassments mounted. At Bien Hoa Air Base near Saigon, a young GVN air commodore, Nguyen Cao Ky, briefed Associated Press newsmen on his flying exploits over North Vietnam and described the land, sea, and air drops of sabotage teams into the DRV. For practical purposes, he had thus declassified the most sensitive U.S.-GVN activity, OPLAN 34A. At the same time, the *Saigon Post*, an English language daily, began a campaign of complaints against the U.S. government for not warmly backing the "March North" program.[58] Not only did leaders along the Potomac River take Khanh seriously, but so did those along the Red River in the DRV; they made their capital city ready. In mid-July the British Consul General reported from Hanoi that air raid shelters appeared to be under construction there, some in public parks.[59] Clearly, the DRV was anticipating war.

With the situation deteriorating rapidly, internationalists dispatched a cable on July 26 to the U.S. embassies in both Saigon and Vientiane. "Pri-

marily for reasons of morale in South Vietnam and to divert GVN attention from proposals to strike North Vietnam," it said, the United States
was planning "air attacks on VC supply lines in the Laotian Panhandle."
Two days earlier, in fact, McGeorge Bundy had informed Johnson that he
and others hoped to placate Khanh with some small military action. In
other words, in order to limit the war on a larger scale, the internationalists
were willing to enlarge it on a smaller scale.[60]

During the first week of August, three American-engineered covert
operations, all occurring within close proximity and timing of each other,
culminated in North Vietnamese and U.S. ships firing at one another. On
July 31 South Vietnamese naval craft began another series of OPLAN 34A
missions, bombarding DRV installations on the North Vietnamese islands
of Hon Me and Hon Ngu. On August 1 and 2 Laotian T-28's furnished by
the United States strafed and bombed two North Vietnamese villages in
Nghi An province near the Laotian border. Twelve hours after the naval
bombardment began, the destroyer U.S.S. *Maddox* began a De Soto patrol
off the DRV coast. By August 2 it had steamed several kilometers east of
the island of Hon Ngu. Sighting a number of DRV junks massing near the
island, the captain of the *Maddox* put out to sea—but only to find himself
ordered back. He resumed his patrol track, and as he reached waters near
the island of Hon Me on the afternoon of August 2, three North Vietnamese torpedo boats pursued the *Maddox* at high speed. Having decided their intent was hostile, the U.S. ship opened fire, and the DRV
boats returned fire with torpedoes. By evasive action and effective fire,
the *Maddox* along with aircraft from the carrier *Ticonderoga* drove off the
DRV boats, sinking one in the process.

The *Maddox* withdrew to refuel at Yankee Station off the coast of
South Vietnam, where she joined another destroyer, the U.S.S. *C. Turner
Joy*. Johnson ordered both ships back onto De Soto patrol duty. Immediately after the first Tonkin Gulf encounter, Rusk cabled Ambassador
Taylor that the administration believed "that present OPLAN 34A activities
are beginning to rattle Hanoi, and *Maddox* incident is directly related to
their [DRV] effort to resist these activities. We have no intention yielding
to pressure."[61]

The two warships resumed patrol on August 3, again cruising near
Hon Me island, but turning out to sea as evening approached. At a little
past midnight on August 4 South Vietnamese naval craft continued
OPLAN 34A raids by shelling DRV installations at Cua Ron and Vinh Son.
The De Soto patrol commander, Captain John Herrick, aboard the *Maddox*, reported that his patrol had intercepted DRV radio communications
that, according to his on-board analysts, showed DRV officials agitated
and convinced that both De Soto and OPLAN 34A performed as one opera-

tion. Ominously to Herrick, these communications suggested that the DRV was preparing a counterstrike.

Within hours of Captain Herrick's report, at 7:40 p.m. to be exact, destroyer personnel reported observing surface radar contacts approximately 36 miles to the northeast and closing. When the radar contacts persisted, both destroyers engaged those targets and also received aircraft support flying from the deck of the *Ticonderoga*. When these August 4 reports later became the center of a major debate, key destroyer personnel insisted that the engagement had occurred, but hard proof was difficult to furnish. Even on August 4 there were some in U.S. Navy circles who suggested the possibility of a radar malfunction. This possibility was reported to the White House within a few hours of the attack, and Johnson instructed McNamara to recheck the radar reports. But by then the President had already launched his own political boats.[62]

After DRV torpedo boats had engaged the *Maddox* on August 2, Johnson had rejected maximalist recommendations for retaliatory air strikes. But on August 4, after receiving news of the second engagement, he called a secret White House meeting, to which he invited his old Senate colleagues Richard Russell, George Aiken, William Fulbright, Bourke Hickenlooper, Mike Mansfield, Leverett Saltonstall, Charles Halleck, Everett Dirksen, and Frances Bolton, along with House Speaker Sam Rayburn. The Senators were joined by key administration internationalists, including Rusk, of State; McNamara, of Defense; McCone, of the CIA; and Wheeler, of the Joint Chiefs. Johnson craftily threw the meeting into a state of unease by accusing "someone" of leaking news of the meeting to the media. Halleck rose to the bait, declaiming "I did not tell a damn person." Johnson then withdrew the charge from any member present. Hickenlooper compared the situation to the Cuban missile crisis. After several briefings by his internationalist team, Johnson won all but one Senator to his position. The lone holdout was Mike Mansfield, the senior Senator from Montana. As Johnson mapped out his domestic battleground he came to believe that the circumstances called for a resolution that would approve his handling of the incidents in the Gulf of Tonkin and pledge that "the United States is . . . prepared, as the President determines, to take all necessary steps, including the use of armed force, to assist any member or protocol state (South Vietnam, Cambodia, Laos) of the Southeast Asia Collective Treaty requesting assistance in defense of its freedom." Vague as the language was, that was how the President wanted it.[63]

To get his resolution Johnson prepared to do battle on two fronts. On the first front, that of congressional opinion, Johnson had gained the support of key Senators in the secret meeting of August 4. When the Senate and House took up the resolution, he had his Ambassador to Saigon on hand, ready to confront critics with first-hand reports. The most outspoken of the few critics, Senator Wayne Morse, of Oregon, attacked Taylor's testimony sharply. Morse knew that the South Vietnamese had bombarded the two DRV islands prior to the first Tonkin engagement, but Taylor would not admit to having specific knowledge of that evening's targets. Morse said he believed that these on-going raids were the beginning of an escalation of the war to the North, and he asked the retired general if that was a fair assessment. In reply, Taylor affirmed the old internationalist position: the raids were counterstrikes in retaliation for illegal DRV activities. Senator Morse said he did not deny illegal activity by the DRV, but repeated that his main concern was illegal GVN activity sponsored by the United States. The West Pointer held his ground while Morse relentlessly tried to outflank him. Taylor finally threw the Senator off guard by denying that any U.S. advisers had accompanied raids into the DRV, but stating that he, as a citizen, would approve of Americans' joining these raids if the American government, even by indirection, determined that it would further American national security policy.[64] When the debate concluded, Morse had not convinced his colleagues. On August 7 the resolution passed the House of Representatives unanimously, and the Senate by a vote of 88 to 2. On August 10, with Johnson's signature, it became Public Law 88-408.

On his second front, that of public opinion, Johnson had his eye on the November elections. To obtain the political advantage at home against his Republican challenger for the presidency, Barry Goldwater, Johnson had another plan. He would present himself to the public as a man of peace who spoke softly but carried a big stick—a stick he had not hesitated to use against communist threats to the peace in Southeast Asia. On this front, his strategy also seemed to work. Both before and shortly after the Tonkin naval engagement, the Gallup Poll had asked citizens, "Do you think the United States is handling affairs in South Vietnam as well as could be expected, or do you think we are handling affairs there badly, or do you have no opinion?" Before, 52 percent had answered "as well as expected," 38 percent answered "badly," and 10 percent answered "no opinion." After, the corresponding figures were 71 percent, 16 percent, and 13 percent.[65]

With victory on both domestic fronts, Johnson moved to obtain the military advantage abroad. He ordered implementation of CINCPAC OPLAN 37-64. This plan, as McNamara explained it to a joint session of the Senate's Foreign Relations and the House's Armed Services Committees, included the following: transfer of an attack carrier group from the Pacific coast to the western Pacific; movement of intercepter and fighter bomber aircraft into South Vietnam; movement of fighter bomber aircraft into Thailand; transfer of intercepter and fighter bomber squadrons from the United States to advance bases in the Pacific; movement of an antisubmarine force into the South China Sea; and the preparation for movement of selected Army and Marine Forces. Johnson felt empowered to make these moves based on the resolution he had signed into law.

So that American public law would be understood in Hanoi, however, the internationalists used a Canadian citizen, thereby also dragging an unresponsive Ottawa government into the American strategy for the Southeast Asian rim. No sooner had the Canadians assigned J. Blair Seaborn as their representative to the International Control Commission than Lodge proposed him to Rusk as an intermediary between the United States and the DRV. Rusk confirmed this double-tasking on a visit to Ottawa on April 30; and in a cable sent in early May Lodge suggested it would be well "for Seaborn to tell Ho if the U.S. has to choose between enlarging the war and withdrawing, we will enlarge." Events convinced the Hanoi leadership of this fact. When Seaborn met Phan Van Dong in the DRV capital after the Tonkin engagement, Dong angrily informed him on August 13 that "if war comes to North Vietnam, it will come to the whole of Southeast Asia."[66]

Initially, both Peking and Moscow released their reactions to the Gulf of Tonkin strikes through the state media. The American Consul General in Hong Kong, which was the U.S. listening post for "China watchers," reported that PRC Cantonese broadcasters accused the United States of fabricating the incident "to expand the war in Indo-China and to send armed force to areas near the DRV from Taiwan and Hong Kong." Moscow's response was muted, for at least two reasons: Khrushchev was away, somewhere in the Volga region; and the United States and the USSR had just reached an accord on sharing desalinization technology. In some embarrassment, the editors of Moscow's television "News of the World" attached a brief report of the Tonkin attacks to the end of a scheduled program devoted largely to extolling the benefits of Soviet-U.S. friendship.[67]

Although U.S. actions in the Tonkin Gulf did not drive a wedge between Moscow and Peking, they created a split in the opinion of U.S. internationalists. The core issue was whether to resume the OPLAN 34A raids, the Laotian counterstrikes, and the De Soto patrols. In Saigon, General Khanh insisted on resuming and enlarging all three, while Ambassador Taylor and his mission, as well as General Westmoreland, agreed that initially only the Laotian counterstrikes should be resumed. CINCPAC and the Joint Chiefs, maximalists though they were, agreed with Taylor and Westmoreland; they were concerned that their South

Vietnamese allies might lead them into a greatly expanded war. In fact, Westmoreland worried that the United States might lose control of Laotian air strikes to adventurers in the GVN–Joint General Staff hierarchy. He hoped that by having the recommended U.S. advisers present on all cross-border operations, and by giving the United States sole control over FARMGATE air operations, the United States could rein in any such adventurers. Calling the Vietnamese plan for Laos an "overly ambitious scheme," Westmoreland nevertheless argued that the Khanh government needed encouragement in its stalled war effort inside South Vietnam. Khanh's arguments in favor of resuming De Soto patrols and OPLAN 34A raids matched those for restarting Laotian operations: all these activities would increase DRV war weariness while raising GVN morale.[68] But the U.S. military wanted at least a short halt in De Soto patrols and OPLAN 34A raids.

Public support for the Tonkin actions raised the morale of some members of the Johnson administration, but others worried. Even CIA analysts, mostly of Tory persuasion, had never shared the military's enthusiasm for these expanded operations, specifically targeted or not. Their field personnel in Vietnam reported that counterstrikes brought no major effective military return for the required political investment. Internationalists in the NSC and the State Department, such as Mike Forrestal and Averell Harriman, shared some of the CIA's misgivings. Secretary of State Rusk also felt uneasy about a quick resumption.

Given this hesitation to restart all three operations, Johnson temporized by ordering a "short holding phase"; this, his internationalists reasoned, would make the communist side look responsible for any escalation that occurred. The "holding phase" applied mainly to De Soto patrols and new OPLAN 34A operations, for the President approved resupplying saboteurs already in the DRV. Johnson refused to countenance the presence of U.S. advisers in cross-border operations into Laos, but he approved intensive air reconnaissance of the Laotian panhandle and the DRV. Ominously for those internationalists who wanted to take and hold "the high moral ground," the President also approved of the use of napalm in Laos, at the discretion of Ambassador Unger in Vientiane.[69]

This "holding phase" could not last long in a house divided. Previously Johnson had made it clear to his personal war manager, McNamara, that he wanted nothing less than full support in funds, personnel, and equipment for his field commanders; no American military men should die because of old equipment. Now —having had their short halt in operations, and in order to protect the U.S. expeditionary force of advisers—Westmoreland, Taylor, Sharp, and Wheeler stated that they needed to collect intelligence, block infiltration of enemy forces and supplies, and counterstrike the DRV at each turn. In their assessment, this was what the De Soto patrols and OPLAN 34A raids, combined with Laotian cross-border operations, had granted them. The CIA, however, soon challenged this military assessment. In a Special National Intelligence Estimate released on September 8, CIA analysts concluded that "at present the odds are against the emergence of a stable government capable of effectively prosecuting the war in South Vietnam." The day following this report, with which the United States Intelligence Board concurred, CIA Director John McCone issued a bleak estimate of what advantages could be gained from pressuring the DRV.[70] His CIA analysts argued against a return to counter-strikes—which they thought were provocative raids upon the North—at least until some hopeful signs appeared in the southern struggle.

On the same day that McCone issued the Special National Intelligence Estimate, McGeorge Bundy wrote a memorandum in which he told President Johnson that a consensus worked out with Maxwell Taylor was "the best we can design for the central purpose of thickening the thin fabric of the Khanh government in the next two months"—that is, until the November elections. Bundy foresaw what his chief wanted—no substantial escalation before October, and cautious actions continuing until November. But he warned Johnson also of the inevitable price of politically motivated postponement: "You should know that in the longer perspective nearly all of us are agreed that substantially increased pressure against North Vietnam will be necessary if we are not to face the prospect of a gradual but increasingly inevitable break-up of our side in South Vietnam."[71] Ambassador Taylor shared this assessment, agreeing with Bundy. As early as August 18, Taylor had tied the international war to the national election, and suggested that the United States "prepare to escalate against NVN with January 1965 as target date." Though he hoped to hold out until that date, in his diary Taylor admitted to himself that the Khanh government might fall before then. If Khanh failed, that, in Taylor's opinion, would force the United States to strike at the DRV before November in order to hold Khanh's "government together and avoid collapse of morale."[72]

After reviewing this divergent advice, LBJ decided on September 10 to temporize again, this time on the side of his field commanders. As always, he set conditions. First, he authorized CINCPAC to resume De Soto patrols promptly; these patrols, however, were to steam well outside the DRV's newly proclaimed 12-mile limit and were to be clearly dissociated from OPLAN 34A maritime operations. The President asked that selected destroyers operate at least in pairs with air cover from the carriers, and with on-board antisubmarine warfare equipment. If U.S. warships had to return to these waters, he was determined not to lose one. Second,

Johnson agreed to let the Saigon government resume certain OPLAN 34A operations as soon as the first De Soto patrol came off station; approved operations included maritime raids, air resupply, and propaganda leaflet drops, but not air strikes. Third, President Johnson approved a resumption of Laotian operations, but without U.S. ground advisers on cross-border raids. All these instructions were put into National Security Action Memorandum 314, signed by McGeorge Bundy on September 10, 1964.[73]

Whig minimalists, such as Mike Forrestal, fumed that McGeorge Bundy mistakenly had sided with the military maximalists. In two memoranda on September 22, Forrestal tried to redirect the process. First, he wrote to Ambassador Lewellyn Thompson, at State, blaming the Tonkin affair on mismanagement of the De Soto patrols and OPLAN 34A timing. As a minimum, Forrestal suggested, there should be a Washington-level coordination and approval process centered at either the NSC or State, but not at the JCS. Next he wrote to Bundy, enclosing a memo from Harriman to Rusk, that recommended postponement of the De Soto patrols. Forrestal concurred with Harriman, but to no avail.[74]

When Forrestal lost, Admiral Sharp, who was then the CINCPAC, solidified the maximalist victory by alerting the fleet. Sharp had his own conditions to add to those specified by the Commander-in-Chief. He ordered SP2 aircraft cover for De Soto patrols in order to illuminate all vessels that approached within 5 nautical miles of the destroyers. He stressed the importance of obtaining photographs of suspect or hostile vessels during hours of darkness and daylight. Further, Sharp authorized stationing a submarine in the Gulf of Tonkin. If he had to order his fleet elements to hostile waters, he was going to be prepared to win any naval battles above, on, or below the surface, and to have photographs to prove it.[75]

This was how Johnson's Southeast Asian war came to North Vietnam. The fact remains, of course, that the DRV had carried its war to the southern half of Vietnam before Johnson began to escalate and enlarge it. Neither antagonist understood the motives of the other, mainly because the Washington-Hanoi impasse rested on differing interpretations of Indochinese history. Ho Chi Minh and the Lao Dong party leadership believed they had won, on the battlefield, the second phase of a multiphase Indochinese war. They felt, however, that on the peace-field of Geneva in 1954, where diplomats—most of them non-Vietnamese—replaced soldiers, they had been cheated of full victory. They decided then not to allow any group to repeat this procedure in the third phase of the Indochinese war. (Phase one was the 1941–45 struggle against the Japanese, who had replaced the French; phase two was the 1945–54 struggle against the French, who had returned; and phase three was the current struggle with the Americans.)

But Lyndon Johnson, and the internationalist leadership in both U.S. parties, had decided by 1964 that the Lao Dong party, a Leninist-style elite, had cheated the old Viet Minh anticolonial groups out of the true fruits of victory, and had brought a harsh and repressive government to power in Hanoi's half of the truncated state. Given the weak, non-democratic regimes in Saigon, Johnson and his internationalists feared that Ho Chi Minh would cheat his way to victory in the South unless there was a U.S. commitment to block him; and they were determined to block any possible win by the DRV in this third phase of the war.[76] With this in mind, Johnson conducted his Southeast Asian war secretly in 1964, largely because of his view of political requirements at home. Ho Chi Minh also conducted his Southeast Asian war secretly, but he did so because of his view of political requirements abroad.

After he was elected in his own right in November 1964, Johnson, al-ways something of a Texas Tory, responded favorably to his maximalist advisers. Ho Chi Minh (not in need of election cover) had already re-sponded favorably to his own maximalist advisers' call for escalation, thereby stealing the march on Johnson. By 1965 American combat units were fighting against Viet Cong and North Vietnamese Army units, whereas before that time American advisers had been limited to assisting ARVN troop units in their firefights with opposing southern Viet Cong forces. By 1965 the air war had escalated, with the DRV the target for the ROLLING THUNDER air assaults. But the President had set the pattern well before November 1964. Only quantitatively did his secret preelection moves differ from his postelection war-hawking. Johnson insisted that he was helping South Vietnam fight off an aggressor, and that he had limited the fighting to Vietnam alone. Therefore, he never recognized ei-ther the war's civil dimension or its larger regional dimension.

The Sanctuary States: The Philippine Islands and Thailand

The four new nations of old imperial French Indochina were the major battleground for Johnson's Southeast Asian war. But he stationed air and naval fleets in two other countries: in the Philippine Islands at Clark Air Force Base and Subic Bay, and in Thailand at Korat, Udorn, and Nakhom Phanom. Interestingly, the fleet elements that Johnson ordered back into the Gulf of Tonkin in September 1964 steamed from sanctuaries at Subic Bay. And Clark Air Force Base became a major replacement and repair airdrome for forward-based aircraft. The use of the bases did not call for serious negotiation with the Philippine government, since these had been established long before American military involvement in the Southeast Asian war.[77]

Moreover, according to an analysis completed by State Department intelligence officers in April 1964, both the Philippines and Thailand had reasons to fear any neutralization of South Vietnam. These analysts characterized South Vietnam as the critical buffer state blocking the spread of China's influence through its protégé, North Vietnam. Neither academics nor State Department officials at this time referred to a Southeast Asian domino theory, according to which state after state would fall once South Vietnam was unbuffered. Instead, a checkerboard analogy was used, with the PRC jumping over strong anticommunist states as it pushed south along the Pacific basin rim. In the assessment completed by Thomas Hughes, the Director of Intelligence and Research at the State Department in 1964, neither the Philippines nor Thailand wanted to find a PRC ally at its flanks or rear.[78]

Thailand proved the more reluctant of these two allies, and wooing that country required political and financial incentives. Winning rights to bases in Thailand opened the back door to Laos and, through Laos, the back door of the DRV. Maximalists had a precedent for seeking these rights: in 1962 Kennedy had swiftly introduced U.S. combat troops into Thailand as a signal in the Laotian negotiations. (Senator Mansfield had criticized this move, as he would soon criticize Johnson's Thai moves.) And as most American internationalists analyzed it, the Southeast Asian situation had deteriorated so badly that even minimalist Whigs could opt to lift the limits and approve Johnson's Thai maneuvers. Furthermore, the internationalists did not envisage the proposed U.S. military presence in Thailand as susceptible to dismantlement in the short term.[79] Suddenly Ambassador Graham Martin, in the U.S. embassy in Bangkok, found himself part of a larger limited war. In a May 17 cable, Secretary Rusk asked him to assess, without first consulting the Royal Thai Government, what the Thai reaction would be if the Johnson internationalists sought to bring U.S. ground and air forces onto Thai soil during the next ten days. Again, the internationalists posed the inquiry in terms of the Laotian problem.[80]

By August the internationalists in Washington had won a substantial Thai victory. U.S. ground combat units did not arrive, but there were support units for air control and intelligence gathering, as well as aircraft and pilots, established at positions up-country from Bangkok. Internationalists began a multi-million-dollar investment in computers, code breakers, and automated control for the most esoteric of new technical weapons. Udorn and Nakhom Phanom became the research and development testing ground for space-age weaponry.

The U.S. Air Force, flying from bases in Thailand under the code name IGLOO WHITE, "seeded" the Ho Chi Minh Trail with Air Delivered Seismic Intrusion Detectors (ADSID) and Acoustic Sonobuoys (ACOU-BUOY's). An aircraft "on station" would receive their signals and relay them automatically to computers at Nakhom Phanom. The computers targeted and dispatched aircraft to bomb the locations. This was devastating to the trail network and the North Vietnamese logistical forces. Interestingly, Bernard Brodie, premier defense intellectual in postwar America and the scholar who was RAND's first strategic heavyweight, erred when he concluded that in this war the U.S. military did not initiate new weapons and new strategies for their employment.[81] They did. But new weapons do not necessarily win wars, as Germany had discovered with jet fighters and V2 rockets in World War II. Nevertheless, despite growing evidence that even high-technology weapons could not completely seal the logistical leaks along the damaged trail, McNamara's internationalists campaigned hard for their use. Before long, the demands of controlling this new generation of weapons meant that the Thai-U.S. border bases had to go on a 24-hour war footing, with CINCPAC complaining that his Thai counterparts, in the midst of the August Tonkin crisis, worked only 13 hours to the American 24.[82]

Command and Control

As the war expanded, military internationalists found that this ad hoc enlargement of the war zone posed thorny problems of command and control. General Westmoreland, for example, discovered that Ambassador Martin did not want him to visit Thailand—given what Martin and others predicted the international press would make of such a visit—even though Westmoreland also commanded U.S. forces in Thailand. This remained a military-diplomatic impasse.[83] Ambassador Maxwell Taylor, however, who had little tolerance for impasses, invited Martin and Unger to an ad hoc conference in Saigon on September 16. There he outlined the structure of a unified command to mount effective military operations in Southeast Asia; it would be composed of military forces from four sovereign states—the United States, South Vietnam, Laos, and Thailand (he had already placed Cambodia in the enemy column). Taylor proposed a Political-Military Southeast Asia Coordinating Committee, to be housed in Saigon, that would report to the U.S. State and Defense Departments. Although this body would control military forces of several foreign states, those states would not themselves be represented on the committee. In Taylor's scheme, the political members would be the Deputy Chiefs of Mission of the U.S. embassies in Bangkok, Vientiane, and

Saigon, under the chairmanship of his own deputy, Alex Johnson. The military members would be General Westmoreland and senior U.S. military representatives from the office of CINCPAC and the 7th Fleet, with Bangkok and Vientiane represented by the senior U.S. military officer assigned to those respective capitals.

This proposed committee, its name shortened to SEACOORD, became the subject of a feud in September and October. Rusk, in a cable to Taylor and other Ambassadors, approved mildly of regional coordination so long as its existence remained "completely confidential, since we do not wish [to] give any impression at this time [of the] establishment of [a Southeast Asian] political and military command structure in Saigon." But Rusk frowned on the prospect of any large number of officials traveling to Saigon for meetings. Admiral Sharp, too, was uneasy about SEACOORD, fearing the loss of his command turf to a super-committee controlled by Army Generals—the sort of thing Navy Commanders had endured in World War II, when General MacArthur dominated the South West Pacific Command.[84] Washington-based internationalists were not happy with Taylor's proposed SEACOORD either, and they were in a position to get what they wanted. The opening of direct satellite communications between Washington and Saigon put them in a position to go beyond Taylor's actions, and seek instantaneous results according to their own war designs.

So Taylor fumed in Saigon; for him, this communications cure had become worse than the disease. He tried to control F-105 jets from Korat, Thailand, when they flew air cover missions over YANKEE TEAM operations in Laos. But Ambassador Martin cabled his disapproval when he learned that Taylor planned to order YANKEE TEAM sorties from Korat to the cross-border operational area of the Laotian panhandle. And it was not Martin alone who blocked Taylor's plan (which had received Westmoreland's full support).[85] It was the President, too, because his solution for war-coordination problems also reflected his penchant for centralizing. When the communications revolution enabled Washington planners to take over as field commanders, they began to design even the tactics. Figuratively, they flew the planes, sailed the ships, and marched the soldiers about their larger battlefield of Southeast Asia.

Bombing, Raiding, or Mining

From 1961 until 1964 the war's geographic limits were expanded by small Niebuhrian steps, causing only minor disagreements between Whigs and Tories. But after 1964 the issue of overt strikes within North Vietnam split their ranks. For different motives, Whig and Tory maximalists suggested three types of strikes: bombing from the air, raiding on the ground, and mining or blockading from the sea. Their agenda even gained the approval of unilateralists in Congress, Senators like Goldwater, and in the military, Generals like Le May, famous for his suggestion that the United States should bomb the North Vietnamese back to the Stone Age. Whig and Tory minimalists were appalled at their maximalist colleagues' alliance-of-convenience with internationalism's enemies, the unilateralists. Strangely, the minimalists fought hardest against mining or blockading, which under the Niebuhrian criterion of damage limitation would have caused the least loss of life and property. Besides meeting this criterion, mining or blockading also offered a more likely possibility of meeting the effectiveness criterion, the criterion of statesmanship. To be effective, the selected action should fulfill the basic task better than other recommendations; and the basic task should be essential to a limited victory. In this situation, neither condition was met.

Instead of picking a task that would lead to limited victory, minimalists kept insisting on the primacy of retaliation. They should have reflected on the fact that Churchill had not brought victory closer in 1940 by terror-bombing Berlin in retaliation for the London blitz, nor had he added to British honor by seeking revenge of the worst kind, indiscriminate killing. Bombing might have boasted British morale temporarily, but alone and incorrectly targeted it could not contribute to victory for London—nor could it now for Saigon.[86]

So, rather than trying to apply the standard of effectiveness by mining or blockading, minimalists went along with the recommendation for bombing. To be effective, bombing would have to accomplish the basic task better than the other two options; and the basic task was to curtail the flow of supplies going south. While no one action or combination of actions could stop *all* infiltration, bombing was not the answer. Contrary to much conventional wisdom, all the forces fighting against Saigon and Washington could not "live off the land." Pure Viet Cong units, those not saddled with infiltrated northern-born replacements, could do so; but the regular forces of the North, the People's Army of Vietnam (PAVN), could not. And as PAVN units grew into divisional-size units operating throughout the South, neither the military arm of the Viet Cong, the People's Liberation Army (PLA), nor the Viet Cong infrastructure could supply them. Moreover, the North not only had to supply the forces, but starting in 1965 had to resupply them continuously.[87]

To stop this resupply posed immense problems. But by careful analysis, U.S. logistical experts identified three bottlenecks in the flow of PAVN supplies: the port of Haiphong, the rail link to the People's Republic of China, and a few mountain trails into Laos such as the Mu Gia and Aideo

Passes. To the extent that these three routes were left to function, the PAVN could disperse its supplies widely; and the more widely they were dispersed, the more targets an attacker would have to strike; and striking a multitude of targets would result in a magnitude of destruction unwarranted by McNamara's "cost effectiveness" criterion. At certain times of high frustration minimalists relaxed their opposition to bombing the passes and rail links. But they remained adamant in their opposition to closing the port, the point of greatest congestion, and the route that could be eliminated with the least destruction. The reason was not that they were unaware of logistical strategy. It was that they feared drawing the war's limits too close to what Peking and Moscow might consider their own vital interests. At best, the minimalists were making an educated guess in a game of global chess. Since ultimately nuclear weapons could be brought into play, and since Chinese armies stood next door, minimalists could approve taking only pawns and an occasional knight; to check or checkmate remained taboo. But at the time, the game's maximalists pointed out that Peking and Moscow had to play by the same chess rules. Thus if Hanoi represented a vital Leninist chess piece, Saigon represented a vital Lockean chess piece.

From this impasse, each side maneuvered to see how close it could come to the limits of the other's tolerance. American documents summarizing the military constraints in the war, for the most part collected in the form known as *The Pentagon Papers*, illustrate this problem. One example surfaced prior to the 1968 Tet offensive. On May 19, 1967, John McNaughton allowed his colleagues within the enlarged Office of the Secretary of Defense (OSD) to read a draft presidential memorandum he had written. Initially, he repeated the minimalist error in choosing a rationale for actions against the North, particularly bombing. To him the primary purpose in bombing the North remained retaliation and improving "the morale of the people in the South." The secondary goal was "to add to the pressure on Hanoi"—a purpose so unspecific as to be ineffective by any test. As the third, McNaughton listed the one purpose—denial of substantial logistical support to PAVN units in the South—that made strategic sense. Colleagues quickly saw McNaughton's dilemma. By reversing his list and giving his last rationale top priority, they could see his admission of failure: implicitly he had confessed that bombing dispersed supplies—the limited bombing option that he had supported—could not have a major impact on the rate at which supplies were reaching PAVN and mixed Viet Cong units in the South. (In fact, McNaughton could not imagine any option that would do this.)[88]

Knowing that maximalists believed other actions, which he had not supported, could bring effective results, McNaughton countered with a hypothetical question: "Why not escalate the bombing and mine the harbor and perhaps occupy southern North Vietnam—on the gamble that it would constrict the flow, meaningfully limiting enemy action in the South, and that it would bend Hanoi?"[89] In other words, there were three options. Option one was to escalate the current bombing program over the North. Option two was to mine the harbors of the North. Option three was to occupy southern North Vietnam. McNaughton then assessed the risks inherent in each one.

Of the first option, "intensified air attacks against the same types of targets," he said, "We would anticipate [that it] would lead to no great change in the policies and reactions of the Communist powers."[90] In fact, both minimalists and maximalists generally shared this assessment.

In weighing the risks of exercising the second option—mining harbors—McNaughton admitted that "it would place Moscow in a particularly galling dilemma as to how to preserve the Soviet position and prestige in such a disadvantageous place." He considered that the Soviet Union "might, but probably would not, force a confrontation in Southeastern Asia—where even with minesweepers they would be at as great a military disadvantage as we were when they blocked the corridor in Berlin."[91] But he went on to surmize that Chinese Leninists might "read the harbor-mining" as a sign that the United States planned to occupy the North. If so, "China might decide to intervene in the war with combat troops and air power, to which we would eventually have to respond."

McNaughton's assessment of the third option—occupying southern North Vietnam—recalled the Korean War nightmare: "To U.S. ground actions in North Vietnam, we would expect China to respond by entering the war with ground and air forces." Worse, he expected the Soviet Union to "generate a serious confrontation with the United States at one or more places of her own choosing."[92]

A year before these calculations were discussed, McGeorge Bundy had assured Canadian diplomats involved in possible peace overtures that the United States "had no intention of bombing the cities of Hanoi and Haiphong, or mining the Haiphong harbor." To be precise, Bundy agreed that the sensitive Chinese "might well react if they concluded that it had become our objective to destroy North Vietnam or eliminate the Communist regime there." Bundy left no doubt that by the word "react," he meant direct military intervention.[93] To avoid this, he and others tried to expand the war a little, but not too much. They hoped to compromise, to straddle between too little and too much, whatever that entailed. Of course, the possibility remained that they had calculated incorrectly from the start.

From February 1965 to March 1968 the Johnson compromise meant bombing the North. The planners of this campaign, known as ROLLING THUNDER, tried hard to set limits that the Leninists could clearly discern, in the form of five special zones. Bombing was to be prohibited in a buffer zone in China, prohibited within a 10-mile radius of Hanoi and a 4-mile radius of Haiphong, and restricted within a 30-mile radius of Hanoi and a 10-mile radius of Haiphong.[94] This design succeeded in preventing the Chinese and the Russians from intervening in force. But it failed to bring effective results. And, by everyone's estimate, the destruction it brought about was enormous; there were 304,000 tactical and 2,380 B-52 sorties (a sortie being one mission or attack by a single plane), with 634,000 tons of bombs dropped.[95]

As winning the war within tight limits became more difficult, the limits were progressively loosened, but before long even maximalists found good reasons for caution. One reason outranked all others. On May 20, 1967, the Joint Chiefs of Staff issued a memorandum, JCSM 284-67. One of its last sentences read as follows: "Should the CHICOMs [Chinese communists] intervene overtly with major combat forces in Vietnam, it might be necessary to establish a strategic defense in South Vietnam and use tactical nuclear weapons against bases and LOCs [lines of communication—roads, bridges, railroads] in South China."[96] In response to this warning, which could be read as a prediction of Armageddon, internationalists of both persuasions kept insisting that the United States and South Vietnam do nothing to provoke the entry of Chinese armies into the combat. One result of their insistence was that the whole mission of U.S. forces in South Vietnam was redesigned—or, to put it less charitably, left to improvisation.

An Improvised Mission

U.S. military units had disembarked in South Vietnam designed, equipped, and trained to fight a reenactment of World War II. Soon they found it difficult, if not almost impossible, to adjust that kind of training to the new requirements of low-intensity combat—the war designers' term for counterguerrilla warfare.

One example should suffice. By 1967, three U.S. Army Infantry Divisions—the 1st, the 9th, and the 25th—surrounded Saigon. The designers at MACV positioned the 1st to the north of the city, the 25th to the west, and the 9th to the south. Each division—approximately 18,000 soldiers organized into nine maneuver battalions that could be controlled by any of three brigades—arrived replete with heavy equipment originally designed for combat against heavily armed Soviet divisions, rather than the lightly armed Viet Cong guerrilla units. This posed the greatest problem for the 9th Division, stationed south of Saigon in the province of Long An, a province that Ambassador Lodge told General Westmoreland resembled Maine politically—as Long An goes, so goes South Vietnam.[97] Long An not only was densely populated but also was a lush floodplain of rice paddies, a terrain abhorred by heavily armed military units for obvious reasons. Actually, U.S. Army designers had tried to forecast the division's role in Vietnam when it was reactivated at Fort Riley, Kansas, on February 1, 1966. They had placed it under the Reorganization Objective Army Division (ROAD) system, so that it could form units to meet particular combat demands, using improved mobility and increased firepower. If that were not change enough, the 9th Division discovered in Vietnam that it had to place one entire brigade in boats. They renamed the brigade the Riverine Force.[98]

Obviously, the capacity to improvise is an asset, not a fault. But designers cannot expect unlimited flexibility from their designs; and they should calculate that a design's efficiency probably will decline as the improvisation becomes more radical. Still, the change in organization was the lesser of two major problems in improvisation for this particular war. The greater problem—the changed mission that the designers gave the U.S. armed forces—proved to be something in which the military could not improvise.

Surely the most radical military improvisation imaginable would be to take large combat units composed of civilian-soldiers under the control of professional noncommissioned officers (NCO's) and commanded by a professional officer corps, send them to a foreign land, a place already torn apart by civil war, and ask them to become the major nation-building instrument for one of the parts. But that is precisely what the designers did—and it did not work. Why did they try?

The answer, basically, is that when internationalists found themselves averse to using military units in their major mission of destroying the enemy's military units, they looked for new missions. Yet even when given innovative new units, they misused them.[99] For example, the 1st Air Cavalry Division—a unit that could airlift a full brigade of almost 6,000 soldiers in its own helicopters and drop them on top of the enemy—was designed and brought to Vietnam. That division could have chased an enemy until it destroyed it, but it did not. Instead, the 1st Air Cavalry did what the other big units did: it chased the enemy back to the border of its own tactical area of operations (TAO) and then halted—even when the other side of the TAO lay inside South Vietnam. The VC and PAVN units, discovering that their enemy had decided to protect only certain parcels of real estate, watched from across national borders and, when inside South Vietnam, straddled divisional and corps borders.[100]

But only at the beginning were U.S. divisions underemployed as real estate security guards. The war designers soon decided to place them at the center of an expensive nation-building design. In calling for civic action and military pacification, that design came to be something that William James would have approved calling the "moral equivalent of war." In hopes of leading the United States away from what Darwinians asserted to be the natural aggressiveness of human animals, James had insisted that a constructive substitute for the distraction of war could be found in large civic tasks.[101] Little could he have imagined that half a century later, for reasons very different from his, the largest civic task imaginable, nation-building, would be assigned to combat troops who were simultaneously fighting a war—a substitution that should amaze those Darwinians of our own time, the sociobiologists.[102]

Most critics have assumed that pacification and civic action were a sort of sideline to the main war effort in Vietnam. Further, many of them have argued that it should have been central. In fact, pacification *was* central, but the central actors were not trained for the task. For example, U.S. Army units could and did seal off village after village searching for Viet Cong soldiers—trying, step by step, to make each village secure. But it was common knowledge that U.S. troops could not distinguish a Viet Cong or PAVN Vietnamese from a loyal or ambivalent South Vietnamese unless he or she was firing a Soviet-manufactured AK47 rifle at them. If an American soldier had been given a color photograph of the ten most-wanted Viet Cong, he would have said that they all looked alike—short orientals with black hair, wearing black pajamas, perfectly representative of millions of identical peasants. To overcome this obstacle, American units brought Vietnamese interpreters along with them. But to assume, for example, that a bilingual youth from urban Nha Trang assigned as an interpreter to a constantly moving U.S. Army unit could recognize an outsider among the villagers of a hamlet south of An Loc was wishful thinking, to say the least. One might as well expect a streetwise teenager from Newark to identify the Democrats in a grange meeting of North Dakota wheat farmers.[103]

Folly of this order had to have powerful proponents. Professional NCO's and officers knew that their assignments were ill-suited to their abilities or the abilities of their charges. The task called for paramilitary units with training in police and intelligence functions. If an army was needed to support such units, the ARVN could have served. But McNamara, racing to get the job done, told the U.S. military to do it. He found no lack of military personnel who replied "can do." Unfortunately, more often than not, they could *not* do. Their belief in the idea of progress, a belief in which they were trained and which they optimistically expressed in the "can do" attitude, had trapped the American officer corps in much the same way that traditional belief in élan had trapped the pre–World War I French officer corps, with tragic results. Apparently, an office corps that tends toward pessimism would better serve twentieth-century national interests.

Once McNamara realized that his officer corps could not build a nation, he convinced Johnson that he knew someone who could: Robert Komer. To ensure that everyone understood, McNamara convinced Johnson to sign National Security Memorandum 362, which said, "Pacification (revolutionary development) will be integrated under a single-manager concept."[104] Making Komer, a civilian, a MACV deputy did not win the hearts and minds of the American military. McNamara had to learn that the hard way; Johnson knew it instinctively.

To make matters worse, Komer acted as if he considered himself a General. But Westmoreland, his boss and Washington's favorite "can do" General, decided that it was possible to bring Komer "on board" without an MACV palace revolt. Even Westmoreland, however, found Komer (whom Lodge called "Blowtorch") hard to command. Trying to keep him under surveillance, Westmoreland asked for a trusted General, George Forsythe, to serve as Komer's deputy. Forsythe first heard of his appointment when an unknown civilian named Komer telephoned him from the White House and told him to pack his bags and join him in Saigon, where he, Komer, was going "to be Westy's deputy and run the war for him."[105] While West Point Generals are more relaxed than their Prussian counterparts, they have their limits. When some MACV Generals heard that Komer, whom they suspected of being a Leninist political commissar, was sending cables to the White House—cables unauthorized by MACV, in which Komer asked the President to order Westmoreland to do certain things—the MACV Generals wanted Komer's head. Even the South Carolina cavalier in Westmoreland became a momentary fire-eater.[106] Komer got the message.

What did Komer accomplish? Unfortunately very little. The cause of this failure was the fact that Komer's pacification program gave field units well-meant but inappropriate tasks. In total missions, the figures indicate an amazing effort. To summarize that effort, we may cite two examples from the work of the U.S. Air Force, the service with the fewest personnel in South Vietnam. In 1966, members of the 3rd Tactical Fighter Wing at Bien Hoa Air Base heard that the local elementary school needed school furniture. Accordingly, they donated used bomb-fin crates, delivered them to the schools, and disassembled them into pieces usable as desks and benches. And in 1968 at Pleiku Air Base in the central highlands, airmen initiated several farm instruction programs. Using their own surplus lumber, they showed Montagnard villagers how to build chicken coops and grain bins. With true American ingenuity, they somehow obtained enough vegetable seeds from the United States to plant more than 80 acres of vegetables for these same villagers. Some critics have called Americans in Asia "sentimental imperialists," but the better term, at least in Vietnam, would be "romantic rustics."[107]

Unfortunately, the war was neither sentimental nor romantic, but simply cruel. One would expect American Marines to know that intuitively, but Marine historians have produced an entire book celebrating their civic-action contributions. One of their commanders in Vietnam, General Lewis Walt, who later wrote a devastating critique of the war designers, contributed $9,000 in 1966 to Buddhist schools and orphanages. The money came from the III Marine Amphibious Force's (MAF) Civic Action Contingency Fund.[108] Marine units from MAF, operating with ARVN units, also engaged in Country Fair operations. Taking villagers by surprise in the morning, the Marines would lead them to areas where they could identify them while feeding them and showing them movies; meanwhile, troops would search the empty village for telltale signs of the Viet Cong. *A Rumor of War*, one of the better novels about Vietnam, fictionalizes similar operations.[109] Finally, when off duty, members of the 3rd Marine Division Band and Drum and Bugle Corps presented free concerts for the Vietnamese. Encouraged by their reception, they "began to include music appreciation along with the English classes being taught in an attempt to appeal to the Vietnamese."[110] Surely there is something flawed in the larger design of a war that encourages a Marine to teach music appreciation in a combat zone.

The U.S. Army, of course, brought numerous battalions to fight in Vietnam. Each Army division has its own official history, and some also have been the subject of research by scholars outside the Defense Department. A scholar who followed the U.S. 25th Infantry Division around Hau Nghia province—figuratively, through the documents—has concluded that "there was probably not a single month during their entire stay in Hau Nghia that some 25th Division units were not engaged directly in support of the pacification campaign." In fact, "during the rainy seasons of both 1966 and 1967 such operations were the major effort of the entire division."[111]

Mixing civic action and pacification became easy. To secure and to build appeared to go together: on one side soldiers had their rifles, on the other their hammers and nails. While they could perform both tasks, the building task was not their primary one. Several U.S. Army officers concluded their careers (for example, Sam Wilson) or their lives (for example, John Paul Vann) working for AID, trying to win the war by nation-building.[112] They lost their war just as their comrades commanding troop units lost theirs. More fundamentally, William James had been wrong from the start: there is no moral equivalent of war. But the design improvisers like Komer and Westmoreland insisted that there was, and that American enlisted men and women would carry it out. Most of these men and women performed to the best of their abilities, only to watch the Viet Cong and PAVN units capture their moral-equivalency handiwork. For in limiting the geographic area of the Vietnam intervention, the internationalist designers of the war had also limited the ability of their military to intervene effectively, as others had designed it to do.

PART TWO

POLITICAL CONSTRAINTS

Les Aspin, Staff Assistant to President Kennedy's Council of Economic Advisors, 1963:

"Vietnam changed the whole focus up here," says Rep. Les Aspin, the Wisconsin liberal who recently was elected Chairman of the House Armed Services Committee. "Whole areas that up to then had been the most bipartisan—defense, the CIA, foreign policy—suddenly became the most partisan."

Wall Street Journal, Mar. 11, 1985, p. 14.

Zbigniew Brzezinski, Member Policy Planning Council at State Department, 1966–68:

"Would victory have averted a shattering blow to U.S. self-confidence, the most precious asset the country has? Zbigniew Brzezinski, President Carter's national security adviser, thinks so. 'Defeat fragmented the cohesion of a generation of policy members,' he says, and helped create a national pessimism of which there are still traces."

Wall Street Journal, Mar. 11, 1985, p. 14.

CHAPTER FOUR

Vietnam and the Failure to Govern

SOME GOVERNMENTS RISE, some fall, and some are installed. The proposition that governments rise and fall because of decisions made by their own citizens had been an essential assumption of American foreign policy since the birth of the republic. After World War I, Wilson made nonintervention in the internal affairs of another nation one of his Fourteen Points. To practice global politics in the Wilsonian mode, moreover, a state had to act openly, not clandestinely.

In the global politics that World War II created, Tory and Whig internationalists modified these venerable concepts. In special circumstances, they decided, some governments could be installed by outsiders. Internationalists had a reason for this caveat. With the extraordinary rise of U.S. global power following the close of hostilities in 1945, the internationalists wanted to harness the American giant to missions that required a global reordering.[1]

An earlier American attempt at limited global reordering based on a Lockean rationale—Wilsonian altruistic internationalism—had failed.[2] But that did not daunt the post-Roosevelt internationalists, for they believed in an internationalism based on self-interest. Their internationalism had its limits, but in each decade following the war those limits were pushed back. As many scholars have noted, the New Deal and Fair Deal reformers considered themselves pragmatists, practical people who could reform both national and international politics. In the foreign arena they believed that pragmatism rooted in self-interest would allow them to avoid the fatal flaw of Wilsonian policy, its pure altruism.[3] Internationalists of both persuasions—Whig and Tory—shared this belief.

The Whigs continued to view the final goal of U.S. foreign policy as encouraging the rise of liberty on a global scale. Envisaging a new order that stressed political liberty, they set themselves the tasks of helping other states write constitutions, conduct free elections, and establish an independent fourth estate. In other words, the Whigs wanted general political modernization. In order to promote it, they borrowed from John Locke's work the part they could project into global politics. For Whigs, liberty was mainly political. For example, Ambassador Henry Cabot Lodge, a Whig Republican who served under two Democratic Tories, Presidents Kennedy and Johnson, writes that "although we were all aware that Vietnam had no Western democratic traditions, we reached the conclusion that an effort to bring about government under a constitution would have a salutary effect."[4] Thus Lodge encouraged legal specialists to give help that the Vietnamese needed in order to write their constitution. Two of these people, Professors Albert P. Blaustein and Gisbert H. Flanz, took to the challenge with vigor. Flanz had helped draft the South Korean constitution in the 1950's, and Blaustein was to make a new career for himself in the 1960's giving constitutional advice to the Vietnamese.[5]

The Tories agreed with these Lockean assumptions, but for different reasons. The projection of political liberty onto global politics smacked to them of Wilsonian altruism unless most of the essential economic groundwork had already been laid. The Tories stressed that economic liberty was a necessary prior condition for political liberty. The tasks they set themselves to achieve in other states included currency reform, movement away from subsistence agriculture and toward a market economy, establishment of light industries such as textiles, the creation of transportation and communication links that would encourage a national market, and other reforms favored by economic modernization theory.

Tories intended to pursue their vision of global order "by imparting to other parts of the world the means that we [the United States] have developed for raising the standard of living."[6] To create abundance became their mission for America. If an expanding economy had made democracy possible in America—by meeting the demands of new American voices without the need for a radical redistribution of wealth—then an expanding world economy should make political liberty possible throughout the world. Thus Secretary of Defense Robert McNamara, a Tory internationalist, could write, "There can, then, be no question but that there is an irrefutable relationship between violence and economic backwardness."[7] McNamara's Tory colleague, Secretary of State Dean Rusk, was equally committed to changing economic conditions in Vietnam before helping the Vietnamese change their political conditions. Instead of buying bullets for Vietnam, Rusk wanted to buy beans. Rusk hoped that, like Jack's fabled bean, they would grow to bear a gigantic weight.[8]

Whig and Tory factions within the internationalist camp chose not to battle each other over the primacy of political or economic liberty. They maintained a united front against the return of their chief nemesis, American unilateralism. Moreover, most of the time there was enough room for maneuver; each faction could work at promoting the kind of liberty each preferred; and a shared pragmatism helped them compromise on differences. Moreover, many internationalists, being neither pure Whig nor pure Tory, could tolerate mixed and divergent opinions so long as these did not devolve into unilateralism.

One such hybrid internationalist, Walt W. Rostow, joined the Kennedy administration, and in the Johnson administration rose to be the President's National Security Adviser. Author of the controversial *Stages of Economic Growth*, Rostow was an economist who represented the Massachusetts Institute of Technology in the heavily Harvard-dominated Cambridge group of advisers in the JFK and LBJ years. One might suspect that he was a Tory who pushed mainly economic measures, but in fact Rostow often was heard to utter Whig sentiments. He wrote his boss, Secretary of State Dean Rusk, the following comments concerning Vietnam: "Among the urban elites there is a strong and growing impulse to participate in political life. . . . If this is so we must try to create a situation where . . . they [the government] accept and dramatize a civilian-led political nursery, starting with work on the constitution, leading soon to an honestly elected Parliament of perhaps limited power."[9]

However, both Whig and Tory internationalists recognized the danger of forcing seventeenth-century English political theory on twentieth-century global politics. While Lockean principles had triumphed in the domestic politics of Anglo-American and some continental European nations, most internationalists in the 1960's found global politics distinctly Hobbesian.

Political Intervention Through Covert Action

Without much hesitation, American internationalists felt competent to define what was a correct government in Lockean terms. But how to encourage the establishment of correct governments posed a complex problem. They could try legal incentives, such as education programs, technical assistance, and diplomatic arrangements. If these failed, they could try illegal incentives, such as bribes or blackmail. As a measure of last resort, and in secret, internationalists could support a coup that promised to install a government that they could push toward the Lockean ideal.

This acceptance of the American-supported coup as an instrument of policy shows how far and how quickly American internationalists had distanced themselves from Wilsonian altruism. In little more than a decade, a position had been reached that was exactly opposite that of their predecessors. Of course, even President Wilson had been willing, under specific conditions, to intervene in the political life of certain Latin American states. But although he could easily approve of the fall of the Czar and the overthrow of the Ching dynasty, Wilson would not consider encouraging a coup against the leader of an allied country. The new internationalists would, however; for experience in World War II had transformed their view of covert intervention.[10] They believed that if any of the powerful Western democracies had acted against the weak Hitler of 1936–37 by helping anti-Hitler forces to stage a successful coup, the world would have been spared the bloodbath of 1939–45. The same applied to the lesser Axis tyrants, Mussolini and Tojo. Although America and its allies prevailed militarily over the Axis dictators, other dictators remained; one of them, Stalin, had been a major war ally. In fact, postwar U. S. internationalists saw all Soviet leaders—Stalin, Khrushchev, Brezhnev—as dictators who resembled either Hitler or the Kaiser.[11] And they were dictators who appeared impervious to outside coup attempts, as lesser tyrants did not.

In the monopolar world of American preeminence from 1945 to 1950, lesser tyrants—Perón, Franco, Farouk, Batista, and Somoza—maneuvered in a shadow world of American toleration. In the bipolar world of 1950–70, both the United States and the USSR, for reasons of state, tolerated various minor dictators. In the multipolar world since 1970, other major powers also have tolerated the small fry. Regarding Eastern Europe, a special case, world powers have tolerated Soviet-installed dictators because they (the powers) have hesitated to upset the hegemony in that region of the last great European land empire, the USSR.

Between approximately 1950 and 1970, in the bipolar world dominated by the United States and the USSR, both "the United States and the Soviet Union intervened in the internal politics of the countries between them, but under a frequently impeccable judicial camouflage."[12] Both states practiced the art of the coup, especially in the arena beyond their own recognized spheres of influence. The Soviet Union initiated that pattern in its 1948 Czechoslovakian manipulations. But American internationalists learned quickly; by the 1960's, the United States had sponsored coups in Iran, Guatemala, and Zaire. As one scholar has noted, "In the ideological confrontation which developed after the war . . . honourable men of great ability served their countries by engaging in activities of a kind unjustifiable by any criteria other than the most brutal kind of *raison d'état*, and by the argument that their adversaries were doing the same."[13]

In order to match Soviet successes of the late 1940's, U.S. internationalists needed an organizational structure for conducting Cold War coups. They secured the foundation for such a structure when Congress passed and their President signed into law the 1947 National Security Act. By sponsoring this successful legislation, the internationalists provided legitimacy for three new bureaucratic organizations that were soon to emerge: the Department of Defense (DOD), the National Security Council (NSC), and the Central Intelligence Agency (CIA).[14] The CIA was for internationalists the organization of last resort, an instrument that they could use covertly and only to deal with circumstances that otherwise might force war upon the world.

Although the Office of Strategic Services (OSS), created in World War II, had given a few people some experience in supervising a modern intelligence agency, most American leaders knew little about it. The OSS was dissolved when the war ended in 1945; and until 1947 the most that a still-learning, budget-restricted Truman administration would approve in the way of intelligence organization was a residual OSS nucleus called the Central Intelligence Group. This consisted mainly of a few key cadres from the OSS, such as Richard Helms and James Angleton, and a few other advisers—Allen Dulles, for example, who had left OSS to return to the law firm of Sullivan and Cromwell.

With the birth in 1947 of their own intelligence agency, some "old hand" internationalists, along with new recruits, quickly filled the top positions. From law came Allen Dulles, from industry John McCone, and from academia Richard Bissell—who, as an instructor at Yale, had either taught, hired as teaching assistant, or had as colleagues the two Bundy brothers and the two Rostow brothers. Also from academia came a former Harvard law professor, Robert Amory, Jr., and two political science professors, Ray Cline, of Georgetown University, and Lyman B. Kirkpatrick, of Brown University. From the seminary came William Sloane Coffin, later Chaplain of Yale University; from an art museum came Dartmouth Professor of English Thomas Braden; and from government itself came careerists such as the 1964 CIA Saigon mission chief, Peer De Silva.[15] All these men possessed talent, energy, and dedication. The directors of the newest agency in Washington never complained of a shortage of creative people.

If there is a career of one powerful internationalist that marks the distance traveled from pre–World War II self-righteousness about the "dirty" world of spying to a postwar tolerance of clandestine operations, it is that of Henry L. Stimson. During Stimson's first cabinet-level service as Secretary of State in the 1920's, he decided that intelligence-gathering activities were not cricket, not sporting, not gentlemanly, for "gentlemen do not read other gentlemen's mail." During World War II, as Secretary of

War, Stimson had learned to turn the other eye and read nongentlemen's mail, if not with relish, then with disdain.[16]

For the new Stimson and other postwar internationalists, the constraint against reading other gentlemen's mail applied now only to citizens of nations like Great Britain, in which a Lockean reordering had long since been accomplished. In the Hobbesian remainder of the world, and especially in nations friendly to Soviet Russia, there were no gentlemen; and so internationalists not only read the mail of others but also forged it, bribed with it, and if all else failed, used it in arranging coups.[17]

No presidential memoir, not Truman's, Eisenhower's, or Johnson's; no CIA director's own remembrances, such as Allen Dulles's *The Craft of Intelligence*; and no investigative reporting, such as Thomas Powers's *The Man Who Kept the Secrets: Richard Helms and the CIA*, indicates that the influential internationalists lost any sleep in debates with conscience. They had convinced themselves, in the words of Allen Dulles, that "we [the United States] cannot safely limit our response to Communist strategy of take-over solely to those cases where we are invited in by a government still in power."[18]

The Espionage Cult

Was the consensus of the American public on their government's use of espionage generally positive, neutral, or negative in the 1960's? If they had known the facts, would most Americans have objected to it? One way to seek an answer is to look at how public opinion is expressed in the folk culture, especially in folk art. The dominant form of folk art in the United States at mid-century was the motion picture. And after President Kennedy assured Ian Fleming's millionaire status by publicly admitting that his light reading, often called "escape reading" in the 1960's, included the English author's spy thrillers, the motion picture industry created a cult hero in the person of James Bond. Sequel followed sequel. Bond as folk hero outlived the youth of the actor who played the role; fans accepted younger replacements in order to keep their hero operating.

A critic could point out that the youthful Bond carried a British passport—and a British license to kill. But the American entertainment media, after all, had often borrowed folk heroes from British writers. The detectives, sleuths, and spies abounding in U.S. books, television shows, and motion pictures included Conan Doyle's Sherlock Holmes and Agatha Christie's Hercule Poirot. But Bond overshadowed these earlier Anglo imports and became a transatlantic model for the pop culture's view of international intrigue in the American Camelot of the 1960's. And Bond was not a negative symbol. As Sir Galahad and other knights represented "the good guys" of another myth in another Camelot, so Bond—in *Dr. No*, *From Russia with Love*, *Goldfinger*, and dozens of other films—repeatedly triumphed over evil in American movie palaces.

In fact, *Casino Royale*, not *Dr. No*, introduced Bond to Americans, and they saw it on television, not in movie theaters: October 21, 1954, marks the date when CBS's "Climax Mystery Theatre" gave ordinary Americans their new Galahad.[19] The first of the Bond films was *Dr. No*. It premiered at the London Pavilion on October 6, 1962, at some risk, given that United Artists awaited the verdict of tough London critics before launching the film in the American market. Its producers at United Artists had planned "to banish the film to the U.S. drive-in circuit in Texas and the Midwest." They had not even scheduled a New York or Hollywood premiere. Nevertheless, the monarchs of British filmdom attended the opening in England, along with social leaders such as J. Paul Getty. Most important, the London critics were kind; Derek Hill in *London Scene* noted: "*Dr. No* has the kind of rock hard competence more usually associated with Hollywood." The Fleming group was launched. A *News of the World* correspondent called *Dr. No* "magnificent mayhem." Even the intellectual critics succumbed. Penelope Gilliatt, of the *Evening Standard*, "noted the snobbish and brutal character of Ian Fleming's hero but spotted, with approval, the element of self-mockery in the film." To beat its competition into print, *Time* magazine published its review even before the American release of *Dr. No*.[20]

The second Bond film surpassed *Dr. No*. On August 23, 1963, *From Russia with Love* completed its shooting schedule; two months later it opened at London's Odeon Theatre. Again Gilliatt led the praise, calling Bond "a voice of the age." The film became an amazing box-office success, making its cost back in Britain alone. Free publicity helped; *From Russia with Love* was on Kennedy's reading list. One Bond historian notes that "what political writer Hugh Sidey had cooked up as an interesting example of what a President read, was actually a windfall for the Bond people." This writer notes also that "with encouragement from the White House, paperback publishers began to spread Ian Fleming's novels across America and sales began to rise spectacularly." As the third Bond film began to enter production, *From Russia with Love* became the top money-making film in Britain, and book sales in Britain and the United States indicated a "massive interest" in Bond. The third Bond blockbuster, *Goldfinger*, opened in the United States in December 1964, and within weeks broke every box office record in New York and Los Angeles as well as London. American theater managers ran the film around the clock while begging for re-release of the first two.[21]

Rental income presents a fair measure of a film's impact in popular culture. The Bond films were an inexhaustible gold mine, generating millions of dollars in earnings decade after decade. Assuming that film earnings represent wide distribution throughout the popular culture, the spy-as-hero was generating ticket sales of the same magnitude as the cowboy and the private detective. The actor who played him became a superstar. In the 1960's Sean Connery joined John Wayne and Clint Eastwood as one of the top ten box office attractions.[22]

When one considers that motion pictures and television are the dominant art forms of the twentieth century, and that Americans dominated both, in the way fourteenth-century Italians dominated painting and fifth-century Greeks dominated sculpture, it becomes clear that the iconography of this century is on celluloid and tape. Even as the figures of Washington and other early national leaders dominated revolutionary American iconography in paintings and sculptures, so James Bond, Dirty Harry, Shane, and others—even though fictional characters—dominated post–World War II American iconography. Even among these icons Bond stood out as a superstar. Every Bond film has made more money than its predecessor. In 1987, Eon Productions, the British company that produces the Bond films, estimated that they "can now virtually bank on $100 million gross off every $30 million invested per feature." Iconography can pay handsomely. With a new actor playing Bond, *The Living Daylights* opened to headlines like "Bond Knocks 'em Dead at Nation's Box Offices"; it earned $11 million in 1,728 theaters in its first weekend of release. With this 1987 release, the fifteenth screen adventure for Agent 007, United Artists announced the best three-day gross for any Bond film, surpassing the previous best, set by *A View to a Kill* in 1985, of over $10 million in three days.[23]

The Bond mania spread from popular cinema to other aspects of folk culture. In France an advertising campaign spread James Bond toiletries throughout the world. The Italians renamed Bond "Mr. Kiss Kiss Bang Bang" and planned various Italian imitations. In the United States the 1964 Sears catalog started a merchandising bonanza in Bond toys. In Japan, where Bond was "hugely popular," Sean Connery was mobbed by 007 fans when he arrived to shoot footage for the fifth Bond film, *You Only Live Twice*. The earlier Bond had driven Aston Martin sports cars (an interesting free advertisement for a British motor producer); Toyota Automobile Corporation offered to create a special version of their GT sports car complete with Japan's first convertible top in honor of Bond.[24] The Oscar committee did not forget 007; the fourth film won the gold statue for special effects. That 1965 film had cost $5.6 million, six times the cost of *Dr. No*.

Did Bond influence American popular culture of the 1960's? Some have thought so. "It is safe to say that the cinematic exploits of James Bond, Agent 007, have become firmly rooted in American popular culture," wrote Carl F. Macek. Spy novels, helped along by the Book-of-the-Month Club, came to join spy films as a major part of the folk culture.[25]

Was Bond the master spy depicted and received in the folk culture of the 1960's in a positive manner? Yes. Folk culture contains three levels, which might be labeled lowbrow, middlebrow, and highbrow. Bond is the quintessential lowbrow hero. In American popular culture during the 1960's, Bond competed with both middlebrow and highbrow novel-to-motion-picture heroes, all derived from the world of espionage. The middlebrow heroes played by George Segal in *The Quiller Memorandum* and Michael Caine in *Funeral in Berlin* took a more sophisticated approach to espionage than Bond. Their producers released those films in 1966, and the latter—authored by Fleming's middlebrow competitor, Len Deighton (whose *Ipcress File* also played film palaces in the 1960's)—received the imprimatur of a Bosley Crowther review in the *New York Times*.[26]

Creating the most sophisticated spy remained for the imagination of John Le Carré. One could argue that Le Carré directly challenges the romantic spy images of Fleming and others. In fact, Le Carré's spies embody Niebuhr's moral men in immoral societies. Nevertheless, they are activists, spying for the least bad side. When Richard Burton appeared in Le Carré's *The Spy Who Came in From the Cold* (1965), highbrow taste met highbrow antihero. Now even intellectuals could feast unashamed at the espionage table. And Hollywood actually could dare to nominate Richard Burton as best actor for his work in that picture—for this was not a "movie" but a "film." Nor did highbrow fascination with espionage pass from fashion as the 1960's ended. As late as the 1980's public-television audiences fell for Sidney Riley, real life antihero of the elegant miniseries *Reilly, Ace of Spies*. Adding to sales of books about spies, William F. Buckley began writing his own espionage series.

This glamorization of espionage had an influence that extended beyond popular culture in the 1960's, to reach the policy-making elite. During the decade in which Bond entered American pop culture, both Kennedy and Johnson appointed George Ball, a leading Whig internationalist, to positions from which he could observe the CIA at work. His assessment is a measured one: there is justification for an intelligence agency in America, but it ought to be more limited in power than the one he knew.[27] In making his assessment, Ball uses the language of the popular culture: "What many CIA recruits looked forward to as experiences in the pattern of James Bond turned out, on a number of occasions, to be dubious escapades cooked up by a bureaucracy out of touch with the real world, recalling the writings of John Le Carré." Acknowledging that "as an intelligence-gathering and analytical organization, the CIA has displayed great competence," Ball nevertheless writes that the CIA's "less than perfect record in operations was vividly demonstrated by the fantastic debacle of the Bay of Pigs, which was not scripted by Ian Fleming but by Evelyn Waugh." An Under Secretary of State wrote this. In the same vein, a former CIA director, William Colby, writes that the CIA was not meant to be an "elite corps of slick, daring James Bond operators."[28]

Various academics have confirmed the connection between popular and elite attitudes. John Cawelti, professor of English literature, has written that "even scholars and critics professionally dedicated to the serious study of artistic masterpieces often spend their off-hours following a detective's ritual pursuit of a murderer or watching one of television's spy teams carry out its dangerous mission." With many books, magazines, films, and television productions containing espionage themes, Cawelti finds that they represent an "artistic and cultural phenomena of tremendous importance." He suggests three "turning points in the evolution of popular literature—Conan Doyle's Sherlock Holmes, Mario Puzo's Don Corleone, and Ian Fleming's James Bond." Cawelti sees Bond as a superhero living "a special form of moral fantasy" in which Bond was the enforcer, "the bureaucratic killer, the man with an official number that gives him license to kill."[29] A sociologist has written that the media have created a "good guy–bad guy" mentality that "spills over into domestic and international politics." A historian has suggested that media personalities themselves can become social commentators through their work.[30] For example, Chaplin's little tramp—a work of individual creation—commented on domestic politics; Sean Connery's superspy—a work of collaborative invention—commented on international politics.

Allen Dulles understood this long before academics wrote about it. As CIA director in the 1950's, he encouraged spy-as-hero novels, sometimes going so far as to offer plots to writers such as Helen MacInnes. Richard Helms, a successor to Dulles at the CIA, enjoyed Fleming's spy-as-activist but detested Le Carré's spy-as-intellectual. In the 1960's Helms gave E. Howard Hunt permission, as a CIA employee, to publish his forty spy-as-hero novels, though most of them did appear under pseudonyms. Furthermore, Bond-as-hero survived both the debacle in Vietnam and the Watergate scandal. At the 1985 premiere of the film version of *A View to a Kill*—a film that cost $30 million to produce—the Mayor of San Francisco, overjoyed that her city had been the locale for much of the film, proclaimed May 22 James Bond Day. When, as late as 1986, Michael Howard, a serious strategist and scholar, reviewed a major historical work on intelligence agencies, the *New York Times Book Review* editors headlined his piece "Cowboys, Playboys and Other Spies," and explicitly connected the work under review, a history by a Cambridge University Fellow, to the popular culture. Howard suggested that British intelligence-collecting had improved since the withdrawal of "cowboys" and the arrival of "professionals," explaining that "we have moved from the world of John Buchan via that of Ian Fleming to that of Len Deighton and John Le Carré."[31]

Of course, the popularity of espionage is not evidence that either elite or popular opinion approved of its misuse. The assassination of a head of state is quite different from the interrogation of defectors. And interrogation might be approved, but not interrogation through torture, physical or mental. But this much is clear: by the 1960's internationalists inhabited a national arena that tolerated the CIA, and this toleration allowed a wide scope for what could be accomplished through the CIA. Given that a cult of espionage makes popular heroes of spies, in the same way that a cult of athleticism makes popular heroes of athletes, it is not surprising that American Presidents used and abused this agency in the Vietnam war.

Complex as the CIA's Vietnam activities became, it is not impossible to unravel two specific cases for closer scrutiny: the coup against the Ngo family (see Chapter 5 below) and the CIA field reports of 1964 (see Chapter 6 below). Before doing so, however, it is necessary to outline the internal Vietnamese political struggles of the postwar years. In those struggles, two unique intelligence organizations played an important role in the rise, fall, and installation of Vietnamese governments. For Saigon this intelligence organization was a traditional extended family; for Hanoi it was a revolutionary party.

Vietnamese Neo-tribalism

South Vietnam in 1954 stood as a quasi-state, left rudderless after the collapse of imperial French rule. One close observer, Chester Cooper, called its creation the "birth of a non-nation."[32] Greater Vietnam, balanced on the edge of the Pacific basin rim, was split in two in 1954. After this division—handiwork of the world's great powers—the single most important desire among the majority of Vietnamese in both parts of the fatherland was for unification.[33] Unfortunately, the patron-client relationship of the United States to the southern half and of the USSR to the northern half thwarted this desire, for each patron had its own global agenda. Each superpower wanted its client to prevail in any unification scheme; failing that, each was prepared to support indefinitely its half of a divided state.

Both patrons could offer their clients a version of nation-building. Both thought their offer of nation-building assistance would absorb the energies of this most energetic people. Indeed, though the political aims were far different, the Soviet and the American plans for nation-building had grown to resemble each other; both were blueprints for technical assistance in economic planning. Such technocratic solutions did not, however, inspire Vietnamese unifiers; the patrons had guessed incorrectly.

What the patrons thought the Vietnamese would want was not what the Vietnamese wanted. Although forced to accept a postponement of unification, the Vietnamese did so unhappily, and they still considered unification inevitable in the long run. Lockean and Leninist ideas about economic planning remained for the Vietnamese basically imported theories, for they were driven by a more basic motive.[34] Neither "modern nationalism" nor "peasant nationalism" is a term that gets at the roots of the single-minded Vietnamese concern with unification; one that does is "neo-tribalism."

Vietnamese neo-tribalism was not a sort of primitive nationalism but something quite the opposite: a form of primordial identity-by-blood. There were, of course, some in mid-twentieth-century Vietnam who preached what modern political theorists would call nationalism, but these were a few small urban groups who, through French, Japanese, Russian, and Chinese contacts, had imported the ideological necessities for various modes of modern nationalism.[35] Despite the importation of such urban-based theories, most Vietnamese remained at heart village-based peasants, inhabiting a peasant-dominated society. In 1955 the country was approximately 15 percent urban and 85 percent rural.[36] The war later drove more rural residents into the coastal cities, but they existed there as city hostages, not true city dwellers. Thus it would be fair to say that although the Vietnamese village of the 1960's was in a state of transition—given the impact of wars, revolutions, and foreign incursions—it was still the dominant form of social and political organization. That form still took its shape and coherence from attitudes we may call neo-tribal.

Peasants had very limited horizons; to travel to a neighboring village remained a rare treat; to travel to a provincial capital was a privilege granted to a very few; and to visit Saigon or Hanoi an unreasonable dream. A French scholar has described a typical village in Vietnam as one "enclosed within a thick wall of bamboo and thorny plants; the villagers used to live behind a kind of screen of bamboo, or perhaps it was more like living within the magic ring of a fairy tale." He suggests that they supplied "their needs from the surrounding fields, they kept to themselves behind their common protection, away from strangers, away, even, from the state."[37] That was written in 1952. A little more than a decade later an American scholar wrote about these same peasants: "Villagers often remark that they do not know fellow villagers from other hamlets—they may know them by sight, but they have never spoken . . . [and] the effect of the dispersion is compounded by the fact that there are no real focal centers to attract sizable segments of the village populations."[38] Of course there were some exceptions; certain recently established, relatively affluent villages in the Mekong Delta had peasants who could look beyond the village, if seldom beyond the province. But generally speaking Vietnam remained a land of island-villages.

It remained so because these villages were so diverse in religious, linguistic, and regional loyalties. There were at least ten religions among the South Vietnamese alone: Mahayana Buddhist, Theravada Buddhist, Roman Catholic, Confucianist, Hoa Hoa, Cao Dai, Moslem (Cham), Protestant (Montagnard), ancestor worship, Montagnard (animist).[39] Even without counting the religions of Chams and Montagnards (since they were non-ethnic Vietnamese), there were many gods around; a modern Vietnamese Richelieu could find no one church around which to build a state. Even language, that essential human tool, was fractured: "No fewer than eight language options were theoretically available to Vietnamese of the early twentieth century."[40] Finally, regionalism also posed a divisive problem. One anthropologist notes that the three major regions of prepartitioned Vietnam—Tonkin, Annam, and Cochinchina—had very little in common. He suggests that two (Tonkin and Cochinchina) were like "baskets hanging from the same long pole (Annam)."[41]

In a peasant community that was so thoroughly fractured, the only commonality that remained was a tribal one—identity through race. One clue to this pattern of tribal identity shows up in the way that peasants identified differences. The most basic distinction was between insider and outsider—between us and them, between belonging and not belonging—and this had been going on for centuries. In historical sequence, the outsiders were first the Chinese; then, when the Vietnamese aggressively pushed south, the Cham and Cambodian tribes; after this came the French; later the Japanese; and finally, in the 1960's, came the American and Soviet patrons. Outsiders all, their presence had to be tolerated until circumstances allowed the Vietnamese insiders to expel them.[42]

The task for twentieth-century Vietnamese leaders was fairly simple in the abstract. They had to learn how to connect the ancient insider-outsider struggles to the problems of the 1960's in such a way as to unite the extended Vietnamese tribe. Modern abstractions—nation, citizen, comrade—could not do this. Instead they settled on the concept of fatherland—*to quoc* in Vietnamese—for although relatively new, the term encapsulated the concept of racial unity that Vietnamese inherited.[43] Fatherland denotes paternity. Of course, concepts such as countryman (*dong bao*) and even citizen (*quoc dan*) were not unknown, but these suited urban elites better than the peasant majority. Even the Vietnamese word for people, *dan*, originally meant "children of the ruler" and now implied only common ethnic identity; in urban centers alone did it imply "citizen." Thus "individuals might not have had a 'State' (*nha nuoc*) to identify with, but they did have an idealized total community."[44]

Both Vietnamese contestants for leadership, Ho Chi Minh and Ngo Dinh Diem, seem to have had an inkling that peasants could imagine an idealized community, a fatherland. For example, Ho used the term fatherland in numerous speeches, proclamations, letters, appeals, and reports. On September 2, 1945, in writing a short Vietnamese Declaration of Independence, which he modeled on the American document, Ho used the term in three separate paragraphs.[45] This does not mean that Ho and others did not use other metaphors for Vietnam. They did, especially when addressing party cadres, urban elites, foreign dignitaries, and the global media. In fact, "fatherland" appeared reserved for internal consumption, especially peasant consumption.[46]

It is important to add that the term fatherland was not limited to use in the tribal contest between two leaders. Whoever translated the Boy Scout Oath into Vietnamese, for example, also must have wanted to reach the large Vietnamese tribe, for one Vietnamese version went "On my honor I promise before God [according to my religion] to do everything possible to revere the Fatherland."[47] A generation of youth trained in repeating such oral commitments was sure to produce some dedicated young people willing to spread the tribal call, and to evoke patrimony as justification for ejecting the new outsiders.

It is also important to emphasize what it means to say that the Vietnamese rural people were peasants. We distinguish peasants from preliterate toilers of the soil; and we should also distinguish peasants from farmers. Farmers "participate fully in the market" and "commit themselves to a status game set within a wide social network," whereas "the major aim of the peasant is subsistence and social status gained within a narrow range of social relationships."[48] Historically there have been several categories of peasants: a poor peasantry, a middle peasantry, a free peasantry, and a tactically mobile peasantry. This last category is probably a good one under which to sort the population that formed the "basis for rebellion in Vietnam," in that its members moved about the country, at least within the provinces of their birth.[49]

Whatever the composition of this peasant base, it constituted the majority within the extended Vietnamese tribe. And that tribe had grown, as one anthropologist reports: "Vietnam is estimated to have sustained a population between 6 and 14 million in 1820; it had 30.5 million inhabitants in 1962."[50] Since neo-tribalism based on racial identity emerged as the strongest transregional value in Vietnam, the person who could manipulate it most effectively would be the one who could best lead the peasantry to rebellion.

In 1954 two men—Ho Chi Minh and Ngo Dinh Diem—were contenders for the role of chieftain.[51] Both had struggled with outsiders, and both were raw tribalists with the correct credentials: they hated the past French colonial regime; they hated the recent Japanese occupation; and they quietly hated the new superpower patrons of the 1950's and 1960's— Russians and Chinese concentrated in the Tonkinese North, Americans and French in the Cochinese South. The Chinese in the North represented the traditional Asian intruders; and the French in the South, the newer Western intruders—with the Soviets and Americans as late additions.

Ho Chi Minh and Ngo Dinh Diem began their personal battle in 1945. Before they began to fight, the two antagonists met. The encounter was reminiscent of a scene in Schiller's play *Mary Stuart*, in which a southern and a northern queen battle over the destiny of an island that had not yet become one state. Ngo Dinh Diem, like Mary, was a prisoner; unlike Mary, he had been reprieved from the axe. He came to be a prisoner in September 1945, when Viet Minh agents captured him, blocking Diem's attempts to warn Emperor Bao Dai against supporting Ho Chi Minh. While a prisoner Diem learned that the Viet Minh had shot both his brother, Ngo Dinh Khoi, and Khoi's son. Six months later the Viet Minh escorted him to Hanoi to confront Ho Chi Minh. Their meeting was not a success, for Diem blamed Ho for the murder of his relatives, even though Ho denied any role in the affair.

Ho offered Diem a role in the future government, but Diem refused, and Ho allowed his antagonist to go free. In 1960, when Ngo Dinh Diem told the story of this meeting to Stanley Karnow, he was not able to paint more than "an almost sympathetic portrait of Ho." Further, Vietnamese Communist party propaganda chief Hoang Tung told Karnow in 1981 that "considering the events that followed, releasing Diem was a blunder."[52] Clearly, the killing of his brother, given the strong Ngo family bonds, made any rapprochement between the two tribalists impossible. All that remained was for one to win, the other to lose—tribal combat.

Both men had talent, energy, and ambition—if marred by xenophobia. Most important, by nature both inclined toward petty tyranny, not alone from the urge to self-advancement but also from a preference for strong central authority with which to reorder the greater tribe. Both leaders appeared to be incorruptible as individuals, both ruled via force and terror, and both possessed a small base of power. In Hanoi, Ho Chi Minh led a Leninist party that gave him a modern mechanism for channeling Vietnamese neo-tribalism into a struggle for national independence. In Saigon,

Ngo Dinh Diem led a coalition of Roman Catholics (ex-northerners as well as southerners) and other southern groups that gave him a traditional mechanism for pursuing the same goal.

Neither witnessed the unification of their fatherland, as both were dead by 1975. Diem died by a murderer's hand in 1963, Ho of heart failure in 1969. Neither had been installed by a foreign patron, although both accepted foreign patronage—Ho that of the USSR and the People's Republic of China, Diem that of the United States. It is true that having had influential foreign contacts had harmed neither man. Diem's contacts included Senator Mansfield and Cardinal Spellman, while Ho's included Chou En-lai and Vyacheslav Molotov. Neither leader had ever been the choice of the departing French, and both had stressed this in reinforcing their anti-French credentials.[53] But Paris quickly lost its pre-1954 preeminence in the post-1954 succession crisis. In things political, Lockean and Leninist internationalists replaced defeated French colonialists. The French, having ruled the Vietnamese for nearly a century, did, however, bequeath the Vietnamese contenders two French versions of an outsider's culture. For both Ho and Diem practiced creeds not indigenous to the Vietnamese tribe; Catholicism and Marxism were alien faiths. In order to imagine how foreign creeds operated in the context of Vietnamese tribal history, one would have to be able to envision Moses as a high priest of Isis while he functioned as leader of the tribes of Israel. Ngo Dinh Diem's Catholicism (a medieval legacy from preindustrial France) and Ho Chi Minh's Marxism (a modern grant from post-Enlightenment France), rested uneasily upon the Vietnamese tribe's historical experiences. But even with these marks of the outsider upon them, each contender at first managed to overcome this tribal taboo against the new, the unknown. Both rose to the challenge of neo-tribalism's demands, the ideology of their personal creeds thus bending to ambition's call.

The Rise of Ho Chi Minh

Between 1945 and 1954, Ho Chi Minh captured part of the anti-French movement, especially its large umbrella organization, the Viet Minh. From 1954 to 1960 he took command of the northern half of the tribe by eliminating his competitors, especially his previous non-Leninist allies in the Viet Minh front. After 1960 he began to gain control over the extended tribe, first by capturing the chief's role within the National Front for the Liberation of South Vietnam (NLF), second by fighting a costly guerrilla war in the southern half. After Ho's death in 1969, the Leninist party in Hanoi, his creation, mounted a conventional invasion of the South and eliminated its political competition within the NLF.[54]

Capturing the chief's position in the Viet Minh and then in the NLF illustrated Ho's tribal good sense, as well as his effective organization and enormous will to power. Both organizations possessed a fairly broad base within the extended tribe, and Ho's leadership in both assured final victory for his elite group of tribal retainers. He had risen to the chieftainship by palace coups, as did his chief competitor, Ngo Dinh Diem. But Ho Chi Minh freely left the palace to visit the peasants, which Ngo Dinh Diem seldom felt safe enough to do.

Ho's chief military strategist, Vo Nguyen Giap, remembers many cold nights in the Vietnamese mountains in 1941 when a fire would draw the rebels to its warmth. On such occasions, Ho, "as if telling folk tales," would narrate a global history that linked Vietnamese experiences to larger events.[55] Extending this role as bard, Ho composed a poem, "The History of Our Country from 2879 B.C. to 1942" (typed on his own portable typewriter but disseminated chiefly by the Viet Minh in oral training classes). In his poem Ho carefully stressed the crucial role of the peasants led by the Tay Son family, in their defeat of those ancient outsiders, the Chinese.[56]

The mountains, the fires, the rebel band around its chief—these were the ingredients that E. J. Hobsbaum warmed to as he studied archaic forms of rebellion in the nineteenth and twentieth centuries. In Vietnam the rebels fit his description of a prepolitical people who had not yet found "a specific language in which to express their aspirations about the world."[57] Ho Chi Minh brought them such a language. He and his top advisers, such as Vo Nguyen Giap, were not themselves primitive rebels. But their followers were: as they sat by a mountain fire in 1941, they probably dreamed of a rice planting and a harvest, and proclaimed their willingness to die for the tribal fatherland.

Grand designs may have existed in the minds of Ho and his lieutenants, but such designs had to pass through a filter in order for young men and women, those who would risk death, to connect them to their daily lives. One historian, Robert Middlekauff, has suggested that such filters are parochial: as in the American revolution, ordinary people risked their lives because their friends were doing so, in defense of their common way of life.[58] Others have suggested an obvious parallel with China's experience: war brought by outsiders (the Japanese), combined with years of occupation and exploitation (by the same Japanese) that led to a devastating famine. In addition, some scholars have stressed the unique role of a Leninist party.[59] Vietnam exemplified all these patterns. Whatever his intellectual creed, the leader who rode the tiger of Vietnamese peasants' hatred and revenge gained the right to try to become the new chieftain.

The Vietnamese peasantry were the critical group that fought in this rebellion. For example, there were five gradations of leadership of the National Liberation Front—the national leadership, zonal leadership, provincial leadership, district leadership, and village leadership. The national leadership was led by the "Lenin of the NLF," Nguyen Van Hieu, and the Central Committee Chairman, Nguyen Huu Tho, who was "the best known NLF figure in Vietnam." Both played essentially political roles. Politicians also dominated the zonal level. Rebels who fought, as opposed to politicians who talked, were located at the next three levels. In 1966 peasant leaders within the NLF were concentrated at the levels of province, district, and villages. Of the vice chairmen of district committees in twenty Mekong Delta provinces, eight were peasants. A Viet Cong defector confirmed these figures, claiming that "most of the cadres are peasants, most of the party members are peasants, most of the military commanders are peasants."[60] It was these peasants who died for their fatherland.

The Rise of Ngo Dinh Diem

Not all toilers of the soil chose the same contender. Some chose Ho Chi Minh's opponent, Ngo Dinh Diem, who was as wily as Ho Chi Minh. Both were survivors, both combatants, both eager to lead the greater Vietnamese tribe. Ngo Dinh Diem began his rise in May 1953, when he left the Maryknoll seminaries in New Jersey and New York, which had hosted him for two years, and moved in with the Benedictines of Saint André-les-Bruges in Belgium. Operating from this Belgian monastery Diem made adroit use of his younger brother, Ngo Dinh Luyen, to capture the leadership of the anti-Leninist Vietnamese organizations in Paris. But Paris was not Saigon. Then, with another brother, Ngo Dinh Nhu, acting as the family's advance man, Diem returned to Saigon on June 25, 1954, his anti-French credentials still intact. Initially Emperor Bao Dai—the French puppet living in a villa on the Côte d'Azur—blessed Diem's return and made him Prime Minister. But even with the Emperor's blessing, it was necessary to fight again for the chieftainship with the other non-Leninist, anti-French Vietnamese residing in the South. As he had in Paris, Diem succeeded. Next, he had to neutralize Bao Dai, whom Diem saw as an agent of the French. Outmaneuvering the nonresident Emperor proved no major obstacle after Ngo Dinh Diem had exiled the Emperor's Chief of the Army Staff, General Nguyen Van Hinh, a man who had flaunted his disloyalty to the Prime Minister.

A more troublesome challenge came from the private armies of southern religious sects: the Cao Dai, an ad hoc mixture of Confucianism, Buddhism, spiritualism, and Catholicism; and the Hoa Hao, a fundamentalist Buddhist splinter group. In addition, Diem had to destroy Saigon's mafia, the Binh Xuyen river pirates, who had simply bought the Saigon municipal police from Bao Dai in 1954 for over a million dollars. By this sale, the Emperor had given them control of gambling, prostitution, and opium in Saigon and its environs. Diem dealt with the sects by ruling through rewards and punishments. Against the gangsters he launched his new army, with a moral vengeance for which his family became notorious.[61] The family's moral rectitude was again displayed, for example, when, later in Ngo Dinh Diem's rule, his sister-in-law Madam Nhu launched a campaign to eliminate prostitution, although she knew quite well that the new patrons, the Americans, were frequent users of the brothels of Saigon and other urban centers.[62]

Having come this far, Ngo Dinh Diem had to consolidate his power in the South before meeting Ho Chi Minh for the last battle, a type of ancient challenge in which the tribe allows two hero-contenders to do battle for their allegiance. But the field of battle would be uphill for Ngo Dinh Diem, because his patron, unlike Ho Chi Minh's, was Lockean; and American Whig internationalists demanded that their client legitimize his rule through a bargaining process of electoral politics. Amazingly, their client agreed, and constitutionalism was accepted in South Vietnam.

But what kind of constitutionalism was it? Ngo Dinh Diem appointed the committee that wrote the southern constitution, and the resulting document reflected his own mandarin preference for a strong executive.[63] Ho Chi Minh had created a strong executive through a Leninist organization, and Diem tried to achieve one through a Lockean organization. But there was a crucial asymmetry between the two arrangements. Whereas Ho Chi Minh was a Leninist, Ngo Dinh Diem was not a Lockean. He was not a Leninist either; he was a page turned back to the time prior to the recent outsiders, for Diem existed as a traditional mandarin in an age when that type of Vietnamese tribal leader was rapidly becoming extinct.[64]

Though mandarin in his vision of the proper social order, in practice Diem was Tammany Hall at its worst. He ruled through bargains, trades, deals, bribes, harangues, and threats—often threats of exile or worse. He offered patronage, not programs. If his Whig internationalist patrons insisted on programs, such as legal reforms, Diem would build them on patronage within a system that few Americans understood. Whig internationalists could understand the obvious, and that much Diem gave them. For example, in his National Assembly between 1956 and 1959, there were ten different parties or movements with which a deputy could affiliate.[65] Through these representatives, urban elites were allowed to bargain with their last mandarin.

But who could bargain with the vast tribal membership of peasants? Ngo Dinh Diem tried. He knew that there were Boy Scouts in his portion of the tribe, and that folk tales and songs still lingered in the memory of southern peasants. So he took a 1945 song that had served as a rallying cry against the French—Luu Huu Phuoc's "A Call to Youth"—and, after changing the title and some of the words, declared it the official song of the South. Diem also set up several mass organizations, notably the Women's Solidarity Movement, the Association of War Martyrs' Families, and Republican Youth and Women.[66] But these efforts were not enough. It was evident to most that Ngo Dinh Diem seldom left the palace to make contact with the people in ways that would encourage the allegiance of many primitive rebels and zealots; and his opponent was doing exactly that.

Still, in 1957 the race for the chieftainship was far from resolved. Ngo Dinh Diem's position in the South appeared fairly stable, especially as compared to the instability of 1955, his first full year in Saigon. David Halberstam wrote that "Diem acted forthrightly and courageously in the early years of his government." Chester Cooper seconded Halberstam's assessment, especially when he compared Ngo Dinh Diem's government to others emerging around the world.[67] But Halberstam quickly joined the swelling ranks of Whig critics, especially those in journalistic circles, who found Ngo Dinh Diem's continuous abridgement of political rights intolerable.

While some Whig internationalists began to condemn the mandarin in Saigon, Tory internationalists remained committed to supporting him although working to moderate his policies. A historian argued "that the strength of the Communists and their determination to unify the country under Ho Chi Minh justified temporary dictatorial measures against them if democracy was to have a chance in the South. . . . Only thus could the people have been offered the choice between Communism and the better government that the anti-Communist West expected Diem to create." And even this writer qualified his Niebuhrian manifesto: the dictatorship must remain "temporary" and the dictator must create a "better government." This constituted a heavy task. Other academics also supported Diem. Hans Morgenthau, a political scientist with influence to match Niebuhr's, having witnessed the lack of freedom of speech and press in Saigon's half of Vietnam, nevertheless stated that "considering the enormity of the task which confronts Diem, it would be ill-advised to be squeamish about some of the methods he used."[68]

Traditional Mandarin Versus Revolutionary Mandarin

By 1957 Ho Chi Minh in the North and Ngo Dinh Diem in the South had consolidated enough power to prepare for the final struggle—over the unification of Vietnam. This could not be achieved through compromise; there had to be a winner and a loser. To the patron states involved, this meant that one patron's ideological frontier would be extended at the expense of the other's. And the more energy and prestige each patron invested in this peripheral Southeast Asian land, the less willing each became to absorb even a temporary setback.

In client-patron quarrels, Ho Chi Minh had one solid advantage over Ngo Dinh Diem. While neither of Ho's patrons, the Soviet Union and the People's Republic of China, appeared eager to push him into a war for liberation in the South, neither acting alone could forbid it.[69] The Sino-Soviet split granted Ho Chi Minh a margin of maneuverability that Ngo Dinh Diem lacked. The Franco-American split, especially after de Gaulle's return to power in 1958, never offered Ngo Dinh Diem such opportunities. After 1954 France never again possessed even partial coequality in South Vietnam. And there could be no real hope that any American-supported government in Saigon would liberate the North by force, because U.S. Whig and Tory internationalists could and did forbid it, thereby making it obvious to all southern leaders that they would have to be content with half a country.

The leader of the house of Ngo did have one advantage that later Saigon chiefs never had: he was never a puppet. Unlike those who replaced him, Diem insisted that he was an ally, not a client, and on several occasions demonstrated this belief by his independent actions. But even he could not attack the North. Leaders of Saigon governments had to limit their horizons, to sustain their hold on half a banner; their only hope was that a democratic evolution might some day bring the northern half back into their fatherland. Hanoi's leaders were under no such constraint.

This was not the only way in which the contest was skewed in favor of the North. There also existed the political preference of the opposing patrons for special types of organizations. Both of Ho Chi Minh's suspicious patrons, China and Russia, offered similar models of a Leninist, single-party government. With such a government the Hanoi regime could force total compliance upon its mainly Tonkinese segment. In contrast, Ngo Dinh Diem's one suspicious patron, the United States, demanded political toleration for dissenting non-Leninist groups within the South. An increasingly suspicious Ngo family found that this Lockean demand conflicted with their ability to rule, for it made it difficult for them to force compliance upon their mainly Cochinese and Annamese segments. Down to the collapse in 1975 of the Thieu regime, their successors would experience the same difficulty.

Whereas the southern leader had to tolerate mixed opinions on subjects political, the northern leader—buttressed by strong central-party control—did not. An unusual event had also helped eliminate Ho Chi

Minh's compliance problem: at the time of partition in 1954, a sizable portion of Ho's noncomplying population voted with their feet—not for Whig liberty, but for traditional authority. The fortunate ones obtained space on U.S. warships that Washington officials had ordered to assist in the evacuation. Approximately 750,000 Tonkinese, mostly Catholics, resettled themselves south of the 17th parallel in the first year following partition.

In a reverse migration, some 30,000 to 100,000 tribal members moved North—not for Leninist equality, but to escape dire poverty. The majority came primarily from the Phu Yen, Binh Dinh, and Quang Ngai coastal plains, a desolate land of destitute peasants. They were joined by a small minority of Viet Minh members and communists, who now feared for their lives.[70] Both southern and northern tribal leaders tolerated the provisions of the Geneva Accords that allowed for these two migrations—which clearly had very little to do with Locke or Lenin.

The Geneva Accords of 1954 provided for Vietnam-wide elections to be held in 1956. When Ngo Dinh Diem refused to hold elections in the South, he eliminated any hope that the Vietnamese fatherland could ever be united by ballot. The blame for this failure has fallen in part on Diem and the Eisenhower administration. But the real responsibility lay with the Whig and Tory internationalists, Republican and Democrat alike, who supported U.S. national security policy in Vietnam. For example, the junior Senator from Massachusetts, John F. Kennedy, argued that Democratic party internationalists, especially Tories like himself, should take the position that neither "the United States nor Free Vietnam is ever going to be a party to an election obviously stacked and subverted in advance, urged upon us by those who have already broken their own pledges under the agreement they now seek to enforce."[71]

There is a more down-to-earth explanation for the failure of elections to take place. In 1956 Ngo Dinh Diem had not yet finished consolidating power on his own turf, while Ho Chi Minh had; in fact, Ho already was repositioning his forces so that he could try to start consolidating power on his antagonist's home ground. Furthermore, the leaders of the People's Republic of China deemed elections a waste of effort and easily pressured Ho Chi Minh to forget about them. In the United States, circumspection forced Kennedy to suggest Tory economic competition in lieu of Whig election contests.[72] Apart from this, the blood feud between the two contending chieftains and their retainers, and the ideological hostility that existed between their superpower patrons, was enough to make a peaceful solution to the conflict almost impossible.

By 1960 Ho Chi Minh, having already established a South Vietnamese branch office of the Vietnam Communist party, called for reunification of the greater Vietnamese fatherland. Then, on December 20, 1960, the National Front for Liberation of South Vietnam (NLF) was established. Its membership embraced both agents of Hanoi and southerners dissatisfied with Ngo Dinh Diem's rule; and both groups believed they represented the southern cause. Who controlled the NLF? It seems clear that it was not simply "Hanoi's creation." Certainly primitive rebels were not fighting for Lenin (or Locke), and it would have been unwise to confuse them with sophisticated imported theories. But it is clear also that Ho encouraged the appearance of the NLF as a patriotic coalition while his agents, gradually and incrementally, were acquiring power within it—so that by the mid-1960's the NLF was not really "acting independently" of Hanoi. Conclusive evidence of Hanoi's role came when two Viet Cong leaders published their memoirs: Nguyen Thi Dinh in 1976, and Truong Nhu Tang in 1985 (Tang was a former Viet Cong Minister of Justice who had to flee Vietnam by boat).[73] It would be fair to state that the NLF fronted for many for most of its existence, but it fronted for Hanoi in the end.

While the NLF lasted, it required an organizational base to facilitate relations with Hanoi. This was accomplished through the Fatherland Front (Mat Tran To Quoc), founded in April 1961. In October 1962 its leaders met with northern leaders in Hanoi, and they issued a joint communiqué calling for "reunification of the Fatherland."[74] Thereafter, the civil war in the South became, in the main, a war to win adherents for the North among the peasantry, especially among the primitive rebels.[75]

In summary, by the late 1950's two possible leaders of a unified Vietnam—Ngo Dinh Diem and Ho Chi Minh—began their final struggle. Beneath the surface they fought a neo-tribalist battle to become the new chief. One headed an extended family, the other a political party. As organizations, the family was traditional and the party was revolutionary. Both family and party served their respective leaders as intelligence networks. And among the many American organizations that assisted the American ally, South Vietnam, the CIA played a paramount role. At least initially, its leaders favored supporting the traditional Ngo family in order to facilitate the CIA view of orderly growth combined with modest change.

CHAPTER FIVE

The Fall of the House of Ngo

AMERICAN INTERNATIONALISTS agonized over whether to support revolution or reform in global politics. Although averse to colonialism, they had an even greater animus toward communism. In Vietnam, since the French represented colonialism and Ho Chi Minh represented communism, Americans supported Ngo Dinh Diem even though internationalists knew he was neither a Lockean revolutionary nor a reformer, but simply an anticommunist, anticolonialist nationalist who was also a traditional Vietnamese authoritarian. And because the United States followed a moderate reform strategy that emphasized defensive tactics (and allowed only limited use of offensive tactics), Ngo Dinh Diem found himself at a military disadvantage within his half of Vietnam. This did not mean that his ally had inconvenient moral scruples: coups, sabotage, raids, and subversion were all permissible. In fact, American-aided covert attempts to foster a northern fifth column for Diem failed badly. His biggest problem remained that he lacked what Ho Chi Minh had: a powerful, diplomatically recognized organization (the National Liberation Front, or NLF) based in his opponent's half of the fatherland. Consolidation of his power allowed Ho Chi Minh to speak to the fatherland as the single northern voice. But consolidation made Ngo Dinh Diem only the most powerful voice among several southern voices. And because he had the bad luck to be under the tutelage of the United States—that Whiggish republic where he had lived in exile but which he had never come to understand—Diem had to go on fighting to consolidate power at home. Unfortunately for him, the NLF proved resistant to the tactics he had employed against his opponents in 1956—the Cao Dai, Hoa Hao, and Binh Xuyen sects, Saigon intellectuals, remnants of pro-French connections, and restless Army officers.

Early in 1962, Ngo Dinh Diem talked with Sir Robert Thompson, the British expert on counterinsurgency (who had recently visited President

Kennedy and his advisers). It was obvious to Thompson that Ngo Dinh Diem had "to devote much of his time and energy to manipulating the army commands in order to retain control and maintain his position." Thompson concluded from this that "all efforts to encourage him to broaden the base of his government and attract more popular support were meaningless in a situation in which the reality of political power lay not with the people but with the army." Ngo Dinh Diem seemed to realize this better than his critics, and commented that "successful generals were always retired." According to Thompson, Diem said that "any successor, if he wished to maintain an effective government, would have to be twice as repressive as he himself had been." Diem concluded this interchange by recalling the Bourbon death cry: "Aprés moi le déluge!"[1]

On August 7, 1963, four months before his murder, Ngo Dinh Diem granted a 5-hour interview to Marguerite Higgins.[2] He suggested that "procedure applicable to one culture cannot be transplanted wholly to another culture." Most of his trouble, he thought, came from "a certain type of Occidental who is wont to assume almost unconsciously that the East has everything to learn from the West and little or nothing to give in return." Diem believed that the West suffered from an assumption of superiority based on achievements in the physical sciences and the type of progress those achievements brought, and therefore had "a tendency to regard, as a general inferiority, the inferiority of the Oriental in material efficiency."[3]

More to the point, Ngo Dinh Diem understood the clash between the Whig ideal of Lockean liberty and his own traditional ideal of mandarin discipline. He told Higgins, for example, that the American "press and radio mock the idea of discipline and respect for authority and glorify so-called civil liberties and the right to criticize and the need for political opposition, but this country is in a life-and-death struggle." Besides, Diem added, "even Western democracies suspend civil liberties during war emergencies." Honest elections he thought impossible also. "How could they be [honest] when most villagers [85 percent of the population] and many city dwellers could not even read the names on their ballots, much less understand such concepts as constitutionalism, consent of the governed, secret ballots, checks and balances, and other features of democratic government?" He thought that "in time and with practice, the people might eventually be able to work such a system, but not soon and especially not in the midst of the current turbulence."[4]

Higgins and other American journalists in Vietnam knew what Ngo Dinh Diem meant by "the current turbulence." Some suggested that it had begun as early as January 11, 1956, when Diem signed a law that allowed him to imprison and place under house arrest any person he deemed dangerous to the state. In 1959 he signed Law 10, which permitted military courts to impose the death penalty or life imprisonment for numerous acts that he, Ngo Dinh Diem, considered contrary to the welfare of the state. The repeal of this law became one of the Kennedy administration's chief concerns in 1963, when the summer riots began in Vietnam's urban centers.[5] But local Vietnamese had been protesting it for over three years; on April 26, 1960, eighteen nationally respected South Vietnamese, including former cabinet members, had placed their own lives at risk by signing the Manifesto of the Eighteen (or Caravelle Manifesto), in which they asked for the repeal of Law 10. The signers were not communists; they simply wanted reform.[6] But because they represented only unorganized urban elites, they lost. In the midst of war, their hopes for a Vietnamese fatherland housing Lockean ideals were as forlorn as those of the Whig internationalists. Ngo Dinh Diem turned a deaf ear to their appeal. Other groups complained and received the silent treatment, or were silenced. Others attempted coups, and they too failed.

As it happened, all opposition plotters would fail until they received a green light from the American patron. And that signal would be slow in coming, for the Americans were prepared to tolerate violence that seemed associated with the modernization of their client. Among internationalists, even Whigs accepted the Tory view that no "significant social, economic, or political reform takes place without violence or the imminent likelihood of violence."[7] In Vietnam, violence had become routine. There is no evidence that before 1962 any major American internationalist objected to this situation. For example, Frederick E. Nolting, the American Ambassador before Henry Cabot Lodge, supported the Ngo family. General Paul Harkins, the senior U.S. military person in Saigon, seconded him in this. Most significantly, however, the senior CIA representative—in 1963, John Richardson—supported the Ngo mandarinate's intelligence apparatus.

This apparatus, as critical as it was to American designs, remained under the control of the House of Ngo—specifically, under Ngo Dinh Nhu, one of Diem's brothers. As an organization it could function both as an intelligence agency, like the CIA, and as an internal security agency, like the FBI. The United States stressed the first function, but Ngo Dinh Nhu stressed both. To Westerners he recalled Dostoyevski's and Verdi's dark Grand Inquisitors and Arthur Koestler's modern inquisitor of darkness, Gletkin. But no one questioned Nhu's effectiveness, not even Thomas Hughes, the chief of the State Department's intelligence arm. Hughes briefed Secretary Rusk about the effective, but ruthless, operations conducted by Nhu.[8] Richardson's most important task was to maintain contact with Ngo Dinh Nhu and support him with funds, equipment, and training. With this assistance Ngo Dinh Diem constructed his Special Forces, supposedly an elite combat unit but in fact a palace guard. Whether it was a combat unit or palace guard did not bother Richardson. He and his bosses assisted the mandarin's inquisitor for years. Ngo Dinh Nhu's power was such that he could deal directly with the U.S. mission. He did not have to go through his brother and the U.S. Ambassador; he could go directly to Richardson.

This arrangement gave Tory internationalists the upper hand in determining Vietnam policy. Their influence depended on two conditions: Ngo Dinh Nhu would be the most influential member of his brother's government, and the CIA would be the most influential member of the country team in the U.S. embassy in Saigon. These conditions survived the 1950's and continued into the early 1960's even with the violence both conditions generated. To ride out the violence while changing Vietnam from the economic bottom of Abraham Maslow's hierarchy—that was the Tory agenda for handling Vietnam. Whig internationalists could fume over abridged political rights at the pinnacle of a Maslowian hierarchy as they saw it in Vietnam, but Tory internationalists were confident of victory for themselves and their recalcitrant Whig friends "in the long haul." Tories and Whigs did not differ on the acceptability of authoritarianism; both wished for its demise. But on the question of how to promote its demise, Whigs preferred a frontal attack and Tories a flanking attack.

The end of Tory predominance in Vietnam policy-making began in the ancient capital of Hué on May 8, 1963, when a group of Buddhists began displaying a banner celebrating the 2,527th anniversary of the Buddha's birth. The government in Saigon had forbidden the flying of religious banners, although Ngo Dinh Diem's own brother, Archbishop Ngo Dinh Thuc, ordered Vatican flags flown in Hué to celebrate the twenty-fifth anniversary of his own consecration—a celebration started a few days before the Buddhists' celebration. Apparently Thich Tri Quang, a key Buddhist leader in the Hué area, refused to send Archbishop Thuc a congratulatory telegram.[9] Partly in revenge for this slight and partly for reasons of state, the Ngo family in Saigon then ordered Hué officials to enforce the ban on religious flags, but by then only Buddhist flags were flying; the Catholics had finished their celebration. When the crowd of Buddhists refused to take down their banner, the Deputy Province Chief, Major Dang Xy, who happened to be a Catholic, ordered his men to fire blanks at them. When this failed to disperse the crowd, his soldiers fired live ammunition and killed nine Vietnamese. News of this incident sparked unrest in other cities—here again, even Buddhist unrest was mainly an urban phenomenon. Initially, Ngo Dinh Diem made minor concessions.[10] When these failed, he unleashed his brother the inquisitor, Ngo Dinh Nhu, to crush the opposition.

With Nhu in charge, the Buddhist movement had a widely hated target. Vietnamese who practiced Buddhism only nominally or not at all now supported the demonstrators. Collective grievances dating from 1954 suddenly coalesced to form a movement. Many of these grievances had nothing to do with Buddhism, and certainly nothing to do with Whig views of freedom of religion. In fact, there is no evidence that Ngo Dinh Diem had any sort of antireligious policy. As a matter of private conscience he cared little about someone else's religion, but, like his opponent in Hanoi, he did not trust its political manifestations.

It is true, of course, that Ngo Dinh Diem favored Catholics; and true also that he bargained with Hoa Hao, Cao Dai, and other religious sects—though not for religious reasons. Within his government he had many politicians who happened to be Buddhists. Vice President Nguyen Ngoc Tho, for example, was a Buddhist, but his Buddhism had not gained him his office. The kind of politics Ngo Dinh Diem practiced meant making deals to gain support. The Vice President and other Buddhists had to bargain with chips other than their religion because they could not deliver the support of a Buddhist bloc. Without a coherent Saigon faction you could not play the Saigon political game. Ngo Dinh Diem simply found no organized Buddhist faction that could bargain or deal with him for a larger share. Politics, not religion, was the key issue.[11]

Buddhist Politics

Reviewing the political incidents of 1963, George Carver writes: "Bit by bit a plethora of incidents, events, practices, and policies—many of them almost certainly unintentional or accidental—laid the groundwork for a 'religious issue' on which non-Communist but also non-Catholic opposition to Diem could, and eventually did, focus." He adds that the opposition "had been gradually building up almost from the day Diem took office." Carver occupied a unique post from which to make this assessment, because when Richard Helms became Director of the CIA in 1966, he appointed Carver to replace Peer De Silva as Special Assistant for Vietnamese Affairs.[12]

After Diem's murder none of the many military leaders who succeeded him ever published documents indicating a policy of religious oppression—for the simple reason that there had been no such policy. If anything, the traditional Confucian court at Hué historically had held the Buddhists in low esteem, prejudiced as the court was against Buddhism. But Diem employed talented Buddhists, something the court tried to avoid. The opposition to Diem swelled because the Ngo brothers had failed to grant the Buddhists an even larger share of the political rewards—a larger role in making national policy, a greater share in the new wealth brought by the Americans, and a special role for their religion in state affairs. Harsh as it may sound, these political spoils were what the radical Buddhist leaders wanted. Even after the murder of their alleged religious oppressor—by which they achieved their ostensible aim, the fall of the House of Ngo—Buddhist urban leaders with media contacts continued their civil disobedience. They had motives beyond the political, of course; they acted partly out of Buddhist pride, solidarity, and indignation. But once these feelings became inflamed, radical Buddhists so inflated their political demands that the new government in Saigon—composed of the Buddhists, Catholics, and generals who had "saved" them from Diem—finally had to crush them.[13]

In increasing their demands, the radical Buddhist leaders learned to use the modern media. After a series of June riots and demonstrations, their representatives (acting much like advance media and public relations agents) informed the American press of a dramatic event planned for June 11, 1963. In the courtyard of the Xa Loi Pagoda, in downtown Saigon, a crowd gathered to initiate a dramatically new use of the media. On the arrival of the venerable Quang Duc, a circle formed around him. The seventy-year-old bonze seated himself on a cushion, assuming the posture of contemplation. Another monk approached and doused him with gasoline. The venerable one then struck a match and set himself afire. With his act, self-immolation became a political weapon. Malcolm Browne, of the Associated Press, captured the death on film, and prints of his negatives appeared around the world.[14]

Instead of trying to douse this political fire by offering a major compromise, Diem left the situation to his chief police official, his brother Ngo Dinh Nhu. This was bad enough, but Madame Nhu soon added fuel to the fire: appearing on American television, she spoke of barbecued monks, said she clapped her hands in applause at such suicide, and even suggested that the journalist David Halberstam should follow the Buddhist's example. Since Halberstam wrote for the *New York Times*, her venom went right to the heart of American Whiggism, with disastrous results for those she presumed to protect. To American viewers she was the personification of the Dragon Lady, cruel yet beautiful.

Tory internationalists struggled to hold the American course steady, but their luck did not hold. Ambassador Nolting was on a regularly scheduled leave in the midst of the crisis stirred by the Buddhist tactics, and his deputy chief of mission, William Trueheart—with a true Whig distate for the Ngo Dinh Diem of 1963—did nothing to stabilize events. A flurry of "for Trueheart from Hilsman" messages immediately dominated the cable traffic in and out of the U.S. embassy in Saigon. On June 11 a cable authorized Trueheart "to tell Diem that unless GVN [Saigon] is willing to take effective action . . . within the next few days the U.S. will find it necessary publicly to state it cannot associate itself with the GVN's unwillingness to meet the reasonable demands of the Vietnamese Buddhist leaders." Five days later Trueheart, having contemplated a Saigon without Ngo Dinh Diem, nervously cabled: "Notwithstanding that my misgivings about the Ngo family including Diem have greatly increased during last two weeks, I am still not—repeat not—impressed by the competition." Suddenly it looked as though Saigon's Whig had lost his nerve. With a possible defection by Trueheart in mind, Hilsman instructed his colleague in a cable of June 19 to proceed with "a very hard-hitting approach to Diem."[15] Even with a somewhat reluctant Trueheart, the damage to U.S.-Saigon relations was severe. Nolting rushed back to support the pro-Diem forces at the Saigon embassy, but no one could repair the damage.

Unknown to Nolting, President Kennedy—though a Tory internationalist himself, and worried about the domestic repercussions of any Vietnam debacle—had long been considering a shake-up in Saigon. In November 1961 McGeorge Bundy had suggested to JFK that he replace Nolting, but Rusk opposed the idea. Bundy also had badgered his boss to find a new senior military man for Saigon, and he had a candidate in George McGhee, whom he dubbed "the victor of Greece," a reference to the American assistance in that civil war of Truman's time. Again someone resisted, this time the American military aristocracy.[16] With change in mind but facing resistance everywhere, Kennedy moved with caution; to secure bipartisan support, he sprinkled his administration with Republicans—Douglas Dillon, Robert McNamara, John McCone—and tried to keep Tory and Whig factions in balance.

The Whig Ascendancy

In June 1963, when Kennedy appointed a patrician Republican, Henry Cabot Lodge, to replace Nolting as Ambassador to Saigon, his balancing act faltered. He knew Lodge only as a Boston Brahmin, not as a man with strong Whig credentials. It was, in fact, Rusk who had first suggested Lodge as Nolting's replacement. As soon as Lodge took control of the embassy, he placed his Whig stamp on it and on those employees he allowed to remain on the embassy staff. For example, by October Lodge had arranged for the recall of the CIA's John Richardson.[17] And Lodge found himself connected to an important Whig team at the State Department: Under Secretary of State Averell Harriman and Assistant Secretary of State Roger Hilsman. All were troubled about Vietnam.

In Vietnam Diem appeased some critics by a radio speech of July 18 in which he promised minor concessions concerning the Buddhists' right to fly religious flags. But this gesture was too late and too feeble, and it enraged his brother Nhu, who called a meeting of leading Generals to discuss the possible need for a change of government. The CIA could not discover whether Diem knew of this meeting, but according to their report the younger brother told the Generals "that if he believed the government, meaning Diem, was becoming servile to the United States, he himself would lead a coup d'état."[18] With no base in the peasantry to which to retreat, Ngo Dinh Diem prepared to endure a siege by the Buddhists—which he fully expected to win. The second Buddhist suicide by flame came on August 5. Nolting departed from Saigon for his new assignment on August 20, and the third self-immolation occurred in Hué the next morning. Nolting assumed he had Ngo Dinh Diem's promise to try conciliation, but five days after his departure Nhu's troops, trained and equipped by the CIA, struck urban pagodas throughout the South.

On the way to his new assignment Lodge had stopped in Hawaii, so neither he nor Nolting was present in Saigon when Nhu's forces raided the pagodas. Under these circumstances, State Department internationalists felt they had to protest. Their statement, drafted by Harriman, was full of the acid indignation of aroused Whiggism: "The action represents a direct violation by the Vietnamese Government of assurances that it was pursuing a policy of reconciliation with the Buddhists." The bulletin concluded by informing the culprits that "the United States deplores repressive actions of this nature."[19]

Lodge arrived in Saigon the day after the pagoda raids. One of his first actions was to visit two Buddhist monks who had taken refuge in the offices of the U.S. Agency for International Development. While he was talking with the monks, Diem's Ambassador to Washington, who was tied to the Ngo family as the father of Madame Nhu, resigned his post and at the same time denounced his daughter. All but one member of his staff followed his example. As if this were not enough, the Foreign Minister resigned also, shaving his head like a monk to assure that his gesture would be understood as a response to government actions against Buddhists. Lodge soon discovered that Ngo Dinh Nhu had directed his secret police (disguised as airborne troops) and Colonel Le Quang Tung's Special Forces to carry out the raids. But U.S. officials had reported already that the South Vietnamese regular army was the culprit, and the Voice of America had broadcast that version. Needless to say, South Vietnam's military leaders fumed over this charge, and Lodge had to see to it that the Voice of America corrected its story. But larger problems remained.

The previous June, the *New York Times* had reported that U.S. Air Force transport aircraft had ferried South Vietnamese troops to Hué in order to quell the Buddhists. To counter the impact of this article, Robert McNamara, though still a firm Tory supporter of a reformed House of Ngo, guessed the political mood at the White House and informed Kennedy that he, as Secretary of Defense, had instructed General Harkins "that no U.S.-owned aircraft will be used to transport troops incident to the present Buddhist troubles in Vietnam." On June 5, 1963, to make sure he was understood, McNamara sent every major military command in the Pacific a copy of these instructions.[20]

Another problem grew out of the American funds that the CIA and others had been giving to Ngo Dinh Nhu's Special Forces. Once Lodge learned of these funds, he successfully lobbied the Kennedy administration to have them cut off. This action was intended to force Nhu to release control of his Special Forces, which Lodge called "a formidable force [which] man for man appears to have a big edge over an ordinary military outfit." To wrest control from Nhu and return it to Vietnamese Army generals, Lodge sent General Richard Stilwell to negotiate with Colonel Le Quang Tung, the Chief of Special Forces.[21] The negotiations were noisy, but Stilwell did not budge. Now even Tory internationalists were willing to use one of their weapons in hopes of causing Ngo Dinh Diem to dismiss his brother: with encouragement from allies in the Senate, the Tories managed to get $150 million a year in economic aid for Vietnam cut from the Commodity Import Program.[22]

Nothing worked. Ngo Dinh Diem would not budge. Obviously he thought the price was too high. Expelling his brother would violate a great taboo against disloyalty within the family, the most important unit within traditional society. Together they had stood, together they would fall. If they fell a new government would have to be installed, and the United States—as a deeply involved patron—would play a decisive role in the process.

The Green Light for a Coup

Each of the four key Whig internationalists who helped to orchestrate the end of the House of Ngo—Henry Cabot Lodge, Averell Harriman, George Ball, and Roger Hilsman—has published an account of it.[23] For frankness and detail, Hilsman's version is the most useful, but all four are drawn upon here to reconstruct the story of the coup. It appears that within a few days following the pagoda raids a group of senior Vietnamese military officers, using covert channels, contacted Lodge. In simple terms, they wanted assurances that the United States would support them if they could stage a successful coup. Lodge cabled Washington for instructions and received two cables in reply. The first contained an unclassified press advisory clearing the South Vietnamese military of responsibility for the attacks on Buddhists. The second, to which the drafters applied a defense classification, was very carefully phrased. Hilsman describes it as saying, in effect, that Washington "would certainly be prepared to work with Diem without Nhu, but that was up to the Vietnamese"; and that whereas the United States would take no part in planning or acting, "if action were taken, an interim, anti-Communist military government could expect that American support for the war effort would continue."[24] When he had this message passed to the dissident South Vietnamese officers, Lodge was clearly giving them the green light for a coup.

This second cable split the ranks of the internationalists. It was drafted by Whigs—George Ball, Averell Harriman, Michael Forrestal, and Roger Hilsman—on Saturday, August 24. But approvals were hard to obtain; President Kennedy was in Hyannisport, Secretary Rusk was in New York, and both Secretary McNamara and CIA Director McCone were on vacation. The drafters managed to contact only the first two, who seemed to approve. But when the National Security Council met on Monday, August 26, Kennedy was annoyed to find his advisers arguing about the second cable. McNamara—who by this time dominated the cabinet and any NSC meetings he attended—was furious.[25] Opposing McNamara meant defying Camelot's star knight, and, on the issue of supporting a coup, McNamara refused to budge. He believed in exerting heavy pressure on Diem, but not in changing mandarins. Backed by other Tories—General Maxwell Taylor and the CIA's John McCone—McNamara, in Hilsman's words, believed that "a certain amount of authoritarianism" was necessary if the Vietnamese struggle was to be settled on the United States' terms.[26]

After considering McNamara and McCone's position, the President, at heart a Tory internationalist himself, said he wished he had a chance to give a more ambivalent answer to the Generals.[27] Just such a chance appeared, for the South Vietnamese Generals held back. Their reluctance probably had many causes. Lodge reportedly said that perhaps, like others, they were afraid to die. Also, there was evidence that Ngo Dinh Nhu had spies everywhere. On September 1 his English-language newspaper, *The Times of Vietnam*, printed a long exposé headlined "C.I.A. Financing Planned Coup d'Etat."[28] Even more important was the fact that two Generals who knew that a coup was being planned remained loyal to Ngo Dinh Diem. They were General Ton That Dinh, military governor of Saigon and the surrounding III Corps, and General Huynh Van Cao, commanding IV Corps south of Saigon. Cao had helped save the regime during the 1960 coup attempt; a coup without him and Dinh might lead to a bloodbath.

While the plotters were hesitating, in early September Kennedy used a television interview with Walter Cronkite to present the essentials of a Tory resolution—a settlement that would leave Ngo Dinh Diem in power. Admitting that "in the past two months the [Vietnamese] government has gotten out of touch with the people," Kennedy faced the key issue when he stated that "the repressions against the Buddhists, we felt, were very unwise." Cronkite persisted and asked if there existed a good chance that the United States and the South Vietnamese could win the war. "With changes in policy and perhaps with personnel," Kennedy answered, the Saigon government could win, but "if it doesn't make these changes, I would think that the chances of winning it would not be very good." [29] By suggesting changes Kennedy was, diplomatically, calling for the removal of Ngo Dinh Nhu and the appointment of more Buddhists. In the days following this broadcast, Kennedy received support from the Congress. Rising on the Senate floor to support the President, Senator Frank Lausche (Democrat from Ohio), Chairman of the Far East Subcommittee of the Senate's Foreign Relations Committee, found himself seconded by Frank Church (Democrat, Idaho) and Frank Carlson (Republican, Kansas) when he called for a possible "change of personnel" in Vietnam. [30]

But Ngo Dinh Diem did not make any of the changes hinted at by Kennedy or the Senators. Under pressure he did what he had always done: he rigidly held his position. In the meantime university students joined the demonstrations in Saigon. As jails filled, more Vietnamese awaited their turn to have Ngo Dinh Nhu's forces arrest them. School children demonstrated, and parents had to beg to obtain their release. Leading Buddhists took refuge in the U.S. embassy. Frustrated by their inability to persuade Diem to compromise, Tory internationalists wanted Lodge to threaten him personally, but Frederick Nolting, Lodge's predecessor, advised Kennedy against it. He reminded the President that his own predecessor as Ambassador, Elbridge Durbrow, had insisted that Ngo Dinh Nhu be made to leave the country, but that it was Durbrow and not Nhu who had been expelled. [31] Kennedy understood.

That was September. October was worse. Those in Saigon who wanted a coup needed assurances that the American light flashed by Lodge in August remained green. In fact, it did. During September and October, CIA cables concerning coup plans, cables which had begun to flow on July 8, began to inundate Washington in-boxes. [32] Lodge was responsible

for the autumn flood. In an early September "Eyes Only" cable to the Sec
retary of State, he told Dean Rusk that "the time has arrived for the U.S.
to use what effective sanctions it has to bring about the fall of the existing
government and the installation of another." But Lodge qualified this advice in curious ways. He said, "I do not doubt the military judgment that
the war in the countryside is going well now." He admitted that U.S. involvement "would arouse the xenophobia which is always latent here."
And, having no likely candidate in mind to lead a new government,
Lodge worried that "we do not want to substitute a Castro for a Batista."
Rusk replied with a cable that began, "Highest level meeting September 11 discussed your 478 [cable] and draft[ed] State Department plan for
multiple pressures, public and private, to remove Nhus from scene."
Again, the Tory Secretary seemed willing to move only against Nhu and
his wife, not against Diem. To reinforce Rusk, JFK sent his own "Eyes
Only" cable to Lodge; it said, "Your 478 [cable] is a major paper and has
stirred a corresponding effort."[33] This encouragement notwithstanding,
Lodge yet had to get the message to the plotters. As Ambassador, he
could not do it himself; that would be impolitic. But he had a man who
could—Lucien Conein.

Conein—a Saigon-based CIA agent on loan from the military, where
he held the rank of Lieutenant Colonel—had the right credentials. He
knew Indochina from OSS assignments there at the end of World War II.
He had assisted in the attempts to set up an anti–Ho Chi Minh underground network in the North before implementation of the Geneva Accords. (Together with the CIA's Ed Lansdale, who had helped President
Ramón Magsaysay mount successful operations against the Hukbalahap
insurrection in the Philippines, Conein had succeeded in a few sabotage
strikes in the North, but Ho Chi Minh soon destroyed intelligence networks he had set up.) Finally, he had been a friend of General Tran Van
Don for eighteen years. Don was a key plotter in the coup. For these reasons, Lodge told McGeorge Bundy, Conein was essential to U.S. involvement in a successful coup. Lodge insisted on that point because Bundy
and the NSC staff had grown increasingly nervous as the coup-planning
advanced. Bundy even began writing and sending out cables to the CIA
in Saigon under his own signature.[34] A botched coup was not for him.

In October 1963, Conein "sat with the generals." In CIA terms, this
meant that dealing with the Generals became his mission. Lodge vouched
for his bona fides to one of the coup Generals.[35] Yet Lodge cabled Kennedy
on October 30, 1963, that there was little the United States could do to
influence those Generals, who might or might not decide to stage a coup.
McGeorge Bundy replied for Kennedy: this opinion was unacceptable;

Tories would not accept Lodge's view that the United States had little influence in Saigon politics.[36] Lodge got the message, and he sent Conein to influence the coup.

Meetings between Conein and various generals sometimes took place outside of Saigon. On October 2 he met with General Tran Van Don at the seaport of Nha Trang. A few days later he saw General Duong Van Minh in the capital. As late as October 28 he met again with General Don, this time in a Saigon dentist's office. The question was always whether the American green light was still on, and Conein's answer was always in the affirmative. Lodge knew the purpose of these meetings. The internationalists in Washington knew, and sent Lodge confirmation of their concern. Bundy said Washington awaited a "D-day"—a move by the plotters that would "turn out to be real." And he told Lodge that the "President wants you to know of our concern."[37] Hence one concludes that Kennedy knew.

The Countercoup

Ngo Dinh Nhu also knew. He had survived to become the inquisitor, after all, because he knew more than others did. The CIA had tutored him and helped him set up an intelligence apparatus. The CIA was now ordered to support a different team, but it could not withdraw the resources it had already given him. Furthermore, Nhu had experience in dealing with what he considered U.S. duplicity. In the wake of the 1960 coup attempt against his brother, he had dealt with William Colby, John Richardson's predecessor as CIA station chief in the U.S. embassy. Colby writes that Nhu, furious upon discovering that the CIA had prior knowledge of the coup and had remained neutral, spoke as follows: "All nations conduct espionage, and this is not a matter to get upset about. But what no nation can accept, and our government no less, is interference with its political authority and processes." Nhu then demanded the ouster of the CIA agent who had been in contact with the plotters; Colby agreed, and that agent departed.[38] Now, in late 1963, Nhu faced the challenge of a repeat performance. How could he, for a second time, force the United States to accept Ngo family terms? The answer, he decided, was to stage a countercoup.

Ngo Dinh Nhu's ingenious countercoup plan called for two initiatives, to be taken in sequence. The first initiative was political. Its purpose was to frighten Americans into thinking that the Ngos would make a deal with Ho Chi Minh. Ngo Dinh Nhu conducted behind-the-scenes talks with French and Polish representatives from the International Control Commission who flew to Saigon from Hanoi at his invitation. The Polish representative, Mieczyslaw Maneli, met with Ngo Dinh Nhu twice, once on August 25 and a week later on September 2. Maneli, a Marxist intellectual who finally discovered that Leninists usually take over a Marxist state, later defected to the West and was persuaded to write his memoirs, in which he chronicles the fall of that southern institution, the Ngo family, and the reaction to it by Hanoi Leninists. According to him, the northern leaders recognized the problem as organizational—one could no longer rule Vietnam through a traditional institution—and they were willing to negotiate with the Ngo brothers about a new system of rule. In October Saigon came alive with rumors that the House of Ngo alone might negotiate the fatherland's future with Hanoi's claimant.[39] As Saigon buzzed with stories of a possible rapprochement—many of them spread by Nhu's agents—Washington became the object of international paranoia. In the midst of this Potomac confusion, Ray Cline rushed a CIA report to Bundy and his NSC staffers. Cline reported how Nhu had planted the story of a possible Saigon-Hanoi-Paris effort to arrange peace without U.S. participation with Joseph Alsop of the *Washington Post*.[40]

When this political part of the plan neared completion, the second initiative was to start. This was the military part of the plan, and it had two stages—Bravo 1 and Bravo 2. In Bravo 1, General Ton That Dinh and Colonel Tung were to launch a phony coup in Saigon a few days after October 26, Vietnam's national holiday. The troops used in Bravo 1 were to appear to be disloyal subordinate units operating with a mix of police and other forces all under the leadership of junior officers. Bravo 1 would lead to the destruction of property and the death of some Vietnamese and some Americans. The two Ngo brothers, as if fearing for their lives, would flee to Cape St. Jacques (Vung Tau), a resort southeast of Saigon. In Bravo 2, General Dinh and Colonel Tung would attack the city using other troops to dislodge the supposedly anti-Ngo police units and goon squads who had carried out Bravo 1. When General Dinh had "restored order," the brothers would return from their coastal hideaway as heroes.[41]

Clever, careful, cruel—but it did not work. General Dinh, his ego bruised by Diem's refusal in September to appoint him Minister of Interior, betrayed the Ngo brothers by informing the Generals plotting against the House of Ngo about Nhu's Bravo plan. Next, Nhu discovered that the opposition had moved up the date for their coup, so he did the same; but the anti-Diem forces were able to move first. On November 1 they struck. Admiral Harry Felt, U.S. commander for the Pacific basin, was in the presidential palace paying a courtesy call to Ngo Dinh Diem when news of the coup began to come in; he barely had time to get out. In the next hour or so, the brothers tried everything. They made calls to loyal units.

They demanded that the coup leaders come forward to talk. Ngo Dinh Diem even telephoned Lodge; the authors of the *Pentagon Papers* report this conversation as follows:

> Diem: Some units have made a rebellion and I want to know, what is the attitude of the U.S.?
>
> Lodge: I do not feel well enough informed to be able to tell you. I have heard the shooting, but am not acquainted with all the facts. Also it is 4:30 A.M. in Washington and the U.S. Government cannot possibly have a view.
>
> Diem: But you must have some general ideas. After all, I am a Chief of State. I have tried to do my duty. I want to do now what duty and good sense require. I believe in duty above all.
>
> Lodge: You have certainly done your duty. As I told you only this morning, I admire your courage and your great contributions to your country. No one can take way from you the credit for all you have done. Now I am worried about your physical safety. I have a report that those in charge of the current activity offer you and your brother safe conduct out of the country if you resign. Had you heard this?
>
> Diem: No. [And then, after a pause] You have my telephone number.
>
> Lodge: Yes. If I can do anything for your physical safety, please call me.
>
> Diem: I am trying to re-establish order.[42]

Once it became clear to them that they stood alone, the brothers fled the palace. They traveled by Land Rover to the waterfront, where they jumped into a Citroen and drove to a Chinese merchant's home in Cholon, the Chinese section of Saigon. This choice of help in an emergency was significant. Because Ngo Dinh Diem had failed to win support among the primitive rebels of his fatherland, he could find no sanctuary with them; in his time of need, he had to turn to outsiders, the Chinese.

Murder in the Cathedral

Two of the Vietnamese military plotters, Tran Van Don and Nguyen Cao Ky (each of whom, with U.S. support, later attempted to rule in Ngo Dinh Diem's place), have provided details of their roles in the coup. As soon as the coup leaders discovered the palace empty, the Ngo brothers phoned in to surrender. The plotters traced the call to the Cholon house, but the brothers had moved again, this time to a small Catholic church, from which they called again, agreeing to surrender. An American-furnished armored personnel carrier was sent to the church. Out of it stepped Colonel Duong Ngoc Lam, the head of the Civil Guard, a man known and trusted by the brothers. Behind him in another vehicle rode General Mai Huu Xuan, one of the original plotters. General Duong Van Minh, who was to lead the next government, had already ordered General Xuan to kill both brothers, so Xuan ordered a Major to do so. The brothers, having surrendered, were taken inside the closed carrier, in which they thought the escorts were to give them safe passage back to the palace.[43] There, the Major shot his President in the head and then shot the younger Ngo brother, who was also stabbed repeatedly by other escorting officers. The Whig internationalists, worried that murder might occur, had tried to forestall it, but they failed.[44]

The death of Ngo Dinh Diem was not unlike the death of other autocrats caught in the ideological crossfire between Lockean and Leninist dogmatists in their global attempts to reorder other fatherlands. Even the novels of this period use this for their plots. In his novel *The Autumn of the Patriarch*, Gabriel García Márquez captures the tragedy of a nationalist leader turned autocrat by force of his heritage and tradition. In Márquez's Latin American setting the death of the patriarch becomes the only solution. In his novel *The Coup*, John Updike captures the comedy of American outsiders turned into inept coup-makers by force of their Lockean assumptions. In Updike's African setting the American outsiders are in competition with Leninist outsiders who are no better than they at staging a coup. But the botched Saigon coup of 1963 did not even serve as the plot for a novel. Nor did it unduly discourage the internationalists; in 1964 the American country team in Brazil were accomplices in a coup that succeeded. And in 1965 CIA station chiefs in Zaire and Indonesia influenced two coups that brought new governments to power in both of those strategic states.[45]

Did Whig internationalists in the United States help bring down Ngo Dinh Diem's government? Let us consider the evidence provided by the key American actors. To begin with, on the day of the murders Lieutenant Colonel Conein of the CIA gave the plotting generals $42,000 to pay their troops. Later that night, at the insistence of Lodge, Conein called on the new autocrat, Duong Van Minh, or "Big Minh," and asked him to supply a plausible reason for the death of the mandarin. Minh replied that Ngo Dinh Diem had committed suicide. Conein, a Catholic, was not convinced that the Catholic President of South Vietnam had committed suicide in a church, and he told Minh of his misgivings once the Generals released this suicide explanation.[46] Upon hearing of this, Lodge was not satisfied that Conein had impressed the Generals with the niceties they should have observed in playing a Pontius Pilate role for the media and the public. The next day, with Conein beside him, Lodge met with Genrals Don and Le Van Kim and "asked whether they were planning a statement which would absolve themselves from the assassination of Diem and Nhu." The two blandly agreed this was an idea that might help them, at least among outsiders. General Don relates how he and General

Minh made a public display of calling on President Diem's niece in Saigon. They assured her that the deaths "occurred as an unfortunate incident during the coup." Both offered to help with the funeral arrangements. Having no further use for Conein, Lodge soon let him go, but not before sending the CIA Director, John McCone, the following accolade: "I wish particularly also to set down the valuable services rendered by Lt. Col. Conein, whose contacts with the General's group were of priceless value to us and whose tireless and accurate reporting and transmission have been of the greatest benefit."[47]

Lodge has always denied his complicity in any plot, although he received most of the blame. The authors of the *Pentagon Papers* succinctly stated that the United States "variously authorized, sanctioned, and encouraged" the coup against their client.[48] Not so, states Lodge, for "the coup of November 1 was essentially a Vietnamese affair." Lodge maintains that this had to be true: "Because of our lack of involvement in the intricacies of Vietnamese political life, we could not have started the coup if we had wanted to." More important, he maintains that the United States could not "have stopped one once it started." Lodge admits that "our policy, under instructions from President Kennedy, was 'not to thwart' a coup." He bases this defense on later cables that supposedly modified that first green-light cable.[49]

Given the years Lodge has had in which to construct a convincing case, it is remarkable that he has not succeeded. Almost all those involved agree that he managed the Saigon embassy closely and exercised all his powers to influence events in the city. For example, when William Colby, then head of CIA's Far Eastern Division, accompanied Robert McNamara to Saigon in late September in a Tory attempt to stave off disaster, Lodge prevented Colby from seeing either Ngo brother.[50] If Lodge could block Colby in this way, he certainly could have persuaded Kennedy to order Lucien Conein off the coup case—or had him recalled, as he had done with John Richardson.

The account of Under Secretary of State George Ball is the least defensive of those offered by the ex-plotters. Initially he was a "reform" Whig, convinced that global conditions could be changed only at the speed a particular government could accept changes enforced by aid from outside. Ball was frightened by what he saw as the desire for quick results among "reconstruction" Whigs; he feared that if they had their way, they would make radical intervention a policy regardless of the situation—and that could lead to chaos. But in the matter of Vietnam policy, continuing pressure from colleagues led Ball to a painful reappraisal of his position. He said at one point, "We were rapidly discovering that the tiger we were backing in Vietnam was more of a Tammany tiger than a disciple of Thomas Jefferson."[51]

Of course Ball was correct; even Ngo Dinh Diem himself never tried to convince anyone that he took as his model the sage of Monticello. What Ball overlooked was the fact that Tammany tigers understood politics; a group could make a deal with them, especially if it could make offers they could not refuse. Not being a politician in the tradition of George Plunkett, from New York's old Tammany, Ball had a Whig aversion to political deals of the Tammany variety. In Ball's reading of American history, it had been reform Whigs who had corrected the worst aspects of Tammany politics. And Ball was unwilling to tolerate internationally the political practices his reform predecessors had fought against nationally, even if some "honest graft" might help a few of the less fortunate.

In seeking advice, Ball found willing advisers. One of the most vocal among them, John Kenneth Galbraith, had visited Saigon at Kennedy's request. Upon his return, Galbraith told Ball "in unambiguous terms that Diem was an insurmountable obstacle to success." As Ambassador to India, Galbraith gave Kennedy the same negative view of the House of Ngo.[52] As reconstructionists pressured them to approve a coup, reformers were held back by their experience of cognitive dissonance: to sponsor or assist in a coup would contradict their most cherished ideals. Ball admits as much: "Encouraging coups, of course, ran counter to the grain of American principles." But then he discovered his way around those principles. Like others, he changed one critical part of his belief system about Vietnam. Ball decided that "Diem's legitimacy was dubious at best; we had in effect created him in the first place." If by Lockean standards as Ball understood them, Ngo Dinh Diem was no longer a legitimate ruler, helping to overthrow him could not be an illegitimate action.

Ball went beyond theorizing. When the Whig reconstructionists sent their cable to Lodge on Saturday, August 24, they had instructed him first to warn Ngo Dinh Diem of a possible coup and "give Diem reasonable opportunity to remove the Nhus." In his Sunday cable of reply, Lodge requested "permisson to go directly to the generals, without first telling Diem." At this point Ball surrendered: "I approved a telegram authorizing this change in procedures, which I cleared with Mike Forrestal [at the NSC], who was acting for a briefly absent Mac Bundy." After the coup, Ball supported Lodge in insisting that it was "a thoroughly indigenous operation, Vietnamese in origin and Vietnamese in every respect."[53]

Averell Harriman, in his memoir, is both less frank and less defensive. In a cryptic paragraph he says that "the situation became so acute that Diem was forced out by a military coup on November 1, 1963." He notes that "in the confusion of their capture, he and his brother were killed by a junior officer." He concludes, "These events deeply shocked President Kennedy."[54] But Harriman misconstrues even Kennedy, as we shall see.

Kennedy's Failure

Kennedy's role in Ngo Dinh Diem's murder remains controversial. Certainly he must share some responsibility for it; the question is how much. Arnold Wolfers, a colleague of both Niebuhr and Morgenthau, places questions like this in a Weberian context. He insists that we listen "to the nonperfectionist who demands of man not that he follow a code of absolutist ethical values—what Max Weber calls the 'natural law of absolute imperatives'—but that he make the best moral choice that circumstance permits." Dismissing those he calls ethical perfectionists, Wolfers notes that nonperfectionist moralists in the Western world condone the acts of those who kill in self-defense, in executing a criminal, in war, and "possibly in the case of tyrannicide." But he insists that nonperfectionist statesmen and private individuals alike are morally required to consider the options open to them and to select "the one which under the circumstances promises to produce the least destruction of value or, positively speaking, points toward the maximization of values."[55] By perfectionist standards, Kennedy's actions before the coup would make him an accomplice, at least in Anglo-Saxon terms—and in the America of the 1960's there were still many perfectionists who held to Anglo-Saxon definitions. But internationalists almost consistently were nonperfectionists. For them, this coup posed three questions. Was the situation in Vietnam one that warranted such action? Was Ngo Dinh Diem a tyrant? Was this coup one that would entail either the least possible destruction of value or some maximization of value? Tories said no, Whigs said yes.

In T. S. Eliot's *Murder in the Cathedral*, King Henry II asks, in frustration, if no one would rid him of a meddling priest. Once the king flashed his emerald light, several "no ones" murdered Thomas à Becket, the Archbishop of Canterbury, in his cathedral. Eliot and some historians condemn Henry as an accomplice to that murder. The green light Kennedy continually allowed his Ambassador to flash did rid him of a meddling mandarin, but Diem's murder in front of a church made Kennedy's critics view him as an accomplice. Although the authors of the *Pentagon Papers* shied away from placing the guilt for Diem's "sudden, bloody, and permanent end," they do assert U.S. "complicity in the coup" and suggest that the coup "only heightened our responsibilities and our commitment in this struggling, leaderless land." [56]

Should Kennedy have known that U.S. interests would be damaged by this coup? Indeed he should; he possessed substantial evidence that Diem was the strongest of the Vietnamese nationalists who had been able to survive the battles of Saigon factional politics. (There were a few other factional leaders with nationalist credentials, but Kennedy did not know of them.) JFK allowed his nation to back the overthrow of an allied leader, and he did so without having in mind a candidate who could hope to survive the ensuing chaos. Even the Ambassador who pushed the President toward a coup had sent him a cable in October warning him that after a coup "a succession of fights for control of the Government of Vietnam would interfere with the war effort." [57]

Questions of personal complicity aside, how could this happen? The answer, in general, must be that Kennedy's advisers were confused and divided on a basic question: What is a legitimate U.S. intervention abroad? Unfortunately, intervention meant many things to many Americans. For example, to George Ball it meant that the United States should have covertly intervened in France before World War II in order to help the French anti-Nazi media alert Frenchmen to the danger they faced; to George Kennan, it meant that the United States ought to intervene covertly in the Western European elections of 1948 to check the spread of Leninism. These opinions did not provide definitions, but most Americans agreed on one point: in a just cause, foreign interventions were permissible if they were legal. And to be legal an intervention had to be invited, or requested, by a foreign government. Internationalists knew that invitations to intervene often came from nondemocratic oligarchs, but nevertheless they were willing to serve their country by working with them.

Internationalists would simply hold their noses over certain offenses, but they could be outraged when these offenses became massive affronts to basic human rights. They could become outraged enough to intervene without an invitation—that is, by extralegal means. Initially uneasy about this, the internationalists discovered an explanation, or a corollary, for their use of means that were unlawful for themselves and their fellow citizens. Raised to believe in rule by law and not by men, their lawgivers had sent them into a world that held the reverse to be true. That was the world in which they had to operate, that outside world where chaos prevailed. To operate there often meant assisting rulers who did things that by any code would be considered illegal and immoral. Yet to walk away seemed cowardly, leaving the most helpless to a cruel fate. Therefore most internationalists persevered, allaying their qualms with the belief that they could change the forces that ruled abroad into a rule by law. To do this they had either to convince foreign oligarchs to change, or to force the changes. Both of these they were willing to do, but the latter only after the former had failed. The light at the end of the internationalist tunnel remained their version of a state reordered by Lockean intervention. And, though some were inclined to act faster than others, all were prepared to force the arrival of that light if necessary.

This might have been mere rationalization for some internationalists, but not for the majority. Most internationalists honestly believed they could find a justification for their most difficult actions in the Niebuhrian injunction to select between undesirable options—which often was their only option. Refusing to remain uninvolved, they took the consequences of choosing a lesser evil. But Niebuhr had set conditions for making that choice. For example, if a coup were to be selected, it should have a good chance of bringing to power a more effective ruler or government. And the net result should be a good chance of bringing a better life to those who were ruled. Here the internationalists had Machiavelli, in addition to Niebuhr, as a guide. Machiavelli denies that all worthy ends justify morally dubious means, but he suggests that some do. Like Niebuhr, he insists that the justification for morally dubious means depends on the necessity of the case. By this caveat both Niebuhr and Machiavelli meant that, in a given situation, there might be no morally acceptable means to bring about the constructive end being sought. Under these conditions, and having exhausted all other options, certain Americans chose the coup as the means of last resort.

Believing that these special conditions obtained in Vietnam, the Whigs to some extent exchanged Niebuhrian positions with the Tories. On the question of limiting the geographical extent of the war, the Tories remained maximalists and the Whigs minimalists. But on the subject of the coup against Diem, Whigs believed that there was much to be gained and comparatively little to be lost, whereas the Tories believed the reverse. But even Whigs understood that any coup required a candidate for the succession, a candidate with a good chance to survive.

Kennedy, we now know, did not have such a candidate. Nor did the South Vietnamese Army have an officer corps that could function as an oligarchy. In addition, Kennedy had domestic political problems. Elected by the narrowest of margins, and aware of the limits of his mandate, he never believed he could innovate in Vietnam. Kennedy did not think, for example, that he could make a major change in the direction of U.S. policy, such as pursuing a neutralist solution with the help of an ever-willing France.[58] Yet in spite of the national limits on his ability to maneuver, in international politics he had more than enough power to forcefully urge the ally in Vietnam to moderate his methods. But Kennedy equivocated in using this power and instead fell into a late-forming Whig trap—the desperate option of supporting an uncontrolled coup.

Kennedy and his advisers had no inhibitions about intervening in the internal affairs of a client state. But among American internationalists it was the unwritten rule that the intervener must select, from a hierarchy of extralegal methods, the least offensive method for advancing a just cause. If building a free and independent South Vietnam was a just cause, then internationalists hoped to attain it by the best means if possible, but by the least odious means if necessary. Existing in a national environment of Lockean order, their dissonance level rose a bit when they viewed the international scene, which they saw as mainly Hobbesian disorder. The dissonance rose significantly when internationalists tried to bring order out of chaos by extralegal means, and it rose even higher when they perceived that their Leninist competition was using all means fair and foul to promote an order that went counter to the American view of human destiny.[59] And so, although they did assume that their leaders would resort to extralegal means in cases of apparent necessity, they also expected them to choose the least offending methods—and to do so with consistency. To Lockean internationalists it might be a brutal and bloody international order; nevertheless, there existed no excuse for unmitigated villainy in battling it.

But if an internationalist decided to resort to limited villainy in unusual times for the sake of a worthy ultimate outcome, that leader must stick to the chosen villainous plot; for to change one's Henry VIII tactics for Arthurian ones in the midst of a critical situation could mean disaster. In the interest of the long-range good, limited villains needed to be consistent in their villainy.

As an actor in the international arena, Kennedy had some notably consistent predecessors. He noted that it was Churchill who saw the flaws in democracy, the best worst form of government yet tried, and that it was Roosevelt who succeeded in doing what Senator George Norris had attempted, with a filibuster against the Armed Ship bill, to keep him from doing.[60] Internationalists believed that these two Tory heroes had proved their consistency in two challenges.

Churchill, in order to conceal his success in breaking a Nazi code, allowed German bombers to penetrate to the cathedral city of Coventry and bomb its citizens. He knew that civilians were the target, but refused to warn them because it might signal to the Germans that he was "reading their mail." He maintained a consistent approach to his unusual times. Churchill also had learned how to be consistent from people like Kennedy's own father, who, as the American Ambassador in London, had made political life consistently miserable for both Churchill and Roosevelt by suggesting that the United States stay out of the European war that he, Kennedy, predicted Britain would lose.[61] And if Churchill could be firm, so could his Atlantic friend, Roosevelt. This friend—the man Churchill wrote to under the code name "a former naval person"— began in 1940 to allow British intelligence agents to establish a counter-espionage network based in New York City, something he knew to be in violation of U.S. laws. Although Roosevelt saw the grievous harm in breaking the law, he never backed away from his decision, since doing so would have imperiled the British and risked losing a critical advantage over the Nazis.[62] Here and in other situations, this Dutch-American aristocrat from the Hudson River Valley played his role consistently.

Since internationalists believed that Vietnam in the 1960's raised some of the same difficult questions faced by American leaders in the early 1940's, they believed that a consistent application of limited extralegal methods might be required on certain occasions. It is obvious that President Kennedy thought the times were comparable; that is the general theme of his book *Why England Slept*. And like Churchill and Roosevelt before him—not to mention his two immediate predecessors, Truman and Eisenhower—JFK possessed a Lockean mechanism for escaping dissonance as well as the Niebuhrian mechanism. It was to be found in one of Locke's explanations, called the prerogative of the sovereign—a doctrine for unusual methods in unusual times. Basically, it meant that the sovereign could use extralegal means if necessary during a time of crisis, if doing so served the best interest of the subjects. Applying this doctrine to a foreign intervention required a broad reading of Locke, but that presented no problem for internationalists.

Before a leader exercises the prerogative of a sovereign he should understand the nature of the problem his actions aim to solve. In 1963 Kennedy faced a problem of political chaos in a client state, a chaos that had two causes. The proximate cause was the Ngo family and the secondary cause was the politics of urban Buddhists. Kennedy misjudged both. Reflecting on Kennedy's misreading of the powerful pull of the traditional family unit on the Ngo brothers, it becomes difficult to understand how he failed to note certain similarities to his own ambitious political family, unflattering though this comparison might have been.[63]

The Family in Politics

Both the Kennedy and the Ngo families had one brother acting as statesman and one as enforcer. If the Ngos had gone to Harvard and bathed and sailed at Hyannisport before going into American politics, and if the Kennedys had attended colonial lycées and bathed and sailed at a town renamed Cape St. Jacques by the French colonizers, rather than the reverse, perhaps the political results would have remained somewhat similar. Even as it was, RFK's efforts to jail James Hoffa by any means within his grasp, or the Attorney General's request to wiretap phones in order to jail organized crime lords—the American version of Saigon's Binh Xuyen gangsters that the Ngo family had destroyed—were measures the younger Ngo brother could appreciate more readily than could some Lockeans. The important difference between the two police officials, and more generally between the two families, was not in any personal circumstances but in their societal contexts.

The Kennedy family lived in a society that was both ordered and modern, whereas the Ngos lived in a society that was neither: Vietnam was a traditional society in chaotic transition. The Kennedy brothers could relax and play touch football while an admiring America watched. But in Vietnam a football could contain plastic explosives, and the Ngo brothers knew that it was best never to be in the same place at the same time, lest one bomb eliminate the two pillars of the House of Ngo. Besides, touch football requires established rules that define right and wrong conduct in the game. The Vietnam in which the Ngo brothers lived was in the process of replacing old rules with new ones. It was like the fictional African country described by V. S. Naipaul in *A Bend in the River*, where the people had reverted to tribalism after the departure of the colonial government. One of Naipaul's characters, trying to explain the situation to an outsider, says it is not that there is no right and wrong in the country; there is only no right. Half the rules were missing.[64]

In Vietnam, Ngo Dinh Diem needed a persistent friend to force him to find the missing half of the rules that concerned his public duty. Basically, to succeed in this required mastering his family. By the 1960 elections, John Kennedy had learned how to master his own family. He let Robert Kennedy fight against the choice of Lyndon Johnson as candidate for Vice President, and take a hard loss—a family defeat.[65] John Kennedy could do this because he, the head of both a prominent family and a political party, had chosen the larger group as the more important politically. In America, it is usually possible to have both family duties and public duties, and enjoy the rewards of both. That is why, more often than not, American political life lends itself to melodrama, while other states—including Vietnam—more often face tragedy. Two examples starkly illustrate the options the Ngo family faced. Taken from Greek literature and French history, respectively, they show ruling families letting family concerns become entangled with the concerns of state-formation—exactly the problem faced by Ngo Dinh Diem.

Among the classic Greeks one royal family that was in transition from one level of rulership to another, caught the imagination of great dramatists—Aeschylus, Sophocles, and Euripides. In ancient Greece the House of Atreus ruled over the city of Mycenae. The royal couple had mostly daughters—Chrysothemis, Iphigenia, and Electra—and but one son, Orestes. The father, and king to his people, was Agamemnon; his wife was Clytemnestra. Agamemnon had a brother and fellow king, Menelaus, who lost his wife, Helen, sister of Clytemnestra, to a Trojan prince. For brotherly love, family pride, exciting adventure, rich plunder, and a host of less subtle reasons, brother supported brother, fellow Greek kings supported their own, and all went to war.

A fatal choice appeared when the two Greek brothers and their allies assembled. Mysteriously, unfavorable winds held their warships to the Greek coast. In order to obtain favor with the gods who controlled the winds, the priests demanded a royal sacrifice—the life of Agamemnon's youngest daughter, Iphigenia. Agamemnon, having earlier accepted the public duty of leading the Greeks to Troy, now found his stars crossed. His private duty as father demanded that he protect his own flesh and blood, but his public duty required that he sacrifice her. He had to choose, and fate forced on him his own destruction. But he chose public duty over private, leadership of his people over leadership of his family. He could not satisfy both. Neither could Ngo Dinh Diem, who, following his own Asian tradition, possessed the Hindu classic the *Mahabharata*, an epic struggle of two families, the Pandavas and the Kauravas, whose feuds took precedence over the problems of the state and thus destroyed that state.[66]

Approximately 2,000 years later, members of another ruling family, one belonging more to history than to dramatic literature, mingled their own internal arguments with the greater dissent among their people. In the seventeenth century, Louis XIII, head of the French ruling house of Bourbon, was forced to choose between public duty and family duty. His adviser Cardinal Richelieu, "the king's secular inquisitor," urged him to choose a policy for the good of the state; at the same time, the Queen Mother was urging a policy beneficial to the House of Bourbon. One scholar has written that the day Louis XIII said "I am more obligated to the state" may be called "the birthday of the modern state." Others have agreed that "the claim of the state and of the nation have to be assisted by the monarch against the more parochial claims of family, class and clan."[67]

Ngo Dinh Diem was by no means the only twentieth-century leader whose problems of state-formation resembled those of France. In the formation of Zaire, Mobutu Sese Seko faced many of the same disputes. Mobutu had to master family, clan, and past tribal connections in order to follow his new vision of a great chief ruling a great state—his fatherland ruled by a native Big Man.[68] And American postwar statesmen had to learn to work with Mobutu as well as Diem. It was not only scholars who saw the parallel between the political problems of the Vietnamese House of Ngo in the 1960's and the French House of Bourbon in the seventeenth century. In a 1963 *Saturday Evening Post* article entitled "Edge of Chaos," an American journalist made exactly that comparison.[69]

Kennedy's failure to analyze Diem's problems led to an American policy that vacillated between force and statecraft. If Kennedy had begun in 1961 with a policy of statecraft—teaching Ngo Dinh Diem to loosen family ties while incorporating larger units of Vietnamese society into the process of both power and responsibility—he might have helped Diem avoid the problems of 1963. He might have started by using the remnants of the Viet Minh party—now renamed the Dai Viets—which had rejected the Leninist reordering of the North. But Diem did not try to maneuver them into his orbit, and thus gained nothing except potential enemies and a slow strangulation by the family tether.

Failing to take the high road of statecraft consistently in 1961, Kennedy failed also to take the low road of force consistently after the crisis broke in 1963. To contain the crisis while maintaining Diem in power, Nhu had to go; and orderly departure was much to be preferred over chaotic flight. If he wanted this result, Kennedy should not have allowed Lodge to give the coup-plotters a green light; instead, Lodge should have flashed a red light on Ngo Dinh Diem until he got rid of his brother. Kennedy did not have to demand, as the priests did of Agamemnon, a bloody sacrifice of kin; but he did need, at a minimum, to ensure that Diem emulated Louis XIII's decision to put the state first, by seeing to it that Nhu departed.[70]

Although Ngo Dinh Diem could have refused to do so, he might have given in if nudged the right way. After all, he had almost exiled Madame Nhu at the suggestion of Ambassador J. Lawton Collins. He had also been warned that his brother might try to overthrow him and send him into exile. Diem responded by doubling his watch on Nhu, thereby further straining family trust.[71] Kennedy possessed the power to move Diem, but failed to apply it in the consistent manner that might have brought about Nhu's departure.

Many Americans did not know how easily their government could arrange such departures or returns, but Kennedy knew. The CIA, having mastered the travel business, could give first-class treatment to ex-dictators, junta chiefs, double agents, and fallen allies. Unnumbered Swiss bank accounts, new personas scripted with Bond-like efficiency, safe houses in which to store defectors while CIA specialists literally grafted new identities onto old ones—all this and more the magicians at

CIA headquarters in Langley, Virginia, could provide. However, for Ngo Dinh Nhu, a less drastic option was available.[72]

He could have been posted abroad, say, as Ambassador to Franco's Spain. Kennedy himself had sent troublesome people to foreign posts. For example, after clashing with both Kennedy and McNamara, Admiral Robert Anderson, the Chief of Naval Operations, was made U.S. Ambassador to Salazar's Portugal. Unfortunately, exile as a means of statecraft was not something Diem used. (Those who ruled Saigon after Diem's murder did learn to use it. For example, in February 1965 Generals Ky and Thieu ousted General Khan, sending him into exile as an Ambassador-at-Large. In July 1966 Ky and Thieu obliged General Chanh Thi to pay for assisting the Hué Buddhists in their last rebellion not with his life but with a generous exile in the United States.) But Kennedy failed to try to teach Diem the niceties of such devices.[73]

If the Ngo brothers had objected that Nhu's exit under pressure would weaken the government, a staged kidnapping, well within CIA abilities, was not impossible. Since their contact man, Conein, had found it possible to meet surreptitiously with coup-plotters for three months, obviously he could have arranged to meet Ngo Dinh Nhu once. With American aircraft departing from Saigon daily, Nhu could have been gone before he was missed, like the Dai Viet chief, Truong Tu Anh, who simply vanished one night.[74] The uproar that would have followed, like all else in Saigon politics, soon would have subsided. In those days, personages appeared and disappeared, in Saigon as in Hanoi, usually for the same reasons.

Kennedy operatives might have taught Ngo Dinh Diem how to go on ruling without other members of his family. In time, two more Ngo brothers, both sources of disturbance to public life in South Vietnam, might have been eased out. One of them, the Bishop of Hué, could have been called to Rome—for religious reasons, it would seem—by Kennedy's request to the Vatican. To accomplish this Kennedy might have had to use Boston's Cardinal Cushing to outmaneuver the powerful Cardinal Spellman, vicar of the New York archdiocese and friend to the Saigon Bourbons.[75] And Ngo Dinh Can could have been made to give up the satrapy of Annam for some permanent ambassadorship of Diem's choosing. The last of the brothers, Ngo Dinh Luyen, was a French-educated engineer who had lived in France before and had never been a controversial political figure. Diem's brothers were not his only problem, but until he removed this immediate cause of chaos the others could not be solved.

In all of this Kennedy would have had to be disingenuous; he might have found it necessary to imply to the brothers that Nhu could return once the Buddhist affair had been forgotten. In any case, Kennedy would have had to work consistently to help the elder Ngo find support in institutions other than his own family.

Religion and Politics

Had the Ngo family been scattered around the globe by such means, the Buddhist crisis probably would have diminished. It almost certainly would have done so if the elder Ngo had combined brotherly departures with a political settlement that was significant for moderate Buddhists. At that time, the most desirable method for diffusing the crisis was to incorporate moderate Buddhist leaders within larger institutions. Radical Buddhist leaders might not have accepted such a compromise; if not, they probably would have been crushed as they were in 1965, when Johnson backed Prime Minister Nguyen Cao Ky against radical Buddhists, who then collapsed even though they had used more fiery suicides against Nguyen Cao Ky than against Ngo Dinh Diem in 1963.[76]

The first Buddhist crisis of 1963 was the secondary cause of the chaos in Vietnam. As with the primary cause, the Ngo family, Kennedy also misjudged this. It was not that he was trapped by Whig advisers into believing that the Buddhist crisis amounted to a simple case of religious persecution; even Hilsman, who usually takes the dimmest possible view of the Ngo regime, argues that the crisis came out of a dispute over power, not over theological issues.[77] In other words, urban Buddhist leaders objected to their underrepresentation among the political factions of Saigon and in smaller centers such as Hué. Southern politics were conducted by "factions without parties" and "factions within parties," with the Buddhists underrepresented in both.[78]

As an urban political problem, the Buddhist crisis affected less than 20 percent of southerners. In Vietnam, as elsewhere, Buddhism was not an organized religion; it had no hierarchy, in Western terms, and took a casual approach to religious training.[79] But Buddhism was native in a way that French Catholicism was not. Hilsman suggests that within a South Vietnamese population of approximately 14 million, about a million and a half were Roman Catholic, about 2 million were members of one or another of the sects (such as Hoa Hao), and approximately 4 million were active, practicing Buddhists. The remainder—the vast majority of Vietnamese—were nominal Buddhists. Hilsman explains the position of these nonactive, nonpracticing Buddhists by reference to the father of Madame Nhu, Vietnamese Ambassador Tran Van Chuong, who explained "that for purposes of ceremonies of birth, marriage, and death,

he would call himself a Buddhist, but for all other purposes that Westerners associate with religion—ethics and spiritual meaning—he would call
himself Confucian."[80]

Since the Buddhist turmoil apparently never reached the countryside,
it can be seen as an urban phenomenon that affected less than 20 percent
of the population. By being localized it could be handled not by soldiers
but by statesmen—not by threats but by bargains. No one seriously believed that this disorganized, ancient religion was a communist front. In
fact, evidence suggests that Whig internationalists knew that the Viet
Cong was the one group that had not even rallied to the side of the Buddhists, let alone infiltrated it to any degree.[81] If Ngo Dinh Nhu had gone,
and had been followed later by other family members, those who had
rallied to the cause of the radical minority within Vietnam's Buddhist majority doubless would have lost their enthusiasm—Ngo Dinh Nhu having
been their target and his departure their success. Then a bargain to share
power could have been made with moderate Buddhist leaders.

These complexities should not have been overlooked by Kennedy, as
they apparently were in a September 10 meeting of the NSC at which he
received evidence about the Buddhist situation. Earlier McNamara had
suggested dispatching General Victor Krulak (on what Hilsman characterized as a "McNamara Special") to visit several Vietnamese locations
between September 6 and 10—Hilsman had suggested that a State Department official, Joseph A. Mendenhall, accompany Krulak; this was not
easy to arrange, since McNamara wanted Krulak to depart within 90
minutes. After a short delay in the departure time, both Americans raced
through Asia at Olympic speed. On their return their bosses brought
Krulak and Mendenhall before another session of the NSC. Krulak,
having talked with eighty-seven American military advisers in the field,
summarized his findings by stating that the political situation continued
to affect the war, but not greatly. Mendenhall spoke next. He had visited
Saigon, Hué, and Danang, as well as several provincial towns where he
had talked chiefly to Vietnamese he had known before. He summarized
his findings by stating that civil government barely functioned, so greatly
was it affected by the political crisis. Kennedy simply looked at both jet-
age messengers and asked quizzically if they had both visited the same
country.[82]

Protagonists immediately took sides: Nolting noted Mendenhall's
known anti-Ngo family bias, and John Mecklin, chief of USIA activities in
Saigon, stated that in order to save the situation American ground troops
should be committed in force. The real problem, however, was Kennedy,
who failed to recognize that both messengers were reporting the truth.
He could not comprehend that two conditions existed at the same time:

the war, while not going well, was proceeding more or less as it had before the crisis; and the cities, always centers of unrest, were simply more unrestful than before. Therefore the real problem that Kennedy and Ngo Dinh Diem faced amounted to an unusual level of urban unrest; solving the problem meant bringing the cities back to their normal state of unrest. That alone would not win the war or even offer a compromise, but without it there existed no hope for any solution acceptable to Ngo Dinh Diem or Kennedy.

To be sure, the Buddhist crisis would not have been easy to solve. It was not the suicides by fire, tragic as they were, that required action. What had to be done was to get rid of Nhu and then to design a bargain that would give certain Buddhists a share of power. But which ones? Among Vietnamese Buddhists, disunity was the norm. There were at least fourteen different subdivisions within their own leadership. A few possessed political talent. One of these, the monk Tri Quang, had even persuaded Lodge that he would be a good candidate for membership in any government that followed Ngo Dinh Diem. Perhaps Lodge was ready to be persuaded. Hilsman had previously released a cable to Lodge; it noted that because North Vietnam "has two monks in national assembly," it "might be very effective gesture for GVN (Saigon) to permit several monks [to] run and win seats in August National Assembly elections."[83]

Tri Quang may have appealed to Lodge, but he did not appeal to the other monks. When the heads of eleven of the Buddhist subdivisions met in the early spring of 1964, agreeing to stop bickering, they chose Tam Chau to be their leader in secular affairs, because they worried that Tri Quang was too much of a rebel. First, in May 1963, on the night of the disturbances, he had toured Hué in a sound truck stirring up the people against Ngo Dinh Diem. In August of that year, having moved to Saigon, Tri Quang chose to flee to the U.S. embassy following Ngo Dinh Nhu's raids on the Xa Loi temple. In May 1966, during the final Buddhist crisis, Stanley Karnow interviewed Tri Quang in his political headquarters in the Dieude temple, an ornate structure located near Hué's Perfume River. Here the saffron-robed monk, Vietnam's version of Savonarola, issued political directions to his acolytes. This struck Karnow as inconsistent with his view of what monks did; he compared it to a situation in which Cardinal Spellman might have tried to manage a New York mayoralty campaign from an alcove in St. Patrick's Cathedral. After Hanoi won the war in 1975, the Leninists, less hospitable to monkish bravado, banished Tri Quang to a monastery. As late as 1984 it was reported that "severe repression of the Buddhist opposition has led to many immolations."[84]

Leninists could banish monks to monasteries; mandarins would have done likewise, except for their Lockean patrons. Reform, always more difficult than revolution, required compromise. If one could strike a bargain with the Hoa Hao and Cao Dai, one could also deal with Buddhists, difficult though it might be. With Ngo Dinh Nhu banished, such a bargain might beguile moderate Buddhists into quiet suspicion. Over time, if Ngo Dinh Diem kept his word, Buddhism might become another bulwark against the Leninists from the North. As one scholar noted in 1968, "If Buddhist monks broaden their allegiances from their local temple and monastery to a national Buddhist movement—each of these developments is a broadening of loyalty and in that sense presumably a contribution to political modernization." [85]

Although Kennedy could not comprehend it, monks did play a political role throughout southern Asia. In Sri Lanka in 1956, for example, monks traveled from village to village pronouncing a dire warning: to vote for the United National Party (UNP)—the Westernized, urban, Roman Catholic elite that dominated the minority government—meant to vote against the Buddha. The government fell. By 1965, however, the UNP had learned to bargain with the non-Westernized majority and again it formed a government. In another Buddhist-dominated state, Burma, monks in 1960 rallied to U Nu "and became his most effective propagandists in the towns and villages of Burma." [86] U Nu won.

Instead of perceiving the politics behind the screen of burning incense and tinkling bells, Kennedy's advisers, led by him, attempted to fathom the mysteries of the religion itself. In no case is this more evident than with Chester Cooper. As a member of the OSS in World War II, he had served in the China-Burma-India theater; in 1954 he had been an American delegate to both the Geneva Conference on Indochina and the Manila Conference that established SEATO. In 1961 and 1962 he was a delegate to the Geneva Conference on Laos; in 1963 he was in Saigon; and in 1964 he was invited to the White House by Bundy to serve as the NSC Assistant for Asian Affairs.

Cooper's honesty about his own failings must have been refreshing to his colleagues, as refreshing as it has been to readers of his book *The Lost Crusade*. Yet in his eagerness to understand Buddhism, he represents the well-meaning American misled by an alien culture—even when, as in the Vietnamese situation, Buddhist philosophy was not the root problem. He admits that "the air in my office and my home was heady with discussions of Hinayana or Theravada Buddhism (which stressed individual salvation) and Mahayana Buddhism (which emphasized the need to help others as well as oneself to achieve Nirvana)." What did he learn from such discourse? "In the course of my pursuit of the elusive key to understanding the bonzes, I was told of a study done by two Thai psychologists for the National Institute of Mental Health" in which "the burden of the study was that Buddhist monks had an alarmingly high incidence of schizophrenia as a consequence of their efforts to bridge the gap between the real world and the world of isolation and meditation."[87]

To try to understand only why some monks were committing suicide was to avoid the real problem. After all, the Buddhist leadership, represented by monks such as Tri Quang, did not commit suicide; what was their position? Furthermore, self-immolation was hardly as new as many in Kennedy's government thought. It occurred among Chinese Buddhists from the fifth to the tenth centuries, and reappeared in Thailand at Wat Arun in 1790 and in 1817. One honored the Buddha by burning a candle. A story in the Mahayana scriptures, the *Saddharmapundarika Sutra*, illustrated how this simple idea could be magnified: a Bodhisattva, after eating incense and drinking oil for twelve years, bathed in oil and set himself on fire as an offering to the Buddha.[88]

Instead of studying religious fables that honored the Buddhist past, Cooper and Kennedy should have looked for the political meaning of Tri Quang's night of driving and broadcasting from a sound truck in Hué. But fables were in fashion as clues to "culture." Cooper even admits to a panicked search for an interpreter of fables: "Finally the State Department dispatched to Saigon the only Buddhist Foreign Service Officer on active service [he was then serving in Hong Kong] to see if he could penetrate the fog." Cooper adds that Lodge also "prided himself on another asset—his uncle was a Buddhist."[89] Lodge should have recalled his father, that indestructible unilateralist Lodge Senior, rather than any Buddhist uncle. At least his father knew politics.

Kennedy's job as President was to know politics, both national and international. In the Vietnam crisis he failed the political test. Robert Kennedy purportedly said that "President Kennedy's favorite quotation from Dante was that the hottest corner of hell was reserved for those who preserved their neutrality in times of moral crisis."[90] During his involvement in the Ngo coup, although the President had not preserved his own neutrality, he did learn that those who stoked the furnace of international politics distributed the heat equally between neutrals and activists. Failing to know politics, Kennedy failed to know statesmanship, at least in regard to Vietnam. He failed to help build institutions there that held the promise of permanence. As one scholar has suggested, "What distinguishes statesman from politician, then, is not necessarily higher intelligence or loftier motives but an awareness of [the need for] building institutions according to political designs."[91]

Others noted the importance of that challenge to assist new states in building their institutions. Speaking of economic assistance, Harlan Cleveland insisted that "the most useful measuring rods in development are those which measure the building of institutions, rather than those which measure only production, trade, or national income." He added, "We know that technicians who leave institutions behind are good technicians, and [that] technicians who just leave techniques are bad technicians—even if everybody loves them and they are fairly dripping with cultural empathy."[92] Chester Bowles, twice Ambassador to India (under Truman and Kennedy) and former Governor of Connecticut, concurred. He insisted that "true development" was not only economic and social but "political as well . . . political in terms of domestic institutions which create an informed and constructively motivated citizenry."[93] Kennedy failed to meet the conditions of either Cleveland or Bowles.

To summarize our discussion of political intervention by the United States in South Vietnamese politics, we may say the following. By 1963 certain internationalists tired of what they considered Tory procrastination in forcing a change in the authoritarian practices of the Saigonese leader of the House of Ngo. In the summer of 1963, a clash between Vietnamese Buddhists and Roman Catholics forced American leaders to reconsider the goals of their intervention in Vietnam. Frustration mounted. President Kennedy did little to forcefully persuade his ally, Ngo Dinh Diem, to rely less on his family as a government institution by building a political party to serve in public roles. The results were tragic. In 1905, another New England Brahmin, Henry Adams, had said that "America has always taken tragedy lightly," and that "Americans ignore tragic motives that would have overshadowed the Middle Ages."[94] In a last-minute plan to assist in the coup against Diem in 1963, the Whigs outmaneuvered the Tories. But the coup they sponsored became a tragedy of uncontrolled dimensions.

CHAPTER SIX

The Politics
Behind Saigonese Coups

THE PREVIOUS CHAPTER dealt generally with the politics behind the military coup aimed at the family of Ngo Dinh Diem; the general
theme of this chapter is that of the politics behind the military escalation
aimed at Ho Chi Minh's forces. The first was a Kennedy problem, the second belonged to Lyndon Johnson; the solutions each President chose exemplify American political interventions abroad in the 1960's. Looking
back at 1963, Roger Hilsman has written, "The best that could be hoped
for if the Diem regime was removed would be that, like Egypt, Vietnam
would find her Nasser the second time around—or the third—or the
fourth."[1] What a melancholy conclusion: the best this Whig could hope
for, after years of struggle, was that perhaps a Vietnamese Nasser would
take control.

Tory internationalists quickly condemned the coup against Diem, a
coup they perceived as folly of the highest order. They made three main
arguments: (1) the American national security system was not working;
(2) there was now no functioning government in Saigon, simply a vacuum in leadership that Washington had created; and (3) the Whigs were
willing to seek political liberty only, and only for the few—the urban
elites—at the expense of the many, whereas Tories saw peasant demands
for economic reform as the main problem of the war.

The Tories' first argument has been disputed.[2] But in Vietnam, at
least, it is clear that in key respects the American national security system
did *not* work. The results of the coup against Diem are proof of that. Of
more concern to us here, the coup did not have the backing of the Central
Intelligence Agency: on the record, the Director, John McCone, the Far
Eastern area chief, William Colby, and the recent Saigon station chief,
John Richardson, all strongly opposed it.[3] McCone later explained that
"after analyzing all of the potential leaders of Vietnam, I could see no one
on the horizon [of whom we] could say that if the focal authority was

transferred from Diem to this man, then conditions would immediately improve." Also he warned President Kennedy personally "that removal of Diem would result in not one coup, but several coups—political turmoil that might extend over several years." Kennedy had worried about this prospect from the time he took office, and in 1961 had asked both Rusk and McNamara to look back to the 1940's to see "what we did in Greece." Kennedy wanted to know "how much money and how many men" had been used there to secure a pro-Western, non-Leninist government. While he was considering a Tory economic approach of the sort applied to Greece, the President received a nine-page cable from John Kenneth Galbraith, proposing a political approach of the sort applied to Korea. Galbraith, writing from New Delhi, argued that "Korea represents the only model that holds out any promise." He said that although Diem "was a significant figure in his day . . . he has run his course"; that he could not "be rehabilitated"; and that the only solution must be to drop Diem. It should be added that Galbraith, a political economist, was by no means a political idealist of the Whig variety. In the same month that he sent Kennedy the cable recommending that Diem be dropped, Galbraith sent JFK a memorandum that concluded: "Intrigue, nepotism, and even corruption might be accepted, for a time, if combined with efficiency and visible progress. When they accompany paralysis and steady deterioration, they become intolerable."[4]

Neither Galbraith nor McCone could suggest a replacement for Diem. McCone worried that, with Ngo Dinh Diem gone, no viable candidate existed in the Lockean-supported camp; and McCone's forebodings, incidentally, were expressed only as private advice. But, if the U.S. national security system were to work, key internationalists at CIA, DOD, Treasury, and State should have made their recommendations through the clearinghouse of the NSC, so that the President could have all suggestions reviewed. His policy choice could then be implemented by the appropriate government agency; and the appropriate agency for handling a coup was the CIA.

But this coup fell to others, others who were novices. Lodge exemplified the amateur spy. William Colby has written that "the American decisions . . . were made by the White House, not by the CIA." He says that his instructions to the CIA in Saigon were to "work totally under the direction of Lodge," and that these instructions "were followed to the letter, as both Lodge and the White House later confirmed." Lodge made this clear when he cabled McGeorge Bundy that "CAS [CIA-Saigon] has been punctilious in carrying out my instruction," and that "I have personally approved each meeting between General Don and [CIA agent] Conein, who has carried out my orders in each instance explicitly." One key figure who would not cooperate was General Harkins. Lodge had deliberately kept him ignorant of the coup plans, and when Harkins heard of them in late October he exploded in an "Eyes Only" message to General Taylor. He told Taylor that when Lodge had asked him to concur in the coup by adding his name to a joint message back to Washington, he had refused. When the NSC staff realized that Harkins was both uninformed and unenthusiastic, they panicked. Moreover, Lodge had scheduled a visit back to the United States; this raised the chilling possibility that the coup might take place while Lodge was away, leaving an unknowledgeable and unwilling Harkins as the senior U.S. representative in Saigon. Acting for the President, McGeorge Bundy therefore ordered Lodge to brief Harkins immediately on all coup plans.[5]

If the system had been working, the internationalist President would have ordered CIA professionals to conduct the coup. Instead, amateurs conducted it, and JFK received an amateur's reward. Lodge, Harriman, Hilsman, and Kennedy simply took a chance that their sally into espionage would succeed in bringing a more stable government to power in Saigon. It did not; it failed with disastrous results. Critics admit that this coup "marked a middle watershed in U.S. policy." For the system to work, they maintain, leaders would have had to pursue the core goal—containment of the communists in the North—with consistency. An amateur coup could hardly qualify, for it raised too many questions. Who would be the new leader of South Vietnam? What were the new leader's goals? Did these goals match the American ones? None of the Americans involved knew the answers. And as conditions in Saigon deteriorated, still no one knew.[6]

Lodge's own words negate his early optimism. He states that "in 1964, when I was still on duty in Saigon, the team of General Don and General Minh which had overthrown Diem had themselves been overthrown by General Khanh in a coup which seemed to take everyone by surprise—including the Americans." These Americans included Lodge, the Ambassador who had helped install these Vietnamese generals as political leaders, and the patron whose tolerance was necessary in order for them to remain in power. They were Lodge's clients, they lived in close proximity in a smallish city, and yet they lasted in their new jobs less than four months before Khanh overthrew them. Khanh became the next U.S. client, but the United States could not sustain him, either; he was overthrown in February 1965. Lodge writes that when he "returned for a second tour in the summer of 1965, I found the Saigon government in a state of grave instability and turmoil. . . ; the changes of prime ministers could only be described as kaleidoscopic." Interestingly, General Nguyen Cao Ky, a key player in these Vietnamese-American games of revolving leadership chairs, entitles one chapter in his memoirs "1964: The Year of the Seven Coups."[7] Yet the fact that Lodge and other Whig internationalists were collaborators in these disasters never got through to Lodge.

When Lodge resigned as Ambassador in 1964, the Tories got their chance to try to control the political chaos in Saigon. It was clear that the United States now had no dependable clients in Saigon; but some effort to make the system work was essential. In place of Ambassador Lodge, the Whig, President Johnson, the Tory, installed his own kind of Ambassador, General Maxwell Taylor. Taylor was the ideal Camelot general— intelligent, articulate, and handsome; he wrote books, played tennis, and had survived national service at Pentagon and White House levels.[8] His Tory credentials passed inspection. Yet Taylor could not place Pandora back in the Saigon government box that the Whigs had helped open. His cables brim with frustration and fury over this issue. His anger boiled over in one famous dressing-down that he administered to the key Vietnamese generals.[9] Still, the coups continued.

A Tory internationalist like Kennedy, Lyndon Johnson could hardly contain his own fury. From the start he had opposed the coup against Ngo Dinh Diem. When he had met the mandarin during a tour of Asia in 1961, the then Vice President had publicly hailed Diem as the Winston Churchill of Southeast Asia—the highest compliment a Tory could pay. Privately, LBJ told Kennedy that he found Ngo Dinh Diem a man of "admirable qualities" but remote from his people and "surrounded by persons less honorable than he."[10] Beyond the hearing of his Harvard-educated chief, Johnson used the saltier slang of west Texas. When journalist Stanley Karnow asked the Vice President if he truly believed that the elder Ngo brother was the Winston Churchill of Southeast Asia, Johnson roared, "Shit, man, he's the only boy we got out there."[11]

CIA director John McCone seconded his new chief's logic: "Diem may be a sonofabitch, but he's our sonofabitch."[12] What Johnson and his Tories wanted was not just another SOB, but *their* SOB; Whigs who objected could get out. Thus Lodge left the embassy, and Hilsman soon took himself off to Columbia University. But even with Hilsman gone and others soon to depart, the Tories failed to reestablish control. One scholar of coup d'états has suggested that "in Saigon the U.S. embassy is generally recognized as a greater source of power than the presidential palace."[13] Then why was a Tory on the order of Maxwell Taylor, U.S. Ambassador in Saigon, unable to wield that power? The answer, largely, is that Whiggism does not vanish with the Whig; somehow it goes on dominating American attempts to think seriously about complex cultures that do not share Lockean assumptions.

An example of this endemic Whiggism—Whiggism of the sort characterized in the third argument of the Tory internationalists—may be found in the State Department planning that went on after the coup. Hilsman and other departing Whigs, under the protective wing of Averell Harriman, insisted "that Vietnam was a political problem of winning the allegiance of the people rather than a military problem." This sounded like the pre-coup Hilsman; he had agreed with State Department analysts who "argued that the idea that government existed for the benefit of the people, that a government could really *care*, was as revolutionary in most of Asia as anything the Communists had to offer."[14] Tories insisted that when Whigs used the phrase "benefit of the people," Whigs meant only the noisy urban minority, the only group Tories thought Whigs cared about when they wrote that "a government could really *care*."

But the Leninists did not offer "caring." Instead, they were feeding, watering, clothing, sheltering, medicating, and educating the peasant majority under a ruthless political system totally opposed to the openness of the Lockeans. The jails, torture chambers, and graves created by Ngo Dinh Nhu gave up their walking wounded and decomposing dead after the Lockean coup; but the jails, torture chambers, and graves created by the forces of Ho Chi Minh remained hidden behind a Leninist veil. What the Whigs refused to recognize was that the only Niebuhrian choices open to them in finding a Vietnamese leader to support were variations of Inquisitors and Leninists.

Taylor tried a Tory choice or two. They failed. By September 1964, Johnson had not found his SOB. In frustration he blurted out to the American people that he, the patron, did not know who the client or clients were: "And we have now had four or five governments [in Saigon] in the last year—I can't tell you who runs the Government here, much less who runs it in Vietnam."[15] It was surely a historical first; South Vietnam became the first ungoverned puppet to pull its own strings. Things could get worse, and they did. Though in similar circumstances anyone else would have been discredited, Henry Cabot Lodge was not; the name alone carried enough cachet to survive several debacles. Once the Tory Taylor failed, Lodge the Whig went back where angels should have feared to tread—went back by Tory invitation. As he had done in 1963 after Kennedy offered him the Saigon post, so in the spring of 1965 Lodge again consulted with the Republican oracle at Gettysburg. Eisenhower once more gave him the green light, saying, "You have unique qualifications."[16]

What those unique qualifications were remains a mystery; perhaps they were his persistence in fighting for freedom. If so, what Lodge failed to learn was that the English who first applied Whig principles never fought to export them. But their ex-colonists did so with a vengeance. Lodge writes that upon his return as Johnson's envoy, he set himself the task of presenting the South Vietnamese the gift of a Western-style constitution. Patrician optimism would not die: "The job of electing delegates to a constitutional convention, drafting a constitution, and then bringing its adoption about might be catalytic."[17] Never losing hope, the Whigs wished away reality, trying to leap to the top of Maslow's need-hierarchy and thereby fulfill most needs in one giant effort. Unfortunately, in 1964, getting a constitution was the lowest-priority need in Vietnam.

Hilsman himself reported that during the very year when Lodge was talking constitutionalism, the Viet Cong assassinated 1,895 South Vietnamese and kidnapped 12,778 others.[18] *That* was catalytic. These assassinations and kidnappings bled off what remained of a southern body politic. In 1962, assassinations and kidnappings had amounted to 11,407; in 1963 they fell to 9,335; but in 1964 they climbed back to 11,349.[19] What medication to apply and whom to send in as doctor remained unsettled problems in the South. For Tories such as Taylor, the medication became a tincture of economic and military measures; for Whigs such as Lodge, the tincture was made up of political and military measures. And both sets of internationalists discovered their doctors in military careerists from Saigon barracks.

Who were they? After the murder of Ngo Dinh Diem the doctoring governments of the South basically were composed of shifting coalitions of military officers. In 1969, toward the end of America's involvement in Vietnam's long war, a final coalition gelled, stable at least by comparison with the kaleidoscopic confusion Lodge had earlier reported. But by then it was too late, for the politics of Washington replaced the politics of Saigon; Washington wanted out of the war. And tardiness was only one reason for the final political debacle. What was the other?

The Rise of Saigon's Bakufu Governments

In part, the final failure of U.S. policy lies in the nature of these doctoring coalitions. To call them juntas would confuse them with old-fashioned Latin American militarists; to call them a manifestation of bureaucratic authoritarianism would confuse them with new-fashioned Latin American militarists. Nor does the classic use of the term "military praetorianism" define these armed Asian coalitions. No officer rose from any of these coalitions to become a caudillo as did Franco in Spain. Coalition members were not professional soldiers in the American military sense; nor were they revolutionary military leaders in the Israeli or Chinese communist military sense.[20] Not to be able to label them implies an inability to understand them.

Labels are useful only if they add precision; the above labels do not.[21] What these Saigon groups resembled most closely was an earlier version of Asian government by military elites. In Japanese history particularly we can discover a label that is perhaps more suitable than any other to the Vietnamese coalitions. These Saigon warriors represented a new *bakufu* (or "tent") government, like those that vanished from Japan in the late nineteenth century. There were, of course, important differences. In Saigon, the bakufu was only one among many Vietnamese institutions. And although it remained powerful so long as it received modern weapons from outsiders, the bakufu in Vietnam did not draw strength from classic national traditions in the manner that it had for the Japanese. A historian of Japanese bakufus calls it "a hybrid state held together by feudal bonds at the top and by bureaucratic means at the bottom."[22] In Saigon there was no feudal system at the top, and no bureaucratic means at the bottom. To succeed, Japanese bakufus had depended on a military caste; to succeed, a Vietnamese bakufu would have to depend on primitive rebels. But a primitive rebel from the countryside would find no place in the Saigon bakufu, not even at the bottom where the dying was done. Only retainers and cronies crowded the tent. Nevertheless, while their Tory patrons took to economics and their Whig patrons to politics, the Vietnamese bakufu took to war.

It is true that Ho Chi Minh, too, possessed an elite organization that by definition did not include the masses, let alone primitive rebels. The northern Leninists did not have a military caste, intent as they were on creating a classless society. But they did have a revolutionary army. Yet it was not this army that did most of the dying in the southern lands in the early years of combat. It would seem that these northern contenders possessed nothing unique in comparison to their southern antagonists; if so, why and how did success crown their efforts? In fact, Ho Chi Minh did possess one unique institution. While American Lockeans were watching the leaders in Saigon fumble with a traditional institution, a semiroyal family, Vietnamese Leninists in Hanoi had organized themselves around a modern institution, the Leninist party, with its iron discipline and tight organization. As an organization it was able to motivate and mobilize the primitive rebels, and for Leninists it was the crucial weapon.[23]

How successful was the organization-as-weapon in Vietnam? Between 1964 and 1968, the RAND Corporation conducted interviews with 2,400 Vietnamese who were familiar with the northern organization. From a test group of 53 Vietnamese who had originally fought and worked against the Saigon government—25 who were cadre and 28 who were soldiers; 26 who were from South Vietnam and 27 who were from North Vietnam; 30 who were POW's and 23 who had defected—one RAND analyst tried to discover why the Viet Cong fought successfully.

He found three reasons: "(1) party organization and ideology, (2) the cadre-leaders, and (3) a primary group of soldiers with strong and homogeneous values."[24] From similar evidence another author argues that the Vietnamese primitive rebels, turned into soldiers, had no strong political beliefs; he stresses that it was the party organization that tapped peasant socialization, awakening it and giving it motivational force.[25] It is obvious that as an organization the Saigon bakufu did not achieve what this Leninist organization accomplished. Nor did the Ngo family.

In fact, had Sir Lewis Namier studied Saigon in the twentieth century along with London in the eighteenth century, he would have noticed a similarity between the politics of the accession of Saigon governments and the politics of the accession of George III.[26] In both situations, factions contended for place in majority coalitions. Under the Ngo family, Saigon lived with a mixture of civilian and military factions vying for favor; after establishment of bakufus, the diversity of contenders gradually tapered off, so that eventually military factions predominated. In contrast, the variety and scope of Hanoi politics virtually disappeared overnight, as one monolithic institution replaced all factions.

If the bakufus in Saigon had no organizations capable of fighting in civil struggles while simultaneously building a nation, the United States did. For the internationalists had constructed a neo-Leninist organization in the CIA. It could effectively alert internationalist leadership to crucial client failings. Though the conventional wisdom has it that these alerts did not take place, in fact they did. Nevertheless, one scholar writes that "two presidents were led into disastrous military adventures based largely on miscalculation by intelligence agencies communicating at the top misleading pictures of the situation in Cuba, the Dominican Republic, and Vietnam."[27] The Presidents referred to must be Kennedy and Johnson, and one of the intelligence agencies, the CIA (named in the same paragraph).

That author's assessment disregards the evidence of the CIA's role in Vietnam. The record shows that in fact, CIA officials repeatedly warned both Presidents of an impending disaster in Vietnam. Their reports went to Kennedy and then Johnson, as well as to that critical new institution within the American national security state, the National Security Council. These reports came from an organization that would have pleased Lenin and saddened Locke. The latter would not necessarily have bewailed the fact that the organization comprised an elite, a vanguard. But its powerful scope and secrecy, combined with its esprit within and reputation without, would certainly have concerned him.

As an organization the CIA succeeded—often it accomplished what James Bond accomplished. Bond symbolized the simplifications of a popular fantasy: he served just causes, but fate forced him to meet them on unjust terms. This is what justified his limited use of illegal methods. Thus, some of Camelot's sun shone on the CIA, as the popular culture of the 1960's added spies and astronauts to the iconography that already included cowboys and detective heroes. Along with NASA, the CIA exemplified the technocratic revolution in business and government management, and it did effectively what it was designed to do.[28]

In Vietnam the CIA accomplished its assigned mission of keeping the President informed of the facts. Once Diem's murder and Kennedy's assassination had made their impact, CIA Director John McCone wrote his new boss a startling letter, which could not have misled anyone. He told Johnson that between Secretary McNamara and himself the only substantive difference was that he, McCone, felt "a little less pessimistic" on the Vietnam situation, and that there were "more reasons to be pessimistic than to be optimistic about prospects of our success in South Vietnam." McCone gave several reasons for his pessimism. He said, "There is no organized government in South Vietnam at this time [December 21, 1963]," and saw as ominous "the lack of an outstanding individual to lead" the country. He thought the political stability of the new bakufu was subject to serious doubt: "Conflicts of ambition, jealousy, difference of opinion over policy matters all are possible, could develop serious schisms, precipitate further dissension and coup attempts, all of which will affect the war effort against the VC." McCone concluded that "there are more reasons to doubt the future of the effort under present programs and moderate extensions to existing programs (i.e., harassing sabotage against NVN, border crossings, etc.) than there are reasons to be optimistic about the future of our cause in South Vietnam."[29]

McCone wrote this letter after reading McNamara's report of a trip to Saigon on December 19 and 20. McNamara trusted his own field research best, and it became part of his technocratic revolution at the Defense Department to leave his desk and go see for himself. Instantaneous media coverage brought the average citizen a living room war, and satellite communications brought higher headquarters down to the platoon level; but the ability of the Secretary of Defense to visit the scene of battle on less than 24 hours' notice brought to Washington a new sense of immediacy and personal involvement in the war. No sooner had McNamara returned to the capitol, than he composed a letter full of pessimism to his Commander-in-Chief, a Texan who did not like to lose.[30] To Johnson, a

Tory internationalist himself, it appeared as if his two Tory allies, McCone and McNamara, were forecasting an Alamo for Vietnam. Indeed they were doing just that.

McNamara's pessimism was even deeper than McCone's. Like the CIA Director, he saw the new Saigon bakufu as the primary weakness in the system. Upon meeting this military committee in Saigon, McNamara, according to General Tran Van Don, coldly asked, "Who is the boss here?" Surprisingly, even to the general, no one answered. That alone convinced McNamara that this new institution was a weak substitute for the discarded Ngo family. But all problems did not originate with the Vietnamese, according to the Pentagon boss. The second major weakness he observed was the U.S. country team—that is, the Ambassador and all the key American military and civilian officials in Saigon. McNamara claimed that this most important group lacked "leadership, has been poorly informed, and is not working to a common plan." He located the prime cause in the person of the Whig Ambassador. "Above all, Lodge has virtually no official contact with [General] Harkins." McNamara criticized Lodge for "dispatching reports with major military implications without showing them to Harkins" and said he "does not show Harkins important incoming traffic [cables]."[31]

The Whigs were not caught off-guard by these reports. Already somewhat apprehensive about a backlash from their erstwhile Tory allies, they sent an emissary to LBJ to explain and defend their position. The emissary was Michael V. Forrestal, son of the first Secretary of Defense, James V. Forrestal and a man almost raised by the Harrimans following his father's suicide. Since 1961 Michael Forrestal had held the Whig frontier on the National Security Council. Even Hilsman had recognized the younger Forrestal as a member of an "inner club" in the earlier Kennedy days.[32] Knowing that McNamara, one of Forrestal's father's successors, planned to descend momentarily on Saigon to pass judgment on the bakufu and their war, the Whigs tried to outmaneuver him.

At the NSC, Forrestal prepared a memorandum that Johnson could use "in giving guidance to the Secretary."[33] Guiding McNamara would prove to involve more than Forrestal envisaged, for the Secretary of Defense was one Camelot player that Johnson really admired (at least before the war began to go badly and McNamara became the loose cannon-of-peace on the warship deck). Nevertheless, Forrestal gave it his best. He suggested that McNamara's mission have as its major task "to focus the attention of the Vietnamese generals on their first priority problem, the immediate restoration of administrative [political] initiative in the provinces." He failed to understand that bakufus fought first and administered seldom; Whig political administration and reform remained more foreign to the bakufus than they had been to Ngo Dinh Diem. Forrestal informed the new President also that "it would be worthwhile exploring the possibility of larger-scale operations against selected targets in the North," and further suggested that "Secretary McNamara might also direct our own military and intelligence people to cooperate on devising a significant capability to strike at selected targets in North Vietnam."[34] This Whig advice came less than three weeks after Kennedy's assassination. Apparently Whigs remained prepared to play Niebuhrian poker and raise the ante. In other words, if now they were losing on a small scale they were willing to try to win on a larger scale—to expand the war in order to make free even more Vietnamese.

As it happened, neither Forrestal nor Johnson forced an agenda on McNamara, who flew to Saigon, made his inspection, and returned to write the pessimistic report described above. Johnson, at his Texas ranch for the holidays, had to choose between the escalation against the North suggested by Whig maximalists and the escalation in the South suggested by Tory minimalists. As the President was deliberating, McGeorge Bundy cabled Johnson's aide, General Clifton, with two ideas for short-term compromises. One consisted of a draft New Year's cable to the bakufu, assuring them of support but requesting that they take charge of a multi-front agenda. The other consisted of a morale-boosting cable for the embattled Lodge. The bakufu received their New Year's praise just in time to be overthrown: General Minh and his committee were out; General Khanh and his committee arrived. Lodge lasted a while longer, and Taylor took time to replace him.[35] All these changes proved temporary. In time, the Khanh bakufu would go and Lodge would return.

The CIA View of Vietnam, 1964

One change was not temporary, and it had important consequences. In his letter to Johnson, McCone had promised to send a number of his "old South Vietnamese hands" to Vietnam in order to develop "the necessary covert resources of native case officers and agents to inform us concerning the effectiveness of the MRC [bakufu] and the public acceptance of the new government." The agents indeed were sent, but before they could organize and report details on the Minh bakufu, the committee disappeared in a coup. The only CIA success here came in their reporting of the changing of tent governments, over which they had no control. The new bakufu originated in the field, so far from Saigon that it had a leader who was commanding troops of I Corps, in the area bordering the Leninist lands of the North. The American in closest contact with the new bakufu chieftain, General Khanh, happened to be his senior U.S. Army adviser, Colonel Jasper Wilson.[36]

This Colonel cabled news of the coup to CIA Saigon—in the intelligence lexicon, CAS Saigon, meaning "controlled American source." Khanh had told Wilson, who told CAS, that a neutralist coup might occur in Saigon unless he, Khanh, could promptly stage his own coup. Khanh saw the major enemy not as Diem's followers in Saigon but rather as the mandarin in Paris, Charles de Gaulle. The CIA agents warned by cable that a recent returnee from Paris, Lieutenant Colonel Tran Dinh Lam, might be a French agent with the ability to spend several billion piasters to install a neutralist government. Nevertheless, because these CIA agents did not yet know Khanh well, they were unwilling to evaluate the likelihood of his staging a coup.[37] CIA Saigon cabled Washington internationalists, alerting them to the possibility of a coup attempt by General Khanh. Before the printer had disgorged this warning cable, another cable from the CIA Watch officer, this one of higher precedence, arrived at the White House International Situation Room. The terse message confirmed that "move now underway by northern 1st Corps commander, General Khanh . . . to change composition of ruling military revolutionary council"—in other words, a coup.[38] By the following day all uncertainty ended—a new bakufu was born.

After this, the CIA did not hesitate to guess at the implications of Khanh's coup. First, agents reported that the unity of the Vietnamese Armed Forces would "be seriously strained by the current coup d'état." Second, and of long-range importance, they said that although this bakufu would remain "pro-American, anti-communist, and anti-neutralist," Vietnamese public reaction "cannot now be judged."[39] If they could not judge the local reaction, neither could they guess how the President would react. Johnson had to readdress his New Year's greetings—from Minh to Khanh. And since the NSC files on Vietnam, which are the source of the majority of original documents cited in this study, contain almost no documents penned by Johnson, that handwritten note of February 2 to Khanh makes a poignant impression. In the last sentence of this short, two-paragraph letter, Johnson promised to help Khanh "increase the confidence of the Vietnamese people in their government."[40] LBJ was looking for a friend to stay the course.

Unfortunately, the President could not help the new bakufu gain the confidence of the peasants, particularly the remaining primitive rebels who had not gone over to the other side. CIA specialists gave Johnson and his National Security Council the bad news about the new leadership's reception by the people within weeks of his February greetings to

Khanh. By that time these CIA agents had written reports based on field-work. A cable they sent to Washington on February 10 exemplifies the difference between reports covering Saigon salon factions and those covering working-level groups in the countryside. This CIA report covered Binh Long province in the II Corps area north of Saigon. First, agents reported that "local reaction to the new coup leaders is one of disgust." To illustrate, they described the reactions of a group of Vietnamese who had listened to a communal radio as the new bakufu chieftain announced his policies. When he finished, these locals "remained silent for a few moments, then spat on the floor and walked out." As if that were not enough, the next sentence ran, "The comment most frequently heard locally is, 'What was wrong with General Minh's government?'"[41]

But Binh Long represented only one province in one corps area, and there were four corps areas covering the South. Did CIA reports for other corps areas contain more optimistic reports for the Johnson team? Not if one looks carefully. On February 14 the CIA reported worse news from I Corps in the far north, the corps commanded by the new bakufu chief before he took over in Saigon. The opening sentences of the I Corps cable contained the most optimistic analysis, and it was enough to frighten even a hardened veteran of Texas political struggles: "The war is not progressing favorably in I Corps area." It went on: "Since last summer, I Corps has had three commanders, Thua Thien province five chiefs, Quong Nam province three chiefs, and Danang city five police chiefs." In fact, CIA case officers reported, "in some provinces virtual collapse of administration was prevented only by the presence of MAAG [American military] sector advisors."[42]

Johnson's remaining hope for political light at the end of his Vietnamese tunnel received its coup de grace on February 18, with the arrival of the CIA team's country-wide analysis. "Tide of insurgency in all four corps areas appear to be going against GVN [the Khanh bakufu]"; this was the first sentence in subparagraph 1a, and each following subparagraph began with worse news than the one before. Thus, "National level direction of all programs appears to be weak to nonexistent" was followed by "Strategic hamlet program . . . at virtual standstill," which was followed by "There is no evidence of any particular GVN appeal to youth or students and as a matter of fact GVN propaganda mechanism in toto is largely moribund."[43]

These reports of hopelessness came within the first thirty days of the Khanh bakufu's existence. The Johnson administration probably hoped for better news by summer, but, if so, it hoped in vain. The CIA report of July 29 contained worse news. By then it appeared that Khanh was mounting a political "March North" campaign in order to expand the war and "bring about greater U.S. involvement" in part because "internal maneuvering against Khanh continues." The preceding week's CIA summary also had given bad news: "No significant progress was apparent in the government's counterinsurgency program."[44] And August brought no relief. Khanh celebrated the Tonkin Gulf attack by repeating himself on one issue: "The people of North Vietnam must be liberated." More ominously, he attacked one of the few anticommunist political parties that had considerable standing. This party, the Dai Viet, contained many former Viet Minh fighters who rejected the Leninist leadership of the North. According to Khanh's press secretary, Colonel Pham Ngoc Thao, their efforts to build a mass following worried Khanh.

Several leading Generals belonged to the Dai Viet: General Thieu, who held the Chief-of-Staff position on the Joint General Staff, and the commanders of the 5th, 7th, and 9th Divisions near Saigon. Ominously for the Khanh faction, General Khiem, the Minister of Defense within the bakufu, "has been rumored to have Dai Viet ties and to be involved in coup plotting." Foreign Minister Quat, formerly a member of the Dai Viet faction in the North, also had influence in Saigon, as did Nguyen Ton Hoan, Deputy Premier for Pacification and leader of the southern faction of the Dai Viet. Apparently to appease the Dai Viets, Khanh accepted the resignation of Trang Le Quong, who was the Vietnamese pacification coordinator (and the counterpart of William Sullivan on the American side). The Americans considered Quong "one of the more qualified appointees on the Southern Vietnamese pacification council." From this perspective, it would seem that Khanh bought temporary political peace in Saigon at the high cost of losing a competent Vietnamese who could have helped him in his long-range struggle.[45]

In this early August report, which noted Khanh's attempt to promote a march North, the CIA also cited evidence that some Dai Viets were enamored of a more startling scenario. These Dai Viets leaked their plan when, in late August 1964, Defense Minister Khiem, on a tour of Malaysia, "referred publicly to the eventual need for U.S. combat troops in Vietnam."[46] Khiem, one of the Dai Viets, shocked internationalists in Washington. Johnson, with his eye on the American elections in November, was planning to secure his own victory over Goldwater by beating him over the head with a peace platform. Press releases about a fighting role in Vietnam for U.S. troops was the last thing Johnson wanted to receive from Saigon officials.

In the middle of August Khanh decreed a state of emergency and curtailed all civil liberties. Among other actions, he censored all media and began to seize "harmful publications." Whig internationalists watched in horror as Khanh and his bakufu resorted to the tactics of Ngo Dinh

Diem—and for that matter, of Ho Chi Minh. Khanh also had inherited Diem's political war with the Buddhists, a problem that he had to face when he traveled to their Hué stronghold on August 9.

And there were other problems: Khanh continued to worry about a coup, particularly now that he planned to have anyone suspected of "harming the national economy" tried by military courts and made subject to immediate execution. Further, after the Gulf of Tonkin air strikes, Khanh had encouraged "widespread euphoria and imaginative speculation on future American actions." The CIA analysts, however, saw this as creating another political hazard: when the southerners realized that the Tonkin raids were a one-time-only demonstration, it "could produce despair and frustrations creating new pressures on and within Khanh's" bakufu. So while the air strikes bolstered Johnson's image as a candidate of limited peace against the machismo of Goldwater as the candidate of expanded war, Khanh got only a temporary reprieve.[47]

In August the Tory Ambassador in Saigon, Maxwell Taylor, now desperate for a solution, took the advice of some Whig maximalists and recommended widening the war. In Washington his old Tory ally, McNamara, fought the suggestion, siding with those Whig minimalists who feared that an unlimited war would result. McGeorge Bundy, acting as the chief clearing agent in the National Security Council, warned Johnson of the Tory split. On August 13, in a thirteen-page memorandum for Johnson, Bundy started the section entitled "Essential Elements in the Situation" by stating that "South Vietnam is not going well."[48]

Things were going worse by August 30, when CIA analysts reported that Khanh's press officer, Colonel Pham Ngoc Thao, now planned to stage a coup of his own in order to bring a younger bakufu to power—by younger, he meant Colonels instead of Generals. Thao was a political time bomb. Some important Vietnamese Generals considered him a high-ranking Viet Cong agent. He was a practicing Catholic and had the backing of the Catholic hierarchy in Saigon. Yet he had helped plot the downfall of the Catholic Diem less than a year earlier. Buddhists, especially Thich Tri Quang, distrusted him, and Thao's success would assure Buddhist violence on a large scale. Finally, the southern Dai Viet would not have tolerated the colonel because of his checkered past, including his 1956 defection from the Viet Minh and his status as protégé under Diem's brother Bishop Ngo Dinh Thuc. Clearly, Thao was a disaster waiting to happen. (After 1975, the worst fears of many were confirmed. Thao, or "Albert" as he was known to other Viet Cong agents, turned out to be one of several NLF agents who had served in several bakufus.)[49]

Although Thao's coup failed to materialize, worse news was on the way. The first paragraph of a September 28 CIA cable warned that "the signs of deterioration are so many and so clear, in our view, that the odds now favor a continuing decay of South Vietnam[ese] will and effectiveness in coming weeks, sufficient to imperil the political base for present U.S. policy and objective[s] in South Vietnam." Acting Director of the CIA, Lieutenant General Marshall A. Carter, thought this report so important that he dispatched a special copy with a covering memorandum to McGeorge Bundy at the National Security Council. Each paragraph of the memo, which was appropriately titled "Deterioration in South Vietnam," rang with defeat. For example: "The deluge of adversity being reported out of South Vietnam raises the question whether we may be on the verge of some sudden calamity." And: "The likely pattern of this decay will be increasing South Vietnamese defeatism, paralysis of leadership, friction with Americans, exploring of possible lines of retreat with the other side."[50]

These predictions of doom came from the CIA, the senior U.S. intelligence agency. Did other American intelligence agencies, using different sources, take a more optimistic view? Apparently not. The State Department had its own analysts in its Bureau of Intelligence and Research, directed in 1964 by Thomas L. Hughes. In a July 17 report to his boss, Dean Rusk, Hughes suggested that "Khanh has become increasingly aware of the difficulties he faces in implementing his counterinsurgency program, to say nothing of restoring lost momentum." Hughes informed Rusk also that Khanh's frustrations were political, stemming from recent threats to his position by important military officers and key civilian officials. He concluded his report by warning Rusk that Khanh hoped to use a direct miltiary commitment of U.S. forces more as a means of stabilizing his Saigon bakufu than as a means of waging a winning war.[51] We must conclude, then, that neither diplomats nor CIA analysts misled Kennedy or Johnson. The remaining U.S. intelligence agencies were those managed by the military services. What did their reports say? In the main, military intelligence report writers limited themselves to estimates in the narrower range of military matters. For example, Colonel Wilbur Wilson, the III Corps Senior Military Adviser, produced many examples of frank field reporting. On April 10 he wrote to his Saigon bosses that the progress of the GVN in constructing New Life Hamlets—the new name for the old strategic hamlets—was insignificant.

In their own reports, CIA analysts could—and did—use such military reportage, as well as evidence furnished by Defense Department agencies and State Department estimates. For instance, CIA reports of July 1, 8, and 15 include references to ground operations, prisoner of war interrogations, air support activities, and Army of Vietnam desertion rates.[52] In no sense could the military evidence in these reports have communicated "misleading pictures of the situation." Who could have given such "misleading pictures" to Presidents Kennedy and Johnson if not their intelligence agencies? The truth is that no individual or group did so. Quite the contrary; the intelligence reports contained striking evidence of impending disaster. It is true, however, that at least two Johnson aides— neither a professional intelligence officer—tried to sugarcoat the sour news. They were Maxwell Taylor and McGeorge Bundy. On July 15 Taylor cabled the President that "deterioration resulting from GVN paralysis following two coups has generally halted." Trying to emphasize the positive, he claimed to see "blood flowing back into GVN provincial veins." But from the complete diagnosis in Taylor's cable, the patient appeared more dead than alive.[53] Similarly, on the next day, McGeorge Bundy gave the President a note to which he attached the CIA report on Vietnam for the week of July 8. Bundy told Johnson, "I cling to my own impression that the overall situation is marginally better than it was a month ago." Now this could hardly reassure a President who, if he read the attached report, would find hard evidence of the cancer: "With few exceptions, pacification program makes little progress," "Disclosure of land reform provisions arouses landowners."[54]

Johnson's War

Johnson launched and lost a war by playing poor politics. Playing politics with war is an unfortunate by-product of holding four-year elections for the top position in the U.S. government. Others have played it. but they played good politics, if good means winning. Lincoln and the American Civil War, and the second Roosevelt and World War II are two obvious examples. In light of the many debates that scholars have chronicled concerning just and unjust wars, it is evident that for a war to be just, there must first of all be a decent chance of winning.[55]

By January 1, 1965, no such chance existed in Vietnam, at least not under prevailing conditions—conditions that were often the fault of the United States. Yet Johnson had sat and watched opportunities drift by as he planned his own political victory. Once installed, he launched his war. Now he erred again, in allowing a large conventional war to dominate American "forecraft," that part of statecraft that deals with the conduct of war. Johnson could have used a good Leninist adviser, someone who could make clear that objective reality in the Vietnam of 1964 showed a correlation of forces working against Washington and Saigon. To hope to change this correlation required patience and precision. The American eagle, singed but not fatally burnt, had to find the vulnerable point of the little dragon of North Vietnam.

Since the Vietnamese struggle was a militarized mass insurrection that a dedicated elite had planned, the point within South Vietnam at which the elite connected to the mass was critical. Severing this link became the task—a task requiring precision. If the war were to be contained within South Vietnam, then this vital point—the Viet Cong infrastructure (VCI) as an operating political organization able to contact the peasants—had to be destroyed. Viet Cong military units represented the muscles; the VCI represented the brain. The VCI were what Karl von Clausewitz would have called the enemy's center of gravity, his hub of power and movement on which everything depended and therefore the point against which all force should be applied. By 1964 there was little time remaining for such a precise application of force. Unfortunately, being traditionalists, Johnson and his advisers believed with Clausewitz that war was the continuation of politics by other means. But Vietnam was not a traditional war, and a nontraditional Leninist view would have suggested that for a militarized mass insurrection, politics was the continuation of war by other means. Johnson, the quintessential politician, understood this when it came to Austin and Washington, but not when it was Saigon and Hanoi. His decision to concentrate on military means rather than political means meant a long war, costly in casualties. Defeating enemy military units alone could not end the insurrection because the political connection that those units had through the Viet Cong infrastructure remained unsevered, thus able to raise new units, at least prior to 1968. The discredited Diem of the House of Ngo had earlier directed a program—the strategic hamlet program—that, if faulty, nonetheless held political promise for severing the connection. But Johnson had an election battle to fight and win in 1964; too late would Washington and Saigon return to a variation of that promising beginning. After his triumph over Goldwater, LBJ reportedly told his chairman of the Joint Chiefs, General Earle Wheeler, that now the Chiefs could have their war.[56] But it was not Wheeler's war, it was Johnson's; and it cost a national fortune to lose.

Narrow as was Johnson's interpretation of containment, he pursued it with the illusion that he could prevail. His view of a rigid perimeter defense against all Leninist attempts to break out was part of his inheritance from NSC-68, even though the world of 1964 was quite different from that of 1950. In a chapter that is generally favorable to Johnson, one historian suggests that Johnson "inherited the assumptions of the cold war and the conflict in Vietnam, though he did not question them."[57] Again the system did not work, for if it had, important decisions about Vietnam would have been made "without illusions about the odds for success."[58]

Johnson spent billions of dollars and millions of lives going from de facto military defeat in 1964 to de jure political defeat in 1968.

Not only did he do this deliberately, but he also turned the national security system into an adjunct for his election campaign, a special committee for the reelection of the President. The NSC, premier organization of the internationalists as of their creation of the National Security State in 1947, became in 1964 not a clearinghouse for national security affairs but one of many campaign locations to assist in the election of Johnson. Although it is not unusual for Presidents to use their appointees for electoral purposes, wholesale distortion of the mission of government units is malfeasance. Three examples will illustrate the distortion that Johnson promoted.

The first example involves the NSC staff. On July 31, 1964, William Bundy and Mike Forrestal reported to the NSC on their reelection work— work that took the form of a five-page draft for an unclassified statement "of the Administration's position on expanding the war in South Vietnam." Having been asked to perform this campaign work by McGeorge Bundy, Forrestal and Bill Bundy gave Bill's brother McGeorge the requested draft on the assumption that it would "be in the hands of the major campaigner and speaker," as part of the "overall campaign arsenal." The two drafters fretted over the problem of how to make expansion of the war seem "clearly less attractive than our present policy, but at the same time not so unattractive that we [would be] tying our hands if we should ever decide we had to do it." Peace now and war later— that was their election strategy. The two authors were undecided about whether Johnson's campaign "should further accentuate the fact that North Vietnamese support is indeed crucial to the [Viet Cong] effort in the south and that there is indeed a [North Vietnamese] sanctuary involved here."[59]

The second example involves the NSC Director. On August 20, McGeorge Bundy wrote a memorandum for Johnson concerning Senator Hubert Humphrey's California campaign speech on Vietnam the previous Sunday. Bundy told Johnson that the NSC 'gave him a lot of help on [the speech], and it got a good play out there." Bundy reminded Johnson that "this was done pursuant to a request of yours" and that "the Senator was very responsive to all our suggestions and comments."[60] By October 17 Johnson was sending McGeorge Bundy news clippings about the impending election. On that date he gave Bundy a clipping from *The News Dispatch* of Leannette, Pennsylvania. The clipping quoted a local Republican, Bennett S. Chapple, of U.S. Steel Corporation, who maintained that "we are at war as far as I'm concerned." What Chapple didn't know, even though he had a son serving in Vietnam, was that he would have to wait until after November for Johnson to go to war.[61]

The third example of Johnson's distortion of government functioning involves one of his major field representatives—representatives on whom the NSC depended for accurate information. On August 18, 1964, General Maxwell Taylor, Johnson's Ambassador in Saigon, said he believed that the situation had deteriorated to the point where he would have to recommend escalation against the North; but he added that perhaps he could wait until January 1, 1965, to use more force. By September 6, with the situation worsening, Taylor cabled that he believed Johnson could wait for escalation only until December 1. In his own daily chronicle the Ambassador wrote, "No George Washington in sight."[62] This is only one of several indications that the manner in which Johnson forced his own domestic political concerns on his Ambassadors and Generals kept them from offering unqualified advice.[63]

Should Johnson have known he was going to lose his war in Vietnam? Indeed he should; he possessed substantial evidence that to ignore his ever-changing client and to concentrate only on his own domestic political agenda made a winning strategy for the war impossible. Did he have too shaky an electoral mandate to arrange a neutralist solution with the help of France? Not at all; after he trounced Goldwater in 1964 he had more support at home, on both left and right, than any President in modern times—including Nixon, who was to talk peace in Asia four years later.

Given the political constraints inherent in an internationalist view of national security policy, was Johnson's war in Vietnam essential for the doctrine of containment to work? Not according to George Kennan, principal author of that doctrine. In 1947 Kennan believed that only certain key geographic locations required defending.[64] Contrasting with this point-defense idea was the concept of perimeter defense—the notion expressed in NSC-68—namely, that it was necessary to defend all locations on the perimeter of a global arc of containment. Thus, in the classic Whig terms of NSC-68, "the assault on free institutions is worldwide now, and in the context of the present polarization of power a defeat of free institutions anywhere is a defeat everywhere."[65] This was the interpretation of containment that Johnson had inherited, and his use of it in Vietnam proved disastrous for himself and his country. Kennan had advised Truman internationalists to adopt the more realistic point-defense interpretation at the time in which America was the world's only superpower. If a more flexible interpretation was all the United States could afford then, how could one possibly assume that the nation could afford the more costly perimeter interpretation when the Soviet Union forced bipolarity into international politics? How could one even consider the idea in the late 1960's, when both the United States and the USSR began their respective adjustments to the multipolar world? By that time both global actors had found Vietnam a costly political proposition.[66] The only remaining question between them was: Which power would lose the most? Johnson's rigid loyalty to the perimeter defense, a strange affinity for a congenital Tory, assured that the big loser would be the United States.

In summary, American intervention in the politics of South Vietnam was a failure. Initially, American internationalists granted South Vietnam a minimum of assistance. They supported the early Saigon leadership of Ngo Dinh Diem, hoping for steady improvements on all fronts—military, economic, and political. While far from perfect, Ngo Dinh Diem achieved some modest successes. Anxious to increase the rate of these successes, however, key Whigs in both the Kennedy and Johnson administrations initiated extensive plans to modernize the political institutions in the southern half of this ancient and proud land. They wanted quick results, speed being of the essence given the four-year cycle of American politics. Political designs poured forth. Now it so happened also that the proud inhabitants of Vietnam had designs for their own future, a future that placed very little emphasis, if any, on Western-style elections, courts, free press, and so on. The Vietnamese chose their own institutions, most often a mix of the old and the new.

In their failure neither Whig nor Tory internationalists understood that they were dealing with a problem of institutions. The mandarin and his family were a traditional institution, the Leninist and his party were a revolutionary institution.[67] The Americans wanted a mix of both—a reforming institution. But a bakufu, basically a military institution, was not a reforming institution, and was most unlikely to become one. American interventionists were correct, in fact, in believing that modernization involved a mixing of traditional and modern; in the bakufu, however, they had fostered, however inadvertently, the wrong institution, because even a military that helps modernize its own state will often block the arrival of what Americans had told themselves all other national groups wanted—a democratic state that protected their political liberty.[68]

PART THREE

ECONOMIC CONSTRAINTS

McGeorge Bundy, National Security Adviser, 1961–66:

"If I had to pick just one lesson, it would be: Ask yourself ahead of time about any adventure: How much is this game worth? We should also have asked more sharply what our prospects were." *Wall Street Journal*, Jan. 14, 1985, p. 8.

Cyrus Vance, Secretary of the Army, 1962–63; Deputy Secretary of Defense, 1964–67; Secretary of State, 1977–80:

"It teaches us a lesson about understanding people involved in situations where we are contemplating intervention. We really didn't understand the Vietnamese, how they reacted to actions. We assumed they would react in a Western way to the bombings. And that simply ignored the realities of that society." *Wall Street Journal*, Jan. 14, 1985, p. 8.

CHAPTER SEVEN

Vietnam—An Economic Design

BOTH PRESIDENTS Kennedy and Johnson bear responsibility for the U.S. debacle in Vietnam.[1] Although the two Presidents tolerated Whig political plans, they preferred Tory economic solutions, placing their hopes in the Agency for International Development (AID), the new Tory agency for global reordering. Mirroring the willingness of Whig internationalists to intervene in the domestic politics of other nations, Tory internationalists readily intervened in the domestic economies of the same nations. Both Whig and Tory internationalists were determined to fulfill Maslow's hierarchy of needs, Whigs by starting at the political top, Tories at the economic bottom. Whigs used the CIA as their agency of last resort; the Tories, however, consolidated various plans inside their agency of first choice, AID.[2]

Yankee intervention in the Vietnamese economy did not bring the results the initiators desired any more than did that of the Whigs. Since political intervention was covered in the preceding section, none of the details need reappear here. In quick summation, that section contains a description of three types of intelligence agencies employed for political control—for the southern leader, the extended family was the traditional intelligence agency; for the northern leader, the Leninist party provided a revolutionary intelligence agency; and for the two American leaders, the CIA was a democracy's attempt at an intelligence agency. The organizational form of Ngo Dinh Diem's intelligence agency worked against his attempt to govern South Vietnam; although a semiroyal family could function as an intelligence organization in traditional society, the times of the last mandarin were revolutionary ones that required revolutionary organizations. Failing to heed the history of his own church—which, faced by the revolution of the Reformation, reorganized and used the revolutionary organs of the Counter-Reformation—Ngo Dinh Diem confronted the northern revolutionary party with his traditional family apparatus, and lost. In contrast, Ho Chi Minh's intelligence agency, basically the elite Leninist party, was an excellent instrument for revolution. The northern leader did not fail to heed the history of his own creed, which since 1917 had faced the attempts by Lockean activists—counterrevolutionaries to Leninists—to substitute reform for revolution. Ho Chi Minh, therefore, met his southern adversary armed with the knowledge that in modern times revolution was often easier to accomplish than reform.[3] For Ho Chi Minh this again proved to be true. The American intelligence agency too worked with a fair amount of success. What did not work was the national security system, of which the CIA was only one part.

One can also review the economic competition by comparing three organizations. As in the political sphere, so in the economic Ngo Dinh Diem relied on his family, Ho Chi Minh on his party; but Kennedy and Johnson, rich with bureaucratic state organs, preferred the AID to the CIA.

Reform From the Bottom Up

In 1947 the first Tory internationalists commenced building a two-tiered economic approach to the Lockean-Leninist competition. The first tier of economic containment entailed isolating the Soviet Union outside the Western commercial system. The second tier involved granting foreign aid, especially to that part of the globe that was neither Lockean nor Leninist. Of the two, the first task was less complex; because the Soviets imposed most of their isolation on themselves and their Leninist satellites, the strategy of containment was made easier for the United States to implement. Although George Kennan did not emphasize an economic rationale for his containment strategy, others did. And once internationalists adopted the strategy of containment as theirs, they broadened its definition. In other words, the strategy had a life of its own.[4] Under such guidance economic containment of the Soviet Union followed the uneven and haphazard history of Soviet-American economic relations.

Two periods, 1917–20 and 1947–50, mark the low ebbs in the first fifty years of Soviet-American economic relations. For the early years of the Soviet state the capitalist powers attempted to isolate what they considered to be a Russian aberration. Their *cordon sanitaire* involved economic isolation, but in less than seven years this economic isolation became economic cooperation. Alone among the major powers of the 1920's, the United States continued to refuse to recognize the Soviet government, but this did not frustrate economic cooperation. In 1924 the Soviets incorporated the Amtorg Trading Company under the laws of the State of New York, and Washington officials were keenly aware that Amtorg represented an official organ of the Soviet state.[5] Lobbying for diplomatic recognition of the USSR, business interests in the United States approached both Secretaries of State Frank Kellogg and Henry Stimson, arguing that "the West needed Russia's vast resources." One of those interested businessmen happened to be the young Averell Harriman. The motivation for America's eventual recognition of the Soviet government was not monolithic; other reasons coexisted with economic ones, such as the realpolitik of two of Roosevelt's advisers, Secretary of State Cordell Hull and Ambassador Joseph Grew, in Tokyo, both of whom hoped that recognizing the Soviet government would enable them to use the USSR to block Japan in Asia. Nevertheless, diplomatic recognition in 1933 followed the economic contacts of 1924. The Soviets next won most-favored-nation status as early as 1937, but it was an unusual arrangement. Fearful that the USSR would only sell and not buy, the United States insisted that the USSR agree to buy a certain dollar amount each year. This the Soviets did.[6] Given the postwar reversals in Soviet-American economic relations, it is worth remembering that the United States created the Export-Import Bank to facilitate Soviet trade.

After World War II the critical issue for internationalists in American contacts with Soviet officials was the future of their trade agreements. From economic contacts with the West, the Soviets desired mainly machinery, equipment, and technology transfers. It was this last category that worried internationalists. After 1947 the United States tried to keep items of high technology (such as the latest computers) from going out of the West and into the Soviet military. But this technology transfer debate dates from 1917; at various times Lenin proposed and Trotsky supported the idea of concessions or leasing-zones within the USSR, zones where foreigners might invest. With these investments would come the latest technology, something for which even Lenin would compromise.[7] But Stalin's rise to power put an end to the idea of leasing-zones.

Since Soviet trade with the West did grow during the interwar years, the important question for historians is, What happened after World War II to the numerous economic agreements—many of them on specific items such as the tonnage of coal the Soviets would ship to the United States—so that by 1947 U.S.-USSR economic relations were almost back at 1917 levels?[8] The answer is that the internationalists allowed these agreements to lapse in the immediate postwar years because these Americans believed that postwar Soviet conduct ran counter to U.S. interest; therefore they did not plan to reward the Soviets by granting them the economic bonus they wanted—entry into the U.S. market. In the fifty years of U.S.-USSR economic relations from 1917 to 1967, the year 1947 marked a low point in economic contact, and part of the explanation for this decline is the advice given by U.S.-based economists familiar with

Soviet budgets.[9] As early as 1946, economists working for the U.S. government, people like Gregory Grossman and Alexander Gerschenkron, warned internationalists about Stalin's economic hopes—his first postwar Five-Year Plan. It was no state secret; the Kremlin had copies published in English for foreign distribution. For Grossman and Gerschenkron it was a plan for rearmament, plain and simple. It was also plainly a copy of Stalin's first five-year plan of two decades before. Equally obvious was the fact that the Soviets were rebuilding exactly what they had had before the war, unlike the West Germans, French, Italians, and Japanese, who, in the wake of the war's destruction, took the opportunity to modernize their industries. This mistake by the Soviets was all the worse in view of their hopes to compete with the United States in the postwar economic arena. After Stalin published his plan most U.S. actions were reactive.

Several observations help to put Soviet-American trade patterns in perspective, especially the decline in trade. First, compared with other nations' trade with the U.S., Soviet trade with America never had amounted to much. Second, after the war a decline in the movement between the two nations of goods associated with lend-lease was to be expected, that program having been designed for temporary wartime assistance. Third, the United Nations Relief and Rehabilitation Agency (UNRRA), which was mainly assisted by the United States, also had completed its emergency postwar shipments to the USSR. Nevertheless, economic issues became an important part of the postwar Soviet-American debate; economic containment joined political and military containment among the goals of U.S. internationalists.

The economic containment policy drew its strength from various sectors. In March 1947 Senator Ralph Flanders, a prominent member of the Committee for Economic Development, introduced a joint resolution to embargo all trade with the Soviet Union—trade based on private arrangements as well as government agreements—until the Soviets had fulfilled American perceptions of the Yalta and Potsdam Agreements. Flanders ardently called for economic war against the Soviets and stated that the "present means of bargaining were economic." In the House a call for economic retaliation, in the form of a joint resolution, came from Congressman William Colmer (a member of the House Special Committee on Post-War Economic Policy and Planning). Under its licensing power, the United States moved in 1947 to cut off oil shipments to the Soviet Union. The Truman administration added steel products to the embargo, thus cutting off any American locomotives after May 1947. They added railway freight cars to the embargo in June. "Export controls were, of course, a logical concomitant of the containment doctrine," and were effective because "exports to Russia in the fourth quarter of 1949 amounted to only

$200,000, as compared to the quarterly average of $88,000,000 in 1946."[10] A portion of the latter figure is accounted for by UNRRA shipments; nevertheless trade did decrease, even discounting that portion. And it was the internationalists within the Truman administration who encouraged and led much of the congressional sentiment for economic containment of the Soviet Union.

Legislative sentiment became law in 1948 when Congress assisted Truman in creating the Coordinating Committee–Consultative Group, better known as CoCom. As an international regime to coordinate a Western embargo policy toward the Communist bloc, CoCom discovered a Soviet-created trading bloc, the Council for Mutual Economic Assistance, or CMEA, dominating Eastern Europe. Initially, the U.S. definition of embargoed strategic goods triumphed at CoCom, especially after the U.S. Congress, in the Mutual Defense Export Act of 1951, stipulated that all U.S. aid to states that exported strategic and even nonmilitary goods to communist nations would be curtailed. Until their postwar economies recovered, the Europeans and Japanese took this warning seriously. By the 1960's CoCom had become a troublesome organization for American Atlanticists, owing to the recovery of the trade-hungry Western European economics and the requirement for a unanimous vote on all embargo decisions. But it remained an instrument of trade control, and in the first decade of its existence CoCom served as a weapon to apply economic pressure against the Leninists, especially under President Truman.[11]

Nor was the press unaware of the influence that economic pressure had in Truman's national security policy. On March 12, 1947, James Reston, writing in the *New York Times*, warned internationalists that their foreign policy was contingent on the use of money to correct what they perceived to be foreign problems when in fact solutions might demand more than economic answers. For Reston the financial cost in 1947 of U.S. aid in the Greek civil war held implications for the future, especially if the Greek case became the model for U.S. interventions abroad. Regardless of Reston's warning, Truman gave his active support to economic intervention.[12] By the end of 1947 it was clear that both Congress and the administration, with business approval and press knowledge, had launched a policy of economic containment of the Soviet Union. Add to this the fact that a Gallup poll in the fall of 1947 indicated that the public approved of this policy by an overwhelming majority (71 percent), and the sweep of the internationalist's triumph is apparent.[13]

But could policies associated with economic containment persist? Once the initial acrimony over the breakup of the Grand Alliance of World War II passed, might not American business leaders and others demand a more pragmatic, flexible policy toward a possible Soviet market, a policy that would have the bonus of human contacts associated with the exchange of goods? Measuring the prospective durability of any policy is difficult. If, however, several government agencies adopt a policy and reorganize their bureaucracies around the goals of that policy—as opposed to the policy's being personified in one powerful individual—then the policy is likelier to endure under pressure. That is what occurred in the late 1940's, and the Truman administration bequeathed the results to its successors.

In a modern nation decisions of state are not made by one person. Instead, decision-making is a complicated process involving many people with differing views who may or may not reach a consensus. Subsequent antagonists may recast the previous arguments at the next policy level. These countervailing forces, moreover, are not permanent but instead form and reform in momentary coalitions to face specific issues. Key concerns can thus be eliminated in the early stages and not be forwarded to higher-level policymakers.

Two features of the governmental decision process are particularly notable here. The first is the powerful force that organizational units of modern government generate from their very existence. It can be found at work in the behavior of organizations and in their ability to sustain themselves. "Most of the behavior is determined by previously established procedure" because the "existing organizational routines for employing present physical capabilities constitute the range of effective choice open to government leaders confronted with any problem."[14] The second feature is a sense of loyalty, pride, and self-justification. More often than not decisionmakers will tilt their opinions along lines set by the bias of whatever department or agency they represent. In policy recommendations at low- and middle-level ranges, the staffers often identify a certain policy with either protecting or advancing their own and their agencys' professional growth and well-being.[15]

An example of the first pattern—the inherent force of organizations—concerns the creation in 1941 of a new job at the State Department, Assistant Secretary of State for Economic Affairs. That job combined in one office all the previously established economic procedures and routines. In the wake of the creation of that powerful position, State Department leaders instituted distinct positions for economic officers at major U.S. embassies, officers who would supervise the embassies' economic sections, as political officers supervised the political section. All these economic officers could be assigned tasks by the Assistant Secretary of State for Economic Affairs. Dean Acheson, returning to government service in February 1941, was the first to fill the assistant secretaryship. Acheson recognized the nebulous charter of the new title and office, but in what he called "my search for a function" he soon created his own power center at the State Department. Through the economic officers he welded his office to offices in all U.S. embassies. So important did his new office become that Acheson made it central to two chapters in his memoirs—"Economic Warfare at Home" and "Economic Warfare Abroad."[16] The State Department that Harry Truman inherited in 1945 thus possessed a strong, functioning segment dedicated to the protection of American economic interests as perceived by State Department bureaucrats.

The State Department was not alone in reorganizing to meet global economic problems: two other departments also indicated by their actions that they were undergoing a similar organizational change. The Treasury Department with its Morgenthau Plan and the War Department with its JCS 1067 Plan—both of which included economic planning for postwar Germany—indicated that they had organizational interests in foreign economic policy. In short order all three departments—State, Treasury, and War—began to compete over economic planning abroad.

But the State Department had reorganized for economic war earliest. It created the first bureaucratic procedure for hot war that could be redesigned for cold war. State's failures and successes from World War II trained its bureaucrats in the hardships of economic warfare. During World War II when Franco's Spain threatened to become a problem, the State Department had discovered economic weapons. To obtain U.S. policy goals in Spain "the principal method was economic coercion and concession." In 1944 when Juan Perón kept Argentina friendly to Hitler's Germany, the American government went into action. The United States imposed punitive economic sanctions, armed Brazil in case of war with Argentina, and pressured Great Britain into reducing ties with Buenos Aires. Chile only narrowly escaped Secretary of State Cordell Hull's Argentine policy. To keep António Salazar's Portugal a bonded ally the "United States and Britain were paying high prices for Portuguese tungsten and threatening economic sanction if Portugal did not cut off its export of the mineral to Germany." Even in America's recognition of Vichy France, economic aspects came to the fore, since by driplets of economic aid the United States tried to "encourage the Vichy regime to resist further concessions to Hitler."[17]

Having succeeded in most of these wartime measures—each success adding to a standing operating procedure (SOP)—when it came time to discuss U.S.-USSR postwar relations, the State Department bureaucrats involved recommended to Secretary of State Byrnes that he sugarcoat all American demands with the possibility of a large loan to the Soviets. No one was surprised when Truman's Assistant Secretary of State for Economic Affairs, William Clayton, agreed with the new Secretary of Commerce, Averell Harriman, that a loan to the Soviets was a "concrete bargaining lever for use in connection with the many other political and economic problems which will arise between our two countries."[18] Each of their subordinate bureaucrats had told them this was so. Nor was it surprising that the Soviets would dodge such a package deal.

But what of the second feature of governmental decision-making? Did internationalists, divided by loyalty to their separate agencies, fight for bureaucratic turf, thereby limiting the parameters of the debate on economic containment? Fight they did. Acheson chronicles some of the debate. He recalls how "our vigorous Cabinet men—Henry Morgenthau, Jesse Jones, Henry Wallace—were empire-builders, impatient with what seemed to them State Department fussiness and diplomatic obstruction." Acheson watched and wailed, for "the result of the conflict of these forces was altogether predictable: more and more the State Department fought desperately for a shrinking place."[19]

The invasion of the War and Treasury Departments into areas that old State hands had thought of as classically their own domain was noted as far away as the office of Minister-Counselor to the U.S. embassy in Moscow. As reported by George Kennan, it was a fantastically ignorant cable from the Treasury Department that spurred him to send his memorable "long" telegram. "It should be remembered," he wrote later, "that nowhere in Washington had the hopes entertained for postwar collaboration with Russia been more elaborate, more naive, or more tenaciously (one might almost say ferociously) pursued than in the Treasury Department."[20] It was Harry Dexter White who represented the Treasury Department's vested bureaucratic interest in economic policy vis-à-vis the Soviets. White insisted to Secretary Henry Morgenthau that U.S. trade with the Soviets would increase substantially after the war.[21]

Nor were Treasury officials the only ones to keep the staff at the State Department and the diplomats at America's Moscow embassy on their guard. After reading the lend-lease legislation, the Navy Department insisted that all lend-lease vessels in Soviet custody be returned. In a memorandum to Secretary of Defense James Forrestal from Secretary of State George Marshall, the old general outlined the diplomatic damage of this demand: "This Government has declared as surplus and sold vessels of some of the types lend-leased to the Soviets, for example, mine sweepers have been sold to Greece and Turkey." He warned Forrestal that "the result of the Navy Department proposal will have an unnecessarily adverse political effect upon our relations with the Soviet Union without compensating results."[22] But the Navy persisted, and the Soviets did return the ships. Although Secretary Marshall attempted to moderate the lend-lease demands of other departments, the powerful pull of bureaucratic parochialism limited the consensus he obtained. For example, the 1974 *Foreign Relations of the United States* covers the Soviet Union in 229 pages, of which 64 cover War and Navy Department struggles with the State Department to make the Soviets return lend-lease items piece by piece. Even a Senator who earlier had opposed lend-lease stated that, while you could get lend-lease back at the end of hostilities, it was like getting chewing gum back after it had been chewed. Chewed or not, Navy and War wanted it back.

As if this were not enough, even Secretary of the Interior Harold Ickes desired a portion of State's domain. To his fear that American domestic oil reserves were nearly exhausted, Ickes's bureaucratic organizational answer was the Petroleum Reserve Corporation. Interior's vested interest, so it seemed to State Department bureaucrats, displayed itself in grandiose plans that appeared to threaten the State Department's responsibility over foreign policy. If economic containment of the Soviet Union was to be a major component in President Truman's national security policy, the State Department wanted the major role of implementing this policy.

Yet even Truman approached economic containment slowly. In 1945 the possibility of applying economic pressure to the Soviets did not have his support, nor was it generally popular.[23] In 1945, when Ambassador Harriman (attending the United Nations Conference in San Francisco at the invitation of Secretary of State Ed Stettinius) warned a conference of newspaper reporters and commentators about Soviet intrigues, a number of those present stalked out in protest. A pronounced sympathy for the Soviets could be detected easily in the congressional debates of 1945. That the atmosphere had changed by 1946 was highlighted by the negative reaction to Henry Wallace's speech on September 24, 1946, at Madison Square Garden, a speech felt by many internationalists to show Wallace's naïveté about Soviet motives. By March 6, 1947, Truman made his position on Soviet motives clear in a speech to an audience at Baylor University; by then Truman had come to see economic power as a major determinate of postwar international relations.[24]

Examples of the use of economics as a threat after 1947 abound. In the American-Soviet discussions on postwar Korea, for example, economics dominated the American agenda. U.S. negotiators demanded, that no reparations be taken from Korea, and that both sections of the nation be treated as one economic unit. American negotiators stressed Korean economic problems—the need for an exchange of electric power from North Korea to South Korea and the reverse exchange in rice, in addition to a general exchange in raw materials, fuels, industrial equipment, and chemicals.[25] But the U.S. insistence on viewing Korean problems in isolated economic terms was not to Soviet taste. Stalin, having made known to Churchill and Roosevelt at Teheran his general aspirations for a stronger Soviet position in postwar Asia, made no attempt to change his plans by accepting an American economic answer in Korea.

Stalin's emissaries understood that an economic plan offered by an ex-ally committed to a free trade policy most likely would result in a Korea dominated by the institutions of the free trade state rather than by the institutions of a state-trading nation similar to the Soviet Union. Not that the rhetoric of free trade frightened the Soviets; instead, they feared the manner in which Americans translated free trade into policy. First, it was the nature of American-style international free trade to emphasize the kind of national private sector for which the Soviets had no sympathy. Second, most states trading with the United States in 1947 would need U.S. loans in order to recover or build the items to be traded. The state receiving aid would be required to open its national economic books to obtain the loan, because of Western accounting rules concerning the assisted nation's receipts, debits, and planned expenditures—items the Soviets considered state secrets, but items that free traders demanded to see in order to approve loans. This alone made the Soviets balk at cooperation in such ventures.

Many of Truman's appointees planned to employ free trade policy to penetrate new and old markets. A successor to Acheson as Assistant Secretary of State for Economic Affairs, William Clayton, became the leading voice in the free trade argument. Clayton spoke on numerous public occasions, always preaching the litany of free trade, American-style. He astutely foresaw the assistance to be gained by cultivating pro-trade press leaders. He even gave his old cotton firm advice on the good investment possibilities in the devastated Italian cotton textile industry.[26] His policy gained early congressional support, and the *Congressional Record* for 1945 is replete with American free trade philosophy: "We are living in a new world, a world in which thinking men know that mutually beneficial international trade is essential to our prosperity and to the prosperity of the other nations of the world."[27]

Truman's advisers hoped to incorporate all of Korea into a new Asian prosperity zone. But Soviet planners set their view of an Asian security zone like a boulder in the path of the American plan. No compromise was possible, even though Truman's negotiators offered several. For example, according to a letter first drafted by Dean Acheson for the President to send to Edwin Pauley in Tokyo, and then toned down in its anti-Soviet aspects by Clark Clifford, U.S. negotiators were to offer the Soviets two compromises on Korea, compromises not easily won among interested Americans. Truman told Pauley that "by making possible the formulation and execution of liberal reforms such as land redistribution and the nationalization of certain industries, which are desired by a majority of Koreans, this policy should also help to broaden the basis for an understanding with the Soviets."[28] The Soviets, however, remained unimpressed by what they considered American tokens in the form of land redistribution and selected nationalization. The Political Adviser to the U.S. XXIV Corps predicted this failure. As an observer of U.S.-Soviet negotiations, he had watched the attempts to sell U.S. economic policy fail to impress the Soviets.[29]

This failure preceded the first Asian war of containment, the Korean War. The limited victory that followed proved to internationalists the worth of limiting that war and fighting it collectively (concepts that internationalists would later hope to see vindicated again in the Vietnam struggle). Of even greater importance, once negotiations with the Soviets failed and war followed, was the postwar creation of an economic unit of productivity in the truncated south of Korea, an economic "miracle" of no minor means.[30] This later caused internationalists to hope that South Vietnam could duplicate the South Korean economic success. Though the Korean economy did not commence its rapid and uneven growth until the 1960's, its founders had built the base for this growth in the 1950's. What Tories hoped to accomplish in South Vietnam was to compress the time required to repeat there the South Korean success, even with a hot war to fight simultaneously.

They reasoned that productive, growing economies located along the global containment arc would create a more powerful counterforce to Leninist expansion than numerous expensive military units standing guard along the border. The positive image of the Korean model for Vietnam should not be overlooked. On a small scale Korea tested the concepts of internationalism—collective security seemed to work, the war had limited goals, and after the war political stability in South Korea led to the successful economic transformation of the lower half of that Asian peninsula. But before the Truman internationalists could commence the economic transformation of much of the globe, it was necessary to complete economic containment of the Soviet Union. As their Korean negotiation with the USSR unraveled, the other end of the containment arc became snared in the Berlin crisis. The Soviet blockade of that city represented a type of economic containment in reverse. The idea of an interconnected containment arc existed in the imaginations not only of American internationalists and their foreign allies but also of their opponents on the other side of the arc. And clashes along its perimeter seemed to both camps to be connected to the global Lockean-Leninist struggle. Ho Chi Minh noted this adversarial arc, giving the internationalists a reverse picture of who played the positive role: "Lenin's popularity and doctrine are closely linked to all the successes of the camp of peace and democracy which stretches from the Elbe River to the Pacific Ocean, and from the arctic poles to the tropics."[31] Reversing the American Lockeans, this Vietnamese Leninist envisioned his camp as being crucial to containing American-led attempts at penetration, one of the deepest being West Berlin.

With occupied Berlin giving three non-Leninist states a deep point of penetration within the Leninist empire, Stalin reacted in an area where he was strong. To counter his attempts to strangle the Western penetrators economically, certain influential Americans suggested economic countermeasures to Truman. General Lucius Clay called for "enactment of stringent regulations which would make Soviet use of ocean canals, bunkering facilities, and other facilities, under our and British control, difficult if not impossible."[32] The New York World Telegram on November 11, 1948, echoed this classified Clay report in an article by General William J. Donovan titled "General Donovan Outlines Global Plan to Halt Russians Without Shooting." Donovan proposed closing the Kiel, Panama, and Suez Canals and the Dardanelles to the Soviets while waging economic warfare by stopping the "100,000 tons of crude rubber going to Russia every year from Singapore by way of Holland."[33] As the director of America's first intelligence agency, the OSS, Donovan was a person whose opinions mattered. These recommendations for economic sanctions, coming from official and unofficial sources, though not adopted, illustrate the willingness of key internationalists to suggest fairly extreme measures to effect economic containment. Understandably therefore, the measures that did become policy, while compromises compared to the harsher recommendations, in themselves were fairly rigid.

How rigid? No loan for the Soviets, but Britain received one; no cancellation for the Soviets of their lend-lease bill, but other allies found Washington more flexible; no reparation for the Soviets from the Western zones of Germany, but France helped itself in its zone.[34] Each of these denials has to be qualified. First, regarding loans: The Soviets refused any conditions that might go with loans and even refused an unconditional Swedish offer of a loan engineered by Gunnar Myrdal. Second, regarding lend-lease: The Soviet bill amounted to $11 billion, and, as with all the Allies, most of the lend-lease bill was forgiven. The complete Soviet bill came in five parts: items consumed, which were the bulk and were forgiven; items in the pipeline when hostilities ended, which were debated; civilian capital stock, which was acknowledged by the Soviets as a debt as late as the time they negotiated with Nixon for a return to a most-favored-nation status; items sunk by Germans, which were not billed; and small naval vessels, which the Soviets returned. Third, regarding reparations:

In the area of reparations from Germany, the Soviets took plenty— legitimately and illegitimately, before, during, and after VE-Day.

All this occurred with Truman officials aware—because of the reporting from the U.S. embassy in Moscow—that the Soviet Union in 1947 was "undergoing serious economic difficulties."[35] Whether these economic difficulties would remain a problem into 1948, with the internationalists guessing that they could use them in motivating Soviet leaders toward compromises, was the question behind a *New York Times* article early in 1948, "Economic Needs of Soviets Regarded as Its Motivation." But both Truman's advisers and the *Times*'s editors guessed wrong.[36]

Not that the Soviets were not needy; they were. But a man ruled them, a man that U.S. Ambassador Charles Bohlen ranked "high on the list of the world's monsters." Ruling by ironfisted terror, Joseph Stalin squeezed the required finances for recovery from his empire, both Soviet and Eastern European, thereby avoiding compromises with his Lockean adversary.[37] But without these compromises, paricularly in the economic sphere, the United States contained the USSR economically while the USSR excluded the U.S. economically.

Clifford as Economic Theorist

That arrangement came to suit the early internationalists. Because it took time to consolidate their various 1947 victories, such as the passage of the National Security Act, economic containment sealed one aspect of Soviet-American relations.

Clark Clifford, the man who moderated much of the postwar national security debate, played a critical role in both organizational and bureaucratic politics. Clifford was arguably more than a Special Counselor, or legal adviser, to the President. Before the creation of the position of National Security Adviser, Clifford performed the functions later assigned to that position. Even after retiring from government to private practice, he remained available to later Presidents for advice and, in a crisis, for active service. In fact, over a decade after his service under Truman terminated, a crisis at the time of the 1968 Tet battles brought him from private life to replace Robert McNamara as Secretary of Defense, a post in which he served unhappily.

Long before being recalled by Johnson, Clifford made it his business to learn everything he could about the Soviet Union in order to keep his first presidential boss, Truman, informed. Eclectically he pursued the most remote pieces of evidence.[38] And his legal training soon clashed with George Kennan's diplomatic training. Dean Acheson often had to be the referee. For example, upon reading Truman's draft message to Congress requesting assistance for Greece, Kennan "thought it too strong" while Clifford "thought it too weak." Acheson used the prestige of General Marshall, who was in Moscow at the time, to find a suitable compromise. In this instance, it was Clifford who withdrew his objections.[39]

Clifford listened to all arguments; also he questioned each piece of evidence. Lacking George Kennan's years of service in Soviet-U.S. relations, Clifford became an autodidact. If Kennan, through his "Sources of Soviet Conduct," holds first place as the architect of political containment, and if Paul Nitze, through his work on NSC-68, is the leading architect of military containment, then Clifford's memorandum "American Military Firmness Versus Soviet Aggression," gives him first place as the architect of economic containment.[40] This does not mean that any of the three, in stressing particular aspects of containment, failed to mention the triad of containment choices—political, military, and economic. In other words, Clifford, like Kennan and Nitze, envisioned a U.S. policy that would tap all of America's strengths while avoiding her weaknesses.

Clifford's memorandum reads like a legal brief. He addresses points in an orderly fashion, raising first those that he would dismiss. Having eliminated certain arguments, he concludes his brief with a short series of recommendations: "Providing military support in case of attack is a last resort; a more effective barrier to communism is strong economic support."[41] But erecting economic barriers against the Soviets did not satisfy Clifford; it meant possessing only a negative policy, a policy of denial. If an economic approach to the Lockean-Leninist competition had any hope of gaining congressional and popular support, it must be two-tiered, comprising a positive as well as a negative thrust. Holding the Soviets behind an arc of economic isolation became the negative task; economic aid to those states on the non-Soviet side of the arc fulfilled the positive requirement: "Trade agreements, loans, and technical missions strengthen our ties with friendly nations and are effective demonstrations that capitalism is at least the equal of communism." On this point Clifford repeated himself for emphasis: "The United States can do much to ensure that economic opportunities, personal freedom and social equality are made possible in countries outside the Soviet sphere by generous financial assistance." He went further by reminding Truman that "our policy on reparations should be directed toward strengthening the areas we are endeavoring to keep outside the Soviet sphere" and that U.S. "efforts to break down trade barriers, open up rivers and international waterways, and bring economic unification of countries, now divided by occupation armies, are also directed toward the reestablishment of vigorous and healthy noncommunist economies."[42]

Clifford believed that the measures taken had already brought beneficial results. He told Truman that "the Soviet Union recognizes the effectiveness of American economic assistance to small nations and de-
nounces it bitterly by constant propaganda." As early as 1946, Clifford,
positive of the benefits to the United States, proposed making it possible
for the Soviet Government to obtain U.S. economic aid and trade.[43] It
pleased him to see that the first major positive economic program, the
Marshall Plan, offered participation in the American largesse to the East
Europeans and Soviets. Later Johnson would offer a similar economic
deal to the Hanoi leadership, only to receive the same negative reaction
that had greeted Harry Truman twenty years earlier.

Vandenberg as Economic Legislator

If Clifford held first place among Truman's White House staff in the
coordination of foreign economic policies, his counterpart in the legislature was Republican Senator Arthur H. Vandenberg, of Michigan,
Chairman of the Foreign Relations Committee. Vandenberg, more than
any other individual, sold the Congress on the positive program inside
the two-tiered economic containment strategy. He had not always been
so zealous; to the contrary, convincing Vandenberg that something positive could result from foreign aid had meant overriding a lifetime antipathy. But once convinced, he made a formidable ally. A late convert to
internationalism, Vandenberg, like most converts, worked fanatically in
his conversion of others.

Vandenberg's conversion came about over a short, nine-month period.
Between the time James Reston wrote a *New York Times* article about a $20
billion, four-year European recovery plan—an article that shocked the
Senator into telephoning Reston to tell him he was out of his senses, for
"no administration would dare to come to the Senate with a proposal like
that"—and March 1, 1948, when Vandenberg rose in the Senate to open
debate on just such a plan, the conversion had taken place. Vandenberg's
conversion took place in the chambers in which he conducted hearings
on the proposed economic legislation.[44]

Vandenberg's speech on the floor of the U.S. Senate caused a sensation. To packed galleries and with House members lining the Senate
walls, his 1-hour-and-20-minute, 9,000-word address, which had been rewritten seven times by the Senator, appeared as Vandenberg's baptism
into his new faith of internationalism. The convert insisted on a pragmatic catechism: "In the name of intelligent American self-interest it [the
legislation] envisions a mighty undertaking worthy of our faith." What

type of an undertaking? "It is an economic act—but economics usually control national survivals these days." What were its goals? It "seeks peace and stability for free men in a free world" but "it seeks them by economic rather than by military means." This search could "mean as much to us as it does to them" by fighting "economic chaos which would precipitate far-flung disintegration."[45] By this speech and the energy he invested in defending his new faith, Vendenberg succeeded in obtaining the bill's passage, even against tactical attacks by the man many members called Mr. Republican, Senator Robert Taft. Helping fend off Taft became the privilege of young Senator Henry Cabot Lodge, later Ambassador in Saigon for both Kennedy and Johnson.[46]

Truman and Eisenhower as Economic Executives

Once Republicans relented and accepted aid as a weapon in the self-interest of Americans, a change in viewpoint that Vandenberg started and Dwight Eisenhower completed, that two tiers of economic containment were needed became a bipartisan assumption about economic competition with Leninism. While holding the Soviets at bay internationalists hoped to reorder global economies. Eisenhower's role in the consolidation phase of American internationalism cannot be overstressed; his fundamental achievement in foreign affairs rests on his incorporation of internationalism into the mainstream of the Republican party.[47] While many postwar Democrats measured their post–Franklin Roosevelt candidates against that war chief's giant reflection, Republicans measured their post–Dwight Eisenhower candidates against that chief warrior's great aspect. And both FDR and Ike had understood the value of economic incentives, at home and abroad.[48]

In this economic setting one assumption won acceptance even though no evidence existed to support it. The assumptions behind aid to European nations and Japan rested on the calculated risk that, since the investment in human capital had already occurred in those states, Lockean reordering required only reconstruction of the physical plants. Since the populations inhabiting these two geographic areas possessed sophisticated political cultures that previously had struggled with the upheavals of industrial society, internationalists assumed that the resumption of postwar politics in the regions meant Lockean politics. The argument that an updated version of a type of Lockean politics would continue in Britain and France once their postwar economies again functioned persuaded internationalists. Western Germany and Japan, former enemy states with less experience under Lockean assumptions, initially appeared problematic. But the success with these two states caused both wings of American internationalism to assume that they could also inculcate such Lockean changes beyond Western Europe and Japan.

Global assumptions of this sort rested on weak foundations. Economic assistance might entrench old-fashioned despots, autocrats, or tyrants, changing them into modern totalitarians rather than Lockean reformers. Aid might finance an elite of ruthless absentee landlords and make them ravenous modern exploiters. An assisted polity might enter the modern arena by adopting mass politics, a politics in which charismatic figures of either the radical left or the radical right might replace traditional tyranny with modern megalomania.[49]

Not recognizing the possible negative implications of their global vision, internationalists pressured Truman to expand his initially limited view of regional assistance into a program of global aid. Truman succumbed to their pleas. In his inaugural address of 1949 he covered four points, the last of which fulfilled the global aspirations of internationalists, especially those of a maximalist inclination within Tory ranks: "Fourth, we must embark on a bold new program for making the benefits of our scientific advances and industrial progress available for the improvement and growth of underdeveloped areas . . . by making available to peace-loving peoples the benefits of our store of technical knowledge in order to help them realize their aspirations for a better life." How would internationalists accomplish this? By the means best understood to Americans: "We should foster capital investment in areas needing development." Thus was born the United States Technical Assistance Program.[50]

The United States Technical Assistance Program had undergone earlier private testing in America. Previous foreign assistance was an expression of American philanthropy, a generous giving to others. Historically, both philanthropy and technical assistance abroad had originated mainly in the private sector. In fact, commencing in 1813 with a Baptist mission in Burma, American intervention in Asia came about through evangelical churches and their schools. But after World War II Americans saw federal agencies overwhelming their private efforts, replacing it with a vast public mission designed to bolster a key principle of the national security state.[51] That the United States could go beyond assisting industrial peoples was not the flaw in their plan; the mistake was to assume that those aided, including the nonindustrial, would somehow undergo a metamorphic change politically, resulting in their final development as Lockean citizens. Historically, results of the church missions in Asia had not been promising, and still were not even in 1947. Evidence indicated that many earlier Asian recipients of private church assistance had failed to become Christians. Why then should modern Asian recipients of public agency assistance become Lockeans, regardless of the economic sermons preached?

Nevertheless, Truman's administration bequeathed this untested but accepted assumption to Eisenhower's, where it had converts. Eisenhower basically made the seemingly temporary Truman revolution permanent. With Ike's support, economic aid as a Lockean weapon triumphed. He, like Truman before him, had to fight. He, like the man from Independence, won some battles and lost others. In his battles Eisenhower gave interviews to the League of Women Voters, as well as writing letters to such influential private citizens as Charles Percy, of Chicago.[52] The programs, although painful for some Republicans, became a permanent feature of internationalism American-style.

The popular Ike went as far as granting aid to independent Leninists, such as Yugoslavia's Josip Tito. As early as 1953 Ike took command of an American counteroffensive to what Walt Rostow calls the 1953 Soviet economic offensive, which was a Soviet attempt to use aid as a weapon against the United States in the Third World. In 1954 Eisenhower signed legislation known as Public Law 480, by which internationalists made available to developing countries surplus food and fiber by sale, loan, or grant. In 1957 he supported a program of long-term "soft" loans, assistance repayable in local currencies. When critics in his own party insisted that he drop foreign aid and rely on trade only, he rejoined that he would have both—trade and aid allowed Eisenhower to grant opposing camps partial victories.[53]

Determined to build bureaucratic institutions from these victories, Eisenhower in 1954 created the Council on Foreign Economic Policy. He appointed former Budget Director Joseph Dodge as the chairman. Later, Clarence Randall replaced him and remained at that job until 1961, at which time Kennedy abolished this economic council and placed its tasks within the National Security Council—winner in the 1960's of the turf battle over who would control foreign economic policy. But before Kennedy did this, Dodge and Randall served with what Eisenhower called "selected Cabinet officers and the heads of other appropriate agencies." Eisenhower instructed this group "thereafter [to] coordinate continuously" our foreign economic policy. Later, when his foreign economic programs appeared to falter in 1957, Eisenhower sent Congress a special message, on the same day that he appeared on national television telling Americans how much they needed "mutual security programs in waging the peace." The audience heard their President warn that on the "economic front" of foreign affairs and mutual security, "the perils can be just as great as in the military arena."[54] By that time Eisenhower had eliminated the phrase "foreign aid," replacing it with "mutual security." To many of his party stalwarts, foreign aid translated as the Democratic dole for aliens. To block their attacks, Eisenhower always stressed the mutual self-interest in assistance, in which the United States received by giving.

Assistance to other nations covered only part of what was, by the end of Eisenhower's eight years as chief supervisor of the covenant with power, an economic success for the Lockeans. They had succeeded; a type of embedded liberalism dominated global economics. Lockeans influenced the new international regimes in ways that satisfied them. Following the conference at Bretton Woods, New Hampshire, in 1944, global traders accepted the U.S. dollar as the world's currency, something as good as gold, $32 to an ounce. International regimes grew around the dollar—a monetary regime in the International Monetary Fund (IMF), a trading regime in the General Agreement on Tariffs and Trade (GATT), etc. Any one regime nested with ease within other regimes, each clustering a certain number of issues within its purview. These new economic regimes were made up of "sets of implicit or explicit principles, norms, rules and decision-making procedures around which actors' expectations converge in a given area of international relations." These principles, norms, and rules were Lockean in spirit, and therefore made the dollar a weapon as well as a currency.[55] If need be, to fight a Lockean war the dollar could be inflated, which move would force all global holders of dollars to help pay for the combat. But Eisenhower did not inflate; he could leave that to Johnson. Instead, Ike chose the less risky road: he gave only moderate amounts of economic assistance.

In Eisenhower's presidency aid to the South Vietnamese commenced; it flowed directly to their Saigon government instead of to the previous French colonial apparatus. Also, by early 1954 Eisenhower had to face inquiries from the press concerning the possibility of his dispatching more than economic aid to Vietnam, perhaps even U.S. combat troops. He shot back, "We provided technical assistance, we provided money, we provided equipment," and he made it clear that this completed the list of what he would and had provided.[56] But the press corps persisted. Reasoning that journalistic frontal attacks would not dislodge the old General, reporters skirmished around his flanks to see if that would unnerve him. They began their flank attacks by quoting the powerful Democrat who ruled over the U.S. Senate—Lyndon Baines Johnson.

And as early as 1954 LBJ had played politics with Vietnam, enmeshing international politics with domestic politics, even Texas politics. In one case that surfaced at two different Eisenhower press conferences, the President was forced to discuss the imminent closing of a local Texas tin smelter. To Eisenhower's dismay the ambitious Senate Majority Leader had evoked national security as a reason why this Texas tin smelter should not close—somehow a possible loss of Vietnam to the West would interfere with the availability of the tin resources of Southeast Asia, an eventuality against which domestic resources should be developed. Eisenhower patiently rejected this thesis and the Texas rescue mission. But Johnson and Texas politics aside, by 1957 Eisenhower faced more important issues than connecting Lone Star tin with Vietnam.

In Eisenhower's first term the French debacle in Indochina had raised the paranoia level of many internationalists, but by Eisenhower's second term a pro-American Saigon regime had reduced these levels. Starting on May 8, 1957, President Ngo Dinh Diem of South Vietnam paid a three-day state visit to Eisenhower. The official communiqué from the two leaders highlighted several subjects, key among them being agrarian land reform and long-range economic plans. On these plans Kennedy and Johnson would rest their hopes for a solution to their problem with Vietnam, one of many states to receive economic attention in the Lockean economic tug of war with the Leninists. In that sense, Vietnam did not present an aberration in American internationalism; it was the logical continuation of American economic national security policy from at least as far back as 1947. And Vietnam remained a minimalist issue. Ngo Dinh Diem and South Vietnam hardly appear in the papers of John Foster Dulles; and in two volumes of memoirs, *The White House Years*, Eisenhower mentions Ngo Dinh Diem once. Reportedly John Kennedy was amazed at Eisenhower's failure to mention South Vietnam. JFK told Walt Rostow, "Ike never briefed me about Vietnam." He should not have been surprised. Ike, unlike JFK and LBJ, considered Vietnam a minimum U.S. problem in a world of maximum U.S. concern. But priorities soon changed.[57]

The Invasion of the Market Mechanism in Vietnam

Although American internationalists commenced their global economic interventions in the middle of the twentieth century, outsiders had begun intervening in the Vietnamese economy in the middle of the nineteenth century, thereby creating the conditions for the revolutionary upheaval in Vietnamese society that U.S. interventionists inherited. Knowledge of those previous failures and successes is a precondition for understanding the economic transformation that both Kennedy and Johnson hoped would stabilize Vietnam.

The Vietnamese economic revolution and the forces it unleashed originated with the basic alienation of the land, that is, the introduction by the French of commercial agriculture and commercial mining, or agromineral extraction. This radical change in the manner in which Vietnamese used the land, making the land a commodity for commercial gain, took place in stages, starting with the French economic rationalization of their Indochinese empire in the last third of the nineteenth century. French and Vietnamese sources have recorded this economic transformation, in similar detail but with interpretations differing.[58]

Whatever the nationality of the scholar—American, French, Vietnamese—there exists general agreement that this economic rationalization created the conditions for revolt. Moreover, the upheaval that followed probably would have occurred regardless of whether a postwar global struggle between Lockean and Leninist antagonists had existed. Even without Ho Chi Minh or Ngo Dinh Diem, a radical change in Vietnamese society would have come about once any innovators replaced traditional subsistence agromineral extraction with its revolutionary commercial counterpart. The introduction of capitalism meant the incursion into the economic body of Vietnamese everyday life of a microbe as virulent as any force humans have created. In any challenge capitalism would outclass political nationalism, religious fundamentalism, or ideological secularism. But it also created more wealth faster than any other economic mechanism. To capture this powerful force, to ride this tiger of change, each of the contenders had to adapt to it and the profound disruptions it brought to Vietnamese life. Since the part played by French capitalism is critical to any understanding of the American economic role in the Vietnam of the 1960's, a summary follows.

The histories of five main agromineral products—rice, rubber, coal, tin, and zinc—capture the nature of French market penetration of the traditional Vietnamese economy. As a commercial product each of the five has a geographic center—the first two, both agricultural crops, dominated the Vietnamese south; the last three, all mineral extracts, dominated the Vietnamese north.

Rice as Politics

Rice is the great cereal grain of Asia. For Vietnamese it was their daily staple, a wet staff of life without which famine threatened. Among the many benefits to early Vietnamese of contact with Chinese culture, irrigated wet-rice cultivation ranks beside river-dike engineering and Confucianism.[59] Yet it meant something more. With rice as its cereal grain Vietnam became a hydraulic civilization. In short, these most energetic people began to concentrate their energy on moving and measuring, in addition to damming and diking, large amounts of water. The choice of rice itself meant something further, for when capitalist agriculture struck Vietnam's wet-rice traditions, rice proved to be, among the great cereal grains (such as wheat, barley, rye, corn, and oats), the most difficult to commercialize; thus changes in the traditional mode of cultivation—for example, the replacement of human labor by farm machinery—proved most difficult to rationalize as economies of scale.[60]

French commercial agriculture also attacked the basic cultural norm of Vietnamese hydraulic civilization, that norm being cooperation. Because a hydraulic civilization is a culture "that involves large-scale and government-managed works of irrigation and flood control," this type of civilization's "organizational key device [is] cooperation." Lenin and his European followers misunderstood societies organized as hydraulic civilizations, as did Locke's intellectual descendents, who were also hard-pressed to conceive of a modern version of such a society.[61] In fact, European-trained Leninists and Lockeans alike misunderstood the critical core value of hydraulic civilization, its cooperative base. Lockeans introduced the market mechanism's core value, competition, which attacked aspects of traditional civic cooperation. Leninists introduced the state mechanism's core value, collectivization, which also attacked the traditional aspects of civic cooperation as understood and defined in the daily life of peasant-dominated Vietnam. Cooperation, competition, collectivization—these defined in turn traditional Vietnam, Lockean Vietnam, and Leninist Vietnam. Two alien creeds fought one traditional creed; one alien creed won.

Before the triumph of collectivization, the French had introduced the market. In order to rationalize their colonial lands in economic terms, the French had to introduce into Vietnam the legal instruments of French capitalism. They began with the land itself, transforming its use through two interconnected devices, the land survey and the land register. In precolonial Vietnam, village families and the local council of notables decided issues of land use, especially communal rights on those public lands held in perpetuity for the use of the village's inhabitants. These communal lands tended to increase as a village aged, because the corporate village inherited land without heirs and also placed under a communal status a portion of all newly developed land. The emperor in Hué, moreover, depended on communal lands as an income base for assessing village taxes. To be effective the imperial tax lists, the *dia boa*, depended on the cooperation of the village notables acting as intermediaries. Villages paid taxes; their inhabitants served in the military and performed compulsory labor services—especially on dike-building. In return, the emperor was responsible for defense against foreign incursions; he also supervised the vast array of intervillage dams and canals, and authorized the conquests of the South, an expansion known as *Nam-tien*.[62]

Transforming these traditional customs into the modern practice of proprietary rights was a revolutionary change. Suddenly land could be bought, sold, rented, and used as collateral for loans. The French commenced their land upheaval in Cochinchina, where in 1863 they ordered replacement of all customary deeds and titles by French substitutes; by 1885 they had forced the same revolution in land-holding onto Annam and Tonkin.[63]

By the 1930's this French revolution in Asia had made its impact. Thus control over the *dia boa* passed to a colonial administration, the officials of said institution maintaining public records of land registration down as far as the district level. The old division between familial and communal lands (*cong dien*) disappeared; a colonial degree of 1903 permitted the alienation of communal lands as authorized by the French resident superior, and a decree of 1923 recognized the proprietary rights of anyone who had occupied communal lands for at least twenty years. By any other name this was confiscation. Being confiscation, it had a purpose; Vietnam-as-colony was to pay for itself. The colonial administration hoped that these payments would come from the land, said land's productivity furnishing the capitalist ingredient for commerce—large yields of rice. Added to rice would be the commercial harvest of latex from the rubber plantations. To obtain both rice and rubber in the abundance necessary meant a radical transformation of Vietnamese villages. Yet not all villages, or all regions, underwent the same degree of upheaval.

In Tonkin and Annam, as opposed to Cochinchina, strong traditional village organization partially blocked change; some villages in the first two regions successfully resisted the French encroachments, though all lost to one degree or another. By 1931 communal land constituted only 20 percent of the total cultivated surface in Tonkin, 26 percent in Annam, and a bare 2.5 percent in Cochinchina.[64] Confiscation had worked.

France experienced two different reactions to confiscation of communal lands, one foreign and one domestic. Like Vietnam—but unlike the United States, which became a state almost simultaneously with the capitalist revolution in agromineral extraction—France possessed its own version of peasant traditionalism. The French version took the form of feudal obligations. Changing these took centuries. The change began by "the progressive disappearance of collective obligations from regions where they had formerly been dominant, and the introduction of new techniques." In Vietnam the French colonial government introduced both forms of change, and succeeded there while the government in Paris was failing in its attempts to introduce similar changes in French agricultural customs. For example, in 1889 French peasant reaction to their government's attempt to abolish the collective grazing on meadows was immediate: they forced Paris to retract the edict and to reinstitute the ancient practice as a legal right.[65] With this success they postponed their own agricultural transformation. Of course, Vietnam's peasants had less power to preserve their patrimonial privileges than did their French counterparts.

Abroad as at home, communal land privileges required repayment in real terms—civil labor over a number of days. The change broke the linkage: no privileges, no repayment. But since empire required payment, the colonial government co-opted the role of emperor; with their new system came not only the privilege of competing in the French market but also the duty of working for it. Because French imperial administrators, like the Vietnamese emperor's mandarins before them, required pools of labor for civic tasks, in 1881 the French abolished the old imperial corvée by establishing a similar labor requirement but with a French name, *prestations*. These were labor dues owed by all Vietnamese under fifty-five, each to give five days of free labor for general public purposes. As this did not fulfill the labor requirements for all civic tasks, the corvée for local public purposes remained, and by 1897 it meant an added thirty days per peasant.

Concurrently with the codification of these land and labor decrees, French citizens and collaborating Vietnamese stampeded in a massive land grab. In one account, by 1930 French citizens had received 256,800 acres in Tonkin, 415,948 acres in Annam, and 1,498,055 acres in Cochinchina. These figures increased only slightly by the time the colonial regime collapsed. Before this collapse France commenced the transformation of Vietnamese society.[66] Americans came to know mainly this new, transformed Vietnam. Overwhelmed by French high culture, Americans saw France-in-Asia through France's lovely city plan for Saigon, the colorful waterfront the French built at Haiphong, and the French-owned cafés of Hanoi, all surrounded by an indigenous people scrambling to attend colonial lycées where, after reading Molière and Montesquieu, then Pascal and Proust, they would place their hopes on passing the *bac*, the French examination necessary for university acceptance.[67] In other words, the Americans did not know the Vietnam that existed before the French.

In fact, in the very name French Indochina, Americans emphasized France. Not that this was a mirage; Saigon, before the French transformed it into the Paris of the Orient, existed as several miles of straw huts strung closely together on the banks of a river, the Song Saigon. In like manner the great northern entrepôt that France created in Haiphong had existed as a native village with a market as late as 1874, located on the right bank of the Song Cau Cam. And the Hanoi of the 1930's reminded observers of Lyon or any number of French cities sprawled near riverine transport hubs.[68] Both the new cities and the new canals were built by French engineers and financed by French overseas capital.

French engineers made Cochinchina, mainly a region of marshlands before they arrived, into a waterborne civilization; and the new villages of the South, more open than their northern counterparts, were concentrated among these southern waterways.[69] In fact, digging global waterways engaged the French imagination, becoming their version of nineteenth-century high technology. Having laced their European lands with a web of waterways, they went on to triumph at Suez (but failed at Panama). Now with Indochina's great river systems beckoning—the northern Red and the southern Mekong—they dug with a vengeance. If Rome is known by its imperial legacy of roads, then France should be known by its big ditches. Neither the French language nor the French legal system ever had the same impact as French engineering, for this struck deepest at the inherited routines of Vietnamese agriculture, hence at the majority of Vietnamese.

And change that life they did. In Cochinchina alone the French expanded the area under rice cultivation from 1,289,340 ares to 5,434,000 acres. Rice exports from Saigon reflected this explosion; these exports rapidly climbed from 284,000 tons in 1880 to 1,548,000 tons in 1937. Rice-cultivated lands in that one region increased 421 percent; the rice exported from Saigon increased by 545 percent.[70]

As a footnote to this rice revolution, a second cereal grain—cultivated by the Vietnamese as a secondary food crop for several centuries—suddenly rose in this century to second place in their foreign trade. Many Americans, caught in the last decade of the Vietnamese economic upheaval, were surprised to find corn, in lieu of rice, in the famous crab soup of Saigon restaurants. Corn appeared in the export figures as well. From 1899 to 1903 corn exports averaged 170 tons. The average for the period from 1909 to 1913 rose to 88,000 tons; in 1932 it rose again to 298,000 tons. By 1937 it reached 575,000 tons. The great bulk of these corn exports passed through Saigon.[71] Rewarded by these cash crops, the French again altered the traditional Vietnamese relationship with the land. In the South they focused on new lands, particularly lands south of the Song Bassac. By the last years before World War II, the French had dug in that one area 4,000 kilometers of canals, as well as having reclaimed 4,940,000 acres of marshlands.[72]

In the North the French focused on established fields, particularly on increasing the productivity of land long cultivated. This required dike networks to canalize the more turbulent northern river systems, especially the giant Song Red. After the flood and famine of 1927 the French reworked the system. In fact, they built forty times the number of dykes built by the Vietnamese emperors. As a result, rice production increased by approximately 60 percent in this region. In 1933, before the rebuilt system was in place, the yield per hectare (2.47 acres) for one annual crop averaged 500 to 600 kilograms of rice. With French irrigation and drainage applied, two crops could be drawn from the same soil with an increase of between 1,800 and 2,000 kilograms per hectare. Great dykes guarded this two-crop land; one scholar described these Tonkinese dykes as "one of the greatest systems in the world."[73]

The French, of course, having created, had to maintain this system of dykes and canals for irrigation, transportation, and flood-control. Between 1921 and 1930 French engineers annually oversaw the dredging of an average of 7,233,000 cubic meters of soil. By 1930 the French had dredged 165,000,000 cubic meters of soil. Compare this to the Suez and Panama canals: the total estimates for their construction, enlargement, and maintenance by 1930 was 260,000,000 cubic meters for the former and 210,000,000 cubic meters for the latter.[74]

What did all this mean? Mainly that Vietnam, particularly, Cochinchina, became a profusely productive rice bowl. The rice harvest of the South so far exceeded indigenous requirements that it became the great Vietnamese export. Vietnam began to furnish part of Japan's critical food imports in addition to meeting a portion of China's huge nourishment needs.

The Chinese connections within Vietnam's rice commerce played a crucial role in placing these outsiders within the French-induced market system. Not only did China absorb 50 percent of Vietnam's rice exports, but also the Chinese community within Vietnam controlled almost all of this commerce. The Chinese came to dominate rice commerce through close family ties, making the Chinese outsiders the most powerful group within the Vietnamese merchant class. In other words, the market strengthened one class, the merchants, while weakening another class, the village notables. This had happened elsewhere in Asia, but in Vietnam it added outsiders, the Chinese and the French, who won in the market while many Vietnamese lost—and this market was their fatherland. Having taken to this market as if born to commerce, the Cholon-based Chinese owned the junks and barges for rice transport, held contacts within the villages, and loaned money to the rice farmers, who used their future crop as collateral.[75] Although these merchants gained power during the French period, they also had the flexibility to change politics when Ngo Dinh Diem replaced the European outsiders. For Ngo Dinh Diem the Chinese connection was an alliance of convenience; but, combined with his other problems, it blocked him from connecting himself to the destiny of the Vietnamese peasantry. Given their numbers, they were Vietnam.

But Vietnam-for-the-Vietnamese was not the rallying cry of the French; Vietnam-for-the-market was. With regard to rice production, despite the great difficulties in commercializing this grain, the market mechanism triumphed.

The Green Hell of Rubber

This story repeats itself for rubber, except for the fact that as a crop the French introduced it. More precisely, in 1897 a French naval pharmacist named Raoul dispatched 2,000 heveca rubber plants from Malaya to Vietnam. The recipients in Saigon planted them, and an industry grew from these experimental stations near Saigon.[76] Rubber prices fluctuated within the world market, in much the same manner as the prices of other export crops. Vietnam, being on the periphery of the world economy, had to accept the roller coaster effect of these fluctuations.

From a high of 82 cents a pound in 1913 the world rubber price fell precipitously to 16 cents in 1921. So steep a decline required the Banque de l'Indochine's intervention. This saved the plantations.[77] With regard to the world price, however, France could do little alone. But the British Colonial Office would accomplish much: Under the Stevenson Plan, the Malay States and Ceylon, together representing 60 percent of world rubber production, reduced harvests. As a result of this action and of growing world demand, the price quoted in New York for rubber rebounded to 73 cents a pound in 1925. The years from 1925 to 1929 were the heyday for French rubber profits. Between those years some successful Vietnamese plantations reported that their dividends exceeded 160 percent of the initial capital investment. With profits like these, new lands opened and capital rushed to fill the needs of the market. Land under cultivation for rubber expanded from 37,050 acres in 1925 to 222,856 acres in 1929, for a total investment of 700 million francs.[78]

The bullish market in rubber did not last, however; by 1932, with the world now in depression, rubber prices fell to 3 cents a pound. Again the powerful Banque de l'Indochine rushed to the rescue, convincing the leadership in Paris to subsidize rubber investments.[79] In the meantime the British moved again, this time in the London agreement of 1934, in which the British government joined with the French and Dutch governments to divvy up the international rubber market. These three European states controlled 99 percent of world rubber production. France scored in London; its quota, at 30,000 tons per year, exceeded by 100 percent its then-current production. In 1938 France renegotiated and won a 60,000-ton quota. Prices returned to normal and production reached the new quota by 1938. This meant that in 1930, 14,607 tons of Vietnamese rubber reached the market; by 1936, 41,314 tons (worth 244 million francs); and by 1938, 60,000 tons. By 1937 rubber again followed only rice and corn among Indochina's important contributions within the world economy.[80]

By these rubber arrangements, France recouped more than it invested. In 1940 its Indochina empire stood fourth in world rubber production—following Malaya, the Dutch East Indies, Ceylon. It was ahead of Thailand. Among the top nine, Indochina outproduced them all in the most critical area, tons per acre. Its rate stood at .22 tons per acre, while Thailand hovered at .13 tons per acre and even Malaya reached only .18 tons per acre. Apparently the use of grafted trees in lieu of the nongrafted variety accounted for this French success.[81] This success won global markets for French Indochina. As an example, in the year 1935 the plantation owners sold France 11,062 metric tons, the United States 9,166 metric tons, Japan 2,813 metric tons, Germany 1,717 metric tons, Italy 303 metric tons, and Czechoslovakia 61 metric tons.[82]

The rewards of this economic success fell into the hands of French colonialists, while the hardships of the system fell onto the backs of Vietnamese workers, traumatizing many. Unlike rice production, rubber production had not developed within traditional Vietnamese village life. It was foreign to village agriculture, a crop the French brought into Vietnam. Furthermore, the best location to grow it within Vietnam—the highly prized rubber lands called the *terres rouges*, in northwestern Cochinchina—lay outside the areas where most villages were and where new settlements might normally be established. But in much the same way that the red earth of Georgia became King Cotton's home, so the red earth of Cochinchina attracted the giant French five of Imperial Rubber— Michelin, the Société des Terres Rouges, the Société des Caôutchoucs de Padang, the Société des Plantations d'Avieng, and the Société Financière Française et Coloniale.[83] In one decade the force of the market had remade the face of the jungle.

Initially the French cleared an area of grey soil in three provinces near Saigon. When the planters moved toward the red soil lands, establishing their first plantation, the Suzannah, in 1905, they found no local Vietnamese workers. The non-Vietnamese people of the area, the Moi, refused the offer of backbreaking wage slavery. Hence the planters imported Tonkinese from the overpopulated North.[84]

At best, living conditions remained primitive. Workers were corralled into dormitory pens—crowded, dirty, steaming. Being located in a malaria-ridden area did not help. Failing to drain the plantation area, to install proper sanitation, to feed a proper diet, and to medicate the sick compounded the malaria threat. Often working an average of 11 1/2 hours a day, the worker lived in accommodations that were something between a prison compound and a slave quarter. Thousands died.

Death was often the penalty for the worker who tried to escape; by this means the executioners hoped to deter others who might tempt fate for freedom. Punishment for lesser crimes ranged from thrashing on the buttocks with a rod to beating on the head with a club. Women too received beatings, even when pregnant. Those who ordered those beatings knew that the trauma often caused the women to miscarry.[85] One need not question why the workers called their strange new locales, the plantations, *dia nguc tran gian*—hell on earth. As happened elsewhere in agromineral extraction, including France itself, the introductory period took a huge toll of labor; capital accumulated via worker productivity, often regardless of human cost.[86]

It would not be unfair to say that there were similarities in labor practice between the pre-revolutionary Indochinese South, particularly on the red earth plantations, and the antebellum American South. Slavery manifests itself in many forms other than chattel. To compare cotton plantation slaves with rubber plantation workers suggests that the system in Vietnam had a heavy impact on the Vietnamese families involved in the production of commercial latex. It did. For many decades planters transported only male workers, bringing them from the North to the southern plantations; hence no family life existed. But eventually the men brought women. Both women and their children, quickly absorbed into the labor force, worked at the same tasks as the men. In fact, children helped their mothers until their tenth birthday, at which time the planters assigned the children their own quotas.

By 1946 women made up 60 percent of those bound over to rubber production, although as late as 1944 they had made up only 10 percent. One explanation for this appears to lie in the desertion rate of Vietnamese men in 1946, for here the Viet Minh found a willing group of primitive rebels awaiting any Vietnamese rebellion. The plantations also created a few Leninists for the North, revolutionaries such as Tran Tu Binh. The rubber plantations garnered a new Vietnamese name in this period: *lo sat sinh*, or slaughterhouses.[87]

Death Valley Minerals

The application of the market mechanism to mineral extraction did not reverse the killing toll on labor. Productivity increased, and forced labor bore the costs. Whether in the coal mines of Hon Gay in Tonkin or in the tin mines of Nam Patene in lower Laos, the workforce consisted

mainly of Tonkinese. For the distant mines of Laos, the Tonkinese working there coined a name, "death valley." Tonkinese in their native coal
region registered a similar despair, calling their mines "hell."

Almost 90 percent of Indochina's mineral extraction occurred in Tonkin.[88] The Vietnamese and Chinese had extracted minerals from Tonkin
before the French came, but were limited by their methods of extraction,
the modest need for the product, and the cost of transportation. The Vietnamese kings received tax revenues from 123 mines. After the French
conquest things changed. Formed in 1884 the Commission des Mines
offered French mining companies large tracts of mineral lands in Tonkin.
In 1902 the Service des Mines commenced surveys to discover new deposits of minerals. In coal alone production astonished investors, reaching 509,000 metric tons by 1913. This expansion continued; in 1923 production topped 1,057,000 metric tons, and by 1938 it reached 2,355,000
metric tons. Vietnamese coal came in both categories, bituminous and anthracite. Large French concessionary companies such as the Société Française des Charbonnages du Tonkin and the Société Française Charbonnages du Dong-Trieu operated in these rich coal fields.[89]

The major coal basin formed an arc from the bays at Fai Tsin Long and
Along to the Song Da Bach, a length of 150 kilometers and a maximum
width of 12 kilometers. Depth ranged from 5 to 80 meters. The Service
des Mines suggested there was an almost inexhaustible supply. Open-pit
mining meant ready access, and the river, road, and train systems meant
easy transport. Exports zoomed. If Cochinchina became a rice bowl,
Tonkin became a coal bowl. Tonkin, by the mid-1920's, was East Asia's
largest exporter of coal; Japan and China were its biggest customers.
While mining broke backs, mainly Tonkinese backs, the French began the
introduction of machines, thereby again increasing productivity.[90]

Early tin mines were concentrated in or near the Tonkinese Pia Quac
mountain range; early zinc mines, in the limestone deposits of northern
Tonkin. Production of both increased under the French, who also began
mechanization of these mines. By 1938–39 Vietnam and Laos ranked
sixth as global exporters of tin ore. In that same year Tonkin by itself
ranked eleventh among global exporters of refined zinc.[91]

A Market Summary

These five agromineral extracts constituted only a segment of the varied Vietnamese economy. Others included the French-built rail and road
systems; the cottage industry of lace-making for export to France; textile
and forest products for internal and external markets; a small chemical

industry; an electric power industry; and a building-materials industry. The French even roasted coffee beans from their own Vietnamese-grown crops. With all this activity came trade unions and strikes, such as the Nam Dinh cotton-weaver strike of 1924.[92]

In other words, before the Americans came to intervene in this developing market economy, three major features distinguished it. First, the Vietnamese economy remained agriculturally based, but this was not subsistence agriculture as before the French. Instead, commercial agriculture, reflected mainly in rice, dominated policy in the agricultural area. Rubber planters employed no more than 40,000 Vietnamese at any given time. Second, the slice of the Vietnamese economy dedicated to mineral production or industry remained small. The number of Vietnamese employed in mining at any given time was no higher than 45,000. All other industries absorbed no more than 86,000.[93] These figures represent the estimates before World War II. Up to that point there still existed a fatherland, though changed by the introduction of alien market forces. But before the full impact of the changes could be felt, war began. For Vietnamese history the Japanese-Allied conflict of 1941–45 marked only the first segment of their warring-states period. Coming at mid-century, the Vietnamese war contained four segments: the Japanese invasion, the French return, the American intervention, and the battles for control after the United States departed. Since France went to war in Europe in 1939, the year 1938 was the last prewar year for which the French kept detailed statistics on the Vietnamese economy. Given that few major improvements occurred after 1938, that year's data show the major changes the market had made in the lives of the Vietnamese people. With adjustments, the 1938 statistics reflect the nature of the economic infrastructure—war-battered, slightly aged, partially repaired—that the two Tory internationalist Presidents inherited in the 1960's.

The third major feature that distinguished the Vietnamese economy, its concentration into larger units, led to a shrinkage in the overall number of entrepreneurs striving, failing, and rebuilding their businesses. For example, by 1930, two companies monopolized anthracite coal, the Société Française des Charbonnages du Tonkin, with 72 percent, and the Société Française des Charbonnages du Dong-Trieu, with 25 percent. In rubber production there existed 1,007 separate plantations in the early 1930's, but by the last years of that decade the large plantations, those above 200 hectares—approximately 154 plantations—produced all the latex.[94] But the real devastation came through concentration in paddy land, the rice-producing base of this new market economy. Suddenly peasants found themselves placed in one of several new subgroups.

These groups included, in order of descent, tenant farmers (*nguoi linh mau ruong*), sharecroppers (*ta dien*), and wage laborers (*tho gat cong*).[95] While some Vietnamese continued to own their own rice lands, more and more did not. As consolidation reduced the number of small farms, mines, and industries, especially the few Vietnamese ones, a group vital to the success of any U.S. Lockean intervention grew smaller and less influential in the politics of Saigon and the economy of South Vietnam.

CHAPTER EIGHT

The Good Earth:
The Wealth of This Nation

JOHN F. KENNEDY INHERITED both the American setting for global economic intervention (dating from Harry Truman through Dwight Eisenhower) and the Vietnamese setting of economic change (dating from the colonial French administration through Ngo Dinh Diem). He had to decide what to do with this inheritance. As an American internationalist, Kennedy meant to intervene. Of Tory persuasion, he wanted to use mainly economic means to obtain results abroad. His speeches during the 1960 presidential campaign make this clear. For Kennedy, aid was an economic weapon, wielded in the Cold War to punish those favoring the Leninist superpower and to reward those favoring the Lockean superpower.

Interestingly, Kennedy thought like a banker; his favored aid vehicle remained the Development Loan Fund. In 1960 he explained this preference in a question-and-answer period following a speech in Portland, Oregon. Kennedy said that he approved of the fund's granting of "loans at low rates of interest for long periods of time to assist these countries which are underdeveloped so that they [can] secure the basic means of production"; in this way, "they can begin to build their economies."[1]

After his election Kennedy appointed George W. Ball as Undersecretary of State for Economic Affairs, the assignment once held by Acheson and Clayton. Ball was amazed by the energy of Kennedy's other economic advisers. He discovered that "the young movers and shakers of the Kennedy Administration . . . had, if anything, a surfeit of theories regarding the economic development of the Third World." As foreign economic surrogate for Kennedy, Ball had to play midwife at the birth of Kennedy's superagency, the U.S. Agency for International Development (AID), the bureaucratic behemoth destined to coordinate and direct his economic competitions with the Leninists. Working together with his Undersecretary, the President, assisted by an informal group of new appointees, prepared the Presidential Message to Congress of March 22, 1961. At the un-veiling of his aid plan, Kennedy employed a favorite device—a challenge for the decade. For Kennedy, if in a decade the United States could place a human on the moon, then in a decade Americans might develop the non-Leninist globe. At least Kennedy's rhetoric implied this to the Con-gress: "For we are launching a Decade of Development on which will depend, substantially, the kind of world in which we and our children shall live."[2]

Building an Economic Agency for Intervention

One week following this challenge to the Congress and citizenry, Kennedy established a Task Force on Economic Assistance, giving it a broad charter. Membership included George Gant, of the Ford Foun-dation; Theodore Tannenweld, Jr., formerly the government's Assistant Director for Mutual Security; and Professor Max Millikan, of the Massa-chusetts Institute of Technology—to name but a few. Five months later, the Congress challenged back. Approving legislation that established Kennedy's superagency, AID, the Congress dared Camelot to conquer global underdevelopment. But before the new agency could begin the conquest, it had to swallow several old agencies and programs—the International Cooperation Administration, the Department Loan Fund, and others. In order to accomplish these tasks the administrator of AID was given the rank of Undersecretary of State, reporting directly to the State Department.

Once Kennedy had the mission, he had to locate the right person for the task. As he had done before, he employed his brother to screen candi-dates. In this manner JFK found his man, Fowler Hamilton, a Democrat who understood Kennedy's affinity for moderate Republicans and busi-ness leaders. Hamilton consulted with Thomas Watson, of IBM; through that consultation Hamilton chose as his deputy a Republican executive at Proctor and Gamble, Walter Lingle, Jr. Watson also helped Hamilton re-cruit other businessmen as AID Mission Directors abroad. Hamilton ob-tained the services of Ed Hutchinson, of RCA, "to run Africa." Repeating that success, Hamilton convinced William Gaud "to run the Near East and South Asia regions." He had known Gaud during World War II, having met him in Kunming, China, where Gaud dispatched American lend-lease to Chaing Kai-shek.[3]

Hamilton filled his new agency with "old hands," especially veterans from the previous lend-lease programs in China. Nor did Watson suggest all the key players; Ed Reischauer, Kennedy's Ambassador in Japan, rec-ommended Seymour Janow. He had worked for Hamilton "at the Board of Economic Warfare," and Hamilton had known Janow when he "was out in India and China with the Air Force." In that lend-lease setting, Janow held a position in Kunming with the U.S. Foreign Economic Administration. At the time Janow was recruited for AID, he owned an engineering firm in Asia. After some prodding, Janow accepted the assignment of running the Far Eastern side of AID.

Soon after Hamilton made these appointments, one social scientist interviewed fifty-four AID officials. He identified the tension that existed between the ideal mission as stated in the *AID Program Guidance Manual*—the development "of a community of free nations cooperating on matters of mutual concern, basing their political systems on consent and progressing in economic welfare and social justice"—and the AID officials' view of their daily mission—support for anticommunist, pro-American political stability. Tension did not exist in all areas; but in some, like Vietnam, it quickly exacerbated the task of economic intervention, both at local and national levels. Fortunately, however, Hamilton had completed assembling his team before these problems arose.[4]

With his key personnel in place, Fowler Hamilton could respond to direct assignments from Kennedy—who sent Hamilton right off to Vietnam in the wake of Maxwell Taylor and Walt Rostow's inspection trip in late October 1961. In Saigon, Hamilton met Ngo Dinh Diem, the recipient of a new kind of lend-lease. The Saigon leader reminisced with his visitor about Eisenhower's positive response to the 1954 Saigon cable requesting aid—this positive response, according to Diem, was "a miracle" that had saved the Ngo family. Hamilton found this vigorous Vietnamese sincere in his appreciation.[5]

On his return to Washington, Hamilton discovered that an unexpected sense of crisis prevailed about what the assistance program would include. Up to October 1961, assistance to Vietnam had consisted mainly of military items. This did not mean that Hamilton's staff had slighted the AID effort to Saigon's civilian sector. Quite the contrary; however, AID officers in Saigon, when working with South Vietnam's civil problems, performed mainly agricultural extension work. This did not satisfy Kennedy; he ordered an extensive new program on a rush basis.

As Kennedy ordered, so Hamilton obeyed. His first act should have alerted internationalists to the dimensions of the impending disaster. In Hamilton's own words: "Thus, we diverted two shiploads of rice that were on their way to Calcutta and shoved them into Vietnam."[6] What had the large U.S. agricultural assistance program accomplished if the United States still had to furnish rice to Saigon? At one time shipping rice to Saigon would have ranked with carrying coals to Newcastle. But the situation had changed; in 1961 the rich rice bowl of South Vietnam gaped empty before it could fulfill all the demands placed on it. Studying rice production figures requires care; as elsewhere with cereal grain production, numerous reasons exist for bumper and bad harvests.

An excellent source for South Vietnamese rice data exists in the bi-annual supplements to the *Economic Bulletin* of the National Bank of Vietnam. According to these national bank reports, rice production varied for any comparative period. For example, production declined from 3.4 million tons in 1956–57 to 3.2 million tons in 1957–58, a difference of 200,000 tons. By 1959–60 the reverse had occurred; rice production increased to 5.3 million tons, compared to the 3.9 million tons of 1958–59. Several reasons existed for the increased yields—better insecticides, more irrigation, newer fertilizers.[7] These indicate how the large American agricultural program had assisted the Vietnamese. And of course weather always helped or hurt; in 1958–59 and again in 1959–60 it helped. But in 1961 and 1962 the weather became another enemy, along with the political enemy who had redoubled his efforts to capture that critical mass, the possible peasant rebel. In fact the authors of the bank report blame both: the bad weather in September and October 1960, and what they reported to be the worst security problem in several years.[8]

An appropriate motto for guerilla wars in rice-dominated peasant cultures might be, As goes the rice, so goes the war. In Vietnam the rice had started to go to the Viet Cong.[9] And for a reason. In developing an economic infrastructure the Ngo family had concentrated on the urban areas, building a light industrial base on top of what they had inherited from the French. In contrast, the Viet Cong concentrated on the rural areas, building a second economy that rivaled that of the Saigon government.

This is not to say that the Saigon leadership had no economic success. In fact it enjoyed a number of early urban successes. By 1961 textile production already had increased; the National Bank, which included jute products under textiles, reported an expansion in textile production of 35 percent. Electric energy production also increased, by 7 percent, as did commercial fishing, by 6 percent, along with gains in commercial fowl production—chicken up 53 percent, duck, 13 percent. Others remained stable, some decreased.[10] Clearly the Saigon leadership had put much effort into these sectors.

Exact data on Hanoi's success remain elusive, but in Long An province there was one good example. Here in 1960 lived approximately 350,000 Vietnamese who double-cropped rice in the soil of the rich Mekong Delta, a land approximately 2 feet above sea level. The annual rice harvests netted 260,000 tons, more than half of which were exported. Hanoi's surrogates imposed a program of Leninist-style land reform; they added a tax that could be paid in rice. Initially, until September 1963, their success went unnoticed by Americans. Then, two months prior to Kennedy's assassination, members of the JCS and NSC staffs began to debate the gravity of the Long An situation, though the JCS staffers made light of it.[11] But the story would not remain buried.

So serious became the issue of Long An province that Mike Forrestal, one of Lyndon Johnson's staff members on the NSC, wrote Johnson a memorandum (less than two weeks after Kennedy's assassination) in which he deplored the failure to pacify a province that stretched from the Cambodian border to the sea. Long An acted as the gateway from Saigon south to the rich rice lands of the Mekong, a gateway vital for reaching peasants concentrated in the great delta area. And already a rich province had begun perceptibly to change hands; as Saigon's influence declined, Viet Cong influence increased. At this difficult time the Americans merely watched.[12]

Although both sides made impressive gains, Hanoi's gains were among the central mass of the population while Saigon's gains took place along the periphery. One could argue that the Viet Cong infrastructure, later known to Americans as the VCI, depended more on their rice-tax collectors than on their soldiers. The rice tax and the information-intelligence functions formed the base of the Leninist party's southern apparatus. While the Saigon government, with its American advisers, could kill the soldiers of the apparatus, to eliminate the financial and intelligence-collecting element remained a fundamentally different problem. Moreover, not only did production-control figures for rice bode ill, but also the figures for rubber, another vital export crop, showed the continuing tendency toward the large concentrations that had figured prominently in the late colonial period. In 1961 small plantations continued to decline. In 1959 they had produced 9.7 tons of rubber; in 1960 the figure declined to 8.4 tons; and in 1961 small plantations produced only 8.3 tons. In comparison, large plantations (those above 500 hectares) produced 70.8 tons in 1961.[13] And these large plantations paid both a Saigon tax and a Viet Cong tax, hoping thereby to avoid the war.

The complex nature of the Vietnamese economic struggle evaded the Kennedy team. Reacting to daily gains and losses, they found it difficult to make substantive impacts. According to Frank Coffin, a man Kennedy had recommended to Hamilton for a major AID job, "The barometer of progress on these fronts fluctuated violently." Before joining AID, Coffin had served four years in Congress, with membership in the House Committee on Foreign Affairs. He recognized the limitations—both foreign and domestic, economic and political, bureaucratic and rational—for what AID might and might not accomplish. As a mimimalist, Coffin quoted Niebuhr to coworkers.[14] But Kennedy wanted quick results, a type of damn-the-torpedoes, full-speed-ahead approach. In 1956 Senator John Kennedy had been the sternest critic of crisis management in U.S. aid programs. What Kennedy wanted in 1956 was long-range, consistent aid plans. In that year the Senator criticized the national leadership suggesting that "Vietnam would in all likelihood be receiving more attention from our Congress and Administration, and greater assistance under our aid programs, if it were in imminent danger of Communist invasion or revolution."[15] In other words, the Vietnamese needed aid before a crisis occurred, not afterwards.

By 1961 President John Kennedy felt compelled to manage his national security policy, at least the Vietnamese portion, by becoming a crisis supervisor. What he never understood about U.S. policy in Vietnam was that it mistakenly emphasized the urban political-economic sector, which was peripheral to the national scene. Urban politics came first, followed by urban economics; U.S. field representatives simply found little time for rural problems—except for one. And that one, land reform, became their undoing. This is not to deny the importance of urban control; it simply did not outrank the central problem of rural loyalty, something on which the Hanoi leadership, even when facing its own struggles over urban versus rural precedence, never stopped concentrating.[16]

The Michigan State University projects represent an early yet typical example of this urban usurpation. Extending a research project at the Government Research Bureau of that university, a four-person team traveled to Vietnam in the fall of 1954. By the time the team began serious work, Ngo Dinh Diem (by then in power in Saigon) had retained Professor Wesley R. Fishel, a member of the team, as a consultant. On the basis of university recommendations, the Diem government negotiated two technical-assistance contracts in the spring of 1955—one with the East Lansing campus, the other with Eisenhower's Foreign Operations Administration—which were to last two years. The Saigon government renegotiated the contracts through 1962; therefore Kennedy's superagency inherited these projects.[17]

What did AID inherit? Two worthwhile projects, but both on the periphery. Both of them—one in public administration, the other in police administration—reflect the American penchant for orderly processes. Unfortunately, these are not guerrilla goals; guerrillas gather people, not paper. In a seventy-one-page report summarizing eight years of work by a team of 200 people, the authors cover counterinsurgency in one short paragraph.[18]

Nevertheless, at least one aspect of the police project held some direct application for countering insurgency, the key South Vietnamese problem. The project's director suggested helping South Vietnam organize a sûreté, or internal security service. His suggestion did not pass unnoticed. As early as 1961, Ambassador Fred Nolting cabled Dean Rusk to suggest that the Secretary support CIA Saigon in its plans to establish a "Special Branch" of the sûreté, a branch that was to penetrate the Communist party and to help "bolster government authority throughout [the] country."[19] The Saigon government indeed needed a good internal security service, for Hanoi had infiltrated it from top to bottom. Even General Paul Harkins's gardener had performed Viet Cong missions.[20] But gardeners came and went; peasant spies persisted.

The French had instituted a sûreté in Vietnam in 1875, but the French version had a bias for blocking anticolonial movements.[21] By 1956 South Vietnam needed a new internal security mandate in order to counteract Hanoi's efficient security apparatus. But Ngo Dinh Diem turned over his sûreté to his brother Ngo Dinh Nhu. Nhu used it to protect the Ngo family in their personal political feuds in the southern cities more than he did to compete with Hanoi for peasant loyalty. After Diem's murder, after the countryside took precedence over the city, and by the time an internal security organization had come into existence, it was too late. By then Johnson and the coup-infested Saigon generals had effectively lost the struggle—at the very time certain controversial programs, such as the CIA-directed Phoenix program, were having some success fighting the internal security war and the economy that supported the insurgents.[22]

Saigon leaders never imagined how extensively the United States planned to intervene in their economy. Slowly at first, but gathering force as each project spawned new ideas, the American economic intervention overwhelmed the Vietnamese. The Yankee public philanthropists proposed solutions to problems the Vietnamese did not know they had. Hurriedly, designs came and designs went. A "boom town" atmosphere grew in the large coastal cities of the South as they began to experience the full impact of American economic ingenuity. Again, the U.S. military became the conduit for much of this, especially large public works projects such as port and airport construction, most of it paid for with AID funds.[23] Therefore, AID intervention received the personal attention of Ngo Dinh Diem. When the Ngo brothers disliked specific American plans, they attacked them. The younger brother demanded that AID plans support the official Vietnamese plans—meaning those of his family. When the two plans differed, Nhu attacked via the press, often the French press.

Manipulating American aid in a manner that satisfied the political ends of the Ngo family called for skill and determination, two qualities Ngo Dinh Nhu possessed. As he manipulated these projects he and his presidential brother knew that the agricultural sector, not light or heavy industry, loomed as the critical battleground with Hanoi. Nevertheless, for both brothers, Saigon and urban politics in general took so much time and energy that little remained for the peasant-dominated countryside. The time the brothers did spare for the countryside often unfortunately was dedicated to big, showplace experiments. One such project, the strategic hamlets, for a time drained what little energy they were willing to apply to the rural problem.

Approved by presidential decree on February 3, 1962, the strategic hamlet program (*ap chien luoc*) represented Ngo Dinh Diem's flawed but promising method for upsetting his enemies' southern center of gravity. In this Asian adaptation of Carl von Clausewitz, Ngo Dinh Diem hoped to disconnect his masses from the dedicated Hanoi elite who had planned a mass revolutionary war in the South. Strategic hamlets were to be made physically defensible by the construction of a defense perimeter around each one. The inhabitants were to be trained and armed. Diem conceived of these strategic hamlets as intensified population control centers, safe islands in an ocean of insecurity. The South Vietnamese Army was to patrol that ocean, thus denying the Viet Cong contact with the peasants. Tories liked the plan, for it would offer the peasants physical security, which was, as a human right, the first priority for Tories. Previously the Ngo brothers had experimented with prototype strategic hamlets called "agrovilles." Finding that American enthusiasm knew no bounds when it came to the agrovilles—in 1961 Kennedy himself wrote to President Diem that agrovilles were important because "security requirements must, for the present, be given first priority"—the brothers agreed to an expanded program, especially since the Americans would pay.[24]

In implementing the strategic hamlet program Saigon's sense of speed for once matched and indeed overtook the furious pace set by the United States. Even Ambassador Lodge approved of this program. In response to a report that reached the White House in October 1961, about the deficiencies of Long An province's strategic hamlet program, Lodge, joined by General Krulak, an unlikely Washington ally in this instance, made a strong case for supporting the strategic hamlet program while insisting that all was well in Long An. The enthusiastic Krulak was able to reassure McGeorge Bundy that between January and September 1963, there had been a 300 percent growth in the number of Long An's strategic hamlets. Buildings, yes, but what of the peasants' security rights, their ability to live and to defend themselves in these hamlets? Even Britain's counterguerrilla hero, R. G. K. Thompson, always favorable to the basic plan, worried about the great speed with which Saigon implemented the program across the country. So did the Joint Chiefs of Staff, but the House of

Ngo was trying to catch up with the Leninists. Faults there were in abundance with the strategic hamlet program, but the Leninists nevertheless recognized the danger and took appropriate measures. Destruction of strategic hamlets became their first priority.[25] However, before this struggle reached a peak, the House of Ngo, forever torn between urban and rural problems, turned its attention from the rural and refocused on the ever troublesome urban base.

By accident, one of William Colby's anecdotes about Ngo Dinh Nhu, from the period when Colby and Nhu were expanding the agroville program into the strategic hamlet program, illuminates the competing urban and rural agendas. As the senior CIA representative in Vietnam, Colby possessed direct entrée to the Ngo family's chief intelligence official. Sitting in his Saigon office, Ngo Dinh Nhu talked constantly to Colby about the rural problem, in the end supporting Colby's idea of what both governments later labeled strategic hamlets. In 1960 Colby and his associates outlined an experiment. The small Montagnard community of Buon Enao, outside Bon Me Thuot, appeared ideas as a test locale, located as it was in a comparatively safe area.

Colby had deliberately designed a joint project, one that would weld together security issues with social and economic issues. On the security side he wanted the civilians at Buon Enao, once trained by Vietnamese and American Special Forces, to defend themselves, with the emphasis always on the Vietnamese side. The symbol for Americans was obvious— Vietnamese minutemen. The concept of inhabitants defending their homes appealed to both allies. Colby believed this feature of self-defense would spread like an ink spot, remaining always defensive but denying the enemy entrée to the peasants of Vietnam. Also, both allies hoped the plan would release the South Vietnamese army from the onerous chore of static village defense. The plan grew, and Colby had his minutemen, known as Citizen Irregular Defense Groups, or CIDG's in bureaucratic shorthand. But minutemen on defensive night patrol were only one plank in Colby's joint platform. The other involved AID projects. For example, at Buon Enao a technical assistance team conducted a sanitation survey, separating the water supply from sewage waste. They then dusted the log houses of this Rhode tribe of Montagnards with DDT. And besides giving the men training with American carbines, they taught the women first aid, something of use beyond its military application.[26]

Colby's anecdote concludes: "On one of the first trips he [Ngo Dinh Nhu] had ever made to the countryside—other than those to the hill palace of Dalat—he came to Buon Enao to see for himself and, as a result, approved the expansion of the program not only in the Highland area, but to a number of other villages along the coast and in the Delta as well."[27]

One could talk about the countryside or travel to it; the Ngo brothers talked, while their enemy traveled. For Nhu, a key presidential adviser, to have waited so late to percolate among the peasants—the trip Colby mentions took place in the autumn of 1960—resulted in a regime wedded to a peripheral arena, the urban setting. And in this setting the outsiders dominated—the French with their hold on the large rubber plantations, the Chinese with their hold on the rice trade, and the Americans with their hold on AID funding. In those days when one looked for the Vietnamese within their urban economy one could hardly find them; they scarcely existed in positions of influence. In the main, urban Vietnamese did the working, not the influencing. In opposition to this city climate of outsider control, an observer could find the Vietnamese in the rural economy. There they worked, and they influenced. At a minimum they controlled their little island communities within the sea of rice. But who had influence over the powerful village leaders within these island communities? Both the Hanoi and the Saigon leadership tried to persuade this local leadership to participate in larger causes. One succeeded, the other failed.

One reason for this has to do with luck, good and bad. Internationalists never ceased bragging about "their" success in rural Taiwan. Unfortunately the Ngos did not have in their own country the luck that Chiang Kai-shek found waiting for him in exile. Once the Nationalists retreated to the relative safety of the island of Taiwan, the Americans pressured them to redistribute the land that belonged either to the defeated Japanese or local Taiwanese, neither of whom could launch a guerrilla movement. To redistribute, the Nationalists reclaimed Japanese holdings and, under American pressure, gave government securities for the locally owned lands. With nowhere to go with Taipei securities, the local owners invested them, thereby becoming accidental entrepreneurs helping to fuel the economic miracle of modern Taiwan.[28] What Taiwan gained—a stable agricultural sector and a booming export sector—eluded unlucky South Vietnam.

Did the Ngo family remain indifferent to the countryside, allowing the strategic hamlet and other rural projects to fail? Had the Ngos authorized these programs only as sops for the Tory internationalists who waited impatiently to intervene in the backyard economy of Vietnam? The evidence does not support that charge. If anything, the Ngo family found itself tied to the urban arena for many reasons, some not even of their own making, one of which originated with the Whig internationalists who insisted on intervening in Saigon politics. This intervention—in the name of transplanting pluralist politics to alien places—kept the Ngos on a full-time schedule shoring up their regime. The politics of survival in

Saigon required complete dedication. Hanoi's leadership had settled that problem; Saigon leaders never did, in fact could not, because they had to court Whiggish Americans.

The Ngos stayed in their urban palace trying to manage their one patron and balance the two contradictory American goals of political modernization and economic modernization. Luck came to Ho Chi Minh; he managed two patrons, often with contradictory goals. But when Chinese goals opposed Russian ones, Hanoi's leadership gained flexibility in emphasizing rural over urban choices—or vice versa if Hanoi saw an advantage. In fact Hanoi's leadership refused Chinese advice, regarding their southern maneuvers, to give up trying to influence the urban part of South Vietnam and fall back instead on protracted guerrilla war Chinese-style.[29] They were enabled to snub the Chinese by firm Soviet approval of their designs on southern cities. Nevertheless, they found themselves, by force of circumstances, having to concentrate first on the rural problem. And when they struck at the southern peasant base, they did so with a fairly safe party apparatus in the face of a fairly unsafe family apparatus under the Ngo clan.[30]

In fact, at times Diem feared Colby and Nhu's large-scale strategic hamlet program. He envisioned them arming possible rural communists. In order to calm Diem's fears, the two senior intelligence colleagues suggested that they would select Catholic villages first. Colby relates how a priest of one of these Catholic villages led a discussion at a village diocesan retreat "in which the priests talked about the comparative effectiveness of the American carbine versus the Russian AK 47 (rifle)."[31] But arming Catholic priests hardly reassured the non-Catholic peasant masses.

Arming priests remained a minor issue. But the AID office in Saigon—the United States Overseas Mission (USOM)—raised a major issue. Its staff planned a more radical change radiating from the urban areas to rural Vietnam. As early as 1957 Vietnamese officials, under the Ngo brothers' strict guidance, had attempted to attract foreign investments into South Vietnam. In a sixty-five page brochure, the Vietnamese Industrial Development Center invited outsiders to invest in rice, rubber, sugar cane, forest products, coal (discovered near Nha Trang), and associated electrical power investments. The government promised that they would allow the remittance of profits and the repatriation of the initial capital after five years. The following quote illustrates the type of investment allure the authors hoped to create: "The spectacular growth of Greater Saigon, whose population has increased from 500,000 in 1944 to 1,900,000 in 1957, calls for the establishment of an industrial commercial network closely linked to all international markets."[32] USOM approved and funded this attempt to find investors.

When illustrating where these investors might find an attractive financial return, the brochure's authors pointed to rubber. While rubber exports increased, imports of fabricated rubber products also grew. Why not fabricate such items in or near the source of supply? The authors of the report suggested this solution. But Saigon needed more than investors. What South Vietnamese planners needed was a developmental institution much like the old Japanese *zaibatsu*, which in fact was a developmental conglomerate. Saigon could have turned to the South Korean economic model: following the Korean War, the South Koreans had used a modified *zaibatsu* to spark their development. Or South Vietnam could have used the weaker Taiwanese model of private business groups, the *quanxi chiye*. Whether one used the Japanese or the Korean term—in Korean it is *chaebol*—South Vietnam required a similar institution. Institutions were not the only necessary ingredients; ideology also helped South Korea, Japan, and Taiwan develop competitive economies. Sharing an Asian communitarianism with their sister states of the northwestern Pacific basin—much of it derived from classical Chinese culture—South Vietnam only needed to foster a certain amount of individualism in order to have a coherent ideology consistent with a competitive market economy.[33] That this began to occur can be seen in the achievements of Vietnamese living overseas after 1975.

South Vietnam also needed a planning agency stronger than their Development Center, something more on the order of Japan's Ministry of International Trade and Industry or, more in line with their size, South Korea's Economic Planning Board. Instead, under the influence of the Americans, South Vietnam built a national Chamber of Commerce. As late as 1971, AID was publishing brochures titled "Vietnam in Brief: General Information for Businessmen." If South Vietnam wanted to join the new trading system of the emerging Pacific basin, then its economic model should have been the losers of World War II, Japan and West Germany, and not the winners, the United States and the USSR. And a rubber *zaibatsu* was one place to commence the making of a trading state. Yet by 1960 the ever-increasing defection of rubber workers made even Saigon AID officials nervous. From 1960 to 1964 the percentage of male workers declined. What prospective investors in South Vietnam weren't told was that rubber production did not have a rosy future as long as the war continued, for Viet Cong recruiters found converts on rubber plantations. AID officials confirmed this: "Because of the war situation, from 1964 to date surveys cannot be conducted (on the rubber plantations)."[34] And if AID officials could not survey, even high-risk investors would not invest.

Not only high-risk investors avoided the war zones; so did AID officials. In May 1964 Dean Rusk took note of the fact in a private cable to Ambassador Lodge.[35] Replying to this cable, which stung him and his AID team, an indignant Ambassador fired back at the Secretary of State with six pages explaining, among other things, why he did "not believe it is possible for USOM [Aid-Saigon] to operate where Viet Cong terror strikes hardest."[36] In the earlier cable Rusk had charged the Saigon-based AID leadership with avoiding the countryside for the city, the one relatively safe city.

As if he desired the Secretary to recant, Lodge inventoried his economic achievements. Among these he included classrooms, educational supplies and equipment, rural trade and agricultural schools, rural and village wells, mobile health units, hospitals, district health centers, village maternity and health stations, surgical units, rural road construction, and rural health programs that had vaccinated millions of people against smallpox, cholera, plague, and malaria. Lodge referred also to plant protection services for over 8 million farmers, including distribution of 5 million copies of plant protection literature; to rat eradication; and to an increase, due to the hog and corn program, of 1 million in the hog population over a three-year period ending in 1964. He wanted the Secretary personally to know that fish fingerling distribution increased to 24.5 million in 1963, commercial fish production went from 221,043 tons in 1960 to 342,775 tons in 1963, motorization of fishing junks increased from 2,689 in 1960 to 10,210 in 1963, and that USOM had constructed thirteen pisciculture stations and fourteen marine-fish landing facilities. Lodge reminded Rusk that USOM had "underway extensive programs for improved varieties of corn, rice, sweet potatoes, and sugar cane in addition to making substantial strides in the central lowlands provinces in improving agricultural products as a result of fertilizer application." Lodge even took credit for radio communications by informing Rusk that "Washington records would indicate the number and installation of hamlet, village, and district radios."[37]

Basically Lodge told the truth; U.S. economic intervention did reach the rural areas. In fact, it could hardly have failed to do so given the large American effort. But Lodge failed to see the Achilles' heel of his own argument. In the majority of the programs Lodge inventoried, his Saigon team had in fact supervised delivery to the rural areas. But, when daylight disappeared, the teams disappeared, returning to their urban centers, often the coastal French-built cities of colonial days. As late as May 1964, when Lodge sent his cable, USOM was able to staff only a scattering of rural affairs teams at the province level, even though Lodge promised to staff such teams heavily enough to "have a minimum of two rural affairs officers in each province as soon as current vacancies have been filled."[38] Lodge did not mention the district level, that crucial level between village and province.

The Great Debate: Land Reform

At village and district levels this nocturnal abdication by USOM and Saigon personnel often meant that the Viet Cong took as much nighttime credit for these numerous improvements as did Lodge's daytime deliverers. When programs lay open to co-option, co-opt the Viet Cong did. For example, in a controversial monograph, one AID employee argues that—at least in the critical rice bowl drained by the Mekong—U.S.- and Saigon-sponsored land reforms, once working, became co-option targets of the Viet Cong. Adding to the urban versus rural argument, Saigon leaders tried to fill the gaps at village and district levels with Revolutionary Development (RD) cadres who "were mainly urban, educated, and petit bourgeois"—a type of Cultural Revolution from the right. With the city dwellers' contempt for peasants, the RD cadres often helped to alienate the people who farmed the reformed plots.[39]

Among scholars the efficacy of land reform as a counterinsurgency tactic remains a source of controversy. The same quarrel prevailed during the Kennedy-Johnson decade; in fact, a split occurred in Tory ranks— maximalists were willing to work with Whig minimalists for a limited land-reform program and minimalist Tories opposed it.

At this point it is necessary to make a fine distinction within the category called Tory internationalist. While American Tories of the 1950's and 1960's, at least those helping to make national security policy, are not exact copies of Anglo-American Tories in the previous two centuries, there are enough similarities. The term Tory is associated with landed gentry, and rightly so. Whether this be the landed aristocracy or the more humble village squire, nevertheless, a government plan to redistribute land by confiscation would neither be welcomed by Tories nor obtain Tory approval. By the middle of this century most American public figures that one might label Tory seldom depended on the land as their major source of income, but they remained attached to the ideals associated with land ownership. They had become lawyers (Acheson, Clifford, Rusk), bankers (Dillon), business managers (McNamara), and professionals of a host of other sorts. Although these people might buy a ranch in Texas (LBJ) or a home in Virginia horse country (JFK), their real income derived from the likes of television and radio stations (LBJ) or a trust based on a stock market portfolio (JFK). Nevertheless, these "high" Tories could not bring themselves to favor radical land reform programs; that usually meant land redistribution by confiscation, at least in their eyes. Even "low" Tories found it difficult to support such a plan.

One need only remember the American Civil War to understand this. In that struggle, once the military issue was settled, the real revolutionary issue emerged. Should former slaves be given, along with the Whig gift of political liberty, the gift of economic liberty in the form of the land they had helped make productive? To confiscate those plantation lands of the old South, redistributing them to the enfranchised slaves, meant the acceptance of truly revolutionary means. As is well known, this plan the winning American Northerners did not accept.

Years later, when Tory internationalists came to influence American national security policy, they, like their Whig colleagues, had a preferred agenda. One might call this the agenda of liberal capitalism. That is, if they deemed intervention abroad necessary, they preferred to intervene in the area of the foreigner's economy. Tory internationalists' intervention involved building a private business sector. Therefore, they approved of technology transfers that either built or improved certain parts of an industrial and commercial infrastructure such as textiles, metallurgy, and chemicals. Preferring to work through the recipient's private sector, they were prepared to assist mixed private-public and some entirely public ventures. In other words, they hoped to fund foreigners who sounded like local Alexander Hamiltons translating their version of Hamilton's "Report on Manufacturers" into the local language.

But when it came to land-related issues, the Tories hesitated. Always ready to help what Americans call "agribusiness," they would help improve the equipment of a rice mill, but were unwilling to redistribute the rice lands whence the miller obtained the rice. Always ready to help increase cereal yields, they would help substitute "miracle rice" for low-yield varieties, though not redistribute the ownership of this improved yield. Always willing to build dams for irrigation of fields and rural electrification for farm use, Tory internationalists would furnish the engineers for the construction of the dam, but not redistribute the water rights that made the land productive. In fact, in 1965 AID officials dedicated one of their largest projects in Vietnam to rural electrification.[40] Whether the Vietnamese rural sector was furnished with cheap electrical power or not, "high" Tories were willing to wait when the issue was land redistribution. Wait for what? For wealth to move away from land, as it had done in Western Europe, North America, and Japan.

But Whigs were not willing to wait; and some "low" Tories, tiring of the minimalist agenda of their "high" Tory friends, joined with some

Whigs in arguing for a limited land-reform program. Whigs guessed correctly that the land issue was less an economic than a political one. For this view they had good historical credentials; a Virginian and Whig aristocrat, Thomas Jefferson, had hoped to secure American democracy for all time by basing it on yeoman farmers. In much the same manner, these later American Whigs and their reluctant "low" Tor; allies hoped to secure a Vietnamese yeoman democracy.

One must also be careful in the use of the historic term Whig. In the British setting the historic Whigs were also landed aristocrats. But they moved more quickly than did Tories into the mainstream of the industrial revolution, cutting more of their real and ideal ties to the land. In the American case, Whigs, from their first political appearance, were associated more with merchants and the towns, despite notable exceptions such as Thomas Jefferson. Therefore, Whig internationalists should not be contrasted with Tories as an antibusiness group. That they were not. In fact, both Whig and Tory internationalists favored developing the private sector, but the two groups had different agendas within that sector; the Whig agenda, with its penchant for radical measures that worked against large accumulations of wealth, earned a reputation for hostility to business in general.

Whigs were willing to redistribute land so that the numerous new landowners would become small businessmen. While Tories would applaud these ends as ideal, many could not approve of the means. Fearing that redistribution could become a means for other ends beyond land policy, many Tories would not make the plunge into uncharted seas. In the twentieth century, given that Vietnam was a place where land continued to be the source of most wealth, most Tories feared that a tidal wave might follow in the wake of a successful land reform program. Ever mindful of Niebuhr, they chose caution over chance. They knew of few historical examples of nations whose main source of wealth was land that had changed land policies in one generation and managed to avoid simultaneous social typhoons.

Similar to other tenets of American internationalism, land reform as a global goal of national security policy emanates from those first, tentative post–World War II clashes between Lockean and Leninist reorderers. Special tools, weapons, or programs became the means by which internationalists implemented the strategy of containment. As I argued above, economic containment as a part of global U.S. strategy meant two things: first, isolating the Soviet Union at the periphery of the Western commercial system and, second, granting foreign aid in competition with the Leninists. By the 1960's trade between the West and the Soviet Union had increased incrementally, but the United States controlled or influenced much of this trade. The foreign aid competition also had grown by the 1960's. Dean Rusk emphasized both of these trends in economic containment in his first two years as Secretary of State.[41] And certain policies were used by both sides in the competition.

Land reform was one such policy. One architect of land-reform-as-weapon resided in the Truman State Department as Assistant Secretary for Economic Affairs. In October 1951, this incumbent, Willard L. Thorp, wrote the internationalists' land reform testament, "Land and the Future," presenting it first as an address in Madison, Wisconsin, for the Conference on World Land Tenure Problems. Within four months the State Department published his and Secretary Acheson's addresses—a busy Acheson highlighting the subject's importance by taking time to appear in Wisconsin—as *Land Reform: A World Challenge*. This book set the global Lockean agenda for rural economic intervention.[42]

Acheson set the tone. Comparing American private farms with Soviet collectivized farms, the Secretary praised the first while condemning the latter. Finding a global model in the American experience, Acheson told his audience how "in our own country, almost from the very beginning of our national existence, we have regarded our family-sized farms, our homestead laws, our laws relating to farm credits as being of fundamental importance to the prosperity and stability of the entire nation." Clearly Acheson was the quintessential Tory internationalist. Essentially he was praising farmers who bought farms and improved them by their labors. One could not read his speech as a plea for land redistribution, especially not land confiscation. In opposition to this American ideal, Acheson denigrated Soviet land confiscation, charging that it brought "worse oppression than before." To make explicit that the United States would intervene to establish the American model farm, Acheson cited the Lockean success in occupied Japan, "where, under General MacArthur's leadership, a land policy was instituted under which 84 percent of the farmers are now full owners of the land they cultivate, in contrast to some 30 percent six years ago."[43] Though the force ordering the Japanese to change land policies was MacArthur, not the market, Acheson chose not to mention that aspect.

What details Secretary Acheson failed to list, Assistant Secretary Thorp supplied. Thorp's more detailed address, especially the section labeled "U.S. Interest in Land Problems of Other Nations," signaled the interventionists to commence their rural missions. To see that these speeches contained policy direction does not mean that one must read them as literal directives. Much was there for show, for rhetorical flourish, for posturing against a perception of different Soviet postures. Yet enough substance remained to form a base, a base on which a U.S. global land reform policy could grow.

And grow it did. By the Kennedy-Johnson decade a new career field had come into existence—agricultural economics. In academic circles modernization theory had come to hold center stage in the social sciences, with the agricultural technocrats staffing much of the bureaucracy at AID.[44] What did technocrats contribute to the struggle over land policy? One example best illustrates the manner in which they isolated an issue from its habitat to study it, as if in fear of contaminants. Acknowledging how little they knew about the real desires of the rural Vietnamese, Kennedy technocrats designed a survey, the "Rural Income Expenditure Sample Survey" (RIES). Johnson technocrats went on to conduct this survey in June and July 1964, and USOM announced that the survey represented "the first known attempt . . . to secure basic data of income and expenditure patterns which would be broadly representative of the Vietnamese rural population." Local school teachers did the interviewing while Provincial Statistical Agents of the Ministry of Rural Affair supervised. The Ministry's Agricultural Economic and Statistics Service selected the sample population, attempting to cover twenty-nine provinces. The Americans said they needed the data; the Vietnamese said they would furnish the data.[45]

What did they find out? Average peasant income was one discovery; it turned out that the average Vietnamese peasant earned an annual income amounting to U.S. $42. Poor and in debt—58 percent of all RIES households reported having debts—they spent their limited resources in three major categories: 56 percent for food, 12 percent for housing, and 9 percent for clothing. What did the peasants desire most? The techocrats discovered the obvious. In their own words, "What respondents said they would do if they had a lot of money is the unmistakable dominance of the choice 'buy land'."[46] To buy land seemed a noble goal even to "high" Tories.

From this Tory-like choice of "buy land" the Whig step appeared clear, at least clear to the maximalist technocrats. To furnish land, in a land with little land not already owned and occupied, meant redistributing it under the label of land reform. This "high" Tories refused to do; they also rejected the rationale for it. Furnish land and you furnish loyalty, said the Whigs. Yet the opposite sometimes occurred. To furnish land, seed, fertilizer, credit, farm education, and new techniques had sometimes meant to stoke peasant disloyalty and even rebellion. This the Whig technocrats only slowly came to understand.

In a controversial RAND Corporation publication, Edward J. Mitchell claimed to tell the Whig technocrats what they did not want to hear. By way of his research Mitchell became in the 1960's a major figure in the policy debate over land reform. His RAND study was republished in several influential journals, but as a RAND publication it had immediate circulation in Washington. In other words, Mitchell set the agenda for the land reform debate. He suggested how the best-made plans often lead to the events most feared—rebellions. Assuming that Americans would intervene in the rural economy with the purpose of assuring rural stability, hence security for the Saigon government, Mitchell insisted that his evidence indicated that "a secure province in South Vietnam is one in which few peasants operate their own land, the distribution of land holding is unequal, no land redistribution has been carried out, large French landholdings have existed in the past, population density is high, and cross-country mobility is low."[47]

Mitchell's argument implies that as intervention corrects each of these situations—as many peasants come to own their own land, as the distribution is equalized, as land is redistributed, and so on—one may increase the likelihood of ending up with an insecure province, insecure from the point of view of Saigon's leaders. Thus Mitchell stirs up the old argument about whether modernization causes revolution or revolution causes modernization.[48] Some evidence from Vietnam suggests that extreme land reform proponents—Whig maximalists—worked for the most radical form of revolution possible in Vietnam; Hanoi's efforts seem much tamer in retrospect. Without hesitating, Whig maximalists wanted to accelerate the market mechanisms's impact in the daily life of the South Vietnamese.

Mitchell argued persuasively that much of Vietnam's peasantry supported rebellion, those supporting it having tasted some equality. Hungering for more, they consumed more, and the more they consumed, the hungrier they grew. From the half-hungry, the half-fed rebellion spread. What the French had begun the Americans completed. The market mechanism contained the possibility of revolution; in Vietnam it released its force. The problem was not that the intervention by Whig maximalists was unsuccessful; on the contrary, the problems arose because of their success.

Unlike some RAND authors, technocrats themselves, Mitchell did not lack a sense of historic comparison. Using historical examples, he suggested that other peasantries had displayed similar tendencies. He cited, for one, England's civil war of Roundheads versus Royalists, in which the King's government mainly retained the loyalty of the less populous and more backward peasantry of the west and north, while the economically advancing peasants of the south and east often joined the rebellion. In an example from a century later, Mitchell recalled the choices of French peasants: those for the great revolution were the half-fed of the Île-de-France; those against were the half-starved of the Vendée. In citing these famous peasant defections, Mitchell noted Alexis de Tocqueville's warning that "history is full of such wonders," for "it is not always by going from bad to worse that a society falls into revolution."[49]

Did South Vietnamese rural society generally proceed from bad to better economic conditions circa 1956–66? Yes it did. Populations of farm animals may be cited as visible signs of rural wealth. The number of pigs in 1957 totaled 2,564,000, and in 1966 they totaled 3,254,000. For the same years cattle totals went from 688,000 to 1,013,000; buffalo totals climbed from 544,000 to 751,000. Chicken totals, growing from 7,484,000 to 19,980,000, and duck totals, from 5,157,000 to 13,939,000, nearly tripled.[50] One cannot conclude that any agency evenly distributed these gains; but the peasant who owned more pigs and ducks suddenly owned a greater stake in any rebellion that might touch these pigs and ducks.

Nevertheless, does any evidence exist that a goodly number of these half-fed, newly enriched Vietnamese peasants followed their English and French precedessors into rebellion? Were they in fact tactically mobile peasants (those able to move from one job to another, at least within a province), touched by the market, land reform, and the ever-present war? A pervasive case exists for this view. First, along with the gains that the census indicated for farm animals, the general economic indicators for crops displayed fairly large gains from 1958 to 1963. Suddenly this declined. For example, rice production grew from 4,235 tons in 1958 to 5,327 tons in 1963, but declined to 4,337 tons by 1966. Corn repeated this curve with 29 tons harvested in 1958, 37 tons in 1963, and 35 tons in 1966.[51]

Unfortunately a farmer can neither move his unharvested crops with him nor shelter them from destructive aerial spraying, something he can do for his family or his Whig liberties. Although peasants continued to lose an increasing part of their crops to the Viet Cong, these were not the only human locusts. Two other RAND authors estimated that by 1967 almost 325,000 villagers had lost their crops to U.S.-Saigon crop destruction programs.[52] In October of the same year, authors of an Air Force study concluded that few peasants understood the crop destruction program, and that the Viet Cong, who grew only about 1 percent of their own food anyway, were exploiting the situation to their advantage. Worse followed: the Air Force authors admitted that, because of the recent U.S.-Saigon crop destruction programs, some of these peasants had joined the Viet Cong.

Crop destruction programs had a strange history, dating from 1961, when Dean Rusk helped convince Kennedy of the worth of such operations. Once Kennedy approved them, Robert McNamara kept his boss apprised of the results. In the early years both Rusk and McNamara hoped to avoid "food denial," concentrating instead on "clearing road-sides, power lines, railroads and other lines of communications, and the area adjacent to depots, airfields and other field installations." But as the war went from bad to worse, so followed the defoliant operations. From such operations the two Tories later found themselves losing a human crop to that other harvester, the Viet Cong.[53]

Not only did peasants often lose some of their winnings to aerial spraying, but many lost all their fixed assets, new and old, in the forced relocations sponsored by the United States and Saigon. Creating refugees in mass—almost 1 million by 1967—these operations resembled collective punishment. In January 1967 the Viet Cong–controlled village of Ben Suc was evacuated by Saigon authorities, who moved 6,106 villagers with their livestock, but not their crops. Commenting on Ben Suc, even General William Westmoreland admits that the operations had not succeeded as a model relocation effort.[54]

Saigon and Washington officials tried to derive a positive result from the refugee relocations. For them, the relocations meant either the refugees' voting with their feet for Saigon-controlled areas or Saigon's volunteering to remove the peasants to areas safe from Viet Cong harassments. State Department officials like Undersecretary of State Nicholas Katzenbach and pacification specialists like Robert Komer praised the relocation efforts, envisioning them as denying the enemy shelter, food, and new recruits.[55] All this supposedly led to a safe and contented peasantry. Yet when Washington officials read the field interviews with peasants, they often discovered disgruntled and disappointed people. Worse yet, the government often and unwittingly had resettled the Viet Cong infrastructure with the peasants. But at the same time, the free-fire zones that were made possible by the peasants' departure delighted those who had to conduct big-unit warfare. As the big-unit war increased, so did the number of "volunteer" refugees. Unfortunately, in this way you could win the war while you lost the revolution.

Big-unit warfare—that is, the maneuvering and countermaneuvering of battalion-sized units—often caused as many civilian casualties as military ones, especially when the maneuvering battalion was an American one or, by 1965, a South Vietnamese one organized by a U.S. adviser on a firepower-rich American model. The refugees repeatedly reported this to interviewers. For example, in 1965 General Harold K. Johnson, Army Chief of Staff, commissioned a Vietnam study in which the authors, after reading numerous transcripts of refugee interviews, concluded that "bombing and artillery fire, in conjunction with ground operations, are the immediate and prime causes of refugee movement into Saigon controlled urban and coastal areas."[56] In addition, within the Mekong Delta area of Ding Tuong province, 54 percent of the refugees interviewed in 1966 blamed artillery and aerial bombardment as the reason they had to move; not unexpectedly, they saw Saigon and Washington as the cause of their grief. In a survey conducted the following year 65 percent of the interviewed refugees—this sample drawn from the entire southern IV Corps area (the Mekong Delta)—blamed their forced relocation on Saigon's and Washington's bombardment.[57] One lapsed member of the Viet Cong reconfirmed this evidence: "The truth is, of these people moved to [Saigon] controlled areas, it was not only because their crops had been sprayed with chemicals," but because "their areas had been hit by bombs and mortars."[58]

The IV Corps area covered most of the lands of Cochinchina and all of the Mekong Delta. Here 70 percent of the South Vietnamese population resided; here French market agriculture had its greatest influence; here Vietnamese traditions had their weakest hold; here Americans and Vietnamese had worked the hardest to intervene economically; and here winners and losers reversed positions depending on the erratic combat surrounding their daily lives. And most important, here many peasants had fed themselves and their families. Even if only half-fed, they were better off than peasants outside the Mekong Delta. Data gathered by the National Institute of Statistics in Saigon from April 1962 to March 1963 indicates that rice consumption in Saigon averaged only 318 grams of rice per capita per day; in central South Vietnam it averaged 432 grams per day; but in the Mekong area it averaged 472 grams per day.[59] Nevertheless, while the data from the delta region reflects fairly widespread, although small, economic gains, a significant number of delta peasants—higher than the relative numbers from other, less well off regions—did join the rebellion, mainly during the mid 1960's.

Here one should not infer a direct cause-and-effect relationship. Multiple causes produced the one effect, the peasant portion of the rebellion. One of these many causes was land reform. Even if unconvinced by Mitchell's study, one can understand that the redistribution of wealth in any society causes as many (if not more) unpredicted as predicted results. Some peasants may have supported the Saigon government in part because of gains from land reform; others may have supported the Viet Cong regardless of their gains. Indeed, some apparently supported the government despite the losses suffered through land reform, while others seemed to support the Viet Cong although suffering losses associated with land reform.

Land Reform Viet Cong Style

Significantly, the Viet Cong suffered some of the same unpredictable results when they instituted land reform. Placing land reform high on their agenda, they raced to apply what they promised, as opposed to Ngo Dinh Diem and his American advisers, who were slow to implement what they promised. Employing the detective methods of George Rudé (who had researched the Paris police records from the beginning of the great French rebellion of 1789), Jeffrey Race looked into the police records in several Mekong Delta villages from the beginning of the Vietnamese rebellion, circa 1960. After discovering a report of June 13, 1960, dealing with Viet Cong land reform problems in the Can Duoc police files, Race detected that land reform squabbles, often leading to violence, entered the police dossiers on a recurring basis.

In the report of June 13, the authorities accused a Mr. Vo of "accepting land distributed by the Viet Cong on the night of April 11, 1960." In July they arrested a Mr. Lai "on a charge of following Viet Cong agitation in a land dispute." In August they reported that "a platoon of armed Viet Cong called a meeting of the residents of Binh Loi and Binh Thuac hamlets" in which the Viet Cong forced local government officials to swear to desist from instituting government land reform plans.

These enforcers also "forbade landowners to recover land from their tenants" and forbade those who had just bought land to evict "the current tenant or to allow anyone else to work the land." In September the local police recorded how four Viet Cong, armed with rifles and submachine guns, came to the house of another Mr. Vo, in Binh Cong hamlet, at 8 o'clock at night and ordered him "to return a piece of land (which Mr. Vo is currently working)" to another person in Binh Chanh hamlet.

In October the police noted in their records that the Viet Cong at 8 o'clock one night had taken a Mr. Truong, of Long Tri village, to a people's trial. Because he had purchasd 2 hectares of land and farmed it himself after dismissing the previous tenant farmer, the Viet Cong charged Mr. Truong with disregarding their repeated demands that he return the land to the previous tenant. Finding him guilty, they promptly took him "to a place approximately 300 yards away and shot him."[60]

Their shooting of farmers is a good indication that even the Viet Cong had problems with land reform. In fact, Leninists as well as Lockeans experienced such disappointments, especially in the first years following the latest land redistribution, a redistribution that often caused winners and losers to fight each other: "Thus, in settling agrarian problems, while trying to meet the needs of poor peasants, we [the Viet Cong] should absolutely avoid encroaching on the rights of middle peasants by taking their land for distribution to poor peasants." But the Viet Cong admitted that they had done this.[61] Having completed an analysis of the rural population, the Viet Cong identified five subdivisions—landlord (*dia chu*), rich peasant (*phu nong*), middle peasant (*trung nong*), poor peasant (*ban nong*), and landless peasant (*co nong*). The position of any peasant on this hierarchy depended on the amount of land that peasant worked.[62] Unfortunately assisting one often harmed another.

If land reform caused the Viet Cong problems in the initial stages, it also plagued them after their inaugural period. Evidence for this comes from the interrogations of captured Viet Cong cadres. For example, in a military operation in 1962 government forces captured a Viet Cong party member identified as Mr. Le Van Chan, former Viet Cong Deputy Secretary of the Interprovince Committee for Western Nam Bo. In 1962 he represented the second highest ranking party political cadre captured by Saigon's forces.

Knowing a great deal about Viet Cong land redistribution, Mr. Le Van Chan chronicled many of its successes and failures. One particular failure remained "the middle and rich peasants, who do not like the communists, because the communists hurt their interests; they are not permitted to charge interest and rentals as before, and if they want to hire laborers they are accused of exploitation." Why not oppose the Viet Cong openly? Chan answered, "They don't like the communists [but] they don't dare oppose them, because, if they oppose the communists, they must go to live in a government area" such as Saigon, where, among other things, they could not afford the cost of living.[63] Not only could they not afford the urban cost of living, these peasants also found it difficult to afford the Viet Cong cost of living: "As the pace of the war increased, those who had received land had to pay for the war, for wherever the Party mentioned land it also mentioned politics." Le Van Chan went on to claim that "only by sending their [peasant] sons into the army [the Viet Cong] and paying taxes could the war be won, and only by winning the war could they keep their land." He admitted that these taxes could strain a peasant's ability to pay: "Although sometimes their taxes to the Party are five or seven times those to the government [Saigon] . . . they pay them in order to keep the land."[64]

The Mekong Peasant

Working mainly with the northern delta province of Long An, Jeffrey Race's field research not only confirms this general picture of the Mekong peasant's regional experience but also complements Gerald Hickey's field study of one Long An village. The favorite regional specimen for twenty years of intensive research, the Mekong peasant dominated Vietnam rural studies. The peasant-based research of Mitchell, Race, Hickey, and others covers the first of the three parts of this period, the Ngo years, from 1955 to 1963. The second part (1964–68) consists of the years between the Gulf of Tonkin Resolution and the Tet offensive. Robert L. Sansom updated the information of the region for that period when he published his field research. Sansom worked for USOM Saigon in 1966, and with the assistance of Charles Cooper (the Economics Officer in the American embassy in Saigon), Sansom continued his field research into 1967. Following Sansom's work, Charles Stuart Callison updated much of the literature of American field research among Vietnamese peasants in the final part of the twenty-year research period, 1969 to 1975.

In addition to these individual contributions in field research, the U.S. government sponsored some important research on Vietnamese land reform. Interestingly, government agencies in the 1960's helped to create an expanded market for "think tanks"—private institutions that marketed research concerning public policy issues. Most of these institutions, like the RAND Corporaton, hired academically trained specialists who preferred policy analysis to teaching. Many RAND scholars committed themselves to the four assumptions of internationalism—collective security, limited war, political intervention, and economic containment. Henry S. Rowen typifies these research entrepreneurs. Prior to his appointment as Deputy Assistant Secretary of Defense for International Security Affairs in 1961, he had worked at RAND, with a year stopover at Harvard. In 1967 he returned to RAND as its president. Later in his career, Rowen joined the CIA staff. And RAND was not the only research institution to serve the government's needs. Three of the top institutions signed the most contracts for Vietnam-related research: RAND ranked first, followed by the Washington-based Institute for Defense Analysis (IDA) and the northern California competitor of RAND, the Stanford Research Institute (SRI).[65]

The latter two also contracted with federal agencies—IDA with the Advanced Research Projects Agency of the Defense Department and SRI with AID—to furnish major studies of Vietnamese land reform. Multivolume efforts, both IDA's *The American Experience with Pacification in Vietnam* and SRI's *Land Reform in Vietnam* represent fairly technical attempts to employ limited data for general policy analysis. Because they had a countrywide perspective, the authors did not limit themselves to the unique problems of the delta region. Both research projects also possessed three features not common to most university research. First, the authors had access to data not available to everyone at the time; in fact, at first the U.S. government classified the IDA report. Second, the policy-making recipients of the reports actually read them, exchanging copies and opinions on the contents. By these reports internationalists hoped to keep open their bridges to the intellectual community, a community from which many of them came. Third, the senior authors had influence beyond the immediate projects; for example, Chester L. Cooper (who had served both JFK and LBJ) led the IDA research effort.

In their final form both the IDA and SRI reports show the transition from the French, through the Ngo family, to the American domination of Vietnamese land policy. The authors stress that in each period the new group learned from their predecessors. The American fell heir to two previous attempts to alter traditional Vietnamese land tenure. In 1956, building on the French system, Ngo Dinh Diem, under the strong influence of Eisenhower's special envoy, General J. Lawton Collins, promulgated Ordinance 57, limiting ownership of land to 100 hectares.[66] This was a policy that even "high" Tories could accept, easing as it did the problem of rich, absentee landowners—often living as far away as Paris. Both IDA and SRI authors admit that Ordinance 57 had a positive if limited impact. For example, Hickey notes that the government distributed to former tenants the excess holdings of a landlord with more than 100 hectares (323 to be exact) in Khanh Hau village.[67] Suddenly the number of peasants who owned land in Khanh Hau increased, as did the productivity of their new land.

Having acknowledged limited successes similar to the one in Khanh Hau, the IDA authors underscored the political hazards of any more radical land redistribution scheme. Ngo Dinh Diem, who ruled through factions, could not afford to alienate one of his chief supporting factions—urban land owners: "Much of Diem's personal base of support rested with wealthy Saigon land owners whom Diem was reluctant to antagonize." Again, the Saigon leader associated himself with village outsiders—first the Chinese and Catholics, then the absentee landlords. Despite this limitation, land redistribution did begin, although slowly: "The number of tenant farmers receiving land under Diem's various land reform ordinances was only a little over 100,000—or less than 10 percent of the total countryside."[68] The necessary actions to improve on this record required more effort than the Ngo family felt it could give. But the maximalists disagreed, insisting that Saigon leaders could do more. In the Mekong Delta alone, an area consisting of 2.3 million hectares of rice land, "about 1.2 million hectares were held by 2.5 percent of the owners, many of whom had thousands of hectares of land."[69]

With the Ngo family's political problems mounting by 1962, and finally with Diem's fall in 1963, rural reform changed. Cooper's group argues that "from 1962 to mid 1968, scant attention was paid to land reform by Saigon and Washington officials," although much attention was given to it by the Viet Cong. The IDA report indicted the "high" Tories because, from 1960 through 1965, "AID did not have even one full-time official concerned with this question [land reform] on its Saigon staff."[70] But William Bredo, head of the SRI team, discovered that this period in land policy represented new interest, not a lack of interest. American agrarian technocrats and their Saigon allies now were concentrating their rural efforts on improved technology—that is, new fertilizers, better strains of hogs and poultry, "miracle" rice—all in lieu of reform.[71] This the "high" Tories could approve.

During this period of technology substitution, Mitchell's RAND study received a warm official welcome. Even worse for the land reform advocates, just as they began to beat back Mitchell's offensive, Charles Wolf, Jr., published an attack on the accepted wisdom of winning "hearts and minds." Wolf, an economist with RAND, argued rather that a well-organized insurgency could win even without popular support. Appearing in the *Yale Review*, his article was "circulated in the U.S. Mission in Saigon in early 1967 and received widespread attention."[72]

So contagious did this anti–land reform counterattack seem that David Halberstam took note of it in the popular press, labeling it a revisionist attack. With so much at stake, the pro–land reformers appealed to the general public. Jeffrey Race fought back in 1970, making it a clear issue in an article in *The Far Eastern Economic Review* titled "The Battle Over Land." Other author-combatants rushed into the fray—Roy L. Prosterman, Frances Starner, John D. Montgomery, and MacDonald Salter.[73] Both Prosterman and Salter were AID officials, but, even while serving, they joined the public debate.

Actually the swing to a Whig maximalist interpretation of land reform began as early as late 1965. It was marked by the appointment of a land reform adviser to the USOM staff and, according to Cooper, the decision of AID officials to commission the 1967 SRI study.[74] Also, a new team arrived in Saigon; for upon Lodge's final departure a professional foreign service officer took charge of America's Saigon embassy. Ambassador Ellsworth Bunker brought with him the controversial Robert Komer, a late convert to land reform.[75]

As Cooper's team illustrates, by 1968 a number of American officials had become converts to land reform. Earlier, and like Komer before them, they had favored the "forced refugee" program. By 1967 they had second thoughts. The first sign of this came when the "forced refugee" program died. Cooper's team reports that by 1968 "200,000 refugees were to be returned to their native villages and hamlets."[76] The French had learned about land policy in Southeast Asia from the traditional Vietnamese who preceded them, and the Ngo family from the French; but the Americans so often reversed themselves, and had changed official teams even more often, that by this time they were learning from the most recently departed Americans.

Ironically, the evidence supports the conclusion that the maximalist reforms after 1970 began to bear productive results almost simultaneously with the fall of the republic. By February 1975 Saigon officials, under the Land-to-the-Tiller Program, had granted new titles to peasants for 1,136,705 hectares of land.[77] This represents over 45 percent of all rice lands. From 1970 to 1974 South Vietnam's total agricultural production increased by 26 percent, an increase that some scholars directly connect to this large-scale land reform effort.[78] Again, this assessment emanates from field work completed in the early 1970's in four Mekong Delta villages—Khanh Hau, in Long An province; Long Binh Dien, in Dinh Tuong province; Phu Thu, in Phong Dinh province; and Hoa Binh Thanh, in An Giang province.

With inauguration of the Land-to-the-Tiller Program on March 6, 1970, President Nguyen Van Thieu began to orchestrate a land program more radical than the Viet Cong's. Significantly choosing the Mekong market city of Can Tho in which to sign Law 003/70, this last bakufu chieftain "allowed a (landlord's) retention limit of only 15 hectares, and that only where the owners themselves cultivated the land."[79] Maximalists associated these 1970 reforms with what they considered a previous major achievement in rural economic reform in Asia—the land-to-the-tiller programs they had forcefully encouraged in occupied Japan and Allied-dependent Taiwan in the late 1940's and early 1950's.[80]

Several statistical measures exist for charting the impact of those 1970 reforms. Over a decade before, in 1958, Hickey had determined the percentage of thatched roofs in two delta hamlets; Callison refigured the percentage for 1971. Hickey found 85 percent, Callison only 25 percent.[81] Replacing thatch with tile roofing had become a peasant's status symbol. Among pollsters this caused no surprise. In the 1965 Rural Sample Survey the "peasants ranked buying land first and improving housing second."[82] Purchasing this tile or other non-traditional roofing material, such as corrugated metal or pressed cement fiber, required piasters. Peasants accumulated piasters by entering the market. On more than one occasion, entering the Vietnamese market meant innovating; two innovations in the 1960's had an impact on the newly owned land of the 1970s.

In 1962 a Mekong peasant named Van Nam invented a special water pump that another Vietnamese, Pham Van Thanh, reinvented in 1963. In other words, almost simultaneously two Mekong residents—unknown to each other and lacking communication links or patent coverage—introduced a cheap, efficient water pump that individual market peasants—those who produced enough to be able to sell the excess for a profit—could rent or own. Both inventors knew about French dredging machines—Van Nam had worked as a mechanic on one French firm's dredges for twelve years before his return to farming, and Pham Van Thanh had studied these dredges for almost as long. Van Nam limited his contribution by renting his pumps for 40 piasters per hour. Pham Van Thanh, a small-engine merchant in the other Mekong market city, My Tho, quickly capitalized on his version of the invention. A Schumpeterian entrepreneur to warm the hearts of all Tory internationalists, by 1964 he had sold 600 of his new pumps and by 1967 was selling an average of 200 a month. In that year, at the age of twenty-eight, he built a new hotel in My Tho at a cost of 14 million piasters.[83]

Sansom investigated the importance of this pump in two Mekong villages, Than Cuu Nghia and Long Binh Dien. He found that the pump did two things—it increased profits, and it reduced seasonal unemployment because it helped the peasant to obtain water efficiently during the dry season. Interestingly, Sansom found that three major institutions tried to block the introduction of this innovation—the Saigon government, the Viet Cong, and the AID. According to his evidence, each group saw some danger in the invention—Saigon thought the Viet Cong would use the pump to motorize their sampans; the Viet Cong believed Saigon would make money on the deal; and AID, in its own terms, "couldn't recommend an inefficient piece of equipment like that."[84]

Callison identifies both the water pump and "Miracle" rice (IR-8 rice), "which together permitted steady double-cropping with high yields."[85] The peasants initially labeled the new rice—first introduced into the Mekong Delta in 1958—as "Honda rice" because they and their friends were able to buy so many Honda motorcycles after the first harvest. "In an eighteen-month period from 1967 to 1968, Honda Motor shipped a total of 600,000 Super Club (motorcycles) to Vietnam."[86] In fact, Vietnamese import and registration figures for motorcycles indicate a constant demand for this cheap transportation, a demand delayed only temporarily when the war came to an area. Moreover, though the full impact of the transportation revolution came late to Vietnam's peasants, when it did come, peasants traveled as never before. To get them moving, AID gave contracts to both Booz-Allen Applied Research, Incorporated, and the Electro-Motive Division of General Motors Corporation—turning to the former for a management study of Vietnam's highways and to the latter for a production study of diesel engine manufacturing in Vietnam.[87] There was also a growing number of diesel-powered vehicles that moved

Vietnam's peasants on its road system, those movers being for the most part motorcycles, automobiles, and trucks. Peasants moreover had the money to buy these motorcycles. For 1969 the total cost of new motor-bikes imported from Japan was 1.38 billion Vietnamese piasters.[88]

Following the motorcycle bonanza, market peasants renamed the rice "House-Construction rice" (*lua cat nha*) because these market peasants employed the profits from the second harvest for rebuilding purposes. Profits meant the market worked. Introduced by the French, accelerated by the Americans, this Lockean economic triumph came in the Mekong region almost simultaneously with the Leninist military triumph. In the nature of things, power in Asia in 1975 did come from the barrel of a gun.

But the peasants of the Mekong remained. These peasants calculated their own interests; their suitors had to come to them. The peasants watched winners and losers, Leninist and Lockeans, change places. In the early 1960's many Mekong peasants identified their interest with, and hence offered their limited support to, the Viet Cong. By the early 1970's many Mekong peasants identified their interests with those of the Saigon bakufu; thus they offered limited support there. The peasants put their self-interest first, and this made them politically ambivalent. Both Viet Cong and Saigon officials had to admit that whichever side gave the peas-ant land, the peasant took the land. Later, no matter which military force arrived in the village, the peasant would support it. A good example is Long An, which Race and others perceived as pivotal. Race records how "revolutionary (Viet Cong) forces [by 1965] had gained victory in virtually all the rural areas of Long An"; yet within five years some form of change of allegiance away from the victors had occurred. Thus Race concludes that "speaking only of Long An, the revolutionary movement in late 1970 was in a difficult position."[89] Cooper's team agreed: "By the middle of 1970 over 92 percent of the (South Vietnamese) population was living in areas not under Viet Cong or NVA (North Vietnamese Army) control," and "a sharp improvement in local security was particularly evident in areas of MR III (around Saigon) and IV (Mekong Delta)."[90]

The most important test came in the Spring (Easter) Offensive of 1972, in which the Viet Cong gained none of its objectives in the entire Mekong region.[91] Apparently the ambivalent peasants were at this point at least neutral, if not pro-Saigon. Having more now to lose, the peasants also had more to gain. If the war missed their districts, if they evaded Viet Cong or Saigon taxes and drafts, that year they might prosper. But the next year their luck might change, sometimes disastrously and quickly. Therefore, the longer the war endured the greater the likelihood that most peasants would find themselves enriched at one moment and impoverished the next. Out of such peasant experiences came the rural struggle.

Mitchell posited this rural struggle without field research, inviting the criticism that quickly followed. Not only did he dare denounce the sacred cow of land reform, but he claimed to do so scientifically by linear regression analysis. Using six variables, Mitchell claimed to have measured Saigon's control in twenty-six provinces in 1964 and 1965. Recalculating his model by refining the data, a team of RAND specialists denied the association of five variables: their recalculations did not indicate these five as statistically significant. But it did so find the sixth variable. One might argue that this sixth variable lies at the crux of Mitchell's revisionism, for it holds that "greater inequality (in landholdings is associated in 1964 and 1965 with) greater [Saigon] control."[92] Nevertheless, his critics have generally proven their case; Mitchell's regression analysis is riddled with errors. Yet with all the effort expended on this mathematical evidence, the real peasant, too complex to be quantified, eludes even Mitchell's critics.

What the evidence suggests is that this economic intervention had an impact, even though the United States expended little time on economic intervention in the countryside compared with the maximum effort placed on political order in Vietnamese urban centers. This impact varied greatly, usually leading to a subtle mix of opportunities for either Hanoi or Saigon leaders to exploit. Enriching peasants only to impoverish them later; juggling them in a war that went first here, then there; redistributing the land and then next year deciding to resettle the new owners in a "safer" area—no one of these actions in itself produced willing supporters of either Hanoi or Saigon. Enriching the peasants might drive them to choose the representatives of Hanoi; impoverishing them might place them in Saigon's camp. Such results would be the opposite of what internationalists expected.

How either side exploited an actual event determined, more often than not, the way the peasants decided. Exploitation meant leadership, rural leadership, and Hanoi Leninists invested to a larger degree in peasant propaganda than did Saigon traditionalists. Nor should it be overlooked that the northerner needed to win only a few converts, whereas the southerners, for survival, had to win the vast majority. Saigon lost.

Winning, for Hanoi, involved many things, rural terror included.[93] For example, a peasant was richer after an American team dug him a well near a concrete slab (that they had poured and then fenced for him) and taught him how he must douse clean daily the concrete slab upon which his fenced farm animals now resided. These wells, animals, and fences were fact, not fiction. One AID official who served in Danang and Quang

Nam from 1962–64 wrote, among other things, about wells and pigs in his memoirs. Now, in numerous reported cases, Viet Cong political cadres in the villages near Danang and Quang Nam would execute such a newly rich peasant's village chief as an example of the risks of collaboration with the AID enemy.[94] Under this terror the peasant would supply pork to the Viet Cong, even if they attacked the nearby Americans—to whom, in silence, he might still remain thankful.

This tacit appreciation might be sensed only by nearby Americans; occasionally it might extend to the district or province chief, or even to the peasant's faraway government in Saigon. It all depended on whom the peasant blamed for his troubles or blessed for his good fortune. If a Viet Cong military unit later brought the war to the newly enriched peasant's village, the peasant might lose his new pen and animals to the same Americans who had provided them and who now were firing artillery shells or dropping napalm cannisters on the peasant's fenced, clean animals. Perhaps the peasant would later blame the Viet Cong for attracting the war to his village; but perhaps he would blame his old friends, the Americans. Whom he blamed often depended on how either Saigon or Hanoi had exploited him.[95]

In exploitation, Hanoi's Leninist party surpassed its competition—first the Ngo family, later their many Saigon successors. Although in the main rural, South Vietnam did contain some lucrative urban targets for exploitation. In order to cover all contingencies, Hanoi exploited both countryside and city, finding many rural recruits among those who had been relocated in the urban world of the South.

Moreover, in the years from 1958 to 1966 South Vietnam's urban groups, like its rural groups, grew richer, not poorer. For example, textile fabric production in 1958 amounted to only 65,000 meters of cloth; by 1965 it had expanded to almost 200,000 meters. In 1955 only one textile mill existed in South Vietnam; in 1966 there were thirty mills, employing 70,000 persons. Another example is sugar. In 1958, Leland Barrows, Director of USOM Saigon, corresponded with Day and Zimmermann, Incorporated, Engineers, of Philadelphia. They had completed a study of Vietnam's sugar industry, an industry in which they believed "small farmers may work and prosper," which was "further reason for national development to expand the (sugar refining) industry to a level where it will compare formally with other sugar growing countries in the Far East." And expand it did. In 1957 South Vietnam refined only 16,000 metric tons of sugar. By 1966 this figure had grown to 75,000 metric tons.[96] But even as Saigon and Washington organized the capital for these textile and sugar plants, Hanoi was organizing the labor.

Hanoi party officials directed their southern agents to organize the unions in these new industries, reinventing the same types and combination of fronts that they had employed to reach the rural peasantry. Reacting to this Leninist labor threat, Lockeans in the labor movement convinced George Meany to escort Mr. Tran Quoc Buu, president of the Confederation of the Workers of South Vietnam, to the White House. Willard Wirtz and Averell Harriman also hosted him while the President's senior military aide briefed President Johnson for his encounter with South Vietnam's George Meany.[97]

Charismatic Leaders and Their People

Here again the positive results that should have rewarded their initial actions often eluded the internationalists; success instead went to the craftier opposition. Leninist opportunists frequently gathered the revolutionary sprouts that Lockean pragmatists had transplanted. By harvesting the fruits of someone else's labors, Hanoi leaders increased the gains that had come from their own efforts. In other words, the huge influx of American capital, technology, and education did bring results—but not always to those who had initiated the changes.

How does one steal an economic revolution? Though difficult, it is not impossible. Hanoi had made its own gains independent of Saigon and Washington efforts; but also, with amazing success, it managed to appropriate to itself much of what the other two had cultivated. Combined with Hanoi's own gains, this made for a goodly accumulation of credit among both rural and urban people—a powerful advantage for an antagonist who did not need a majority in order to survive in the South, as Saigon did. Such is the difference between Leninist and Lockean politics. A successful theft of someone else's economic intervention depends on a charismatic leader, not on institutions or ideologies. In 1960 two transregional autocrats existed in Vietnam, Ho Chi Minh and Ngo Dinh Diem. Each had strengths and weaknesses, followers and enemies. Both hoped to lead a postcolonial Vietnam by capitalizing on their pan-Vietnamese credentials, which indeed both possessed.

Before this venomous rivalry ended, one political scientist, Lucian Pye, completed field research in which he tried to identify the critical role played by charismatic leaders in building new nations out of old societies in Southeast Asia. His findings suggested that a people in transition out of traditional society might realize their collective sense of identity through the political career of one of their own—that is, the great leader as father figure. Fifteen years after this case study, a summary of the literature on the "new states"—those Third World lands that gained independence after World War II—suggests that in fact autocrats, not institutions or ideologies, played the key role in forming the identity of these nations.[98]

Certainly Ho Chi Minh, as personality-leader-autocrat, played the key role in Vietnam. Both he and Ngo Dinh Diem represented the triumph of the will, the will to power, in modern Vietnamese history. They were event-making leaders who, like Mao Tse-tung, believed that people create history and are not merely the pawns of fate.[99] After Ngo Dinh Diem's murder, no figure of comparable stature existed in Saigon to exploit the weaknesses of the other side, to steal its creations, to co-opt its programs, to abrogate its successes. And opportunities for exploitation did exist. Yet few commentators on Vietnam shifted their critical focus away from southern myths to northern realities, such as Hanoi's maximalist land reform program. Critics of Hanoi also existed, including, amazingly, northern Vietnamese intellectuals who had fought for the Viet Minh victory and were supporting Ho Chi Minh's leadership. One such critic, Nguyen Manh Tuong, appointed professor at Hanoi University, had voiced sharp criticism of the Hanoi Leninist in his address to the National Congress of the Fatherland Front (held in Hanoi in October 1956).

The speaker took considerable risks even at a time when Hanoi leaders were tolerating some divergence in views, their experimental "Hundred Flower" period, then in vogue in Hanoi. Nguyen Manh Tuong reminded his northern audience of "the disastrous effects of the mistakes committed in the Land Reform" and "of all the innocent people killed, not by the enemy, but by our hands." Nor did he spare urban reform: "The same mistakes have not only been committed in Land Reform, but in many other fields," mistakes that "caused the death of innumerable people." What did this mean? It meant that "hundreds and thousands of former public servants and their families who were living on their pensions have starved one after another because they have not been paid for two years." Nguyen Manh Tuong mentioned fellow revolutionaries driven to suicide; he indicted the leadership for the continuing torture. He does not tell us how many died in the northern land reform of the 1950s, though others did. Bernard Fall estimated that northern leaders executed 50,000 landlords. One displaced northerner, Hoang Van Chi, who published his *From Colonialism to Communism* after he reached Saigon in 1955, estimated that the Leninists executed 5 percent of the population.[100]

As the bloodbath interpretation spread, exaggerations grew. Three academics joined the debate. D. Gareth Porter attempted to demonstrate that some Saigon officials had fabricated or mistranslated most of their evidence for a northern bloodbath. When that came to Robert Turner's attention, he refuted Porter. It became a debate of numbers. How many dead landlords equaled a bloodbath? With his careful interpretation of the northern sources, Edwin Moise presents the most reliable estimate of what happened. He assumed that "the main point of the executions lay in their psychological effect," and to have such an "effect on the whole population the Party wanted to have a few executions, but not too many, in each area." Moreover, Moise concludes that, allowing for certain uncertainties, "the most that can be said is that the total number of people executed during the land reform was probably on the rough order of 5,000 and almost certainly between 3,000 and 15,000."[101]

But the Saigon leadership never—despite U.S. attempts to help—exploited these northern weaknesses to the degree that the leaders in the North exploited those of the South. Saigon leaders were reactive, concentrating only on their own urban problems and the chronic instability of the incumbent Saigon regime. Instead of exploiting Hanoi's problems, the South waited to counter-exploit Hanoi's attacks; thus generally they failed to take the offensive. Seldom did they try to steal the rebellion back for Saigon, basically because the Lockean answer remained technocratic and bureaucratic. All Washington and Saigon seemed able to do was to create committees to study the problem.[102] But no one ever stole a rebellion by means of a committee. Only the personality of the rebel chief, be he bandit or thief, could charge the imagination of those who had to do the dying. Hero or false prophet, the rebel chief had to make real in his person that which remained abstract in the ideology. Such requirements had existed in other national struggles, of course, but the unique aspect of wars of national liberation after World War II made charismatic leaders all the more important. This was especially the case if the new states found themselves wooed by either the Americans or the Soviets, with both superpowers rushing to help their friends with technical and economic panaceas. Unfortunately, the technical and economic elite sent by the patron often overwhelmed the client elite. Although this was not true for the Americans, French, Russian, or Chinese revolutions, it did occur in the post-1945 world because of Soviet and American competition in the same economic arenas.

The domination of the domestic elite of a new nation by a foreign elite tends to enervate the new nation, and nowhere more so than in technical matters. The fact that Soviet and American teams often provided the technology for nuclear power plants, petrochemical industries, and national airlines posed a problem for peoples who knew only horse power, whose knowledge of petroleum hardly included chemical derivatives, and whose imagination did not conceive of manned flight. This meant that outsiders made the important contributions to nation-building. Over time this imbalance frequently led to an inferiority complex on the part of the recipient states.

The domestic leader who was strong enough could help block the feeling of collective inferiority in the face of overwhelming technical superiority of the outside elite. To one degree or another, both Ho Chi Minh and Ngo Dinh Diem accomplished this.[103] After the Ngo family's removal, no southern leader arose who could match Ngo Dinh Diem's abilities at this task, let alone those of Ho Chi Minh. The fact that southern bakufus remained as military elites dependent on a foreign political elite was bad enough, but in the more visible field of daily economic transformation, the economic elite, too, remained dominated by a high-technology American elite. While Hanoi's leader struggled—successfully—to present himself to his Vietnamese as the major law-giver and economic Czar, the post-1963 southern leadership often appeared as an acquiescent committee, waiting for the Americans to tell them what to do next. False or true, the perception denied authenticity to the Vietnamese character of Saigon's intervention.

Ngo Dinh Diem had tried, with some success, to stamp an authentic Vietnamese character onto economic intervention. As the Kennedy brothers established a Washington apparatus for assistance, the Ngo brothers set up its counterpart in Saigon. As the Kennedys founded AID and appointed its administrator, Fowler Hamilton, the Ngos created their own Office of Budget and Foreign Aid and appointed Vu Van Thai as the Director General. And as the Kennedys influenced the selection of Frank Coffin for the AID staff, the Ngos named Tran Ngoc Lien as Commissioner General for Cooperatives and Agricultural Credit.

By their speeches, these two Vietnamese officials reveal the Ngo family's concept of development, rural and urban. Vu Van Thai, later a consultant for RAND, stressed the "balanced-growth principle," calling for a balance between geographic sections, between urban and rural, between industry and agriculture.[104] Development had a political and a social importance for a Vietnamese technocrat that preceded pure economic efficiency arguments, which were stressed by the American technocrats. Tran Ngoc Lien went even further than Vu Van Thai; for him agricultural development meant creating cooperatives rather than further profiting rich individual peasants. In other words, American AID internationalists might dream of the global family farm, but Vietnamese would dream of the local farm community.[105]

After the removal of Ngo Dinh Diem, no alternate and authentic South Vietnamese voice spoke up to demand a Vietnamese model of development. Instead, an echo reverberated in the Vietnamese presidential palace, the echo of the U.S. Ambassador's latest suggestion, often an offer of more technical intervention in the economic war. Both Ambassadors Taylor and Lodge recognized the problem of seeming to appear as Viceroys. Lodge even told Khanh that he "was well aware that he (Khanh) must not appear at any time to be under undue American influence" and that he, Lodge, "would always be sympathetic to any gestures he (Khanh) might feel like making to show that this was not the case." Taylor would not go that far, but regardless of the concerns of both, nothing they did improved the reality, especially with congressional and administration experts flooding the country.[106]

The reality haunted General Khanh. At a meeting of his bakufu, the Military Revolutionary Council, in August 1964 he and General Tran Thien Khiem, a leading Dai Viet member, "had a violent verbal exchange." The Dai Viet called Khanh "a puppet of the Americans," claiming "that the people were tired of seeing Americans meddle in internal Vietnamese affairs." The White House received a fifteen-page CIA cable concerning these Vietnamese verbal pyrotechnics. Attached to this cable was a White House note that read, "This is a participant's version of the Vietnamese generals bickering."[107]

Bickering generals caused indignation among American civilian internationalists, especially when the bickering concerned what these civilians described as careerism; this seemed a waste of energy on the part of a beleaguered ally. But the civilians fumed silently. Among American military internationalists, however, the bickering caused an outburst of rage, General Maxwell Taylor being the most outraged of the group. Having held his praetorian temper until December 20, 1964, on which date the Khanh bakufu arrested twenty-two politicians and civilian officials, Taylor summoned General Khanh. Instead Khanh sent four bakufu emissaries—Generals Thieu, Thi, Ky, and Admiral Cang—to Taylor's office, where the American Viceroy rebuked them in the strongest terms he could muster. With his years of experience in receiving and giving the military version of "ass-chewings," Taylor chewed expertly.[108]

In his diary Taylor wrote, "Khanh exploits situation to picture military insulted by Maxwell Taylor." Indeed Khanh did, and they were. Khanh went public; in an interview with a *New York Herald Tribune* correspondent he called Taylor a meddler in his country's politics. Khanh claimed that Taylor and other Americans tried to remake Vietnam in their own image. The night following the insult and the interview, doubling his effort for revenge, Khanh blasted Taylor in a radio broadcast, implying that the Taylor effort to manage him meant the return of colonialism, something as dangerous as communism.[109]

Taylor exploded. Cornering Khanh on his own turf the next day, Taylor "told him we had lost confidence in him and agreed that it would improve matters if he retired." Khanh fumed publicly, declaring "that Vietnamese forces would not fight to carry out the policy of any foreign government." Taylor recorded this in his diary, and then shocked Washington internationalists by informing them, in detail, that he had yelled what they dared only whisper.[110]

Taylor's boss would have been better served if the Ambassador, rather than yelling at his Vietnamese hosts, had tried to explain the underlying problems to a confused national security apparatus in Washington. In summary, the events in Vietnam should have indicated several things to Taylor: that reform often incited insurgency instead of curing it; that effective reforms are often co-opted by the enemy; and that reforms often require charismatic—and often despotic—leadership, rather than a democratic process.

But all Taylor did was yell.

CHAPTER NINE

The Great River:
Developing Vietnam's Economy

FOR HIS AMBASSADOR to yell at subordinates did not bother Johnson; failing to get results did. Taylor's Washington colleagues were doubly dismayed—that he had yelled at the Vietnamese generals and that his yelling, ill-considered as they thought it was, had failed to get results. Taylor thought this unfair, given that earlier, on a trip back to Washington in August 1964, he had told colleagues of his developing distaste for Khanh. On that trip, Taylor had returned to the White House to brief the chief Vietnam architects about the bickering bakufu. Those listening included Johnson, Rusk, McNamara, McCone, and Wheeler—all Tory internationalists. In the background skulked a few battle-weary Whigs, such as William Bundy. The President asked his Ambassador "to compare Khanh and Diem in the people's affections." The General in Taylor shot back, "The people did not care for either one." Following that exchange, Johnson wondered aloud who would follow Khanh, hoping "that it would not be Mac's [Bundy's] friend Mr. Oanh of Harvard."[1] Taylor's dismissal of the idea pleased the President, who, like Lincoln before him, wanted someone who could win the war quickly, a task he did not think Nguyen Xuan Oanh could handle.

At that point in the meeting Taylor treated Johnson to a taste of embassy squabbling. Taylor's chief AID official, James Killen (Director of USOM Saigon), had reorganized AID in Vietnam. Taylor reported that Killen believed the "program had been too much a U.S. program, and too little a matter of real interest and planning by [Vietnamese] officials."[2] Having assumed that directorship in June 1964, Killen busied himself with eliminating appointees of differing opinion, such as the ex-RAND official George Tanham. Rumors of these bureaucratic skirmishes reached down as far as AID field locations in Vietnam. Taylor supported Killen.[3] (That solution did not last. When Lodge returned to Saigon to replace Taylor, he got rid of Killen.)

Neither Johnson nor McNamara was amused to discover that economic intervention was going as badly as military and political intervention. McNamara, as usual, set the tone of this White House meeting by placing his agenda at center stage. He asked "if it were clear that money was no object," and he then "returned to the importance of carrying out the kind of program recommended in the RAND report," a report that dealt more with economic warfare than with military combat. Rusk said that he hoped that cost estimates would not constrain the effort, insisting "that it would be worth any amount to win." In order to make his point, Rusk drew a comparison with the cost of the "anti-Communist struggle in Greece, which worked out at $50,000 a guerilla." The President concurred with Rusk; winning was worth any cost. Both Johnson and Rusk drew support from their advisers, who, in the context of the 1960's and its euphoria for aid projects, also cited Greece to show where U.S. economic assistance had made a major difference in the outcome.[4] In fact, Johnson was incredulous that a RAND author would accuse his administration of scrimping on funds for victory in Vietnam. Johnson repeated to Taylor what he had told Lodge: "In our effort to help the Vietnamese to help themselves, we must not let any arbitrary limits or budget, or manpower, or procedure stand in our way." Earlier he had told Lodge that "the guidance I would like to give to your entire Mission is not to let your thinking be limited by possible budgetary or personnel restraints upon the resources at your disposal to execute our policy."[5]

Thus it happened that the Tories responded to increasing troubles by increasing expenditures. And costs escalated. In August 1963 Senator Mike Mansfield had warned Kennedy that this might occur: "The costs in men and money [for Vietnam] could go at least as high as those in Korea." Mansfield readdressed that warning to Johnson in December 1963. So worried did Johnson become about this important Senate defection that he invited McNamara to suggest a reply. Not one to avoid a clash, McNamara simply refuted the Mansfield premise on the basis of what McNamara calculated would be the duration and size of the American effort in Vietnam.[6]

Another Actor: The Secretary of the Treasury

If McNamara could forget to mention costs, others within the Kennedy-Johnson circle would not. The respective Secretaries of the Treasury found government costs the key item on their agendas, and Vietnam expenditures kept rising. Initially the Yankee aristocrat Douglas Dillon kept the financial tally; he was replaced by the cavalier aristocrat Henry Fowler, once Dillon forced Johnson to recognize that his deter-

mination to resign remained nonnegotiable. Dillon was a highly respected Republican; any Democratic administration housing him held a
trump against malcontents within corporate America. Such a Republican
resignation might rally the enemy party. Johnson knew this. When Dillon, supporting Senator Harry Byrd, insisted that the administration hold
the 1965 fiscal year budget below $100 billion, Johnson sided with Dillon
and against Walter Heller, his Chairman of the Council on Economic
Advisers.[7] Years earlier Johnson had watched the suave Dillon sell Eisenhower's foreign aid packages to Capitol Hill as Eisenhower's Undersecretary of State for Economic Affairs, to which post Dillon had been appointed after serving as Ambassador in Paris. Once back at the State
Department, Dillon had seen Johnson operate in the Congress, where he
was the great pawnbroker of the Senate.

Once Dillon had departed Johnson found that it was easier to relax
with the Virginia version of aristocracy; in Fowler he had a low-key but
talented accountant. Not only had Fowler served under Dillon as Undersecretary of the Treasury, but both men also had participated in numerous National Security Council meetings and ad hoc groups growing from
the NSC. Their attendance was pertinent because of the costly nature of
general economic containment policies vis-à-vis the Soviet Union, and
particularly of aspects such as economic intervention in Vietnam. But
Vietnam was not the only reason. It so happened that forming national
security policies also required expert economic advice.

Fowler had gained his expertise through years of public service. He
worked for the Tennessee Valley Authority before World War II, and during the war he served in London for the U.S. Mission for Economic Affairs, a combined U.S. office of the War Production Board, Foreign Economic Administration, Petroleum Administration, and the War Food
Administration. Following this, Fowler worked on postwar German
problems. A brief return to private law practice ended when Truman
called him back to government service, this time at the National Production Authority, a Korean War equivalent of the War Production Board.
From there Truman moved Fowler again, appointing him Director of Defense Mobilization, a post he retained until the end of Truman's mandate.
Eight years of private law practice followed; then Kennedy asked Fowler,
a Democrat, to serve under the Republican Dillon. Though he accepted
for two years, he stayed for four. He escaped for a short period; Johnson
accepted Fowler's resignation in April 1964, but called him back in March
1965, this time to replace Dillon. He reluctantly accepted.

The epitome of a financier, Fowler readily admitted what the impact
of Vietnam was in financial terms: "The basic impact was to change, you
might say, one hundred and eighty degrees the direction of economic

and financial policy for the federal establishment of which the Treasury was the integral basic part." From "fiscal and monetary stimulation to achieve goals of full employment and a healthy rate of growth," Fowler directed a turn to a "policy of fiscal and monetary restraint designed to keep the economy in tolerable bounds, given the additional economic and financial strains that would be a consequence of an involvement in a war requiring unpredictable increases" in expenditures. Though Fowler felt that the United States could afford the war in financial terms, he stressed that "other things would have to be postponed." Believing "that the American economy couldn't do everything all at once," Fowler thus preached prudence.[8]

Much of the debate concerning Johnson's lack of economic prudence turns on the issue of "guns and butter." Could Johnson afford both the domestic war on poverty and the foreign war in Vietnam? He feared raising the tax rate he had recently got Congress to lower, but clearly the federal budget could not fuel both. Fowler argued for a middle position: Vietnam would rank first, and the Great Society would receive less financing, several projects actually being postponed until the conclusion of the costly war in Vietnam. Johnson, however, gambled on fueling both, and he lost; the loss caused the economic crisis that followed his retreat from the White House. Senator Jacob Javits and others held the President in contempt for this economic mismanagement. Senatorial critics thought it would be prudent either to postpone some domestic expenditures until foreign expenditures fell at the conclusion of hostilities, or to raise taxes high enough to cover costs for both campaigns.[9]

Complex Independence

Beyond the domestic troubles that threatened to limit the conduct of the Vietnam war there were also foreign complications. Two scholars suggest that by the 1960's issues within the international political economy were beginning to constrain even the superpowers.[10] Did this happen? American internationalists did discover that global commitments outside Vietnam influenced their options inside Vietnam. Like Swift's Gulliver during his travels, the internationalists during their globe-trotting were caught by a tangle of lilliputian economic, military, and political threads that made it more difficult for one state to act by itself, even if it was a superpower.[11] When Kennedy or Johnson aides tugged at one thread of this netting, a host of other unexpected threads tightened or loosened. Did this have "costly effects"? Did complex global interdependence manifest itself in America's intervention in Vietnam in the 1960's? Since, as the two scholars believe, "struggles over the governance of economic issues are responsible for much of the increased attention to interdependence," it would seem that global economic issues should have constrained both Secretaries Rusk and McNamara from assuming that a victory would be worth any economic cost.[12] But neither they nor the Presidents they served seemed to recognize any economic constraints. The Treasury printing presses kept printing.

From the beginning of the Kennedy administration global economic issues influenced American internationalists. But to influence is not necessarily to constrain. Two issues illustrate the difference: the balance of payments and the loss of gold. Both kept Dillon busy, for "Kennedy had a very special interest" in both. According to Dillon, Kennedy "talked to economists about it [gold], and was quite interested in this area." His Treasury chief remembers Kennedy as having this "phobia about gold." Worried about the "esoteric area of international monetary business," Kennedy "liked to be kept very closely abreast of what was happening on the balance of payments, literally month-to-month and almost week-to-week." If Dillon dallied, the impatient Kennedy would telephone, inquiring for the latest figures.[13]

Dillon and, later, Fowler had to commence an international rescue of the global monetary system, an American creation of the 1940's. In the early 1960's the two men helped set up Working Party Three, a body established under the Organization for Economic Development "to regularly review, on a multilateral basis, the various financial developments in the so-called balance of payments areas as concerned the member countries."[14] Next they found themselves involved in creating the Group of Ten, a committee that was to rescue the International Monetary Fund (IMF), which had nearly exhausted hard currency funds available to developing countries. "How additional liquidity would be provided for the international monetary system" remained a problem throughout the decade. At the same time that the Working Party Three and the Group of Ten began work, the London Gold Pool market came into existence. In Fowler's view, all this activity "gave rise to a worldwide concern with the international monetary situation and the U.S. balance of payments."[15]

Secretary Fowler thought that what had existed as a "beneficent deficit"—something the United States had tolerated for several years because of the need of other countries for dollars in the early postwar years—had reverted to a destructive deficit once European Central Banks possessed their own convertible currency. After that occurred, the deficits were no longer beneficial. But instead of declining, they rose "going up to 3.9 billion dollars in 1958," again in 1959, and again in 1960. This led "to major outflows of gold." European governments, especially the French, converted over a billion dollars into gold each year for that three-year period.[16]

In finding the delicate balance, such that one solution in one area would not cause an overwhelming reaction at another point in the interconnected global economy, Fowler looked to two possible solutions. "Perhaps the major consideration was to restore and maintain a healthy trade surplus." This "would give us the margin in so called current accounts by which we could meet the very substantial government expenditures outside the United States for security and aid in addition to the greatly increasing quantities of capital"—capital that investors were sending out of the United States for direct or portfolio investments, apart from what tourists spent abroad. The second solution involved the agreement to create the Special Drawing Rights (SDR) as an international reserve in lieu of gold or dollars. By July 1966, after interminable compromises, the Group of Ten, minus the ever-dissenting French Minister of Finance, agreed at The Hague to create the SDR's.[17]

These international rescue missions were causing considerable alarm in internationalist circles by July 1965. To allay fear, Fowler suggested, and Johnson approved, a White House Advisory Commission on International Monetary Arrangements. Chaired by former Treasury Secretary Dillon, it included David Rockefeller, of the Chase Manhattan Bank; Andre Mayer, of Lazard Freres; Walter Heller, former Chairman of the Council of Economic Advisers; Kermit Gordon, president of the Brookings Institution (former Director of the Budget); and Frazier Wilde, who chaired both the Committee on Economic Development and the board of Connecticut General Life Insurance Company.[18] Sharing the economic concerns with the President's Commission, the Joint Economic Committee of the Congress had established an International Monetary Affairs Subcommittee led by Chairman Henry Reuss and Congressmen Robert Ellsworth. Reuss previously had worked in the Chief Price Control Branch Offices of the U.S. military government in Germany, and later served as Deputy General Council to the Marshall Plan office in Paris.[19]

With all of this assistance, both Kennedy and Johnson then tried to bolster the U.S. position within the global economy. In 1961 Kennedy devoted his second message to Congress to the balance-of-payments problem. He sent a similar message in 1963. He also obtained a travel tax aimed at stanching the tourist-dollar hemorrhage. In 1965 Johnson was forced to send a major message to Congress setting forth his own programs for reducing the deficits. He went so far as to suggest "voluntary restraint in the utilization of U.S. capital in direct investment abroad"; but this did not stop the economic bleeding. Suddenly another lilliputian thread jerked the global economy: in the fall of 1967 the British devalued the pound. By March 1968 Washington had asked London to close the Gold Pool temporarily. From this came the two-tier gold system, a mere

Band-Aid for that hemorrhage. Stymied, Johnson experimented, sending the Congress a new "action program" in 1968. As late as January 1968, his Treasury Department, forced by worsening conditions, issued a major report in which it analyzed the whole historical treatment of the balance of payments problem in the United States from the 1950's.[20] More Band-Aids appeared—national and international ad hoc measures for temporary economic stability.

Each of the economic problems influenced both Kennedy and Johnson, though they failed to constrain them; the two Presidents pushed their agendas for Vietnam regardless of costs. The United States, economic behemoth of the 1960's, was the major actor in the global economy. The most expensive American effort in the 1960's was the Vietnam war. For a theory of complex interdependence to be valid for the United States in that decade, international economic forces would have had to constrain the Americans in this war. In fact, they did not. Although the United States shared a complex and close association with the global political economy of the 1960's, it did so not as others did in complex interdependence, but in complex independence. While America often acted like a Gulliver, it was a cooperative Gulliver. This meant that, when it was unwilling to grant other states their demands, this giant could pull more lilliputian strings in the global economy of the 1960's than could its lilliputian partners or enemies. The United States was, in that decade, *the* superpower. And by mismanaging the economy, the United States damaged the economic system that it had put in place in the late 1940's.

The Cost of the Body Count

With these economic convulsions stretching across the decade, how could the United States afford simultaneously a war on poverty, in which to rescue one individual might cost many thousands of dollars, and the other war, in Vietnam, where (according to Secretary Rusk) it might take $50,000 to kill one guerrilla? And how many guerrillas existed? Given that the Viet Cong launched a monsoon, or summer, offensive in 1965 with regimental-sized attacks, internationalists knew the enemy numbered far more than a few thousand. Rusk's own staff published two reports in which the authors conservatively estimated enemy strengths. Analysts agreed that at a minimum the Viet Cong in 1961 had a strength of about 16,000; that the North had regrouped an additional 28,000 southerners in the South between 1959 and 1964, in addition to infiltrating 12,400 northerners in 1964, 37,100 in 1965, 92,287 in 1966, and 101,263 in 1967.[21]

These generally conservative estimates totaled 287,050. What would it cost to kill or capture the entire lot? In 1947 dollars, $14.3 billion. Taking into consideration inflation, which would raise the cost to about $72,800 per guerrilla, the total would be $20.9 billion. But one scholar has suggested that VC/NVA dead between 1965 and 1974 amounted to 444,000. If so, the cost in unadjusted Greek-aid dollars ($50,000) would amount to $22.2 billion—$32.5 billion if adjusted for inflation.[22]

Even these figures fail to reflect the real cost. To arrive at closer cost estimates calls for using a different set of data. Between 1965 and 1972, the years of highest costs and heaviest casualties, the Vietnam conflict cost $135 billion in military expenditures, not counting the $4 billion in economic assistance.[23] If we use a figure of 400,000 dead VC/NVA and a cost of $135 billion, Rusk's real cost per dead guerrilla averages somewhat closer to $337,500 per guerrilla between 1965–72. Now for a moment consider that the average annual income of a peasant in Vietnam was U.S. $42. Because he owned nothing, one could say that this sum represented his net worth alive. But if he joined the Viet Cong his net worth skyrocketed to $337,500. Alive he was worth $42. Dead the peasant was worth $50,000 to Rusk, but the actual cost-overrun on killing per enemy would approach $300,000.

The authors of one congressional committee report maintained that "all of this occurred at a time when the U.S. economic position abroad has become increasingly perilous." Warning that "the U.S. budget deficit for fiscal year 1972 totaled more than $23 billion," the committee report illustrated the complex way internationalists had misjudged Vietnam war costs as well as many connected problems in the international political economy. Reminding Americans of this new circumstance, the committee reported that "our balance-of-trade and balance-of-payments situation has been continuously worsening [during the war] to a point where the President, in mid-August 1971, imposed wage, and other economic controls on the U.S. economy and took other steps which, in effect, have devalued the dollar in the world markets (by approximately 8 percent) and suspended our Government's redemption of dollars with gold."[24]

South Vietnam's Economy

All global economic problems in the 1960's did not spring from American mismanagement of the Vietnam war. Many of South Vietnam's economic problems, for example, currency stability, were the fault of Vietnamese mismanagement. Even as the stability of the U.S. dollar was important in warding off chaos in the global economy, so that of the Vietnamese piaster was crucial in stabilizing the Vietnamese economy. The United States performed a rescue mission in both the global and Vietnamese currency campaigns. As the French and Americans discovered, a flood of francs or dollars into the Vietnamese economy invited chaos. Both Western nations had to install controls.[25]

Worse for the Americans, the shooting war only complicated the economic war against the market's bedfellow, imported inflation. Not only that, Americans found themselves enmeshed also in a plan to strike a blow at the Viet Cong underground economy. This second economy used Saigon's currency, the piaster. In fact the Viet Cong paid "their Main Force troops almost entirely in the 500 piaster note." The Harvard-trained economist and Prime Minister to Khanh's bakufu, Nguyen Xuan Oanh, decided on a blitzkrieg replacement of all the 500-piaster notes in circulation in order to leave the Viet Cong with only the worthless old notes. General Harkins had christened Oanh, who was well known to Americans, with a new name, "Jack Owen." For U.S. officials it stuck. Oanh, or Jack Owen, contacted his agents in London, where the British were printing new notes and packaging them in small footlockers. Next he requested that Taylor supply an aircraft. Intrigued by a plan as bold as any he had carried out when commanding the 101st Airborne Division in the Normandy blitz, Taylor agreed as soon as he received the green light from Washington.[26]

Beyond currency and inflation, the Americans suffered also from other problems that had plagued the French. Since the French had solved some of them, it galled American internationalists that they seemed unable to repeat those successes. The case of rice exports is one example. As indicated earlier, France had made its colony the rice bowl of Asia. But in late March 1964 a joint State-Defense-CIA cable arrived at the U.S. embassy in Saigon; the authors were unhappy about falling rice exports: "We continue concerned about Saigon government activity in rice marketing, and especially in exports." The authors reminded their Saigon embassy colleagues that the "world rice market has an especially rosy future which Vietnam ought to share." Concerned that Vietnamese officials in Saigon might "strangle rice exporting opportunities," they urged the American team to redouble its efforts.[27] Failing to understand that much of the increased rice production went to the Viet Cong, Washington officials fumed at what they considered to be the inept, corrupt, and often lazy Saigon officials.

It did not help matters when, in July 1964, the General Accounting Office (GAO) issued a report highly critical of AID programs in Vietnam between 1958 and 1962. So unhappy did the report make AID supporters that David Bell, of AID's Washington staff, felt compelled to write McGeorge Bundy a two-page letter explaining the corrective measures

AID had already instituted. Bell told Bundy that the GAO critics "exhibited a great lack of recognition of total U.S. objectives and the interdependence of economic considerations and the politico-military complex." [28]

Stymied by these critics, "high" Tories turned from currency problems and rice exports to the one thing they knew they could do as well, if not better, than the French, who had irrigated so much of their colonial garden. These Tories wanted a big hydraulic project. Fearing that their U.S. and Vietnamese counterparts in Saigon lacked the breadth of imagination for such a choice, Washington interventionists made suggestions. They "proposed that the U.S. undertake with Saigon a dramatic and intensive social and economic effort on a single project or area which would highlight as quickly and effectively as possible the opportunity for progress after pacification." [29]

What did that mean? It happened that in the Phan Rang valley of Vietnam a Japanese team was "completing a feasibility study of an irrigation system using runoff from Da Nhim dam which might irrigate 20,000 hectares [49,400 acres]." Since that water was going to waste, Washington wanted to irrigate more land. Internationalists suggested forming a joint American-Vietnamese agency modeled on one they knew existed in Taiwan. While Saigon prepared for this big project, the Tory minimalists also suggested that U.S. embassy officials continue with the intensive village water wells and cisterns program. [30]

A Mekong River TVA

Little did anyone suspect that the President might suggest a project that would overwhelm any previous plans. A hint came in Johnson's speech at Johns Hopkins University in April 1965. With obvious reference to the Marshall Plan—"the American people have helped generously in times past in these works"—Johnson called on all "the countries of Southeast Asia to associate themselves in a greatly expanded cooperative effort for development." He tried to tempt the Hanoi Leninists toward peace by promising to "ask the Congress to join in a billion dollar American investment in this effort as soon as it is under way." As in the Marshall Plan, the enemy could participate under peaceful conditions. After insisting that "we would hope that North Vietnam would take its place in the common effort just as soon as peaceful cooperation is possible," the President awaited their reply. Five days later Johnson received his answer, when the official party newspaper of Hanoi referred to the billion dollars as "bait." [31]

Even though North Vietnam refused to cooperate with him, Johnson stoically named his target—the mighty Mekong River. It would be harnessed by his version of an international Tennessee Valley Authority. Along with this he would create a development bank. For both projects Johnson pushed and shoved Congressmen, finally receiving his Asian Development Bank Act on March 16, 1966. He tied one project to the other at the signing ceremonies, saying, "The Asian Development Bank is the first step of what I conceive to be a very long journey." One can view the creation of this bank in light of three issues. First, it was part of the "North-South" debate, in which rich northern hemisphere states were to help poor southern hemisphere states. Second, it was part of the ongoing American search for Cold War allies in the economic as well as the military battles for South Vietnam. Third, the bank was part of the U.S. attempt "to involve Japan more heavily in assistance efforts."[32] This last attempt dated from the Truman administration; if the United States could lure Japan back to Southeast Asia as a banker, it would lessen the financial drain on the Lockean superbanker.

What was Johnson's second move? "We are taking another [step] today by announcing that we have pledged half of the 24 million dollars that is needed to construct the large Mekong River project, the Nam Ngum tributary project in Laos." He told his audience that "the first phase of the project will include a dam and power station with an installed capacity up to 30,000 kilowatts." Not only could "additional generators up to 120,000 kilowatts" be installed but "an international transmission line, with a link across the Mekong River, will connect the power station with the capital of Laos and northeast Thailand."[33]

Johnson never tired of talking about his Southeast Asian river project. In remarks to Prime Minister and Mrs. Holt, of Australia, to troops of the 101st Airborne Division in Kentucky, and to President and Mrs. Marcos, of the Philippines, LBJ made the Mekong sound like the Mississippi. When given the chance to be near his Asian river, he went. Addressing students and faculty of Chulalongkorn University, Bangkok, the President reminded these Thai intellectuals that "two dams, both here in Thailand, are already supplying water and power as the first part of what was the visionary Mekong development project."[34]

Development dreams die slowly. Departing Presidents often have bequeathed temptation to their successors. Intrigued by the idea of a "buy out," President Nixon ordered his team at the Paris peace talks to raise the ante "to 7.5 billion dollars, of which something like 2.5 billion dollars would be earmarked for postwar reconstruction aid to North Vietnam." Once this was leaked to the press, the media linked Nixon's offer to Johnson's earlier one. American critics noted that Johnson's offer had been made when only 400 Americans had died in combat, while Nixon's offer came after the deaths of 45,000 Americans.[35] Hanoi, with casualties of its own, remained as negative toward Nixon's dollars as it had toward Johnson's, regardless of media, popular, or congressional reaction.

Casualties or no casualties, taming and harnessing the Mekong appealed to Tories once they accepted the magnitude of the task. This project represented a fundamental connection to a past domestic American success. Earlier Albert Hirschman had observed several large development projects.[36] One of these, the Damodor Valley Project, in India, received its funding from the Bank for Reconstruction and Development, better known as the World Bank. American internationalists possessed a near-veto at this bank because of the linkage or proportional voting to percentage of contributions. But this Indian venture intrigued them—a TVA for the subcontinent. Hirschman noted the connection between the national and international valleys. He suggests that, following World War II, "any river valley development scheme . . . was presented as a true copy—if possible, certified expressly by David Lilienthal—of the Tennessee Valley Authority." In fact, Chester Bowles had contacted Lilienthal at Princeton with a White House offer to go to "our most troubled spot in the world." Bowles confirmed that "the President [Johnson] would like to name you [Lilienthal] Ambassador to Thailand, so you could create the atmosphere and steam behind the development of the Mekong River, a big Southeast Asian TVA." Labeling the phenomenon the "TVA model," Hirschman saw the political magic in the connection.[37]

Neither Johnson nor Hirschman was the first to make this connection. It dates back at least to John F. Kennedy, who found the idea congruent with his own interventionist plans. Fittingly, one of his first public references to international TVA's occurred in Tennessee. Addressing a rally in Knoxville, Kennedy told the crowd that "the Tennessee Valley [Authority] has been a source of strength, not only to the Tennessee Valley and not only to the United States, but the Tennessee Valley [Authority] typifies, in my opinion, the kind of domestic program which has far reaching implications around the world." So that his audience would not miss the point of his arguments, Kennedy told the Tennessee voters that "the reason that Mr. Lilienthal works in Iran today is because he worked in the Tennessee Valley." Continuing to connect this southern, Bible-strong valley to valleys around the globe, Kennedy claimed that "when they talk about damming the Jordan River, they talk about making another Tennessee Valley in the Middle East."[38]

Kennedy did not desist upon leaving Tennessee. In Iowa he told the faithful that "project after project had sprung up in southeast Persia, in the Indus River, in Colombia, and all over the world, modeled after what we did in the Tennessee Valley." They heard it again in Billings, Montana; in Cheyenne, Wyoming; in Denver, Colorado; in fact, wherever Kennedy campaigned in 1960 audiences were likely to hear how the Irish Senator planned to make the planet even greener than the emerald isle of his ancestors.[39]

Unfortunately, being politicians, neither Kennedy nor Johnson listened to Hirschman, the economist. He warned that "two river valley development schemes will differ vastly more from one another than two Coca Cola bottling plants." But Hirschman had only an academic audience, while the two Tory Presidents had the media.[40] This latter audience had little patience for the nuances in a Hirschman-style approach, one that basically resembled a cautious Niebuhrian view. Instead, the media focused on the promises of enthusiasts, often going beyond what even they would dare suggest. And the Kennedy-Johnson team did find the TVA-Mekong analogy attractive. Whether Hanoi participated or not, a developed Mekong River Valley, based on a modified Lockean model, might be an economic wall of containment behind which all of Southeast Asia could develop. Comprising developed segments, a Tory world order depended on economic self-interest.

McNamara's Strategy: Economic Warfare

No stronger convert could have inhabited that world than Robert McNamara. As Defense Secretary he wrote *The Essence of Security*, in which he praised both the Mekong Development Project and the Asian Development Bank, finding in them a major part of the essence of American security.[41] Strange as it seemed to many at the time, McNamara's departure from DOD to the World Bank made more sense than this initial appointment as Defense Secretary. By education McNamara was more thoroughly prepared for and by intellect more suited to the bank task than the Pentagon assignment. For their war in Vietnam, what Kennedy and Johnson discovered in McNamara was the epitome of a brilliant manager.[42] Though what both needed was a brilliant strategist, McNamara's penchant remained statistics, not strategy. Smarter than most of his opponents, especially the traditionalists in the senior ranks of the military, he dazzled Washington with his erudition. But his vast knowledge did not result in wisdom when the United States went to war.

McNamara reduced the war to problem sets, data he could manipulate. He would have excelled as the Treasury Secretary or AID Director. Their troops could have furnished him with exact census data, GNP figures, productivity gains, and so forth. Ideally suited for the computer age, McNamara's insistence on counting features of the war—his infamous "body count" of enemy kills and his pacification scheme to color-code villages as to the proportion of inhabitants that remained pro-enemy or pro-Saigon—meant treating war as a science, not as an art.[43] Of course war is neither; "rather it is part of man's social existence." War is chaos, but McNamara wanted to control chaos. In his refusal to tolerate the unknown and the unknowable in warfare, McNamara violated Clausewitz's warning to strategists about "the countless minor incidents—the kind you can never really foresee" that bring "about effects that cannot be measured, just because they are largely due to chance." Clausewitz labeled these effects "friction." One soldier-scholar, working from a careful reading of Clausewitz's *Von Krieg*, compares McNamara unfavorably to the Prussian theorists.[44] Managed or not managed, the war turned McNamara-the-believer into McNamara-the-nonbeliever. McNamara apparently believed in the military aspects of the war in the initial stages under JFK and LBJ because he trusted the results of his data-collecting. Intellectual as he was, his actions followed his beliefs. When he saw his data-collecting system failing him, McNamara stopped believing that the war was winnable militarily. Again his actions followed his beliefs, in this case reversing his earlier position.

This was not the only example of wavering in McNamara's view on military intervention. While he would not comment about his role in Vietnam policy-making until the courts forced him to testify in the 1984 Westmoreland/CBS libel case, McNamara—son of a San Francisco shoe salesman who had only managed to obtain an eighth-grade education—gave a long, three-installment interview on non-Vietnam issues during his stewardship of defense to the *Washington Post*, its owner, Katherine Graham, being an old friend. The second installment revolved around the issue of the first use of nuclear weapons. It had been McNamara's assignment to design a collective security strategy (especially in Europe) for JFK and LBJ, by which they could halt any possible conventional military attack by the Leninists on a NATO ally. McNamara's answer was the strategy of flexible response, "which envisioned the use of nuclear arsenals as a last resort to a halt a Soviet conventional attack." But once the strategy was created, the creator reprogrammed. Confused though it seems, the creator of flexible response did not believe in the first use of nuclear weapons: "In long private conversations with successive presidents—Kennedy and Johnson—I recommended, without qualification, that they never initiate, under any circumstances, the use of nuclear weapons."[45]

But how was flexible response supposed to work if the two internationalists followed McNamara's advice? On this point McNamara was no help. Basically this is because McNamara tended to deny the efficacy of military force in international relations. This did not make him a Clausewitzian pessimist, mainly because the economic battlefield was where, if forced to it, McNamara wanted to wage war. But two Presidents had assigned him the military, not the economic, portion of the problem. As a Lockean reorderer, McNamara had made his own economic convenant with power, relinquishing an annual salary of approximately $600,000 from Ford Motor Company for a annual DOD salary of approximately $25,000. But this was a $25,000 assignment to practice *military* forcecraft if statescraft failed—while someone else received a federal salary to manage *economic* forcecraft if statescraft failed. And neither military nor economic managers were able to reduce the essential military, economic, and political problems of the U.S. involvement in Vietnam to numbers on which one could base systems analysis and obtain useful information. Nevertheless, McNamara decided to implement the non-Clausewitzian doctrine of economic intervention as his offensive doctrine.

Meanwhile, General Westmoreland decided to call forth the old Clausewitzian doctrine of attrition as his offensive doctrine. Interestingly, Westmoreland remembered that the last time great powers had used attrition was in the World War I battles of the Somme and Verdun.[46] Unfortunately, he did not recall what happened to those powers: the winners lost as much as the losers. To make matters worse, in Westmoreland's war his side had to build and destroy simultaneously. At a cost of billions of dollars, one U.S. group struggled to build an economic structure; at a cost of many more billions, the other U.S. group was striving to destroy an enemy infrastructure. Unfortunately the enemy often concealed themselves within the economic structure; this ensured that the big guns of the American military would have to destroy much of the economic structure in order "to save it."

Long An Province: A Test Case

The mission to save Vietnam from itself dominated Washington leadership. The province of Long An figured in many of the rescue missions. Saved on one occasion only to undergo trauma again later, the patient-province expired from the doctor-patron's care. In the first days of Johnson's inherited presidency, McNamara warned Johnson about Long An: "Out of 219 strategic hamlets in Long An Province which had been reported as completed under the Diem regime, only 45 have actually been identified."[47] Following this bad news, in February 1964, both Harriman and Hilsman received embassy cables from the political section in Saigon. A Joint Chiefs of Staff message to Westmoreland had the Saigon diplomats boiling. The JCS had ordered "an immediate concentrated counterinsurgency offensive in Long An province to restore effective [Saigon] control."[48]

Noting the seriousness of the Long An situation, the Saigon-based diplomats strongly suggested that "the utter impossibility of launching" such an offensive was obvious. Here they felt that the peasant, not the enemy military units, would be the target. The diplomats also demanded that Washington recognize that no "quick fix" or short dramatic campaign would change the peasant. They suggested that the United States faced "a long hard pull." [49]

By April the situation had worsened. Finally William Sullivan, a young protégé of Harriman's, dispatched a cable to the Saigon embassy. He noted that "over a consistent period of time" the U.S. embassy had said it was dissatisfied with the situation in Long An province, but that this had not produced any results. Sullivan suggested that Washington wanted someone to do something. [50] At this point Lodge betrayed his own staff. At a June meeting called by Lodge at the Vietnamese Joint General staff compound, he "stressed that success in Long An, for example, would have favorable repercussions elsewhere." So that those attending—Peer De Silva for the CIA, William Westmoreland for MACV, Generals Khanh and Thieu for the Saigon bakufu—would not misunderstand him, Lodge emphasized the need for "a good flashy victory, even if not very big." [51]

Westmoreland suggested more troops. By June he had an agreement with Khanh, blessed by Lodge: "General Khanh agreed with me that a regiment should be moved into Long An as early as practical." [52] Westmoreland stationed a battalion of the U.S. 25th Infantry Division there, later replacing it with the even larger brigade from the U.S. 9th Infantry Division. One could argue that the situation demanded these troop units, that no government could reach the peasant if first the government could not secure that peasant from enemy military harassment. But the manner in which the firepower-rich Americans fought beside their Vietnamese firepower-enthusiast pupils "brought extensive physical destruction and loss of life to the province." And even with his greater firepower, Westmoreland could not give Lodge a going-away present in the form of a quick "good flashy victory, even if not very big." Taylor, after replacing Lodge in July, reported that "Long An can boast little or no discernible progress yet." [53]

Nevertheless one could further defend Westmoreland's use of this firepower. By employing it he took fewer risks and thus sustained fewer casualties. His charge, after all, was to fight while protecting to the maximum the lives of those within his command. Further, the economic and political war in Vietnam belonged to someone else. Though these needed to be interconnected, someone other than Westmoreland was responsible for interrelating them.

Westmoreland did not lose the war, nor did he win it. He was not a bad commander, nor was he especially good. The term adequate suits him; he was what one of the Bundy brothers called a blunt instrument. Like the older Taylor, Westmoreland looked like a Camelot general. But, unlike Taylor, he had no intellectual pretensions. Westmoreland did suffer from an overdeveloped sense of enthusiasm, having caught the "can do" disease. During the bloodletting at the remote mountain battle of Khe Sanh, Westmoreland advised General Wheeler to tell Johnson not to worry. Westmoreland later recalled that this battle "was a real challenge, but I never had any doubt about the outcome." Yet no matter how eager and affable, he could not do what Johnson wanted—win the war in Vietnam (a place Johnson began to refer to as "that damn little pissant country").[54] Westmoreland won battles with the enemy military units; but winning the peasants was out of his reach. He tried. He failed.

Although the failure of the military and political efforts became painfully obvious the longer the strategy of attrition lasted, the economic success, although limited, raced like wildfire through South Vietnam—rewarding first one side, then the other. It should have caused no surprise when a CIA case study of May 1964, "The Situation in Long An Province," concluded that "the popular attitude in Long An reportedly remains one of apparent apathy toward both sides."[55] The rewards and punishments delivered by the market won few permanent adherents to either political creed. Ambassador Taylor, too, was concerned about the number of ambivalent peasants surrounding his mission compound. While commenting on how "peasant attitudes, in [the] Delta especially, seem to be turning against VC, as latter step up heavy taxation, indiscriminate terrorism, etc., and at same time are unable to produce on promises of last several years," he nevertheless forced himself to recognize also that the peasants were also "still far from point of significant commitment to the GVN cause." There was a growing rural apathy.[56]

But Lyndon Johnson could not understand ambivalent or apathetic people. Bill Moyers heard LBJ exclaim, "My God, I've offered Ho Chi Minh $100 million to build a Mekong Valley." He added that "if that'd been George Meany he'd have snapped at it." Robert Komer commented, "LBJ had no particular grasp of foreign culture"; basically "he felt no particular need to delve into what made Vietnamese Vietnamese—as opposed to Americans or Greeks or Chinese." Because Johnson had been a poor man "he saw the Vietnamese farmer as being like the Texas farmer or the Oklahoma farmer." Komer remembers Johnson's stating, "We're going to provide them with rural electricity" and "we're going to provide them with roads and water, and we're going to improve the rice crop."[57] In other words, the President had a dream. Unhappily, for others it turned into a nightmare.

In summary, the French had introduced the market mechanism into the daily life of ordinary Vietnamese, and the American Tories were accelerating its effects. Unfortunately, its revolutionary impact created as many losers as winners. In many ways the Lockean impact on economic life was more revolutionary than was the Leninist's. One need only observe agriculture, the mainstay of a majority of Vietnamese. While Hanoi's communal agriculture was not traditional Vietnam village agriculture, it resembled that more than did the Lockean family farms of revolutionary Americans. And so it went in all areas—rubber, textiles, transportation, irrigation, power plants, and a host of other economic segments. Once the maximalist coalition of Whigs and "low" Tories had won their fight with the "high" Tory minimalists, they pushed for revolutionary changes, especially in land ownership. In a good cause they went beyond the bounds of Niebuhrian caution, and with their successes came their failures. One of the failures to which they contributed was the very loss of the war, for no government could stabilize a nation in the throes of an invasion and a major economic upheaval. And by 1975 it was a classic invasion that brought down the Lockean peasant-pupils, clutching deeds to their redistributed new land, by then spread throughout South Vietnam. Hanoi was soon to ask for the deeds back, Leninists never having seen value in individual property rights.

By 1964 McNamara had usurped the economic role, influencing the Vietnamese economy as strongly as he had its defense sector. Officials outside the Pentagon responded to McNamara's commands, for he was recognized as a financial wizard. Determined to spend himself to victory if necessary, he stamped his personality onto the cables of other officials. For example, a positive AID reply to a Vietnamese supplemental appropriations request reads: "This action being taken at Secretary McNamara's recommendation in order to assure availability of funding for increased needs now foreseen and to remove any possible psychological or political impediment to all-out [Saigon] budgetary, administrative and military efforts." In an effort to control the resulting imported inflation, the authors of this cable and of a second (both sent in May 1964) remind the recipients to curtail luxury imports further. The second cable carried the warning to State Department recipients not to forget the man across the river—"Department [State] pass DOD for McNamara."[58]

Despite the power he wielded as Kennedy's and Johnson's most influential cabinet member, even McNamara could not channel the forces unleashed within the Vietnam war economy. At the close of the nineteenth century, French capitalists had introduced ingredients that started a chain reaction within Vietnamese society, a disturbance that grew into a firestorm from which even the American Tories, "high" and "low," could find no shelter. The Tories of the 1960s, acting through their new organization, AID, accelerated the urban and rural changes in the daily life of the ambivalent masses. Within the twenty years given them to intervene in the economy, some Tories switched their rural emphasis from land reform (Niebuhrian maximalism) to technology substitution (Niebuhrian minimalism) and back to land reform. The emphasis depended on personalities, as "high" Tories avoided endorsing large-scale land reform, seeing in it a Whig attempt to ensnare "low" Tories into political intervention via an economic vehicle. But land itself remained the great issue. And the cost of changing land practices while defending those on the land from attack cost a national fortune. By 1966 South Vietnam received over 43 percent of AID's worldwide development grants.[59]

Whig maximalists finally forced the last military committee, the Thieu bakufu, to reform landholding practices completely, by replacing the traditional agricultural pattern of property ownership with the modern model of the American family farm. Pushing that program to its limits—meaning government confiscation of private lands—this coalition did what even Leninists feared to do. A revolution that southern peasants could understand at last arrived on their soil, but too fast and with too great an impact for both winners and losers. South Vietnam in the 1960's was "a violence-rent agrarian society, in which broad stretches of terrain were under the shifting control of contesting armies." Under such conditions "it was hardly suitable ground for the sort of technical assistance and private investments that the Point Four program had sought to encourage."[60] Truman's Point Four was the forerunner of Kennedy's AID.

But both Whig and Tory intervention came much too quickly, and at the most inopportune time. For while political and economic interventions in another state might complement each other in a competition with Leninism, such a competition required some modicum of stability. A specialist in Soviet affairs notes that after the 1960's even Leninists began changing their view of reordering turbulent Third World economies. This observer insists that, having seen Leninist predictions fail, the Soviets, like their American competitors, had to reformulate their arguments. John Kenneth Galbraith suggests that, by the 1970s, the two powers had reorganized the limits to their influence.[61] In other words, both Leninists and Lockeans realized that the maximum social turbulence their interventions could withstand was a Cold War environment, and even then the outcome was not predictable. In 1970 AID officials had called a conference to study thirty nations that the United States had helped with local land reform programs. Some found that the results were at best mixed. Other conferees were less favorable in their assessments. The idea that by giving aid one would change the recipient no longer had many believers after 1970.[62]

These Soviet and American reviews appeared after the United States began to withdraw from the Vietnam war. As Kennedy and Johnson had accelerated the rate of change in Vietnam's polity and economy, the cold war in Vietnam had nonetheless become an unheralded hot war for Americans—armies were shooting, air forces were bombing, and navies were shelling. In America the effects of this war were destroying the consensus that had held the American elite to certain national security policies. As Whigs and Tories began to fight over the design of their policies in Vietnam, citizens of the American covenant with power watched their covenantors commit what Raymond Aron aptly calls "the suicide of an elite."[63]

More caustic than Aron, James Schlesinger, the senior manager in the Defense Department at the time of final American withdrawal (1973–75) and an unreconstructed Tory, maintains that the withdrawal resulted from a failure of will: "During Vietnam, the nation's supposed elite, possessed by views then fashionable, was set upon by their children saying: 'You led the nation astray.'" Schlesinger believes that the internationalists "didn't have the strength of conviction to do what the older generation of an elite have always done when the younger generation acted up: simply stare back at them."[64]

George Kennan, an unreconstructed Whig, also had little toleration for what he saw as youth's folly, especially what he called the "student left" of the 1960's. Others joined him in a general critique of the Americans of the 1960's. Some saw the prevalent American antipathy toward the war as a failure of nerve.[65] Just such a person was Edward R. Murrow, head of The U.S. Information Agency (USIA). Quoting Shakespeare's *Henry V* to Dean Rusk, Murrow suggested that, in the time following Henry's death, the English lost their Saigon (Paris) and yielded up their Danang (Rouen) not by treachery "but want of men and money."[66] In other words, the new Camelot, echoing the Lancasterian "Once more unto the breach, dear friends, once more," merely updated the language: Send more, spend more. But by 1968, the year of the Tet offensive, fewer wanted to go, fewer wanted to spend.

CONCLUSION

America has always taken tragedy lightly. Too busy to stop the activity of their twenty-million-horse-power society, Americans ignore tragic motives that would have overshadowed the Middle Ages; and the world learns to regard assassinations as a form of hysteria, and death as neurosis, to be treated by a rest-cure. Three hideous political murders, that would have fattened the Eumenides with horror, have thrown scarcely a shadow on the White House.   Henry Adams, *The Education of Henry Adams*

Among these I mention as of special interest the fields of communications, including television and radio; agrovilles, land development, agricultural credit and agricultural extension; extended assistance to road building; continued efforts to expand education, particularly primary and elementary education in the villages; a mobile medical program, and further development of rural medical services; training for rural administration; and plans to assure more and better equipped and trained officials, adequately compensated, especially in rural areas and in the villages. Our basic premise is that these programs be designed with your government to meet your needs and conditions, and that they be carried out by your people, with our assistance where required. . . . Our support of Viet-Nam's independence and development will, as I have assured you in the past, remain among the highest priorities of American foreign policy.

Letter from President John F. Kennedy
to President Ngo Dinh Diem, Aug. 3, 1961

The Design of Defeat

> O God, give us serenity to accept what cannot be changed, courage to change what should be changed, and wisdom to distinguish the one from the other.
>
> Favorite prayer of Reinhold Niebuhr

FOR THE AMERICANS the war in Vietnam was not an accident. It evolved from a global design, a design that, when forced on Vietnam, became an aberration. For the Vietnamese, the revolution was an accident originating with the haphazard, midcentury interventions within their homeland by a number of outsiders—Japanese, French, American. The Vietnamese revolution was long by comparison to what the Americans call the Vietnam war, although, given their lack of strategic patience, the Americans thought it interminable. Worse, they discovered that they had failed. One should not conclude from this that postwar American internationalists routinely failed. They did not. Surprisingly, given the complex nature of global politics, they were generally successful, especially in managing national security tasks.

One might ask by what standards this judgment of success could be measured. Several crude indicators of success result from a trio of questions. First, did American internationalists avoid a war with the Soviet Union? Second, did they remain allied with Western Europe and Japan, with neither hostile toward American interests, that is, hostile enough to join with the Leninists against the United States? And third, did the American version of a global Lockean order result in more successes than failures in underdeveloped segments of the globe? Interestingly, the answers are generally affirmative.[1]

But the big exception remains Vietnam. Why? Partially because the designers of American internationalism—figures such as Clark Clifford, George Kennan, and Paul Nitze—recommended that their colleagues take minimum risks in competing with the USSR, while their successors—men such as Robert McNamara, Roger Hilsman, and Henry Cabot Lodge—recommended taking maximum risks. Whatever the degree of risk, all internationalists relied on a positive attitude toward international collective security, limited-war theory, political intervention abroad, and global economic reordering. Yet, when implemented, clearly any one of the four could cause volatile reactions. Therefore, caution was required; but in making policy decisions concerning Vietnam caution was missing.

Caution would have required patience and forbearance—to avoid overextending commitment, to avoid drawing false analogies with the prewar Munich agreement or the postwar Korean intervention, and to avoid linking local turbulence, indeed all anti-Western events, to conspiracies of Moscow Leninists. Simultaneously, caution also would have called for some action: some commitments required expansion; some "peace in our time" advice, blatantly the voice of appeasement, demanded rejection; and some conspiracies, in fact planned if not assisted by Moscow, required counteraction. To differentiate one from another was difficult but necessary. Knowing where and when to react called for statesmanship. And one of the greatest tests of internationalists' statesmanship was to learn not simply how to win but how to lose small, so that one did not lose large.

Eisenhower was better than most at losing small, even accustomed as he was to winning. He balked at helping Paris, London, or Tel Aviv rid Egypt of Nasser, nor would he help Paris at Dien Bien Phu, though Leninists or their allies might gain a temporary (or permanent) inch or two on Cold War maps.[2] This Kansan was cautious. Did that mean he was not an activist? Quite the contrary; he moved in Lebanon and succeeded. With limited goals and surgical precision Eisenhower applied what force he thought was needed to obtain what he set as minimalist goals; he did the same in Iran and Guatemala. Trying to win, but always prepared for a small loss, Eisenhower with active caution supervised the covenant with power. Whether one approves of his interventions is not the issue. The issue is the scope of his interventions and their objectives.[3]

Unfortunately, neither Kennedy nor Johnson had learned to lose small. To them losing was losing; it had no size. Perhaps it did not in the politics of Boston and Austin, but it did in world politics. Somehow Eisenhower knew this, as did Truman, who was feisty over Korea but prudent over the Chinese civil war. But prudence did not mark the careers of Truman and Eisenhower's successors. Kennedy and then Johnson both saw themselves losing in South Vietnam; rather than cutting their losses, each tried to increase the odds in his favor. As they gambled for higher stakes they trapped themselves.[4] Unexpectedly, their initially small win or loss became a debacle. Activism dominated, making into the main event a local conflict that once had been a sideshow of the global Lockean-Leninist struggle.

Since both Kennedy and Johnson gave public impressions of being activists on all fronts, they believed they could not be inactive in Indochina.

They were wrong—at least about the extent of the action required. On occasion, little or no action is the mark of a statesman, especially when it means refusing to do what might appear at the time to be the right thing. In Vietnam, to paraphrase General Bradley, the United States fought the wrong war (for political modernization) before fighting the right war (for internal security), at the wrong place (in the cities instead of the countryside), and with the wrong timing (the speed with which economic reforms toppled Vietnamese institutions was revolution, not reform). Perhaps if U.S. leaders had limited themselves to one intervention out of three—military, political, or economic—Vietnam still might have been the wrong war, given the nature of Vietnamese problems. However, the decision to intervene on all three levels simultaneously made this the ideal wrong war.

But the question is more complex than this. Not only must statesmen select the right type of intervention; they must in the first place decide whether to intervene at all. For example, in 1956, who intervened with force to help the anti-Leninists in Hungary? Eisenhower commanded the only power that could have helped, and although the Hungarian cause appeared just, he feared that intervention would have risked war with the Soviet Union. Here a small gain risked a larger loss. Therefore, militarily Eisenhower did nothing to save the cause of those who remained fighting in the streets of Budapest. In this situation, what Eisenhower accomplished amounted to a Niebuhrian best choice among unattractive options.[5]

In contrast to Hungary, the nation of South Vietnam had not already fallen within the Leninist orbit. But neither did it completely fall within the Lockean one. In the 1950's it was one of many contested areas, any of which could have tilted toward either orbit, or refused to be a satellite of either. In this and many other ways Vietnam did not resemble Hungary; yet in other ways it did. And, because of the manner in which it did resemble Hungary, the Vietnamese situation forced Kennedy and Johnson to make choices similar to Eisenhower's.

Eisenhower's two Democratic successors indeed did face a more complex issue; nevertheless, their task as statesmen required them, like Eisenhower before, to assess risks. What damage would the United States suffer from a protracted war that might weaken it in the most critical arena of global politics—that is, the struggle with the leading Leninist power, the Soviet Union? Would the U.S. economy, already troubled, be weakened? Would the one, critical, collective security arrangement, NATO, and the one, critical, bilateral arrangement, the Japanese-American Security Pact, both already threatened, be even more so? And most important, would domestic tranquillity, almost always in a state of flux in the

United States, be torn asunder? And in the chaos likely to follow, would American consensus on the four basic strategies of internationalism dissolve, with the public withdrawing its deference to national security experts?[6]

Since democratic elites depend heavily on public acceptance, its withdrawal causes serious problems. The rancorous debate over U.S. policy in Vietnam—a debate both within and outside of American opinion-making elites—assured a public withdrawal of deference. This can be seen in the responses of 2,282 officials who served variously as Foreign Service officers, labor leaders, politicians, clergy, foreign affairs experts outside government, media professionals, representatives of women's groups, and military personnel. The respondents were polled by means of a questionnaire mailed in 1976, the year following the fall of Saigon to Hanoi's forces. From their responses it is obvious that the fighting in Southeast Asia was a watershed event—it shattered the postwar consensus on international affairs among Americans and gave rise to sharply divergent views on the nature of the international system and the appropriate international role for the United States. While the majority "agreed that the credibility of American defense commitments had been seriously eroded as a consequence of the war," the respondents did not want a return to unilateralism; they expressed instead "a general consensus against unilateral action to cope with conflict issues."[7]

Is it fair to expect that the American leaders of the 1960's should have foreseen the likely outcome of their decisions? While it might appear unreasonable to expect statesmen to be seers, by definition they do possess a little of the prophet—enough, that is, to make careful, modest attempts to find a path away from the greatest dangers. This both Kennedy and Johnson failed to do in Vietnam.

This is not to argue that the victory of Hanoi Leninism was inevitable. A decade prior to the Vietnam conflict victory for Leninism in Korea had not been inevitable. It is to argue that the radical reform tendencies of the Americans made victory less likely for Saigon and the forces in the South. Those many miscalculations of the Whigs and Tories contributed heavily to the defeat of the last bakufu. It was a defeat assisted by extremism in American national security policy, an extremism that was centered in the National Security Council of the 1960's. The NSC of that period was a coordinative council that acted like a second State Department—the White House miniature of the original with a staff of "irregulars" who, by virtue of their academic training, found innovative ways to strip policy formation functions from the "regulars," career foreign service officers.[8] Limited-war theory, as applied to Vietnam, was one NSC innovation in policy formation and implementation. Unfortunately, nothing compares with an actual war to test human ability to limit it. Filled with the dead and dying, the test environment itself tries the sternest testers. Stern believers sitting behind Washington desks found that the limits they insisted on for Vietnam, once implemented, resulted in more violence than they ever supposed possible.

Observing the results of their limited war in Vietnam, many Whigs at the NSC were horrified. By their attempts to limit the area of combat, unfortunately these minimalists had managed only to increase its duration and intensity. Whether or not one approves of U.S. military intervention in Vietnam, surely once it took place, the intervention should have been completed as quickly as possible. At the very least, self-interest should have alerted these Whigs to the dangers for their own policies of a protracted war—as in Marshall's famous warning concerning a seven-year limit. In addition, Niebuhrian strategists should have recognized that, within nonnuclear limits, maximum conventional force applied quickly usually results in minimal overall damage. While perhaps sad, it is also unfortunately true.

Tories tended to understand this better than Whigs. However, although they were maximalists—who would enlarge the combat zone to Cambodia, Laos, and parts of North Vietnam if necessary—they allowed the minimalists to confuse them by analogies to Peking's previous reaction in the Korean War. Minimalists—shaken by the realization of their responsibility for the additional violence underway in Vietnam—kept the specter of Chinese intervention constantly in front of the maximalists.[9] Again, whether one agrees or disagrees with the decision to intervene, once engaged in combat, a state cannot be half engaged; that condition can only prolong the conflict and extend the damage. Moreover, Vietnam's borders with Cambodia and Laos were not similar to Korea's Yalu border with industrial Manchuria. In fact, with regard to South Vietnam, the border areas between Vietnam and either Cambodia or Laos met two Niebuhrian tests as permissible combat zones. First, the enemy had already introduced their military into both areas, and thus had been first to incorporate these bordering states into a larger combat zone. Second, these border areas were almost uninhabited, so that if combat had taken place there, destruction would have been limited.

Would these same arguments apply to North Vietnam? In part they would. Maximalist raids, in strength, north of the demilitarized zone as far as the North Vietnamese coastal city of Vinh would have avoided close proximity to Chinese territory. While it might remain questionable whether the Peking regime ever considered their southern border—rural even where settled, but mostly jungle-covered mountains—to be as vital as their northern industrial border with Korea and the Soviet Union,

Vinh was not near enough to threaten it. Everything south from Vinh was outside the Red River Delta. Although the land drained by that river remained a buffer for China, not all of North Vietnam was required for that buffer. Therefore, the land war could have been extended to southern North Vietnam without necessarily involving the Chinese in the combat.

The Chinese question was a constant concern. It need not have been. Internationalists worried that Chinese manpower, if it entered the Vietnamese war, would overcome U.S. weapons—what some call "man-over-weapons." The same argument had been used during the Korean War, but the facts did not validate the argument. In 1951, for example, an interview was conducted with approximately 300 Chinese prisoners captured in Korea. The prisoners indicated that whenever the Chinese PLA (People's Liberation Army) went beyond the borders of China and met an alert, better-armed force, the PLA superiority in manpower was canceled and could even be overwhelmed by the superiority of opposing weapons. In other words, among even well-indoctrinated troops—the soldiers of revolutionary armies—high morale can break down once troops are pounded by the superior, conventional weapons of a smaller force, especially if that revolutionary army is fighting on foreign soil and for a cause other than its own revolution.[10]

For the air war over the North, Vinh—approximately 150 miles south of Hanoi and over 300 miles from the Chinese border—marked the farthest point north that minimalist Whigs such as Paul Warnke (one of Nitze's replacements as Assistant Secretary of Defense for International Security Affairs) wanted to bomb. To Warnke, bombing parts of North Vietnam seemed less likely to cause a Chinese intervention than would ground raids. Perhaps; but it remained less effective also.[11] Effectiveness, obtaining results from actions, appropriately marks the statesman. From a bombing of North Vietnam a statesman would have demanded that his subordinates secure a major objective. Avenging American casualties was not a major objective; closing the French-built entrepôt of Haiphong was. But internationalists hesitated. Yet they could have met the Niebuhrian standard of little or no loss of life and physical damage. How? By mining the harbor. It was patently unrealistic to think that the United States, merely by bombing trails, could destroy enough of the supplies flowing to the enemy. Having watched the French be proved wrong on this count, why repeat the error? In lieu of intensive and destructive bombing throughout much of the North, a statesman would have pushed for intercepting the imported Soviet and Chinese arsenal at critical places, such as the necks of supply funnels.

Nor was Haiphong the only bottleneck. Bridges such as the bridge at Than Hoa were critical structures that funneled tons of supplies over a few crucial points. Likewise, the Mu Gia, Keo Neua, and Bannakai mountain passes into Laos also acted to force the convergence of supplies. Instead of concentrating on these specific targets for effective results, however, the nonstatesmen of the 1960's waited until the numerous porters had scattered the supplies throughout the land. Only then did the Americans give chase. Probably only Americans would dream up the idea of using high-performance aircraft to chase porters who often walked or bicycled their supplies south. And it happened, many times. Johnson's attitude to the bombing is captured in the following quote: "I won't let those Air Force generals bomb the smallest outhouse north of the 17th parallel without checking with me." [12] Clearly Johnson failed to realize that statesmen do not concern themselves with such details. Again, whether one concurred or not with the decision to intervene, surely this was not the manner in which to obtain a quick victory with the least amount of destruction. Here excessive caution was no caution at all.

Amazingly, the internationalists proved this the hard way, and the anti-Niebuhrian extreme way at that. First they called for extensive bombing throughout North Vietnam in their ROLLING THUNDER campaign. [13] This extreme action broke with the Niebuhrian guide, and was simultaneously ineffective and devastating. The internationalists followed this in 1972 with the bombing campaign named LINEBACKER I. Here they had more success, partly because of technical breakthroughs that included pinpoint accuracy gained by television or laser-guided smart-bombs. But more important, targets included specific Haiphong port facilities and rail links to China. And one great success crowned their efforts—U.S. pilots felled the difficult Than Hoa bridge. By September, estimates of supplies arriving in the South showed a reduction from May of 35–50 percent. [14] But loss of life and damage to property could not be avoided in Haiphong even if pilots dropped only smart-bombs. Mining, however, would have resulted in less violence, perhaps none at all. And an accident involving a Russian or Chinese ship would have held no greater risk than a non-smart pilot's hitting them with a smart-bomb.

Navalists such as Paul Nitze understood this. He and Elmo Zumwalt, the later Chief of Naval Operations, preferred that their bosses avoid a major military engagement in Vietnam; thus not all internationalists supported the big-unit war that commenced in 1965. Nitze and Zumwalt, who remained within government as a loyal opposition on that point, at a minimum wanted any big-unit engagement to be as quick and as inexpensive as possible, and as effective as possible. A naval mining of

Haiphong would have been such an action. It would have been no more risky than many other recommendations, and also would have met more of the criteria than most other recommendations.

Instead, geographical arguments ensnared the internationalists, arguments such as the exact location of the Vietnamese-Cambodian border through the midchannel of the Mekong. So also did investigations into hot pursuit of enemy personnel who, while firing at their pursuers, were retreating from South Vietnam to locations inside Cambodia, such as the border village of Chantrea. Without recognizing it, the internationalists had fumbled into deciding to be half in the war and half out of it. But straddling does not substitute for strategy.

And while they straddled, minimalist arguing against maximalist about where the war's limits should be, the internationalists also blatantly mislabeled their actions as part of a collective security response. The blame for this fabrication, more than for any other, rests solely with Lyndon Johnson. But Vietnam was not a test of collective security, regardless of how hard Johnson tried to create the image that it was. By misleading the public, Johnson took the cornerstone assumption of internationalism and denigrated it. Never trusting the American public to understand that American intervention in South Vietnam had begun in the Eisenhower years as a bilateral process, LBJ manipulated the case for intervention.

One might assume that this was of little consequence. In politics, if one cure does not work, another is tried. In fact, Johnson himself tired of collective security after 1965 and acted on a bilateral basis; this was his new "snake oil" cure. Unfortunately, internationalists could not be as cavalier as this Southerner. Their strategies were not last year's fashions, depending on the mood of fickle designers to tack on or snip off assumptions as Paris designers were fond of doing with buttons and bows. They saw honesty and consistency as an issue of public trust.

The dangerous thing about abusing public trust, at least in the United States, is that the public can become as cynical as their cynical abusers. Sooner or later the abuse of public confidence robs authority of its validity. In no way does this mean that a statesman cannot err and yet maintain enough public deference to govern. It is how he errs that matters. Johnson erred; that could be forgiven. Johnson deceived, and his deceptions regarding Vietnam policy could not be forgiven. In fact his deceptions were his undoing, in time even making it difficult for him to justify continued intervention in Vietnam to his closest advisers. For example, Wilbur Cohen, the Assistant Secretary of the Department of Health, Education, and Welfare, surprised Johnson late in his presidency by asking the President to explain to a cabinet meeting, "Why are we in Vietnam?" Cohen recalls that the President took half an hour to answer, "and the answer didn't make any sense to me." Cohen was shocked, believing that "if he [Johnson] had given the answer publicly, he would have been laughed out of court."[15] Such was the price of deception. This deception did not go unnoticed. In 1967, 65 percent of a Gallup poll sample responded that they were sure Johnson was not "telling the public all they should know about the Vietnam war." He deceived, and the people caught him at it. In this deception he damaged the principle of collective security, by letting cynicism replace commitment.[16]

While Johnson might casually change from his 1964 fashion of collective security to his 1965 fashion of a bilateral arrangement, his colleagues, once committed to collective security, could not change as fast. For example, Johnson, having appointed Walt Rostow as his National Security Adviser, found that Rostow continued to campaign for collective security to the bitter end. In mid-1967—with Johnson desperate to raise more troop units in order to support the military's insatiable appetite, an appetite by then unnerving even McNamara—Rostow devised a percentage scheme that he called a "troop community chest operation in Vietnam." Rostow put his calculations in a table that "showed that if each country (Korea, Australia, New Zealand, Philippines, Thailand, Indonesia, Republic of China, Malaysia) dispatched the same percentage of its total armed forces to Vietnam as the United States had done, about 14%, . . . there would now be an additional 70,000 troops in that country."[17] One can only be thunderstruck that the person with the second most critical job within the apparatus of the national security state, second only to the President, for whom he clears the agenda, would be found calculating mirages as late as 1967. But calculate he did.

Obviously, internationalists miscalculated phase three of the long Vietnamese revolution. These interventionists were trying to constrain Leninism at the Vietnamese point on a global arc of containment. But instead of complementing the specific agenda of the people at that global point, much of the American agenda, especially its timing, conflicted with the Vietnamese agenda. The South Vietnamese elites discovered that the American elites wanted to force upon them too much, too soon. Saigon's leaders also never understood the fact that the United States had a global responsibility that obliged it to watch more than one political eruption at a time.

In fact, in geological terms one might say that the two camps, one Lockean and the other Leninist, resembled two giant plates under the constant pressure of global movement, folding and faulting at their sensitive points of contact. Geologists tell us that along the Pacific Ocean's edge is a rim of fire, active volcanoes plus concentrated earthquake activity. Along this rim large pieces of the earth's crust rub against each other, creating violent activity. In like manner, as the two camps rubbed each other raw at their crusty extremities, political and military violence erupted in surrogate wars, revolutions, and general civil strife. In postwar Asia the eruptions that involved Leninists and Lockeans, both local and foreign, occurred in Indonesia when army generals replaced their island Leninists; in Malaysia when the British helped to block the local Leninists; in the Philippines when Americans aided in the struggle against indigenous Leninists; in China when the United States refused to try to halt the winning Leninists; and in South Korea when the United States defeated the invading Leninists. And then there was Vietnam. Such peripheral eruptions could turn into Krakataus. To avoid such calamity each camp hoped to maintain buffer space between itself and the neighboring camp.

For the superpowers, finding a buffer was not easy. In Europe, Soviet and American armies occupied the buffer space that existed between their homelands—the Soviets in Eastern Europe and the Americans in Western Europe. Their respective front lines marked the new political frontiers. In Southeast Asia, their armies did not occupy the buffer space. This buffer problem predated the Soviet and American interest in southern Asia; the Hindu strategist of antiquity, Kautilya, noted it when he wrote about a circle of states. In post–World War II Asia, new battles determined new frontiers; but in a nuclear era, battles had to be fought away from the Lockean and Leninist homelands. Whig and Tory internationalists tried to locate these battles as far as possible from their homeland. Leninist internationalists attempted the same, contesting with the Lockeans where the lines would be drawn. For this task the Cold War combatants needed new military cartographers.[18]

One should not assume that the references to lines, arcs, points, or perimeters marked solely the language of American interventionists. Ho Chi Minh conceived of global strategy in these terms.[19] So did Indian intellectuals in New Delhi. As early as 1951 they used such terms in *The Eastern Economist*. One editor, concerned about Chinese Leninists, stated that "India's McMahon line which separates our defensive apparatus from China also runs now in Vietnam." The New Delhi authors also believed that it might be possible to connect Pacific and Atlantic security: "It may be that the occasion, if ever there is one, for invoking the terms of the Pacific Security Pact may also be the occasion to invoke the North Atlantic Treaty, in which case no difference will be perceptible."[20] On the last point, the one concerning the lack of any perceptible difference between Pacific and Atlantic security, the author erred. He overlooked the essential question of community, something the Americans also overlooked when they turned to collective action in Southeast Asia.

For states to risk collective action, there must exist some recognizable self-interest that is at risk. For Americans in 1947, two manifestations of their self-interest became apparent. One involved a shared political culture with its essentials—political and economic liberty.[21] American opinion-making elites perceived that the loss of these liberties in another state threatened a later loss at home. This made it obligatory for more than one state to share the costs involved in protecting these liberties. About this the internationalists were hardheaded. For instance, by the 1960's they recognized that, in the economic dimension, alliances such as NATO furnished a collective good, namely, security. Since some NATO states, chiefly the larger and richer members, believed they had more to secure, these same states paid more proportionally for their security.[22] And when American internationalists added cultural and political dimensions to the economic dimension, they simply compounded the glue that held diverse parts together, especially when under strain. The internationalists of the 1960's knew that even in the best of times the Atlantic-basin culture contained diverse and strained components. Nevertheless, the 1960's became the age of Atlanticism, at least among American internationalists. By the 1980's much of this American enthusiasm had cooled, especially after the vigorous economic growth in the Pacific basin. But in the 1960's Atlanticism dominated the American international agenda, and the Atlantic basin represented their premier community.

While the United States shared both a political culture and a political economy with Western Europe, Japan and the United States shared only a single dimension—a political economy. Nevertheless, in both instances the values each member state shared made possible a community alliance. Under stress both alliances, when called upon for collective action, survived. Their opinion-making elites saw this survival as serving their self-interest. This was not true in Southeast Asia, regardless of the designs of the American internationalists.

Clearly collective action, whether taken for security or other reasons, limits the independence of each participating elite. The classical reference for this problem is Jean-Jacques Rousseau's staghunt analogy, to which diverse authors find themselves returning.[23] In short, if all hunters (states), motivated by self-interest, remain together and risk hunger in order to hunt a stag (security), all will benefit from the feast. If one hunter (state) fails to take the risk and instead defects to hunt rabbits, he himself at least will have food—not as much or as tasty, but enough to survive—while the risk that the others will go hungry or even starve increases. With each such defection the risk increases. It is possible that the temptation to defect will be strong; hence defections should be expected. But if the hunters lessen temptation by sometimes having group staghunts and sometimes going on solitary rabbit hunts, collective action will be possible but intermittent. Under ideal conditions, opinion-making elites would understand that consistent stag-hunting would be in their own interest, hence they could avoid temptation, and collective action would be possible on a regular rather than an intermittent basis. It is important to recognize that for collective action to work, a high level of consensus within a community is not necessary. In fact, it has been argued that just the opposite obtains: "Although a symmetric and an asymmetric community might collectively choose similar levels of supply of a host of collective goods, the asymmetric community might be far more successful in generating the political activity to bring about supply."[24]

The problem for Southeast Asia was that it wasn't a community. Convincing oligarchs—those who were Roman Catholic Filipinos with Spanish surnames—to risk their future with a South Vietnamese Confucian elite was not possible. Nor would others in the region risk all—neither royal Buddhist elites in Thailand, nor Muslim civilian oligarchs from Malaysia, nor Muslim bakufu generals from Indonesia. None came forward with an internationalized conception of their self-interest; none wanted to go on staghunts that locked them to the future of Confucian Vietnam. Obviously they did not enjoy the prospect that any Greater Vietnam, be it Lockean or Leninist, would become the major military power in their region.[25] They, more than outsiders, knew the Vietnamese as the region's Prussians. A fact unnoticed outside Southeast Asia was not overlooked by Southeast Asian leaders: pugnacious Vietnam, unlike conquered China and Russia, had defeated the invading Mongols. The Vietnamese had never forgotten this and were delighted to remind those who had. Americans had not forgotten it: they never knew it. But they soon learned that their creation, SEATO, did not hold back the Tonkinese Mongols.

Amazingly, as SEATO crumbled, another organization was created. But it was not organized by the Atlantic-based outsider. It was a Tory outsider who first took note, in strategic terms, of this regional association.[26] Robert McNamara watched while Southeast Asian oligarchs discovered that they were in the midst of the creation of a one-dimensional community based on the developing political economy of their region. The royal Thai government was instrumental in recognizing the birth of this community. Thai oligarchs, both royalist-civilian and military, helped organize the Association of Southeast Asian Nations (ASEAN), which came to life in the Bangkok declaration of August 8, 1967. Americans were not invited to join ASEAN, nor were the Vietnamese. By 1967 the Americans were too dangerous to be invited to join. Willing to save a state from itself by destroying it if necessary, the Americans had the will and the money to help a state rebuild. But the states in ASEAN did not desire to undergo the initial destruction. Therefore, they did quietly what the Americans had tried to do noisily. Behind the Mekong—the American position was in front of the great river—ASEAN began to build the Tory dream, but to build slowly. Expanding economies, doused with a minimum of Lockean assumptions, sprang up, in their own regional way, to block the spread of Leninist assumptions.[27]

Unevenly at first, Asian economic leaders began to attack poverty, disease, illiteracy, and despair. But they began by granting their people the basic right to security—the first task of any government.[28] Because modernization could uproot the teak trees of their cultures, the regional oligarchs moved cautiously, unimpeded by the short time limits by which Americans measured change. Unlike the ASEAN leaders, Americans assumed that transplanting Lockean institutions was like rooting ivy from cuttings—quick and simple. In fact it was more like waiting for an acorn to turn into an oak—slow and complex. It was as if ASEAN leaders had heeded the warning that "modernization, whatever else it involves, is always a moral and a religious problem."[29] For example, in Vietnam modernization began to change the relationship between family members, between neighbors, between peasants and the soil, between employees and their places of work. A modern son or daughter could choose to leave the family home, to make his or her own career, to find a mate. A modern neighbor could be declared owner of the once-common water rights, could insist on other neighbors' paying for the right to use the water, could sue in court if payment were late or not made. A modern peasant could use his farm as collateral to buy modern equipment such as a water pump, could rent this equipment to other farmers, could become a business-farmer and buy other farms in distress. A modern employee could strike, could open his own business in competition with his old employer, could form a legal partnership with others who were previously strangers. All of this and more went to the core of a civilization's past moral and religious beliefs, often changing and distorting them.[30]

But the internationalists demanded quick results, whatever the distortions. Without caution, the Johnson administration, threatened by revolt from within and defeat from without, finally rejected the guidance of Niebuhr. In particular, the Whigs became extremists. Determined to make the Vietnamese free even before they were secure, they confirmed Rousseau's prediction "that whoever refuses to obey the general will shall be compelled to do so by the whole body. This means nothing less than that he will be forced to be free."[31]

Allen Whiting demonstrates the American application of Rousseau by quoting from a speech by a senior member of the Truman administration, Francis Matthews, as reported by *Time* magazine. *Time* did not miss the opportunity to bring the Secretary of the Navy's message to millions of Americans when it reported that he spoke to a crowd of 100,000 Americans on August 25, 1950. In this speech, covered by the national and international media, the Navy Secretary advocated "instituting a war to compel cooperation for peace." He suggested that Americans "would become the first aggressors for peace."[32] More sober minds rejected his concept of a military crusade for peace. Men like George Marshall (who more than any other individual had managed the U.S. share of victory in World War II) saw the extremism in what was essentially a call to universal arms. But later leaders did not. Somehow, once committed in Vietnam, activists within the national security membership decided to respond to Matthews's challenge in the 1960's even though it had been dismissed by mimimalists in the Truman administration.

Coming as it did in the third month of the Korean War, Matthews's speech was in the demagogic tradition, a tradition not unknown even in Lockean democracies. While wiser leaders prevailed against Matthews—whom they exiled to Ireland as U.S. Ambassador—one must recognize that the missionary spirit in American politics sometimes can be as destructive as it is sometimes constructive. It is most destructive when it entices wise leaders to forget their wisdom, and to universalize the American or Lockean experience. When carried to an extreme, something as innocent as Tory or Whig security assistance programs become pernicious. In fact, the extremism of Tory and Whig programs for South Vietnam was one of the major causes of the final disaster. Yet early postwar Whigs and Tories rejected the obvious extremism of Matthews and others. And there were other extremists. For example, Truman had to retire General Orville Anderson, Commandant of the Air War College, for joining the Ambassador to Ireland in his calls for wars for progress and peace.[33] But somehow the later internationalists could not see the same faults within their own more subtle arguments.

Until the intervention in Vietnam, internationalists had frowned upon extremism. Initially they had entertained fairly modest ambitions in Vietnam. Unhappy to see their French ally expend so much blood and treasure in their vain effort to reestablish its sway in the Pacific basin, internationalists hoped for a compromise. But they badly wanted this compromise to come short of a local Leninist's winning the wreckage left by a French collapse. In the 1950's, when careful, when with patience and forbearance, they had learned to moderate those impulses that could influence a nation to use extreme measures, American internationalists did follow Niebuhrian moderation. But by the 1960's they had lost their way, at least in Vietnam.

Initially, postwar American leadership succeeded in blending military, political, and economic designs into a coherent, global policy. As inter-nationalists the leaders represented a covenant between merit and power. They saw the mission of this covenant as a competition with Leninist con-spiracies. At a quickening pace after 1947, the United States became ac-tively engaged in most regional disputes, in part because Leninists were intervening in global politics, but also in part because internationalists themselves believed in intervention whether others had intervened or not. In intervening, internationalists worked for a Lockean rather than Leninist reordering of the world's political economy. This reordering con-test resulted from postwar changes that regrouped the prewar, multi-polar world into a world led by two states of continental dimension— hence the tepid bipolar world of Soviet and American combat. In other words, in the postwar era, American security specialists created a na-tional security state in order to conduct what some of them called liberal interventions. In creating this state internationalists held shared images of the world.[34] In fact, from the onset of the Lockean-Leninist struggle these shared images allowed a diverse combination of individuals from both major parties—Democratic and Republican—to practice a coherent statecraft that continued regardless of changes in White House occu-pants, or Kremlin retainers.

The coherence finally broke down, however, when it came to inter-vention in Vietnam. U.S. statecraft faced major problems when both Whig and Tory ranks suffered internal splits over fundamental policy matters. These internal splits added to the tensions in policy-making caused by the basic split between Whig and Tory approaches.

The basic agenda of Whig internationalists was to reshape Saigon's political order, to eliminate authoritarianism from Saigon's politics. But the Whigs were split on the question of timing. Some Whigs were able to tolerate the political authoritarianism of Ngo Dinh Diem, hoping to re-form him in place, but others despaired, turning to reconstruction of Vietnamese politics (a coup) as a last hope. The Tories were dissatisfied with most Whig efforts because Tories viewed the resulting political up-heaval as interfering with Tory efforts to reform the Vietnamese economy. Therefore, the speed of political change was an issue that mainly split Whig ranks.[35] Those who wanted to proceed slowly with the changes in Saigon's politics were a category of reform Whig while those who stressed speed were reconstruction Whigs.

Whig internationalists, even with their minor differences healed, did not usually dominate the making of U.S. national security policy toward Vietnam; the Tories did. Therefore, the split in Tory ranks was the most critical. The Tory agenda was simple; first change the internal economic order and you create citizens with a vested interest in fighting on the

Lockean side of any war. Political reordering could wait; in fact, many Tories thought that a certain amount of political rigidity was necessary in order to stabilize the government during the turmoil of economic change. But changing the economic order was not simple; and Tory views on how to proceed diverged.

While South Vietnam's economy was more advanced than the economies of many Third World states of the 1960's, nevertheless most of its wealth still came from rice agriculture. In this productive Southeast Asian rice bowl the land was not evenly distributed. In fact, the need for economic reordering in the mid-twentieth century was the long-term result of disruptions in traditional patterns of land ownership that the French colonial rulers had created by introducing the market mechanism. Later American and South Vietnamese leaders inherited a peasantry that had already begun to experience the trauma of alienation from the land. Within South Vietnam's economy, Tories faced two choices associated with land policy: they could wait to see how successfully economic assistance would shift the major sources of wealth from land and agriculture to manufacturing and commerce (a condition under which, Tories believed, wealth would be more widely dispensed, or at least would be earned by merit), or they could move quickly themselves to seize and redistribute landed wealth. The former choice attracted "high" Tories, who abhorred the idea of state confiscation, an evil that they believed others had promoted in the guise of modern land reform programs. "Low" Tories, on the other hand, impatient with what they perceived as slow-footedness in their "high" colleagues, were attracted by the moderate position of limited land redistribution, one of those major dislocations that Joel Migdal suggests results in a strong state. And so they quarreled over the design of their respective interventions.

With Whig and Tory coalitions rising and subsiding on an issue-by-issue basis, for Lockeans to achieve political or economic reform in another state became difficult at best, impossible if it meant rushing. To reform meant to progress, at least to American internationalists. In the experience of Americans, progress had meant willingness to bear burdens during the period of national reform.[36] In an age of international reform, American reformers faced even more difficult problems in trying to replicate their national success. In this new age of reform two major export-models of reform competed, one Lockean, the other Leninist. What made it easier for both American and Soviet elites to win domestic support for international reform was the fact that the potential recipients—those who would have to bear the burdens of reform—were not the reformers' own population.

The history of international reform in Vietnam confirms the diagnosis that, in comparing reform with revolution, the former is far harder to accomplish. To recast Michael Ignatieff's view of *King Lear*: there "is a truth in the brutal simplicities of the merciless" revolutionary that "the more complicated truth of the merciful" reformer is helpless to refute. But the argument that reform, in the guise of modernization, breeds revolution is difficult to prove for Vietnam.[37] But also it is not clear that the reverse is true—that revolution causes reform. In Vietnam both were at work simultaneously.

Although the French began the modernization of Vietnam, that transformation intensified under the Americans, the more so because it took place in the midst of a war, so that the U.S. military, instead of the South Vietnamese military, was the agent that conducted the programs. What modernization accomplished was to help produce a field of contenders for leadership of the nation, political personalities, each of whom advanced his particular alternate claim of political legitimacy. Revolution resulted when these claims clashed (revolution here being defined as a militarized mass insurrection). Politics and personality were the two key ingredients in the Vietnamese nation-building process. In fact, charismatic leadership was the critical element in the revolutionary mixture. In Vietnam it was the charismatic leader to whom people turned in moments of anxiety and distress, as that figure, by sheer force of personal magnetism, negated established rules and structures, or validated systems or norms, or, failing in these two, became a prophet who revealed and ordained "a unified view of the world derived from a consciously integrated and meaningful attitude toward life."[38]

By stressing individuals (the method of history) over systems (the method of the social sciences), the uniqueness of the American experience in Vietnam becomes clearer. One concentrates "on the contents rather than the container."[39] This method connects people through organizations to events—it connects John Kennedy to the NSC coup against Ngo Dinh Diem; Lyndon Johnson to the deceptions of his administration in the pre-election-year activities of 1964; Ambassadors Henry Cabot Lodge and Maxwell Taylor to the State Department's failure to coordinate political activity between Washington and Saigon; General William Westmoreland to the unsuitability of Military Advisory Command Vietnam as the agent for nation-building and pacification; Secretaries Robert McNamara and Dean Rusk to the failure of the NSC apparatus to design a realistic strategy; and Secretaries Douglas Dillon and Henry Fowler to the economic patchwork of the Treasury that for so many years put off facing the financial crisis fueled by the war.

The Vietnamese pattern can be seen to repeat the American one—Ngo Dinh Diem was connected to events through his family, a traditional political organization; Ho Chi Minh through his party, a revolutionary organization; and General Nguyen Khanh through a bureaucratic organization derived from his bakufu. It is difficult to assess the leadership of these three Vietnamese. Some scholars tend to condemn all three, spotlighting their many weaknesses. Other specialists err in another way; they praise the winner and condemn the losers. In truth, each of the three had his weaknesses and strengths. Evaluating the balance between the positives and negatives is difficult. Only a fatalist would assign the victor the spoils—thereby allowing Ho Chi Minh most of his strengths but few of his faults, while recognizing the faults but none of the strengths of Diem and Khanh.

Any attempt to make a balanced judgment of contemporary authoritarian leaders, whether from the left or right, is highly controversial. The Whig tradition, so dominant in Anglo-American circles, strongly biases the argument against twentieth-century autocrats. Most of us tend to set aside unjust or illegal acts of the autocrats of the distant past—Henry VIII, Louis XIV, Frederick the Great, Peter the Great; and the compelling reason for our doing so seems to be the success of each autocrat in his own nation-building process.[40] With the passage of time even modern Whigs forgot the transgressions against Anglo-American liberties of men such as Pitt during the Napoleonic Wars and Lincoln during the American Civil War. The injuring autocrat of the present often stands convicted on one injustice by global public opinion, and then all his deeds, both constructive and destructive, are blighted. Though justifiably debited for misdeeds, he should be credited for his contributions. Only in this way can the fully formed historical personality emerge. Fortunately for the Vietnamese, they were led neither by great saints nor by great sinners. Instead, as in most nations, mere mortals contended for the right to rule. Unable to settle disputes amicably, the Vietnamese contenders warred instead. Of the three, two were evenly matched. Because his cause lost, Ngo Dinh Diem is condemned by many critics as a petty tyrant; because his prevailed, Ho Chi Minh is often praised as a peerless leader. Neither assessment is accurate.

The generally pejorative assessement of Ngo Dinh Diem makes it only the more difficult to compare his strengths and weaknesses. As Shakespeare so astutely had Mark Antony note about a Roman oligarch, "The evil that men do lives after them, the good is oft interred with their bones." In the literature authors usually characterize Ngo Dinh Diem as Vietnam's last mandarin—a title chiefly used to convey hostility. The original meaning, however, comes from the Chinese and is not pejorative, in that these public officials were the rulers of traditional Vietnam. That is, the mandarin symbolized the Vietnamese past. Now, as a Vietnamese traditionalist, Ngo Dinh Diem was not an American puppet, but he was an authoritarian leader, by both inclination and training. The traditional Vietnamese elite selection-process had efficiency, not equality, as its goal. A modern approximation of a mandarin elite, in fact, would be the French graduates of grand écoles, especially the "ENACS" from the École Natonale d'Administration.[41] In much the same manner as this French elite, Vietnamese mandarins such as Ngo Dinh Diem represented a historical approach to leadership selection. In the Chinese-influenced Orient, the mandarin elite ruled by benevolent authoritarianism—and it was a meritocracy in one key aspect, the testing for entry.

It is helpful, in comparing and contrasting Saigon's Diem with Hanoi's Ho, to avoid being excessively judgmental, while still recognizing their obvious flaws. Both contenders, bachelors with little interest in worldly possessions, appear ambitious to the point of ruthlessness. As Vietnamese, both had fought to eliminate foreign domination, be it Chinese, Russian, Japanese, French, or American. When cornered, each took what assistance necessity demanded. But, despite being servants to none, both men did play client to stronger patrons. Although in this role both played falsely, both also remained true to the ideal of an independent Vietnam. But how did peasants view an independent Vietnam?

The peasantry, too, rejected all outsiders, but this was not simply another form of peasant nationalism; for the Vietnamese peasant, it was far more. What one might call nationalism in the early 1960's was but an urban veneer—concealing, ignoring the majority, most of whom were nonmarket peasants. Without the market mechanism, modern nationalism could not exist for this majority. Although outsiders had inserted the market mechanism among them, it had not affected the centers of peasant life by the time the two leaders began their contest. The gradual demystification of their rural world confused Vietnamese peasants, but it did not send them rushing into the commercialization of social relations; rather, most of them resisted the secular and utilitarian call of the market.

The main audience for Ngo Dinh Diem and Ho Chi Minh during their battle for the tribal chieftainship was the traditional Vietnamese, both urban and rural. The two contenders fought vigorously and viciously for the loyalty and support of this population, Ngo Dinh Diem concentrating on the cities and Ho Chi Minh on the countryside. Worldly as were both contenders, they continued to address their fellow Vietnamese as a kinship group.[42] This kinship group respresented a type of tribalism in the

Vietnamese people that was reflected in their response to the primordial call of a fatherland. But both major contenders were dead before the battle for leadership was won.

While the stress on individuals is vital to understanding the American experience in Vietnam, it is also important to understand key groups of people and key agencies. On the American side, certain federal organizations dominated national security. Among them were the Departments of Defense and State, the Central Intelligence Agency, the National Security Council, and the Agency for International Development. Because the first two are gigantic bureaucracies, it is necessary to concentrate on the key subsections through which leaders made policy. At DOD the key subsection was the Office of the Secretary of Defense (OSD), where Congress and the President located policy-making; at State there were two vital subsections—the Policy Planning Staff during the time of Kennan and Nitze, and the Office of the Undersecretary of State for Economic Affairs during the tenures of Acheson, Clayton, Dillon, and Ball. Internationalists dominated all of these organizations and initiated their programs, beginning in 1947 with DOD, CIA, NSC, and State. Looking at the organizational procedures, memory, and loyalty that formed the basis of bureaucratic politics prior to the 1960's, the evidence indicates that the entrenched procedures of these agencies influenced many U.S. decisions about Vietnam. In other words, the security policies of the late 1940's and early 1950's took root within the national security apparatus, and Vietnam policy came to be one manifestation of these earlier decisions.

More particularly, three key thinkers in the early postwar period, sharing a set of common beliefs and possessed of powerful intellects, devised the components of the containment policy, a policy to contain the great Leninist adversary, the USSR. They incorporated the doctrine of containment into ideas that the bureaucracy could implement. Their written policy statements were dispersed by their President, and the thoughts contained within them came to have a life of their own, passing almost unchanged from one decade to the next. The trio of advisers were Paul Nitze, George Kennan, and Clark Clifford. The four strategies that internationalists devised from the containment policy were these: First, these internationalists broke ranks with their predecessors by stressing the need for long-term, collective security commitments. Second, if conflict with Leninists were to occur, the internationalists insisted that it be conducted under their new strategy of limited war. Their antagonism remained generally cold; but when hot, it had to be limited. Third, when the antagonism was cold, the United States could intervene in the politics of selected states, with the intention of drawing the states into the Lockean orb. Thus states were to be rescued from local or foreign Leninists. Fourth, they believed that injection of the market mechanism was a means of re-ordering the economic base of a foreign state, again to carry that state to the Lockean side of the containment arc and thereby to deny Leninists an ally on the other side of the arc. When it came to incorporating these strategies into policy, the three thinkers each emphasized a different aspect of the overall containment policy. Nitze was most responsible for articulating a policy emphasizing military containment; Kennan emphasized political constraints; and Clifford added economic emphasis. While emphasizing particular aspects of containment, all three men of course remained aware of the triadic nature of the overall containment effort.

That triad of constraints was important in Vietnam; important also was the combination of people and their organizations. By combining both, one can see how Vietnam policy was more than a series of military engagements, which is the least important way of explaining this war. The combination shows the war for what it was, a test of the entire national security system. The argument has been made that this system worked, but this is a narrow argument that suggests that all the system could do was to act like a communications link for political reports. In this argument the national security officials only reported political success or failure; they had no capacity to influence either. In this closed system the only important decisionmakers were Washington politicians.

But the national security system was an open one, one that individuals beyond the White House influenced in dramatic ways. Ambassador Lodge in Saigon, planning to assist an NSC attempt to direct a coup with a foreign military committee—that is only one stark example. It is true that the NSC staff tried to keep the system's Washington decisionmakers informed concerning this possible coup. But when key Whigs forced a decision favorable to the coup, many system participants did not believe "all important decisions were made without illusions about the odds for success." Furthermore, the fact that a major series of decisions concerning land reform programs was made at lower levels of the system, does not substantiate the claim that "virtually all views and recommendations were considered."[43]

Private research institutes also influenced policy. They sold their intellectual services within the market. By the 1960's many existed, with three of them doing much of the national security research—the RAND Corporation, the Stanford Research Institute, and the Institute for Defense Analysis. To understand their positioning within an open system, where their members contributed to decisions, is to understand how "knowledge factories" had direct influence on Vietnamese policies—influence that could enter the system from the bottom, the middle, or the top. Two other organizations—invisible in most studies of major events such as the Vietnam War because of their newness or smallness, and because their work is associated with classified information—made a major difference in policy decisions. The two, one public, the other private, are the National Security Council and the Council on Foreign Relations. Because of their unique memberships and situations, each had power to influence events.

Beyond what these organizations covered, two subjects within the overall security system caused the greatest confusion. One was misunderstood, the other almost unmentioned. The first was intelligence collection; the second was the financial complexity of the war, especially its influence on the domestic Vietnamese and American economies and its repercussions in the international economy.

When one says American intelligence, the CIA springs to mind. As a postwar creation of the national security state, the CIA was accepted by Americans once elite and popular opinion began to recognize that intelligence collection, within bounds, was a proper role for government. This agency was not an aberration; it did not lack popular legitimacy, nor did professional CIA personnel misrepresent or miscalculate the evidence they collected about Vietnam (hence supposedly misleading Presidents Kennedy and Johnson). The CIA neither recommended nor controlled the coup against Ngo Dinh Diem. Nor does evidence indicate that the CIA predicted any upturns in the war following that coup. Not only the CIA, but also other American intelligence units, controlled by the CIA's bureaucratic competitors in the State and Defense Departments, corroborated the negative estimates about the Saigon governments and the possibilities of a military victory between 1963 and 1965. CIA agents reported what they saw in Vietnam in those years; their field reports establish that the CIA, from field to federal level, did not misrepresent or miscalculate the war, at least not during the critical years from 1963 to 1965. It is also clear that senior CIA field representatives, people such as William Colby, John Richardson, and Peer De Silva, influenced local policies in Saigon in many subtle ways, ways that often did not require coordination with Washington politicians.

In assessing the financial part of the system, it is necessary to bring the participants—people such as Douglas Dillon, Henry Fowler, Fowler Hamilton, and Frank Coffin in Washington and their equivalent colleagues and counterparts in Vietnam, both American and Vietnamese—into any discussion of their organizations. This war, a war previously considered a political-military struggle, was as much an economic war as it was either political or military. Moreover, the scale of the economic intervention was enormous.

The war was costly for both Vietnam and the United States. Reducing the expenditures to cost per Viet Cong, or North Vietnamese body-count, a grisly way to state costs, reveals at least the cavalier manner in which the internationalists of the 1960's—particularly Secretaries Rusk and McNamara and President Johnson—squandered a national fortune. Inflated costs led to inflation, especially in a war economy like Vietnam's. The inflation spread to the U.S. economy, but Johnson preferred to temporize rather than underwrite the expensive political costs required to correct the financial hemorrhage. True, U.S. economic problems were associated with the nation's unique role in the larger postwar global economy; but Vietnam only complicated matters and made the situation worse.

It has been suggested that the complex interdependence of the global economy of the 1960's constrained the United States. Though it hurt, it did not constrain, especially with regard to the intervention in Vietnam under Johnson. Since the financial burden of the war, once manifested, quickly made itself widely apparent, should not the structure of trans-governmental politics have forced Johnson to act more responsibly? Could not other investors in the international economy have made the cost of continuing the war unbearable? Fundamentally this is the problem with the theory of complex interdependence as applied to the cost of Vietnam; it fails to predict the behavior of superpower actors, at least that of Johnson in the 1960's. And his was the critical administration for that war. Theorists admit as much quietly by sidestepping the Vietnam connection. Instead, they refer generally to the international monetary politics of the 1960's.[44] But the United States was at the center of said politics at that time, and, simultaneously, Vietnam was at the center of American monetary politics.

No one can skirt the centrality of the U.S. economy to the global economy or the centrality of Vietnam to the economic issues of the Johnson administration. Although the South Vietnamese economy was complexly dependent on the U.S. economy, the American economy was not dependent on the global economy, nor were the two interdependent.[45] Instead, the U.S. economy was connected to the global economy in a complex, independent way. Nothing constrained Johnson's printing presses as he tried to buy himself out of losing a war. The fact that he failed does not prove that he was constrained by an interdependent global economy, an economy that acted through multiple channels as a powerful countervailing force against irrational or irresponsible states, even superpowers. From the simple fact that Johnson's bequest of economic problems caused financial headaches for those who inherited them we cannot infer that while he was causing them they simultaneously constrained him. Where a scholar might best employ the concept of complex interdependence for the 1960's is in the realm of political economy—say, with respect to France and Germany ten years after joining the Common Market—instead of the realm of national security, with respect to Vietnam and the United States in the 1960's. This is because national security issues often confound economists' demand for rational actors as that term is used in classical economies. The case of Vietnam certainly confounds.

The South Vietnamese economy was the target of interventions by both Lockeans and Leninists, and their many actions fall into two categories, rural and urban. In either case, the purpose of intervention could be either substitution or reconstruction. Substitution meant making an extant economic structure more productive and efficient; reconstruction meant transforming a structure into another kind of structure. An example of substitution in the urban category is the program of the early 1950's to replace older manufacturing technologies in much of the Vietnamese textile industry. These substitutions were innovations that had been successfully applied by others, usually in newly industrialized countries. An example of substitution in the rural category occurred when American agricultural experts supplied newly developed hybrid rice to the Vietnamese. With innovations such as these, Americans repeated their earlier successful feats of technology transfer in Asia, especially in South Korea and Taiwan.

While substitution often caused short- and long-range shifts in the local power structure, it was far less disruptive than programs of reconstruction, which could cause upheavals. Reconstruction in Vietnam was also either rural or urban, but it had two levels, pervasive reconstruction and specific reconstruction. Pervasive reconstruction came about when interventionists attempted to change such basic social structures as land ownership. When that changed, the distribution of wealth changed. Therefore, in the competition between the Viet Cong and Saigon governments over land reform, whoever won would bring a pervasive alteration of the basic structure of peasant life. Architects of the other level of reconstruction attempted to change only one feature, usually a national resource, such as the Mekong River, into a monumental regional development project. The former was a case of thinking small, the latter of thinking big. Interestingly, the results tended to be reversed; small thinking fed more directly into big events such as revolution, while big thinking usually caused modest changes, at least at the beginning. Both levels of reconstruction escalated the revolution and were difficult and damaging for both the reconstructors and their recipients—doubly so when combined with military and political intervention.[46]

Military and political interventions are determinants of only a minority of society's winners and losers, usually small political groups in the capital city. A majority of ambivalent people usually exists outside these political groups. As large pockets around which the war flows, they do not concern themselves directly with the politics of war, its winners or losers. The Vietnamese peasants were an ambivalent majority, and mobilizing them, while not easy, often occurred as a by-product of a small but pervasive economic change.[47]

In Vietnam the economic effort altered the one part of the structure that had furnished what little wealth the peasant majority possessed. Land represented that wealth. Land reform did two things—it added a multitude of new recruits to the military struggle and swelled the ranks of the ambivalent, making things equally miserable for the American reformer and the ever-changing Vietnamese winners and losers. In fighting the Leninist land reformers, Lockeans consistently failed to recognize that Leninists instituted reforms to achieve political control, not economic efficiency. In like manner, Leninists consistently failed to understand the efficiency arguments of Lockean agriculture.

American reformers in Vietnam, be they Whig or Tory by program, thus can be viewed as generally unhappy with their situation. Among many predicaments, two dominated their agenda—the Buddhist crisis of the Kennedy administration and the nation-building crisis of the Johnson administration. While Whigs such as Roger Hilsman recognized the Buddhist crisis as political and not religious, nevertheless they found it impossible to channel the issue in a manner by which they could obtain a political compromise. Unable to accomplish such a political compromise, Kennedy Whigs drifted into the unhappy political predicament of having to support a coup.

The nation-building predicament was a part of the larger military problem. For the civilian leadership gave the American military an inappropriate task, a mission often called pacification or nation-building. The results, even allowing for military accomplishments, nevertheless indicate the folly of asking a high-technology military (organized and trained to defeat the Soviet Red Army) to readjust, not simply to counter-insurgency tactics but also to nation-building techniques. This was not the only strategic blunder involving military planning. Ranking next to it was the folly of misapplying the theory of collective security in Southeast Asia, and following these was the error of misjudging the minimum requirements of limited-war theory, especially as applied to a war at China's southern gateway.

To argue that collective security alliances had a special meaning for American internationalists is not the same as arguing that all alliances, like durable marriages, must rest on shared values, be they political, economic, or cultural. In fact most have been the opposite—mere temporary marriages of convenience—but in the postwar period the United States was most unwilling to enter that type of pre–World War II relationship. The American people required more than power politics if they were to go into the international marriage market. Atlanticism had made the difference clear; it gave the postwar generation their first successful wooing abroad. Postwar Japan was the second success. After Europe and Japan the United States never again succeeded at this task, especially not in Southeast Asia, though failure there was not caused by want of effort.

As if this were not bad enough, it became necessary to draw limits around the Vietnamese conflict. The military was unable and unwilling to explain to the civilians that within certain limits it was possible for the enemy to win. So drift set in, and the one task for which the American military was suited—to help defeat conventional invaders—came to be its secondary mission. When wisdom wanders, defeat beckons. And beckon it did. Suspecting defeat, senior members of the American officer corps wanted little to do with this war; if ordered to intervene, the most they expected to do was to help the South Vietnamese gain their rights to security. But as war-associated troubles mounted, desperate Washington officials demanded that the military play a leading role in securing political and economic rights as well.

Human rights do not exist in a vacuum, disconnected one from the other, or from the specific historical setting that gives them meaning. Nor does one set of rights necessarily outrank any other. It is not possible to defend "the thesis that all economic rights take priority over all other rights, a thesis as crude and implausible as its sometime rival, the thesis that all political rights take priority over all other rights." This simple dichotomy can be "misleading in several aspects."[48] As late as 1977, an American diplomat tried to avoid this dichotomy when explaining U.S. human rights policy. But it was not an easy task. Cyrus Vance relied on a trichotomy, thus correcting some of what is simplistic in the dichotomy. This former Kennedy-Johnson internationalist, by 1977 Secretary of State for President Carter, placed his three categories in a Tory order of priority, giving first place to security rights, second place to economic rights, and last place to political rights.[49]

It is easy to fault Vance's hierarchy, but not simple to offer an alternative. One is forced by the nature of the problem to argue generally that in certain situations there exist "some economic rights over which no other rights have priority."[50] One also tends to include security rights within any short list of critical economic rights. Yet at the same time one understands the close connection among all three categories of rights, a connection that suggests their basic equality even if we allow for the limited priority of a small set of economic and security rights.

Recognizing the possibility of a limited priority makes it easier to see how the three categories of rights fit in with the intervention in Vietnam. Observation of Vietnamese daily life in the 1950's reveals that the struggle to institutionalize security rights as social building-blocks dominated Vietnamese development; economic rights rested on security rights, and political rights topped the structure. Each level in this vertical structure thus depended on the level below. But by the 1960's numerous building-blocks at the base of Vietnamese society began to crumble when the blocks came under pressure from the Americans, who then tried to brace the crumbling foundation. The foundation crumbled because some American internationalists had decided to speed up the process of modernization by hastily and drastically rearranging the institutional blocks at the middle and top of South Vietnam's new society. In the process Americans failed to give even a limited priority to security rights. The uppermost blocks remained in constant jeopardy, and the middle level was hardly more stable. Conditions deteriorated when Washington and Saigon began redesigning the upper structure before anyone had finished bracing the lower sections. This topsy-turvy approach to reconstruction presumed that a war-weary population would be satisfied to receive liberty before libation, freedom before food. To make the situation worse, not only did construction reversals occur, but military operations often destroyed the already fragile superstructure—then the leaders who had ordered the destruction would direct the military to rebuild. And internationalists wanted the impossible—to rebuild a new society, not simply to spruce up the old physical plant.

Building and rebuilding meant constant intervention. When Americans intervened they hoped to design a new society better equipped to fulfill the needs of its membership. At least that motivated the majority of internationalists. That they and their philanthropic designs were often unwanted and unwelcome—and that they themselves had not entered public service believing it correct policy for one state to intervene in the internal affairs of another—caused them to suffer cognitive dissonance. In this situation, individuals became less anxious if they came to believe they were performing a difficult but necessary service that at a minimum represented what Reinhold Niebuhr would recognize as the lesser of two evils.

This description does not fit all internationalists in all situations, but it fits the majority involved in Vietnam. Nor did they all see their work as a lesser evil; in fact many saw it as falling within the tradition of American philanthropy abroad.[51] Before World War II, most philanthropic aid came from private individuals and private organizations whose chief aim was disaster relief. After 1945, public individuals and public organizations predominated, and their aim also was disaster relief, but to this was added the goal of eliminating the causes of disasters. The attempt to achieve this goal, an effort that internationalists often thought required intervention in order to force reforms, went well beyond the earlier aims of American philanthropy. By observing the actions of key Americans concerned with South Vietnam, one can view the war as in itself an attempt to force a vision of a better society, hence to force an extension of this new philanthropy. To justify this vision it was necessary to present a type of political sermon that could convert a generous but ambivalent American public. The internationalists found their means in the anti-Leninist jeremiads they preached to postwar Americans, often suggesting that America should impose reform upon the entire globe.

To force reform in Vietnam was costly, especially in personal terms. Not only was it burdensome; also it created victims. The majority were Vietnamese; some were Americans, including many internationalists. These internationalists received the least attention as victims, partially because they inflicted their own wounds—that is, their dissonance never completely vanished. Some critics see the claim of dissonance as another way to rationalize the mistakes of the past; but one cannot sustain the argument that, as a group, internationalists in each decade after World War II could recruit new members by appealing to such a rationalization. In the main, the leading participants believed their actions promoted reform, a type of global public philanthropy to relieve what were, in fact, terrible conditions. Their individual dissonance lessened once it became possible to view interventions like the one in South Vietnam as a continuation of the American philanthropic tradition, a continuation orchestrated by the government as Lockean reform of the international order.

Concerning Vietnam there existed no conspiracy among the Kennedy and Johnson elite. Most said openly what they believed privately about the intervention. Nor does this imply that there was a conspiracy within groups who opposed Vietnam policies. An explanation of the Vietnam tragedy does not require villains. Ordinary human error produced and enlarged tragic consequences. This came about as the American experience slowly became the only experience, the highest good, for internationalists dealing with Vietnam. But given the condition of South Vietnam in the postwar world, the American experience was irrelevant. Unfortunately, given the condition of the United States in the postwar world, the earlier Vietnamese experience was irrelevant. Because of the lack of patience in the America of the 1960's, the "can do" mentality of its brash, bold leaders, momentary defeat could not deter these Americans; defeated at one level, they just raised the stakes, thus fueling what would bring final defeat—extremism. Both the "can do" leaders and their opponents became extremists. Having chosen the lesser of two evils—an authoritarian regime in South Vietnam instead of a larger Vietnam united forecefully by the Leninist regime in Hanoi—Lockean internationalists failed to note that, as they raised the stakes, their lesser evil became the greater evil. In other words, it is impossible to save a people by first destroying them. The principle of proportionality condemns such extreme measures.[52] But somehow the Americans did not note their drift into extremism until they were well past the midway point of the intervention.

Some will find it difficult to conceive of philanthropy, even philanthropy combined with self-interest, as leading to war. One should remember that the initial assistance to South Vietnam began at a time when the struggle there seemed but a minor internal feud. But once public philanthropic aid was underway, public servants acted upon the normal human desire to perpetuate and enlarge their domain. As their handiwork became a chief target for the enemy in the growing struggle, the Lockeans' response intensified.

As public servants the greatest number of Lockean internationalists were not elected officials. But it is possible to conceive even of the officeholding minority, men such as Johnson, as having multiple motives for their actions in Vietnam. First, they believed they needed to win the war to avoid losing office in subsequent elections. Second, they believed that winning the war, with all its faults, was at least better than the alternative. Third, elected interventionists believed, in the main, that Americans were in the war to help the South Vietnamese build the U.S. version of the good society; hence it was a form of self-interested philanthropy.

What about the internationalists who did not hold office? They were the majority, and were relatively unaffected by elections. These decision-makers were presidential appointees, career bureaucrats, and military officers. If their party lost an election the appointees just marked time in Washington and New York law firms and investment banks, at "think tanks" such as the Brookings Institution, on the Council on Foreign Relations, at universities, or within the civil service or military ranks. Some, like Cyrus Vance and Zbigniew Brzezinski, later returned; others began a new life, as Robert McNamara did at the World Bank. Career bureaucrats and military officers remained, their futures safe. Philip Habib at State, William Colby at CIA, and General Westmoreland at DOD—all rose in their positions even while South Vietnam, a nation with which they had associated their careers, was going under.

One cannot, therefore, sustain the often-repeated argument that the chief reason Washington officials continued the war was that losing it would cause them and their party to lose control in national politics. Internationalists in the main were not party stalwarts; and, as a mixed group, the majority of whom were not elected, they had not lost control in national security affairs since 1947, regardless of presidential and congressional elections. But, although the internationalists did not lose control of the machinery of the state (at least of its national security machinery), they did lose control of "the central hallmark of a politics of interest—rational calculation."[53] The U.S. failure in Vietnam confirms that assessment.

Moreover, the evidence fails to support the argument charging that public explanations hid private understandings—that is, that the war protected American business interests in Southeast Asia. The recurrence of that explanation is remarkable given the fact that it cannot be sustained. Indeed the reverse was more often true: "In the American interventions after the Second World War, however, economic goals and the stability of the social system in general were, ultimately in Vietnam, sacrificed to an ideological vision."[54] In the hands of Tory developmentalists, the general concept of "ideological vision" as applied to Vietnam meant using economic constraints as tools and weapons in a financial battle with the Hanoi Leninists. This is a very different economic explanation of motives and policies from the one used by economic determinists who infer that America fought the war in Vietnam to control the natural resources in Southeast Asia. In fact Americans fought that war for many reasons, but for that one least of all.[55] And they lost for many reasons, a few of which were connected with their extremism in the defense of liberty— liberty being defined as security, political, and economic rights. After the enthusiasm of the 1960's receded, it became difficult to convince a later generation that Americans had fought the big war of the 1960's for any ideals. But they did. Nor could one convince that same generation that ideals could lead to extremism. But it happened. Innocent ideals can lead toward extreme visions more readily than might be supposed. For example, one scholar has suggested that the idea of self-government and the idea of national self-determination have "been the greatest contribution of the United States to the progress of international relations in modern times." Not content with this innocent claim, the scholar presses his idealism to an extreme that holds the possibility of tragedy: without these two Whig principles there would be, he says, "no hope for lasting peace or for progress throughout the world."[56]

This claim simply is not true. One can cite various periods—the Rome of the Antonines, the Ming dynasty of China, the Abbasid Califate, pharaonic Egypt under the Ramseses, and Incan and Mayan America—to show times of some peace, prosperity, and progress that did not depend on Whig principles. In other words, the guiding principles for human destiny were and remain diverse and complex. Even the optimistic Immanuel Kant wrote *Perpetual Peace* without claiming as much for his dream of confederation as did Americans of the 1960's for their visions. For Kant it was enough that each group within the confederation be allowed its own version of a free society—with or without progress as defined by Atlantic-basin modernists.

When Kant's concepts are applied to the period 1945–70, the issue of American national security raises three questions. Is there a difference between the American competitive covenant with power and the Soviet noncompetitive configuration of power? In a brutish world must a state be a brute? Can a democracy conduct a national security policy? Yes, no, yes.

The postwar American covenant with power worked within a Kantian confederation of democratic states; each had differences, but each tolerated the uniqueness of its confederates. At a minimum they did not go to war with one another. Sections within the Soviet configuration did, however. Between the Atlantic confederation and the Soviet consolidation existed a peace marked by tension, with minor outbreaks of violence between their respective allies at the periphery. This general peace obtained in part because, given the problem posed by nuclear weapons, senior partners on either side were oriented toward a status quo. Threats to the status quo would diminish the possibilities of peace. Evidence of an orientation toward the status quo can be seen in a state's learning to accept losses; the Soviet removal from Egypt in 1972 and the American withdrawal from Vietnam in 1973 are but two examples among many. However, the attraction of changing the status quo continues strong for the (Kantian) Atlantic confederation of today because of its low tolerance for nonrepresentative states inside or outside of the confederation.[57]

Strong leaders are not by necessity brutes, for strength need not be expressed as brutality. Nor is compassion weakness, in state or leader. Tolerance, patience, and fairness need not be restricted to national politics; they can serve also as international guides. Most postwar presidents, at their best, aimed for a mixture of strength and compassion—nationally and internationally.

Democratic states can conduct coherent national security policies. Between 1947 and 1961 the United States succeeded in doing so, even given particular problems and failures. Only when leaders began to make assumptions about the universal applicability of Lockean goals and strategies did failure begin to outweigh success.

Fearing that one person's progress can be another's prison, wise leaders abjure universal formulas. Unfortunately, this was not what American leaders in Vietnam did. Having succeeded on one part of the globe at one historic period, they were tempted to universalize their good fortune. When that temptation became a desire to force "the good" onto others, the world became less safe than before.[58]

By pushing reform beyond reasonable limits, Americans turned out to be the real revolutionaries in Vietnam. Preaching their jeremiads about the Cold War, they tried to make the South Vietnamese free, politically and economically, but killed many in the process. The maximalist Whigs worked hardest at this task. Starting simultaneously at the top and the bottom of Vietnamese society, they tried to fulfill for the Vietnamese all of Maslow's needs. Noble dreams perhaps, but all for naught. William McNeill, ruminating on these failures, suggests that it is necessary for Americans to adjust their myths about the ways of the world: "Recognition of humanity's cultural pluralism might, indeed, allow us to react more intelligently to encounters with other peoples than is likely to happen when we are either aggrieved and surprised by their persistent, willful differences from us, or else remain self-righteously impervious to the possibility of learning something useful from people who diverge from us in enduring, conspicuous ways."[59] Preceding yet going beyond McNeill's advice was that of a Prussian historian. Otto Hintze advised the oligarchs of Bismarck's northern model of a Roman Empire that preconditions existed for representative government. These preconditions existed at least for the few such governments the world would come to know in modern times—a period during which the military states of the North Atlantic basin risked representation, thus helping to usher in their great transformation from authoritarian to representative politics.[60] Unfortunately, McNeill's and Hintze's wisdom was not guiding the devout Tory and Whig interventionists when they acted in the Vietnamese crisis of 1963–65. Advice, even historic experience, was something they did not heed in Vietnam unless it confirmed what they planned.

Better they had taken the advice of Isaiah Berlin. In his introduction to a work on nineteenth-century revolutions, Berlin suggests that basic Maslowian needs must be provided for first: "[What] the vast majority of peasants in Russia (or workers in Europe) needed was to be fed and clothed, to be given physical security, to be rescued from disease, ignorance, poverty and humiliating inequalities." As for political rights— votes, parliaments, republican forms—Berlin believed that these were "meaningless and useless to ignorant, barbarous, half-naked and starving men . . . and merely mocked their misery."[61] But in Vietnam, confronted with an enemy actively pushing its political agenda on the people, the internationalists felt pressed to work for their own version of political reform even before they could accomplish the portion of Berlin's list that accorded with minimalist Tory priorities—namely, the assuring of physical security. This momentous decision, more than any other aspect of the American intervention in Vietnam, was responsible for the disastrous end of the war.

REFERENCE MATTER

Notes

Full authors' names and publication data for works cited only in short form in the Notes are given in the Bibliography, pp. 397–410. The following abbreviations are used in the Notes:

AES American Embassy Saigon
AIDL,RV Agency for International Development Library, Rosslyn, Va.
CINCPAC Commander-in-Chief of the Pacific
CINCPACFLT Commander-in-Chief of the Pacific Fleet
DOD Department of Defense
HSTL Harry S. Truman Library
JCS Joint Chiefs of Staff
JFKL John F. Kennedy Library
LBJL Lyndon B. Johnson Library
MACV Military Advisory Command Vietnam
NSFV National Security File Vietnam
SecDef Secretary of Defense
State State Department
USIA United States Information Agency
VCUCB Vietnam Collection, University of California, Berkeley

Introduction

1. Peter Scholl-Latour, *Death in the Rice Fields: An Eyewitness Account of Vietnam's Three Wars 1945–1979* (New York, 1979); C. Johnson, *Revolution and the Social System,* 29–69; Lawrence Stone, "Theories of Revolution," *World Politics,* 18 (Jan. 1966), 159–76; William Kornhauser, "Revolutions," in Roger W. Little, ed., *Handbook of Military Institutions* (Beverly Hills, Calif., 1971), 384. According to C. Johnson, the Vietnam struggle was a militarized mass insurrection, our century's creation in which a dedicated elite deliberately plans mass revolutionary war.

2. Maurice Matloff, *Strategic Planning for Coalition Warfare, 1943–1944* (Washington, D.C., 1959), 5. In the United States the longer the war and the

more casualties, the less support; see Mueller, *War, Presidents and Public Opinion*, and Russell F. Weigley, "Dissent in Wars," in Alexander DeConde, ed., *Encyclopedia of American Foreign Policy*, 3 vols. (New York, 1978), 1: 253–67.

3. Ronald Syme, *The Roman Revolution* (Oxford, 1939), 346; Erich S. Gruen, *The Last Generation of the Roman Republic* (Berkeley, Calif., 1974), 502; Aron, *The Imperial Republic*; C. Wright Mills, *The Power Elite* (Oxford, 1956); Osgood et al., *Retreat from Empire?* Darrell P. Hammer, in *The U.S.S.R.: The Politics of Oligarchy* (Boulder, Colo., 1986), 1–2, notes that Lenin called his government "a full-fledged oligarchy." In contrast to Hammer, Robert A. Dahl suggests that the U.S. government represents a polyarchy. See Dahl's *A Preface to Democratic Theory* (Chicago, 1956), 63–89.

4. Amaury de Riencourt, *The American Empire* (New York, 1968), 94–95; Dean Rusk, quoted in Graff, *The Tuesday Cabinet*, 135. Also see Claude Julien, *L'empire américain* (Paris, 1968).

5. "Every perceptive European visitor to America perceives that, in a society lacking Europe's aristocratic and medieval distinctions, the captain of industry is a hero-type for adult men and women"; Graham Hutton, quoted in Jonathan Hughes, *The Vital Few*, expanded ed. (Oxford, 1986), dedication page.

6. Gardner, *A Covenant with Power*; Samuel Flagg Bemis, *The Latin American Policy of the United States* (New York, 1943), 219; Robert H. Ferrell, *Peace in Their Time* (New York, 1952), 225.

7. Degler, *Affluence and Anxiety*.

8. Leuchtenburg, *A Troubled Feast*.

9. Here "elite" is used in a neutral sense, not as a pejorative term. Membership remained open to converts, internationalism in its postwar membership being more of a meritocracy than anything else. You could be a poor boy from Cherokee County, Georgia, like Dean Rusk, or a New England Cabot or Lodge, like Henry Cabot Lodge. You could be a Kansas lad, like Clark Clifford, or a Wall Street figure, like Douglas Dillon. Because of what George Liska calls "the always qualifying social background in the United States," American national elites represent "highly diversified and only weakly hierarchical group pluralism," which makes it difficult for any elite so constructed to "wrest particular and fleeting advantages from the tendency of pluralism to settle into deadlock among interest groups." See Liska, *Career of Empire*, 211; Richard S. Kirkendall, "Elitism and Foreign Policy," in DeConde, *Encyclopedia of American Foreign Policy*, 1: 302–9; Heinz Eulau and Moshe M. Czudnowski, *Elite Recruitment in Democratic Politics* (New York, 1976), 118–19; Giovanni Sartori, *The Theory of Democracy Revisited* (Chatham, N.J., 1987), 141–48. Eulau and Czudnowski show a decline of lawyers and an increase in Ph.D.'s by 1964.

10. William E. Borah, "The Case for Non-Entanglement," in Robert Goldwin and Harry Clor, eds., *Readings in American Foreign Policy* (Oxford, 1971), 412–22. Borah remained in the U.S. Senate from 1907 to 1940. From 1924 to 1932 he chaired the Senate Foreign Relations Committee. To William E.

Leuchtenburg, Borah represents a transitional figure, a "vestigial internationalist who looked to the power of public opinion and to the instrumentality of international law to maintain peace and secure justice"; Leuchtenburg, *The Perils of Prosperity: 1914–1932* (Chicago, 1958), 117.

11. Iriye, *From Nationalism to Internationalism*, 235; Charles Lindblom, *The Policy-Making Process* (Englewood Cliffs, N.J., 1968), 26–27.

12. The terms national security and national security state are given primacy in Yergin, *Shattered Peace*, 193–220.

13. Acheson, *This Vast External Realm*, 128.

14. Franz Schurmann, *The Logic of World Power* (New York, 1974), 61, 67.

15. Herbert McClosky, "Personality and Attitude Correlates of Foreign Policy Orientation," in James N. Rosenau, ed., *Domestic Sources of Foreign Policy* (New York, 1967), 51–109, quotations at 106–7.

16. Morris Janowitz, *The Reconstruction of Patriotism* (Chicago, 1983), 11. Fred Kaplan suggests that LeMay "distrusted and disliked most foreigners"; Kaplan, *The Wizards of Armageddon*, 93.

17. Jack Plano and Milton Greenberg, *The American Political Dictionary*, 7th ed. (New York, 1985), 494 (definition of isolationism); Geoffrey Perrett, *Days of Sadness, Years of Triumph* (Madison, Wis., 1985), 190. While Williams aimed his comments at those who called the 1920's and 1930's an isolationism era, Lippmann aimed his comments at those who saw the entire American past in isolationist terms. See William Appleman Williams, "The Legend of Isolationism," *The Shaping of American Diplomacy* (Chicago, 1956), 2: 657–63; Walter Lippmann, *U.S. Foreign Policy: Shield of the Republic* (Boston, 1943), 16–20, and *Isolation and Alliances: An American Speaks to the British* (Boston, 1952), 8–16.

18. Unilateralism did not fade away; see Charles Krauthammer, "A Triumph of American Unilateralism: Reykjavik and the End of Days," *The New Republic*, Nov. 1986, 22–28.

19. Europeans translated U.S. globalism as "the world was their oyster"; see Carlo Maria Santoro, *La perla e l'ostrica: Alle fonti della politica globale degli Stati Uniti* (Milan, 1987).

20. George Washington, "The Farewell Address," in Goldwin and Clor, *Readings in American Foreign Policy*, 125–29.

21. Kennan, "The Sources of Soviet Conduct," 566–82.

22. "NSC-68," Apr. 14, 1950, in *Foreign Relations of the United States: 1950* (Washington, D.C., 1950), 1: 243–44; Samuel F. Wells, Jr., "Sounding the Tocsin: NSC68 and the Soviet Threat," *International Security*, 4 (Fall 1979), 116–38; Fred Kaplan, "Our Cold-War Policy, Circa 1950," *New York Times Magazine*, May 1980, 34; Paul Y. Hammond, "NSC68: Prologue to Rearmament," in Paul Y. Hammond, Warner Schilling, and Glen Snyder, *Strategy, Politics and Defense Budgets* (New York, 1962), 273–378.

23. Paul Y. Hammond, *Resource Limits, Political and Military Risk Taking and the Generation of Military Requirements*, RAND Corp. P-3421-1 (Santa Monica, Calif., 1966), 21–26.

24. William M. Leary, "History of the CIA," in Leary, ed., *The Central Intelligence Agency*, 38–40.

25. *Ibid.*, 38. Years later Kennan testified that CIA covert activities "did not work out at all the way I had conceived it." Kennan also testified that covert activities would be approved very infrequently, only when no other option appeared possible. See *Final Report of the Select Committee to Study Governmental Operations with Respect to Intelligence Activities*, 95th Cong., 2d sess., 1978, S. Rept. 94-755, 31.

26. Clifford, "American Military Firmness versus Soviet Aggression," 9–13. The original document is in a bound volume, *American Relations with the Soviet Union: A Report to the President by the Special Counsel to the President*, Sept. 23, 1946, Conway Files (OSS), HSTL.

27. Yergin, *Shattered Peace*, 214.

28. "Oral History of C. Douglas Dillon," taken by Paige Mulhollan, June 29, 1969, and "Oral History of Henry H. Fowler," taken by David McComb, July 31, 1969, both in LBJL.

29. Martin P. Claussen, ed., *Numerical Catalog and Alphabetic Index for the SWNCC/SANACC Case Files* (Wilmington, Del.: Scholarly Resources Inc., 1978, microfilm).

30. Senate Committee on Naval Affairs, *Unification of the War and Navy Departments and Postwar Organization for National Security, Report to Secretary of the Navy James Forrestal* (Eberstadt Report), 79th Cong., 1st sess., 1945.

31. Huntington, *The Common Defense*, 153–55.

32. Matloff, *American Military History*, 531–32; Ries, *The Management of Defense*, 143–45.

33. *Documents of the National Security Council: 1947–1977; Minutes of the National Security Council with Special Advisory Reports; Documents of the NSC: First Supplement;* and *Documents of the NSC: Second Supplement* (Frederick, Md.: University Publications of America, 1980, 1981, and 1983, microfilms); Henry M. Jackson, ed., *The National Security Council: Jackson Subcommittee Papers on Policy Making at the Presidential Level* (New York, 1965).

34. Destler, *Presidents, Bureaucrats and Foreign Policy*, 19, 96–118; Dean Acheson, "The Eclipse of the State Department," *Foreign Affairs*, 49 (July 1971), 593–606; Henry Trofimenko, "Review Article: Struggle for the Turf," *World Politics*, 37 (Apr. 1985), 403–15.

35. Destler, *Presidents, Bureaucrats and Foreign Policy*, 130; Michael Wright, "National Security's New Insiders," *New York Times Magazine*, Mar. 3, 1985, 58–62; Simon Serfaty, "Brzezinski: Play It Again, Zbig," *Foreign Policy*, no. 32 (Fall 1978), 3–21; Richard Pipes, "Who Should Direct U.S. Policy Toward Moscow?" *National Security Record* (The Heritage Foundation), no. 83, Sept. 1985, 5–6.

36. JFK did not despair of "Rusk's unobtrusive modesty"; he simply wanted the job for himself. "At no time, press reports to the contrary, did the President regret having selected him"; Sorensen, *Kennedy*, 271.

37. Charles Lindblom, "The Science of 'Muddling Through,'" *Public Administration Review*, 19 (Spring 1959), 79–88, and his "Still Muddling, Not

Yet Through," *Public Administration Review*, 29 (Nov.–Dec. 1979), 517–26; Bowles, *Promises to Keep*, 441, 551, 575–76.

38. Edwin Borchard, "Shall the Executive Agreement Replace the Treaty," *Yale Law Journal*, 53 (Sept. 1944), 644–83; Myres S. McDougal and Asher Lans, "Treaties and Congressional-Executive or Presidential Agreements: Interchangeable Instruments of National Policy: I & II," *Yale Law Journal*, 54 (Mar. 1945), 181–351, 534–615; Edwin Borchard, "Treaties and Executive Agreements—A Reply," *Yale Law Journal*, 54 (Mar. 1945), 616–64; Walter LaFeber, "The Constitution and United States Foreign Policy: An Interpretation," *Journal of American History*, 74 (Dec. 1987), 695–717; George Southerland quoted on 711; Raoul Berger, "Executive Privilege versus Congressional Inquiry," *UCLA Law Review*, 12 (Aug. 1965), 1287–1364, and *Executive Privilege: A Constitutional Myth* (Cambridge, Mass., 1974); Louis Fisher, *Constitutional Conflicts Between Congress and the President* (Princeton, N.J., 1985), 272–83.

39. Krasner, *Defending the National Interest*, 15, 278; Levin, *Woodrow Wilson and World Politics*, 4; Larry G. Gerber, *The Limits of Liberalism* (New York, 1983), 2–3, 348. It was Louis Hartz who first suggested that U.S. diplomacy, in combating the Russian Revolution and its leader, Lenin, was dominated by "an impulse to impose Locke everywhere"; Hartz, *The Liberal Tradition in America* (New York, 1955), 10–13, 308.

40. Alvin Z. Rubinstein, *Soviet Foreign Policy Since World War II: Imperial and Global*, 2d ed. (Boston, 1985), 309.

41. Dimitri Simes, "The Military and Militarism in Soviet Society," *International Security*, 6 (Winter 1981–82), 123–43; Rubinstein, *Soviet Foreign Policy Since World War II*, 74; Adam B. Ulam, *A History of Soviet Russia* (New York, 1976), 32; Michael S. Volensky, *Nomenklatura: The Soviet Ruling Class* (New York, 1984); Pierre M. Gallois, "The Soviet Global Threat and the West," *Orbis*, 25 (Fall 1981), 649–62; James Willard Hurst, *Law and Markets in United States History* (Madison, Wis., 1982), 22–30, 34, 62, 74, 99; H. L. A. Hart, *The Concept of Law* (Oxford, 1961).

42. Rusk, "Trade and Exchanges with Communist States," in his *The Winds of Freedom*, 235–56; V. G. Solodnikov and V. V. Bogoslovskij, *Non-Capitalist Development* (Moscow, 1976); Stephen Clarkson, *The Soviet Theory of Development* (Toronto, 1978); Arthur Klinghoffer, *Soviet Perspectives on African Socialism* (Cranbury, N.J., 1969); V. M. Kollontai *et al.*, "Theory and Practice of the Non-Capitalist Way of Development," *International Affairs*, no. 11 (Nov. 1970), 11–15.

43. P. E. Aldrich, "John Locke and the Influence of His Work in America," in *Proceedings of the American Antiquarian Society* (Worcester, Mass., 1879), 9–39; Henry May, *The Enlightenment in America* (Oxford, 1976), 33, 38, 79–80, 83, 98, 185–86, 292–93; Bernard Bailyn, *The Ideological Origins of the American Revolution* (Cambridge, Mass., 1967), 27; Merle Curti, "The Great Mr. Locke: America's Philosopher, 1783–1861," *Huntington Library Bulletin*, 11 (Apr. 1937), 107–51.

44. Minh, *On Revolution*, 281–89. No international Leninists had to recite Lenin weekly. They had enough ideology to get along, and the rest—Leninist

attitudes—were soaked into their bones. See Robert Conquest, *Present Danger: Towards a Foreign Policy* (Stanford, Calif., 1979), 12. The reverse was true for Americans, in that Lockean attitudes were soaked into their bones.

45. John Locke, *Two Treatises of Government*, ed. Peter Laslett, rev. ed. (Cambridge, 1965), 2: 344; Alan Ryan, *Property and Political Theory* (London, 1984), 47–48; V. I. Lenin, *The State and Revolution* (New York, 1926), 197–99; Thomas P. Bernstein, "Leadership and Mass Mobilization in the Soviet and Chinese Collectivization Campaigns of 1920–1929 and 1955–1956: A Comparison," *China Quarterly*, 31 (July–Sept. 1967), 1–47, and his "Problems of Village Leadership After Land Reform," *China Quarterly*, 36 (Oct.–Dec. 1968); M. Lewin, *Russian Peasants and Soviet Power: A Study of Collectivization* (Evanston, Ill., 1968); James R. Millar, ed., *The Soviet Rural Community* (Urbana, Ill., 1971).

46. Neal Wood, *John Locke and Agrarian Capitalism* (Berkeley, 1984), 100–3; Pike, *History of Vietnamese Communism*, 100–1; Canh, *Vietnam Under Communism*, 31–35.

47. Neal Wood, *The Politics of Locke's Philosophy: A Social Study of "An Essay Concerning Human Understanding"* (Berkeley, 1983), 101–9; Lenin, *What Is to Be Done*, 171–72. Locke's politics were the politics of religion; party for him meant religious party, not political party. As the philosopher of what Christopher Hill calls the "transition from parish to sect," Locke argued for toleration of most competing religious parties, which came to mean toleration for the secular religion—politics—and its parties. See Christopher Hill, *Society and Puritanism* (London, 1969), 477; John Locke, "A Letter Concerning Toleration," in *Great Books of the Western World* (Chicago, 1978), 6. For discussion of how the "operational code of Leninism" mattered or didn't matter for Soviet leaders and their allies after World War II, see Joseph L. Nogee and Robert H. Donaldson, *Soviet Foreign Policy Since World War II* (New York, 1984), 32–39.

48. Stephen F. Cohen, *Rethinking the Soviet Experience: Politics and History Since 1917* (Oxford, 1985), 55, 152. Some argue that Leninism tried to legitimate a party while Stalinism tried to legitimate a person. Others say that both failed because neither party or person gained legitimacy. Since Stalin's time the leaders of the USSR are, at a minimum, authentic representatives of their political system.

49. Earl C. Ravenal, a unilateralist libertarian who worked for McNamara, published *Defining Defense: The 1985 Military Budget* (Washington, D.C., 1984) and *NATO's Unremarked Demise* (Berkeley, 1979).

50. *Webster's Seventh New Collegiate Dictionary* (Springfield, Mass., 1965), 934, 1016. My use of "Whig" as a subcategory of internationalism in the postwar United States owes a great deal to H. Butterfield's *The Whig Interpretation of History*. Especially important is his emphasis on political manifestations of liberty. For a critique of a Tory interpretation of history see Jennifer Hart, "Nineteenth Century Social Reform: A Tory Interpretation of History," *Past & Present*, 31 (July 1965), 39–61.

51. Alonzo L. Hamby, *Liberalism and Its Challengers: FDR to Reagan* (Oxford, 1985), 5; George F. Will, *Statecraft and Soulcraft: What Government Does* (New York, 1983), 146; James MacGregor Burns, *Roosevelt: The Lion and the Fox* (New York, 1956), 235–37; Hartz, *The Liberal Tradition in America*, 178–200. Anglo and American Tories were not all aristocrats or upper middle class; see Eric A. Nordlinger, *The Working Class Tories* (Berkeley, 1967).

52. Richard Abrams, "American Anticommunism and Liberal Internationalism," *Reviews in American History*, 10 (Sept. 1982), 454–67; Schurmann, *The Logic of World Power*, 116. Waltz, *Man, the State, and War*, 103, subdivides Abrams's liberal internationalists into interventionist liberals and noninterventionist liberals.

53. Paul Seabury, "Realism and Idealism," in DeConde, *Encyclopedia of American Foreign Policy*, 3: 856–66; George Kennan, *American Diplomacy 1900–1950* (Chicago, 1951), and "Morality and Foreign Policy," *Foreign Affairs*, 64 (Winter 1985–86), 205–18; Charles Krauthammer, "The Poverty of Realism," *The New Republic*, Feb. 17, 1986, 14–22.

54. Max Weber, *From Max Weber: Essays in Sociology* (Oxford, 1946), 243–67; Arthur Schweitzer, *The Age of Charisma* (Chicago, 1984).

55. Memo from Alvin Friedman to McGeorge Bundy, "Proposed Unclassified Statement by Mr. Vance before House Armed Services Committee on August 18, 1964," Aug. 17, 1964, NSFV, box 7, Vietnam Memos, vol. 16, LBJL; Cyrus Vance, "The Human Rights Imperative," *Foreign Policy*, no. 63 (Summer 1986), 3–19.

56. Maslow, *Motivation and Personality*, 107; Jeanne Knutson, *The Human Basis of the Polity* (Chicago, 1972); Maslow, *The Psychology of Science*, 55, 67, 69, 116, 144; *Toward a Psychology of Being*, 155–60; and *The Farther Reaches of Human Nature*, 40–51. For Maslow's influence in the 1960's see Patricia Springborg, *The Problems of Human Needs and the Critique of Civilization* (London, 1981), 184–94. In order to see the danger of assigning human needs based in one culture to another culture, see Ignatieff, *The Needs of Strangers*, 11. Ignatieff does suggest that all humans have some basic needs, needs they must seize if necessary (53).

57. Edward O. Wilson, *Sociobiology: The New Synthesis* (Cambridge, Mass., 1975), 550, and his *On Human Nature* (Cambridge, Mass., 1978), 71–97. I would compare the Tory view to the view of some sociobiologists like Wilson; i.e., I would say that in cave society all were of Tory inclination in the sense of concentrating their energies in fulfilling basic needs. Only after dominating their environment could the first Whig cave folk suggest a higher order of human needs. And only in a very few historic cases did Whig fulfillment occur.

58. Richard Henry Tawney, *The Acquisitive Society* (New York, 1920), 184.

59. Hilsman, *To Move a Nation*, 433.

60. Churchill, quoted in Kennedy, *Profiles in Courage*, 264.

61. AES cable from Henry Cabot Lodge to State, Sept. 16, 1964, NSFV, box 8, Vietnam Cables, vol. 18, LBJL.

62. "Oral History of C. Douglas Dillon," taken by Mulhollan, 24–28.

63. Nitze, "Eight Presidents and Their Different Approaches to National Security Policymaking," 31–63.

64. Abrams, "American Anticommunism and Liberal Internationalism," 467.

65. Herbert A. Simon, *Administrative Behavior* (New York, 1976); Alexander George, "Adaption to Stress in Political Decision Making," in G. V. Coelho et al., eds., *Coping and Adaption* (New York, 1974); Ernest May, *Lessons of the Past* (Oxford, 1973); Robert Jervis, *Perception and Misperception in International Relations* (Princeton, N.J., 1976); Irving Janis and Leon Mann, *Decision Making* (New York, 1977), 25–28 (quotations).

66. Miller, *Lyndon*, 462.

67. Irving L. Janis, *Victims of Groupthink* (Boston, 1972), 101–35; Nelson Polsby, *Political Innovation in America: The Politics of Policy Initiation* (New Haven, Conn., 1984), 76–77; L. Berman, *Planning a Tragedy*, 79–129. Janis states (135) that "it seems highly probable that group dynamics exerted considerable influence on the decisions of the policy-makers who escalated the war in Vietnam." In fact some group dynamics influenced internationalists when they believed internationalism was under assault, particularly domestic assault. But this does not mean that they were unwilling or unable to question and debate various options concerning Vietnam. Also see James J. Best, "Who Talked to the President When? A Study of Lyndon Johnson," *Political Science Quarterly*, 103 (Fall 1988), 531–45, and David M. Barrett, "The Mythology Surrounding Lyndon Johnson, His Advisers, and the 1965 Decision to Escalate the Vietnam War," *Political Science Quarterly*, 103 (Winter 1988–89), 637–63.

68. Robert Axelrod, *The Evolution of Cooperation* (New York, 1984), 153–54. The father of game theory and one of RAND's chief early players was John von Neumann; see Kaplan, *The Wizards of Armageddon*, 63–67.

69. John McNaughton, quoted in *The Pentagon Papers*, Senator Gravel Ed. (Boston, 1970), 3: 696.

70. Festinger, *A Theory of Cognitive Dissonance*, 204–6, and his *Conflict, Decision and Dissonance*; Milton Rokeach, *The Nature of Human Values* (New York, 1973), 217; Robert Putnam, *The Beliefs of Politicians* (New Haven, Conn., 1971), 4, 5–6, 125–28, 147–49; William Safire, "Cognitive Dissonance," *San Francisco Chronicle*, Sept. 3, 1985, 49; Ithiel De Sola Pool, "Political Alternatives to the Viet Cong," *Asian Survey*, 7 (Aug. 1967), 555–66; Hannah Arendt, "Lying in Politics," in her *Crises of the Republic* (New York, 1969), 35. Pool suggests that Viet Cong cadres from middle or rich peasant families suffered from cognitive dissonance because they resented the discrimination the Viet Cong exercised against them and their families. The question of bombing civilian targets caused dissonance for many internationalists from World War II to Vietnam; see Ronald Schaffer, "American Military Ethics in World War II: The Bombing of German Civilians," *Journal of American History*, 67 (Sept. 1980), 318–34, and the replies to it, "American Military Ethics in World War II: An Exchange," *Journal of American History*, 68 (June 1981), 85–92; Lee Kennett, *A History of Strategic Bombing* (New York, 1982).

71. Larsen, *Origins of Containment*, 24–65.

72. Milton J. Rosenberg et al., *Attitude Organization and Change* (New Haven, Conn., 1960); J. Stacy Adams, "Reduction of Cognitive Dissonance by Seeking Consonant Information," *Journal of Abnormal and Social Psychology*, no. 62, 1961; Philip E. Tetlock and Charles McGuire, Jr., "Cognitive Perspectives on Foreign Policy," in Samuel Long, ed., *Political Behavior Annual: 1986* (Boulder, Colo., 1986), 147–79. For the Dulles study see David J. Finlay, Ole R. Holsti, and Richard Fagen, *Enemies in Politics* (Chicago, 1967), 25–96. For political science and psychology dealing with deterrence theory see Robert Jervis, Richard Ned Lebow, and Janice Gross Stein, *Psychology and Deterrence* (Baltimore, Md., 1985), 24–25, 52, 55, 79, 81, 83–84, 126, 133.

73. Walter Lippmann, *The Public Philosophy* (Boston, 1955), 144–45; Arthur Schlesinger, Jr., "National Interests and Moral Absolutes," in Ernest W. Lefever, ed., *Ethics and World Politics* (Baltimore, Md., 1972), 21–42.

74. Acheson, *Present at the Creation*, 461; Karnow, *Vietnam*, 14; Schlesinger, "National Interests and Moral Absolutes," 23; Ernest W. Lefever, *Ethics and U.S. Foreign Policy* (New York, 1957), 19, 22, 52, 99, 101, 128; *The Papers of Adlai E. Stevenson: 1952–1955*, ed. Walter Johnson (Boston, 1974), 4: 42, 229–30, 305; Felix Frankfurter Papers, Library of Congress; R. Fox, *Reinhold Niebuhr*, 269, 281–83; Hamby, *Liberalism and Its Challengers*, 146–47, 162–63; David W. Noble, *The End of American History* (Minneapolis, Minn., 1985), 65–89; Massimo Rubboli, *Politica e Religione Negli USA: Reinhold Niebuhr e il suo tempo* (Milan, 1986).

75. Wolfers, *Discord and Collaboration*; Kenneth W. Thompson, *The Moral Issue in Statecraft* (Baton Rouge, La., 1964); H. Butterfield, *Christianity, Diplomacy and War*. Niebuhr, on the dust jacket of Thompson's book, states that "Thompson makes a telling refutation of both pure perfectionism and moral rigidity posing as moral idealism."

76. Hans J. Morgenthau, "The Influence of Reinhold Niebuhr in American Political Life and Thought," in Harold R. Landon, ed., *Reinhold Niebuhr* (Greenwich, Conn., 1962), 99–109; Gordon Harland, *The Thought of Reinhold Niebuhr* (Oxford, 1960), 163–213. Harold Brown cites Morgenthau in his *Department of Defense Annual Report for Fiscal Year 1982* (Washington, D.C., 1982), ix.

77. Waltz, *Man, the State, and War*, 18–40. In 1954, Dean Rusk and Kenneth Thompson, of the Rockefeller Foundation, invited both realist professors and practitioners to a small conference in Washington, D.C. Attending were Walter Lippmann, Hans, J. Morgenthau, Paul Nitze, Arnold Wolfers, James Reston, William T. R. Fox, Reinhold Niebuhr, Don K. Price, and Dorothy Fosdick—plus Rusk and Thompson. Later, Professor Fox, Director of the Institute of War and Peace Studies at Columbia University, hosted a series of meetings at Columbia. The group grew to include Morton Kaplan, Ken Waltz, Arno Mayer, Warner Schilling, Glenn Snyder, Robert Tucker and Charles P. Kindleberger. Fox had their papers published. One volume contains essays by Nitze, Waltz, Niebuhr, Kindleberger, and Morgenthau: William T. R. Fox, ed., *Theoretical Aspects of International Relations* (Notre

Dame, Ind., 1959). However, realism and neorealism have not triumphed over other interpretations. See Robert Keohane, ed., *Neorealism and Its Critics* (New York, 1986), and Joseph S. Nye, Jr., "Neorealism and Neoliberalism," *World Politics,* 40 (Jan. 1988), 235–51.

78. Christian pessimists included Martin Wight, Karl Barth, Paul Tillich, and Dietrich Bonhoeffer. See Howard, *The Causes of Wars,* 51–52.

79. Niebuhr, *Moral Man and Immoral Society,* 258, 267; Alexander Hamilton, *Pacificus,* no. 4, July 10, 1793; Reinhold Niebuhr, *The Irony of American History* (New York, 1952), 37–42. Aldous Huxley, in the same decade as Niebuhr's *Moral Man and Immoral Society,* refused to disconnect man from society; see his *Ends and Means* (London, 1937), 320–21.

80. Winston Churchill, *The Gathering Storm* (Boston, 1948), 320.

81. Bundy, *The Strength of Government,* 106. Years later Bundy, in reviewing Kissinger's *White House Years,* suggested that sometimes it is necessary for good men to do nothing; see McGeorge Bundy, "Vietnam, Watergate and Presidential Powers," *Foreign Affairs,* 58 (Winter 1979–80), 397–407.

82. Henry Allen, "War Is Hell, Movies Aren't," *Washington Post National Weekly Edition,* Feb. 9, 1987, 25; Tim O'Brien, *Going After Cacciato* (New York, 1975); Larry Heinemann, *Paco's Story* (New York, 1986).

83. Baker, *Nam;* Pratt, *Vietnam Voices;* Santoli, *Everything We Had;* Bernard Edelman, ed., *Dear America: Letters Home From Vietnam* (New York, 1985); John Keegan, *The Face of Battle* (New York, 1976); Kinnard, *The War Managers,* 10, 24–25, 48, 54–55, 59, 99–108, 169–85. The Historical Division Headquarters, U.S. Marine Corps, Washington, D.C., has stored thousands of interviews with Marines who served in Vietnam. For discussion of militarized mass insurrection see C. Johnson, *Revolution and the Social System,* n. 1.

84. Ellis, *Armies in Revolution,* 1–9; Mark A. Kishlansky, *The Rise of the New Model Army* (Cambridge, 1979); Amos Perlmutter and Valerie P. Bennett, eds., *The Political Influence of the Military* (New Haven, Conn., 1980), 3–24.

85. Isaiah Berlin, *Four Essays on Liberty* (Oxford, 1979), x, 170.

86. Hartz, *The Liberal Tradition in America,* 308; Perry Miller, *Errand into the Wilderness* (Cambridge, Mass., 1956), 6; Sacvan Bercovitch, *The American Jeremiad* (Madison, Wis., 1978), 4.

Chapter 1

1. Brodie, *Strategy in the Missile Age;* Perkins, *America's Quest for Peace,* 49–90; Ernst B. Hass, *Tangle of Hopes* (Englewood Cliffs, N.J., 1969), 269–82.

2. "Oral History of Paul Nitze," taken by Dorothy Fosdick, July 7, 1964, 1, LBJL; Truman, *Memoirs, vol. 2, Years of Trial and Hope, 1946–1952,* 307; David Holloway, *The Soviet Union and the Arms Race,* 2d ed. (New Haven, Conn., 1983), 18–25.

3. Karl Jaspers, *The Future of Mankind* (Chicago, 1961), 1–13; Bernard Brodie, *The Absolute Weapon* (New York, 1964).

4. Keohane, *After Hegemony,* 31–46.

5. McNamara, *The Essence of Security,* 9.

6. In fiscal year 1980 nuclear forces accounted for 13.4 percent of the defense budget, in 1981 only 13.7 percent, and in 1982 up to 15 percent. This was also the case in the 1950's, 1960's, and 1970's. See Harold Brown, *Department of Defense Annual Report for Fiscal Year 1982*, appendices, Chart C-4.

7. Lodge, *The Storm Has Many Eyes*, 204–5, 223–24, 226, 249.

8. *Public Papers of the Presidents of the United States: John F. Kennedy, 1963* (Washington, D.C., 1964), 497–98.

9. *Ibid.*, 516–21. Also see Deutsch, *Political Community at the International Level*, 27, 33–34, 41–42, and Karl W. Deutsch *et al.*, *Political Community and the North Atlantic Area* (Princeton, N.J., 1957).

10. J. G. A. Pocock, *The Machiavellian Moment: Florentine Political Thought and the Atlantic Republican Tradition* (Princeton, N.J., 1975), 423–24, 460–61, 544–47; John Dunn, *The Political Thought of John Locke: An Historical Account of the Argument of the Two Treatises of Government* (Cambridge, 1969), and "The Politics of Locke in England and America in the Eighteenth Century," in John W. Yolton, ed., *John Locke: Problems and Perspectives* (Cambridge, 1969), 45–80; Calleo, *The Atlantic Fantasy*, 100–22; Charles de Gaulle, *Unity*, vol. 2 of his *Complete War Memoirs* (New York, 1955–60), 172; Robert K. Merton, *Social Theory and Social Structure* (New York, 1957), 421–22.

11. Almond and Verba, *The Civic Culture*, and their *The Civic Culture Revisited*, 31–32; Alexis de Tocqueville, *Democracy in America* (New York, 1969), 287; James Ceaser, "Alexis de Tocqueville on Political Science, Political Culture, and the Role of Intellectuals," *The American Political Science Review*, 79 (Sept. 1985), 656–72.

12. The multivolume study (Princeton, N.J.) comprises Lucian W. Pye, ed., *Communications and Political Development* (1963); Joseph LaPalombara, ed., *Bureaucracy and Political Development* (1963); Robert E. Ward and Dankwart A. Rustow, eds., *Political Modernization in Japan and Turkey* (1964); James S. Coleman, ed., *Education and Political Development* (1965); Pye and Verba, eds., *Political Culture and Political Development* (1965); Joseph LaPalombara and Myron Weiner, eds., *Political Parties and Political Development* (1966); and Leonard Binder, James S. Coleman, Joseph LaPalombara, Lucian Pye, Sidney Verba, and Myron Weiner, eds., *Crisis and Sequences in Political Development* (1971). See also Lowell Dittmer, "Comparative Communist Political Culture," *Studies in Comparative Communism*, 16 (Spring–Summer 1983), 9–24.

13. Lucian W. Pye, "The Politics of Southeast Asia," in Almond and Coleman, eds., *The Politics of the Developing Areas*, 65–152; Alex Inkeles, "Convergence and Divergence in Industrial Societies," in M. Atlir, B. Holzner, and Z. Suda, eds., *Directions of Change: Modernization Theory, Research, and Realities* (Boulder, Colo., 1981), 3–38; Grosser, *The Western Alliance*, 330–32; Wilbur E. Moore, *World Modernization: The Limits of Convergence* (New York, 1979); Michael Ellman, "Against Convergence," *Cambridge Journal of Economics*, 4 (Sept. 1980), 199–210; William Form, "Comparative Industrial Sociology and the Convergence Hypothesis," *Annual Review of Sociology*, 5 (1979), 1–25; R. Alan Hedley, "Work Values: A Test of the Convergence and Cultural Di-

versity Thesis," *International Journal of Comparative Sociology*, 21 (Mar.–June 1980), 100–9; Neil J. Smelser, *Theory of Collective Behavior* (New York, 1963), 28 (quotation).

14. Ruth Benedict, *The Chrysanthemum and the Sword* (Boston, 1946); Du Bois, *Social Forces in Southeast Asia*; Dick Wilson, "The Pacific Basin Is Coming Together," *Asia Pacific Community*, Fall 1985, 2–11; St. Munadjat Danusaputro, "The Prospective Changes in the Pacific Ocean," *The Indonesian Quarterly*, 14 (July 1986), 313–39, John Hay quoted on 313.

15. Brown, *Department of Defense Annual Report for Fiscal Year 1982*, 26; George F. Will, *The Pursuit of Virtue and Other Tory Notions* (New York, 1982), 165–67; James R. Huntley, *Uniting the Democracies: Institutions of the Emerging Atlantic-Pacific System* (New York, 1980).

16. Destler, *Presidents, Bureaucrats and Foreign Policy*, 114; McNamara, *The Essence of Security*, 8.

17. Millis, *Arms and Men*, 117–88.

18. Betts, *Soldiers, Statesmen and Cold War Crises*, 35.

19. Ries, *The Management of Defense*, 188.

20. Westmoreland, *A Soldier Reports*, 74–77; Sharp, *Strategy for Defeat*, 87, 96,198, 230; memo from Mike Forrestal to President Kennedy, Jan. 28, 1963, and memo from McGeorge Bundy to President Kennedy, Feb. 4, 1963, both in NSFV, box 197, Vietnam Memos, vol. 1, JFKL.

21. Ries, *The Management of Defense*, 189–90.

22. Hitch and McKean, *The Economics of Defense in the Nuclear Age*; Enthoven and Smith, *How Much Is Enough?*, xiii. The Hitch and McKean book was basically rewritten as *Elements of Defense Economics* and republished by the Industrial College of the Armed Forces, Washington, D.C., in 1967.

23. Aaron Wildavsky, *The Politics of the Budgetary Process*, 4th ed. (Boston, 1984), 142.

24. Enthoven and Smith, *How Much Is Enough?*, 251–62; Art, *The TFX Decision*; Charles de Gaulle, *Memoirs of Hope: Renewal and Endeavor* (New York, 1970), 220; Harold Macmillan, *At the End of the Day: 1961–1963* (London, 1973), 283, 340, 356–62, 366, 372, 373, 454, 461, 469, 535–45; Sorensen, *Kennedy*, 564–74.

25. AES cable to State, "For the President from Lodge," Feb. 22, 1964, and the reply, State cable to AES, "For Ambassador from Secretary," Feb. 28, 1964, both in NSFV, box 2, Vietnam Cables, vol. 4, LBJL.

26. Robert N. Anthony, *Planning and Control Systems: A Framework for Analysis*, Harvard Graduate School of Business Administration—Studies in Management Control (Cambridge, Mass., 1965); Herbert York, *Race to Oblivion* (New York, 1970), 22–23.

27. Dickson, *The Electronic Battlefield*, 20–54.

28. Weigley, *The American Way of War*, 288–390.

29. Gaddis, *Strategies of Containment*, 91.

30. Destler, *Presidents, Bureaucrats and Foreign Policy*, 225.

31. "Oral History of Paul Nitze," taken by Fosdick, May 22–July 7– July 11, 1964, JFKL (quotations on p. 1); "Oral History of Paul Nitze," taken

by Dorothy Pierce (McSweeny), Nov. 20–Dec. 26, 1968, LBJL; Nitze, "Eight Presidents and Their Different Approaches to National Security Policymaking," 31–63. Also see Talbott, *The Master of the Game.*

32. Nitze, "Eight Presidents and Their Different Approaches to National Security Policymaking," 40. Also see DOD memo from Paul Nitze to the "Tuesday Luncheon" group, Sept. 8, 1961, and memo from JCS Chairman General Lyman Lemnitzer to SecDef, Aug. 24, 1961, both in NSFV, box 194, JFKL.

33. Zumwalt, *On Watch,* 35.

34. Paul Nitze, "The Strategic Balance Between Hope and Skepticism," *Foreign Policy,* no. 17 (Winter 1974–75), 136–56, and "Living With the Soviets," *Foreign Affairs,* 63 (Winter 1984–85), 360–74.

35. MacArthur, *Reminiscences,* 385–440.

36. Brodie, *The Absolute Weapon;* William W. Kaufmann, "Unlimited Weapons and Limited War," in Kaufman, ed., *Military Policy and National Security;* Osgood, *Limited War,* and *NATO;* Henry A. Kissinger, *Nuclear Weapons and Foreign Policy* (New York, 1957).

37. MacArthur, *Reminiscences,* 440.

38. Niebuhr, *Moral Man and Immoral Society,* 44, 110.

39. Niebuhr, quoted in Acheson, *Present at the Creation,* 461.

40. *The Papers of Adlai E. Stevenson: 1952–1955,* ed. Walter Johnson (Boston, 1974), 4: 229.

41. George C. Marshall, "Testimony Before the Armed Services and Foreign Relations Committees," in Guttman, ed., *Korea,* 45–52; J. William Fulbright, *The Crippled Giant: American Foreign Policy and Its Domestic Consequences* (New York, 1972).

42. Omar N. Bradley, "Testimony Before the Armed Services and Foreign Relations Committees," in Guttman, *Korea,* 53–58. Senator Lyndon Johnson heard this testimony, plus the testimony of General MacArthur, whom he questioned about the limits of this war.

43. Stanley L. Falk, "The National Security Council under Truman, Eisenhower, and Kennedy," *Political Science Quarterly,* 79 (Sept. 1964), 403–34; Keith C. Clark and Laurence J. Legere, eds., *The President and the Management of National Security: A Report by the Institute for Defense Analyses* (New York, 1969); Alfred D. Sander, "Truman and the National Security Council: 1945–1947," *Journal of American History,* 59 (Sept. 1972), 369–88; I. M. Destler, "National Security Advice to U.S. Presidents: Some Lessons from Thirty Years," *World Politics,* 29 (Jan. 1977), 143–76; Anna Kasten Nelson, "President Truman and the Evolution of the National Security Council," *Journal of American History,* 72 (Sept. 1985), 360–78.

44. Memo from James B. Webb, Bureau of the Budget, to President Truman, Aug. 8, 1947, Clark Clifford Papers, box 11, HSTL. Also see the oral history interview with Webb located in the files of the HSTL.

45. Memo, undated, Sidney W. Souers Papers, box 1, HSTL; Sidney W. Souers, "Policy Formulation for National Security," *American Political Science Review,* 43 (June 1949), 534–43.

46. John Foster Dulles, "Notes, Commission on a Just and Durable Peace,"

Nov. 8, 1945, John Foster Dulles Collection, box 84, Mudd Archives of Princeton University.

47. "Oral History of Paul H. Nitze," taken by Fosdick, July 7, 1964, 2.

48. *Ibid*. The Council on Foreign Relations had more than its New York headquarters and its quarterly journal through which it influenced U.S. policy; it also staffed an active Washington office. See Strobe Talbott, *Deadly Gambits* (New York, 1984), 331.

49. "Speech by Dwight David Eisenhower," *New York Times*, Oct. 9, 1952.

50. Cutler, *No Time for Rest*, 311.

51. Clark and Legere, *The President and the Management of National Security*, 55–70; Alexander George, *Presidential Decisionmaking in Foreign Policy* (Boulder, Colo., 1980), 150–58.

52. M. Bundy, quoted in Senate, "Report of the Jackson Subcommittee," in *Inquiry on National Policy Machinery, II, Studies and Background Materials* (Washington, D.C., 1961), 1337. Jackson was a unilateralist; see Talbott, *Deadly Gambits*, 16.

53. Clark and Legere, *The President and the Management of National Security*, 79; Richard Smoke, *War: Controlling Escalation* (Cambridge, Mass., 1977), 5, 9, 25, 43–44, 275, 285.

54. Rostow, *The Diffusion of Power*, 284–87, 482, 502.

55. Whiting, *China Crosses the Yalu*, 92–94.

56. *Ibid.*, 116–17.

57. Memo on NSC stationery from Jim Thomson to Mr. Bundy, July 21, 1964, NSFV, box 6, Vietnam Memos vol. 14, LBJL. An attached note reads: "Attached is INR's note on the most recent Chicom reactions to our SEA actions. Allen Whiting is following the decibel count and wording very closely against the backdrop of signals sent in the Korean War and offshore island crises." In this same file see memo from the Director of Intelligence and Research to the Secretary of State, Subject: "Peiping Plays Up Warnings on Indochina," July 20, 1964.

58. Rostow, *The Diffusion of Power*, 286; Westmoreland, *A Soldier Reports*, 298–99, 412–13, 466–67; Palmer, *The 25-Year War*, 177, 183; Krepinevich, *The Army and Vietnam*, 261–68.

Chapter 2

1. Gaddis, *Strategies of Containment*, 153; Acheson, *Present at the Creation*, 731–32.

2. Both resolutions are republished in Guttman, *Korea*, 5–13.

3. John Kee and Dean Rusk, quoted in House Committee on International Relations, *United States Policy in the Far East: Part 2*, vol. 8 (Washington, D.C., 1976), 491.

4. Leonard Mosley, *Dulles: A Biography of Eleanor, Allen and John Foster Dulles and Their Family Network* (New York, 1978), 307–8; Townsend Hoopes, *The Devil and John Foster Dulles* (Boston, 1973), 487. Also see the oral histories by Nitze in both the JFK and LBJ Presidential Libraries; Huntington, *The Common Defense*, 20.

5. James C. Thomson, Jr., "How Could Vietnam Happen?" in Richard Abrams and Lawrence W. Levine, eds., *The Shaping of Twentieth-Century America* (Boston, 1965), 683–94. Even with the loss of many China experts— those experts on Asia remaining at the State Department were expected to watch all the Asian rim, leaving Indochina to two "desks," the French desk officer and the China desk officer—continuity marked the internationalist years after World War II regardless of party affiliation, even when the rhetoric was the most venomous. The Dulles-Rusk relationship is a case in point. See Halberstam, *The Best and the Brightest*, 419.

6. Acheson, quoted in House Committee on International Relations, *Military Assistance Program, Part 1*, vol. 5 (Washington, D.C., 1976), 229.

7. Kennan, *Memoirs*, 497–528. Also see John Lewis Gaddis, "Was the Truman Doctrine a Real Turning Point?" *Foreign Affairs*, 52 (Jan. 1974), 386– 402; David McLellan, *Dean Acheson* (New York, 1976); Policy Planning Staff Paper 43, "Considerations Affecting the Conclusion of a North Atlantic Security Pact," Nov. 24, 1948, in *Foreign Relations: 1948* (Washington, D.C., 1950), 3: 286.

8. Acheson, *Present at the Creation*, 728–29.

9. Ambrose, *Rise to Globalism*, 81. Not only did the United States avoid the heavily populated rim of Asia, but its president, FDR, while avoiding battle there, held strong views about the area, especially Indochina. See Gary R. Hess, "Franklin Roosevelt and Indochina," *Journal of American History*, 59 (Sept. 1972), 353–68.

10. U.S. Department of State press release, "Statement by the Honorable John Foster Dulles, Secretary of State, Before the House Foreign Affairs Committee," Apr. 5, 1954, no. 178, John Foster Dulles Collection, box 84, 8, Mudd Archives of Princeton University.

11. U.S. Department of State press release, "Address by the Honorable John Foster Dulles, Secretary of State, Before the California State Chamber of Commerce, San Francisco," Dec. 5, 1958, no. 730, John Foster Dulles Collection, box 132, 2–4, Mudd Archives of Princeton University.

12. NSC 48/1, "The Position of the U.S. with Respect to Asia," Dec. 23, 1949, and NSC 48/2, "The Position of the U.S. with Respect to Asia," Dec. 30, 1949, both in U.S. Department of Defense, *U.S.–Vietnam Relations, 1945–67* (Washington, D.C., 1971), 7: 226–64, and in Thomas H. Etzold and John L. Gaddis, eds., *Containment: Documents on American Policy and Strategy: 1945–50* (New York, 1978). The appeal of an iron triangle—Taiwan, Japan, South Korea—has not evaporated from U.S. strategy as the anchor for U.S. policy in Northeast Asia. See A. James Gregor and Maria Hsia Chang, *The Iron Triangle: A U.S. Security Policy for Northeast Asia* (Stanford, Calif., 1984).

13. Michael Schaller, "Securing the Great Crescent: Occupied Japan and the Origins of Containment in Southeast Asia," *Journal of American History*, 69 (Sept. 1982), 392–414; Michael Schaller, *The American Occupation of Japan: The Origins of the Cold War in Asia* (Oxford, 1985).

14. C. Johnson, *MITI and the Japanese Miracle*, 200 (quotation); Takafusa

Nakamura, *The Postwar Japanese Economy: Its Development and Structure* (Tokyo, 1981), 35–48.

15. McNamara, quoted in U.S. Department of State, Historical Studies Division, Research Project no. 747, "Chronology on Vietnam," Nov. 1965, NSFV, box 38, NSC History of Gulf of Tonkin, Presidential Decisions, vol. 1, LBJL.

16. H. Johnson, *Challenge*, 16. There is a copy of this work in Army Historical files, Washington, D.C.

17. State cable to multiple embassies, Nov. 19, 1961, and AES cable to State, Jan. 23, 1963, both in NSFV, box 197, JFKL.

18. State cable, May 30, 1964, NSFV, box 5, LBJL; memo from Dean Rusk to President Johnson, Subject: Third Country Aid to Vietnam, June 15, 1964, NSFV, box 5, Memos, vol. 12, LBJL.

19. State cable from President Johnson to multiple embassies, July 2, 1964, NSFV, box 6, Cables, vol. 13, LBJL.

20. State cable from Dean Rusk to Ambassador Lodge, May 1, 1964, NSFV, box 4, Cables, vol. 13, LBJL.

21. Memo from William H. Sullivan to McGeorge Bundy, Subject: Third County Aid to Vietnam, June 24, 1964, NSFV, box 5, Memos, vol. 12, LBJL.

22. Lodge denied having any feud with Harkin in his cable to State, Oct. 5, 1963, NSFV, box 204, JFKL.

23. AES cable to State, "For Rusk and McNamara from Lodge," Apr. 29, 1964, p. 1, NSFV, box 3, Cables, vol. 4, LBJL; AES cable to State, "For Rusk and McNamara from Lodge," May 14, 1964, sec. 3, p. 3, NSFV, box 3, Cables, vol. 9, LBJL.

24. Memo to President Johnson from Carl T. Rowan, Director of the U.S. Information Agency, Aug. 24, 1964, NSFV, box 17, Memos, vol. 16, LBJL. See also *Public Papers of the Presidents of the United States: Lyndon B. Johnson, 1963–64* (Washington, D.C., 1965), 2: 937–38. Lodge later toured the United States in support of the administration's role in Vietnam; see "Memorandum to the President from McGeorge Bundy," Oct. 23, 1964, NSFV, box 9, Memos, vol. 20, LBJL.

25. Incoming cable from A. Harriman, U.S. embassy, London, to State, Mar. 20, 1964, NSFV, box 3, Vietnam Cables, vol. 6, LBJL; Westmoreland, *A Soldier Reports*, 69, 274; State cable to AES, "For Westmoreland and Zorthian from Manning and Sylvester," June 19, 1964, NSFV, box 5, Vietnam Cables, vol. 12, LBJL.

26. State Historical Studies Division, Research Project no. 747, "Chronology on Vietnam"; incoming cable from U.S. embassy, Bonn, to State, May 11, 1964, NSFV, box 4, Memos, vol. 8, LBJL.

27. CINCPAC cable to MACV, Dec. 7, 1962, and letter from John Kennedy to Doctor Luther Terry, Mar. 7, 1962, both NSFV, box 197, JFKL; AES cable from Henry Cabot Lodge to State, May 4, 1964, p. 2, NSFV, box 4, Cables, vol. 8, LBJL.

28. AES cable from Henry Cabot Lodge to State, May 19, 1964, p. 2, NSFV, box 4, Memos, vol. 9, LBJL; Generals Stanley R. Larsen and James L. Collins, Jr., *Allied Participation in Vietnam* (Washington, D.C., 1975), 164–65.

29. Joint State–DOD cable, Mar. 18, 1964, NSFV, box 2, Cables, vol. 5, LBJL.

30. Incoming cable from E. O. Reischauer, U.S. embassy Tokyo to State, Mar. 19, 1964, NSFV, box 2, Cables, vol. 5, LBJL.

31. AES cable from Henry Cabot Lodge to State, Mar. 9, 1964, NSFV, box 4, Cables, vol. 8, LBJL.

32. Larsen and Collins, *Allied Participation in Vietnam*, 120–25; Claude A. Buss, *The United States and the Republic of Korea* (Stanford, Calif., 1981), 80; U.S. Congress, Senate, Committee on Foreign Relations, Subcommittee on United States Security Agreements and Commitments Abroad, *United States Security Agreements and Commitments Abroad, Part 6, Republic of Korea: Hearings*, 91st Cong., 2d sess., Feb. 1970, 1717; U.S. Department of State, *United States Treaties and Other International Agreements*, vol. 5, pt. 3, 2368–74.

33. AES cable from Maxwell Taylor to State (information copy to U.S. embassy Tehran), July 18, 1964, NSFV, box 6, Cables, vol. 16, LBJL.

34. *Public Papers of the Presidents: LBJ, 1963–64*, 2: 886.

35. Larsen and Collins, *Allied Participation in Vietnam*, 19.

36. *Ibid.*, 2. In fact, on Sept. 15, 1945, Chiang Kai-shek had requested that General Albert Wedemeyer help him transport his Chinese 52nd Army from Haiphong to Darien, Manchuria, a task that fell to Admiral Thomas Kincaid's 7th Fleet.

37. AES cable from CIA to State, Mar. 15, 1964, NSFV, box 2, Memos, vol. 5, LBJL.

38. AES cable from Henry Cabot Lodge to State, Sept. 3, 1964, NSFV, box 8, Cables, vol. 17, LBJL.

39. State cable from Dean Rusk to Maxwell Taylor, AES, July 20, 1964, p. 5, NSFV, box 38, NSC History of the Gulf of Tonkin, Presidential Decisions, vol. 1, LBJL.

40. State cable from Dean Rusk to Maxwell Taylor, AES, July 23, 1964, p. 5, NSFV, box 38, NSC History of Gulf of Tonkin, Presidential Decisons, vol. 1, LBJL.

41. "Oral History of Michael Forrestal," taken by Paige Mulhollan, Nov. 3, 1969, LBJL.

42. Memo from W. Averell Harriman to Secretary Rusk (copies to Ball and Forrestal at White House), Sept. 22, 1964, NSFV, box 9, Memos, vol. 18, LBJL. In a Gallup Poll taken from July 23–28, before the Gulf of Tonkin incident, 52 percent expressed a view that the United States was handling the Vietnam conflict as well as could be expected, 38 percent expressed a view that it was handled badly, and 10 percent had no opinion. In a poll taken from August 6–11 the figures approving jumped to 71 percent, the percentage disapproving fell to 16 percent, and those with no opinion rose to 13 percent. See *The Gallup Poll: Public Opinion 1935–1971, Survey 696K* (New York, 1972), 3: 1899.

43. AES cable from Ambassador Taylor to State, Nov. 14, 1964, NSFV, box 10, Cables, vol. 21, LBJL.

44. Cooper, *The Lost Crusade*, 266.

45. *Ibid.*, 266–67.

46. Larsen and Collins, *Allied Participation in Vietnam*, 22–23.

47. *Ibid.*, 23; Richard A. Hunt, "America's Allies in Vietnam: Problems of Recruitment and Command, 1965–1968," *Asian Perspective*, 6 (Spring–Summer 1982), 123–32; Peter King, ed., *Australia's Vietnam: Australia in the Second Indo-China War* (Winchester, Mass., 1983).

48. *Gallup Poll: Public Opinion 1935–1971*, interview dates July 23–28, 1964, survey 695, question 18, 1896–97.

49. M. J. Peterson, *The General Assembly in World Politics* (Boston, 1986), 11–13; for Article 52 see p. 43. It was during the 1960's that the U.S.-led coalition in the United Nations lost its majority to a coalition of African, Asian, and Latin American states. Disenchantment soon followed.

50. Senator Mike Mansfield (D-Montana), commencement address, Michigan State University, June 10, 1962, NSFV, box 1, Vietnam Memos, vol. 2, LBJL. For Mansfield's memo to LBJ see the same file under Dec. 7, 1963. Also see a second letter from Mansfield to LBJ dated Feb. 1, 1964. For a sample of the LBJ team's refutation of Mansfield see the same collection for a Jan. 7, 1964, memo from Robert S. McNamara to the President.

51. Memo from Director of Intelligence and Research, to Secretary of State, Subject: Reactions to Neutralization of Southeast Asia, Apr. 6, 1964, NSFV, box 4, Memos, vol. 8, LBJL.

52. Dean Rusk, quoted in State, Historical Studies Division, Research Project no. 747, "Chronology on Vietnam."

53. On British attempts at peace negotiations see "Oral History of Chester Cooper," taken by Paige Mulhollan, interview 2, July 1969, 29–33, LBJL. For the Vietnam connection to NATO, especially de Gaulle's role, see Grosser, *The Western Alliance*, 237–43. The French position was well-known in Saigon. See AES cable to State, Apr. 15, 1964, box 3, NSFV, cables, vol. 7, LBJL.

54. Mansfield, commencement address, 12. Mansfield had a few of Senator Borah's qualities. While part of the U.S. delegation that helped organize SEATO, Mansfield seemed to distance himself from what organizations like SEATO or NATO meant; see Rostow, *The Diffusion of Power*, 396.

55. Melvyn P. Leffler, "Strategy, Diplomacy, and the Cold War: The United States, Turkey, and NATO, 1945–1952," *Journal of American History*, 71 (Mar. 1985), 807–25.

56. State cable from Dean Rusk to AES, Sept. 5, 1964, NSFV, box 8, Cables, vol. 18, LBJL.

57. Memo from McGeorge Bundy to Robert McNamara, May 12, 1964, NSFV, box 4, Memos, vol. 8, LBJL. Eugene Zuckert, Secretary of the Air Force, speedily answered Vinson on May 13; see letter from Zuckert to Vinson, May 13, 1964, NSFV, box 4, Memos, vol. 9, LBJL.

58. Note from President Johnson to McGeorge Bundy, Oct. 17, 1964, NSFV, box 9, Memos, vol. 20, LBJL.

59. Charles Krauthammer, "The Poverty of Realism," *The New Republic*, Feb. 17, 1986, 14–22.

60. Stephen M. Walt, *The Origins of Alliances* (Ithaca, N.Y., 1987).

Chapter 3

1. "Oral History of Lt. General Victor H. Krulak," taken by Benis M. Frank, June 12, 1970, 195, filed at the Historical Division Headquarters, U.S. Marine Corps, Washington, D.C. The classified volume of this history, covering Krulak's covert DOD-CIA tasks in Vietnam, is not yet declassified.

2. State cable from Dean Rusk to Ambassador Lodge, AES, May 21, 1964, NSFV, box 4, Vietnam Cables, vol. 9, LBJL.

3. Memo from SecDef Robert McNamara to President Johnson, Dec. 21, 1963, and memo from Mike Forrestal to President Johnson, Dec. 11, 1963, both in NSFV, box 1, Memos, vol. 2, LBJL. (General Krulak authored the options mentioned by McNamara; see the oral history cited in n. 1 for this chapter.)

4. Letter from Senator Mike Mansfield to President Lyndon B. Johnson, Subject: Southeast Asia and Vietnam, Dec. 7, 1963, NSFV, box 1, Memos, vol. 2, LBJL.

5. Scott, *The Moral Economy of the Peasant,* 67; Popkin, *The Rational Peasant,* 172–74.

6. U.S. Department of State, Historical Studies Division, Research Project no. 747, "Chronology on Vietnam," Nov. 1965, NSFV, box 38, NSC History of Gulf of Tonkin, Presidential Decisions, vol. 1, LBJL; intelligence note from Director of Intelligence and Research to Secretary of State, "Khanh's Claims on Increased North Vietnamese Infiltration," July 17, 1964, NSFV, box 6, Memos, vol. 14, LBJL.

7. MACV cable to JCS, Jan. 8, 1964, NSFV, box 1, Cables, vol. 2, LBJL.

8. AES cable from Ambassador Lodge to State, Mar. 9, 1964, NSFV, box 2, Cables, vol. 5, LBJL.

9. AES cables to State, Mar. 13 and Mar. 16, 1964, NSFV, box 2, Cables, vol. 5, LBJL; AES cable from Ambassador Lodge to State, Mar. 15, 1964, NSFV, box 2, Cables, vol. 5, LBJL.

10. DOD memo from Paul Nitze to "Tuesday Luncheon" group, Sept. 8, 1961, and memo from Chairman of JCS to SecDef McNamara, Aug. 24, 1961, NSFV, box 194, JFKL; CINCPAC cable to JCS, Dec. 5, 1963, NSFV, box 1, Vietnam Cables, vol. 1, and memo from SecDef McNamara to President Johnson, Dec. 21, 1963, NSFV, box 1, Cables, vol. 2, LBJL.

11. Cable from SecDef McNamara to AES, July 23, 1964, NSFV, box 6, Cables, vol. 14, LBJL.

12. AES cable to State, Sept. 12, 1964, and State cable from Dean Rusk to Ambassador Lodge, AES, Sept. 11, 1964, NSFV, box 8, Cables, vol. 17; U.S. Embassy, Phnom Penh, cable from Herbert Spivak to Dean Rusk, State, July 29, 1964, NSFV, box 6, Cables, vol. 14; all in LBJL.

13. JCS cable to CINCPAC, Sept. 10, 1964, and CINCPAC cable to MACV, Sept. 30, 1964, NSFV, box 8, Vietnam Cables, vol. 18, LBJL.

14. MACV cable to National Military Command Center, Oct. 23, 1964, NSFV, box 9, Vietnam Cables, vol. 20, LBJL.

15. Memo from Robert Johnson to Walt Rostow, Sept. 7, 1961, NSFV, box

194, JFKL; State, Historical Studies Division, Research Project no. 747, "Chronology on Vietnam"; MACV cable to JCS, Mar. 21, 1964, NSFV, box 3, Vietnam Cables, vol. 6; MACV cable to CINCPAC, May 8, 1964, NSFV, box 3, Vietnam Cables, vol. 8; all in LBJL.

16. MACV cable to JCS, Mar. 21, 1964, NSFV, box 3, Vietnam Cables, vol. 6, LBJL.

17. Memo from Mike Forrestal to McGeorge Bundy, Apr. 1, 1964, NSFV, box 3, Cables, vol.6, LBJL; Broughton, *Thud Ridge*, 94–96.

18. State cable to AES, May 16, 1964, NSFV, box 4, Cables, vol. 8, LBJL.

19. AES cable to State, Apr. 7, 1964, NSFV, box 3, Cables, vol. 7, LBJL.

20. AES airgram to State, Apr. 9, 1964, including letter from General C. Youngdale to AES, Apr. 7, 1964, with attached report of 13th Reconnaissance Technical Squadron, Mar. 4, 1964, NSFV, box 3, Cables, vol. 7; also AES cable to State, May 23, 1964, NSFV, box 4, Cables, vol. 9; all in LBJL.

21. AES cable to State, Sept. 10, 1964, NSFV, box 8, Cables, vol. 12, and 2nd Air Division (Ton Son Nhut Air Base, Republic of Vietnam) cable to Pacific Air Force, Sept. 5, 1964, NSFV, box 8, Cables, vol. 18, both in LBJL.

22. AES cable to State, May 23, 1964, NSFV, box 4, Cables, vol. 9, LBJL.

23. Two MACV cables from MACV to National Military Command Center, Washington, D.C., Oct. 27 and 29, 1964, NSFV, box 9, Cables, vol. 20, LBJL.

24. Malcolm Caldwell and Lek Han Tan, *Cambodia in the Southeast Asian War* (New York, 1973), 146–205.

25. Letter from John Kenneth Galbraith to President Kennedy, Nov. 8, 1961, NSFV, box 195, Memos and Reports; letter from Averell Harriman to President Kennedy, Nov. 11, 1961, NSFV, box 195, Memos and Reports; memo from Walt W. Rostow to President Kennedy, Nov. 14, 1961, NSFV, box 195, Memos and Reports; memo from State to President Kennedy, Nov. 11, 1961, NSFV, box 195, Memos and Reports; memo from President Kennedy to Secretaries of State and Defense, Nov. 14, 1961, NSFV, box 195, Memos and Reports; AES cable from Ambassador Nolting to State, Aug. 12, 1961, NSFV, box 194, Vietnam Cables; all in JFKL; R. B. Smith, *An International History of the Vietnam War*, vol. 2, *The Kennedy Strategy*, 115–34.

26. Langer and Zasloff, *North Vietnam and the Pathet Lao*, 9–59; Pike, *People's Army of Vietnam*, 46–47.

27. EYES ONLY CINCPAC cable from Admiral Felt to State, for McGeorge Bundy at White House, Dean Rusk, George Ball, Averell Harriman, and Roger Hilsman at State, John McCone and Richard Helms at CIA, and ACTION JCS, Dec. 5, 1963, NSFV, box 1, Cables, vol. 1, LBJL.

28. EYES ONLY State cable from Dean Rusk to AES, for CINCPAC Admiral Felt and Ambassador Lodge, Dec. 6, 1963, NSFV, box 1, Cables, vol. 1, LBJL. Also see Marek Thee, *Notes of a Witness: Laos and the Second Indochina War* (New York, 1973).

29. Memo from Robert S. McNamara to President Johnson, Mar. 13, 1964; letter from Roger Hilsman to Dean Rusk, Mar. 14, 1964; and memo from McGeorge Bundy to President Johnson, Mar. 18, 1964; all in NSFV, box 2, Memos, vol. 5, LBJL.

30. Incoming cable from American embassy Vientiane, to State, May 2, 1964, NSFV, box 4, Cables, vol. 8, LBJL.

31. Memo from Mike Forrestal to McGeorge Bundy, May 5, 1964, NSFV, box 4, Memos, vol. 8, LBJL.

32. Outgoing State cable to American embassies Saigon, Bangkok, London, Paris, New Delhi, Moscow, Ottawa, CINCPAC, Apr. 19, 1964, box 3, NSFV, Cables, vol. 7, and incoming cable from Leonard Unger, American embassy Vientiane, to State, May 11, 1964, NSFV, box 4, Cables, vol. 8, both in LBJL.

33. AES cable from Henry Cabot Lodge to State, May 7, 1964, and State cable to AES, May 18, 1964, both in NSFV, box 4, Cables, vol. 8, LBJL.

34. CIA intelligence information cable, May 30, 1964, NSFV, box 5, Cables, vol. 10, LBJL.

35. Personnel and confidential letter from Senator Mike Mansfield to President Johnson, June 9, 1964, NSFV, box 5, Cables, vol. 11, LBJL.

36. CIA cable, undated, titled "Intelligence Information Cable," sanitized Sept. 14, 1976, NSFV, box 6, Cables, vol. 13, LBJL. In fact Klusmann escaped.

37. Memo from McGeorge Bundy to President Johnson, Aug. 13, 1964, NSFV, box 7, Memos, vol. 15, LBJL; EYES ONLY memo from Mike Forrestal to John T. McNaughton (OSD/ISA), top secret, Sept. 23, 1964, NSFV, box 8, Memos, vol. 17, LBJL.

38. CINCPAC cable from U.S. Grant Sharp to JCS, Aug. 19, 1964, NSFV, box 7, Cables, vol. 16, and CINCPAC cable from U.S. Grant Sharp to JCS, Sept. 24, 1964, NSFV, box 8, Cables, vol. 18, both in LBJL.

39. JCS cable to CINCPAC, Apr. 30, 1964, NSFV, box 3, Cables, vol. 7; CINCPAC cable to JCS, May 23, 1964, NSFV, box 5, Cables, vol. 10; CINCPAC cable to JCS and Commanding General Special Warfare Center, Ft. Bragg, and CO Special Forces Group Okinawa, June 2, 1964, NSFV, box 5, Cables, vol. 11; AES cable from Henry Cabot Lodge to State, May 4, 1964, NSFV, box 4, Cables, vol. 8; all in LBJL. See also Eliot A. Cohen, *Commandos and Politicians: Elite Military Units in Modern Democracies* (Cambridge, Mass., 1978).

40. State cable to American embassies Saigon, Vientiane, Bangkok, Sept. 9, 1964, NSFV, box 8, Cables, vol. 17, LBJL.

41. Senate Committee on Foreign Relations, Subcommittee on U.S. Security, 91st Cong., 1st sess., Oct. 20, 21, 28, 1969, Hearings; U.S. Department of State, "For the Press," no. 131, June 5, 1968; Ministry of Foreign Affairs of Laos, *White Book on the Violations of the 1962 Geneva Accords by the Government of North Vietnam* (Vientiane, 1969); John Prados, *Presidents' Secret Wars* (New York, 1986), 281–82.

42. U.S. Department of State, "Working Paper on the North Vietnamese Role in the War in South Vietnam," reprinted in *Vietnam Documents and Research Notes*, no. 37, May, 1968, LBJL.

43. Joseph G. Goulden, *Truth Is the First Casualty* (Chicago, 1969), 86; Westmoreland, *A Soldier Reports*, 106.

44. Ridgway, *The Korean War*, 75; Matthew B. Ridgway, "Indochina: Disengaging," *Foreign Affairs*, 49 (July 1971), 583–92.

45. AES cable to State, "For the President from Lodge," Feb. 20, 1964,

NSFV, box 2, Cables, vol. 5, LBJL. For Ridgway's views on the subject of sanctuaries see his *The Korean War*, 146.

46. Memo from SecDef Robert McNamara to President Johnson, Mar. 13, 1964, NSFV, box 2, Cables, vol. 5, LBJL.

47. AES cable from Henry Cabot Lodge to State, Mar. 18, 1964, NSFV, box 2, Cables, vol. 5, LBJL.

48. Memo from Mike Forrestal to McGeorge Bundy, Mar. 18, 1964; memo from W. Y. Smith to McGeorge Bundy, Mar. 17, 1964; and Rollen Anthis, quoted in memo from W. Y. Smith to McGeorge Bundy, Mar. 17, 1964; all in NSFV, box 2, Cables and Memos, vol. 5, LBJL.

49. White House cable to AES, Mar. 15, 1964, and AES cable to State, Mar. 13, 1964, both in NSFV, box 2, Cables and Memos, vol. 5, LBJL.

50. Memo from Mike Forrestal to McGeorge Bundy, May 5, 1964, The White House, NSFV, box 4, Memos, vol. 8, LBJL. See Associated Press news summary for M. Bundy, July 22, 1964, NSFV, box 6, Cables, vol. 14, and MACV cable to JCS, Aug. 15, 1964, NSFV, box 8, Cables, vol. 18, as well as CINCPACFLT cable to JCS, July 12, 1964; CINCPACFLT cable to JCS, July 11, 1964; and JCS cable to CINCPAC, July 8, 1964, all in NSFV, box 6, Cables, vol. 13, LBJL.

51. JCS undated "Rules of Engagement, De Soto Patrol," NSFV, box 8, Memos, vol. 17, LBJL; on the Hainan Island incident, see the Reuters dispatch from Peking "Peking Reports Hainan Airfight with U.S. Planes," Jack Langguth's article "One MIG Seen on Fire," and John W. Finney's "U.S. Unsure on MIGs," all in *New York Times*, Apr. 10, 1965, 1, 3; Jack Langguth, "U.S. Jets Wreck Bridge in North," *New York Times*, Apr. 11, 1965, 1, 6; "Two on Navy Jet Lost in Friday MIG Clash," *New York Times*, Apr. 12, 1965, 2. Also see Thies, *When Governments Collide*, 4–5, 8–14, 295–300, 406–7, 409–13; Jack S. Levy, "Misperception and the Causes of War: Theoretical Linkages and Analytical Problems," *World Politics*, 36 (Oct. 1983), 76–99; Thomas Schelling, *The Strategy of Conflict* (Oxford, 1960), and *Arms and Influence* (New Haven, Conn., 1966). Both of Schelling's books are influential.

52. AES cable to State, May 2, 1964, and JCS cable to CINCPAC and MACV, May 9, 1964, both in NSFV, box 4, Cables, vol. 8, LBJL.

53. Draft memo for discussion, June 10, 5:30 P.M., NSFV, box 5, Cables and Memos, vol. 11, LBJL.

54. EYES ONLY AES cable from Henry Cabot Lodge to Dean Rusk, State, Jan. 12, 1963, NSFV, box 5, Cables and Memos, vol. 11, LBJL.

55. See the three memos cited in n. 48 for this chapter; quotation is from memo for meeting on June 15, 1964, 6 P.M., NSFV, box 5, Memos, vol. 12, LBJL. Also see Ernest May, *Lessons of the Past* (Oxford, 1973); Robert Jervis, *Perception and Misperception in International Relations* (Princeton, N.J., 1975).

56. State cable from Dean Rusk to AES, July 20, 1964, NSFV, box 38, Presidential Decisions, vol. 1; AES cable to State (concerning Khanh), May 14, 1964, NSFV, box 4, Cables, vol. 9; State cable to AES, May 14, 1964, NSFV, box 4, Cables, vol. 9; all in LBJL.

57. CIA weekly report, July 29, 1964, NSFV, box 38, Memos, vol. 14; and

AES cable from Maxwell Taylor to State, July 25, 1964, NSFV, box 38, Cables, vol. 14; both in LBJL.

58. Associated Press news summary of Nguyen Cao Ky briefing, prepared for McGeorge Bundy, July 22, 1964; and AES cable to State, July 29, 1964, both in NSFV, box 6, Cables, vol. 14, LBJL.

59. AES cable to State, July 21, 1964, NSFV, box 6, Cables, vol. 14, LBJL.

60. State cable to American embassies Vientiane and Saigon, July 26, 1964, NSFV, box 38, Presidential Decisions, vol. 1; memo from McGeorge Bundy to President Johnson, July 24, 1964, NSFV, box 6, Cables, vol. 14, LBJL. See John Burke and Fred Greenstein et al., *How Presidents Test Reality* (New York, 1989), to compare 1954 with 1964.

61. State cable from Dean Rusk to Ambassador Taylor, AES, Aug. 3, 1964, NSFV, box 7, Cables, vol. 15, LBJL.

62. The best original source for the Tonkin Gulf naval engagements is a series of memos, notes, and summaries compiled by the NSC staff for White House use. Their LBJL numbers are 38, 26, 26a, 27, 28, 29, 30, 31, 32, 143, 188, 187b, and 190, all in NSFV, box 38, Memos, vols. 1 and 2. Also see Jim Stockdale and Sybil Stockdale, *In Love and War: The Story of a Family's Ordeal and Sacrifice During the Vietnam Years* (New York, 1984), 3–36; Galloway, *The Gulf of Tonkin Resolution*.

63. "Notes Taken at Leadership Meeting on August 4, 1964," NSFV, box 38, Memos, vol. 1, LBJL; L. B. Johnson, *The Vantage Point*, 118.

64. State cable to AES, September 12, 1964, NSFV, Cables Vol. XVII, Box 8, LBJL; this cable contains a copy of Taylor's testimony, which he requested once he returned to Saigon.

65. *The Gallup Poll: Public Opinion 1935–1971*, Survey 696K (New York, 1972), 3: 1896–99; Mueller, *War, Presidents and Public Opinion*, 208–13. Mueller labels Tonkin Gulf opinion as a "rally-round-the-flag-variable" and compares the role of this variable in the two Asian rim wars (Korea on the northeast Pacific quadrant and Vietnam on the southeast Pacific quadrant) to its role in the "swings" in public opinion on the two American Presidents Truman and Johnson.

66. AES cable from Henry Cabot Lodge to State (info Ottawa), May 4, 1964, NSFV, box 8, Cables, vol. 8, LBJL; Thies, *When Governments Collide*, 47–48.

67. Incoming cables from American Consul General Hong Kong and American embassy Moscow, to AES, Aug. 6, 1964, NSFV, box 7, Cables, vol. 15, LBJL.

68. MACV cable from General Westmoreland to JCS, Aug. 16, 1964, NSFV, box 8, Cables, vol. 18; AES cable from Ambassador Taylor to State, Aug. 9, 1964, NSFV, box 7, Cables, vol. 15 (Khanh's position); AES cable from Ambassador Taylor to State, Aug. 27, 1964, NSFV, box 7, Cables, vol. 16, all in LBJL.

69. EYES ONLY State cable to American embassies Saigon, Vientiane, and CINCPAC, for Ambassadors and Admiral Sharp, Aug. 14, 1964, NSFV, box 7, Cables, vol. 15; and White House memo for the record of Aug. 10 meeting in

Cabinet Room, Aug. 13, 1964, NSFV, box 39, Presidential Decisions, vol. 3, both in LBJL.

70. Special National Intelligence Estimate: 53–64, "Chances for a Stable Government in South Vietnam," Sept. 8, 1964, and CIA memo on communist reaction to increased U.S. pressure against North Vietnam, Sept. 9, 1964, both in NSFV, box 8, Memos, vol. 17, LBJL.

71. Memo from McGeorge Bundy to President Johnson, Sept. 8, 1964, The White House, NSFV, box 8, Memos, vol. 17, LBJL.

72. Maxwell Taylor, "Chronology of Events While Ambassador to the Republic of Vietnam, July 1964–July 1965 (MDT)," 2, in Maxwell Taylor's Papers, box 52, folder E, Library of the National Defense University, National War College, Ft. McNair, Washington, D.C. Also see Taylor's book *Swords and Plowshares* and his oral history at the LBJL.

73. National security action memo no. 314, from the White House to Secretaries of State and Defense, signed by McGeorge Bundy, Sept. 10, 1964, NSFV, box 39, Presidential Decisions, vol. 3, LBJL.

74. Memos from Mike Forrestal to Ambassador Lewellyn Thompson and to McGeorge Bundy, Sept. 22, 1964, NSFV, box 9, Memos, vol. 18, LBJL.

75. JCS cable to CINCPAC and Fleet commands, Sept. 26, 1964, and CINCPAC cable from Admiral Sharp to Fleet commands, Sept. 26, 1964, both in NSFV, box 9, Cables, vol. 18, LBJL.

76. George McT. Kahin and Robert Scalapino, "Excerpts from National Teach-In on Vietnam Policy," in Raskin and Fall, eds., *The Vietnam Reader*, 289–306; "The NSC Working Group Paper on Vietnam" (CIA-DIA-INR Panel), Section I: Intelligence Assessment, Nov. 13, 1964, 1–16, NSFV, box 44, Memos, vol. 9, LBJL; memo from McGeorge Bundy to President Johnson, Nov. 28, 1964, NSFV, box 45, Memos, vol. 4, LBJL; memo from NSC (National Security Council) to Rusk, McNamara, McCone, Wheeler, Ball, and McGeorge Bundy, "Issues Raised by Paper on Southeast Asia," Nov. 24, 1964, NSFV, box 48, Memos, vol. 3, LBJL; Lodge, *The Storm Has Many Eyes*, 211–12.

77. CINCPAC cable to the JCS and Fleet commands, Sept. 26, 1964, NSFV, box 9, Cables, vol. 18; also CINCPAC cable to JCS, Aug. 14, 1964, NSFV, box 7, Cables, vol. 15, both in LBJL.

78. Memo from Thomas Hughes to the Secretary of State, Apr. 6, 1964, NSFV, box 4, Memos, vol. 8, LBJL.

79. Memo from McGeorge Bundy to President Johnson, Mar. 18, 1964, with attached letter from Roger Hilsman to Dean Rusk, Mar. 14, 1964, NSFV, box 4, Memos, vol. 8, both in LBJL.

80. State cable from Dean Rusk to Graham Martin, U.S. embassy Bangkok, May 17, 1964, NSFV, box 4, Memos, vol. 8, LBJL.

81. Bernard Brodie and Fawn Brodie, *From Crossbow to H-Bomb* (Bloomington, Ind., 1962), 280; Dickson, *The Electronic Battlefield*, 84–90.

82. CINCPAC cable to JCS, Aug. 14, 1964, NSFV, box 7, Cables, vol. 15, LBJL.

83. AES cable to State, Aug. 29, 1964, NSFV, box 7, Cables, vol. 16, LBJL. Graham Martin became the U.S. Ambassador in Saigon a decade after Taylor

resigned the job. Martin was the last; Saigon fell as he fled. See Willenson, ed., *The Bad War*, 47–49, 100–102.

84. State cable from Dean Rusk to Maxwell Taylor and other American Ambassadors in Bangkok and Vientiane, plus CINCPAC (Admiral Sharp), Oct. 7, 1964, NSFV, box 9, Cables, vol. 19, LBJL.

85. AES cable to American embassy Bangkok, Sept. 25, 1964, and American Embassy Bangkok cable to AES, Sept. 23, 1964, both in NSFV, box 8, Cables, vol. 17, LBJL; Westmoreland, *A Soldier Reports*, 543.

86. *The Pentagon Papers*, Senator Gravel Ed. (Boston, 1971), 4: 483; Kenneth P. Werrell, "The Strategic Bombing of Germany in World War II: Costs and Accomplishments," *Journal of American History*, 73 (Dec. 1986), 702–13. Also see Mark Clodfelter, *The Limits of Air Power: The American Bombing of North Vietnam* (New York, 1989).

87. Pike, *People's Army of Vietnam*, 46–49.

88. *The Pentagon Papers*, Senator Gravel Ed., 4: 483–84.

89. *Ibid.*

90. *Ibid.*, 485.

91. *Ibid.*

92. *Ibid.* McNaughton came to Saigon and ridiculed Westmoreland and his air commander, General Joe Moore, for trying to get permission to bomb SAM-2 sites under construction before Hanoi could use them. McNaughton claimed that "putting them in is just a political ploy by the Russians to appease Hanoi"; quoted in Westmoreland, *A Soldier Reports*, 120. In his *China and Vietnam: The Roots of Conflict* (Berkeley, Calif., 1986), 49, William J. Duiker indicates that the PRC warned Washington not to send troops across the 17th parallel into North Vietnam.

93. McGeorge Bundy, quoted in Herring, *The Secret Diplomacy of the Vietnam War*, 203–4.

94. James Clay Thompson, *Rolling Thunder: Understanding Policy and Program Failure* (Chapel Hill, North Carolina: University of North Carolina Press, 1980), 79.

95. C. Berger, *The United States Air Force in Southeast Asia*, 89.

96. *The Pentagon Papers*, Senator Gravel Ed., 4: 492.

97. Westmoreland, *A Soldier Reports*, 208.

98. Fulton, *Riverine Operations*, 51–80.

99. The best source for official Army films of units that served in Vietnam is the Department of Army Pamphlet #108-1, Department of Army Headquarters, Washington, D.C., Jan. 1979.

100. The designers did employ the 1st Air Cavalry Division in its new role late in the war: acting with ARVN units, one designer asked the 1st Air Cavalry Division to move into Cambodia in April 1970. See Tran Dinh Tho, *The Cambodian Incursion*, Indochina Monographs (Washington, D.C.: U.S. Army Center of Military History, n.d.), 73.

101. James, "The Moral Equivalent of War," 267–96.

102. Edward O. Wilson, *On Human Nature* (Cambridge, Mass., 1978), 99–120.

103. After the American phase of the Indochina war ended, the U.S. Army published a series of monographs written by important ARVN officers. In one, *Pacification,* the author, a Brigadier General, admits that the Vietnamese pacification leaders, whom he observed closely from his position on the Joint General Staff, were mainly recruited "from among the educated urban petty bourgeoisie"; Tho, *Pacification,* 193.

104. Memorandum 362, quoted in Cooper *et al., The American Experience with Pacification in Vietnam,* vol. 3, *The History of Pacification,* 260.

105. Komer, quoted in Westmoreland, *A Soldier Reports,* 215.

106. *Ibid.* The political label "fire-eater" originated prior to the American Civil War. It designated particular South Carolinians of hot temper who demanded war rather than compromise. See Bruce Catton, *The Coming Fury* (New York, 1961), 9, 158, 199, 337–38.

107. C. Berger, *The United States Air Force in Southeast Asia,* 294; James C. Thomson, Jr., Peter W. Stanley, and John Curtis Perry, *Sentimental Imperialists: The American Experience in East Asia* (New York, 1981), 4–19.

108. William D. Parker, *U.S. Marine Corps Civil Affairs in I Corps, Republic of South Vietnam: April 1966–April 1967* (Washington, D.C., 1970), 14; L. Walt, *America Faces Defeat.*

109. Parker, *U.S. Marine Corps Civil Affairs in I Corps, Republic of South Vietnam,* 14; Caputo, *A Rumor of War.*

110. Parker, *U.S. Marine Corps Civil Affairs in I Corps, Republic of South Vietnam,* 14.

111. Eric M. Bergerud, "The War in Hau Nghia Province, Republic of Vietnam, 1963–1973" (Ph.D. diss., University of California, Berkeley, 1981), 379. It is pacification for nation-building that Colonel Harry G. Summers, Jr., opposes. He sees it as the "wrong" U.S. Army mission—one that should have been given only to the ARVN. He suggests that the U.S. Army did not try to perform that mission in the Korean War for the same good reasons that pertain to Vietnam. See his *On Strategy,* 172–73.

112. Sheehan, *A Bright Shining Lie,* 494–97.

Chapter 4

1. Robert A. Divine, *Second Chance: The Triumph of Internationalism in America During World War II* (New York, 1967).

2. Krasner, *Defending the National Interest,* 15, 278; Levin, *Woodrow Wilson and World Politics,* 4.

3. John Morton Blum, *V Was for Victory* (New York, 1976), 302–23, and his "Limits of American Internationalism, 1941–1945," in Leonard Krieger and Fritz Stern, eds., *The Responsibility of Power* (Garden City, N.Y., 1967); Richard Hofstadter, *The Age of Reform* (New York, 1955), 317–24.

4. Lodge, *The Storm Has Many Eyes,* 215.

5. The Albert P. Blaustein Papers, 12 vols., Pike Collection, VCUCB.

6. David M. Potter, *People of Plenty: Economic Abundance and the American Character* (Chicago, 1954), 139.

7. Robert S. McNamara, speech given in Montreal, Quebec, May 18, 1966, quoted in *New York Times*, May 19, 1966, 11.

8. Rusk, *The Winds of Freedom*, 180.

9. Memo from Walt W. Rostow to Secretary of State Dean Rusk, Sept. 14, 1964, NSFV, box 9, Memos, vol. 18, LBJL.

10. Ball, *Diplomacy for a Crowded World*, 216; Frederick S. Calhoun, *Power and Principle: Armed Intervention in Wilsonian Foreign Policy* (Kent, Ohio, 1986). One entire chapter in Ball's book illuminates the Whig predicament: "The Right of Privacy of Nations," 211–30. Ball never tired of this subject, sometimes changing sides depending on the war and the decade. See George Ball, Ray S. Cline, William Colby, Daniel Patrick Moynihan, John Stockwell, *et al.*, "Should the CIA Fight Secret Wars? Overt Talk on Current Action," *Harper's*, Sept. 1984, 33–47.

11. Les K. Adler and Thomas G. Paterson, "Red Fascism: The Merger of Nazi Germany and Soviet Russia in the American Image of Totalitarianism, 1930's–1950's," *American Historical Review*, 75 (Apr. 1970), 1046–64; Donald Kagan, "World War I, World War II, World War III," *Commentary*, Mar. 1987, 21–40; Miles Kahler, "Rumors of War: The 1914 Analogy," *Foreign Affairs*, 58 (Winter 1979–80), 374–96.

12. John Dziak, *Chekisty: A History of the KGB* (Lexington, Mass., 1987); Raymond Aron, "From American Imperialism to Soviet Hegemonism," Washington Quarterly, 2 (Summer 1979), 8–22, quotation on p. 11.

13. Howard, *The Causes of Wars*, 30. Also see Walter LaFeber, *America and the Cold War, 1945–1966*, 2d ed. (New York, 1972), 156; Robert Engler, *The Politics of Oil* (Chicago, 1961), 205–6; Ronald M. Schneider, "Guatemala: An Aborted Communist Takeover," in Thomas T. Hammond, ed., *The Anatomy of Communist Takeover* (New Haven, Conn., 1975), 573–74; Cole Blasier, *The Hovering Giant: U.S. Responses to Revolutionary Change in Latin America* (Pittsburgh, Pa., 1976), 161–62; Stephen Schlesinger and Stephen Kinzer, *Bitter Fruit* (New York, 1982); Senate Select Committee to Study Government Operations with Respect to Intelligence Activities, *Covert Action in Chile, 1963–73*, 94th Cong., 1st sess., 1975; Staff Study 94-1.

14. P. Hammond, *Organizing for Defense*, 227–32; Destler, *Presidents, Bureaucrats and Foreign Policy*, 10–15; Keith C. Clark and Laurence J. Legere, eds., *The President and the Management of National Security: A Report by the Institute for Defense Analyses* (New York, 1969), 3–9 and 55–98; Matloff, *American Military History*, 531–32; Huntington, *The Common Defense*, 33–47; Ries, *The Management of Defense*, 111–14.

15. R. H. Smith, *O.S.S.*, 367–76. Also see Robin W. Winks, *Cloak and Gown: Scholars in the Secret War* (New York, 1987), and Jeffreys-Jones, *The CIA and American Democracy*.

16. David Kahn, *The Code-Breakers* (New York, 1967), 5, 360 (quotation). Also see Corey Ford, *Donovan of O.S.S.* (Boston, 1970), 5; De Silva, *Sub Rosa*; James Bamford, *The Puzzle Palace* (New York, 1982).

17. In 1948 McGeorge Bundy acted as biographer to Stimson in *On Active*

Service in Peace and War (New York, 1948). Bundy helps to explain the pre–World War II Stimson when he suggests that Stimson followed the principle that the way to make men trustworthy is to trust them. Therefore, Stimson, as Secretary of State, closed down the State Department's Section 8 of Military Intelligence. By 1921 Section 8 had broken the Japanese diplomatic codes, thereby allowing American gentlemen to read other gentlemen's mail, if they so desired.

18. Lyman B. Kirkpatrick, Jr., *The Real CIA* (New York, 1968); A. Dulles, *The Craft of Intelligence*, 217. President Carter's CIA director, Stansfield Turner, did indicate his reluctance to employ covert means to obtain certain ends. But this was long after the Vietnam war was a memory, and even then Turner hid his dislike by stressing "how little it [covert action] can actually accomplish on its own"; Stansfield Turner, *Secrecy and Democracy: The CIA in Transition* (Boston, 1985), 278.

19. Rubin, *The James Bond Films*, 1.

20. *Ibid.*, 23–24.

21. *Ibid.*, 34–35, 37, 55.

22. The initial rental earnings on the movie *Goldfinger*, released in 1964, amounted to $22.5 million; for *Thunderball*, released in 1965, they increased to $27 million. See David Pirie, ed., *Anatomy of the Movies* (New York, 1981), 109, 222.

23. Michael Kammen, *A Season of Youth* (New York, 1978); see esp. Chap. 3, "Revolutionary Iconography in National Tradition," 76–109; Michael Vermeulen, "Timothy Dalton: New 007 Running Scared," *San Francisco Chronicle*, Datebook Sunday Section, July 26, 1987, 19 (quotation); "Bond Knocks 'em Dead," UPI, *San Francisco Chronicle*, Aug. 3, 1987, 51; Bruce Handy, "It's a James Bond World," *San Francisco Chronicle*, Oct. 18, 1988, B3. With the arrival of Timothy Dalton in 1987, there were four actors who had played Bond—Sean Connery, George Lazenby, Roger Moore, and Dalton. In another revolutionary period the icons were often classical (Hercules) or composites of ideal types (Marianne); see Lynn Hunt, *Politics, Culture, and Class in the French Revolution* (Berkeley, Calif., 1984), 87–119.

24. Pirie, *Anatomy of the Movies*, 45, 57, 58, 78, 79. For another view of Bond as a symbol see Umberto Eco, ed., *The Bond Affair* (London, 1966), and Raymond Benson, *The James Bond Bedside Companion* (New York, 1986), 27–29.

25. Carl F. Macek, review of Bond, in *Magill's Survey of Cinema* (Englewood Cliffs, N.J., 1981), 654; Pauline Kael, *Kiss Kiss Bang Bang* (Boston, 1965), 8, 189, 221. Macek and Kael were not the first to note the American preoccupation with violence and murder, be it sanctioned or unsanctioned. See David Brion Davis, *Homicide in American Fiction* (Ithaca, N.Y., 1968). For the role of the Book-of-the-Month Club in American middlebrow culture see John Shelley Rubin, "Self, Culture, and Self-Culture in Modern America: The Early History of the Book-of-the-Month Club," *Journal of American History*, 71 (Mar. 1985), 782–806. This book club helped launch a spy-as-hero fiction in the postwar United States. For example, their editor's making John Le Carré's *A Perfect Spy* (New York, 1986) his fifth main selection reinforced the already

popular cult of espionage. Also see Dwight Macdonald, "Masscult and Midcult: II," *Partisan Review*, no. 27 (Fall 1962), 592.

26. Bosley Crowther, "Funeral in Berlin," *New York Times Film Reviews: 1959–1968* (New York, 1959), 3, 653.

27. Ball, *Diplomacy for a Crowded World*, 226. Whether to limit, but still to keep, an intelligence agency continues to be a matter of debate. See Stanley Hoffmann "Under Cover or Out of Control," *New York Times Book Review*, Nov. 29, 1987, 3, and Robert M. Gates, "The CIA and Foreign Policy," *Foreign Affairs*, 66 (Winter 1988–89), 215–30.

28. Ball, *Diplomacy for a Crowded World*, 226; Colby and Forbath, *Honorable Men*, 184.

29. John G. Cawelti, *Adventure, Mystery, and Romance* (Chicago, 1976), 1, 31, 32, 39, 40, 51, 67.

30. Wilensky, *Organizational Intelligence*, 150; Lawrence W. Levine, "William Shakespeare and the American People: A Study in Cultural Transformation," *American Historical Review*, 89 (Feb. 1984), 335–46. Also see Thomas Powers, *The Man Who Kept the Secrets: Richard Helms and the CIA* (New York, 1979), 54–55. Also see how Will Wright employs arguments similar to Wilensky's and Powers's, using cowboy or western films, in *Sixguns and Society: A Structural Study of the Western* (Berkeley, Calif., 1975), 185–94.

31. *San Francisco Chronicle*, May 23, 1985, 1; Michael Howard, "Cowboys, Playboys and Other Spies," *The New York Times Book Review*, Feb. 16, 1986, 66–67.

32. Cooper, *The Lost Crusade*, 115–43.

33. For an example of the Vietnamese emphasis on unification see Ho Chi Minh's speech on the occasion of the tenth anniversary of the Democratic Republic of Vietnam, in his *For a Lasting Peace, For a People's Democracy* (Hanoi, Dec. 1955).

34. For North Vietnamese rejection of patron models see Le Duan, *On the Socialist Revolution in Vietnam* (Hanoi, 1961), 3: 56–57. For South Vietnamese problems with their patrons and their models see AES cable to State, "For the Secretary from Lodge," May 29, 1964, NSFV, box 5, Cables, vol. 10, LBJL.

35. Marr, *Vietnamese Anticolonialism*, 271–77; Eric R. Wolf, *Europe and the People Without History* (Berkeley, Calif., 1982), 76; William Pfaff, "Tribalism Is Dynamite, to Be Handled with Caution," *International Herald Tribune*, June 5, 1987, 4. I use "neo-tribalism" to refer to a rural population without a national attachment except through race, a population that does live in a type of isolation, political autonomy, and self-sufficiency even though these three characteristics are under stress and collapsing. See Theodor Shanin, ed., *Peasants and Peasant Societies* (New York, 1971), 255, 341.

36. *Encyclopedia Britannica* (Chicago, 1980), Macropaedia, 19: 149.

37. McAlister and Mus, *The Vietnamese and Their Revolution*, 31. McAlister worked with June Guicharnaud, who translated parts of Mus's *Viet Nam: Sociologie d'une Guerre*. McAlister then rewrote the book to obtain the English volume from which this quote is taken. The Frenchman Mus on Vietnamese peasants might remind the reader of the German Marx on French peasants:

"The small peasants form a vast mass, the members of which live in similar conditions, but without entering into manifold relations with one another. In so far as there is merely a local interconnection among these small peasants, and the identity of their interests begets no unity, no national union, and no political organization, they do not form a class"; Karl Marx, *The Eighteenth Brumaire of Louis Bonaparte* (New York, 1963), 109.

38. Hickey, *Village in Vietnam*, 278. Eric Wolf calls some villages "open villages"—those in which market exchange was important; see his *Peasant Wars of the Twentieth Century*, xiii–xv, 176–78. In Vietnam open villages were concentrated in the Mekong Delta; see Murray, *The Development of Capitalism in Colonial Indochina*, 422.

39. Goodman, *Politics in War*, 72. Buddhist leaders were aware of how weak their hold on rural people was. They proposed to Lodge "to send mobile teams of monks to proselytize in rural areas"; AES cable from Ambassador Lodge to State, Mar. 23, 1964, NSFV, box 3, Vietnam Memos, vol. 6, LBJL.

40. Marr, *Vietnamese Tradition on Trial*, 147. Also see Cao Thi Nhu-Quynh and John C. Schaffer, "From Verse Narrative to Novel: The Development of Prose Fiction in Vietnam," *Journal of Asian Studies*, 47 (Nov. 1988), 756–61, and Jack A. Yeager, *The Vietnamese Novel in French: A Literary Response to Colonialism* (Hanover, N.H., 1987).

41. Clifford Geertz, *The Interpretation of Cultures* (New York, 1973), 262–63. Geertz also suggests that the Vietnamese shared one language, which is not correct. As Marr indicates in *Vietnamese Anticolonialism*, there was a multiplicity of languages and several writing systems among peasants and elites.

42. I use the term outsider as Barrington Moore, Jr., uses it. In his usage, fraternity for the peasant "was more a negative notion, a form of localism." Moore's peasant "had no abstract interest in feeding the towns," for "his organic conception of society stopped quite short of altruism." Those who were "outsiders" remained "mainly a source of taxes and debt." But "fellow villagers, on the other hand, even if they too were often creatures to be treated warily, were people with whom it was necessary to work at crucial stages in the agricultural cycle." Moore sees cooperation as the dominant theme inside the group, while hostility and distrust were the dominant themes toward outsiders, with variations in everyday life. See B. Moore, *Social Origins of Dictatorship and Democracy*, 498–99.

43. Marr, *Vietnamese Tradition on Trial*, 119. As Janowitz concludes, "There are nations, highly industrialized ones such as Japan, without effective terms for citizen and citizenship"; Morris Janowitz, *The Reconstruction of Patriotism* (Chicago, 1983), 1–2.

44. Marr, *Vietnamese Tradition on Trial*, 119, 172.

45. Minh, *On Revolution*, 143, 145, 170, 172, 175, 186, 229, 242, 258, 306.

46. *Ho Chi Minh, Selected Writings: 1920–1969* (Hanoi, 1977), 123, 218, 286, 288, 296, 349.

47. Quoted in Marr, *Vietnamese Tradition on Trial*, 82.

48. Wolf, *Peasant Wars of the Twentieth Century*, xiv.

49. *Ibid.*, 290–91.

50. Eric Wolf, "On Peasant Rebellion," in Shanin, *Peasants and Peasant Societies*, 265.

51. Max Weber illustrates the concept of chieftain: "Kingship is preceded by all those charismatic forms which assure relief in the face of extraordinary external or internal distress or which promise success in risky undertakings. In early history, the precursor of the king, the chieftain, often has a double function: he is the patriarch of the family or sib, but also the charismatic leader in hunt and war, the magician, rainmaker, medicine man—hence priest and doctor—and finally, the arbiter. Frequently, each of these kinds of charisma has a special bearer"; Max Weber, *Economy and Society*, trans. and ed. Guenther Roth and Claus Wittich (New York, 1968), 3: 1142.

52. Diem and Tung, quoted in Karnow, *Vietnam*, 216–17.

53. Fall, *The Two Viet-Nams*, 255.

54. For details on Ho Chi Minh's life see Chap. 6 of Fall, *The Two Viet-Nams*, 81–103. For Ho Chi Minh's capture of the northern tribe see Chap. 8 (130–68) of the same work. For the concept of transitional phases in the rise to power of a man like Ho see Huntington, *Political Order in Changing Societies*, 205. For Ho Chi Minh's capture of the Viet Minh see Patti, *Why Vietnam?*, 294–95. For Ho Chi Minh's capture of the NLF see Pike, *Viet Cong*, 217.

55. Vo Nguyen Giap, "Father of the Vietnamese Revolutionary Army," in Hoai Thanh *et al.*, *Days with Ho Chi Minh* (Hanoi, 1962).

56. Marr, *Vietnamese Tradition on Trial*, 284.

57. Hobsbaum, *Primitive Rebels*, 2.

58. Gurr, *Why Men Rebel*, 317–59. Robert Middlekauff, "Why Men Fought in the American Revolution," *Huntington Library Quarterly*, 43 (Spring 1980), 135–48. Ithiel de Sola Pool, "Political Alternatives to the Viet Cong," *Asian Survey*, 7 (Aug. 1967), 555–66. Pool's data came from the Chieu Hoi (Open Arms) program, by which Saigon attempted to get Viet Cong and NVA troops to desert. Saigon had some success and the Viet Cong tried to block the program; see Viet Cong Directive no. 02/CT, Eastern Nambo Party Committee Military Region, Subject: Counter Chieu Hoi (Open Arms) in the Armed Forces, signed by Nguyen Tung, Feb. 15, 1967, Pike Collection, VCUCB.

59. C. Johnson, *Peasant Nationalism and Communist Power*, 195; Frederick Wakeman, Jr., "Rebellion and Revolution: The Study of Popular Movements in Chinese History," *Journal of Asian Studies*, 36 (Feb. 1977), 201–37. Johnson chose to deal with this phenomenon as peasant nationalism while, in the Vietnamese case, the stress is on neo-tribalism.

60. Pike, *Viet Cong*, 216–29; Race, *War Comes to Long An*, 130 (quotation).

61. For the details of Ngo Dinh Diem's victory over the sects see Fall, *Viet-Nam Witness*, 141–59. For a good description of these early days in Ngo Dinh Diem's Saigon see Cooper, *The Lost Crusade*, 120–43. For a short biographical sketch of Ngo Dinh Diem see Karnow, *Vietnam*, 213–39.

62. Goodman, *Politics in War*, 26. For one of the few sympathetic reviews

of Madam Nhu see Colby and Forbath, *Honorable Men*, 153–54: "[She hoped] for the betterment of the lot of women in Vietnam. She was a complex and impressive character. But she had a fatal flaw, a complete lack of tact."

63. Goodman, *Politics in War*, 27.

64. Pike, *Viet Cong*, 60.

65. Goodman, *Politics in War*, 25.

66. Marr, *Vietnamese Tradition on Trial*, 188. Roger Hilsman and William Trueheart later learned how thoroughly institutions such as the Woman's Solidarity Movement supported the mandarin; see AES cable from Trueheart to Hilsman, State, June 8, 1963, NSFV, box 197, JFKL.

67. Halberstam, *The Making of a Quagmire*, 42; Cooper, *The Lost Crusade*, 191. Both Leslie Gelb and Richard Betts, in their *The Irony of Vietnam*, 207, insist that all during the 1950's the elite U.S. press supported the mandarin.

68. Buttinger, *Vietnam*, 11 (quotation); Hans J. Morgenthau, *Vietnam and the United States* (Washington, D.C., 1967), 24.

69. Pike, *War, Peace, and the Viet Cong*, 35–40; Whiting, *The Chinese Calculus of Deterrence*, 247. Whiting worked in the State Department's Bureau of Intelligence and Research under Roger Hilsman.

70. Pike, *Viet Cong*, 83.

71. John F. Kennedy, quoted in Hans J. Morgenthau, "The 1954 Geneva Conference: An Assessment," in Morgenthau's *America's Stake in Vietnam*, 13.

72. Fox Butterfield, "The New Vietnam Scholarship," *New York Times Magazine*, Feb. 13, 1983, sec. 6, 31–32; Morgenthau, *America's Stake in Vietnam*, 13.

73. Le Duan, *Thu Vao Nam (Letters to the South)* (Hanoi, 1985); Pike, *Viet Cong*, 136; Kahin and Lewis, *The United States in Vietnam*, 120; Karnow, *Vietnam*, 237–39; George C. Herring, "Vietnam Remembered," *Journal of American History*, 73 (June 1986), 152–64; Dinh, *No Other Road to Take*; Tang, *A Viet Cong Memoir*. Le Duan, the late General Secretary of the Communist party of Vietnam, makes it clear that he was running the war in the South from 1961 onward.

74. Quoted in Pike, *Viet Cong*, 327–28.

75. Paret and Shy, *Guerrillas in the 1960's*, 49; John Shy, "The American Revolution: The Military Conflict as Revolutionary War," in S. Kurtz and J. Hutson, eds., *Essays on the American Revolution* (New York, 1973), 121–56. Shy alludes to the Vietnamese revolution as he draws his conclusions about the American revolution. See his reference to Lord North's "cost-benefit analysis" and King George's "domino theory," 140.

Chapter 5

1. Memo from William Brubeck to McGeorge Bundy, for meeting between Kennedy and Robert Thompson during the period April 1–4, dated Mar. 19, 1963, NSFV, box 197, JFKL; R. Thompson, *Defeating Communist Insurgency*, 58–59 (quotations), and his *No Exit from Vietnam*.

2. The term "murder," instead of "assassination," is used advisedly.

Those who staged the coup in Saigon had both the unarmed mandarin and his brother in their control before killing them. Chester Cooper, in *The Lost Crusade*, also terms it murder (214).

3. Ngo Dinh Diem, quoted in Marguerite Higgins, *Our Vietnam Nightmare* (New York, 1965), 168–79. Higgins, like David Halberstam and Robert Shaplen, is a journalist who reported on Vietnam in 1963. She was promandarin in 1963; Halberstam and Shaplen were antimandarin in 1963. See Hilsman, *To Move a Nation*, 457, 481, 488, 508, 544.

4. Ngo Dinh Diem, quoted in Higgins, *Our Vietnam Nightmare*, 167–71.

5. State cable to AES, June 8, 1963, NSFV, box 197, and AES cable from William Trueheart to Roger Hilsman, State, June 5, 1963, NSFV, box 127, both in JFKL.

6. Diem and Chanoff, *In the Jaws of History*, 94–95.

7. Huntington, *Political Order in Changing Societies*, 357.

8. Cooper, *The Lost Crusade*, 216; State Department research memo from Thomas Hughes to Dean Rusk, Sept. 11, 1963, NSFV, box 199, JFKL. A moderate description of Ngo Dinh Nhu appears in Colby and Forbath's *Honorable Men*, 155–56: "Nhu was the intellectual, interested in theoretical concepts and political forces. He seemed to be overly fascinated with intrigue." Nguyen Cao Ky calls Ngo Dinh Nhu an "Oriental Richelieu" married to an Asian version of "Lucrezia Borgia"; Ky, *How We Lost the Vietnam War*, 32. Ky was wrong. South Vietnam's problem was that it did *not* have a Richelieu.

9. AES cable to State, June 8, 1963, NSFV, box 197, JFKL.

10. CIA intelligence memo, Office of Current Intelligence, June 3, 1986, NSFV, box 197, JFKL.

11. CIA SECRET special report, "The Buddhists in South Vietnam," June 28, 1963, NSFV, box 197, JFKL; Shaplen, *The Lost Revolution*, 191–93.

12. George A. Carver, Jr., "The Real Revolution in South Viet Nam," *Foreign Affairs*, 43 (Apr. 1965), 387–408. For information concerning Carver's career in the CIA see Thomas Powers, *The Man Who Kept the Secrets: Richard Helms and the CIA* (New York, 1979), 170. Carver's name appeared in articles that Ngo Dinh Nhu's organization planted in the media concerning the unsuccessful 1960 coup attempt; see AES cable to State, July 8, 1963, NSFV, box 198, JFKL. A number of CIA personnel published their interpretations of their CIA-Vietnam years. Two of these books are among the most helpful: Cline, *Secrets, Spies and Scholars*, and De Silva, *Sub Rosa*. For a complete listing see George C. Constantinides, *Intelligence and Espionage: An Analytical Bibliography* (Boulder, Colo., 1983).

13. Colby and Forbath, *Honorable Men*, 224. For a more sympathetic view of the Buddhist political struggle, see Kahin and Lewis, *The United States in Vietnam*, 159–95, and Kahin, *Intervention*, 418–32. For the later crushing of the Buddhist political movement see Westmoreland, *A Soldier Reports*, 169–76.

14. James Aronson, *The Press and the Cold War* (Indianapolis, Ind., 1970), 199; Michael J. Arlen, *Living Room War* (New York, 1966). For the most controversial interpretation of the media's role in the war see Braestrup, *The Big*

Story, 2–7, 26, 446. Even Lodge became upset with the manner in which Buddhist leaders exploited the U.S. press, Buddhist leaders calling the press before each suicide; see AES cable to State, Oct. 5, 1963, NSFV, box 204, JFKL.

15. AES cable from Trueheart to Hilsman, State, June 8, 1963; State cable from Hilsman to Trueheart, AES, June 11, 1963; AES cable from Trueheart to Hilsman, State, June 16, 1963; State cable from Hilsman to Trueheart, AES, June 19, 1963; all in NSFV, box 197, JFKL.

16. Memo from McGeorge Bundy to President Kennedy, "Notes for Talk with Secretary Rusk—Nov. 15," Nov. 15, 1961, NSFV, box 195, JFKL. The pressure by Whigs in the White House to rid themselves of Nolting never ceased. Mike Forrestal wrote a memo to Kennedy in which he suggested that "more vigor is needed in getting Diem to do what we want," a vigor Forrestal said Nolting did not possess; see memo from Forrestal to President Kennedy, Jan. 28, 1963, NSFV, box 197, JFKL.

17. "Oral History Interview of John A. McCone," taken by Joe B. Frantz, Aug. 19, 1970, 16, JFKL. On the subject of Kennedy's appointing of Republicans, see "Oral History Interview with Theodore C. Sorensen," taken by Carol Kaysen, Mar. 26, 1964, 68–69, JFKL. Also see cable from Lodge to State concerning the *Times of Vietnam* story "Saigon CIA Chief Recalled on Eve of Congressional Inquiry," Oct. 7, 1963, NSFV, box 204, JFKL.

18. CIA cable, Subject: Comments on Reports (4) of Ngo Dinh Nhu's Coup Plotting, July 13, 1963, NSFV, box 199, JFKL.

19. Department of State bulletin, Sept. 9, 1963, 398, copy at JFKL.

20. Memo from Robert McNamara to President Kennedy, June 6, 1963; Navy Department cable from CINCPAC to multiple commands, June 5, 1963; both in NSFV, box 197, JFKL.

21. AES cable "To State From Lodge," Oct. 7, 1963, and cable no. 770, undated, "From Lodge To State," both in NSFV, box 204, JFKL.

22. U.S. Information Agency memo from Edward R. Murrow to McGeorge Bundy, Sept. 10, 1963, NSFV, box 199, JFKL. Guenter Lewy states, "The U.S. over several years tried to persuade Diem to get rid of Nhu, but these moves only seemed to consolidate his influence"; Lewy, *America in Vietnam*, 26.

23. Lodge, *The Storm Has Many Eyes*, 205–14; Harriman, *America and Russia in a Changing World*, 112–15; Ball, *The Past Has Another Pattern*, 370–74; Hilsman, *To Move a Nation*, 468–94.

24. Hilsman, *To Move a Nation*, 487; Lodge, *The Storm Has Many Eyes*, 208. Lodge supported Hilsman on his "Diem without Nhu," but he simply did not know how to accomplish it; see AES cable no. 652, "To State From Lodge," Oct. 7, 1963, NSFV, box 204, JFKL.

25. In order to gauge the powerful impression that McNamara gave, see the "Oral History Interview with Chester Bowles," by Robert R. R. Brooks, Feb. 2, 1965, 93–94, JFKL. Also see Halberstam, *The Best and the Brightest*, 301–3. An indication of McNamara's power reflected through the popular culture of the 1960's is the fact that he appeared on the cover of *Time* magazine on three occasions, in 1961, 1963, and 1966. Theodore Sorensen even suggests that Johnson wanted McNamara for Vice President in 1964, that is,

until George Meany and others vetoed it; see "Oral History Interview with Theodore Sorensen," by Larry J. Jackman for the Robert F. Kennedy Oral History Program, July 23, 1970, 4, JFKL.

26. Colby and Forbath, *Honorable Men*, 210–11; Hilsman, *To Move a Nation*, 487.

27. A. Schlesinger, *A Thousand Days*, 991.

28. Shaplen, *The Lost Revolution*, 200. For Ambassador Lodge's remark "Perhaps they are like the rest of us, and are afraid to die," see Halberstam, *The Best and the Brightest*, 325.

29. CBS television interview, Sept. 2, 1963, in *Public Papers of the President of the United States: John F. Kennedy, 1963* (Washington, D.C., 1964), 652.

30. State cable to AES concerning the Senators' remarks, Sept. 6, 1963, NSFV, box 199, JFKL.

31. Weldon A. Brown, *Prelude to Disaster* (Port Washington, N.Y., 1975), 205; Karnow, *Vietnam*, 235.

32. CIA cable, July 8, 1963; CIA cable, Sept. 11, 1963; CIA cable, Sept. 23, 1963; CIA cable, Sept. 28, 1963; all in NSFV, box 200, JFKL.

33. AES cable from Lodge to Rusk, State, Sept. 11, 1963; State cable from Rusk to Lodge, AES, Sept. 12, 1963; State cable from President Kennedy to Lodge, AES, Sept. 12, 1963; all three marked "EYES ONLY—TOP SECRET," all in NSFV, box 199, JFKL.

34. Colby and Forbath, *Honorable Men*, 142; Karnow, *Vietnam*, 283–84; Lansdale, *In the Midst of War*; cable from Ambassador Lodge to McGeorge Bundy, Oct. 25, 1963; and CAS Message, EYES ONLY, from McGeorge Bundy to Ambassador Lodge and General Harkins, Oct. 25, 1963, both in NSFV, box 201, JFKL.

35. Colby and Forbath, *Honorable Men*, 35, 215; cable from Lodge to Bundy, Oct. 25, 1963, NSFV, box 201, JFKL.

36. *The Pentagon Papers*, Senator Gravel Ed. (Boston, 1971), 2: 212–20, 253–54, 257–62, 789–92; EYES ONLY White House cable from McGeorge Bundy to Ambassador Lodge, Oct. 30, 1963, NSFV, box 201, JFKL. In this cable Bundy told Lodge, "We do not accept as a basis for U.S. policy that we have no power to delay or discourage a coup."

37. Lodge, *The Storm Has Many Eyes*, 212; CAS message from Bundy to Lodge and Harkins, Oct. 25, 1963, NSFV, box 201, JFKL. Lodge stated that "during the weeks preceding the coup against President Diem, President Kennedy had instructed me not to tell anyone about the cables I was sending to him and the cables he was sending to me, or to reveal any part of their contents"; *The Storm Has Many Eyes*, 212. Unbeknownst to Lodge, Kennedy might have wanted to stop "the steady flow of all-too-revealing information leaking from Saigon" that "drove Kennedy close to distraction," according to Hilsman, *To Move a Nation*, 514.

38. Ngo Dinh Nhu, quoted in Colby and Forbath, *Honorable Men*, 164–65; Karnow, *Vietnam*, 236.

39. Maneli, *War of the Vanquished*, vii, 115, 122, 137–40, 149–50, 170–81; Colby and Forbath, *Honorable Men*, 214; Shaplen, *The Lost Revolution*, 206.

Gareth Porter believes that these "talks about talks" with Hanoi were sabotaged by the United States because Ngo Diem Nhu and others were serious; Porter, *A Peace Denied*, 44–46.

40. CIA memo from Ray Cline, Deputy Director CIA, to McGeorge Bundy, Sept. 26, 1963, NSFV, box 201, JFKL.

41. Shaplen, *The Lost Revolution*, 204–5.

42. *The Pentagon Papers*, Senator Gravel Ed., 2: 268.

43. Tran Van Don, *Our Endless War Inside Vietnam*, 87–118; Ky, *How We Lost the Vietnam War*, 31–43; *The Pentagon Papers*, Senator Gravel Ed., 2: 264–70; Shaplen, *The Lost Revolution*, 209–10.

44. Lodge, *The Storm Has Many Eyes*, 210. Maxwell Taylor witnessed Kennedy's reaction when told of the Ngo brothers' murders: "Kennedy leaped to his feet and rushed from the room with a look of shock and dismay on his face which I have never seen before"; Taylor, *Swords into Plowshares*, 301. Theodore Sorensen, *Kennedy*, 660, corroborates Taylor's view that "Kennedy was shaken," as does Arthur Schlesinger, who, upon seeing Kennedy shortly after he received news of the murders, found him "somber and shaken"; Schlesinger, *A Thousand Days*, 997.

45. U.S. involvement in the 1964 coup in Brazil is reported in Martin I. Elzy, "Researching American Diplomatic History at the Johnson Library," *Newsletter of the Society for Historians of American Foreign Relations*, 8 (Dec. 1977), 17–22; this newsletter is attached to the finding-aid to the National Security File, LBJL. As the consensus on internationalism unraveled in the post-Tet years, various debates commenced about U.S. aid for foreign coups. See Paul E. Sigmund, "The 'Invisible Blockade' and the Overthrow of Allende," *Foreign Affairs*, 52 (Oct. 1975), 322–39; Paul E. Sigmund (versus Elizabeth Farnsworth), "Chile: What Was the U.S. Role?," *Foreign Policy*, no. 16 (Fall 1974), 126–56; Richard R. Fagen, "The United States and Chile: Roots and Branches," *Foreign Affairs*, 53 (Jan. 1975), 297–313, and Paul E. Sigmund (versus Fagen), in Correspondence section, *Foreign Affairs*, 53 (Jan. 1975), 375–77. From the debate concerning Allende, of Chile, and Diem, of Vietnam, one thing is clear: apparently U.S. leaders were willing to assist in coups against both the left and the right, depending on circumstances at the time. Also see Joseph B. Smith's *Portrait of a Cold Warrior* (New York, 1976), 205–23, for early CIA activity in Indonesia, and John Stockwell's *In Search of Enemies: A CIA Story* (New York, 1978), 136, for CIA activity in Zaire.

46. Senate, Select Committee to Study Governmental Operations with Respect to Intelligence (Church Committee), *Interim Report: Alleged Assassination Plots Involving Foreign Leader*, 94th Cong., 1st sess., 1975, S. Rept. 465, 22; *The Pentagon Papers*, Senator Gravel Ed., 2: 271; Conein-Minh exchange quoted in Karnow, *Vietnam*, 311.

47. AES cable from Lodge to State, Nov. 3, 1963, and AES cable from Lodge to McCone, State, Nov. 2, 1963, both in NSFV, box 201, JFKL.

48. *The Pentagon Papers*, Senator Gravel Ed., 2: 207.

49. Lodge, *The Storm Has Many Eyes*, 209. Lodge remained jealous of his prerogatives. His clash with Harkins over "who got to see whom without

his (Lodge's) permission" had to be solved by Rusk and McNamara; state letter from Rusk to "Dear Cabot," Apr. 30, 1964, with note from Lodge to Rusk, Apr. 23, 1964, and note from Harkins to Lodge, Apr. 22, 1964, NSFV, box 3, Vietnam Memos, vol. 7, LBJL. Also see Colby and Forbath, *Honorable Men*, 212.

50. Colby and Forbath, *Honorable Men*, 212.

51. Ball, *The Past Has Another Pattern*, 370–74.

52. TOP SECRET incoming White House cable from New Delhi to Director of NSC, for the President from Ambassador Galbraith, "Policy in Vietnam," Nov. 21, 1961, NSFV, box 195, JFKL. This is not the only message from Galbraith to President Kennedy; see his SECRET letter, Nov. 8, 1961, NSFV, box 195, JFKL.

53. Ball, *The Past Has Another Pattern*, 370–74. Ball returned to the larger theme of Vietnam in *The Discipline of Power* (Boston, 1968), 310–42.

54. Harriman, *America and Russia in a Changing World*, 115.

55. Wolfers, *Discord and Collaboration*, 50–51.

56. *The Pentagon Papers*, Senator Gravel Ed., 2: 270. The definition of an accomplice, according to Henry Campbell Black, *Black's Law Dictionary*, 5th ed. (St. Paul, Minn., 1979), 16, is "One who knowingly, voluntarily and with common intent unites with the principal offender in the commission of a crime."

57. AES cable from Lodge to NSC, Oct. 25, 1963, NSFV, box 201, JFKL.

58. Kern, Levering, and Levering, *The Kennedy Crisis*, 164–91. One should not assume that Kennedy did not try to find a nonmilitary way out of Vietnam. He authorized Harriman and William Sullivan to open secret talks in Geneva in 1962 with Hanoi representatives. Both men met Foreign Minister Ung Van Khiem and his military assistant, Colonel Ha Van Lau, secretly in Geneva. But nothing came of the meetings. See Isaacson and Thomas, *The Wise Men*, 636.

59. Craig and George, *Force and Statecraft*, 275–76; Robert Jervis, *Perception and Misperception in International Politics* (Princeton, N.J., 1976), 113. Jervis writes one chapter (chap. 11) on cognitive dissonance and international relations.

60. Kennedy, *Profiles in Courage*, 230, 264.

61. Michael R. Beschloss, *Kennedy and Roosevelt: The Uneasy Alliance* (New York, 1980), 191–233.

62. William Stevenson, *A Man Called Intrepid* (New York, 1976), 82–84, 87–89, 94–95. Robert Dallak, *Franklin D. Roosevelt and American Foreign Policy: 1932–1979* (Oxford, 1979), 224–25, admits that "Roosevelt was less scrupulous about constitutional and political processes when combating potential espionage and domestic opponents of his national defense program." Kenneth O'Reilly contends that FDR, possessing no CIA, used and abused the FBI for national security cases. See his "A New Deal for the FBI: The Roosevelt Administration, Crime Control, and National Security," *Journal of American History*, 69 (Dec. 1982), 638–58.

63. It is obvious that both Presidents Kennedy and Diem appointed

trusted brothers to the senior police function within their governments. Both also assisted other brothers in politics: the Vietnamese President gave a second brother control over the region of Annam while the American helped a second brother control the region of Massachusetts from his new seat in the U.S. Senate. Yet another brother became Vietnam's Ambassador to London while a brother-in-law was appointed to the Kennedy administration. Diem had yet another brother who could become his Bishop, although Kennedy had to borrow from outside the family for his priest—a Boston Irish cardinal became his family's personal confessor. Both families had in-laws whom the media glamorized—Madam Nhu and a Hollywood star decorated their respective compounds. Both leaders had also lost their eldest brothers in wars.

64. A. Schlesinger, *Robert Kennedy and His Times*, 283–85; V. S. Naipaul, *A Bend in the River* (New York, 1980), 92. Schlesinger states that the courts, legislature, press, and public opinion acted to balance Kennedy's over-enthusiastic pursuit of crime.

65. Robert Kennedy was not the only urban Democrat disgusted with the choice of Johnson. Arthur Schlesinger, Jr., for example, expressed his outrage about it in a telephone call to Reinhold Niebuhr; Niebuhr, however, counseled forbearance, suggesting that if the democrats were honest and planned to pursue their strong platform on civil rights, perhaps a Southerner who knew racism first-hand could be of great help. Again it is Arthur Schlesinger, in *Robert Kennedy and His Times*, who gives a more pleasant view of the two Kennedy brothers and "the accident" of Johnson as Vice President. Victor Lasky, *Robert F. Kennedy: The Myth and the Man* (New York, 1968), 145–46, is less hesitant to view the choice of Johnson as the result of a brotherly feud; see Lasky's notes on the feud in Chap. 15. For the telephone call to Niebuhr see A. Schlesinger, *A Thousand Days*, 56.

66. Richard Kuhns, *The House, the City, and the Judge* (Indianapolis, Ind., 1962), 86–97; Wallace Gray, *Homer to Joyce* (New York, 1985), 34–35. For a modern retelling of the classic Greek family feud, see Joseph Tussman, *The Burden of Office* (Vancouver, B.C., 1989). For the *Mahabharata* see either Jean-Claude Carriere's dramatization by the same name or the edition edited by J. A. B. Van Buitenen (Chicago, 1973). Antigone faced much the same private-versus-public choice as did Agamemnon. See Michael Walzer, *Obligations* (Cambridge, Mass., 1970), 14.

67. Carl J. Friedrich, *The Age of the Baroque: 1610–1660* (New York, 1952), 215–16 ("birthday" quotation); Gianfranco Poggi, *The Development of the Modern State: A Sociological Introduction* (Stanford, Calif., 1978); Huntington, *Political Order in Changing Societies*, 156 ("parochial claims" quotation).

68. Thomas M. Callaghy, *The State-Society Struggle: Zaire in Comparative Perspective* (New York, 1984), 179, 181, 397–407.

69. Stanley Karnow, "Edge of Chaos," *Saturday Evening Post*, Sept. 28, 1963, 27–37.

70. By following such a formula, or one similar to it, Kennedy would have been operating closer to what Craig and George, *Force and Statecraft*, 271–76, call the nonperfectionist approach, an approach between what they

call the amoral approach and the perfectionist approach. For our purposes, the nonperfectionist approach is the approach of internationalists.

71. Karnow, *Vietnam*, 266. Also see Don, *Our Endless War Inside Vietnam*, 114.

72. Leary, *The Central Intelligence Agency*; Allan E. Goodman, "Dateline Langley: Fixing the Intelligence Mess," *Foreign Policy*, no. 57 (Winter 1984–85), 48–73; Snepp, *Decent Interval*, 13. General Bruce Palmer maintains that "the Agency did a good job in assessing the situation in Southeast Asia during the 1965–74 period" *The 25–Year War*, 163.

73. See Sorensen, *Kennedy*, 608, for Anderson's ambassadorship in exile. See Karnow, *Vietnam*, 450, for General Nguyen Chanh Thi's exile in the United States. See Maxwell Taylor, "Chronology of Events While Ambassador to the Republic of Vietnam, July 1964–July 1965 (MDT)," 10, in Maxwell Taylor Papers, box 52, folder E, Library of the National Defense University, National War College, Ft. McNair, Washington, D.C., for Prime Minister Khanh's exile as Ambassador-at-Large.

74. Diem and Chanoff, *In the Jaws of History*, 43, 48–51. Leninists considered the Dai Viets a threat. Indeed, they reacted to these parties by listing their membership for eradication. In a directive from the Binh Dinh People's Revolutionary Party Central Committee, "Suppression of Counter-revolutionaries in Binh-Dinh Province," July 1, 1972, Pike Collection, VCUCB, the party leader lists as targets "members of reactionary parties positively opposing the Revolution including members of Quoc Dan Dang, Dai Viets and Can Lao Nhan Vi."

75. John Cooney, *The American Pope* (New York, 1984), 240, 245.

76. Karnow, *Vietnam*, 446–50.

77. Hilsman, *To Move a Nation*, 470.

78. Giovanni Sartori, *Parties and Party Systems* (Cambridge, 1976), 82–93.

79. Fred R. von der Mehden, *Religion and Modernization in Southeast Asia* (Syracuse, N.Y., 1986), 67–85.

80. Chuong, quoted in Hilsman, *To Move a Nation*, 469. William J. Duiker maintains that Buddhism "did not play the formative social role [in Vietnam] that it did in other Buddhist societies in Southeast Asia"; see his *The Rise of Nationalism in Vietnam*, 187. Buddhism also did not offer an organizational structure that could be used in the politics of rebellion the way that Islam did in Indonesia; see Karl Jackson, *Tradition, Religion and Rebellion* (Berkeley, Calif., 1979), 418–20. On Jackson's views on Southeast Asian rebellions in general see his "Post-colonial and Counter-insurgency in Southeast Asia," in Chandran Jeshurun, ed., *Governments and Rebellion in Southeast Asia* (Singapore, 1985), 3–52.

81. CIA SECRET special report, "The Buddhists in South Vietnam," June 28, 1963, NSFV, box 197, and State cable to AES, June 3, 1963, NSFV, box 197, both in JFKL. In this cable State told Saigon that it "seems most unlikely that Chief Bonzes are in fact VC."

82. "Oral History of Lieutenant General Victor H. Krulak," taken by Benis M. Frank, June 12, 1970, Historical Division, Headquarters, U.S. Ma-

rine Corps, Washington, D.C., 190–91. Krulak indicates that Kennedy accepted his version, and Maxwell Taylor states that later evidence confirmed Krulak; see Taylor, *Swords into Plowshares*, 296. Hilsman, *To Move a Nation*, 502–3, and A. Schlesinger, *A Thousand Days*, 993, argue against Krulak's view.

83. State cable from Hilsman to Lodge, AES, June 8, 1963, NSFV, box 197, JFKL.

84. *Freedom in the World: Political Rights and Civil Liberties, 1983–1984*, ed. Raymond D. Gastil (Westport, Conn., 1984), 450 (quotation); Karnow, *Vietnam*, 280, 286, 298, 339, 448, 449.

85. Huntington, *Political Order in Changing Societies*, 39.

86. D. K. Rangnekar, "The Nationalists Revolution in Ceylon," *Pacific Affairs*, no. 33 (Dec. 1960), 363–64; Robert N. Kearney, "The New Political Crisis of Ceylon," *Asian Survey*, 2 (June 1962), 19–27; Donald E. Smith, *Religion and Politics in Burma* (Princeton, N.J., 1965), 242 (quotation).

87. Cooper, *The Lost Crusade*, 210.

88. Trevon Ling, *Buddhism, Imperialism and War* (London, 1979), 53–54.

89. Cooper, *The Lost Crusade*, 209, 211. Kennedy would have learned more about the politics of sound trucks if he had read V. S. Naipaul's *The Suffrage of Elvira* (New York, 1958) instead of Ian Fleming's novels about James Bond. Naipaul captures both the comic and the tragic aspects of the democratization of Trinidad, his place of birth.

90. Hilsman, *To Move a Nation*, 15. Kennedy did enjoy quoting from Dante. In fact, he and Franklin Roosevelt chose the same passage to repeat. See *The Speeches of Senator John F. Kennedy*, 112, 172, 205, 284, 374, 396, 427, 469, 487, 770, 913, 1104, 1138. Theodore H. White suggests that both JFK and RFK, when lost for words, would go into what reporters called "the Dante sequence"; see White, *The Making of the President, 1968*, 187.

91. Paul Seabury, *Balance of Power* (San Francisco: Chandler Publishing Company, 1965), 207.

92. Harlan Cleveland, quoted in U.S. Department of State press release, no. 746, Dec. 28, 1962, 6.

93. Chester Bowles, quoted in U.S. Department of State press release, no. 467, July 18, 1962, 6.

94. Henry Adams, *The Education of Henry Adams* (Boston, 1918), 416.

Chapter 6

1. Hilsman, *To Move a Nation*, 486.

2. Gelb and Betts, *The Irony of Vietnam*, 2.

3. Not all CIA personnel opposed the coup—some in Saigon and Washington were for it. See Hilsman, *To Move a Nation*, 499. Also see Halberstam, *The Best and the Brightest*, 324, where he maintains that John Richardson was pro-coup after the pagoda raids. For an overview by a policy participant who observed the CIA's influence in Washington and abroad in the 1960's, see Chester Cooper, "The CIA and Decision Making," *Foreign Affairs*, 50 (Jan. 1972), 221–36.

4. "Oral History of John A. McCone," taken by the staff of the LBJ Li-

brary, 16, JFKL; NSC memo from President Kennedy to Secretaries Rusk, of State, and McNamara, of Defense, Nov. 14, 1961. NSFV, box 195, JFKL; incoming White House cable from Ambassador Galbraith to President Kennedy, Nov. 21, 1961, NSFV, box 195, JFKL; memo from Galbraith to President Kennedy, Nov. 13, 1961, NSFV, box 195, JFKL. Twenty years after the murder of the mandarin Diem, Tory internationalists continued to criticize the decision by the United States; see H. Joachin Maitre, "When Washington Ditched Diem," *Wall Street Journal*, Nov. 2, 1983, 26.

5. Hilsman, *To Move a Nation*, 499–500; Colby and Forbath, *Honorable Men*, 215; AES cable from Ambassador Lodge to McGeorge Bundy, NSC, Oct. 25, 1963, NSFV, box 201, JFKL; EYES ONLY MACV Saigon cable from Harkins to Taylor, JCS, Oct. 30, 1963, NSFV, box 204, JFKL; EYES ONLY White House cable from McGeorge Bundy to Ambassador Lodge, Oct. 30, 1963, NSFV, box 201, JFKL.

6. Gelb and Betts, *The Irony of Vietnam*, 2–86.

7. Lodge, *The Storm Has Many Eyes*, 214; Ky, *How We Lost the Vietnam War*, 45.

8. Maxwell Taylor's published books include *Precarious Security*, *Swords into Plowshares*, *Responsibility and Response*, and *The Uncertain Trumpet*.

9. Taylor, *Swords into Plowshares*, 330.

10. Lyndon Johnson, quoted in A. Schlesinger, *A Thousand Days*, 542–43.

11. Johnson, quoted in Halberstam, *The Best and the Brightest*, 167; Miller, *Lyndon*, 283.

12. John McCone, quoted in Thomas Powers, *The Man Who Kept the Secrets: Richard Helms and the CIA* (New York, 1979), 163.

13. Luttwak, *Coup d'etat*, 26.

14. Hilsman, *To Move a Nation*, 525, 433.

15. *Public Papers of the Presidents of the United States: Lyndon B. Johnson, 1963–64* (Washington, D.C., 1965), 1: 607.

16. Eisenhower, quoted in Lodge, *As It Was*, 170.

17. Lodge, *The Storm Has Many Eyes*, 215.

18. Hilsman, *To Move a Nation*, 525. One need not rely on Hilsman alone for these figures. Viet Cong prisoners and those that defected under the Chieu Hoi program relate case-by-case examples of VC terror—assassinations, kidnappings, etc. See "Terror" file, Pike Collection, VCUCB. Ithiel de Sola Pool, drawing on field interviews other than those in the Pike Collection, obtains the same results. See his "Village Violence and Pacification in Viet Nam," the Edmund J. James Lecture on Government, delivered Feb. 29, 1968, Massachusetts Institute of Technology.

19. Hilsman, *To Move a Nation*, 525.

20. Guillermo A. O'Donnell, *Modernization and Bureaucratic Authoritarianism: Studies in South American Politics* (Berkeley, Calif., 1973); Huntington, *The Soldier and the State*; Morris Janowitz, *The Professional Soldier* (New York, 1960); Amos Perlmutter and Valerie P. Bennett, *The Political Influence of the Military* (New Haven, Conn., 1980).

21. The imprecision of such labels was not lost on middlebrow culture.

New Yorker magazine, a manifestation of middlebrow culture, publishes many cartoons lampooning the military in politics. In one such cartoon a successful coup-coalition of Latin American colonels has received reports that "the *Times* has upgraded us from a 'junta' to a military government"; Joseph Mirachi, cartoon, *New Yorker*, Jan. 2, 1984, 23. Such cartoons made an impact. For fifty years of *New Yorker* cartoons see *The New Yorker: Album of Drawings, 1925–1975* (New York, 1976).

22. Duus, *Feudalism in Japan*, 86 (quotation). See also Jeffrey P. Mass and William B. Hauser, eds., *The Bakufu in Japanese History* (Stanford, Calif., 1985). While Arnold R. Isaacs does not employ the term bakufu, he does state that South Vietnam became so militarized under Thieu (the chief of the last bakufu) that it was "not a country with an army but an army with a country"; see Isaacs, *Without Honor: Defeat in Vietnam and Cambodia* (Baltimore, Md., 1983), 102.

23. Selznick, *The Organizational Weapon*, vi–xvii. While Selznick's classic study refers to Leninists in the general sense, P. Berman's *Revolutionary Organization* is a specific study applied to the Vietnamese Leninists.

24. W. Henderson, *Why the Viet Cong Fought*, 119, 130.

25. P. Berman, *Revolutionary Organization*, 11, 106. See also Paret and Shy, *Guerrillas in the 1960's*, 19; Kuno Knoebl, *Victor Charlie: The Face of War in Vietnam* (New York, 1967). Knoebl watched VC prisoners being questioned. These primitive rebels knew almost nothing about communism (114). Knoebl's conclusions are similar to conclusions Robert Middlekauff draws in "Why Men Fought in the American Revolution," *Huntington Library Quarterly*, 43 (Spring 1980), 135–48. Middlekauff sees colonial Americans as having fought because their friends from town were going to fight. In that great Lockean rebellion few if any fought for grand ideals as understood by intellectuals. They fought for a mix of reasons, like "fighting with their buddies." There is also evidence for this among the Vietnamese. Therefore the struggle for Hanoi and Saigon was to attract "the buddies" to their side.

26. Lewis Namier, *The Structure of Politics at the Accession of George III* (London, 1957).

27. Wilensky, *Organizational Intelligence*, 42. Assessing intelligence failures is difficult but not impossible. See Ernest R. May, ed., *Knowing One's Enemies: Intelligence Assessment Before the Two World Wars* (Princeton, N.J., 1984).

28. Walter A. McDougall, . . . *the Heavens and the Earth* (New York, 1985), 325, 332, 344, 361–88. See above, Chap. 4 n. 23, for U.S. iconography.

29. CIA letter from John McCone to President Johnson, Dec. 23, 1963, NSFV, box 1, Memos and Miscel., vol. 2, LBJL.

30. AES cable to State, Aug. 4, 1964, NSFV, box 7, Memos, vol. 16, LBJL; memo from Robert McNamara to President Johnson, Subject: Vietnam Situation, Dec. 21, 1963, NSFV, box 1, Memos, vol. 2, LBJL. Satellite communications with Saigon were established in August 1964; the seabed cable was finished in January 1965.

31. Memo from Robert McNamara to President Johnson (see n. 30 for this

chapter); McNamara, quoted in Don, *Our Endless War Inside Vietnam*, 133. The authors of *The Pentagon Papers*, Senator Gravel Ed. (Boston, 1971), 1: 260, detail similar concerns that McNamara had about Lodge. In his *The Storm Has Many Eyes*, 213, Lodge published a letter from McNamara that lauds his service—but does not deny the charge.

32. Hilsman, *To Move a Nation*, 6.

33. Memo from Mike Forrestal to President Johnson, Dec. 11, 1964, NSFV, box 1, Vietnam Memos, vol. 1, LBJL.

34. *Ibid.*

35. Cable from McGeorge Bundy to General Clifton, at LBJ Ranch in Texas, Dec. 30, 1963, containing three draft messages, NSFV, box 1, Vietnam Memos and Miscel., vol. 2, LBJL.

36. JCS cable from General Harkins to General Taylor, Jan. 30, 1964, NSFV, box 1, Vietnam Cables, vol. 3, LBJL. Colonel Jasper Wilson's papers are on file at the U.S. Army War College, Military History Institute, Carlisle Barracks, Pennsylvania. George McT. Kahin calls the Khanh coup "The Pentagon Coup," suggesting that Harkins, Taylor, and McNamara gave advanced approval for it. But the evidence is insufficient to sustain his claim. See his *Intervention*, 201–2.

37. White House cable from Jasper Wilson to CAS Saigon, Jan. 29, 1984, NSFV, box 2, Vietnam Memos, vol. 3, LBJL.

38. Cable from CIA Watch Office to White House International Situation Room, Jan. 29, 1984, NSFV, box 2, Vietnam Memos, vol. 3, LBJL.

39. CIA intelligence information cable, multiple addresses, SITREP as of 0725 hour local time, Jan. 30, 1964, NSFV, box 2, Vietnam Memos, vol. 3, LBJL.

40. White House letter from Lyndon B. Johnson to General Khanh, Feb. 2, 1964, NSFV, box 2, Vietnam Memos, vol. 3, LBJL. In *Path to Power: The Years of Lyndon Johnson* (New York, 1981), 198, 664, 716, Robert Caro indicates that LBJ learned at an early age to destroy or modify any unfavorable documentary trace of himself from written files. LBJ also depended heavily on verbal communications—"face to face" discussions and telephone conversations. Consequently, LBJ is missing from a large part of his presidential library collection on Vietnam.

41. CIA report to (among others) Hilsman, Forrestal, Rusk, McNamara, McGeorge Bundy, signed by William Colby, Feb. 10, 1964, NSFV, box 2, Vietnam Memos and Cables, vol. 3, LBJL.

42. CIA report to (among others) Rusk, McNamara, McGeorge Bundy, Maxwell Taylor, Hilsman, Forrestal, signed by William Colby, Feb. 14, 1964, NSFV, box 2, Vietnam Memos and Cables, vol. 4, LBJL.

43. CIA Report to same group as above (see n. 42), Feb. 18, 1964, NSFV, box 2, Vietnam Memos, vol. 4, LBJL.

44. CIA report of July 29, 1964, and CIA report of July 22, 1964, both ˙.ı NSFV, box 6, Vietnam Memos, vol. 14, LBJL.

45. CIA weekly report, Aug. 5, 1964, NSFV, box 8, Vietnam Memos, vol. 15, and CIA intelligence information cable, Sept. 1, 1964, NSFV, box 8,

Vietnam Cables, vol. 18, both in LBJL. For a Vietnamese description of the Dai Viets see Diem and Chanoff, *In the Jaws of History*, 17, 20–26, 44, 51–55, 59–60, 62–63, 71.

46. MACV cable to JCS, Sept. 1, 1964, NSFV, box 8, Vietnam Cables, vol. 18, LBJL. After the coup Khanh "exiled" his former ally Khiem to the United States by making him Ambassador; see State letter from Rusk to President Johnson, Oct. 9, 1964, NSFV, box 9, Vietnam Cables, vol. 19, LBJL.

47. CIA weekly report, Aug. 13, 1964, NSFV, box 7, Vietnam Cables, vol. 15, LBJL (quotation). Also see Richard K. Betts, "Analysis, War, and Decisions: Why Intelligence Failures Are Inevitable," *World Politics*, 31 (Oct. 1978), 61–89; Harvey DeWeerd, "Strategic Surprise in the Korean War," *Orbis*, 6 (Fall 1962), 435, 452.

48. Memo from McGeorge Bundy to President Johnson, Aug. 13, 1964, NSFV, box 7, Vietnam Memos, vol. 15, LBJL.

49. CIA cable to multiple Washington addresses, Aug. 30, 1984, and two CIA cables of Aug. 29, 1984 (cables 315-00570-64 and 314-02346-64), all in NSFV, box 7, Vietnam Cables, vol. 16, LBJL; Tang, *A Viet Cong Memoir*, 56–57. The Viet Cong mole "Albert" served in Washington, D.C., as a South Vietnamese military attaché.

50. CIA letter from Acting Director of CIA, General Marshall A. Carter, to McGeorge Bundy, Sept. 28, 1964, NSFV, box 9, Vietnam Cables, vol. 18, LBJL. In this cable the CIA analysts report on the abortive September 13 coup attempt, the rise of the "young turks"—Generals on their way up as Dai Viets were on their way down—and the CIA's hope for a leader. Hilsman hoped for a Nasser, Taylor for a Washington, and the CIA for a Magsaysay—"No Magsaysay has appeared yet," 4.

51. State intelligence note from Thomas L. Hughes, Director of Intelligence and Research, to Secretary Rusk, July 17, 1964, NSFV, box 6, Vietnam Cables, vol. 14, LBJL; Kahin, *Intervention*, 203–35.

52. Memo from Col. Wilbur Wilson to Chief MAAGV, Apr. 10, 1964, Wilson Papers, Military History Institute, U.S. Army War College, Carlisle Barracks, Pennsylvania; CIA Weekly Reports for July 1, July 8, and July 15, 1964, NSFV, box 6, Vietnam Cables, vol. 13, LBJL. Also see McChristian, *Vietnam Studies*.

53. AES cable from Maxwell Taylor to President Johnson, July 15, 1964, NSFV, box 6, Vietnam Cables, vol. 13, LBJL.

54. Memo from McGeorge Bundy to President Johnson, with CIA weekly report of July 8, 1964, attached, NSFV, box 6, Vietnam Cables, vol. 13, LBJL.

55. M. Walzer, *Just and Unjust Wars*, 299–303; Howard, *War and the Liberal Conscience*, 126–30; "In a World He Never Made: Church and Bomb," *The Economist*, Feb. 5–11, 1983, 18–22. The legal debate is best represented by R. Falk, *The Vietnam War and International Law*, and J. Moore, *Law and the Indo-China War*, 217, 222–25, 436–37, 440–57.

56. Taped interview with former Army Chief of Staff General Harold K. Johnson by the author on Apr. 16, 1981, at his office in the Masonic Lodge, 16th St., Washington, D.C.; Johnson had been Chief of Staff in 1964. He states

that LBJ told his colleague General Earle G. Wheeler, Chairman of the Joint Chiefs of Staff, that the military could have their war after he won the 1964 election. Wheeler was deceased when General Johnson repeated this. Wheeler also apparently destroyed his files when he retired from the JCS; that is the position taken by the official historian at the U.S. Army History Center in Washington, D.C. The LBJL has a fifty-five-page "Oral History of Earle G. Wheeler," taken by Dorothy P. McSweeny on Aug. 21, 1969. In it the General does not confirm or deny this charge; in fact, although critical of Johnson's military strategy, Wheeler apparently became LBJ's friend.

57. John Morton Blum, *The Progressive Presidents* (New York, 1980), 202.

58. Gelb and Betts, *The Irony of Vietnam*, 2.

59. Department of State note from Assistant Secretary William P. Bundy and Mike Forrestal to McGeorge Bundy, July 31, 1964, NSFV, box 6, Vietnam Memos, vol. 14, LBJL. From 1951 to 1969 William Bundy served successively with the National Estimates Board of the CIA (detailed for a time to the NSC Planning Board), as Deputy Assistant Secretary and then Assistant Secretary of Defense for International Security Affairs, and as Assistant Secretary of State for East Asian and Pacific Affairs. From there he went on to become editor of *Foreign Affairs*. See his review article about the NSC process, "The National Security Process: Plus Ça Change . . . ?," *International Security*, 7 (Winter 1982–83), 94–109.

60. Memo from McGeorge Bundy to President Johnson, Aug. 20, 1964, NSFV, box 7, Vietnam Memos, vol. 16, LBJL.

61. Note from President Johnson to McGeorge Bundy, Oct. 17, 1964, NSFV, box 9, Vietnam Memos, vol. 20, LBJL. Also see Robert J. Donovan, *Nemesis: Truman and Johnson in the Coils of War in Asia* (New York, 1984), 176–88.

62. Maxwell Taylor, "Chronology of Events While Ambassador to the Republic of Vietnam, July 1964–July 1965 (MDT)," in Maxwell Taylor's Papers, box 52, folder E, 2–3, Library of the National Defense University, National War College, Ft. McNair, Washington, D.C. Taylor was not the only Ambassador to feel Johnson's interest in his chronology for Vietnam. When LBJ heard on May 14, 1964, that Lodge was "proposing that a sequence of action be initiated in the near future," a sequence that meant "moving against the north," he sent a "For the Ambassador from President" cable in which he told his Republican envoy that "I consider it vital that you and I at all times fully and clearly understand each others' minds and would therefore greatly appreciate it if you would send me urgently your precise present recommendations with respect to the North including the—deleted—the timing, and the degree of visibility of U.S. participation at each stage"; White House cable to AES, May 14, 1964, NSFV, box 4, Vietnam Cables, vol. 9, LBJL.

63. Huntington, *The Soldier and the State*, 459–60. Huntington warns against the creation of Democratic Generals and Admirals and their Republican counterparts. For Huntington the role of the professional soldier in contact with politics must be to give professional advice, not policy advice favorable to those who would fuse the military into politics.

64. For a further explanation of the term particularist see Gaddis, *Strategies of Containment*, 27–29.

65. "NSC-68," Apr. 14, 1950, in *Foreign Relations of the United States: 1950* (Washington, D.C., 1950), 238–40. Also see Paul Y. Hammond, Warner Schilling, and Glen Snyder, *Strategy, Politics and Defense Budgets* (New York, 1962), 267–330. For a critique of the perimeter defense see Hoffmann, *Janus and Minerva*, 332.

66. Keohane, *After Hegemony*.

67. Bertram D. Wolfe, "A Party of a New Type," in Lennard D. Genson, ed., *Lenin and the Twentieth Century: A Bertram Wolfe Retrospective* (Stanford, Calif., 1984), 12–41.

68. Bendix, "Tradition and Modernity Reconsidered," in his *Nation-Building and Citizenship*, 361–434; Ivo Andric, *The Bridge on the Drina* (Chicago, 1977), 136; David E. Apter, *The Politics of Modernization* (Chicago, 1965), 450; Sheldon S. Wolin, "From Progress to Modernization: The Conservative Turn," *democracy*, 3 (Fall 1983), 9–21; Theda Skocpol, "Social Revolutions and Mass Military Mobilization," *World Politics*, 40 (Jan. 1988), 147–68. Interestingly, Samuel Huntington suggests that some military rulers do not block the arrival of democratic politics. Those that do not block it—the Mexicans for example—transform their military juntas into political parties and evolve in that way. See his *Political Order in Changing Societies*, 203, 255–56. The evidence is not clear, except that much depends on the individual case. For example, see Jong-Chun Baek, "The Role of the Republic of Korea Armed Forces in National Development: Past and Present," *Journal of East Asian Affairs*, 3 (Fall–Winter 1983), 292–324; Lucian W. Pye, "Armies in the Process of Political Modernization," in John J. Johnson, ed., *The Role of the Military in Underdeveloped Countries* (Princeton, N.J., 1962), 69–89; Alfred Stepan, *The Military in Politics: Changing Patterns in Brazil* (Princeton, N.J., 1971), 9; William F. Gutteridge, *Military Institutions and Power in the New States* (New York, 1965), 56; John P. Lovell and C. I. Eugene Kim, "The Military and Political Change in Asia," in Henry Bienen, ed., *The Military and Modernization* (New York, 1971), 109–12.

Chapter 7

1. Taylor, *Precarious Security*, 45.

2. "Oral History of Fowler Hamilton," taken by Edwin R. Bayley, Aug. 18, 1964, 5, JFKL. Hamilton was administrator of the U.S. Agency for International Development.

3. Huntington, *Political Order in Changing Societies*, 344–46.

4. Kennan, *Memoirs*, 334, 373–387; George Kennan, "Containment Then and Now," *Foreign Affairs*, 65 (Spring, 1987), 885–90; Lippmann, *The Cold War*, xiii–xiv, 50–51.

5. Memo from Clark Clifford to President Truman, Sept. 24, 1946, Russia II folder, Clifford Files, HSTL.

6. Edward M. Bennett, *Recognition of Russia* (Waltham, Mass., 1970), 78. Also see Report, Executive Agreement Series no. 105, Aug. 4, 1937, Russia I

folder, Clark Clifford Files, HSTL; Robert Paul Browder, *The Origins of Soviet-American Diplomacy* (Princeton, N.J., 1953), 82, 97, 196–97, 198; Mikhail V. Concoide, *Russian-American Trade* (Columbus, Ohio, 1947), 135–37.

7. Antony C. Sutton, *Western Technology and Soviet Economic Development*, 3 vols. (Stanford, Calif., 1973); Richard Day, *Leon Trotsky and the Politics of Economic Isolation* (Cambridge, 1973), 54; Gur Ofer, "Soviet Economic Growth: 1928–1985," *Journal of Economic Literature*, 25 (Dec. 1987), 1767–1833.

8. Memo from Walter Thurston to A. I. Mikoyan, Aug. 6, 1940, Russia I folder, Clifford Files, HSTL.

9. Thomas G. Paterson, "The Economic Cold War: American Business and Economic Foreign Policy, 1945–50," (Ph.D. diss. University of California, Berkeley, 1968), 225–26.

10. *Ibid.*, 226, 227 (Flander's quotation), 232, 234, 240 (quotation). The support for economic containment has never abated. See Louis J. Walinsky, "Coherent Defense Strategy: The Case for Economic Denial," *Foreign Affairs*, 61 (Winter 1982–83), 272–91.

11. Beverly Crawford and Stefanie Lenway, "Decision Modes and International Regime Change: Western Collaboration on East-West Trade," *World Politics*, 37 (April, 1985), 375–402; Michael Mastanduno, "Strategies for Economic Containment," *World Politics*, 38 (July, 1985), 503–529; Angela E. Stent, "Economic Containment," in Deibel and Gaddis, *Containment*, 161–88; David A. Baldwin, *Economic Statecraft* (Princeton, N.J., 1985).

12. James Reston, "Implications of Greek Aid Worry Truman Advisors," clipping from *New York Times*, Mar. 12, 1947, in Foreign Aid UNRA folder, Elsey Files, HSTL; letter from Senator Joseph O'Maloney to Harry S. Truman, May 28, 1945, OF 275-A, Truman Papers, HSTL. Also see the presidential reply of June 2, 1945, in the same file.

13. Paterson, "The Economic Cold War," 236; Robert H. Ferrell, "Truman Foreign Policy: A Traditionalist View," *The Alternative*, 6 (Apr. 1973), 9–29. Not all participants agree that economics played a major role in U.S.-USSR containment in 1947. For an opposite view see the transcript of "Walter S. Salant Oral History Interview," Mar. 30, 1970, 26, HSTL. Salant was a member of Truman's Council of Economic Advisers.

14. Allison, *Essence of Decision*, 78–79.

15. *Ibid.*, 162; James G. March and Johan P. Olsen, *Ambiguity and Choice in Organizations* (Bergen, Norway, 1976), 10–67.

16. Acheson, *Present at the Creation*, 3, 16–17, 39–63.

17. William H. McNeill, *America, Britain and Russia: Their Cooperation and Conflict 1941–1949* (Oxford, 1953); G. Smith, *American Diplomacy During the Second World War*, 29–35 (quotations).

18. Clayton, quoted in Paterson, "The Economic Cold War," 128; U.S. Department of State, *Foreign Relations of the United States: 1946* (Washington, D.C., 1946), 828–29.

19. James MacGregor Burns, *Roosevelt: The Soldier of Freedom 1940–1945* (New York, 1970), 514–15; Acheson, *Present at the Creation*, 39.

20. Kennan, *Memoirs*, 308.

21. Paterson, "The Economic Cold War," 124; Philip J. Funigiello, *American-Soviet Trade in the Cold War* (Chapel Hill, N.C., 1988).

22. George Marshall, quoted in State, *Foreign Relations of the United States*, 691.

23. Clark Clifford, "Reflections on Containment," in Deibel and Gaddis, *Containment*, vol. 1, 46–51.

24. Herbert M. Druks, "Harry S. Truman and the Russians, 1945–1953," (Ph.D. diss., New York University, New York, 1964), 42–43, 193; Harriman, *American and Russia in a Changing World*, 42; Harry Truman, Address on Foreign Economic Policy, Baylor University, Mar. 6, 1947, in *Public Papers of the Presidents of the United States: Harry S. Truman, 1947* (Washington, D.C., 1963), 167–72; John Edelman Spero, *The Politics of International Economic Relations*, 3d ed. (New York, 1985), 348–49.

25. Report on U.S.-Soviet Joint Conference, Seoul, Korea, Feb. 1, 1946, Russia I folder, Clifford Files, HSTL.

26. Ellen Garwood, *Will Clayton: A Short Biography* (Austin, Tex., 1958); William Clayton, speech for new Foreign Service officers, Sept. 3, 1946; speech for U.S. Chamber of Commerce, May 1, 1946; speech for world trade, "Road to Expansion," July 13, 1946, Speech File folder 1946, Clayton Files, HSTL; letter from William Clayton to Charles Pucketts, of the *Chattanooga Times*, July 2, 1945, Chronological folder, July–Sept. 1945, Clayton Files, HSTL; letter from William Clayton to Lamar Fleming of Andersen, Clayton and Company, June 2, 1945, Chronological folder, June 1945, Clayton Files, HSTL.

27. Representative Robertson (of Virginia), remarks in *Congressional Record*, 79th Cong., 1st sess., 1945, 5126.

28. Draft letter from Harry S. Truman to E. W. Pauley, Aug. 1, 1946, Russian II folder, Clifford Files, HSTL.

29. Cable from Political Adviser for XXIV U.S. Corps, Seoul, Korea, to the Secretary of State, Feb. 15, 1946, Russia II folder, Clifford Files, HSTL.

30. Park Chung Hee, *Korea Reborn* (Englewood Cliffs, N.J., 1979).

31. Minh, *On Revolution*, 282.

32. Cable from General Clay, CINCEUR Berlin, to the Secretary of War, Apr. 1, 1948, Russia III folder, Clifford Files, HSTL.

33. General William Donovan, "General Donovan Outlines Global Plan to Halt Russians Without Shooting," *New York World Telegram*, Nov. 11, 1948, clipping in Russia III folder, Clifford Files, HSTL.

34. Report from Ambassador E. W. Pauley to Ambassador I. M. Maisky, July 3, 1945, Records of the U.S. Representative to the Allied Commission on Reparations, Russia I folder, Clifford Files, HSTL. Also see Pauley's letter to Maisky, July 13, 1945, in the same file. The story of possible Soviet reparations from Germany is an interesting one; see Louis Fischer, *The Road to Yalta* (New York, 1972), 198–202.

35. U.S. Department of State, *Foreign Relations of the United States: 1947* (Washington, D.C., 1947), 515.

36. "Economic Needs of Soviets Regarded as Its Motivation," *New York Times*, May 12, 1948, clipping in Foreign Affairs—Russia 1948 folder, Elsey Files, HSTL.

37. Charles E. Bohlen, *Witness to History: 1929–1969* (New York, 1973), 339; Spero, *The Politics of International Economic Relations*, 344–348.

38. A case in point involves the surfacing at top White House levels of the last will and testament of Czar Peter the Great. The following statement to "Dear Clifford" appeared on White House stationery, dated Sept. 21, 1946: "Attached is a copy of the 'political testament' of Peter of Russia that we spoke about. . . . President has a copy." The note ended, "Peter must have been a great guy." This was preceded on Aug. 19, 1946, by a letter from the British Joint Staff Mission to Fleet Admiral W. E. Leahy, Military Adviser to President Truman. It was concise: "I also sent a copy of Rules for the Russian Nation as taken from the Will of Peter the Great, which indicates there is very little change of policy between 1725 and today." The will itself was a three-page rendition of Russian geopolitics circa 1725, with Russia as the power dominating all Europe. There exists no evidence that Clifford interpreted the will literally. But its being in his files indicates Clifford's openness to all opinions. See memo from W. D. L. to Clark Clifford, Sept. 15, 1946, Russia I folder, Clifford File; memo from British Joint Staff Mission to Fleet Admiral Leahy, Aug. 19, 1946, Russia I folder, Clifford File, both in HSTL. Almost thirty years after Clifford first looked at Czar Peter's will, social scientists were still examining documents from Russia's eighteenth-century past for clues to her present politics. See John M. Letiche and Basil Dmytrshyn, *Russian Statecraft: The Politika of Iurii Krizhanich* (London, 1985).

39. Acheson, *Present at the Creation*, 221.

40. Lippmann, *The Cold War*, 9–13; Clifford, "American Military Firmness Versus Soviet Aggression," 9–13. The complete text of the Clifford report is in Arthur Krock, *Memoirs* (New York, 1968), 421–82. Also see Ronald Steel's introduction to Lippmann's book, xiii, xiv.

41. Clifford, "American Military Firmness Versus Soviet Aggression," 12.

42. *Ibid.*

43. *Ibid.*, 13.

44. Vandenberg, quoted in James Reston, "Our History Suggests a Remedy," in Henry Luce, ed., *The National Purpose* (New York, 1960), 114; Immanuel Wexler, *The Marshall Plan Revisited: The European Recovery Program in Economic Perspective* (Westport, Conn., 1983), 50–53.

45. *The Private Papers of Senator Vandenberg*, ed. Arthur H. Vandenberg, Jr. (Boston, 1952), 389–92.

46. *Ibid.*, 392. Some critics might argue that the real innovation in the general congressional attitude to containment policy came not in this European recovery plan but in the earlier legislation to aid Greece and Turkey, another economic program that Vandenberg supported. For that view see Nelson Polsby, *Political Innovation in America: The Politics of Policy Initiation* (New Haven, Conn., 1984), 75–91. But the Greek-Turkish package received "crisis management," limited debate, and for the participants in the debate

the package was an aberration, a one-time plan rather than a formula-setting precedent. In the case of the European recovery plan many participants had a clearer view of the innovative process that it would start, and how it might act as a model for later programs.

47. Ambrose, *Eisenhower*, 2: 625–26; Greenstein, *The Hidden-Hand President*, 46–52.

48. William E. Leuchtenburg, *In the Shadow of FDR: From Harry Truman to Ronald Reagan* (Ithaca, N.Y., 1983).

49. William Kornhauser, *The Politics of Mass Society* (New York, 1959), 5, 40–41.

50. *Public Papers of the Presidents of the United States: Harry S. Truman, 1949* (Washington, D.C., 1964), 114–15. Also see Rotter, *The Path to Vietnam*.

51. Curti, *American Philanthropy Abroad*; Curti and Birr, *Prelude to Point Four*; Joan Jacobs Brumberg, *Mission for Life* (New York, 1980), 4–5, 112–13. As is the case in so many aspects of American history, the roots of American involvement in Asia begin with activities sponsored by American churches. While the popular culture, thanks to Pearl Buck, associates these Asian missions with China and Northeast Asia, it is interesting to note that they began in Southeast Asia.

52. Ambrose, *Eisenhower*, 2: 376–81; "Recorded Interview with Eisenhower by Mrs. John G. Lee, National President, League of Women Voters," Apr. 26, 1954, in *Public Papers of the Presidents of the United States: Dwight D. Eisenhower, 1954* (Washington, D.C., 1960), 24; letter from Dwight Eisenhower to Charles H. Percy, May 20, 1954, in *Public Papers of the Presidents: Eisenhower, 1954*, 503–4.

53. "Memorandum on the Administration of Foreign Aid Programs," Nov. 6, 1954, in *Public Papers of the Presidents: Eisenhower, 1954*, 1020; Rostow, *Eisenhower, Kennedy, and Foreign Aid*, 15; Burton I. Kaufman, *Trade and Aid: Eisenhower's Foreign Economic Policy* (Baltimore, Md., 1982).

54. S. Cohen, *The Making of the United States International Economic Policy* (New York, 1981), 66–70; letter from Dwight Eisenhower to Joseph M. Dodge, Dec. 11, 1954, in *Public Papers of the Presidents: Eisenhower, 1954*, 1097; "Special Message to the Congress on Mutual Security Programs," May 21, 1957, and "Radio and Television Address to the American People on the Need for Mutual Security in Waging Peace," May 21, 1957, both in *Public Papers of the Presidents of the United States: Dwight D. Eisenhower, 1957* (Washington, D.C., 1958), 372–85 and 391–93.

55. John Gerald Ruggie, "International Regimes, Transactions, and Change: Embedded Liberalism in the Postwar Economic Order," in Stephen D. Krasner, ed., *International Regimes* (Ithaca, N.Y., 1983), 195–231; Krasner, *International Regimes*, 2–5, definition of regime (quotation on p. 2).

56. "President's News Conference of April 29, 1954," in *Public Papers of the Presidents: Eisenhower, 1954*, 427–38 (quotation p. 427); Eisenhower, *Mandate for Change*, 332–75. Also see the "News Conference of March 24, 1954," in *Public Papers of the Presidents: Eisenhower, 1954*, 346.

57. "Joint Statement Following Discussion with President Diem of Viet-

nam," May 12, 1957, in *Public Papers of the Presidents: Eisenhower, 1957*, 335–37; John Kennedy, quoted in K. Turner, *Lyndon Johnson's Dual War*, 51.

58. Robequain, *The Economic Development of French Indochina*, 219–42; N. Long, *Before the Revolution*, 4–31.

59. Jeffrey Paige, *Agrarian Revolutions: Social Movements and Export Agriculture in the Underdeveloped World* (New York, 1975), 278–79.

60. Robequain, in *The Economic Development of French Indochina*, describes how one French planter in Vietnam "made the first experiments with mechanized rice cultivation in 1900." It did not work, yet he succeeded as a colonial farmer, for "in the middle of the countryside he set up a rice husking mill which could handle more than 60 tons of rice a day, and a mechanical sawmill." He also owned "his own flotilla of motor barges and succeeded in selling his grain without the help of Chinese middlemen, an unusual achievement" (193). See also Geoffrey B. Hainsworth, ed., *Village-Level Modernization in Southeast Asia: The Political Economy of Rice and Water* (Vancouver, B.C., 1982).

61. Wittfogel, *Oriental Despotism*, 3,6–7, 25–48. Wittfogel distinguishes "between a farming economy that involves small-scale irrigation (hydro-agriculture) and one that involves small-scale government-managed works of irrigation and flood control (hydraulic agriculture)." He came "to believe that the designations 'hydraulic society' and 'hydraulic civilization' express more appropriately than the traditional terms the peculiarities of the order under discussion." This new nomenclature, "which stresses human action rather than geography, facilitates comparison with 'industrial society' and 'feudal society.' . . . By underlining the prominent role of the government, the term 'hydraulic,'" as Wittfogel defines it, "draws attention to the agromanagerial and agrobureaucratic character of these civilizations." See also Germaine A. Hosten, *Marxism and the Crisis of Development in Prewar Japan* (Princeton, N.J., 1986), 127–78, and, for a critique of Wittfogel, see Susanne Hoeber Rudolph, "State Formation in Asia," *Journal of Asian Studies*, 46 (Nov. 1987), 731–46.

62. For details on the changes in land use see Nancy Wiegersma, "Land Tenure and Land Reform: A History of Property and Power in Vietnam" (Ph.D. diss., University of Maryland, 1976). For details on traditional law in Vietnam before the French began to change these codes see Nguyen Ngoc Huy and Ta Van Tai, *The Le Code: Law in Traditional Vietnam* (Athens, Ohio, 1987). For details on Chinese influence on Vietnamese government and law at the time of the French intervention see Alexander B. Woodside, *Vietnam and the Chinese Model* (Cambridge, Mass., 1988).

63. Murray, *The Development of Capitalism in Colonial Indochina*, 65. This is an encyclopedic work.

64. Pierre Gourou, *L'utilization du sol en Indochine* (Paris, 1940), 276.

65. Marc Bloch, *French Rural History: An Essay on Its Basic Characteristics* (Berkeley, Calif., 1966), 197, 198 (quotation), 240.

66. Murray, *The Development of Capitalism in Colonial Indochina*, 66; Karl Polanyi, *The Great Transformation* (Boston, 1944), 223–58B.

67. Virginia Thompson, *French Indochina* (New York, 1937), 219–20. Thompson saw the best and the worst in this "Frenchification" of Vietnam.

68. Donald W. Fryer, "Cities of South-East Asia and Their Problems," in Y. M. Yeung and C. P. Lo, eds., *Changing South-East Asian Cities* (Singapore, 1976), 8–12.

69. Eric R. Wolf, *Europe and the People Without History* (Berkeley, Calif., 1982), 321.

70. Murray, *The Development of Capitalism in Colonial Indochina*, 179.

71. Robequain, *The Economic Development of French Indochina*, 311.

72. Murray, *The Development of Capitalism in Colonial Indochina*, 182.

73. Hitoshi Fukuda, *Irrigation in the World* (Tokyo, 1976), 150–53; V. Thompson, *French Indochina*, 215–19 (quotation p. 217). Also see the Association of Japanese Agricultural Scientific Societies, *Rice in Asia* (Tokyo, 1975). This work contains data on South Vietnam rice production up to the fall of Saigon in 1975.

74. Murray, *The Development of Capitalism in Colonial Indochina*, 178.

75. N. Long, *Before the Revolution*, 103–5. Also see his footnote 18, 118–19.

76. Thomas Schweitzer, "The French Colonialist Lobby in the 1930's: The Economic Foundations of Imperialism" (Ph.D. diss., University of Wisconsin, Madison, 1971), 503–4.

77. Murray, *The Development of Capitalism in Colonial Indochina*, 261; Robequain, *The Economic Development of French Indochina*, 206.

78. Murray, *The Development of Capitalism in Colonial Indochina*, 261–62; Robequain, *The Economic Development of French Indochina*, 206–7.

79. Known in the Far East as the French Bank, the Banque de l'Indochine became a power unto itself. See William Qualid, *Le privilège de la Banque de l'Indo-China et la question des banques coloniales* (Paris, 1923); H. Baudoin, *La Banque de l'Indochine* (Paris, 1903); Donald Lancaster, *The Emancipation of French Indochina* (Oxford, 1961). French-organized banks dominated the French empire. According to one comparative study of these banks, the Banque du Syrie et du Liban played much the same role in French Syria as the Banque de l'Indochine played in French Indochina; see Yahya M. Sadowski, "Political Power and Economic Organization in Syria" (Ph.D. diss., University of California, Los Angeles, 1983), 26.

80. Murray, *The Development of Capitalism in Colonial Indochina*, 265–66 and Robequain, *The Economic Development of French Indochina*, 206–7, 310–11.

81. J. Russell Andrus, *Preliminary Survey of the Economy of French Indochina* (Washington, D.C., 1943), 27. Andrus is typical of the scholar-diplomats of World War II. The State Department hired him to produce studies on his specialty—Southeast Asia. He wrote this study, dated June 2, 1943, for the Division of Economic Studies, Far Eastern Unit, Bureau of Foreign Domestic Committee. Andrus co-edited the "Supplement" to Robequain's often-cited *The Economic Development of French Indochina*.

82. Thomas Ennis, *French Policy and Developments in Indochina* (Chicago, 1936), 147.

83. Robequain, *The Economic Development of French Indochina*, 202–5.

84. N. Long, *Before the Revolution*, 106; Robequain, *The Economic Development of French Indochina*, 204. The term "Moi" translates as "savages."

85. N. Long, *Before the Revolution*, 112–13; Arlene Eisen, *Woman and Revolution in Viet Nam* (London, 1984), 25–30.

86. Original sources on Vietnamese labor remain scarce, as is generally true for other peoples in the first stages of market capitalism. Nevertheless, a few letters from Vietnamese rubber workers do exist. An excellent one appears in N. Long's *Before the Revolution*, 107–12. Another Vietnamese source is Diep Lien Anh, *Latex and Blood: The Wretched Life of the Rubber Plantation Workers in the Red Earth Districts* (Saigon, 1965). Also helpful is Paul Monet, *Les jauniers histoire vraie* (Paris, 1931).

87. N. Long, *Before the Revolution*, 115; Tran Tu Binh, *The Red Earth: A Vietnamese Memoir of Life on a Colonial Rubber Plantation* (Athens, Ohio, 1964). The latter is a short autobiography of a leading communist figure (b. 1907), who became radicalized in his youth, and more so during three years on a French rubber plantation in the South.

88. N. Long, *Before the Revolution*, 116.

89. Murray, *The Development of Capitalism in Colonial Indochina*, 318, 322, 324; Robequain, *The Economic Development of French Indochina*, 249–59.

90. Murray, *The Development of Capitalism in Colonial Indochina*, 323–25.

91. *Ibid.*, 327–30; Robequain, *The Economic Development of French Indochina*, 257–61.

92. Murray, *The Development of Capitalism in Colonial Indochina*, 245, 347–52, 363–64; N. Long, *Before the Revolution*, 102.

93. N. Long, *Before the Revolution*, 102.

94. Murray, *The Development of Capitalism in Colonial Indochina*, 267, 325.

95. N. Long, *Before the Revolution*, 44.

Chapter 8

1. *The Speeches of Senator John F. Kennedy*, 153–54. As he did with Diem, Vietnam, and Southeast Asian revolutions, so JFK did with Nasser, Egypt, and Arab nationalism: he tried to buy them, and with many of the same Americans involved—for example, William Gaud, from AID; Robert Komer, from NSC. See Douglas Little, "The New Frontier on the Nile," *Journal of American History*, 75 (Sept. 1988), 501–27.

2. Ball, *The Past Has Another Pattern*, 208; *Public Papers of the Presidents of the United States: John F. Kennedy, 1961* (Washington, D.C., 1962), 212.

3. "Oral History of Fowler Hamilton," taken by Edwin R. Bayley, Aug. 18, 1964, 2–3, 10, JFKL.

4. *Ibid.*, 11–13; Robert A. Packenham, "Political-Development Doctrines in the American Foreign Aid Program," *World Politics*, 18 (Jan. 1966), 194–235 (quotation on p. 211).

5. "Oral History of Fowler Hamilton," 27–29.

6. *Ibid.*, 29.

7. *Supplément au Bulletin Economique de la Banque National du Viet-Nam* (Saigon), no. 3–4, 1959, 7; *Supplément*, no. 2, 1960, 9; *Supplément*, no. 1, 1961, 5.

8. *Supplément*, no. 1, 1962, 5.

9. A U.S. House of Representatives report of Oct. 12, 1966, suggests that "The Vietcong have for some time had an organization whose purpose is to deny economic resources to Vietnam. For example, the recent shortages of rice in Saigon and other cities have been ascribed, at least in part, to the success of the Vietcong in interdicting shipments of rice from the fertile Mekong delta area"; House Committee on Government Operations, *An Investigation of the U.S. Economic and Military Assistance Program in Vietnam,* 89th Cong., 2d sess., 1966, H. Rept. 42, 35. Also see the declassified J2, MACV, briefing of Apr. 1, 1967, reprinted as Appendix G, "Summary of Briefing on Viet Cong Taxation," in McChristian, *Vietnam Studies,* 166–68.

10. *Supplèment au Bulletin Economique de la Banque National des Viet-Nam,* no. 1, 1962, 6–8. Another source for data is the *Vietnam Report,* published monthly during the 1960's and 1970's by the Vietnam Council on Foreign Relations, which was based in Saigon.

11. Race, *War Comes to Long An,* 125–30; JCS memo from General V. H. Krulak to McGeorge Bundy, Sept. 11, 1963, NSFV, box 199, JFKL.

12. Memo from Mike Forrestal to President Johnson, Dec. 11, 1963, NSFV, box 1, Vietnam Memos, vol. 1, LBJL.

13. *Supplèment au Bulletin Economique de la Banque National du Viet-Nam,* no. 1, 1962, 5.

14. Coffin, *Witness for AID,* 32, 116.

15. John F. Kennedy, "Speech to the Conference of the American Friends of Vietnam: Washington, D.C., June 1, 1956," in Allan Nevins, ed. *The Strategy of Peace* (New York: Harper & Row, 1960), 63.

16. Even Hanoi had problems forcing some of their cadre to grant precedence to the peasants over the proletariat. As late as 1966 the debate raged in Saigon Leninist circles. In the "BA letter" to the Saigon Regional Party Committee and Comrade Ru Anh, Mar. 1966, "BA" stressed the urban emphasis. See Box NLF, General, no. 1, Folder 1966, 11–39, Pike Collection, VCUCB.

17. Guy N. Fox, Chief Adviser, "Final Report Covering Activities of the Michigan State University Vietnam Advising Group: For the Period May 20, 1955–June 30, 1962," Saigon, Vietnam, June 1962, 1, Pike Collection, VCUCB. Robert Scigliano and Guy Fox's *Technical Assistance in Vietnam* (New York: Praeger, 1965) covers most of the same details.

18. Fox, "Final Report," 51.

19. *Ibid.,* 47–48; AES cable from Fred Nolting to Dean Rusk, State, Nov. 16, 1961, NSFV, box 195, JFKL.

20. "Harkins' Gardener Was Communist," UPI, Saigon, Nov. 10, 1963, Box NLF, Operations, no. 1, Pike Collection, VCUCB.

21. Memo from Jack E. Ryan to Howard W. Hoyt, Jan. 10, 1956 (Report no. 1), Subject: Brief History of the Sûreté in Indo-China, Michigan State University Vietnam Advisory Team, Saigon, Pike Collection, VCUCB.

22. By 1970 much of the information covering the highly classified and controversial Phoenix program, a program targeted on eliminating the Viet Cong infrastructure (not its military wing), had become an open U.S. secret. See "Growing Menace to Vietnam: Red Spies in the South," *U.S. News and*

World Report, Dec. 21, 1970, 51–52. For scholarly research on the Phoenix program see Ralph William Johnson, *Phoenix-Phung Hoang: A Study of Wartime Intelligence Management.* This unpublished monograph was completed prior to Johnson's death. A copy is in the Pike Collection, VCUCB.

23. Montgomery, *The Politics of Foreign Aid,* 46, 80, 78–80, 89–92, 100–2. Montgomery spent the years 1958–60 in Vietnam studying the politics of American aid there. Montgomery had derived much of his view from his work on Germany and Japan, where earlier the internationalists had intervened with economic weapons in order to transform the respective polities into democracies. See John T. Montgomery, *Forced to Be Free: The Artificial Revolution in Germany and Japan* (Chicago, 1957). Thus in Vietnam he tested the transfer of his thesis from two developed nations to an underdeveloped one.

24. Letter from President Kennedy to President Diem, Aug. 3, 1961, NSFV, Vietnam Cables, box 194, JFKL.

25. Memo from Robert H. Johnson to Walt Rostow, Sept. 6, 1961, NSFV, Vietnam Memos, box 194; AES cable from Lodge to State, Oct. 19, 1963, NSFV, Vietnam Cables, box 204; Memo from V. H. Krulak to McGeorge Bundy, Sept. 11, 1963, NSFV, Vietnam Memos, box 199; JCS cable to CINCPAC, Mar. 9, 1963, NSFV, Vietnam Cables, box 197, all in JFKL; VC Document 24, "Opposing and Destroying Strategic Hamlets Are One of Our First-rank Essential Tasks," by Tuan-Tu, 1962; VC Document 93, NLF Anti-Pacification Plan—Mid-1962, "With Patience, Determination, Steadfastness, Let Us Oppose and Destroy the U.S.-Diem Strategic Hamlets"; VC Document 3, Indoctrination Booklet, "Methods of Opposing GVN Strategic Hamlet Program," Jan. 1962, all in Pike Collection, VCUCB; R. B. Smith, *An International History of the Vietnam War,* vol. 2, *The Kennedy Strategy,* 168–69.

26. Colby and Forbath, *Honorable Men,* 165–69.

27. Colby and Forbath, *Honorable Men,* 168. One should not forget that both the Hanoi leadership and the Viet Cong strongly reacted to such programs as spraying DDT for malaria eradication. They continued their hostility even after the fall of the House of Ngo. In a directive from the Binh Dinh People's Revolutionary Party Central Committee dated July 1, 1972, in the Pike Collection, VCUCB, they listed as their number one target for eradication the "United States, puppet, French, and Japanese intelligence agents; members of malaria eradication teams; rural pacification cadres; and administrative officials."

28. Pye, *Asian Power and Politics,* 229.

29. For details of Hanoi's balancing act vis-à-vis the Soviet Union and the People's Republic of China, see Eugene Lawson, "Vietnamese-Chinese Relationship During Vietnam War," 107–12, manuscript in Pike Collection, VCUCB; Zagoria, *Vietnam Triangle*; Klaus Mehnert, *Peking and Moscow* (New York, 1963), 441–42.

30. The emphasis on loyalty to the party, regardless of differences between individuals, is a constant theme in Hanoi/NLF/People's Revolutionary party publications. The "BA" letter cited above in note 16 for this chapter has a section II (40–44) appended to it to explain the primacy of party loyalty. The

author of the "BA" letter tried to balance the contradictions of urban versus rural emphasis in the following context: "All efforts are devoted to the establishment of a people's government made up of four classes on the basis of a worker-farmer alliance under the working class leadership for the realization of national independence and distribution of land to the tillers." See Box NLF, General, no. 1, Folder 1966, 41, Pike Collection, VCUCB.

31. Colby and Forbath, *Honorable Men*, 168–69.

32. Government of South Vietnam, *Investing in Vietnam* (Saigon, Mar. 5, 1957), 28–29; copy in the economic periodicals of the Pike Collection, VCUCB.

33. George C. Lodge and Ezra F. Vogel, *Ideology and National Competitiveness* (Boston, 1987), 301–4. Also see Ronald Inglehart, "The Renaissance of Political Culture," *American Political Science Review*, 82 (Dec. 1988), 1203–30 (see p. 1228).

34. Richard Rosecrance, *The Rise of the Trading State* (New York, 1985); Office of Joint Economic Affairs, U.S. AID—Vietnam, *Annual Statistical Bulletin No. 10, Data Through 1966* (published in Saigon by U.S. AID), 9 (quotation), copy in the economic periodicals of the Pike Collection, VCUCB. AID published "Vietnam in Brief: General Information for Businessmen" in Feb. 1971. A copy is in AIDL, RV.

35. State cable from Secretary Rusk to Ambassador Lodge, AES, May 20, 1964, NSFV, box 4, Vietnam Cables, vol. 9, LBJL.

36. Cable from Ambassador Lodge, in Saigon, to Secretary of State Rusk, May 27, 1964, 1, NSFV, box 5, Vietnam Cables, vol. 10, LBJL.

37. *Ibid.*, 1–2 (sec. 1 of six-page cable).

38. *Ibid.*, 3 (sec. 1 of six-page cable).

39. Callison, *Land-to-the-Tiller in the Mekong Delta*, 223–25; Kolko, *Anatomy of a War*, 242–43 (quotation). Callison argues that the NLF tried to convince the peasants via propaganda campaigns that the only reason Ngo Dinh Diem and the later regimes made any land reform effort was that the NLF had done it first, thus forcing Saigon's hand.

40. J. C. Anderson, "National Rural Electric Cooperative Association: Vietnam Rural Electrification, Phase I and Phase II," July, 1965, U.S. AID Report, copy in AIDL, RV.

41. Rusk, *The Winds of Freedom*, 107–26, 235–55. American internationalists found it difficult, as the 1960's progressed, to control Western European and Japanese trade with the Soviets. They continued to try to do so, however, using the Coordinating Committee (CoCom) they had established in 1949 as a mechanism to embargo strategic items.

42. Willard L. Thorp, "Land and the Future," in the State Department publication *Land Reform: A World Challenge* (Washington, D.C., 1952), 54–66. The call for land reform did not fade with the Vietnam War; see William H. Bolin, "Central America: Real Economic Help Is Workable Now," *Foreign Affairs*, 62 (Summer 1984), 1096–1106. In this article Bolin modifed a "low" Tory position by suggesting measures that could, "over time, reduce concentration of property ownership" (1104).

43. Dean Acheson, "World Land Tenure Problems," in *Land Reform: A World Challenge*, 52–53.

44. Examples are available in the form of published AID Discussion Papers. See Dale W. Adams, "The Economics of Land Reform in Latin America and the Role of AID Agencies," Paper no. 21 (Washington, D.C.: Office of Programs and Policy Coordination, AID, State Department, Aug. 1969), 1–31; Charles P. Kindleberger, "AID Discussion Paper #14: Liberal Politics versus Controls in the Foreign Trade of Developing Countries," published by AID's Office of Program Coordination, Apr. 1967. Copies in AIDL, RV.

45. Office of Joint Economic Affairs, U.S. AID—Vietnam, *Annual Statistical Bulletin No. 10, Data Through 1966*, 13.

46. *Ibid.*, 13–14.

47. Mitchell, *Land Tenure and Rebellion*, RAND Memo 5181-ARPA (Santa Monica, Calif., 1967), 31. So controversial a piece soon reappeared in summary form in *Asian Survey*, 7 (Aug. 1967), 1577–80, then in the *New York Times* (Oct. 16, 1967), and then as "Inequality and Insurgency: A Statistical Study of South Vietnam," *World Politics*, 20 (Apr. 1968), 421–38. Mitchell's study is what Christopher H. Achen would call a "quasi-experiment." See Achen's *The Statistical Analysis of Quasi-Experiments* (Berkeley, Calif., 1986), 1–15.

48. Tilly, "Does Modernization Breed Revolution," 453–66; C. Johnson, *Revolutionary Change*, 169–94. Johnson is incorrect, however, when he states (65) that "no noticeable progress" led to the Vietnamese communist revolution of the 1970's. Progress there was, even if only of a material nature. Otherwise Johnson's arguments appear to fit the Vietnam case. For an even larger overview than Johnson's, see Andrew Janos, *Politics and Paradigms: The Changing Themes of Change in Social Science* (Stanford, Calif., 1986). In a more controversial work, Tilly attacks the "huge comparisons" of the social scientists. See Charles Tilly, *Big Structures, Large Processes, Huge Comparisons* (New York, 1984).

49. Mitchell, *Land Tenure and Rebellion*, 22–24; Alexis de Tocqueville, *L'Ancien Regime* (Oxford, 1947), 185. Sansom, in *The Economics of Insurgency in the Mekong Delta of Vietnam*, 232–33 n. 8, argues that the English and French revolutions are not similar to the Vietnamese case and suggests that modern Asian or the Mexican revolutions compare more closely. Hung-Chao Tai, in *Land Reform and Politics: A Comparative Analysis* (Berkeley, Calif., 1974), 430, compares the Vietnamese revolution to the modern Mexican and Asian revolutions, yet he comes to Mitchell's conclusion. Tai also finds "a working of the Tocqueville hypothesis." Also see Gerschenkron, "Reflections on Economic Aspects of Revolutions," 180–204. Regarding the French Revolution, Lynn Hunt, in *Politics, Culture and Class in the French Revolution* (Berkeley, Calif., 1984), 123–48, describes "five Frances" (147) in which some rising groups joined the revolution and some did not, and some declining groups joined the revolution and others did not. For her analysis, literacy, religiosity, and urbanity are added to tax, terror, and emigration rates to indicate the swings in the five regions (139). Hunt works mainly with the period 1792–98 (131), the decade in which winners and losers were trying to adjust to the results of

1789. Regarding these adjusters Hunt finds that "the rhetoric of revolution appealed to the peripheries of the nation, to people who lived in the economic, social, and cultural backwaters" (148). One group that was against the revolution was the Paris barristers; see Michael P. Fitzsimmons, *The Parisian Order of Barristers and the French Revolution* (Cambridge, Mass., 1987).

50. Office of Joint Economic Affairs, U.S. AID—Vietnam, *Annual Statistical Bulletin No. 10, Data Through 1966*, 132; Thomas O. Stephens and William J. C. Logan, *Vietnam Poultry Production Plan* (Washington, D.C., Oct. 1968), copy in AIDL, RV.

51. Office of Joint Economic Affairs, U.S. AID—Vietnam, *Annual Statistical Bulletin No. 10, Data Through 1966*, 16, 95.

52. Russell Betts and Frank Denton, *An Evaluation of Chemical Destruction in Vietnam*, RAND Memo 5446-15A (Santa Monica, Calif., 1967), 21–22, 33.

53. U.S. Department of the Air Force, *Herbicide Operations in Southeast Asia: July 1961–June 1967* (CHECO SEA Report), Oct. 11, (Washington, D.C., 1967), 54–55; memo from Dean Rusk to President Kennedy, Nov. 24, 1962, NSFV, box 195; memo from Robert McNamara to President Kennedy, Nov. 16, 1962, NSFV, box 197, JFKL.

54. Schell, *The Village of Ben Suc*, and his *The Military Half* (both previously published in *The New Yorker*); Westmoreland, *A Soldier Reports*, 153 (his views on Schell's work). For the military details of this large-scale operation at Ben Suc in the Iron Triangle area west of Saigon, see Lieutenant General Rogers, *Cedar Falls J.C.* Also see CINCPAC and Commander of the U.S. Military Assistance Command Vietnam, *Report on the War in Vietnam* (Washington, D.C., 1968), 148.

55. *The Pentagon Papers*, Senator Gravel Ed. (Boston, 1971), 4: 440–41, 507–8.

56. U.S. Department of the Army, Office of the Deputy Chief of Staff for Military Operations, *A Program for the Pacification and Long Term Development of South Vietnam (PROVN)*, Mar. 1, 1966, 100, Center for Military History, Washington, D.C.

57. Jerry M. Tinker, *The Refugee Situation in Dinh Tuong Province* (McLean, Va., 1968), 14; A. Terry Rambo, *The Causes of Refugee Movement in Vietnam: Report of a Survey of Refugees in I and IV Corps* (McLean, Va., 1968), 7.

58. Quoted in U.S. Department of the Air Force, *Herbicide Operations in Southeast Asia*, 55–56. At the time, a debate commenced between scholars like T. G. McGee and Samuel P. Huntington over whether the increased number of urban dwellers worked for or against the defeat of the Leninists. See McGee's "Beachheads and Enclaves," 60–75. What is often overlooked is the fact that Saigon, like other great cities of Southeast Asia, attracted huge numbers of nearby rural people, with or without a war motive for resettlement.

59. Office of Joint Economic Affairs, U.S. AID—Vietnam, *Annual Statistical Bulletin No. 10, Data Through 1966*, 108.

60. Race, *War Comes to Long An*, 124. For an interpretation using old police records see George Rudé, *The Crowd in the French Revolution* (Oxford, 1959).

61. Quoted in Race, *War Comes to Long An*, 125.

62. When comparing these Viet Cong peasant categories with Chinese Communist categories the similarities are striking. See William Hinton, *Fanshen* (New York, 1966), Appendix C.

63. Le Van Chan, quoted in Race, *War Comes to Long An,* 130.

64. James A. Brown *et al., Viet Cong Taxation,* AID Contract no. VN-46, IDA (Washington, D.C., 1969), copy in AIDL, RV; Le Van Chan, quoted in Race, *War Comes to Long An,* 129.

65. One of the most readable histories of RAND is contained in Kaplan's *The Wizards of Armageddon,* 51–124.

66. Price Gittenger, "Agrarian Reform," in Richard W. Lendholm, ed., *Viet-Nam: The First Five Years* (East Lansing, Mich., 1959), 200.

67. Bredo *et al., Land Reform in Vietnam,* 13–15; Cooper *et al., The American Experience with Pacification in Vietnam,* vol. 2, *Elements of Pacification,* 253–55; Hickey, *Village in Vietnam,* 44.

68. Cooper *et al., The American Experience with Pacification in Vietnam,* 2: 255.

69. Bredo *et al., Land Reform in Vietnam,* 8.

70. Cooper *et al., The American Experience with Pacification in Vietnam,* 2: 256–57.

71. William Bredo *et al.,* "Agrarian Reform in Vietnam: Viet Cong and Government of Vietnam Strategies in Conflict," *Asian Survey,* 10 (Aug. 1970), 738–50.

72. Sansom, *The Economics of Insurgency in the Mekong Delta of Vietnam,* 228–41; Charles Wolf, Jr., "Insurgency and Counterinsurgency: New Myths and Old Realities," *Yale Review,* 56 (Winter 1967), 225–41. Sansom records the essentials of a conversation he had in Saigon with Ambassador Lodge and journalist Joseph Alsop in which the influence of Mitchell and other revisionists was obvious.

73. David Halberstam, "Voices of the Viet Cong," *Harper's,* Jan. 1968, 47; Jeffrey Race, "The Battle over Land," *Far Eastern Economic Review,* Aug. 20, 1970, 19; Roy L. Prosterman, "Land-to-the-Tiller in South Vietnam," *Asian Survey,* 10 (Aug. 1970), 759, and his "Land Reform in Vietnam," *Current History* (Dec. 1969), 30; Frances Starner, "Bowing to Revolution," *Far Eastern Economic Review,* 69 (July 2, 1970), 76; John D. Montgomery, "Land Reform in Vietnam," *Orbis,* 12 (Spring 1968), 23; MacDonald Salter, "Land Reform in South Vietnam," *Asian Survey,* 10 (Aug. 1970), 731.

74. Cooper *et al., The American Experience with Pacification in Vietnam,* 2: 258.

75. Robert Komer was an agile bureaucrat. When a policy like that of "forced refugees" lost official favor, he "got ahead of the pack" by switching sides before anyone could identify him with the losing cause. His imposing personality even shows in his publications; see his "Clear, Hold and Rebuild," *Army,* 20 (May 1970), 20–21, and his RAND book *Bureaucracy Does Its Thing.*

76. Cooper *et al., The American Experience with Pacification in Vietnam,* vol. 3, *The History of Pacification,* 281.

77. "Terminal Project Appraisal Report for Land Reform in Vietnam," AID report (Washington, D.C., 1975); Roy Prosterman and Jeffrey Riedinger, "Land Reform Can Be the Marxist's Worst Enemy," *Wall Street Journal*, Oct. 27, 1983, 26.

78. *Agricultural Statistics Yearbook* (Nien Giam Thong Ke Nong Nghiep, Saigon, Ministry of Agriculture, 1970), 33, Pike Collection, VCUCB. Also see Callison, *Land-to-the-Tiller in the Mekong Delta*, 327–29.

79. Callison, *Land-to-the-Tiller in the Mekong Delta*, 81.

80. *Ibid.*, 21–34.

81. *Ibid.*, 112; Hickey, *Village in Vietnam*, 27.

82. Office of Joint Economic Affairs, U.S. Aid—Vietnam, *Annual Statistical Bulletin No. 10, Data Through 1966*, 14.

83. Sansom, *The Economics of Insurgency in the Mekong Delta of Vietnam*, 166–68, 176–79.

84. *Ibid.*, 1975.

85. Callison, *Land-to-the-Tiller in the Mekong Delta*, 113.

86. Office of Joint Economic Affairs, U.S. AID—Vietnam, *Annual Statistical Bulletin No. 10, Data Through 1966*, 177; Tetsuo Sakiya, *Honda Motor: The Man, the Management, the Machines* (Tokyo, 1982), 139. The important thing here is the mobility that cheap motorized transport grants to traditional people in everyday life—mobility both physical and mental.

87. Booz-Allen Applied Research, Inc., "Highway Management Study," vols. 1–3 and Final Report, Sept. 1972, AID Contract no. VN-93; Boris Grunchick, General Motors Corporation Electro-Motive Div., "Final Report: MU45 Interim Diesel Project," 1972, both in AIDL, RV.

88. *Vietnam Statistical Yearbook*, (National Institute of Statistics, Nien-gian Thong-ke, Saigon), vols. 17 (1971) and 18 (1972), AIDL, RV.

89. Race, *War Comes to Long An*, 140, 212, 176.

90. Cooper *et al.*, *The American Experience with Pacification in Vietnam*, 3: 301. Cooper used the controversial Hamlet Evaluation System (HES 70). His team knew it posed serious data problems; see 322–25. Its first version received heavy attacks from researchers like Race, *War Comes to Long An*, 223. Yet even if one discounts the high figures, a researcher is impressed by a marked change in support.

91. Lt. General Ngo Quong Truong, *The Easter Offensive of 1972*, 155, and Col. William E. Le Gro, *Vietnam from Cease-Fire to Capitulation*, 15.

92. Christopher H. Achen, *Interpreting and Using Regression* (Beverly Hills, Calif., 1982); Michael Arnsten and Nathan Leites, *Land Reform and the Quality of Propaganda in Rural Vietnam: Memorandum RM-5764-ARPA* (Santa Monica, Calif., Apr. 1970), 54–65 (quotation on p. 64). The RAND reports represent the critical American thinking on South Vietnam's land reform since the Defense Department contracted for most of these scholarly studies and made available to RAND colleagues classified information not available to others. That these reports had a policy impact is indicated by what happened to RAND Memo RM-4140-PR. On August 17, 1964, having read the memo, General Curtis LeMay, Air Force Chief of Staff, sent a copy with his cover

letter to General Wheeler, Chairman of the Joint Chiefs of Staff. Mr. R. C. Bowman sent a copy to William Bundy to keep him abreast of their military colleagues. Two weeks later another RAND report surfaced in a White House debate between Secretary Rusk, President Johnson, Secretary McNamara, CIA Director McCone, Ambassador Taylor, and others. See memo from General Curtis LeMay to the Chairman of the Joint Chiefs of Staff, Aug. 17, 1964; memo from R. C. Bowman to William Bundy, Sept. 4, 1964; White House memo for the record, Sept. 14, 1964, NSFV, box 8, Vietnam Memos, vol. 17, all in LBJL.

93. At one time it was a matter of serious debate whether the Viet Cong / NLF used terror as a political tool. One side said yes; the other said no, denying that the deaths were anything more than people's justice. The evidence now supports those who held to the affirmative. See the Viet Cong Terrorism File, Pike Collection, VCUCB.

94. William A. Nighswonger, *Rural Pacification in Vietnam* (New York, 1966), 174–75, 185; Hickey, *Village in Vietnam*, 54. In Hickey's study of Khanh Hau he reports that the Viet Cong demanded food from the peasants and kidnapped their village chief, charging him with collaborating with Saigon and Washington appointed officials.

95. This imaginary peasant can be replaced by the peasants whose crops faced the following fate:

"Authority to conduct chemical crop destruction operations, on same basis already approved for Zone D and twelve other zones earlier (Deptel 1357) is granted for New Areas No. 13, 14, 15, and 16, described reftel.

"Comparison of extension of Area No. 5 with MACV map overlay of GVN-controlled areas, dated May 1964, however, shows large part of new area as under GVN control. Before authorization extended to this area, request you reconcile your request with this information.

"Comparison of new areas for crop destruction with Populous Zones Map prepared by GVN and furnished Washington after March Sec Def visit indicates several these areas lie within identified populous zones. Also other discrepancies apparent this map such as northern half of Tay Ninh identified as populous zone. Would appreciate a refined and more accurate Populous Zones Map which indicates where people are on the ground. RUSK"

Apparently, Saigon and Washington leaders wanted to deny the crops in these areas to the Viet Cong. The message required White House clearance before dispatch; both Mike Forrestal and McGeorge Bundy, at a minimum, saw it before its approval. See State cable from Rusk to AES, July 1, 1964 (quotation above), and Memo from Mike Forrestal to McGeorge Bundy, June 30, 1964, both in NSFV, box 6, Vietnam Cables, vol. 13, LBJL. For Viet Cong / NVA use of peasant villages as shields see Military Assistance Command Civil Operations and Revolutionary Development Support (MACCORDS), "A Study of Pacification and Security in Cu Chi District, Hau Nghia Province," May 29, 1968, The Center of Military History, Washington, D.C.

96. Office of Joint Economic Affairs, U.S. AID—Vietnam, *Annual Statistical Bulletin No. 10, Data Through 1966*, 148–50, 153; letter from Mr. Johnstone,

Jr., of Day and Zimmerman, Inc., to Mr. Leland Barrows, USOM, Saigon, Jan. 30, 1958, copy in AIDL, RV.

97. Captured Viet Cong document no. 23, "Programme and Regulations of the Liberation Worker Association," Oct. 1961, and interrogation report of two Viet Cong—Tran Minh Trung and Le Van Triue—on "Organization and Activities of the Workers' Proselyting Section," Apr. 26, 1967, both in NLF, Org. 2, Pike Collection, VCUCB; AFL-CIO letter from Irving Brown to McGeorge Bundy, May 13, 1964; memo from Clifford L. Alexander to McGeorge Bundy, May 18, 1964; memo from Clifford L. Alexander to President Johnson, May 19, 1964, all in NSFV, box 4, Vietnam Memos, vol. 9, LBJL.

98. Pye, *Politics, Personality and Nation Building*, 15–31, 52–53, 288; Clifford Geertz, "The Judging of Nations: Some Comments on the Assessment of Regimes in the New States," *European Journal of Sociology*, 17 (June 1977), 249–53. Also see Jean-Pierre Lehmann, "Dictatorship and Development in Pacific Asia: Wider Implications," *International Affairs*, 61 (Autumn 1985), 591–606.

99. Sidney Hook, *The Hero in History* (New York, 1943); Allan Nevins, "Is History Made by Heroes?" *Saturday Review*, Nov. 5, 1955, 9–10, 42–45; Frederic Wakeman, Jr., *History and Will* (Berkeley, Calif., 1973), 321. Hook does not maintain that heroes make history, only that they can influence the channels in which it flows.

100. Nguyen Manh Tuong, quoted in Senate Committee on the Judiciary, *The Human Cost of Communism in Vietnam*, 92d Cong., 2d sess., 1972, 26–29; Fall, *The Two Viet-Nams*, 156; Hoang Van Chi, *From Colonialism to Communism* (New York, 1964), 225. Nguyen Manh Tuong's speech caused a minor sensation. A copy arrived in Washington via Rangoon and Saigon. In Saigon the leadership had the speech republished in the city press, using it in their war to capture and hold the urban centers. There is no evidence of its distribution to the peasants in large number.

101. D. Gareth Porter, *The Myth of the Bloodbath* (Ithaca, N.Y., 1972); Robert F. Turner, "Expert Punctures 'No Bloodbath' Myth," *Human Events*, Nov. 11, 1972; Moise, *Land Reform in China and North Vietnam*, 216–22.

102. House Committee on Government Operations, *An Investigation of the U.S. Economic and Military Assistance Programs in Vietnam*, 36.

103. One scholar estimates that Ho Chi Minh had to dominate about $330 million in aid from the USSR, the same amount from the People's Republic of China, and $100 million from Eastern Europe. With 2,000 Chinese technicians on duty, the PRC built for Ho Chi Minh twenty-eight sugar-processing plants, fourteen polishing mills, and several consumer goods factories, in addition to rebuilding the Hanoi water works, the postal-telephone-telegraph system, and the rail system. The Soviets kept 300 technicians in the country supplying Hanoi's Lenin with forty-three industrial plants. Both these USSR and PRC contributions occurred between 1955–60, increasing thereafter, shifting as Ho Chi Minh's demands shifted. See Douglas Pike, *History of Vietnamese Communism* (Stanford, Calif., 1978), 106–7, 130–32.

104. Vu Van Thai, "Vietnam's Concept of Development," in Fishel, *Prob-*

lems of Freedom, 69–73; Vu Quoc Thuc, "National Planning in Vietnam," *Asian Survey*, 1 (Sept. 1961), 3–9. Vu Van Thai had an international career that included a consultantship with RAND, where they published his *Fighting and Negotiating in Vietnam: A Strategy*, RAND Memo 5997-ARPA (Santa Monica, Calif., Oct. 1969). He was Saigon's Ambassador to the United States from 1965 to 1967, then he was on the United Nations staff, dealing with economic development. From 1950 to 1954, he was a noncommunist member of the Viet Minh and attended the Geneva negotiations of 1954. He joined the Diem government and served as Director General of Budget and Foreign Aid until he resigned in 1961.

105. Tran Ngoc Lien, "The Growth of Agricultural Credit and Cooperation in Vietnam," in Fishel, *Problems of Freedom*, 177–89. A prediction "in the direction of state socialism" was made for the entire area in 1949 by Cora Du Bois in her *Social Forces in Southeast Asia*, 62.

106. AES cable from Lodge to State, Mar. 26, 1964, NSFV, box 3, Vietnam Memos, vol. 6, LBJL (quotation); White House memo for the record, Subject: Meeting on South Vietnam, Sept. 9, 1964, Cabinet Room, Sept. 14, 1964, NSFV, box 8, Vietnam Memos, vol. 17, LBJL.

107. CIA intelligence information cable, Sept. 1, 1964, plus White House note, handwritten and undated, to Mr. Bundy, NSFV, box 8, Vietnam Cables, vol. 18, LBJL.

108. Maxwell Taylor, "Chronology of Events While Ambassador to the Republic of Vietnam, July 1964–July 1965, (MDT)," 7, in Maxwell Taylor's Papers, box 52, folder E, Library of the National Defense University, National War College, Ft. McNair, Washington, D.C.

109. *Ibid*; Stanley Karnow, *Vietnam*, 382–83.

110. Taylor, "Chronology of Events While Ambassador to the Republic of Vietnam, July 1964–July 1965"; Taylor's cable to State (Embtel 1916) and his memorandum of conversation, both dated Dec. 21, 1964, in his diary, Library of the National Defense Unviersity, National War College, Ft. McNair, Washington, D.C. Also see Taylor, *Swords and Plowshares*, 330–31.

Chapter 9

1. White House memo for the record, Sept. 14, 1964, 4, NSFV, box 8, Vietnam Memos, vol. 17, LBJL.

2. *Ibid*.

3. William A. Nighswonger, *Rural Pacification in Vietnam* (New York, 1966), 199–212. Nighswonger, an AID provincial representative in 1962–64, relates what he experienced of the USOM Saigon struggle. See Chester L. Cooper *et al.*, *The American Experience with Pacification in Vietnam*, vol. 3, *The History of Pacification*, 219, for their views of Killen's reforms. For a view of what George Tanham wanted reformed, see his RAND letter to Walt W. Rostow, Sept. 21, 1961, NSFV, box 194, JFKL.

4. White House memo for the record, Sept. 14, 1964, 5, NSFV, box 8, Vietnam Memos, vol. 17, LBJL. See James Reston, "Implications of Greek Aid Worry Truman Advisers," clipping from the *New York Times*, Mar. 12, 1947, in

Foreign Aid UNRA folder, Elsey Files, HSTL, for an early warning on the implications of the 1947 Greek aid model. Also see Irma Adelman and Hollis B. Chenery, "Foreign Aid and Economic Development: The Case of Greece," *The Review of Economics and Statistics*, 48 (Feb. 1966), 1–19.

5. Draft White House cable from President Johnson to Ambassador Taylor, Apr. 27, 1964, NSFV, box 3, Vietnam Memos, vol. 7, LBJL.

6. Memo from Senator Mike Mansfield to President Kennedy, "Observations on Vietnam," Aug. 19, 1963; letter from Mike Mansfield to President Johnson, Dec. 7, 1963; memo from Robert McNamara to President Johnson, Jan. 7, 1964, all in NSFV, box 1, Vietnam Memos, vol. 2, LBJL.

7. "Oral History of C. Douglas Dillon," taken by Paige Mulhollan, June 29, 1969, 9–11, LBJL.

8. "Oral History of Henry H. Fowler" taken by David McComb, July 31, 1969 (tape no. 5), 1, 5, LBJL.

9. Senate Committee on Foreign Relations, *Impact of the War in Southeast Asia on the U.S. Economy*, 91st Cong., 2d sess., Apr. 15–16, 1970, Hearings, 108; Berman, *Planning A Tragedy*, 147–50.

10. Keohane and Nye, *Power and Interdependence*, 37, 64. See also Robert Keohane, "The Theory of Hegemonic Stability and Changes in International Economic Regimes, 1967–1977," in Ole Holsti *et al.*, eds., *Change in the International System* (Boulder, Colo., 1980), 131–62; David A. Lake, "International Economic Structures and American Foreign Economic Policy, 1887–1934," *World Politics*, 35 (June 1973), 517–43; Charles P. Kindleberger, *The World in Depression, 1929–1939* (Berkeley, Calif., 1973) and his "Dominance and Leadership in the International Economy," *International Studies Quarterly*, 25 (June 1981), 242–54.

11. Stanley Hoffmann, *Gulliver's Troubles or the Setting of American Foreign Policy* (New York, 1968). Hoffman stresses domestic constraints.

12. Keohane and Nye, *Power and Interdependence*, 9, 38. Keohane and Nye do allude to the Vietnam war and its impact on the highly complex U.S. economy (see 18, 29), but it is not one of their case studies. Not every scholar is impressed by the arguments for complex interdependence as a theory. For an opposing view see Kenneth N. Waltz, "The Myth of National Interdependence," in Charles P. Kindleberger, ed., *The International Corporation* (Cambridge, Mass., 1970). Even a convert such as Ernst Haas does not claim that complex interdependence limits international violence. In fact he suggests that in the decades since 1870 the number of wars rose from nine (1875–85) to twenty-six (1976–84). See his "War, Interdependence, and Functionalism," ed. Raimo Vayrynen, *The Quest for Peace* (Beverly Hills, Calif., 1987), 108–26. Also see Hoffmann, *Janus and Minerva*, 57–58.

13. "Oral History of C. Douglas Dillon," 7, 14. For an earlier study of the role of gold in twentieth century international trade and finance see Marcello DeCecco, *Money and Empire* (Totowa, N.J., 1975), and Robert Triffin, *Gold and the Dollar Crisis* (New Haven, Conn., 1960).

14. "Oral History of Henry H. Fowler" (tape no. 3), 20.

15. *Ibid*; Margaret Garritsen de Vries, *The International Monetary Fund, 1966–1971: The System Under Stress*, vols. 1 and 2 (Washington, D.C., 1982).

16. "Oral History of Henry H. Fowler" (tape no. 3), 19.

17. *Ibid.*, 23, 25.

18. *Ibid.*, 25–27.

19. Congressman Henry Reuss was a member of the 84th to the 97th Congresses. In those years he helped write U.S. economic policy, both foreign and domestic.

20. "Oral History of Henry H. Fowler" (tape no. 3), 22–25, 30, 33, and (tape no. 4), 1. Fowler continued to play an active part in advising internationalists even after he left office. See his "America's Role in a Global Economy," *Atlantic Quarterly*, 23 (Spring 1985), 37–43. See also Calleo, *The Imperious Economy*, 21, 26, 35–36, 46, 56, 62, 67–68, 88, 91, 172.

21. Exact figures for troop strengths in each year remain a problem today, because in the 1960's they were derived from fragmentary evidence—captured documents, intercepted transmissions, POW interrogations, etc. And each camp of hawks and doves had their own figures. The figures used here are those the internationalists employed and generally tended to believe. For the Viet Cong figure of 16,000 in 1961, see CIA memo, Oct. 5, 1961, NSFV, box 192, vol. 1, 3, JFKL. For the 28,000 figure see U.S. Department of State, "Working Paper on the North Vietnamese Role in the War in South Vietnam," republished in R. Falk, *The Vietnam War and International Law*, 2: 1183–1204. For the 1964, 1965, 1966, and 1967 figures of 12,400, 37,100, 92,287, and 101,263 see *Southeast Asia Statistical Summary, Office of Secretary of Defense (Comptroller)*, Jan. 18, 1972, table 5, NLF Org. Box, Pike Collection, VCUCB. Owing to the notoriety of the Westmoreland law suit against CBS in 1985, there is some confusion about "who said how many to whom." See Renata Adler, *Reckless Disregard* (New York, 1988) for Westmoreland v. CBS *et al.* In the critical year 1964 all the "whos" seemed to have told all the "whoms" an accurate story. In fact, when Khanh tried to fabricate certain North Vietnamese units in the South, Taylor alerted everyone to Khanh's political manipulations; see AES cable from Taylor to State, July 14, 1964, NSFV, box 6, Vietnam Cables, vol. 13, LBJL. Taylor sent another cable the next day containing a detailed VC Order of Battle from MACV for between 28,000 and 34,000 VC military; see AES cable from Taylor to State, July 15, 1964, NSFV, box 6, Vietnam Cables, vol. 13, LBJL.

22. I obtained the figure of $72,800 by following a suggestion of Gregory Grossman, professor of economics at the University of California, Berkeley. In U.S. Bureau of the Census, *Historical Statistics of the U.S.: Colonial Times to 1970* (Washington, D.C., 1975) series E1-22, there is an implicit price deflation for the GNP for each year. In 1947 it was 74.6, in 1958 100.0, and in 1964 108.8. Lewy, *America in Vietnam*, 453.

23. For the other figures, I consulted House Committee on Government Operations, *U.S. Assistance Programs in Vietnam*, 92d Cong., 2d sess., 1972, H. Rept. 92-1610, 4.

24. *Ibid.*, 5. Also see Bueno de Mesquita, *The War Trap*, 42, 44. Several social scientists have attempted to find better measures of power and apply them to the struggle between the United States and the USSR from 1945 to 1986. Usually they agree that in 1961–68 the United States had the advantage.

See Frank C. Zagare, *The Dynamics of Deterrence* (Chicago, 1987), 146, and Organski and Kugler, *The War Ledger*.

25. AES cable to State, subject: GVN (Saigon) Budget, May 16, 1964, NSFV, box 4, Vietnam Cables, vol. 9, LBJL; AES cable to State, May 23, 1964, NSFV, box 4, Vietnam Cables, vol. 9, LBJL. Also see Walt W. Rostow, *The Diffusion of Power*, 475, and Charles Robequain, *The Economic Development of French Indo-China*, 137–49.

26. AES cable from Taylor to State, for Rusk, info London embassy, July 23, 1964, NSFV, box 6, Vietnam Cables, vol. 14, LBJL. Oanh, an unreconstructed capitalist, survived the fall of Saigon without leaving the country. By 1987, unrepentant yet resurrected, he had a seat in the National Assembly as a noncommunist, and, with some pre-1975 "capitalist cronies," he established a series of commercial banks. See Keith B. Richburg, "Back to Business in Vietnam: The Capitalist Revival in the South is Creeping Northward," *Washington Post*, National Weekly Ed., Aug. 10, 1987, 6–8.

27. Joint State-Defense-CIA cable to AES, Mar. 30, 1964, NSFV, box 3, Vietnam Memos, vol. 6, LBJL.

28. Memo from David E. Bell to McGeorge Bundy, July 15, 1964, NSFV, box 6, Vietnam Memos, vol. 13, LBJL.

29. Joint States-AID cable to AES, July 25, 1964, NSFV, box 6, Vietnam Cables, vol. 14, 1, LBJL.

30. *Ibid.*, 2.

31. L. B. Johnson, *The Vantage Point*, 133–34.

32. *Public Papers of the Presidents of the United States: Lyndon B. Johnson, 1966* (Washington, D.C., 1967), 1: 133; Krasner, *Structural Conflict*, 157.

33. *Public Papers of the Presidents, LBJ, 1966*, 1: 133.

34. *Ibid.*, 2: 328, 348, 459, 557.

35. House Committee on Foreign Affairs, Subcommittee on National Security Policy and Scientific Developments, *The Mekong Project: Opportunities and Problems of Regionalism* (Washington, D.C., May 1972), 59–60.

36. See Hirschman, *The Passions and the Interests*.

37. Hirchsman, *Development Projects Observed*, 21; *The Journals of David E. Lilienthal*, vol. 5. *The Harvest Years—1959 to 1963* (New York, 1971), 162–63.

38. *The Speeches of Senator John F. Kennedy*, 301.

39. *Ibid.*, 310, 335, 338, 342, 381, 525, 545, 586. An African river also attracted JFK; see Thomas J. Noer, "The New Frontier and African Neutralism: Kennedy, Nkrumah, and the Volta River Project," *Diplomatic History*, 8 (Winter 1984), 61–79.

40. Hirschman, *Development Projects Observed*, 21–22.

41. McNamara, *The Essence of Security*, 22; William Clari, "Robert McNamara at the World Bank," *Foreign Affairs*, 60 (Fall 1981), 167–84.

42. In *The Vantage Point*, 20, Lyndon Johnson describes what he saw in McNamara's character: "Brilliant, intensely energetic, publicly tough . . . [he] carried more information around in his head than the average encyclopedia." Later Johnson states that McNamara "told me the World Bank presidency was the one job that deeply interested him so when the time arrived I called in

Secretary of the Treasury Henry Fowler and instructed him to tell the Bank members that our nominee is Bob McNamara." Robert McNamara's talents are best indicated by the man himself. See his article "Time Bomb or Myth: The Population Problem," *Foreign Affairs*, 62 (Summer 1984), 1107–31.

43. See Westmoreland, *A Soldier Reports*, 160–61 for McNamara's tasking in "percentage goals." When JFK, via his brother-in-law, offered the Treasury job to McNamara, he declined it, taking Defense instead.

44. Carl von Clausewitz, *On War*, ed. Michael Howard and Peter Paret (Princeton, N.J., 1976), 119–20, 149; Summers, *On Strategy*. For a critique of Summers's interesting thesis see Russell F. Weigley, "Reflections on 'Lessons' from Vietnam," and Ernest R. May, "Commentary: The Paradox of Vietnam," both in Peter Braestrup, ed., *Vietnam as History: Ten Years After the Paris Peace Accords* (Washington, D.C., 1984), 115–24 (Weigley) and 125–28 (May). An attack on Summers also appears in John M. Gates, "Vietnam: The Debate Goes On," *Strategic Review*, 14 (Spring 1984), 15–25.

45. McNamara, quoted in Charles Mohr, "McNamara on Record, Reluctantly, on Vietnam," *New York Times*, May 16, 1984, A24; McNamara, quoted in Paul Hendrickson, "McNamara" (three-part article), *Washington Post*, May 8, 9, 10, 1984, C1, B1, B1.

46. Westmoreland, *A Soldier Reports*, 153.

47. Memo from Robert McNamara to President Johnson, Dec. 11, 1963, NSFV, box 1, Vietnam Memos, vol. 2, LBJL.

48. JCS cable no. 4893 to Westmoreland plus AES cable to State, Feb. 18, 1964, NSFV, box 5, Vietnam Cables, vol. 4, LBJL.

49. *Ibid.*

50. State cable from William Sullivan to AES, Apr. 10, 1964, NSFV, box 3, Vietnam Cables, vol. 7, LBJL. For an assessment of Sullivan see M. Taylor, *Swords and Plowshares*, 315–16. Also see Halberstam, *The Best and the Brightest*, 115, 457.

51. AES cable to State, "Memo of Conversation at Vietnamese JGS Compound," June 29, 1964, NSFV, box 6, Vietnam Cables, vol. 13, LBJL.

52. MACV cable from William Westmoreland to JCS, June 25, 1965, NSFV, box 5, Vietnam Cables, vol. 12, LBJL.

53. Race, *War Comes to Long An*, 211; AES cable from Maxwell Taylor to State, July 15, 1964, NSFV, box 6, Vietnam Cables, vol. 13, LBJL. The overuse of firepower is what Edward N. Luttwak calls "the dumb-rich style of war"—often the U.S. style. See his *The Pentagon and the Art of War* (New York, 1985), 242.

54. "Oral History of William Westmoreland," taken by Dorothy P. McSweeney, Feb. 8, 1969,13, LBJL; Lyndon Johnson, quoted in Karnow, *Vietnam*, 395. Also see Robert Pisor, *The End of the Line: The Siege of Khe Sanh* (New York, 1982).

55. SECRET CIA letter to White House staff (Mr. Bromley Smith), signed Chester L. Cooper, Subject: Situation in Long An Province, May 15, 1964, NSFV, box 4, Vietnam Memos, vol. 9, LBJL. Enclosed with this letter is a seven-page CIA report on Long An dated May 8, 1964.

56. AES cable from Maxwell Taylor to State, 2, NSFV, box 6, Vietnam Cables, vol. 13, LBJL. Also see Colonel William F. Long, Jr., "Counterinsurgency Revisited," *Naval War College Review*, 21 (Nov. 1968), 4–10; Robert H. Bates, "People in Villages: Micro-level Studies in Political Economy," *World Politics*, 31 (October, 1978), 129–149; Kolko, *Anatomy of a War*, 243.

57. Johnson and Komer, both quoted in Miller, *Lyndon*, 466.

58. Joint State-AID-DOD message to AES, May 5, 1964, and AES cable to State, May 22, 1964, both in NSFV, box 4, Vietnam Cables, vol. 9, LBJL.

59. U.S. AID, *U.S. Overseas Loans and Grants: Obligations and Loan Authorization—July 1, 1945, to September 30, 1976* (Washington, D.C., 1977), 4–6, 82.

60. Nick Eberstadt, "The Perversion of Foreign Aid," *Commentary*, 79 (June 1985), 19–33.

61. Jerry Hough, *The Struggle for the Third World: Soviet Specialist Debates and Their Policy Implications* (Washington, D.C., 1985), and his "The Revolutionary Road Runs Out," *The Nation*, June 1, 1985, 666–68; John Kenneth Galbraith, "The Second Imperial Requiem," *International Security*, 7 (Winter 1983), 84–93. Soviet specialists besides Hough also noted this moderated view reemerging in the USSR in the late 1970's whenever they consulted the Soviet literature on the Third World. See Mark N. Katz, *The Third World in Soviet Military Thought* (Baltimore, Md., 1982); S. Neil MacFarland, *Superpower Rivalry and 3rd World Radicalism: The Idea of National Liberation* (London, 1985); Elizabeth K. Valkenier, *The Soviet Union and the Third World: An Economic Bind* (New York, 1983). Marshall D. Shulman, *Stalin's Foreign Policy Reappraised* (Boulder, Colo., 1985), 268–69, and Marshall D. Shulman, ed., *East-West Tensions in the Third World* (New York, 1986). Also see Melvin Croan, "Last Stages of Leninism," *Problems in Communism*, Jan.–Feb. 1986, 61–66.

62. *Spring Review* (Washington, D.C., 1970); P. T. Bauer, *Equality, the Third World, and Economic Delusion* (Cambridge: Harvard University Press, 1982), and his *Reality and Rhetoric*. *Spring Review* is a U.S. AID conference report on thirty countries in which the United States participated in local land reform projects.

63. Raymond Aron, interview with Jean-Louis Missika and Dominique Wolton, in *Raymond Aron: The Committed Observer or Le Spectateur Engagé* (Chicago, 1983), 238.

64. James Schlesinger, quoted in "Architects of the War in Vietnam Ponder Lessons of the U.S. Defeat," *Wall Street Journal*, Jan. 14, 1985, 8.

65. George F. Kennan et al., *Democracy and the Student Left* (Boston, 1968), 3–20; Gilpin, *War and Change in World Politics*, 319.

66. USIA memo from Edward R. Murrow to Dean Rusk, with copy for McGeorge Bundy at White House, Sept. 26, 1963; NSFV, box 200, JFKL.

Conclusion

1. Bill Warren, "The Postwar Economic Experience of the Third World," in Charles K. Wilber, ed., *The Political Economy of Development and Underdevelopment*, 3d ed. (New York, 1973), 109–33. Both Douglas Pike and Benjamin Ward argue, in their "Losing and Winning: Korea and Vietnam as Success

Stories," *Washington Quarterly*, 10 (Summer 1987), 77–85, that the United States achieved its strategic goals by its intervention in these two Asian wars.

2. George C. Herring and Richard H. Immerman, "Eisenhower, Dulles, and Dienbienphu: 'The Day We Didn't Go to War' Revisited," *Journal of American History*, 71 (Sept. 1984), 343–63. The two authors are less laudatory of Eisenhower than are the current revisionists; however, they do credit his caution (354).

3. Fred I. Greenstein, "Eisenhower as an Activist President," *Political Science Quarterly*, 94 (Winter 1979–80), 575–99; Richard D. Challenger, "The National Security Policy from Truman to Eisenhower: Did the 'Hidden Hand' Leadership Make Any Difference?" in Norman A. Graebner, ed., *The National Security* (Oxford, 1986), 39–75.

4. Fred Charles Iklé, *Every War Must End* (New York, 1971), 83.

5. Dwight D. Eisenhower, *The White House Years: Waging Peace* (New York, 1965), 62, 70, 79, 81–82, 86–87, 107–9, 626. Niebuhr once chastised the early Eisenhower as a libertarian with extreme Cold War views. See Reinhold Neibuhr and Paul E. Sigmund, *The Democratic Experience* (London, 1969), 8.

6. These same questions were posed by the titular head of Johnson's informal "Wise Men" council, former Secretary of State Dean Acheson. He concluded: "Our present domestic discontents and, hence, the domestic problems of government, stem from three sources—the Vietnam war, internal disorder, and the inflation caused by the expense of these troubles plus that of national defense." Acheson thought the rest of America's problems were "subsidiary." Acheson, *This Vast External Realm*, 160.

7. William L. Lunch and Peter W. Sperlich, "American Public Opinion and the War in Vietnam," *Western Political Science Quarterly*, no. 32 (Mar. 1979), 21–44; Gilpin, *War and Change in World Politics*, 227–28; Ole R. Holsti and James N. Rosenau, "Vietnam, Consensus, and the Belief System of American Leaders," *World Politics*, 32 (Oct. 1979), 1–56 (quotations on pp. 23, 45). Holsti and Rosenau discuss the war's destruction of the American consensus about national security policy. Lunch and Sperlich also indicate that Vietnam changed essential ways of doing national politics.

8. Bert A. Rockman, "America's Two Departments of State," in Francis E. Rourke, ed., *Bureaucratic Power in National Policy Making* (Boston, 1986), 335–60.

9. Allen S. Whiting, in the State Department's Office of Research and Analysis from 1962 to 1966, was hired as an expert on Asia. He "watched" China for the China "watchers." See his *The Chinese Calculus of Deterrence*, 181–82, 194–95. After the war Douglas Pike suggested that China never wanted North Vietnam to win anymore than it wanted the United States to win: "The Chinese would have preferred to deal with four separate Indochinese states, including two Vietnams, the southern one preferably left-leaning neutralist but in any case independent of the North"; Pike, *People's Army of Vietnam*, 52–54.

10. George, *The Chinese Communist Army in Action*, 226–27. See Ellis's argument about morale in his *Armies in Revolution*.

11. *The Pentagon Papers*, Senator Gravel Ed. (Boston, 1971), 4: 256.

12. Lyndon Johnson, quoted in Betts, *Soldiers, Statesmen and Cold War Crisis*, 10.

13. J. Thompson, *Rolling Thunder*, 35–82.

14. Lewy, *America in Vietnam*, 410–11; Guenter Lewy, "Some Political-Military Lessons of the Vietnam War," *Parameters*, 14 (Spring 1984), 2–14. In his article Lewy discounts most of the reasons given for defeat in South Vietnam, blaming instead the political and military leadership in Saigon. He is particularly harsh on ARVN. But ARVN held the South together for twenty years (1955–75), perhaps the only institution that, with all its faults, worked at a national level. What Lewy fails to do is to differentiate among several ARVN's—the ARVN of 1955, of 1960, 1965, 1970, and 1975. He also fails to do this for the German army of 1939–40, although he compares the German army to ARVN as an army that was somehow better in defeat than ARVN was. But the German army that defeated France and captured Paris in 1940 was not the same army that retreated to the Rhine in 1944–45. See Heinrich Böll, *A Soldier's Legacy* (New York, 1985).

15. Wilbur Cohen, quoted in M. Miller, *Lyndon*, 490–91.

16. K. Turner, *Lyndon Johnson's Dual War*, 182 (quotation). It is revealing to compare the 1967 Gallup poll to an earlier one. In 1945 a Gallup poll asked, "Do you feel you have a clear idea of what WWII is all about—that is, what we are fighting for?" The affirmative answer approached 80 percent. When the pollsters substituted "Vietnam war" for "WWII" in 1967, only 48 percent of those interviewed answered in the affirmative. See Mueller, *War, Presidents and Public Opinion,* 63.

17. Rostow, quoted in *The Pentagon Papers*, Senator Gravel Ed., 4: 470, 478. John McNaughton, along with Rostow, another advocate of collective security, prepared a similar report. Same source, 469.

18. Thorne, *Allies of a Kind*, 586–633; George Modelski, "Kautilya: Foreign Policy and International System in the Ancient Hindu World," *American Political Science Review*, 58 (Sept. 1964), 549–60. What I mean by "buffer space in Southeast Asia," is similar to what Luttwak means by "buffer" in his *The Grand Strategy of the Roman Empire*, 116. That work can be read at two levels—as a tale of Rome's defensive strategy and as an allegory of a defensive strategy for the United States.

19. Minh, *On Revolution*, 282.

20. "India, China and Viet-Nam," *Eastern Economist*, Nov. 16, 1951, 767; "The Week's Notes," *Eastern Economist*, Sept. 7, 1951, 375.

21. John Curtis Perry, "Asia's Telectronic Highway," *Foreign Policy*, no. 59 (Summer 1985), 40–58. Perry phrases the argument as an optimistic prediction that while North America and Asia "as yet lack the cultural ties that helped forge and then strengthen Atlantic partnerships, they are becoming a community that shares the same advanced technology." Perry envisions a Great Northern Crescent—an arc stretching from San Diego to Shanghai, roughly north of the 32d parallel, on which arc the center of initiative in Pacific affairs now lies. He believes that the "center of gravity of global affairs" will be in that region (41–42).

22. Mancur Olson, Jr., and Richard Zeckhauser, "An Economic Theory of Alliances," *Review of Economics and Statistics*, 58 (Aug. 1960), 266–79.

23. Jean-Jacques Rousseau, *On the Origin of Inequality*, The Great Books Series (Chicago, 1952), 349; David K. Lewis, *Convention* (Cambridge, Mass., 1969), 7, 47; Waltz, *Man, the State, and War*, 167–69; Russell Hardin, *Collective Action* (Baltimore, Md., 1982), 167–69. Also see Marina and Lawrence Finkelstein, eds., *Collective Security* (San Francisco, 1966).

24. Hardin, *Collective Action*, 86.

25. Sheldon W. Simon, "Vietnam: Regional Dominance Arising from the Failure of Great-Power Balances," in R. G. C. Thomas, ed., *The Great-Power Triangle and Asian Security* (Lexington, Mass., 1983), 83–85. Before the arrival of the Europeans, did a trading community exist in the Java Sea, Asia's Mediterranean? At that time was "market Malay" the lingua franca of Southeast Asian port cities, and did these critical cities link commercial elites clustered in entrepôts around the South China and Java Seas, via the region's Gibraltar, the Straits of Malacca, to the Gulf of Siam and the Bay of Bengal? Was this maritime, intraregional system that the Europeans finally destroyed a trade emporium that created the beginnings of a regional community? Some say yes. See Anthony Reid, *Southeast Asia in the Age of Commerce, 1450–1680:* Vol. I, *The Lands Below the Winds* (New Haven, Conn., 1988). Also see Clifford Geertz's review, "A South Sea Renaissance," in *The New York Review of Books*, Feb. 16, 1989, 28–29. This earlier community differed from its modern replacement (ASEAN) in that it traded mainly within the region while ASEAN trades mainly outside the region.

26. McNamara, *The Essence of Security*, 23.

27. Alison Broinowski, ed., *Understanding ASEAN* (New York, 1982), 39–40, 70–91, 201–3, 206–7; Jackson and Soesastro, *ASEAN Security and Economic Development*; H. Higgott and R. Robinson, eds., *Southeast Asia: Essays in the Political Economy of Structural Change* (Boston, 1985); Barnett, *China and the Major Powers in East Asia*, 294–301, 313–17. Also see Larry Diamond, Juan Linz, and Seymour Martin Lipset, *Democracy in Developing Countries: Asia*, vol. 3 (Boulder, Colo., 1989), and Guillermo O'Donnell, Philippe C. Schmitter, and Laurence Whitehead, *Transitions from Authoritarian Rule: Comparative Perspectives* (Baltimore, 1986).

28. Those who would stress the limited role of government—mainly to offer security via police and military—follow in the Anglo-American tradition of John Stuart Mill. But Mill's secured and autonomous beings do not attract praise from all circles. See Giovanni Sartori, *Democratic Theory* (Detroit, Mich., 1962), 298–314. Nevertheless, the principle that the minimum responsibility of any government is the physical security of its populace remained the argument of the U.S. military leaders. In that task, and that task only, they were prepared to assist Saigon.

29. Robert N. Bellah, *Beyond Belief: Essays on Religion in a Post-Traditional World* (New York, 1970), 64.

30. Richard Critchfield, "Science and the Villager: The Last Sleeper

Wakes," *Foreign Affairs*, 61 (Fall 1982), 14–41. Critchfield reiterates Bellah's claim that modernization is a moral and religious problem (23–28).

31. J. L. Talmon, *The Rise of Totalitarian Democracy* (Boston, 1952), 40–42; Jean-Jacques Rousseau, *The Social Contract*, The Great Book Series (Chicago, 1952), 393. It was the internationalists who expanded on Rousseau, willing to move his arguments from national to international politics. In so doing they moved from the moderate political philosophy of seventeenth-century England (Locke) to the more radical views of eighteenth-century France (Rousseau).

32. France Matthews, quoted in *Time*, Sept. 4, 1950, 12, and in Whiting, *China Crosses the Yalu* (Stanford, Calif., 1960), 96.

33. Acheson, *Present at the Creation*, 478.

34. William H. McNeill, *Past and Future* (Chicago, 1954), 72–73; Waltz, *Man, the State, and War*, 103–10; Halperin, *Bureaucratic Politics and Foreign Policy* (Washington, D.C., 1974), 11–12.

35. One could argue that this was not the first time in American experience that Whigs had split over a problem of moral choice. For example, in nineteenth-century America a major domestic quarrel over the question of eliminating the South's peculiar institution of slavery caused Cotton Whigs to break with their colleagues, the Conscience Whigs. The problems of nineteenth-century American Whigs also involved mixing moral choices with practical politics, in this case, national politics. See Charles Sellers, Henry May, and Neil R. McMillen, *A Synopsis of American History* (Chicago, 1963), i, 143, 149, 164, 172, 182. For a more detailed study see Charles Sellers, "Who Were the Southern Whigs?" *American Historical Review*, 59 (Jan. 1954), 335–46. For an example from the northern Whigs, see Ronald P. Formisano, *The Transformation of Political Culture* (Oxford, 1983), 268–301.

36. Richard Abrams, *The Burdens of Progress: 1900–1929* (Glenview, Ill., 1978).

37. Ignatieff, *The Needs of Strangers*, 32. See above, Chap. 8 n. 48.

38. Max Weber, *The Theory of Social and Economic Organizations* (New York, 1964), 328; Pye, *Asian Power and Politics*, 94 (quotation).

39. Waltz, *Man, the State, and War*, 80.

40. A good example of a balanced judgment in the biography by W. W. Tarn, *Alexander the Great* (Cambridge, 1948). Tarn captures the tarnished and untarnished aspects of Alexander's character. The German historians, untouched as they were by Whigism, are more interesting cases. A good example is Gerhard Ritter's biography, *Frederick the Great* (Berkeley, Calif., 1970). Ritter's translator, Peter Paret, takes note of Ritter's shortcomings in his introduction, xii–xiii.

41. Ezra N. Suleiman, *Elites in French Society* (Princeton, N.J., 1978), 57–92. Also see Guy Benveniste, *Bureaucracy*, 2d ed. (San Francisco, 1983), 124–25; Robert M. Spaulding, *Imperial Japan's Higher Civil Examinations* (Princeton, N.J., 1978); John A. Armstrong, *The European Administrative Elite* (Princeton, N.J., 1973).

42. Weber, *The Theory of Social and Economic Organizations*, 181.

43. Gelb and Betts, *The Irony of Vietnam*, 2.

44. Keohane and Nye, *Power and Interdependence*, 115. A scholar sympathetic to Keohane and Nye's theory has suggested the frailty of the theory in a worst-case scenario; see Ernst Haas, "The Frailty of Complex Interdependence," *Jerusalem Journal of International Relations*, 5 (Oct. 1981), 1–13. On U.S. economic independence in the 1960's see Gilpin, *The Political Economy of International Relations*, 136. Complex interdependence seems best to fit medium and small powers, as shown in Peter J. Katzenstein, *Small States in World Markets* (Ithaca, N.Y., 1985), and Peter J. Katzenstein, ed., *Between Power and Plenty* (Madison, Wis., 1978).

45. For an explanation of complex dependence see Fernando H. Cardoso and Enzo Faletto, *Dependency and Development in Latin America* (Berkeley, Calif., 1979). The application of *dependencia* assertions to East Asia is not without debate; see Peter Evans, "Class, State, and Dependence in East Asia," in Frederic C. Deyo, ed., *The Political Economy of the New Asian Industrialism* (Ithaca, N.Y., 1987), 201–26, and, for an opposing view taken from one case study, Thomas Gold, *State and Society in the Taiwan Miracle* (Armonk, N.Y., 1986), 9–17.

46. Montgomery, *The Politics of Foreign Aid*; John D. Montgomery, "The Allocation of Authority in Land Reform Programs: A Comparative Study of Administrative Processes and Outputs," in Norman T. Uphoff and Warren F. Ilchman, eds., *The Political Economy of Development* (Berkeley, Calif., 1972), 449–75; and John D. Montgomery, ed., *International Dimensions of Land Reform* (Boulder, Colo., 1984).

47. Gabriel Kolko prefers the term apathy over the term ambivalent. He also suggests that the peasant in Vietnam was more apathetic toward Saigon than toward the Viet Cong; I suggest that the peasants felt remote from the two combatants, drifting from one side to the other depending on the circumstances. See Kolko's *Anatomy of a War*, 243. Douglas Pike says that "the majority of Vietnamese of middle age or older have been on all sides of all political issues"; quoted in Pye, *Asian Power and Politics*, 243.

48. Henry Shue, *Basic Rights: Subsistence, Affluence, and U.S. Foreign Policy* (Princeton, N.J., 1980), 7. Robert A. Packenham lists "five conditions as the prime correlates or determinants of political development." See his "Political-Development Doctrines in the American Foreign Aid Program," *World Politics*, 18 (Jan. 1966), 194–235 (quotation on p. 195). Where Packenham speaks of political development, Richard Wilson speaks of moral development; see Richard W. Wilson, "Moral Development and Political Change," *World Politics*, 36 (Oct. 1983), 53–75. As Wilson suggests, "the central question of moral development theory is how individuals develop internalized controls over behavior" (p. 56).

49. Cyrus R. Vance, *Human Rights Policy* (Washington, D.C., 1977), p. 1; this is a State Department speech of Apr. 30, 1977. Also see John Ruggie, "Human Rights and the Future International Community," *Daedalus* (Fall 1983), 93–110, and Hoffmann, *Janus and Minerva*, 370–93; Morton E. Winston, *The Philosophy of Human Rights* (Belmont, Calif., 1988).

50. Shue, *Basic Rights*, 8–9. James MacGregor Burns wrestles with the same problem in the following way: "Some—John Rawls, for example, and this author—would grant priority to *liberty* over any other social good, assuming it to be equal liberty. The only value, I believe, that might be elevated over liberty is security, but security would decline in desirability if it guaranteed only survival and not the values such as liberty that make life worth living." See Burns's *Leadership* (New York, 1978), 432.

51. Curti, *American Philanthropy*. Miss Daphne Park, the Principal of Sommerville College, Oxford University, and former British Consul-General in Hanoi from 1969 to 1970 before retiring from the British Foreign Office, suggests that "the Vietnam war was one in which the Americans were fighting not for their own financial or material interests." See Caroline Alexander, "Profiles: Daphne Park", *The New Yorker*, Jan. 30, 1989, 57–71, quotation on p. 67.

52. Walzer, *Just and Unjust Wars*, 119–20, 129–30, 153–56, 211–12, 216, 218, 226–77, 278–80, 318.

53. Krasner, *Defending the National Interest*, 345.

54. *Ibid*. Some economic pressure existed—for example, oil expert William Henderson pushed the JFK-LBJ team to support an independent South Vietnam. See R. B. Smith, *An International History of the Vietnam War*, vol. 2, *The Kennedy Strategy*, 140. But such economic concerns are only one explanation—and not the critical one. Using economic evidence for historical explanations like imperialism requires the recognition of many causes. See David S. Landis, "The Nature of Economic Imperialism," in Kenneth E. Boulding and Tapan Mukerjee, eds., *Economic Imperialism* (Ann Arbor, Mich., 1972), 124–41.

55. Noam Chomsky, *At War with Asia: Essays on Indochina* (New York, 1970), 25. Big business, in the person of Marrimer Eccles, told Johnson and his senior cabinet members (Rusk, McNamara, etc.) in 1965 that the administration had based its Vietnam policy "on fatal errors" and should immediately start "negotiations to end the war," indicating this new policy by an immediate cease-fire. This advance came from an old New Dealer who, as chairman of the Utah Construction Company (and then Utah International) owned millions of dollars in Asian investments in the 1960's. No business voice raised itself against Eccles at this White House dinner. See Jonathan Hughes, *The Vital Few*, expanded ed. (Oxford, 1986), 556. For another view see Paul A. Baran and Paul M. Sweezy, "Notes on the Theory of Imperialism," in Boulding and Mukerjee, *Economic Imperialism*, 156–70.

56. Francis L. Loewenheim, "A Legacy of Hope and a Legacy of Doubt," in Francis L. Loewenheim, ed., *The Historian and the Diplomat: The Role of History and the Historian in American Foreign Policy* (New York, 1967), 7. Also see Paul Seabury's review of this book in *New York Times Book Review*, May 7, 1967, 6.

57. Immanuel Kant, *Perpetual Peace* (Indianapolis, Ind., 1957), 16–20; Kenneth W. Waltz, "Kant, Liberalism, and War," *American Political Science Review*, 56 (June 1962), 331–40; Michael W. Doyle, "Liberalism and World

Politics," *American Political Science Review*, 80 (Dec. 1986), 1151–69; Carl J. Friedrich, *Inevitable Peace* (Cambridge, Mass., 1948), 33–49; Michael W. Doyle, "Kant, Liberal Legacies, and Foreign Affairs," *Philosophy and Foreign Affairs*, 12 (Summer 1983 and Fall 1983), 205–35 and 323–53.

58. Ernst Haas, *Global Evangelism Rides Again* (Berkeley, Calif., 1978), 1–46; James C. Thomson, Jr., "How Could Vietnam Happen?" in Richard Abrams and Lawrence W. Levine, eds., *The Shaping of Twentieth-Century America* (Boston, 1965), 683–94. Thompson served on White House and State Department staffs from 1961–66.

59. William H. McNeill, "The Care and Repair of Public Myth," *Foreign Affairs*, 61 (Fall 1982), 1–13.

60. *The Historical Essays of Otto Hintze*, ed. Felix Gilbert (Oxford, 1975), 305–53; Hannah F. Pitkin, *The Concept of Representation* (Berkeley, Calif., 1967).

61. Isaiah Berlin, introduction to Franco Venturi, *Roots of Revolution* (Chicago, 1960), ix, x. If internationalists did not wish to consult the British Berlin they could have listened to an American advocate of moderation like Robert Dahl, who suggested, in *A Preface to Democratic Theory* (Chicago, 1956), 151, that the American political system "is not for export to others."

Bibliography

Acheson, Dean G. *Power and Diplomacy.* Cambridge, Mass., 1958.
———. *Present at the Creation: My Years at the State Department.* New York, 1969.
———. *This Vast External Realm.* New York, 1973.
Allison, Graham T. *Essence of Decision: Explaining the Cuban Missile Crisis.* Boston, 1971.
Almond, Gabriel A., and Sidney Verba. *The Civic Culture: Political Democracy in Five Nations.* Princeton, N.J., 1963.
———. *The Civic Culture Revisited.* Boston, 1980.
Almond, Gabriel A., and James S. Coleman, eds. *The Politics of the Developing Areas.* Princeton, N.J., 1960.
Ambrose, Stephen E. *Eisenhower,* 2 vols. New York, 1983–84.
———. *Rise to Globalism.* New York, 1976.
Anderson, Benedict. *Imagined Communities.* London, 1983.
Apter, David. *Rethinking Development: Modernization, Dependency, and Postmodern Politics.* Newbury Park, Calif., 1987.
Aron, Raymond. *Peace and War.* New York, 1966.
———. *The Imperial Republic: The United States and the World, 1945–1973.* Washington, D.C., 1982.
Art, Robert J. *The TFX Decision: McNamara and the Military.* Boston, 1968.
Art, Robert J., and Kenneth N. Waltz, eds. *The Use of Force.* Washington, D.C., 1983.
Axelrod, Robert. *Structure of Decision.* Princeton, N.J., 1976.
Baker, Mark. *Nam: The Vietnam War in the Words of Men and Women Who Fought There.* New York, 1981.
Ball, George. *Diplomacy for a Crowded World.* Boston, 1976.
———. *The Past Has Another Pattern.* New York, 1982.
Barnett, A. Doak. *China and the Major Powers in East Asia.* Washington, D.C., 1977.
Bates, Robert H., ed. *Toward a Political Economy of Development.* Berkeley, Calif., 1988.

Bauer, P. T. *Reality and Rhetoric: Studies in the Economics of Development*. Cambridge, Mass., 1984.

Bendix, Reinhard. *Nation-Building and Citizenship*. 2d ed. Berkeley, Calif., 1964.

Berger, Carl, ed. *The United States Air Force in Southeast Asia: 1961–1973*. Washington, D.C., 1977.

Berman, Larry. *Planning a Tragedy*. New York, 1982.

———. *Lyndon Johnson's War*. New York, 1989.

Berman, Paul. *Revolutionary Organization: Institution Building Within the People's Liberation Armed Forces*. Lexington, Mass., 1974.

Berman, William. *William Fulbright and the Vietnam War*. Kent, Ohio, 1988.

Betts, Richard K. *Soldiers, Statesmen and Cold War Crises*. Cambridge, Mass., 1977.

Bingham, June. *Courage to Change*. New York, 1972.

Blaufarb, Douglas S. *The Counter Insurgency Era*. New York, 1977.

Boles, Elizabeth M. "The Challenge of Revolutionary Change to U.S. Foreign Policy." *Conflict Quarterly*, 8 (Fall 1988), 5–25.

Bowles, Chester. *Promises to Keep: My Years in Public Life—1941–1969*. New York, 1971.

Braestrup, Peter. *The Big Story: How the American Press and Television Reported and Interpreted the Crisis of Tet 1968 in Vietnam and Washington*. New Haven, Conn., 1983.

Braudel, Fernand. *Afterthoughts on Material Civilization and Capitalism*. Translated by Patricia M. Ranum. Baltimore, Md., 1977.

Bredo, William *et al. Land Reform in Vietnam: Summary Volume*. Menlo Park, Calif., 1968.

———. *Vietnam as History*. Washington, D.C., 1984.

Brodie, Bernard. *Strategy in the Missile Age*. Princeton, N.J., 1959.

Broughton, Jack. *Thud Ridge*. Philadelphia, 1969.

Bueno de Mesquita, Bruce. *The War Trap*. New Haven, Conn., 1981.

Bundy, McGeorge. *The Strength of Government*. Cambridge, Mass., 1968.

Burns, Richard D., and Milton Leitenberg, eds. *The Wars in Vietnam, Cambodia and Laos, 1945–1982: A Bibliographic Guide*. Santa Barbara, Calif., 1984.

Butterfield, Herbert. *The Whig Interpretation of History*. New York, 1931.

———. *Christianity, Diplomacy, and War*. London, 1953.

Butterfield, Herbert, and Martin Wight, *Diplomatic Investigations*. Cambridge, Mass., 1966.

Buttinger, Joseph. *Vietnam: The Dragon Embattled*. New York, 1967.

Calleo, David P. *The Atlantic Fantasy*. Baltimore, Md., 1970.

———. *The Imperious Economy*. Cambridge, Mass., 1982.

Callison, Charles Stuart. *Land-to-the-Tiller in the Mekong Delta: Economic, Social, and Political Effects of Land Reform in Four Villages of South Vietnam*. Lanham, Md., 1983.

Canh, Nguyen Van. *Vietnam Under Communism, 1975–1982*. Stanford, Calif., 1983.

Caputo, Phillip. *A Rumor of War*, New York, 1977.

Cassen, Robert, *et al. Does Aid Work?* Oxford, 1986.

Cawelti, John G. *Adventure, Mystery and Romance*. Chicago, 1976.

Chanda, Nayan. *Brother Enemy*. San Diego, Calif., 1986.

Cheng, Tun-jen, and Stephan Haggard. *Newly Industrializing Asia in Transi-tion*. Berkeley, Calif., 1987.

"CIA Secret Report on Sino-Vietnamese Reaction to American Tactics in the Vietnam War." *Journal of Contemporary Asia*, 13, no. 2 (1983), 261–71.

Cincinnatus (pseudonym). *Self-Destruction*. New York, 1981.

Clark, Paul G. *American Aid for Development*. New York, 1972.

Clifford, Clark. "A Vietnam Reappraisal." *Foreign Affairs*, 47 (July 1969), 601–22.

———. "American Military Firmness Versus Soviet Aggression." In Thomas G. Paterson, ed., *The Origins of the Cold War*, Lexington, Mass., 1970.

Cline, Ray S. *Secrets, Spies, and Scholars: Blueprint of the Essential CIA*. Washing-ton, D.C., 1976.

Coedès, Georges. *The Making of South East Asia*. Berkeley, Calif., 1966.

Coffin, Frank M. *Witness for AID*. Boston, 1964.

Cohen, Stephen D. *The Making of United States International Economic Policy*. New York, 1981.

Colby, William, and Peter Forbath. *Honorable Men: My Life in the CIA*. New York, 1978.

Collins, Arthur S., Jr. *Common Sense Training*. San Rafael, Calif., 1978.

Collins, James L., Jr. *The Development and Training of the Vietnamese Army, 1950–1972*. Washington, D.C., 1975.

Collins, John M. *Grand Strategy*. Annapolis, Md., 1973.

Cooper, Chester L. *The Lost Crusade: America in Vietnam*. New York, 1970.

Cooper, Chester L., *et al. The American Experience with Pacification in Vietnam*. 3 vols. Washington, D.C., 1972.

Craig, Gordon, and Alexander L. George. *Force and Statecraft: Diplomatic Prob-lems of Our Time*. Oxford, 1985.

Curry, Cecil B. *Edward Lansdale: The Unquiet American*. Boston, 1989.

Curti, Merle. *American Philanthropy Abroad: A History*. New Brunswick, N.J., 1963.

Curti, Merle, and Kendall Birr. *Prelude to Point Four: American Technical Mis-sions Overseas, 1838–1938*. Madison, Wis., 1954.

Cutler, Robert. *No Time for Rest*. Boston, 1965.

Daedalus, issue entitled "A World to Make: Development in Perspective," 118 (Winter 1989), 1–249.

Dawson, Alan. *55 Days: The Fall of Saigon*. Englewood Cliffs, N.J., 1977.

Degler, Carl N. *Affluence and Anxiety: America Since 1945*. Glenview, Ill., 2d ed. 1975.

Deibel, Terry L., and John Lewis Gaddis, eds. *Containment: Concept and Policy*. 2 vols. Washington, D.C., 1986.

Desbarats, Jacqueline. "Population Relocation Programs in Socialist Viet-nam." *Indochina Report*, April–June 1987.

De Silva, Peer. *Sub Rosa: The CIA and the Use of Intelligence*. New York, 1978.

Destler, I. M. *Presidents, Bureaucrats and Foreign Policy*. Princeton, N.J., 1972.

Deutsch, Karl W. *Political Community at the International Level*. New York, 1954.

———. *Political Community and the North Atlantic Area*. Princeton, N.J., 1957.

Devine, Robert A. *The Johnson Years*. 2 vols. Lawrence, Kans., 1987.

Dickson, Paul. *The Electronic Battlefield*. Bloomington, Ind., 1976.

Diem, Bui, and David Chanoff. *In the Jaws of History*. Boston, 1987.

Dinh, Nguyan Thi. *No Other Road to Take*. Ithaca, N.Y., 1976.

Don, Tran Van. *Our Endless War Inside Vietnam*. San Rafael, Calif., 1978.

Doyle, Michael W. *Empires*. Ithaca, N.Y., 1986.

Draper, Theodore. *Abuse of Power*. New York, 1967.

Duan, Le. *The Vietnamese Revolution: Fundamental Problems and Essential Tasks*. New York, 1971.

Du Bois, Cora. *Social Forces in Southeast Asia*. Cambridge, Mass., 1959.

Duiker, William L. *China and Vietnam: The Roots of Conflict*. Berkeley, Calif., 1986.

———. *The Rise of Nationalism in Vietnam: 1900–1941*. Ithaca, N.Y., 1976.

Dulles, Allen. *The Craft of Intelligence*. New York, 1963.

———. *The Secret Surrender*. New York, 1966.

———. *Great True Spy Stories*. New York, 1982.

Dung, Van Tien. *Our Great Spring Victory*. New York, 1977.

Duus, Peter. *Feudalism in Japan*. New York, 1969.

Earle, Edward Mead. *Makers of Modern Strategy*. Princeton, N.J., 1976.

Eayrs, James. *In Defense of Canada*. Vol. 5, *Indochina—Roots of Complicity*. Toronto, 1983.

Eckhardt, George S. *Command and Control 1950–1969*. Washington, D.C., 1974.

Eckstein, Harry. *Internal War*. New York, 1964.

———. "A Culturalist Theory of Political Change." *American Political Science Review*, 82 (September 1988), 789–80.

Eisenhower, Dwight D. *The White House Years: Mandate for Change, 1953–1956*. New York, 1963.

———. *The White House Years: Waging Peace, 1956–1961*. New York, 1965.

Ellis, John. *Armies in Revolution*. Oxford, 1974.

Ellsberg, Daniel. *Papers on the War*. New York, 1972.

Emerson, Gloria. *Winners and Losers*. New York, 1976.

Enthoven, Alain C., and K. Wayne Smith. *How Much Is Enough? Shaping the Defense Program, 1961–1969*. New York, 1971.

Ewell, Julian J., and Ira A. Hunt. *Sharpening the Combat Edge*. Washington, D.C., 1974.

Falk, Richard A. *The Vietnam War and International Law*. 4 vols. Princeton, N.J., 1969.

Fall, Bernard B. "Laos: Who Broke the Ceasefire?" *The New Republic*, June 18, 1962.

———. *Street Without Joy*. Harrisburg, Pa., 1963.

———. *Viet-Nam Witness: 1953–66*. New York, 1966.

———. *Last Reflections on a War*. New York, 1972.

————. *Hell in a Very Small Place.* Philadelphia, 1967.

————. *The Two Viet-Nams.* New York, 1964.

Ferenbach, T. R. *This Kind of War: A Study in Unpreparedness.* New York, 1963.

Festinger, Leon. *A Theory of Cognitive Dissonance.* Stanford, Calif., 1957.

————. *Conflict, Decision and Dissonance.* Stanford, Calif., 1964.

Fishel, Wesley R., ed. *Problems of Freedom: South Vietnam Since Independence.* New York, 1961.

Fitzgerald, Frances. *Fire in the Lake.* Boston, 1972.

Fox, Richard Wightman. *Reinhold Niebuhr: A Biography.* New York, 1985.

Fulton, William B. *Riverine Operations: 1966–1969.* Washington, D.C., 1973.

Gaddis, John Lewis. *Strategies of Containment: A Critical Appraisal of Postwar American National Security Policy.* Oxford, 1982.

Galbraith, John K. *A Life in Our Times.* Boston, 1981.

Galloway, John. *The Gulf of Tonkin Resolution.* Rutherford, N.J., 1970.

Gardner, Lloyd C. *A Covenant with Power.* Oxford, 1984.

————. *Approaching Vietnam.* New York, 1988.

Gelb, Leslie, and Richard Betts. *The Irony of Vietnam: The System Worked.* Washington, D.C., 1979.

George, Alexander P. *The Chinese Communist Army in Action: The Korean War and Its Aftermath.* New York, 1967.

George, Alexander; David Hall; and William Simons. *The Limits of Coercive Diplomacy.* Boston, 1971.

George, Alexander, and Richard Smoke. *Deterrence in American Foreign Policy.* New York, 1974.

Gerschenkron, Alexander. *Economic Backwardness in Historical Perspective.* Cambridge, Mass., 1962.

————. "Reflections on Economic Aspects of Revolutions." In Harry Eckstein, ed., *Internal War*, New York, 1964.

Giap, Vo Nguyen, *People's War, People's Army.* New York, 1962.

————. *The Banner of People's War, the Party Military Line.* New York, 1970.

Gibbons, William Conrad. *The U.S. Government and the Vietnam War.* 3 vols. Princeton, N.J., 1987.

Gibson, James W. *The Perfect War.* Boston, 1986.

Gilpin, Robert. *War and Change in World Politics.* Cambridge, 1981.

————. *The Political Economy of International Relations.* Princeton, N.J., 1987.

Goldman, Eric F. *The Tragedy of Lyndon Johnson.* New York, 1969.

Goodman, Allan E. *Politics in War: The Bases of Political Community in South Vietnam.* Cambridge, Mass., 1973.

————. *The Lost Peace.* Stanford, Calif., 1978.

Graff, Henry F. *The Tuesday Cabinet.* Englewood Cliffs, N.J., 1970.

Gravel, Mike. *The Pentagon Papers.* 4 vols. Boston, 1970.

Greene, Graham *The Quiet American.* New York, 1956.

Greenstein, Fred I. *The Hidden-Hand President: Eisenhower as Leader.* New York, 1982.

Grinter, Lawrence, and Peter Dunn, eds. *The American War in Vietnam.* Westport, Conn., 1987.

Grosser, Alfred. *The Western Alliance: European-American Relations Since 1945*. New York, 1982.

Gurr, Ted Robert. *Why Men Rebel*. Princeton, N.J., 1970.

Guttman, Allen, ed. *Korea: Cold War and Limited War*. Lexington, Mass., 1967.

Halberstam, David. *The Making of a Quagmire: America and Vietnam During the Kennedy Era*. New York, 1964.

———. *One Very Hot Day*. Boston, 1967.

———. *The Best and the Brightest*. New York, 1969.

Hallin, Daniel C. *The "Uncensored War."* Oxford, 1986.

Halperin, Morton H. *Bureaucratic Politics and Foreign Policy*. Washington, D.C., 1974.

Hammer, Ellen J. *A Death in November*. Oxford, 1987.

———. *The Struggle for Indochina, 1940–55*. Stanford, Calif., 1966.

Hammond, Paul Y. *Organizing for Defense*. Princeton, N.J., 1961.

Hannah, Norman B. "Vietnam Now We Know." In Anthony T. Bouscaren, ed., *All Quiet on the Eastern Front*. New York, 1977.

Harriman, W. Averell. *America and Russia in a Changing World*. New York, 1971.

Harrison, Lawrence E. *Underdevelopment Is a State of Mind*. Washington, D.C., 1985.

Hartz, Louis. "The Whig Tradition in America and Europe." *American Political Science Review*, 46 (December 1952), 989–1002.

Hasmer, Stephen T., and Konrad Kellen. *The Fall of South Vietnam*. New York, 1980.

Hay, John H., Jr. *Tactical and Material Innovations*. Washington, D.C., 1974.

Heiser, Joseph M., Jr. *Logistic Support*. Washington, D.C., 1974.

Hellmann, John. *American Myth and the Legacy of Vietnam*. New York, 1986.

Helmer, John. *Bringing the War Home*. New York, 1974.

Henderson, William Darryl. *Why the Vietcong Fought: A Study of Motivation and Control in a Modern Army in Combat*. Westport, Conn., 1979.

Henderson, William, ed. *Southeast Asia*. Cambridge, Mass., 1963.

Herken, Gregg. *Counsels of War*. Oxford, 1987.

Herring, George C. *America's Longest War*. New York, 1979.

———, ed. *The Secret Diplomacy of the Vietnam War: The Negotiating Volumes of the Pentagon Papers*. Austin, Tex., 1983.

Hersh, Seymour. *My Lai 4*. New York, 1970.

Hickey, Gerald Cannon. *Village in Vietnam*. New Haven, Conn., 1964.

Hilsman, Roger. *To Move a Nation*. New York, 1964.

Hirschman, Albert O. *Development Projects Observed*. Washington, D.C., 1967.

———. *The Passions and the Interests*. Princeton, N.J., 1977.

Hitch, Charles J., and Roland N. McKean. *The Economics of Defense in the Nuclear Age*. Cambridge, Mass., 1960.

Hobsbaum, E. J. *Primitive Rebels*. New York, 1959.

Hoffmann, Stanley. *The State of War*. New York, 1965.

———. *Janus and Minerva*. Boulder, Colo., 1987.

Hoopes, Townsend. *The Limits of Intervention*. New York, 1969.

Hopper, E., D. Allard, and O. Fitzgerald. *The United States Navy and the Vietnam Conflict, Vol. I*. Washington, D.C., 1976.

Hosmer, Stephen T. *Viet Cong Repression and Its Implications for the Future*. Santa Monica, Calif., 1970.

Howard, Michael. *War and the Liberal Conscience*. New Brunswick, N.J., 1978.

———. *The Causes of Wars*. Cambridge, Mass., 1983.

Huntington, Samuel P. *The Soldier and the State*. New York, 1957.

———. *The Common Defense*. New York, 1961.

———. *Political Order in Changing Societies*. New Haven, Conn., 1968.

Ignatieff, Michael. *The Needs of Strangers*. New York, 1985.

Inderfurth, Karl, and Loch Johnson. *Decisions of the Highest Order*. Pacific Grove, Calif., 1988.

Iriye, Akira. *From Nationalism to Internationalism: U.S. Foreign Policy to 1914*. London, 1977.

Isaacson, Walter, and Thomas Evan. *The Wise Men*. New York, 1986.

Jackson, Karl D., and M. Hadi Soesastro. *ASEAN Security and Economic Development*. Berkeley, Calif., 1984.

Jackson, Karl D.; and Sukhumbhand Paribatra; and J. Soedjati Djiwandono. *ASEAN in Regional and Global Context*. Berkeley, Calif., 1986.

James, William. "The Moral Equivalent of War." In his *Memories and Studies*. Westport, Conn., 1968.

Jeffreys-Jones, Rhodri. *The CIA and American Democracy*. New Haven, Conn., 1989.

Jervis, Robert. *The Logic of Images in International Relations*. Princeton, N.J., 1970.

Johnson, Chalmers. *An Instance of Treason*. Stanford, Calif., 1964.

———. *Peasant Nationalism and Communist Power: The Emergence of Revolutionary China 1937–1945*. Stanford, Calif., 1962.

———. *Revolution and the Social System*. Stanford, Calif., 1964.

———. *Autopsy on People's War*. Berkeley, Calif., 1973.

———. *MITI and the Japanese Miracle*. Stanford, Calif., 1982.

———. *Revolutionary Change*. 2d ed. Stanford, Calif., 1982.

Johnson, Harold K. *Challenge: Compendium of Army Accomplishments, A Report by the Chief of Staff, U.S. Army*. Washington, D.C., 1968.

Johnson, Lyndon B. *The Vantage Point: Perspectives of the Presidency 1963–1969*. New York, 1971.

Johnson, U. Alexis. *The Right Hand of Power*. Englewood Cliffs, N.J., 1984.

Jordan, Amos A. *Foreign AID and the Defense of Southeast Asia*. New York, 1962.

Just, Ward. *Military Men*. New York, 1970.

Kahin, George McT. *Intervention*. New York, 1986.

Kahin, George McT., and John W. Lewis. *The United States in Vietnam*. New York, 1967.

Kaplan, Fred. *The Wizards of Armageddon*. New York, 1983.

Karnow, Stanley. *Vietnam: A History*. New York, 1983.

Kattenburg, Paul M. *The Vietnam Trauma, 1945–75*. London, 1980.

Kaufmann, William, ed. *Military Policy and National Security*. Princeton, N.J., 1956.

Kennan, George. *Memoirs: 1925–1950*. New York, 1967.

———. "The Sources of Soviet Conduct." *Foreign Affairs*, 25 (July 1947), 566–82; reprinted, along with his "Containment Then and Now," in *Foreign Affairs*, 65 (Spring 1987), 852–68, 885–90.

Kennedy, John F. *Profiles in Courage*. New York, 1955.

———. *The Strategy of Peace*. New York, 1960.

———. *The Speeches of Senator John F. Kennedy: Presidential Campaign of 1960*. Washington, D.C., 1961.

———. *Why England Slept*. Westport, Conn., 1961.

Keohane, Robert O. *After Hegemony. Cooperation and Discord in the World Political Economy*. Princeton, N.J., 1984.

Keohane, Robert O., and Joseph S. Nye. *Power and Interdependence: World Politics in Transition*. Boston, 1977.

Kern, Montague; Patricia W. Levering; and Ralph B. Levering. *The Kennedy Crisis: The Press, the Presidency, and Foreign Policy*. Chapel Hill, N.C., 1983.

Kindleberger, Charles P. *Power and Money*. New York, 1970.

Kinnard, Douglas. *The War Managers*. Hanover, N.H., 1977.

———. *The Secretary of Defense*. Lexington, Ky., 1980.

Kissinger, Henry A. *The White House Years*. Boston, 1979.

———. *Year of Upheaval*. Boston, 1982.

Kolko, Gabriel. *Anatomy of a War*. New York, 1985.

Komer, Robert W. *Bureaucracy Does Its Thing: Institutional Constraints in U.S.-GVN Performance in Vietnam*. Santa Monica, Calif., 1972.

Korb, Lawrence J. *The Joint Chiefs of Staff*. Bloomington, Ind., 1976.

Krasner, Stephen D. *Defending the National Interest: Raw Materials Investments and U.S. Foreign Policy*. Princeton, N.J., 1978.

———. *Structural Conflict: The Third World Against Global Liberalism*. Berkeley, Calif., 1985.

Krepinevich, Andrew F., Jr. *The Army in Vietnam*. Baltimore, Md., 1986.

Ky, Nguyen Cao. *How We Lost the Vietnam War*. New York, 1976.

Lacouture, Jean. *Between Two Truces*. New York, 1966.

Luke, Anthony, ed. *The Legacy of Vietnam*. New York, 1976.

Langer, Paul F., and Joseph J. Zasloff. *North Vietnam and the Pathet Lao: Partners in the Struggle for Laos*. Cambridge, Mass., 1970.

Lansdale, Edward G. *In the Midst of Wars: An American Mission to Southeast Asia*. New York, 1972.

Larson, Deborah. *Origins of Containment: A Psychological Explanation*. Princeton, N.J., 1985.

Leary, William M., ed. *The Central Intelligence Agency: History and Documents*. University, Ala., 1984.

Le Gro, William E. *Vietnam from Cease-Fire to Capitulation*. Indochina Monographs. Washington, D.C., 1981.

Lenin, V. I. *What Is to Be Done: Burning Questions of Our Movement.* 7th ed. New York, 1981.

Leuchtenburg, William E. *A Troubled Feast: American Society Since 1945.* Boston, 1983.

Levin, N. Gordon, Jr. *Woodrow Wilson and World Politics: America's Response to War and Revolution.* Oxford, 1968.

Levine, Lawrence W. "The Historian and the Icon: Photography and the History of the American People in the 1930s and 1940s." In Charles Fleischhauer and Beverly Brannan, eds., *Documenting America: 1935–1945.* Berkeley, Calif., 1988.

Levy, Charles J. *Spoils of War.* Boston, 1974.

Lewy, Guenter. *America in Vietnam.* Oxford, 1978.

Lippmann, Walter. *The Cold War.* New York, 1947.

Liska, George. *War and Order.* Baltimore, Md., 1968.

———. *Quest for Equilibrium.* Baltimore, Md., 1977.

———. *Career of Empire: America and Imperial Expansion over Land and Sea.* Baltimore, Md., 1978.

Lodge, Henry Cabot. *The Storm Has Many Eyes: A Personal Narrative.* New York, 1973.

———. *As It Was: An Inside View of Politics and Power in the 1950's and 1960's.* New York, 1976.

Long, Ngo Vinh. *Before the Revolution: The Vietnamese Peasants Under the French.* Cambridge, Mass., 1973.

Luce, Don, and John Sommer. *Vietnam.* Ithaca, N.Y., 1969.

Luttwak, Edward N. *Coup d'etat: A Practical Handbook.* New York, 1968.

———. *The Grand Strategy of the Roman Empire.* Baltimore, Md., 1976.

MacArthur, Douglas. *Reminiscences.* New York, 1964.

Manchester, William. *American Caesar.* Boston, 1978.

Maneli, Mieczylaw. *War of the Vanquished.* New York, 1971.

Marr, David G. *Vietnamese Anticolonialism: 1885–1925.* Berkeley, Calif., 1971.

———. *Vietnamese Tradition on Trial: 1920–1945.* Berkeley, Calif., 1981.

Marshall, S. L. A. *The Fields of Bamboo.* New York, 1971.

Maslow, Abraham. *Motivation and Personality.* New York, 1954.

———. *The Psychology of Science: A Reconnaissance.* New York, 1966.

———. *Toward a Psychology of Being.* New York, 1968.

———. *The Farther Reaches of Human Nature.* New York, 1976.

Matloff, Maurice. *American Military History.* Washington, D.C., 1969.

Mayers, David. *George Kennan and the Dilemmas of U.S. Foreign Policy.* Oxford, 1988.

McAlister, John T., and Paul Mus. *The Vietnamese and Their Revolution.* New York, 1970.

McChristian, Joseph A. *The Role of Military Intelligence, 1965–1967.* Washington, D.C., 1974.

McGee, T. G. "Beachheads and Enclaves: The Urban Debate and the Urbanization Process in South-East Asia." In Y. M. Yeung and C. P. Lo, eds., *Changing South-East Asian Cities,* Singapore, 1976.

McNamara, Robert S. *The Essence of Security: Reflections in Office*. New York, 1968.

Migdal, Joel S. *Strong Societies and Weak States*. Princeton, N.J., 1988.

Miller, Merle. *Lyndon: An Oral Biography*. New York, 1980.

Millis, Walter. *Arms and Men: A Study of American Military History*. New York, 1956.

Minh, Ho Chi. *On Revolution*. Edited by Bernard Fall. New York, 1967.

Mitchell, Edward J. *Land Tenure and Rebellion: A Statistical Analysis of Factors Affecting Government Control in South Vietnam*. Santa Monica, Calif., 1967.

Moise, Edwin E. *Land Reform in China and North Vietnam*. Chapel Hill, N.C., 1983.

Montgomery, John D. *The Politics of Foreign Aid: American Experience in Southeast Asia*. New York, 1962.

Momyer, William W. *Airpower in Three Wars*. Washington, D.C., 1978.

Moore, Barrington. *Soviet Politics—The Dilemma of Power*. New York, 1950.

———. *Social Origins of Dictatorship and Democracy: Lord and Peasant in the Making of the Modern World*. Boston, 1966.

Moore, John Norton. *Law and the Indo-China War*. Princeton, N.J., 1972.

Morgenthau, Hans J. *America's Stake in Vietnam*. New York, 1956.

Mueller, John E. *War, Presidents and Public Opinion*. New York, 1973.

Murray, Martin J. *The Development of Capitalism in Colonial Indochina: 1870–1940*. Berkeley, Calif., 1980.

Mus, Paul. *Viet Nam: Sociologie d'une Guerre*. Paris, 1952.

———. *Ho Chi Minh, Le Vietnam, L'Asie*. Paris, 1971.

Niebuhr, Reinhold. *Moral Man and Immoral Society*. New York, 1932.

———. *The Children of Light and the Children of Darkness*. New York, 1946.

Nitze, Paul. "Eight Presidents and Their Different Approaches to National Security Policymaking." In Kenneth W. Thompson, ed., *The Virginia Papers on the Presidency: The White Burkett Miller Center Forum 1979*. Washington, D.C., 1979.

Nixon, Richard. *R.N.: The Memoirs of Richard Nixon*. New York, 1978.

Nolting, Frederick. *From Trust to Tragedy: The Political Memoirs of Frederick Nolting, Kennedy's Ambassador to Diem's Vietnam*. New York, 1988.

Oberdorfer, Don. *Tet!* New York, 1971.

Organski, A. F. K., and Jacek Kugler. *The War Ledger*. Chicago, 1980.

Osgood, Robert E. *Ideals and Self-Interest in America's Foreign Relations*. Chicago, 1953.

———. *Limited War: The Challenge to American Strategy*. Chicago, 1957.

———. *NATO: The Entangling Alliance*. Chicago, 1962.

Osgood, Robert E., *et al. Retreat from Empire?* Baltimore, Md., 1973.

Ott, David E. *Field Artillery, 1954–1973*. Washington, D.C., 1975.

Palmer, Bruce, Jr. *The 25-Year War: America's Military Role in Vietnam*. Lexington, Ky., 1984.

Palmer, D. R. *Summons of the Trumpet*. San Rafael, Calif., 1978.

Paret, Peter, and John W. Shy. *Guerrillas in the 1960's*. New York, 1962.

Pastor, Robert A. *Congress and the Politics of U.S. Foreign Economic Policy.* Berkeley, Calif., 1980.

Paterson, Thomas G., ed. *The Origin of the Cold War.* Lexington, Mass., 1970.

————. *Containment and the Cold War.* Reading, Mass., 1973.

————. *Kennedy's Quest for Victory: American Foreign Policy, 1961–1963.* Oxford, 1989.

Patti, Archimedes L. A. *Why Vietnam? Prelude to America's Albatross.* Berkeley, Calif., 1980.

Peers, W. R. *The My Lai Inquiry.* New York, 1979.

Perkins, Dexter. *America's Quest for Peace.* Bloomington, Ind., 1962.

Pike, Douglas. *Viet Cong: The Organization and Techniques of the National Liberation Front of South Vietnam.* Cambridge, Mass., 1966.

————. *War, Peace, and the Viet Cong.* Cambridge, Mass., 1969.

————. *The Viet Cong Strategy of Terror.* Saigon, 1970.

————. *History of Vietnamese Communism: 1925–1976.* Stanford, Calif., 1978.

————. *People's Army of Vietnam.* Novato, Calif., 1986.

Podhoretz, Norman. *Why We Were in Vietnam.* New York, 1982.

Popkin, Samuel L. *The Rational Peasant: The Political Economy of Rural Society in Vietnam.* Berkeley, Calif., 1979.

Porter, Gareth. *A Peace Denied.* Bloomington, Ind., 1975.

Pratt, John Clark. *Vietnam Voices.* New York, 1984.

Pye, Lucian W. *Politics, Personality and Nation Building: Burma's Search for Identity.* New Haven, Conn., 1962.

————. *Asian Power and Politics: The Cultural Dimensions of Authority.* Cambridge, Mass., 1985.

Pye, Lucian, and Sidney Verba. *Political Culture and Political Development.* Princeton, N.J., 1965.

Race, Jeffrey. *War Comes to Long An.* Berkeley, Calif., 1972.

Raskin, Marcus G., and Bernard B. Fall. *The Vietnam Reader.* New York, 1965.

Ridgway, Matthew B. *The Korean War.* New York, 1967.

Ries, John C. *The Management of Defense: Organization and Control of the U.S. Armed Services.* Baltimore, Md., 1964.

Robequain, Charles. *The Economic Development of French Indo-China.* Translated by Isabel Ward. Oxford, 1944.

Rogers, Bernard. *Cedar Falls–Junction City, A Turning Point.* Washington, D.C., 1974.

Rosenau, James N. *Domestic Sources of Foreign Policy.* New York, 1967.

Rostow, Walt W. *The Stages of Economic Growth: A Non-Communist Manifesto.* 2d ed. Cambridge, 1971.

————. *The Diffusion of Power: An Essay in Recent History.* New York, 1972.

————. *Eisenhower, Kennedy, and Foreign Aid.* Austin, Tex., 1985.

Rotter, Andrew J. *The Path to Vietnam: Origin of the American Commitment to Southeast Asia.* Ithaca, N.Y., 1988.

Rourke, Francis. *Bureaucracy and Foreign Policy.* Baltimore, Md., 1972.

Rowe, James N. *Five Years to Freedom.* Boston, 1971.

Rubin, Steven Jay. *The James Bond Films*. New York, 1981.

Rusk, Dean. *The Winds of Freedom: Selections from the Speeches and Statements of Secretary of State Dean Rusk, January 1961–August 1962*. Boston, 1963.

Sansom, Robert L. *The Economics of Insurgency in the Mekong Delta of Vietnam*. Cambridge, Mass., 1970.

Santoli, Al. *Everything We Had: An Oral History of the Vietnam War by 33 American Soldiers Who Fought It*. New York, 1981.

Schandler, Herbert Y. *The Unmaking of a President*. Princeton, N.J., 1977.

Schell, Jonathan. *The Military Half: An Account of Destruction in Quong Ngai and Quang Tin*. New York, 1968.

——. *The Village of Ben Suc*. New York, 1967.

Schemmer, Benjamin F. *The Raid*. New York, 1976.

Schlesinger, Arthur M., Jr. *A Thousand Days*. Boston, 1965.

——. *The Imperial Presidency*. Boston, 1973.

——. *Robert Kennedy and His Times*. Boston, 1978.

Schoenbaum, Thomas J. *Waging Peace and War*. New York, 1988.

Schultz, Richard H., Jr. *The Soviet Union and Revolutionary Warfare: Principles, Practices, and Regional Comparisons*. Stanford, Calif., 1988.

——, ed. *Guerrilla Warfare and Counter-insurgency: U.S.-Soviet Policy in the Third World*. Lexington, Mass., 1989.

Scott, James C. *Comparative Political Corruption*. Englewood Cliffs, N.J., 1972.

——. *The Moral Economy of the Peasant: Rebellion and Subsistence in Southeast Asia*. New Haven, Conn., 1976.

Selznick, Philip. *The Organizational Weapon: A Study of Bolshevik Strategy and Tactics*. New York, 1960.

Shaplen, Robert. *The Lost Revolution*. New York, 1965.

——. *The Road from War*. New York, 1970.

Sharp, U. S. Grant. *Strategy for Defeat: Vietnam in Retrospect*. San Rafael, Calif., 1978.

Sharp, U. S. Grant and William C. Westmoreland. *Report on the War in Vietnam*. Washington, D.C., 1969.

Shawcross, William. *Sideshow: Kissinger, Nixon and the Destruction of Cambodia*. New York, 1979.

Sheehan, Neil. *A Bright Shining Lie: John Paul Vann and America in Vietnam*. New York, 1988.

Smith, Gaddis. *American Diplomacy During the Second World War, 1941–1945*. New York, 1965.

Smith, R. B. *An International History of the Vietnam War*. 2 vols. New York, 1983–85.

Smith, Richard Harris. *O.S.S.: The Secret History of America's First Central Intelligence Agency*. Berkeley, Calif., 1972.

Smith, Roger. *Cambodia's Foreign Policy*. Ithaca, N.Y., 1965.

Snepp, Frank W., III. *Decent Interval: An Insider's Account of Saigon's Indecent End*. New York, 1977.

Sorensen, Theodore C. *Kennedy*. New York, 1965.

Spector, Ronald H. *Advice and Support*. Washington, D.C., 1983.

Stephanson, Anders. *Kennan and the Art of Foreign Policy.* Cambridge, Mass., 1989.

Strange, Susan. "Cave! hic dragones: A Critique of Regime Analysis." In Stephan Krasner, ed., *International Regimes,* Ithaca, N.Y., 1983.

———. "The Persistent Myth of Lost Hegemony." *International Organization,* 41 (Autumn 1987), 551–74.

Summers, Harry G., Jr. *On Strategy: A Critical Analysis of the Vietnam War.* Novato, Ca., 1982.

Talbott, Strobe. *The Master of the Game: Paul Nitze and the Nuclear Peace.* New York, 1988.

Tang, Truong Nhu. *A Viet Cong Memoir.* New York, 1985.

Taylor, Maxwell D. *The Uncertain Trumpet.* New York, 1959.

———. *Responsibility and Response.* New York, 1967.

———. *Swords and Plowshares.* New York, 1972.

———. *Precarious Security.* New York, 1976.

Taylor, Telford. *Nuremberg and Vietnam.* New York, 1970.

Tetlock, Philip E. "Monitoring the Integrative Complexity of American and Soviet Policy Rhetoric." *Journal of Social Issues,* 44 (Summer 1988), 101–31.

Thies, Wallace J. *When Governments Collide: Coercion and Diplomacy in Vietnam, 1964–1968.* Berkeley, Calif., 1980.

Tho, Tran Dinh. *Pacification.* Indochina Monographs. Washington, D.C.: U.S. Army Center of Military History. 1980.

Thompson, James Clay. *Rolling Thunder.* Chapel Hill, N.C., 1980.

Thompson, Robert K. G. *Defeating Communist Insurgency.* London, 1966.

———. *No Exit from Vietnam.* New York, 1969.

Thompson, W. Scott, and Donaldson D. Frizzell, eds. *The Lessons of Vietnam.* New York, 1977.

Thorne, Christopher. *Allies of a Kind.* Oxford, 1978.

Tilly, Charles. "Does Modernization Breed Revolution." In Roy C. Macridis and Bernard E. Brown, eds., *Comparative Politics: Notes and Readings.* 5th ed. Homewood, Ill., 1977.

Tolson, John J. *Air Mobility, 1961–1976.* Washington, D.C., 1973.

Treverton, Gregory F. *The Limits of Intervention in the Postwar World.* New York, 1987.

Trullinger, James W. *Village at War.* New York, 1980.

Truman, Harry S. *Memoirs.* 2 vols. New York, 1956.

Turley, William S. *Vietnamese Communism in Comparative Perspective.* Boulder, Colo., 1980.

Turner, Kathleen J. *Lyndon Johnson's Dual War: Vietnam and the Press.* Chicago, 1985.

Ulam, Adam. *Expansion and Coexistence.* New York, 1968.

United States Department of Defense. *U.S.–Vietnam Relations, 1945–1967.* 12 vols. Washington, D.C., 1971.

Vien, Cao Van. *Reflections on the Vietnam War.* Washington, D.C., 1980.

———. *The Final Collapse.* Washington, D.C., 1983.

Vietnam Settlement: Why 1973, Not 1969? Washington, D.C., 1973.

Wadsworth, James G. *Combat Support in Korea*. Washington, D.C., 1955.

Walt, Lewis W. *Strange War, Strange Strategy*. New York, 1970.

————. *America Faces Defeat*. Woodbridge, Conn., 1972.

Waltz, Kenneth N. *Man, the State, and War*. New York, 1954.

Walzer, Michael. *Just and Unjust Wars*. New York, 1977.

Webb, James. *Fields of Fire*. Englewood Cliffs, N.J., 1975.

Weigley, Russell F. *History of the U.S. Army*. New York, 1967.

————. *The American Way of War: A History of United States Military Strategy and Policy*. New York, 1973.

————. *Eisenhower's Lieutenants*. Bloomington, Ind., 1981.

Westmoreland, William C. *A Soldier Reports*. New York, 1976.

————. *Report of the Chief of Staff of the U.S. Army*. Washington, D.C., 1977.

White, Theodore H. *The Making of the President, 1968*. New York, 1969.

Whiting, Allen S. *China Crosses the Yalu*. Stanford, Calif., 1960.

————. *The Chinese Calculus of Deterrence: India and Indochina*. Ann Arbor, Mich., 1975.

Wiegersma, Nancy. *Vietnam: Peasant Land, Peasant Revolution*. New York, 1988.

Wilensky, Harold L. *Organizational Intelligence*. New York, 1967.

Willenson, Kim, ed. *The Bad War*. New York, 1987.

Williams, William Appleman. *The Tragedy of American Diplomacy*. New York, 1959.

Wittfogel, Karl A. *Oriental Despotism: A Comparative Study of Total Power*. 3d ed. New Haven, Conn., 1957.

Wolf, Eric R. *Peasant Wars of the Twentieth Century*. New York, 1969.

Wolfers, Arnold. *Discord and Collaboration: Essays on International Politics*. Baltimore, Md., 1962.

Yergin, Daniel. *Shattered Peace: The Origins of the Cold War and the National Security State*. Boston, 1977.

Young, Oran. *The Politics of Force*. Princeton, N.J., 1968.

————, ed. *Bargaining: Formal Theories of Negotiation*. Urbana, Ill., 1975.

Zagoria, Donald S. *Vietnam Triangle: Moscow, Peking, Hanoi*. New York, 1967.

Zasloff, Joseph, and MacAlister Brown. *Communism in Indochina*. Lexington, Mass., 1975.

Zumwalt, Elmo R., Jr. *On Watch*. New York, 1976.

Index

Library of Congress Cataloging-in-Publication Data

Hatcher, Patrick Lloyd.
    The suicide of an elite: American internationalists and Vietnam / Patrick Lloyd
Hatcher.
        p.   cm.
Includes bibliographical references.
ISBN 0-8047-1736-2 (alk. paper)
    1. Vietnamese Conflict, 1961–1975—United States. 2. Internationalists—United
States. I. Title.
DS558.H38   1990   89-37829
959.704'3373—dc20   CIP

⊗ This book is printed on acid-free paper